THE World AND ITS People

Silver Burdett Ginn
Parsippany, NJ • Needham, MA
Atlanta, GA   Deerfield, IL   Irving, TX   Santa Clara, CA

PROGRAM AUTHORS

Juan R. García
Associate Professor of History and Associate Dean
   of the College of Social and Behavioral Sciences
University of Arizona
Tucson, AZ

Daniel J. Gelo
Associate Professor of Anthropology, Division of
   Behavioral and Cultural Sciences
University of Texas at San Antonio
San Antonio, TX

Linda L. Greenow
Associate Professor and Acting Chair,
   Department of Geography
S.U.N.Y. at New Paltz
New Paltz, NY

James B. Kracht
Professor of Geography and Educational
   Curriculum and Instruction
Texas A&M University
College Station, TX

Deborah Gray White
Professor of History
Rutgers University
New Brunswick, NJ

CONTRIBUTING AUTHORS

Lillie Johnson Edwards
Associate Professor of History and Director
   of African-American and African Studies
Drew University
Madison, NJ

Akram Khater
Assistant Professor of Middle Eastern History
North Carolina State University
Raleigh, NC

Douglas R. Skopp
Professor of History
S.U.N.Y. at Plattsburgh
Plattsburgh, NY

Silver Burdett Ginn

299 Jefferson Road, P.O. Box 480
Parsippany, NJ 07054-0480

ISBN 0-382-32694-6   7 8 9 10 RRD 05 04 03 02 01 00

CONTENTS

iii

UNIT 3 — THE MIDDLE CENTURIES

UNIT 5

TIMES OF GREAT CHANGE

420

UNIT 6 — TOWARD THE TWENTY-FIRST CENTURY 542

* Found in Summing Up: Geography and You

ATLAS MAPS

MAP ADVENTURES

TIME LINES

GRAPHS, TABLES, CHARTS, AND DIAGRAMS

SKILLS

LITERATURE

The following books are recommended for optional reading and research.

Map Handbook
CONTENTS

When Is a MAP Better Than a Photo?

When astronauts went into space, they saw Earth as no one had seen it before. The photographs they brought back to Earth gave us a new view of our planet. In the 1970s the United States launched satellites into space. These satellites traveled around Earth, sending back pictures of Earth's surface. By fitting together hundreds of these views, a picture map of the United States was put together. How is this photo better than a map? In what ways is it not as useful as a map?

▼ This photograph was taken from about 1,500 feet above Earth's surface.

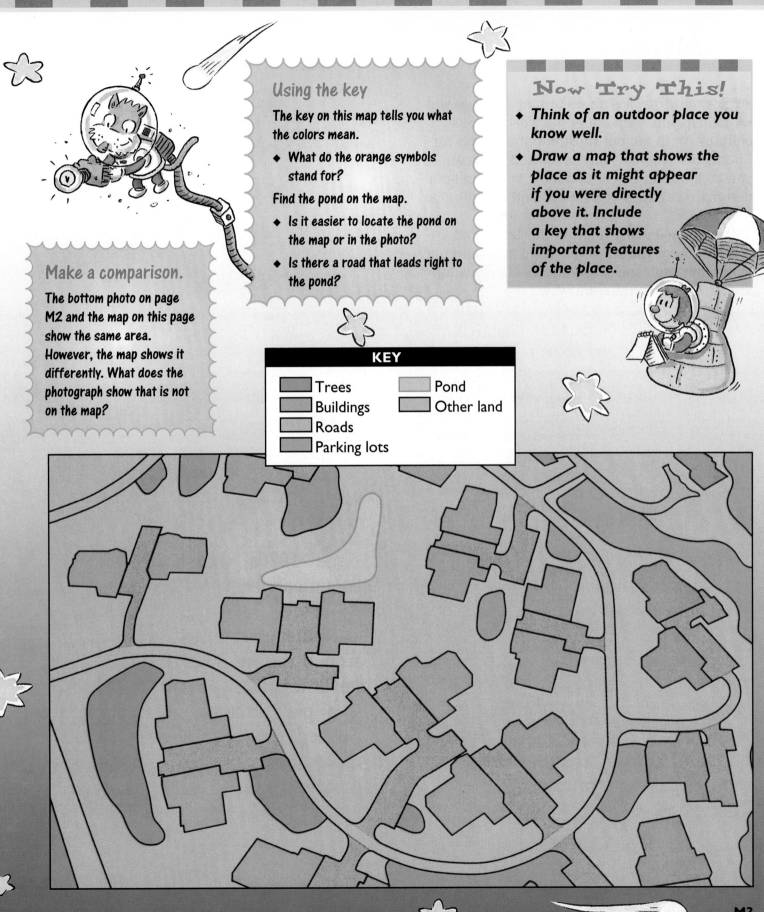

Using the key

The key on this map tells you what the colors mean.

◆ What do the orange symbols stand for?

Find the pond on the map.

◆ Is it easier to locate the pond on the map or in the photo?

◆ Is there a road that leads right to the pond?

Now Try This!

◆ Think of an outdoor place you know well.

◆ Draw a map that shows the place as it might appear if you were directly above it. Include a key that shows important features of the place.

Make a comparison.

The bottom photo on page M2 and the map on this page show the same area. However, the map shows it differently. What does the photograph show that is not on the map?

KEY

Trees
Buildings
Roads
Parking lots
Pond
Other land

MAPS: Make the Most of Them!

Reading maps is an important skill that will help you learn about the world and its cultures. Maps are our most important tools for finding out where a place is located. However, as you look through this Handbook, you'll find out that maps can help you understand other things, too.

You will see many maps in this book, and many of them will show the same outline of our world. But each one gives different information and is useful in a different way.

The Title

In this book, map titles are located at the top of the key. The title tells you what kind of information the map contains.

◆ What is the title of this map?

Key and Locator Map

A box called a key, or legend, explains the symbols on a map. The key often contains a locator map that relates the area in the map to a larger area.

◆ What larger area is shown on this locator map?

The Scale

The scale allows you to tell the distances between places.

◆ How many miles does one inch stand for on this map?

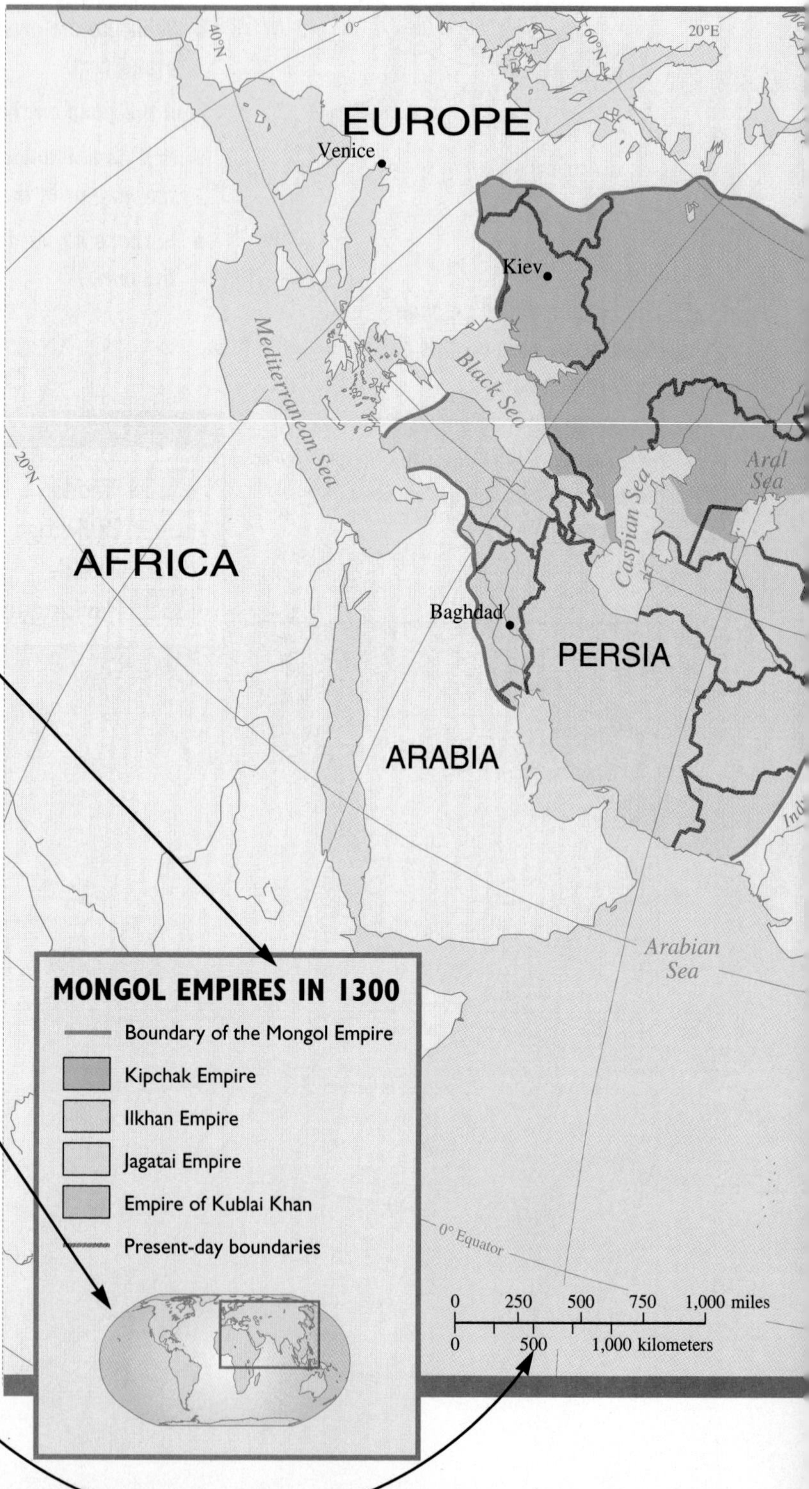

EUROPE
Venice
Kiev

AFRICA

Mediterranean Sea
Black Sea
Caspian Sea
Aral Sea

Baghdad

PERSIA

ARABIA

Arabian Sea

MONGOL EMPIRES IN 1300

—— Boundary of the Mongol Empire

▢ Kipchak Empire

▢ Ilkhan Empire

▢ Jagatai Empire

▢ Empire of Kublai Khan

---- Present-day boundaries

0° Equator

| 0 | 250 | 500 | 750 | 1,000 miles |
| 0 | | 500 | 1,000 kilometers | |

Latitude and Longitude

The latitude and longitude of a place tell its exact location.

◆ Find the 80°E longitude line.

◆ Which line of latitude runs across the Caspian Sea?

Boundaries

The gray lines on this map show boundaries between places.

◆ What do the red lines stand for?

The Compass Rose

This compass rose tells where north is on a map. From that, you can figure out where south, east, and west are.

◆ Is Kiev north or south of Baghdad?

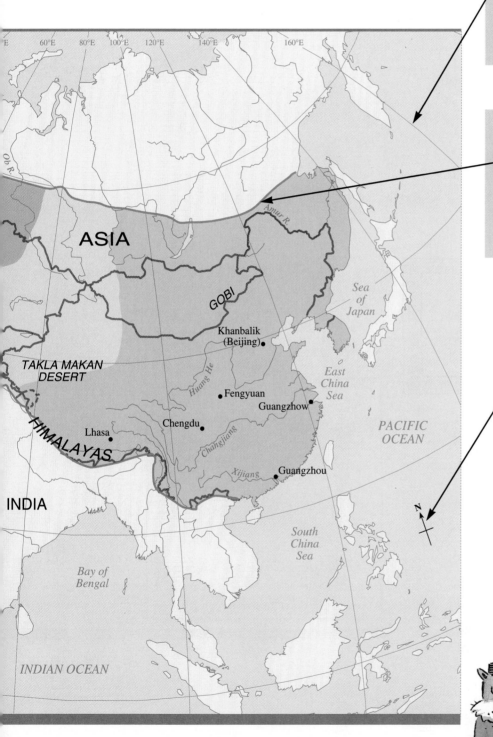

60°E 80°E 100°E 120°E 140°E 160°E

Ob R.

ASIA

Amur R.

GOBI

Sea of Japan

Khanbalik (Beijing)

TAKLA MAKAN DESERT

Huang He

Fengyuan

Guangzhow

East China Sea

PACIFIC OCEAN

Chengdu

Changjiang

HIMALAYAS

Lhasa

Xijiang Guangzhou

INDIA

South China Sea

N

Bay of Bengal

INDIAN OCEAN

Now Try This!

Look at the maps in this book. Locate each of the map parts listed below.

title	key
locator map	compass rose
scale	boundary lines
lines of latitude	

◆ Did you find every map part? Did any one map have all the parts?

An INSET Map: How Can It Help?

If you wanted to tell a friend about a trip you took to Mexico, you could find a map of the country. You would want to tell about what you saw in Mexico City and about driving through Mexico. Your map shows the route you took, but it doesn't show the interesting spots. How can you convince your friend how exciting your adventures in Mexico were?

What you need is a map with **insets**—a main map with one or more smaller maps. Together they show large relationships between areas and details of smaller areas.

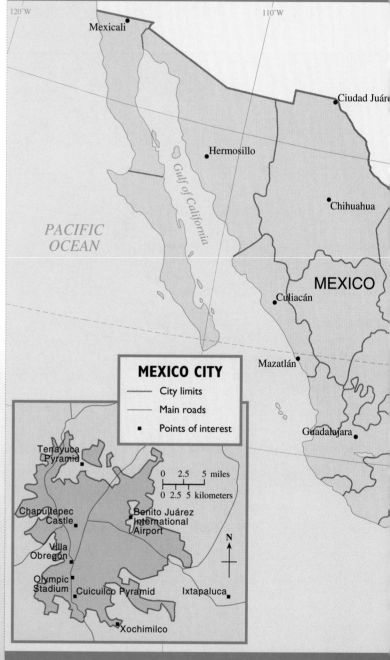

Use the main map.

◆ Find Veracruz on the main map.

◆ Find the Gulf of California, too.

◆ Name the capital of Mexico.

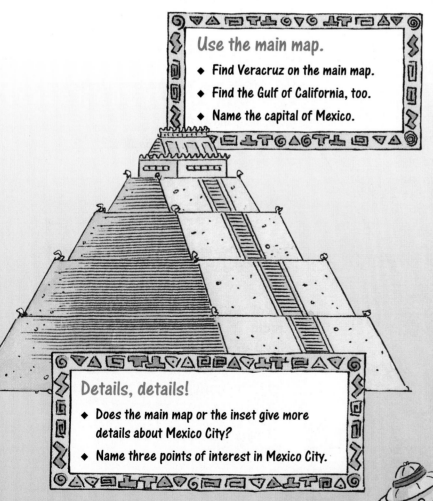

Details, details!

◆ Does the main map or the inset give more details about Mexico City?

◆ Name three points of interest in Mexico City.

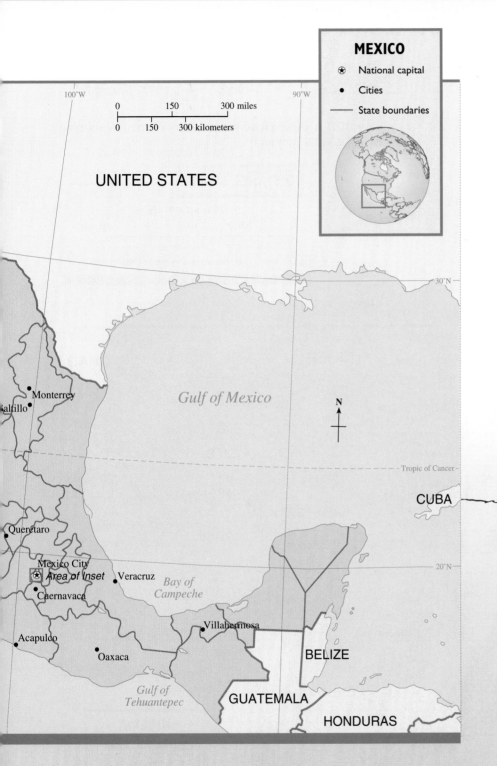

MEXICO

- ⊛ National capital
- • Cities
- — State boundaries

100°W

0   150   300 miles
0   150   300 kilometers

UNITED STATES

30°N

Monterrey
Saltillo

Gulf of Mexico

N

Tropic of Cancer

CUBA

Querétaro

Mexico City
⊛ Area of Inset   Veracruz   *Bay of Campeche*   20°N

Cuernavaca

Acapulco
Oaxaca

Villahermosa

BELIZE

Gulf of Tehuantepec   GUATEMALA

HONDURAS

90°W

Each map has a scale of miles.

- ◆ About how far is it from Mexico City to Monterrey?
- ◆ How far apart are Olympic Stadium and the Benito Juárez International Airport?

See the location.

This locator map relates Mexico to the rest of North America.

- ◆ What can you tell from the locator that you can't tell from the main map?

Now Try This!

- ◆ *Tell two facts about Mexico that appear only on the main map.*
- ◆ *Tell two facts about Mexico City that appear only on the inset map.*
- ◆ *Now find a map that has an inset of a different place and compare the main map and the inset. Tell a group of classmates about the map you chose.*

Can You Read a
DISTANCE SCALE?

Distances on maps are smaller than the real distances on Earth. The **distance scale** shows how much smaller. A certain number of inches on a map stands for a certain number of feet, yards, or miles on Earth. If the map uses the metric system, centimeters stand for meters or kilometers.

On this distance scale, how many miles does one inch stand for? How many inches would show 400 miles? How many kilometers does one centimeter stand for?

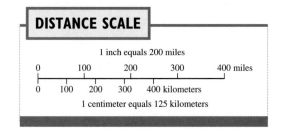

DISTANCE SCALE

1 inch equals 200 miles

| 0 | 100 | 200 | 300 | 400 miles |

| 0 | 100 | 200 | 300 | 400 kilometers |

1 centimeter equals 125 kilometers

Distance between places

How far is it from Abuja, Nigeria, to N'Djamena, Chad?

- To find out, use an index card. Put its top left corner at the beginning of the scale.

- Mark the point where the scale ends. Then mark as many more scale widths as will fit on the card.

- Then place the card so that the straight edge connects the two cities.

- Count the number of marks between the cities. How far apart are they in miles and in kilometers?

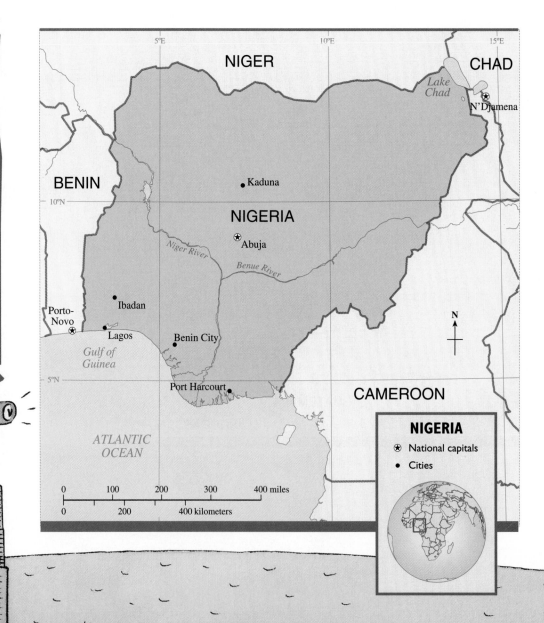

NIGER

CHAD

Lake Chad

N'Djamena

BENIN

Kaduna

NIGERIA

Abuja

Niger River

Benue River

Porto-Novo

Ibadan

Lagos

Benin City

Gulf of Guinea

Port Harcourt

CAMEROON

N

ATLANTIC OCEAN

| 0 | 100 | 200 | 300 | 400 miles |

| 0 | 200 | 400 kilometers |

NIGERIA

⊛ National capitals

• Cities

If a map shows a large piece of territory, a scale of one inch may represent a huge distance. See the map of Africa. If a map shows a smaller area, a scale of one inch will represent a smaller distance. See the map of Nigeria on page M8.

Compare the maps of Africa.

◆ On the map of Nigeria on page M8, how many miles apart are Porto-Novo and Abuja?

◆ How many miles apart are they on the map of Africa on this page?

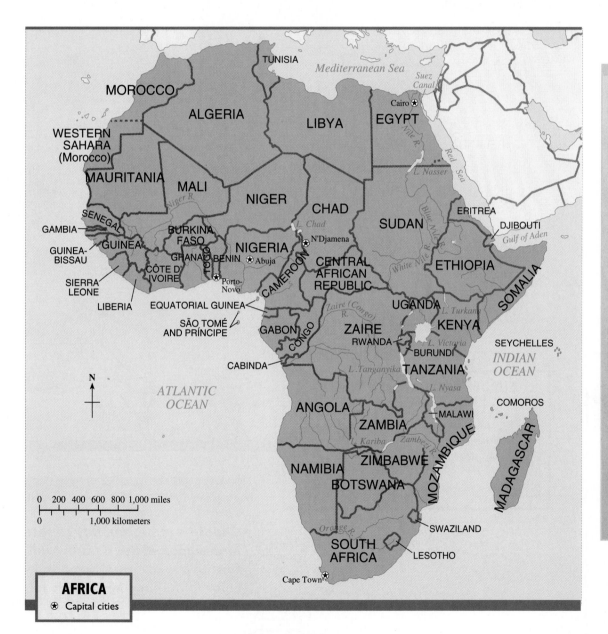

TUNISIA
Mediterranean Sea
Suez Canal
MOROCCO
ALGERIA
LIBYA
EGYPT
Cairo ✪
Nile R.
WESTERN SAHARA (Morocco)
L. Nasser
Red Sea
MAURITANIA
MALI
NIGER
CHAD
Niger R.
SUDAN
Blue Nile R.
ERITREA
SENEGAL
L. Chad
DJIBOUTI
GAMBIA
BURKINA FASO
N'Djamena
Gulf of Aden
GUINEA-BISSAU
GUINEA
NIGERIA
CENTRAL AFRICAN REPUBLIC
ETHIOPIA
White Nile R.
GHANA
BENIN
Abuja ✪
SOMALIA
CÔTE D'IVOIRE
CAMEROON
SIERRA LEONE
Porto-Novo ✪
LIBERIA
EQUATORIAL GUINEA
UGANDA
L. Turkana
SÃO TOMÉ AND PRÍNCIPE
Zaire (Congo) R.
ZAIRE
KENYA
GABON
CONGO
RWANDA
L. Victoria
SEYCHELLES
BURUNDI
INDIAN OCEAN
CABINDA
L. Tanganyika
TANZANIA
N
L. Nyasa
ATLANTIC OCEAN
COMOROS
ANGOLA
MALAWI
ZAMBIA
Kariba
Zambezi
MADAGASCAR
MOZAMBIQUE
ZIMBABWE
NAMIBIA
BOTSWANA
0 200 400 600 800 1,000 miles
0   1,000 kilometers
SWAZILAND
Orange R.
SOUTH AFRICA
LESOTHO
Cape Town ✪

AFRICA
✪ Capital cities

Now Try This!

With a group of your classmates, map your classroom or another room in your school.

◆ First measure the room's length and width, using a yardstick or tape measure. Then decide what scale you'll use to fit the map on a sheet of paper.

◆ Draw the map, being sure to include windows, desks, and other features.

What Doors Does a MAP KEY Open?

To use a map, you must know what its colors or symbols stand for. Cartographers, or mapmakers, gather all the symbols together in one place. This part of a map is called the **key**, or legend.

The map below shows how Europe was divided at the end of World War II. At first glance, it may appear complicated. However, it is easy to "read" if you understand the map key.

First stop: The title

In this book, map titles are located at the top of the map key.

◆ What is the title of this map?

The color is the code.

The colors on the map show that Europe was divided.

◆ Name four countries that were members of NATO in 1955.

◆ What nations were neutral?

◆ What country added a large piece of territory after World War II?

EUROPE AFTER WORLD WAR II

NATO nations, 1955

Warsaw Pact nations, 1955

Areas added by Soviet Union after WWII

Neutral nations

Now Try This!

Choose a map from any chapter in this book. Write a paragraph that tells what every symbol or color in the map key stands for.

How Can a COMPASS ROSE Help You?

The **compass rose** is a small drawing that shows direction on a map. Its tips point to the four **cardinal**, or main, directions: north, south, east, and west (N, S, E, and W). It also shows the **intermediate**, or in-between, directions: northwest, northeast, southwest, and southeast (NW, NE, SW, and SE).

Be a tourist in New Zealand.

From South Island, look for a good place to sail.
- In what direction must you travel?

Sail through Cook Strait for the Tasman Sea.
- In what direction are you sailing?

Start out in Dunedin and travel to the nearest fishing area.
- In which direction are you traveling?

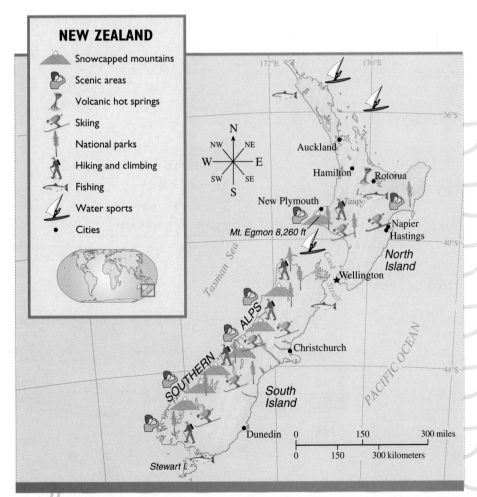

NEW ZEALAND

- Snowcapped mountains
- Scenic areas
- Volcanic hot springs
- Skiing
- National parks
- Hiking and climbing
- Fishing
- Water sports
- Cities

Now Try This!

- *Find a map of your community or of a city you have visited.*
- *Make up some questions that need to be answered by naming cardinal and intermediate directions.*
- *Try your questions out on your classmates. How many students can answer all the questions without making a mistake?*

LATITUDE and LONGITUDE: What Do They Do?

You can locate any point on the surface of Earth if you know how to use lines of **latitude** and **longitude**.

The **equator** is the line of latitude that runs around the center of Earth. It is numbered 0° (zero degrees). The other latitude lines show how far north or south of the equator a place is located. They run east and west around Earth. They are also called **parallels of latitude**.

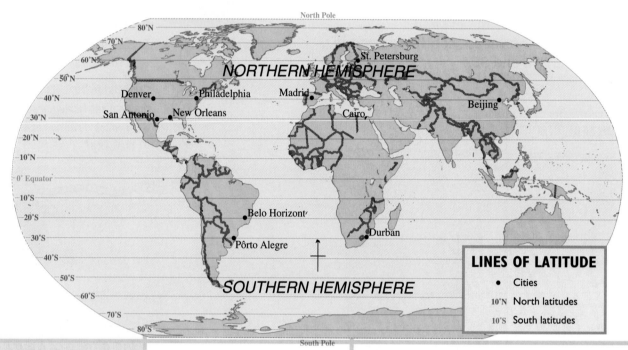

North Pole

80°N
70°N
60°N
50°N
40°N
30°N
20°N
10°N
0° Equator
10°S
20°S
30°S
40°S
50°S
60°S
70°S
80°S

South Pole

NORTHERN HEMISPHERE

SOUTHERN HEMISPHERE

St. Petersburg
Denver
Philadelphia
Madrid
Beijing
San Antonio
New Orleans
Cairo
Belo Horizont
Durban
Pôrto Alegre

LINES OF LATITUDE
- Cities
- 10°N North latitudes
- 10°S South latitudes

Use the parallels.

On this map, parallels of latitude are labeled from 0 degrees (0°) to 80 degrees north (80°N) and 80 degrees south (80°S). The 90°N and 90°S parallels are not shown.

- Cairo is located at 30°N. What cities are at 30°S?

The equator divides.

The equator divides Earth into the Northern Hemisphere and the Southern Hemisphere.

- Which cities on the map are in the Southern Hemisphere?

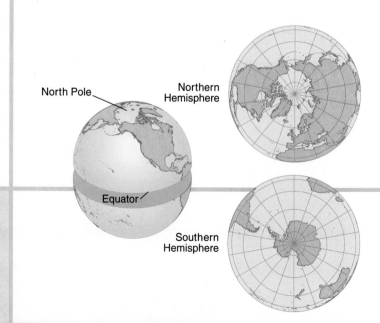

North Pole

Equator

Northern Hemisphere

Southern Hemisphere

The vertical lines on a map that run from the North Pole to the South Pole are lines of **longitude**. They are also called **meridians**. They are numbered from the **prime meridian**. This imaginary line runs through Greenwich, England. Meridians are counted east and west from the prime meridian, which is numbered 0° (zero degrees) longitude.

Lines east of the prime meridian are marked 15°E, 30°E, and so on. West of the prime meridian, lines are marked 15°W, 30°W, and so on. Halfway around the world is the 180° meridian, also known as the **international date line**. This is the point where, at midnight, each day begins. If it is Sunday just west of the line, it is Saturday east of it.

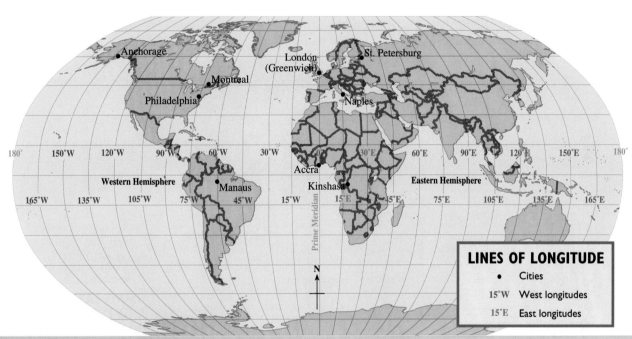

Use the meridians.

◆ **Which cities are located at 15°E?**

◆ **Which cities are located on the prime meridian?**

The prime meridian divides.

The prime meridian and the international date line divide Earth into the Western Hemisphere and the Eastern Hemisphere.

◆ **Is St. Petersburg in the Eastern or Western Hemispheres?**

◆ **What city on the map is in both the Southern and the Eastern Hemispheres?**

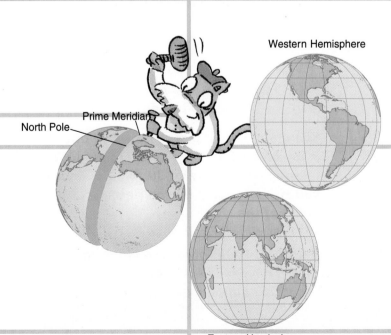

Using Latitude and Longitude

Latitude and longitude are used to give places on Earth exact "addresses." On the map, St. Petersburg, Russia, has a latitude of 60° north. Its longitude is 30° east. The short way to write St. Petersburg's "address" is 60°N/30°E.

Where is it?

◆ What is Philadelphia's "address"?

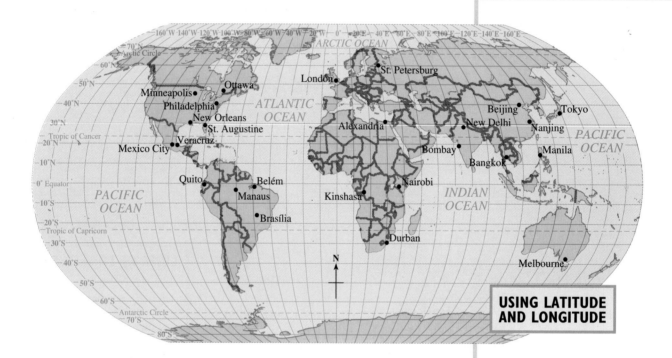

USING LATITUDE AND LONGITUDE

Now Try This!

You are browsing through a world atlas while flying away on vacation. The captain announces: "Passengers, we are at 30°N/30°E. That city below you is . . . ." Before he can finish, you respond with the name of the city.

◆ What city did you name?

◆ Using a world atlas or a globe, make a list of cities that have nice even "addresses," like the one the captain announced.

What's the Purpose
of SPECIAL-PURPOSE Maps?

Precipitation Map

The two most common kinds of maps are **political maps** and **physical maps**. A political map uses color to show nations and states. A physical map shows the natural features of the land.

There are many other kinds of maps, too. Some show where crops are grown, where oil is found, or what countries have a democratic government. These are called **special-purpose maps** because each map has only one purpose.

This special-purpose map is a **precipitation map**. **Precipitation** is moisture that falls to Earth as rain, snow, sleet, or hail. The colors show the average yearly precipitation around the world.

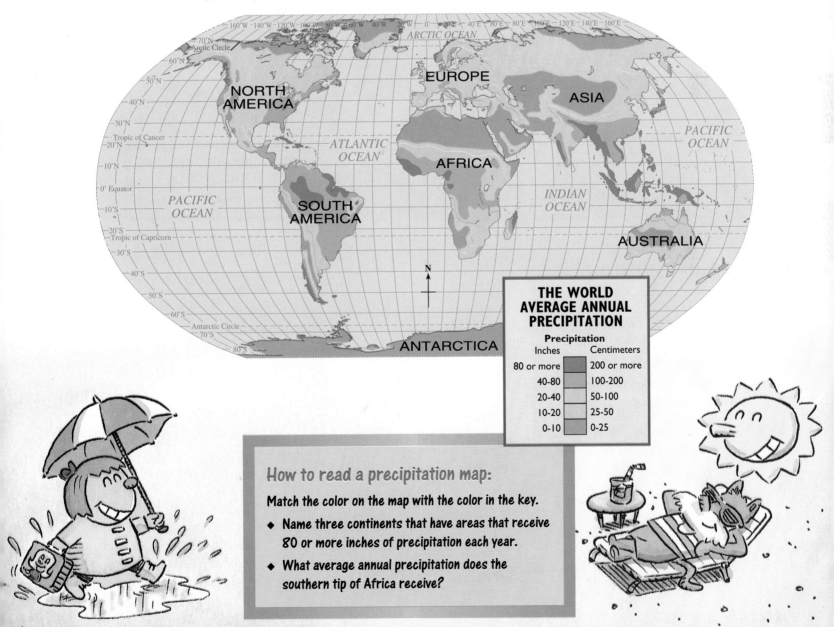

THE WORLD AVERAGE ANNUAL PRECIPITATION

Precipitation

Inches		Centimeters
80 or more		200 or more
40-80		100-200
20-40		50-100
10-20		25-50
0-10		0-25

How to read a precipitation map:

Match the color on the map with the color in the key.

◆ Name three continents that have areas that receive 80 or more inches of precipitation each year.

◆ What average annual precipitation does the southern tip of Africa receive?

Product Map

Some special-purpose maps, called **product maps**, show where resources, such as coal, are found or where crops, such as cotton, are grown.

The map below shows the major rice-producing regions of the world. Did you know that roughly half of the world's people eat rice as their main food? This map shows where rice comes from.

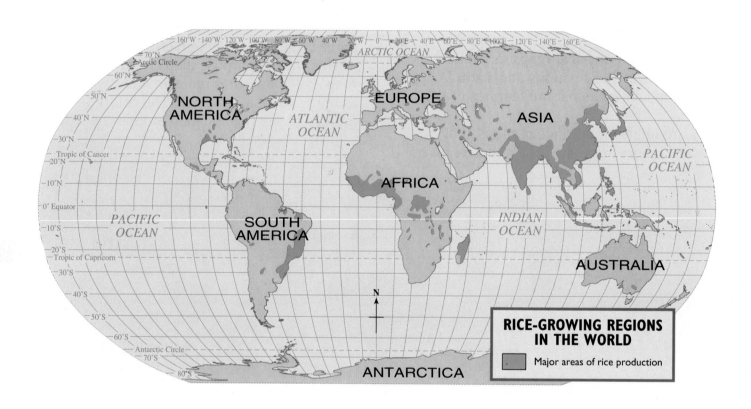

RICE-GROWING REGIONS IN THE WORLD

Major areas of rice production

Where's the rice?

◆ Which continent produces more rice, North America or South America?

◆ Use the Atlas in this book. Find the names of the two countries that produce the most rice.

Put two purposes together.

Use the maps on pages M15 and M16.

◆ Do rice-producing regions receive low, or high, amounts of precipitation?

◆ Find the United States on both maps. How does the amount of precipitation relate to the production of rice in the United States?

Natural Resource Map

The map below is a **natural resource map**. It shows the forested areas of the world. You might be surprised to see forests described as natural resources, but like coal and iron, forests are also provided by nature and are useful to people. Think of all the products you use that come from the trees that are grown in the forests. You can begin with the paper used to make this book!

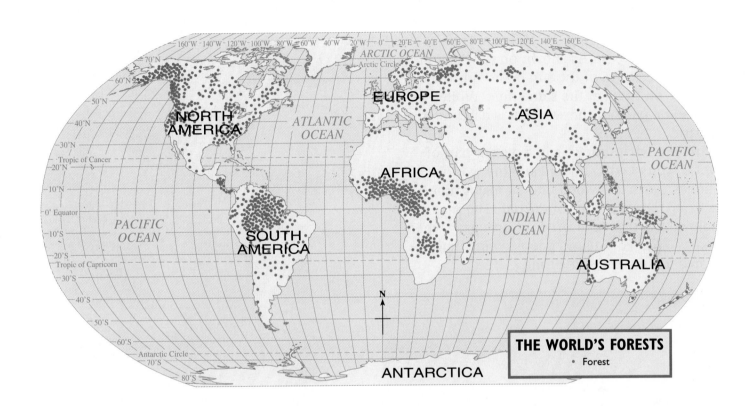

THE WORLD'S FORESTS
· Forest

Make some comparisons.

Use the maps on pages M15, M16, and M17.

◆ Do forests thrive in areas of high or low precipitation?

◆ Follow the Tropic of Cancer and the Tropic of Capricorn across this map and the map on page M16. Compare rice production and forested land in these areas.

Now Try This!

Use a different kind of special-purpose map now. Collect the weather maps from five days' worth of newspapers. Compare the five maps. Did they change from day to day?

Why Do We Need

TIME ZONE
Maps?

Earth moves constantly, rotating on its axis from west to east. As shown on the diagram below, the direct rays of the sun do not hit everywhere on Earth at the same time. While it is night in some parts of the world, it is daytime in other parts.

To find out what time it is in a distant part of the world, you need to understand the world's time zones. Earth is divided into 24 major time zones—one for each hour of the day. The map at the right shows that time zones often zigzag when they cross land. This allows people living in the same area to have the same time.

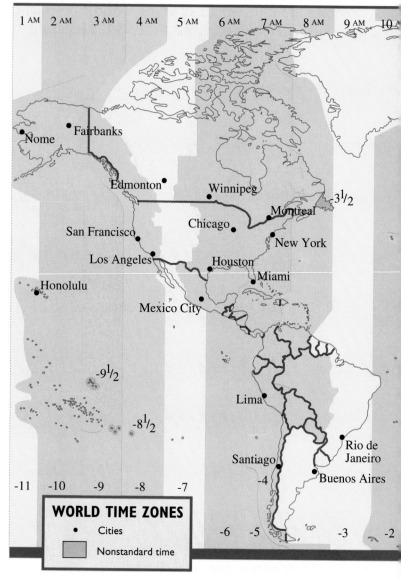

WORLD TIME ZONES

- • Cities
- ▨ Nonstandard time

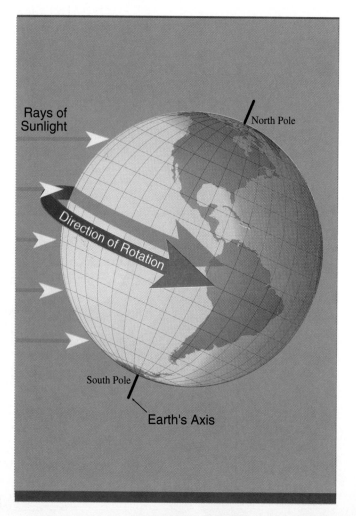

Rays of Sunlight

North Pole

Direction of Rotation

South Pole

Earth's Axis

The prime meridian

All time zones are measured from the prime meridian, which passes through Greenwich, England. When it is noon in Greenwich, the time in other zones is different. How much different depends on how far east or west of the prime meridian the other zone is.

◆ When it is 2:00 P.M. in Greenwich, England, what time is it in Nairobi, Kenya?

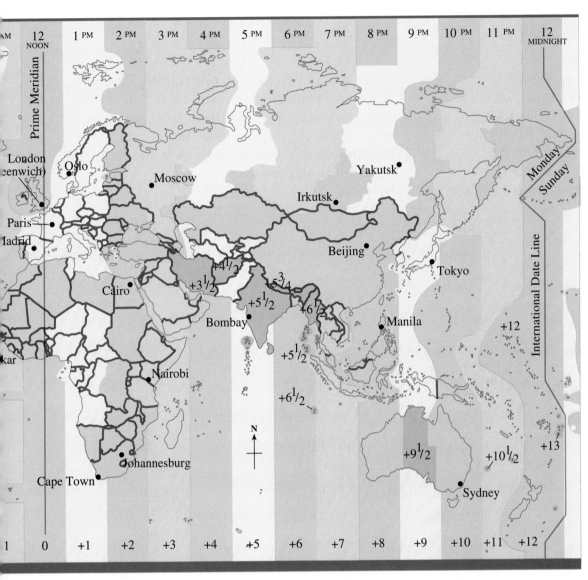

London
(Greenwich)

Oslo

Moscow

Paris

Irkutsk

Yakutsk

Madrid

Cairo

Beijing

+4½

+3½

+5¾

+5½

+6½

Tokyo

Bombay

Manila

kar

+5½

Nairobi

+6½

+12

N

+9½

+10½

Johannesburg

Cape Town

Sydney

+13

12 NOON | 1 PM | 2 PM | 3 PM | 4 PM | 5 PM | 6 PM | 7 PM | 8 PM | 9 PM | 10 PM | 11 PM | 12 MIDNIGHT

1 | 0 | +1 | +2 | +3 | +4 | +5 | +6 | +7 | +8 | +9 | +10 | +11 | +12

Prime Meridian

International Date Line

Monday / Sunday

MONDAY   SUNDAY

International date line

The other important meridian is the international date line, exactly halfway around the world from the prime meridian. It is here that the day changes. When it is Sunday east of the line, west of the line it is Monday.

◆ If you are traveling from east to west on a Thursday, what day is it when you cross the international date line?

Zoom in on the zone.

◆ What time is it where you live when it is noon in Greenwich, England?

◆ Choose any two cities on the map. Figure out the difference in time between them.

Now Try This!

Suppose that you are flying from New York City to London, England. The trip takes seven hours. It is 3:00 P.M. when you leave New York. Write a description of what time you will arrive in London and what you will do after the plane lands.

PROJECTIONS:
Why Aren't All Maps of the Same Place Alike?

As useful as maps are, they all have a drawback. It is difficult to show the curved surface of Earth on a flat map. It is like trying to flatten a rubber ball. Part of the surface always sticks up, causing distortion in showing the surface. Over the years, mapmakers have developed many ways of showing Earth's surface.

These are known as map **projections**. Each projection is useful. However, each distorts, or changes, the shape of Earth in some way. On most maps, the regions near the center of the map are most accurate. Regions farther away from the center are distorted.

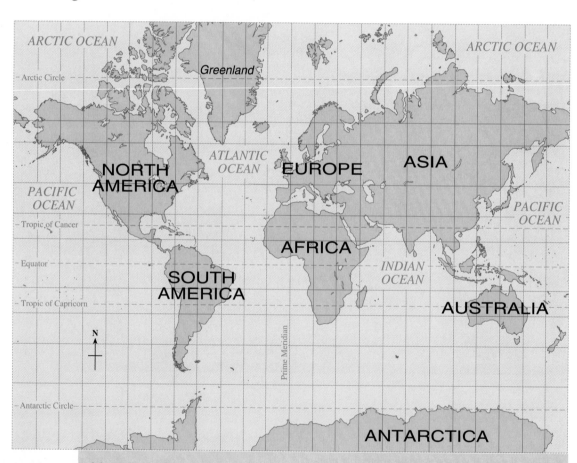

Mercator Projection

A European mapmaker named Mercator created a map in the 1500s that showed direction accurately. The Mercator projection gives an accurate view of land areas near the equator. However, it distorts the size and shape of lands near the Poles.

◆ How is longitude shown on this map? How is it different from longitude on a globe?

◆ Compare the sizes of Greenland and South America on this map. Then look at these places on the map on page M21. Does the Mercator show these two areas accurately?

THE **World** WE **Live In**

What Is It That We All Share?

Let's take a look at the physical world we all share. We'll explore our world and the many ways we learn about our past.

6. **mountain range** A mountain range is a group of connected mountains or steep, high land areas.

7. **mouth of a river** A river mouth is the place where a river flows into a larger body of water.

8. **ocean** The oceans are the entire body of salt water that covers almost three fourths of Earth's surface.

9. **peninsula** A peninsula is a piece of land that is surrounded by water on three sides.

10. **plain** A plain is a broad stretch of level, or nearly level, land.

11. **plateau** A plateau is a large, level area of high land.

12. **source of a river** A river source is the place where a river begins.

13. **strait** A strait is a narrow waterway that connects two larger bodies of water.

14. **tributary** A tributary is a stream or river that flows into a larger river.

15. **volcano** A volcano is a mountain that builds up around an opening in Earth's surface. Under the opening is hot, melted rock.

Photos taken of Earth from outer space seem to show a surface that is very much alike from one place to another. However, the closer one gets to the surface, the more differences one sees. On the surface itself, Earth is a complex, interesting place.

The diagram on these pages shows common forms of land and water. To find out about a certain form, check the number next to its description and find it on the diagram.

1. **bay** A bay is a part of an ocean or lake that is partly enclosed by land.

2. **coast** Coast is land that borders on the sea or ocean.

3. **delta** A delta is an area formed by soil washed downstream by a river.

4. **glacier** A glacier is a large body of ice that moves slowly down a mountain.

5. **island** An island is an area of land surrounded by water.

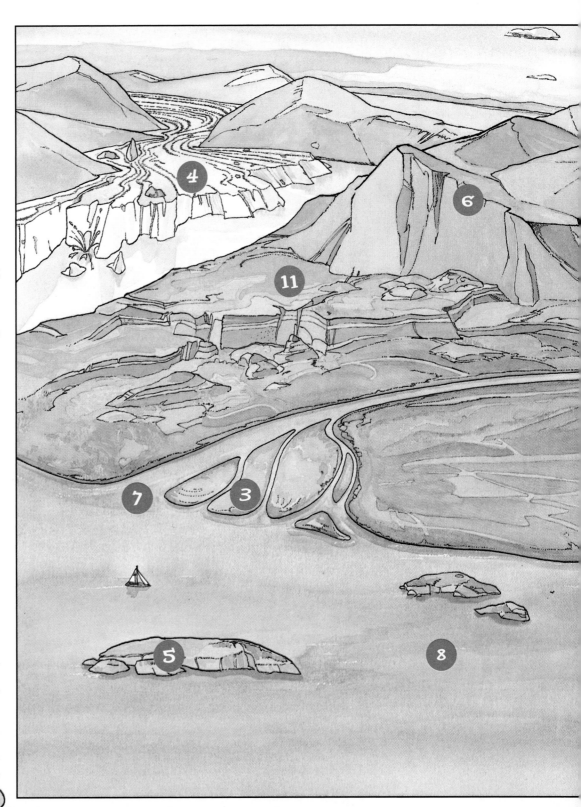

An interrupted projection shows the correct sizes and shapes of land. To do this, however, the oceans are split apart.

◆ Can you measure the distance between the U.S. and Italy on this map?

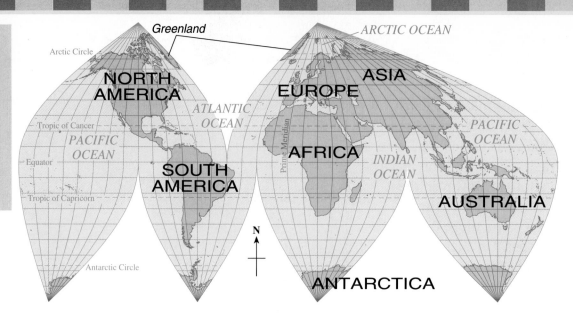

Greenland

ARCTIC OCEAN

Arctic Circle

NORTH AMERICA

ATLANTIC OCEAN

Tropic of Cancer

PACIFIC OCEAN

Equator

Tropic of Capricorn

SOUTH AMERICA

Antarctic Circle

ASIA

EUROPE

Prime Meridian

AFRICA

INDIAN OCEAN

PACIFIC OCEAN

AUSTRALIA

N

ANTARCTICA

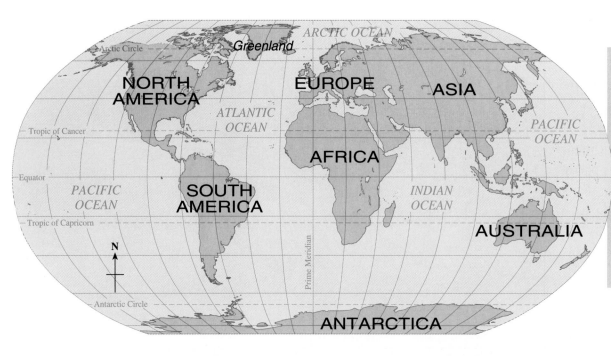

ARCTIC OCEAN

Arctic Circle

Greenland

NORTH AMERICA

ATLANTIC OCEAN

Tropic of Cancer

Equator

PACIFIC OCEAN

Tropic of Capricorn

N

Antarctic Circle

EUROPE

ASIA

AFRICA

PACIFIC OCEAN

SOUTH AMERICA

INDIAN OCEAN

Prime Meridian

AUSTRALIA

ANTARCTICA

Robinson Projection

This projection shows the correct sizes and shapes of most landmasses. It gives a fairly accurate view of the sizes of oceans and of distances across land.

◆ Compare the three projections. How does each one show Greenland?

Now Try This!

If you peel an orange or grapefruit, you can see the problems of making a round object lie flat.

◆ Use an indelible pen to mark the outlines of the continents on the orange.

◆ Now peel the orange, keeping the peel in one piece.

◆ Try to make the peel lie flat. Does it look something like one of the projections on these pages? Which one?

EXPLORE WHAT IS

People's lives are influenced by the location of the place they live. To learn about different groups of people and their cultures, it's helpful to find out as much as you can about the places where the groups live.

▼ How can the boy describe the exact location of a place on the globe? Read page 7 to find out.

CONTENTS

GEOGRAPHY?

You can learn more about maps and about people and the places they live from these books. Read one that interests you and fill out a book-review form.

READ AND RESEARCH

The Eyewitness Atlas of the World **edited by Dr. David R. Green** (Dorling Kinderling Publishing, 1994)
A unique computerized technique produces fine three-dimensional physical maps of the countries of the world. Photos, art, and text present the history, geography, and culture of each region. *(reference)*

Settlements **by Nick Millea** (Thomson Learning, 1993)
You can find out how and why people settled in certain locations around the world. You will learn why some settlements became crowded cities and why some tiny villages never seem to change. *(nonfiction)*

The City **by Rosa Cost-Pau, illustrated by Estudio Marcel Socias** (Chelsea House Publishers, 1994)
Study the various diagrams to see how a city uses its natural resources and deals with waste and pollution. *(nonfiction)*

The Sahara and Its People **by Simon Scoones** (Thomson Learning, 1993)
As the climate of the world's largest desert changes, all living things in the region are threatened. Find out how organizations are supporting the local people to find solutions. *(nonfiction)*

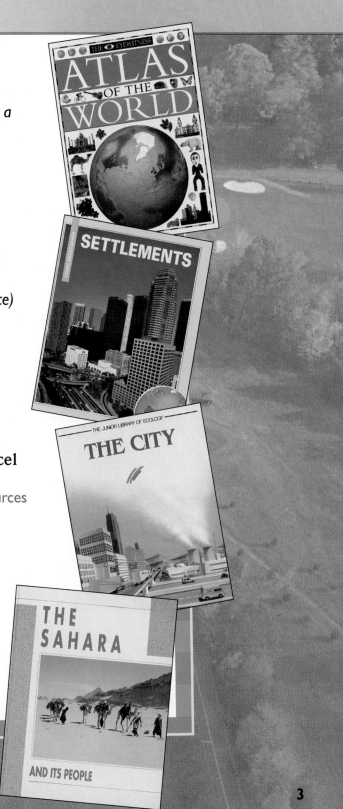

SKILL POWER

Reading Population Density Maps

Knowing how to read population density maps can help you understand where and how people live.

UNDERSTAND IT

Have you ever gone to a crowded stadium, theater, or state fair? How did you feel? Did you like the excitement of having a lot of people around enjoying entertainment? Or did you have an urge to go to a place where there were not so many people?

What you experience in a crowded place is a result of population density—a measure of the number of people in a given area. If a state fair were held on an 80-acre field and 10,000 people were there, the population density would be 125 people for each acre.

EXPLORE IT

The number of people in an area can be shown on a map. Some maps show population density by using dots to represent a specific number of people. Some maps use bands of color to show a population range for an area or region.

Look at the population density map of Great Britain. Each dot represents about 25,000 people. Can you see that most of the densely populated areas in Great Britain are near water?

Areas with mountains often have fewer people living there. Can you guess where there might be mountains in Great Britain by looking at the population density map? Find Great Britain on the physical map of Europe in the Atlas section of this book. Did you make a good guess about the mountain areas?

POPULATION DENSITY OF GREAT BRITAIN

- Cities
- National capital
- 25,000 people

4

Working with a small group or with your whole class, divide the work to create a population density map of your classroom.

Using a tape measure, find the length and width of your classroom. Multiply the two figures together. This will give you the area of your room.

Count the number of people in your classroom. Don't forget your teacher! Divide the number of people by the number of square feet to find the population density of your classroom.

Make a population density map of your classroom, using one figure for each person. You may wish to display the map on the outside of your classroom door.

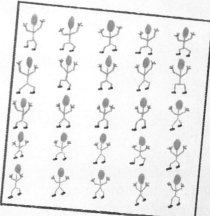

Population Density in Mrs. Smith's Classroom

= 1 person per 18 square feet

To find population density, divide the number of people by the area.

SKILL POWER SEARCH

Find the population density map in this chapter. See how much information you can get from it.

1

Setting the Scene

⭐ **KEY TERMS**

geographer
region
culture region
cartogram

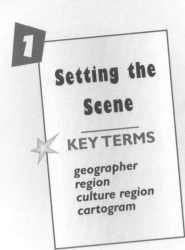

WHERE PEOPLE LIVE

FOCUS *There are billions of people in the world living under a wide variety of conditions. The best way to learn about people and their cultures is to organize them into groups.*

Organizing People Into Groups

Earth, this wonderful planet on which we live, is home to more than 5 billion people. In this book you will learn about these people and their cultures, both past and present. The easiest way to study people is to organize them into groups. As you progress through the book, you will discover that each group of people has its own history and traditions. These are important parts of their culture.

Whenever you organize anything into groups, all members of a group need to have something in common.

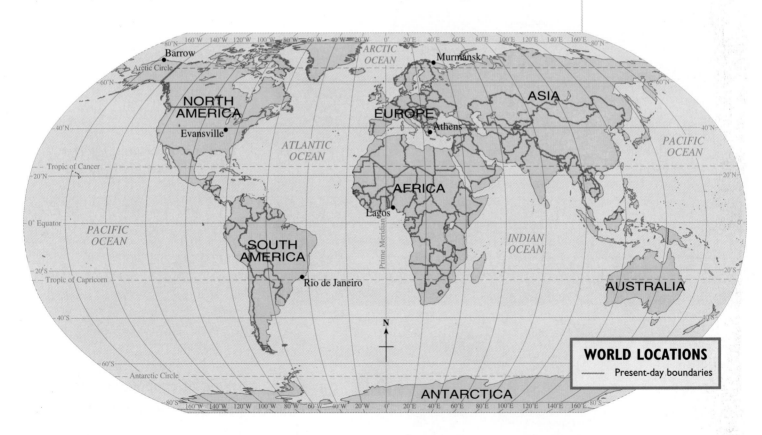

WORLD LOCATIONS

——— Present-day boundaries

 These pictures show the effects of seasonal change on a place.

Geographers often group people according to the kinds of places where they live. To do this, the geographers divide the world into smaller parts called **regions**.

Different characteristics of a place influence the type of culture and traditions that develop there. For example, the grouping of people into a region may be based on such characteristics as climate, geographical features, type of government, language, or religion.

Using Latitude and Longitude

When studying groups of people, it is important to be able to tell where these groups are located. Latitude and longitude are used to describe the location of a place on earth. The map on page 6 shows lines of latitude and longitude. You may wish to refer to pages M12–M14 of the Map Handbook to review latitude and longitude.

To find the exact location of a place, you need to know both its latitude and its longitude. For example, find Athens, Greece, and Evansville, Indiana, on the map on page 6. Notice that both cities are located at the same latitude—38°N. This means that the two cities are the same distance north of the equator. But, as you can see, the cities are not close together. To tell exactly where each city is, you need to include its longitude.

The longitude of Athens is 24°E, while that of Evansville is about 87.5°W. Now you can express the exact location, or address, of each city. The location of Athens is 38°N/24°E; that of Evansville is 38°N/87.5°W.

Grouping by Temperature

One thing that affects the way people live is temperature. In some parts of the world, it is always warm. In other places, it is always cold.

People who live in warm climates have different lifestyles from those of people who live in cold climates. Some ways in which lifestyles differ include clothing, outdoor activities, types of agriculture, and the types of houses people build.

The earth's surface is heated by energy from the sun. The fact that the earth's surface heats unevenly provides a convenient way to divide it into regions—temperature regions.

 ★ *geographer* A person who studies the earth's surface and how living and nonliving things interact with it

★ *region* An area of the earth's surface whose parts have one or more common characteristics

Temperature Regions

The region between 30°N latitude and 30°S latitude is called the tropical region. Millions of people around the globe live in the tropical region. For example, Rio de Janeiro, Brazil (about 23°S), and Lagos, Nigeria (about 6°N), are both in this region. Even though people in these and other low-latitude areas have cultures and languages that differ, they all have one thing in common—the temperatures in these places are warm all year.

Now take a look at places in polar, or high-latitude, regions. One polar region lies between 60°N and the North Pole. The other polar region is between 60°S and the South Pole.

People who live in polar regions have to deal with cold weather all year. For example, in Barrow, Alaska (about 71°N), and Murmansk, Russia (69°N), summers are very cool and winters are icy cold. Ice blocks the lakes and rivers for much of the year. In most of the polar regions, farming is almost impossible. At best, the growing season is very short.

Most people in the United States live in the middle latitudes. The middle latitudes are found between the polar regions and the tropics. These parts of the world are known as temperate regions.

Usually, places in the temperate regions experience distinct seasons. Summers are warm or hot, and

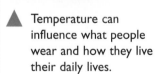

Temperature can influence what people wear and how they live their daily lives.

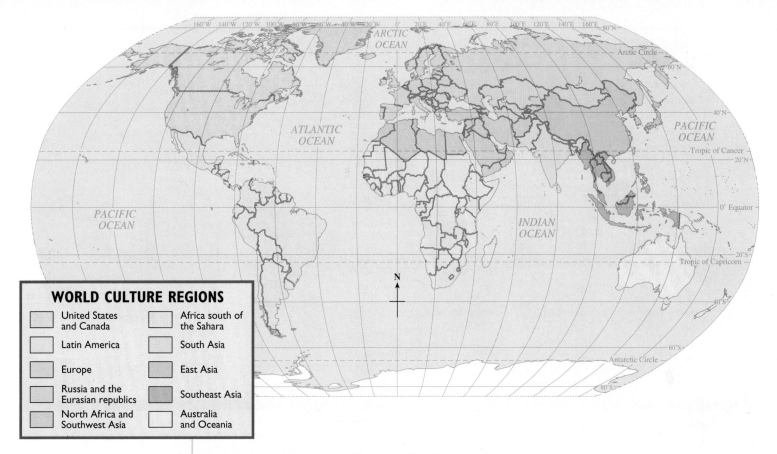

WORLD CULTURE REGIONS

- United States and Canada
- Latin America
- Europe
- Russia and the Eurasian republics
- North Africa and Southwest Asia
- Africa south of the Sahara
- South Asia
- East Asia
- Southeast Asia
- Australia and Oceania

winters are cool or cold. Generally, people's lifestyles, especially their outdoor activities, change from one season to the next.

People in the United States have much in common with people in other middle-latitude countries, such as Argentina. People there grow wheat and raise cattle, just as farmers in the United States do. People in the two countries wear similar clothing and live in similar houses. And they have to adjust to similar seasonal changes in weather.

Culture Regions

One of the most interesting ways to group people is by their culture. The map on this page shows the world divided into **culture regions**.

People living in each of these regions share a similar culture. Many things may unite a people into one culture. People may share a culture based on language, religion, or special customs or traditions.

Culture regions often cross the boundaries of nations and continents. The Latin American culture region, for example, includes all the many nations of South America. But Mexico, Central America, and the island nations of the Caribbean are also part of the Latin American culture region.

The map shows the continent of Africa divided into two culture regions. Most North Africans practice the religion of Islam. They are part of the Muslim culture region, which also includes much of the Middle East.

 culture region   The division of people based on a variety of factors, such as language, religion, or customs and traditions

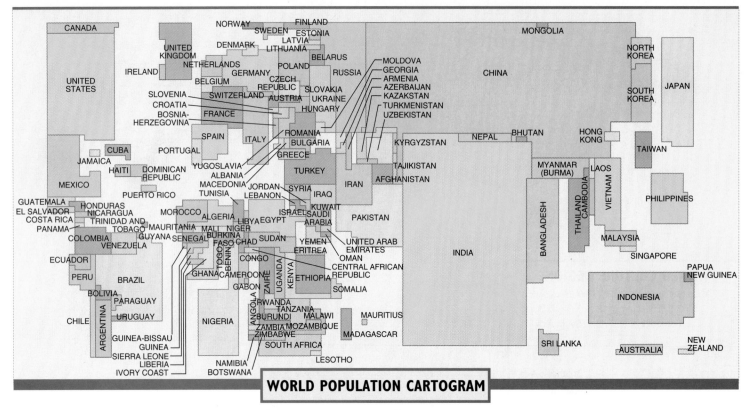

WORLD POPULATION CARTOGRAM

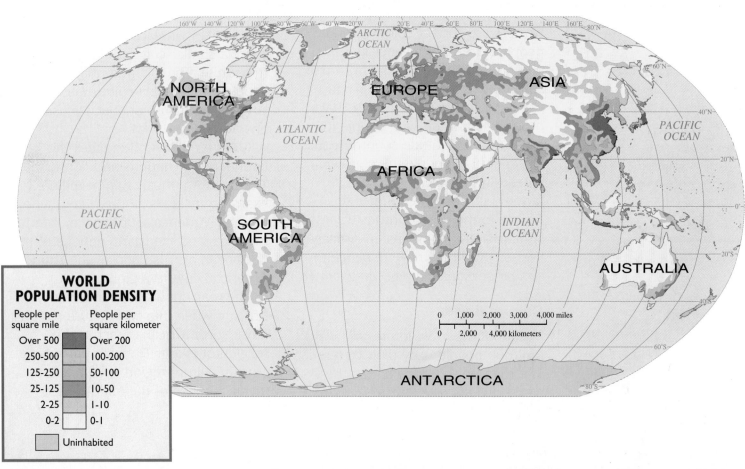

WORLD POPULATION DENSITY

People per square mile	People per square kilometer
Over 500	Over 200
250-500	100-200
125-250	50-100
25-125	10-50
2-25	1-10
0-2	0-1
Uninhabited	

POPULATION DENSITY OF THE CONTINENTS

Continent	Number of People	
	per sq mi	per sq km
Asia	275	106
Europe	82	32
Africa	58	22
North America	47	18
South America	46	18
Australia	6	2
Antarctica	Antarctica has no permanent population	

Africans south of the African desert have different histories, religions, languages, and traditions from those who live in North Africa.

Population—How Many People?

Perhaps the most familiar grouping method used by geographers is to divide the world into large land areas called continents. As the map on page 6 shows, there are seven continents. Except for Australia and Antarctica, the continents are divided into units called countries, or nations.

In order to study the cultures of different countries, it's important to know something about their populations. One way to show where the world's people live is to use a cartogram. The cartogram at the top of page 10 lets you compare the populations of the world's countries.

The size of each country on the cartogram shows how large its population is. For example, on a map that shows land area, Norway is about twice the size of Bangladesh. But on the cartogram, Bangladesh is much larger than Norway. This tells you that the population of Bangladesh is much larger than that of Norway.

Population Density—How Crowded?

Another factor that affects the way people live is population density. Countries with a high population density are crowded. They have a large number of people in relation to the amount of land.

The map on page 10 uses color to show the population density of each country. A cartogram of population density would show Bangladesh as one of the largest nations. It has a population density of about 2,500 people per square mile of land.

How can population density affect people? For one thing, people in very crowded countries often have difficulty making a living. For example, Bangladesh has an average yearly income of about $200 per person. France, with a population density of 275 people per square mile, has an average income of almost $22,000.

Throughout this book you will learn about changing relationships between population densities and cultures. For example, at times when the world was less crowded than today, having a high population density could be an advantage. Today this same condition can present many problems.

⭐ **cartogram** A map in which country size is based on some value other than land area

SHOW WHAT YOU KNOW!

REFOCUS
COMPREHENSION

1. How is the exact location of a place described?

2. What is the difference between a country's population and its population density?

THINK ABOUT IT
CRITICAL THINKING

Two places at the same latitude are likely to have similar climates. Explain why this is not necessarily true of two places at the same longitude.

WRITE ABOUT IT
ACTIVITY

Would you rather live in a place with a high population density or a low population density? Write a brief report explaining reasons for your choice.

PEOPLE AND NATURAL ENVIRONMENTS

FOCUS *The culture that develops in any region is strongly influenced by the environment, especially the climate and physical features of the region.*

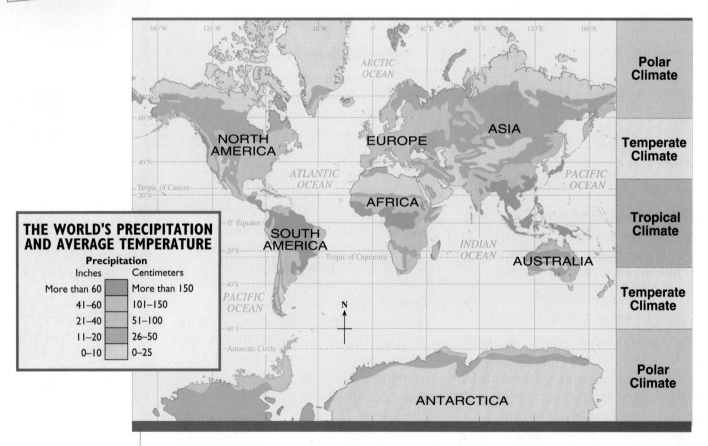

THE WORLD'S PRECIPITATION AND AVERAGE TEMPERATURE

Precipitation	
Inches	Centimeters
More than 60	More than 150
41–60	101–150
21–40	51–100
11–20	26–50
0–10	0–25

Polar Climate

Temperate Climate

Tropical Climate

Temperate Climate

Polar Climate

Climate Factors

Everyone is affected by climate. The ways people dress, the types of houses they live in, and the kinds of work they do all depend on the climate of the place where they live.

The two main factors that determine climate are temperature and **precipitation**. In the last lesson you learned that generally the farther a place is from the equator, the cooler its climate will be. Several other factors affect the amount of precipitation a place receives.

The world has many different kinds of climates. The map above shows world temperature and precipitation patterns. It can help you determine the climate of different places.

⭐ **precipitation** Water that falls from clouds in the form of rain, snow, sleet, or hail

Tropical Climates

Tropical climates are warm or hot year-round. Most tropical climates also have plenty of rainfall. Brazil, in South America; Zaire (zah IHR), in Africa; and Indonesia, in Southeast Asia, all have tropical climates. The heavy rains and heat make trees and other plants grow quickly, forming dense forests.

When trees in tropical climates are cut down, the soil is exposed to the heavy rainfall. This leads to soil erosion, making farming difficult. Farmers in such regions must find ways to protect the soil.

Temperate Climates

Middle-latitude, or temperate, climates range from warm to cool. The amount of precipitation varies. The southeastern part of the United States and much of Europe have cooler winters than tropical areas do. But the warm seasons are long enough for crops to grow. Summers may be warm enough to encourage people to use air conditioning.

Climates in the northern portion of the middle latitudes are somewhat colder. During the winter, snowfall can be heavy. Lakes and even rivers may freeze over. In most of Canada, Russia, and the northern United States, people must wear heavy clothing and heat their houses in the winter. Farmers can grow crops in these climates, but only during the warmest months.

Polar Climates

Very cold, dry climates are found in the polar regions. Snow and ice cover the land for most of the year. So farming is impossible.

People who live in cold climates have learned to adapt to the weather conditions. They fish or hunt for food, work indoors, and wear protective clothing.

Dry Climates

Dry climates are found at all latitudes. Deserts in Africa and the Middle East are very warm. But dry climates are also found in parts of the United States and central Asia, where temperatures are much cooler.

▲ These photographs show typical environments in tropical (*left*), dry (*center*), and polar climate regions (*right*).

erosion   The wearing away of rocks and soil by the action of water, wind, or moving ice

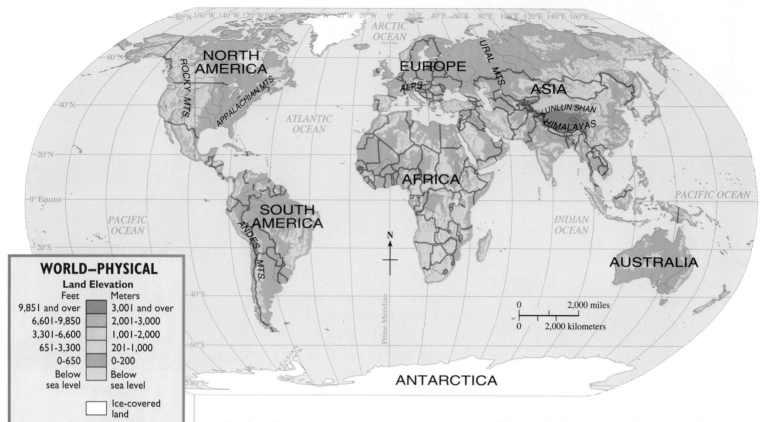

WORLD–PHYSICAL

Land Elevation

Feet		Meters
9,851 and over		3,001 and over
6,601-9,850		2,001-3,000
3,301-6,600		1,001-2,000
651-3,300		201-1,000
0-650		0-200
Below sea level		Below sea level
		Ice-covered land

▼ Physical features of the land include, from left to right, mountains, rivers, plains, and plateaus.

In dry climates, vegetation is sparse and consists mainly of grasses, shrubs, or cactuses. Farmers in dry climates can keep herds of sheep or goats. But to raise crops, farmers have to bring water to their fields through some method of irrigation. In such dry climate regions, everyone must be ready when the rainfall comes. They work together to collect and conserve the precious water.

Physical Features of the Land

Climate is only one of the natural factors that influence people's lives. The physical features of the land create both opportunities and problems for people everywhere.

The earth's physical features include mountains, rivers, valleys, plains, and **plateaus**. These features give each place a unique appearance.

Mountains, Rivers, and Valleys

All the continents have mountains, with high **elevations** and steeply sloped surfaces. People living in mountain regions have found ways to adapt. Long ago, Native Americans in the southwestern United States built villages in the sides of cliffs. In many Asian countries, farmers plant crops on terraces built on steep hillsides.

Mountain areas in the temperate and polar regions are sparsely populated. But in tropical regions, mountains are often the best places to be. The climate changes, becoming cooler and drier the higher you go.

Rivers and their valleys are valuable physical features. Rivers and large streams provide year-round sources of water. When rivers flood, they may cause great destruction. However, as the floodwaters recede, **sediment** is left behind and renews the soil.

Many of the world's earliest civilizations began in river valleys. Farmers along the Nile in Egypt and the Changjiang (CHAWNG jeeahng) in China grew enough food to support a larger population. Having a plentiful food supply meant that fewer people were needed on the farms. This freed people for other kinds of work.

Plains and Plateaus

Plains and plateaus are fairly flat landforms. Farming and construction are easier in these regions than in mountainous areas. Plains are usually at a low elevation. The North European Plain and the Great Plains of the United States are rich farming areas that provide food for millions.

Plateaus usually have a much higher elevation than plains. Some plateaus, such as the Colorado Plateau, are crossed by deep canyons or narrow gorges. Over many centuries, rivers gradually eroded the soil and cut these canyons into the land. This kind of rugged land may be sparsely populated, especially if it is in a dry climate region.

⭐ *plateau*   A large level area that is raised above the surrounding land
elevation   The height or distance above sea level

⭐ *sediment*   Any matter set down by wind or water, such as sand or soil

SHOW WHAT YOU KNOW!

REFOCUS
COMPREHENSION

1. What are the two major factors that determine the climate of a place?

2. How are plains and plateaus similar? How do they differ?

THINK ABOUT IT
CRITICAL THINKING

Compare the climates found near the top and bottom of a high mountain range near the equator.

WRITE ABOUT IT
ACTIVITY

Write a brief paragraph describing the type of climate you live in. Include a description of any seasonal changes that take place.

3

Map Adventure

KEY TERMS

human feature
curator

HOW PEOPLE USE THE EARTH

FOCUS *Land use changes over time as people interact with their surroundings. Communities form and grow, influenced by the physical features and natural resources around them.*

Adventure in Place and Time

You may never experience an earthquake or a volcanic eruption in your life, but you will witness changes in the land. You will even be a part of the changes! Every day, people interact with their surroundings, adapting their behavior to the environment and sometimes changing the environment to suit their needs. Travel through time to see the changes in this landscape.

Map Key

1 **Physical features** Uncut forests and hilly land along the riverbanks are physical features of this landscape. Another feature is the river flowing through the hills.

2 **Human features** Humans make their mark on the landscape by clearing trees for houses and fields. Another **human feature** here is the footbridge that spans the river.

3 **Agriculture** By growing crops and raising animals, humans can make one place their home. Slowly they begin to form communities.

4 **Location** The location of a community plays a large role in its survival. With rich soil and the river as a water source, farms can grow, crops can increase, and people can prosper.

⭐ ***human feature*** The evidence of human presence in an area

A   B   C

5 Resources The community continues to grow through careful use of its natural resources. Here, the river is used to power a mill. The river can also serve as transportation for people and goods to other communities and markets.

6 Development As a community grows, the use of the land changes. Homes and buildings cluster around a town center. Roads that were once dirt paths are widened and extended, and more bridges are built.

7 Population growth Attracted to the resources of the community, new businesses arrive and attract workers who settle in the community. New buildings spring up, and new roads and bridges are constructed.

8 Changing economy The river can now be used to help power a factory and take its goods to market. The land is used for housing and for shops to service the growing population.

9 Urban development The town grows into a city. The town's main street becomes a major highway that connects the city to outside areas. Skyscrapers help create a busy downtown area. More people work and live here. Tunnels are dug for the pipes that carry water, sewage, electric cables, and telephone lines.

10 Land use in the city Though the land is no longer farmed, the city creates open spaces for preservation and recreation. To save energy and reduce pollution, the city provides public transportation. Subway systems reduce crowding on city streets.

MAP IT

You are the **curator** *of the New City Museum. The museum is planning to install a three-dimensional map based on the one shown here. You have been asked to write a brochure that will explain what a viewer is looking at.*

Quickly scan the scenes A-F. Consider the following questions in writing a rough draft of your brochure, "New City—From Past to Present."

1. What physical feature do you see in the center of each scene?
2. How has this feature changed?
3. How did people first change the landscape?
4. How did the river help the community to grow?
5. How can economic growth and an increase in population affect land use in a community?

EXPLORE IT

Take a walk through your neighborhood. Make a list of the physical features and a list of the human features you see. Draw a picture and label the different features you find. Visit your local library to learn how your community's landscape has changed over time.

⭐ **curator** A person in charge of a museum

D   E   F

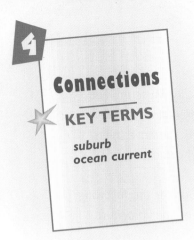

THE PERSONALITY OF PLACES

FOCUS *Places, like people, have certain features and characteristics that help identify them and give them the qualities that make them unique.*

Places Are Like People

In open countrysides, physical features give each landscape its special appearance. Cities are different. People give a city its special personality. In Latin American cities, for example, life centers around plazas, or open squares.

Plazas are often surrounded by important buildings, such as government offices, a cathedral, restaurants, and stores. Friends meet in the plaza to dine, see a movie, or go shopping. The plaza reflects the lively personality of the city.

Plazas Outside the City

Some older cities in the United States, such as New York City, Boston, Chicago, Philadelphia, and New Orleans, have centers similar to Latin American plazas. People still live in the downtown areas of these older cities. After the business offices close for the day or the weekend, people go downtown to theaters, restaurants, and dance clubs.

However, the downtown areas of many American cities, especially younger cities, are often deserted after the workday is over. The buildings

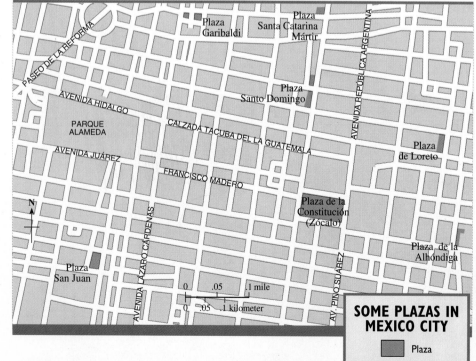

SOME PLAZAS IN MEXICO CITY

▨ Plaza

downtown are mostly offices and stores. People who work in the central city go home to the **suburbs**.

People who live in the suburbs spend much of their time with family and friends at home. They also watch sports events at stadiums or go to shopping malls.

Shopping malls in the United States are very much like the plazas of Latin American cities. Malls and suburbs have become part of the personality of the United States.

Buildings in Different Regions

The personality of a place also shows in the way buildings are

⭐ **suburb** A town, village, or other district on the outskirts of a city

designed and constructed. Naturally, people have used materials they found nearby for building. For example, in northern Europe, where forests are abundant, people have for centuries built their houses of wood.

In regions with hot, dry climates, mud and clay are used for building. The thick, sturdy earthen walls help to keep out the daytime heat and make the inside cool. Streets in such regions tend to be narrow to provide shade.

In wet, tropical regions, the most important function of a building is to keep people dry. Houses are built on wooden stilts, with roofs made of palm leaves to keep the rain out. Large open windows and doors let the air blow through and help keep the house cool.

People throughout the world have built their houses with a variety of materials, including stone, straw, and even ice. As you can see, you can tell a lot about a place simply by looking at the buildings.

▼ The buildings in a region reflect the kinds of materials available and the climate.

For centuries the Khyber Pass has provided a vital link between the Middle East and southern Asia.

Mountain Barrier Passes

The personality of a place or region reflects the exchange of information and ideas between people who live there and visitors from other regions. In the past, certain regions were isolated from the outside world. Physical features such as mountain ranges and oceans served as barriers, restricting the flow of people and ideas into and out of these regions.

In time, people's need to explore and develop trade routes led them to find ways through the mountains and across the oceans. For example, the Hindu Kush mountains stand between the Middle East and southern Asia. As the photograph above shows, travelers used a gap in this rugged mountain range to travel between between present-day Afghanistan and Pakistan. This gap, known as the Khyber (KEYE-bur) Pass, helped in the development of the personalities of these regions.

The traditions and crafts of distant cultures have been spread across a wide region of the Pacific Ocean.

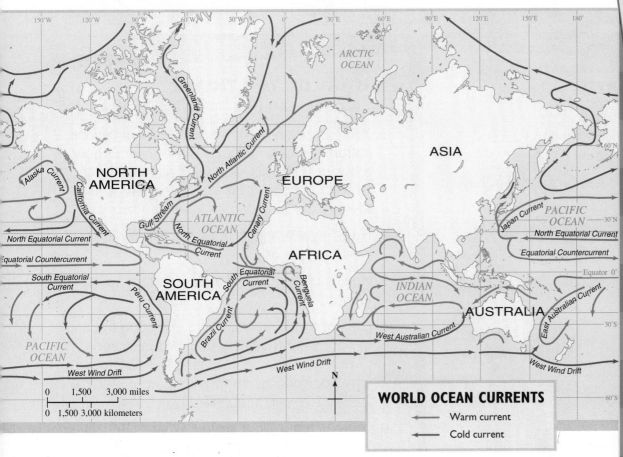

WORLD OCEAN CURRENTS

← Warm current

← Cold current

SHOW WHAT YOU
KNOW!

REFOCUS
COMPREHENSION

1. How do people help give the places they live personality?

2. What can the buildings in a region tell you about the region?

THINK ABOUT IT
CRITICAL THINKING

How might a change in climate bring about a change in the personality of a region?

WRITE ABOUT IT
ACTIVITY

In a brief paragraph, describe the personality of your town or neighborhood.

In North America, pioneers used the Cumberland Gap to cross the Appalachian Mountains. This pass became part of the Wilderness Road, which brought pioneers to settle new areas and helped regions west of the mountains to develop their own personalities.

Ocean Highways

Like mountain ranges, oceans present barriers to people's movement. But ancient sailors of Southeast Asia used **ocean currents** and winds to overcome these barriers. In small wooden boats, they navigated long distances across the Pacific Ocean.

Using these oceanic highways, people eventually traveled between places as far apart as Indonesia and Hawaii, carrying their cultures with them. As a result, people in this large oceanic culture region have similar traditions, foods, and languages.

The map above shows that ocean currents can be either warm or cold. As a result, these currents can influence the climates of coastal regions. For example, even though Norway has a cold climate in places, its west coast has mild winters. That's because the warm North Atlantic Current flows along its Atlantic coast. Cold currents have the opposite effect on other places, such as Chile.

⭐ **ocean current** A narrow band of fast-moving ocean water

SUMMING UP

1 DO YOU REMEMBER . . .
COMPREHENSION

1. What information do you need to express the exact location of a place on earth?

2. What can you say about two places that have the same latitude?

3. Name two ways geographers group people.

4. How does climate affect the way people live?

5. Describe four climate regions.

6. What are the major physical features of the earth's surface?

7. If you lived in a tropical region, why might you want to live in the mountains?

8. How can a growing economy cause changes in the environment?

9. How are many Latin American cities and some older cities in the United States similar? In the United States, how do older cities differ from many younger cities?

10. What two natural barriers have hindered people's movement from region to region?

2 SKILL POWER
READING POPULATION DENSITY MAPS

In this chapter you have learned how to find information on population density maps. Choose a region in the world that interests you and find population density maps of that region in a textbook, encyclopedia, or atlas. Also find out about the region's geography. Make a chart that shows how the geography of the region may have affected its population density.

3 WHAT DO YOU THINK?
CRITICAL THINKING

1. Your community may be made up of several culture regions, including your neighborhood, a business district, and your school district. Describe one of these culture regions and identify the factors that define it.

2. How might a high population density affect the environment of a region?

3. How is the climate of a place related to its latitude?

4. Look at the world map, the climate map, and the population density map. What regions have the fewest people living there? Explain why populations are so low in these regions.

5. If you were designing a building to be constructed in your region, what materials would you plan to use? Explain.

4 SAY IT, WRITE IT, USE IT
VOCABULARY

You have been chosen to give a short talk to third graders about the world's lands and people. Use as many vocabulary terms as you can to write what you will tell them.

cartogram	ocean current
culture region	precipitation
curator	plateau
elevation	region
erosion	sediment
geographer	suburb
human feature	

5 GEOGRAPHY AND YOU
MAP STUDY

1. What is the range of population density in North America?

2. Which country on the continent is least densely populated?

3. Is the United States or Mexico more densely populated?

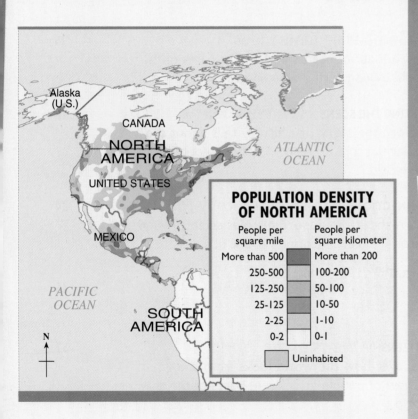

POPULATION DENSITY
OF NORTH AMERICA

People per square mile	People per square kilometer
More than 500	More than 200
250-500	100-200
125-250	50-100
25-125	10-50
2-25	1-10
0-2	0-1
Uninhabited	

6 TAKE ACTION
CITIZENSHIP

You have learned that people can change their environment. Think about the environment around your school. There are probably some changes that would make it better. With a group of friends, think of a project, such as a recycling program or a mural, to improve your school's environment. Present your plan to your teachers and the principal. See if you can bring your project to life!

7 GET CREATIVE
SCIENCE CONNECTION

People can make changes in the land, and so can nature. Find out more about some of the natural forces that affect the land—winds, rain, snow, volcanoes, earthquakes, or glaciers. Make a poster that identifies a force of nature and describes how it can change the environment. Be sure to include captions that explain your drawings. Present your poster to the class.

LOOKING AHEAD
To understand the culture of a group, it is important to know about its past.

What Is History?

History can tell us many things. It can teach us how people developed similar or different ways of thinking and living. Sometimes it can help us learn from the past mistakes of others. Read this chapter to learn about history and the people who study it.

▼ This boy is holding a fossil. Read page 35 to find out how fossils help us learn about the past.

CONTENTS

You can learn more about history and the people who lived it from these books. Read one that interests you and fill out a book-review form.

READ AND RESEARCH

Digging to the Past by W. John Hackwell
(Simon & Schuster Books for Young Readers, 1986)
Digging into the past is not always a simple process. Learn about the men and women who participate in archaeological digs and the work they do to recover delicate artifacts. *(nonfiction)*
• *You can read a selection from this book on page 36.*

Circling the Globe edited by Sue Grabham
(Kingfisher, 1995)
You will find history, geography, and culture described in this concise encyclopedia and atlas. The detailed maps, photographs, and charts will introduce you to many people and places around the world. *(reference)*

Great Lives: Human Culture by David Weitzman
(Simon & Schuster Books for Young Readers, 1994)
Archaeologists and anthropologists search for answers to questions about how people live: their beliefs, customs, dwellings, and art. Read biographical sketches of men and women who have dedicated their lives to this study. *(biography)*

Skill Power Comparing Time Lines

Knowing how to read and compare time lines helps you understand what was going on at different times in history.

UNDERSTAND IT

Do you ever wonder what it would be like to have a time machine? You could go back into history or forward into the future. Think about a time machine that is like a railroad track with a train that stops at stations along the way. You can get off and explore the time at each stop. To go to different places, you can change trains. What time and place would you choose? Would you like to see what your parents were like at your age? Or would you like to see what you will be doing in the year 2025?

EXPLORE IT

Historians don't have time machines, but they do use time lines to show when events took place. A time line is a simplification of historical events. It has a scale like a map, but it shows time instead of distance. Each section of the time line below shows 200 years. A line divides the years B.C. from the years A.D. The abbreviation *ca.* stands for *circa*, which means "about." The break in the time line shows where a period of time has been left out. Events in China are shown on the top, and events in the rest of the world are shown on the bottom.

Use the time line to answer these questions.

- In what year does the time line begin? When does it end?
- Did all free men in Rome have citizenship when paper was invented in China?
- Could the Treaty of Verdun have been printed? Why?
- How many years after Kublai Khan's conquest of China was Tenochtitlán founded?

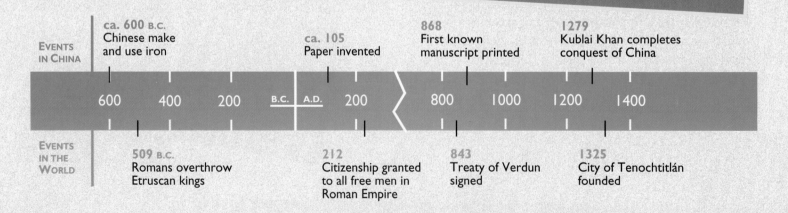

EVENTS IN CHINA

ca. 600 B.C.
Chinese make and use iron

ca. 105
Paper invented

868
First known manuscript printed

1279
Kublai Khan completes conquest of China

600   400   200   B.C. | A.D.   200   800   1000   1200   1400

EVENTS IN THE WORLD

509 B.C.
Romans overthrow Etruscan kings

212
Citizenship granted to all free men in Roman Empire

843
Treaty of Verdun signed

1325
City of Tenochtitlán founded

TRY IT

Make a picture time line of your own life. Begin by making notes about events you remember. Try to collect artifacts of your life, such as photographs, ticket stubs, invitations, letters, or drawings. Decide on the scale for your time line. Then make your time line, describing the events and displaying your artifacts.

If you prefer, select a person, time, or place in history and make a time line on that subject.

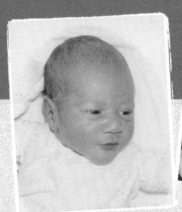

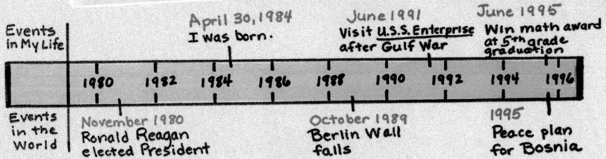

Events in My Life

April 30, 1984
I was born.

June 1991
Visit U.S.S. Enterprise after Gulf War

June 1995
Win math award at 5th grade graduation

1980   1982   1984   1986   1988   1990   1992   1994   1996

Events in the World

November 1980
Ronald Reagan elected President

October 1989
Berlin Wall falls

1995
Peace plan for Bosnia

SKILL POWER SEARCH *You will be comparing time lines throughout this book.*

27

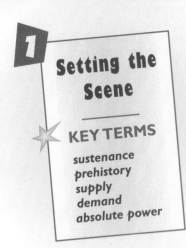

⭐ **KEY TERMS**

sustenance
prehistory
supply
demand
absolute power

HOW WE LOOK AT HISTORY

FOCUS *History is the record of human experience. It reflects the economic, political, social, and religious differences among people.*

How People Are Alike

No two people are exactly alike. Each person has his or her own special qualities. Each has his or her own set of memories, beliefs, ideas, and dreams.

On the other hand, no two people are completely different. We all share certain needs and wants. Some of these needs and wants are physical. Everyone needs food, shelter, and clothing. People everywhere must learn to adapt—or adapt to—their physical environment. It doesn't matter whether the environment is dry or wet, frozen or tropical, wooded or grassy. People everywhere must find **sustenance** from the earth.

Social History

Some needs and wants are social. For example, all people share the need for companionship. They need families and friends—people they can work, play, and raise children with. All through history, people have established communities and traditions that help

group members learn how to behave and help them understand the difference between right and wrong.

Some needs and wants are spiritual. A large number of the people of the world want to be connected with a set of religious beliefs or a spiritual tradition. They take comfort from sharing their beliefs with others in their communities.

Most people also feel a creative impulse that they express in writing, painting, music, or other art forms. All over the world, art galleries, musical performances, and libraries are evidence of the creativity of people.

▼ This family of Turkish farmers shares the same needs for food, shelter, and friends as other people around the world.

⭐ **sustenance** That which sustains life; food or nourishment

Different groups of people find different ways to meet their needs and wants. They build different kinds of houses, wear different types of clothes, make up different definitions of family, and create different works of art. But the underlying needs and wants are shared by everyone. Learning about the ways people meet their needs and wants is what makes the study of history so fascinating.

Oral History Keeps Ideas Alive

There is little doubt that early people passed family beliefs from one generation to another by telling stories. We call this storytelling *oral history* because older members of families told younger members about their memories by talking about events in the past. It is possible that some of our favorite legends began as stories thousands of years ago, but we have no written proof that this is so.

If we say that history began with writing, then history is only about 6,000 years old. That is when the Sumerians in Mesopotamia began keeping records, using symbols on clay tablets. The first full alphabet was developed about 3,500 years ago.

Life before the time when writing began is called **prehistory**. We don't have written evidence of how people lived then. We must piece together their stories from artifacts they left behind—their cave art, tools, weapons, pots, and other bits of evidence.

▲ This Native American painting shows a story-teller passing down family traditions to children.

Economic History

One way to look at history is through the study of economics. Economic history traces such things as the development of trade. Trade began because individuals or communities could not meet all their needs and wants by themselves. It made sense for those with an abundance of goods to trade for the things they lacked. Trading grew because it helped those who engaged in it to thrive.

 prehistory The history before recorded history, as learned from archaeology and other areas of study

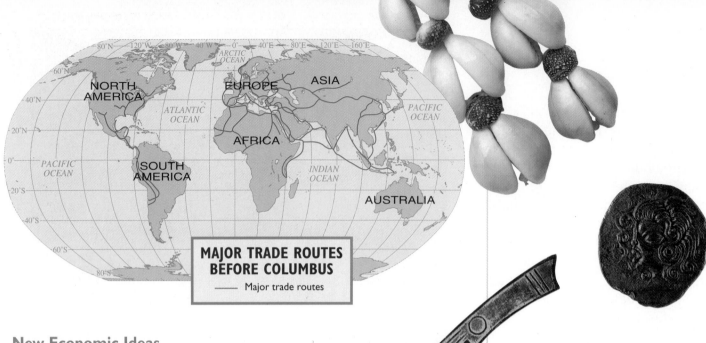

MAJOR TRADE ROUTES
BEFORE COLUMBUS
—— Major trade routes

New Economic Ideas

You can see early trade routes on the map. As trade grew, certain economic ideas emerged. One was an idea that is called the law of **supply** and **demand**. This idea explains why prices vary. If the supply of goods is high and the demand for them is low, the price tends to be low. If the supply goes down and the demand goes up, the price tends to get higher. Successful suppliers are able to provide goods to people who want them at a price people want to pay. Over the years, the law of supply and demand made some people and some nations very wealthy, while others remained poor.

As trade grew, the world became more complicated. Trade between neighbors grew into trade between nations. Governments sometimes played a direct role in encouraging trade. In other cases, governments took over control of foreign trade. In other cases, governments played only a limited role in controlling trade.

---

supply   The amount of goods available for purchase at a given price
demand   The amount of goods people are ready and able to buy at a certain price

▼ Many things—from shells to coins to stone disks—have been used as money.

Historians sometimes explain the fate of societies by examining how their economies were organized. When traders were able to meet the demands of buyers, economies tended to be successful.

Trade Becomes Complex

By the twentieth century, trade had become extremely complex. Nations needed the goods of other nations more than ever before. For better or for worse, expanding trade helped tie the peoples of the world together. Good or bad economic news for one nation often spelled bad or good economic news for other nations.

The growth of world trade means that a teenager in Dallas who buys a sweater may be participating in a global economy. The wool may be from sheep raised in New Zealand, the buttons may be from Africa, and the sweater may have been knit in Taiwan.

All national economic systems have some things in common. For example, they all use money, and they all have some degree of government control or regulation. Still, no two economic systems are identical. The United States economy, for example, is similar—but not identical—to the Canadian economy.

The peoples of every nation must decide which form of economy best meets their needs and wants. Every nation has its own economic system and its own economic history.

Political History

Every society also has its own political history. This form of history tells us how governments were organized and how they changed over time. Throughout the course of history, many different forms of government have been tried.

Early civilizations were often governed by a council of elders. Elders were leaders, usually men, who were considered the wisest people in the community. They made the rules by which the community lived.

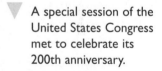
A painting by Anton Alexander Werner shows the opening of the German legislature in the Berlin Palace.

A special session of the United States Congress met to celebrate its 200th anniversary.

A painting of an important battle

some voice in choosing their leaders. Again, these systems had many things in common. Yet each one was unique in some way because each arose from a particular set of historical circumstances or beliefs.

Military History

Conflict has been a constant in history. People, it seems, have always been able to find a reason to fight. The reasons could be economic, political, religious, territorial, or simply for greater glory.

As soon as people started living in groups, there most likely were disagreements. They could have been as simple as two angry people bumping into each other or as complex as one group fighting another over the rights to hunt and survive in an area.

As empires grew, possibilities for disagreements grew as well. Increasing numbers of people gave empires the ability to build large armies. Increasing economic success allowed them to pay for arms and ammunition. The consequences of war became more serious. Military history changed as weapons changed. People went from fighting with clubs and spears to guns and

One Supreme Ruler

As civilizations became more complex, some cultures chose one supreme ruler. That ruler, who often held **absolute power**, might have been called emperor or czar (zahr) or queen or king. It was often believed that such a ruler received his or her power directly from a superhuman source. In China, that belief was called the Mandate of Heaven. In Europe, it was referred to as the divine right of kings. In any case the people had no say in selecting who would rule them.

As political history shows, these systems of absolute power usually failed. They were often replaced by political systems that gave the people a voice in choosing their own leaders. By the end of the twentieth century, most nations allowed people at least

A Japanese helmet inlaid with gold and silver

A jeweled sword ▶

⭐ **absolute power** The power of a ruler that is not limited by a constitution, parliament, or other similar form of government

cannons to missiles and atomic bombs. This change in weapons altered military history. When fighting was done hand to hand, the advantage usually went to the side with the most fighters. But when armies began to use planes and submarines, the balance of power shifted to industrialized nations, which had moved from agricultural economies to manufacturing.

Cultural Expression

The study of history involves more than studying economic, political, and military trends. It requires insights into people's hopes, dreams, and fears.

One way to gain such insights is to study the artistic creations of

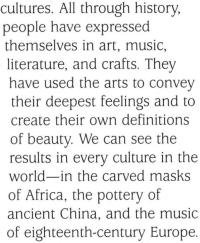

cultures. All through history, people have expressed themselves in art, music, literature, and crafts. They have used the arts to convey their deepest feelings and to create their own definitions of beauty. We can see the results in every culture in the world—in the carved masks of Africa, the pottery of ancient China, and the music of eighteenth-century Europe.

Artistic expression has sometimes been inspired by a love of God or a supreme being. Some of the greatest books in history, such as the Bible and the Qur'an (koo RAHN), describe how people relate to God. The religious impulse has also produced some of history's finest art and music.

We can learn much about ourselves by studying the past. History teaches us that we can use what we have in common to understand one another and ourselves.

◀ *Left,* fashions of 1836 in London; *above,* a Sumerian goddess; *above right,* a scene from a chest found in an Egyptian tomb

SHOW WHAT YOU KNOW!

REFOCUS
COMPREHENSION

1. What are three needs that all people share?

2. Explain the law of supply and demand.

THINK ABOUT IT
CRITICAL THINKING

Why might people have been reluctant to disagree with a ruler they believed to rule by the divine right of kings or the Mandate of Heaven?

WRITE ABOUT IT
ACTIVITY

Find an artistic piece you like—a painting, a poem, a musical piece, or another expression of creativity. Write a few paragraphs telling why you like it.

Connections

KEY TERMS
archaeologist
anthropologist
paleontologist
geologist

LITERATURE
Digging to the Past

PEOPLE WHO STUDY THE PAST

FOCUS *Our knowledge of history depends upon the work of many people who make their living by studying the people, places, and things of the past.*

People Who Dig Into the Past

Through their work, **archaeologists** (ahr kee AHL uh jihsts) teach us about prehistory and ancient history. Much of the time, they have few, if any, written records to guide them. Archaeologists must rely on fragments of evidence, which they uncover by exploring sites of ancient cities or villages. These fragments include such wide-ranging items as tools, seeds, coins, bones, household utensils, and building materials.

In the past 50 years, technology has come to the aid of archaeologists. One problem that archaeologists have faced has been dating the artifacts, or objects made by human work, they find. That problem was solved in 1947 by the development of carbon dating. Because the carbon in organic matter decreases over time, the age of something can be determined by measuring the amount of carbon that remains in it. Other recent technological advances allow archaeologists to see images of the interiors of artifacts without cutting into them.

People Who Study Customs

For many years, archaeologists were primarily concerned with the recovery and preservation of artifacts. However, in recent years, **anthropologists** have begun to influence the way in which archaeologists work. The interests that anthropologists have in the customs and relationships among people are important in reconstructing history. Anthropologists have encouraged archaeologists to look for clues to the behaviors of ancient people.

⭐ *archaeologist* A person who studies the life and culture of the past, especially ancient peoples

⭐ *anthropologist* A person who studies humans, especially the physical and cultural characteristics, customs, and social relationships

▼ Archaeologist Howard Carter recovered fabulous artifacts from the tomb of Tutankhamen in Egypt.

Photography by Egyptian Expedition, The Metropolitan Museum of Art.

People Who Study Fossils

Paleontologists help us understand what life was like in prehistoric times. They do that by studying fossils, or hardened remains, of plants, animals, and humans. These fossils are found under layers of earth and rock that have helped preserve them. Fossils can show how large the earliest humans were, what they ate, what tools they used, and how they lived.

People Who Examine Rocks

Geologists add to our understanding of the past by studying clues in the earth itself. Geologists examine the size, shape, and age of land formations. They gather information about how layers of soil and rock have changed.

From their studies, geologists can provide valuable information about past civilizations. They can describe the climate of previous eras and can detail natural disasters that may have struck early people. These include ice ages, floods, earthquakes, and eruptions of volcanoes.

People Who Look Backward

The main task of historians is to search for the story of human history.

They constantly use what they know now to help them understand people and events of the past. To do this, they often collect information from other sciences, such as the ones mentioned in this lesson. They organize vast amounts of information about the past in ways that we can understand. Their work gives us a window through which we can look at the contributions of people who lived before us.

Above, Reconstructed remains from Jericho, which is believed to be the oldest city in the world; *left,* an artifact from Jericho

Louis Leakey, a British anthropologist, searches for clues at an archaeological site.

paleontologist A person who studies the life forms of the past, especially prehistoric life forms, using animal and plant fossils

geologist A person who studies the earth's crust and the way in which its layers were formed

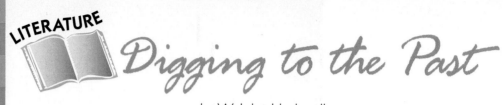

LITERATURE

Digging to the Past

by W. John Hackwell

You might be surprised to know that not all great archaeological finds are made by trained archaeologists. Read about a discovery made by a child.

W. JOHN HACKWELL

DIGGING TO THE PAST

EXCAVATIONS IN ANCIENT LANDS

Just a few years ago, a shepherd boy named Muhammad Adh-Dhib tossed a stone into a remote cave beside the Dead Sea. He heard a sound like pots smashing to pieces. When he climbed in to investigate, he discovered jars and jars of scrolls—now known as the famous Dead Sea Scrolls, regarded by many scholars and historians as the single most important discovery of modern times.

Archaeologists today do not dig in the remains of ancient settlements simply in the hope of discovering treasures such as cult objects, beautiful pottery, or even rare scrolls, important as these finds are. Anthropologists have influenced archaeologists to become concerned with a much wider ancient environment.

Read more about archaeology by checking this book out of your school or public library.

SHOW WHAT YOU KNOW!

REFOCUS
COMPREHENSION

1. Explain the work of archaeologists, anthropologists, paleontologists, geologists, and historians.

2. How is the work of archaeologists and geologists alike and different?

THINK ABOUT IT
CRITICAL THINKING

Using what you know and what you have read in this lesson, explain how anthropologists might influence archaeologists to "become concerned with a much wider ancient environment."

WRITE ABOUT IT
ACTIVITY

Think about a place you would like to know more about. Choose one of the professions in this lesson. Tell how a person in that profession might be able to help you find information you need.

Citizenship

⎯

★ **KEY TERM**

centrism

VIEWS OF THE WORLD

FOCUS *People have different cultures, religions, and political ideals. They inhabit different parts of the earth. These differences tend to influence people's points of view.*

Different Viewpoints

If you look at any serious problem in the world, the chances are good that people will have several points of view about it. Suppose a war breaks out between two countries. Right away, you can see two strong points of view—otherwise, why would there be fighting?

These differences in opinion do not just occur without a reason. They arise from the different economic, political, social, and religious outlooks that people in a country have. In each nation a variety of factors combine to produce a distinct point of view. What happened to people in these countries in the past—from the way they were taught the difference between right

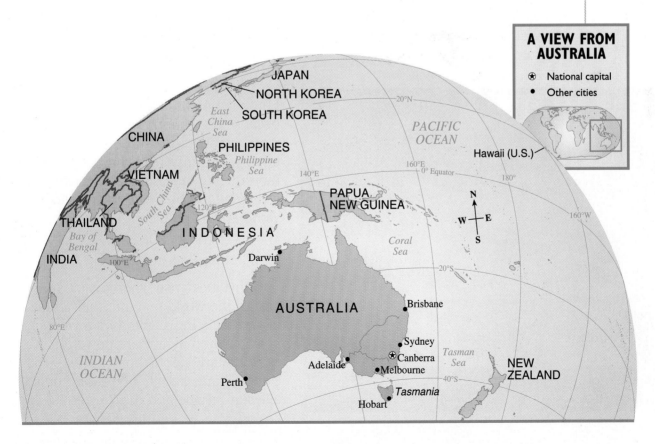

A VIEW FROM AUSTRALIA

⊛ National capital

• Other cities

37

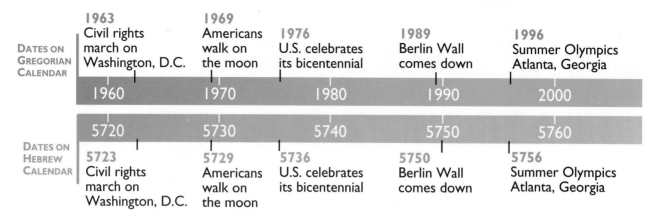

DATES ON GREGORIAN CALENDAR	**1963** Civil rights march on Washington, D.C.	**1969** Americans walk on the moon	**1976** U.S. celebrates its bicentennial	**1989** Berlin Wall comes down	**1996** Summer Olympics Atlanta, Georgia
	1960	1970	1980	1990	2000
	5720	5730	5740	5750	5760
DATES ON HEBREW CALENDAR	**5723** Civil rights march on Washington, D.C.	**5729** Americans walk on the moon	**5736** U.S. celebrates its bicentennial	**5750** Berlin Wall comes down	**5756** Summer Olympics Atlanta, Georgia

▲ This time line shows the same events dated according to two calendars. The Gregorian calendar (*top*) is in general use today.

▼ In 1582, Pope Gregory XIII called scholars together to create a new calendar for the Christian world.

and wrong to the kinds of governments they lived with—affects the way they think. Citizens of a country are influenced by what happened there.

A Central Viewpoint

The idea that the world centers around "us" is called **centrism**. Sometimes the "us" is a country. Or it may be an entire continent. Much of the world in the last century has been dominated by a Eurocentric, or Western, point of view, which has

grown out of the history and culture of Europe and its former colonies.

By looking at Australia, we can think about centrism. What does the world look like from "down under"? Well, to start with, Australians don't think of themselves as down under. That expression comes from Europeans who see Australia as a place that is on the other side of the world. Look at the map on page 37 to see how parts of the world look if Australia, rather than Europe or the United States, is at the center of a map.

To some extent, Australia shares a European point of view. That is because the country was settled largely by Europeans. But, in many other ways, Australians have developed their own unique perspective. That greatly affects how Australians view the world and its problems.

Conflicting Points of View

Difficulties arise when people in one part of the world feel that their point of view is being slighted by a viewpoint favored by a more powerful region. Many people in the West—the United States and its non-Communist allies in Europe and the Western

---

★ **centrism** A way of looking at the world from the point of view of one's own country or region

Hemisphere—think that their ideas should be shared by people everywhere. But in many parts of the world, ideas about democracy, the role of women, and even the calendar do not follow Western ideas. It is sometimes hard for Westerners to realize that not everyone wants what they want.

The Gregorian Calendar

In the West, we measure time using the Gregorian calendar, which was developed to replace an inaccurate old Roman calendar. The abbreviations A.D. (*anno Domini*, or "the year of our Lord") and B.C. ("before Christ"), used in dates, imply that the birth of Christ was a central point in history. But a Buddhist or a Jew would not consider the birth of Christ to be so important.

In fact, there are other calendars in use in the world today. The Chinese calendar begins counting in 2698 B.C. on the Gregorian calendar. The Islamic calendar begins with the date when Muhammad traveled from Mecca to Medina (622 on the Gregorian calendar). The Hebrew calendar begins in 3760 B.C. You can compare dates on the Hebrew and Gregorian calendars by looking at the time line on page 38.

Martin Behaim's "earthapple," the oldest globe in existence, was completed in 1492.

In spite of the existence of all these other calendars, the Gregorian calendar is used around the world for keeping track of time. To avoid ties to one specific religion or culture, many scholars and non-Christians now prefer to use the abbreviation *C.E.* ("common era") to replace *A.D.*, and *B.C.E.* ("before the common era") to replace *B.C.*

Centrist Labels

The way people in the West label regions also shows their centrist views. For example, *Middle East* is a Western term for the area at the eastern end of the Mediterranean Sea. The term only makes sense to someone who is in the West looking east. A less centrist name for the area would be *Southwest Asia.*

Centrism will always exist to some degree. Different people will never view the world in exactly the same way. Yet, in order to live in peace, we must remember that our point of view is not the only one. If we can look at problems from other points of view, we will be better able to see the universal human truths that bind all people together. Differences in ways of looking at things color much of what happens in the world.

SHOW WHAT YOU KNOW!

REFOCUS
COMPREHENSION

1. What does it mean to be Eurocentric?

2. How does the world look different when a map has Australia at its center?

THINK ABOUT IT
CRITICAL THINKING

Use what you know from your own experience to explain the advantages and disadvantages of centrism.

WRITE ABOUT IT
ACTIVITY

Work with a partner to make up a calendar that is based upon events that are important to you.

Spotlight

KEY TERMS

Stone Age
nomad
long house

BEFORE WRITTEN HISTORY

FOCUS *Prehistoric peoples struggled to meet their basic physical needs. Yet, in time, they improved their lives through farming and the creative arts.*

Nomads Become Farmers

The period of prehistory is often called the **Stone Age** because artifacts found from this period are simple tools made of stone. During most of the Stone Age, people were **nomads**. They traveled from place to place, gathering berries, roots, and nuts for food. They also followed herds of animals that they hunted for meat and hides. When food in an area was gone, nomads moved to another area.

Some nomads learned to domesticate, or tame, animals, raise them, and move them in herds. This new way of living was called pastoral migration. People still moved to find food for themselves and pastures for their animals.

Near the end of the Stone Age, people began to settle down. They learned how to plant crops. This change took place over thousands of years in different parts of the world. By the end of the Stone Age, many nomads were farmers.

⭐ **Stone Age** An early period in the history of human beings when stone tools and weapons were used

nomad A person who keeps moving around, looking for food or pasture for his or her animals

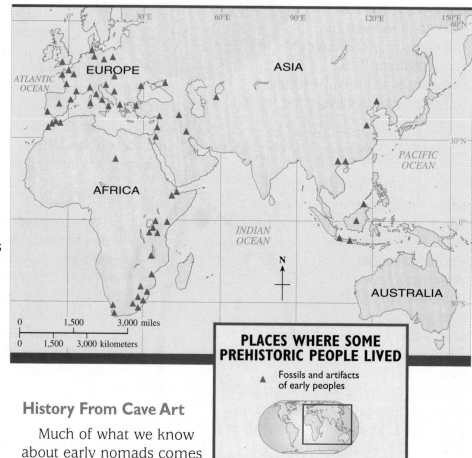

PLACES WHERE SOME PREHISTORIC PEOPLE LIVED

▲ Fossils and artifacts of early peoples

History From Cave Art

Much of what we know about early nomads comes from cave paintings. Near the end of the Stone Age, people drew animals, such as bison or woolly mammoths, on cave walls.

These prehistoric artists used animal hair as paintbrushes. They mixed animal fat with minerals to make paint. They also used sharp flint blades to engrave animal images on hard limestone walls.

▲ Much of what we know about early peoples comes from cave paintings, such as these in Spain.

As time passed, cave art became more sophisticated. Stone Age artists began drawing wild horses, deer, and even sea animals such as penguins. Cave artists also learned to use the natural contours of the stone to create drawings that appeared to be three-dimensional. The map on page 40 shows where important artifacts of Stone Age people have been found.

How Stone Age People Lived

Life was not easy for prehistoric people. They spent huge amounts of time meeting the most basic need—the need for food. Still, prehistoric people found time for other activities. They adorned their bodies with jewelry and developed customs that reflected their religious beliefs. From time to time, they also organized large celebrations in which many people came together to eat, dance, or pray.

Not surprisingly, the specific activities of Stone Age people varied from place to place. Different groups found different ways to meet their needs and wants.

In the Pacific Northwest of North America, for example, the Nootka and Kwakiutl (kwah kee OOT ul) people built **long houses**. In Siberia, on the other hand, people dug homes into the ground. As time passed, Stone Age people found different ways to feed, clothe, and shelter themselves. They also found that they needed to work together with other groups of people to get the most out of life.

▲ This brass and clay pigeon, which dates from 2000 B.C., was found in Hungary.

★ **long house**   A shelter for several families built by some Native American groups

SHOW WHAT YOU
KNOW!

REFOCUS
COMPREHENSION

1. What makes nomads different from other peoples?

2. How have cave paintings helped us learn about people who lived long ago?

THINK ABOUT IT
CRITICAL THINKING

Divide a sheet of paper into two columns. Label the first column *Nomad* and the second column *Farmer*. Under each column heading, write three to five things that tell what you think life would be like for that person.

WRITE ABOUT IT
ACTIVITY

Draw one or more pictures, without words, that would show people in the year 3000 how you live today. On a separate sheet of paper, write a paragraph or two describing your picture.

41

SUMMING UP

1 DO YOU REMEMBER...
COMPREHENSION

1. What is oral history?

2. How do we learn about people who lived in the Stone Age?

3. What are some common reasons for conflict between individuals and between groups?

4. How has science helped archaeologists date artifacts?

5. How have anthropologists influenced the work of archaeologists?

6. What types of information about early life can paleontologists get from fossils?

7. Why is it important to look at problems from more than one point of view?

8. How does the term *down under*, describing Australia, show Eurocentrism?

9. As the Stone Age neared its end, how did many people's way of life begin to change?

10. What tools and materials did prehistoric artists use to create cave paintings?

2 SKILL POWER
COMPARING TIME LINES

Using the time line on page 38, write at least five questions for a classmate to answer. Your questions should require that your classmate use both sides of the time line. Exchange questions with your classmate.

3 WHAT DO YOU THINK?
CRITICAL THINKING

1. Why did so many systems of absolute power fail throughout history?

2. Which gives the most insight into a people's history—economics, politics, military trends, or artistic creation? Give reasons for your choice.

3. Think about the work of archaeologists, anthropologists, paleontologists, and geologists. Which scientist would be able to supply the most information that a historian could use to write about the past? Explain your thinking.

4. Assume that you live in Asia. How might you feel about Eurocentrism in things such as the Gregorian calendar, world maps centered on the West, and ideas of democracy?

5. How would a nomad benefit from changing to a farming way of life?

4 SAY IT, WRITE IT, USE IT
VOCABULARY

Suppose you are part of a scientific team that has discovered a group of people living in Stone Age conditions on a Pacific island. Describe what you and the other scientists in your group might be able to learn about human history in this situation. Use as many of the vocabulary terms as possible.

absolute power	nomad
anthropologist	paleontologist
archaeologist	prehistory
centrism	Stone Age
demand	supply
geologist	sustenance
long house	

5 GEOGRAPHY AND YOU
MAP STUDY

Look at the map of major trade routes on page 30. Then think about your own trade routes. Is there a mall, a shopping center, or a large department store where you and your family like to shop? Make a map that shows how to get there from where you live. Assume that whoever reads your map doesn't know the area very well. Be sure that you show your trade route clearly.

6 TAKE ACTION
CITIZENSHIP

List some conflicts that have taken place in the world between our nation and other countries recently. Use news articles to determine the point of view of each side in the conflict. List the different economic, political, social, or religious outlooks that might have contributed to these points of view. Then, with a partner, take turns, arguing each point of view.

7 GET CREATIVE
LANGUAGE ARTS CONNECTION

Long before the development of writing, people used oral history, or storytelling, to pass down their memories and beliefs. Have a class oral history festival in which you hand down some of the stories that you have heard from older adults in your family or community. Choose stories that reveal something interesting or important about the past. Practice the stories so that you can tell them in a clear and colorful way.

LOOKING AHEAD
The next chapter takes you to the beginnings of recorded history. Read it to learn about life in the Fertile Crescent.

Ancient TIMES

UNIT 2

Where Did It All Begin?

Travel back in time to discover great civilizations. Learn how many of the ideas that shape your life today began thousands of years ago.

CHAPTER 3

THE DAWN OF

Have you ever wondered where writing began? Or who had the idea that a wheel could be used to move things around? Or who first put a group of children together in a room to teach them something? In this chapter you'll learn the answers to these questions.

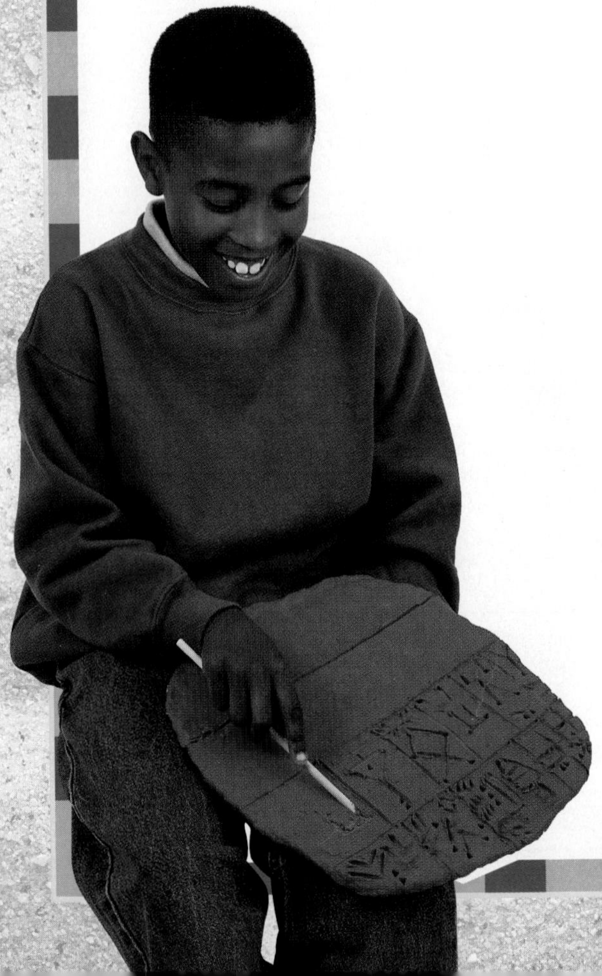

Read page 61 to find out what this boy is doing.

CONTENTS

CIVILIZATION

These books tell about some people, places, and events that make up the rich story of the Fertile Crescent. Read one that interests you and fill out a book-review form.

READ AND RESEARCH

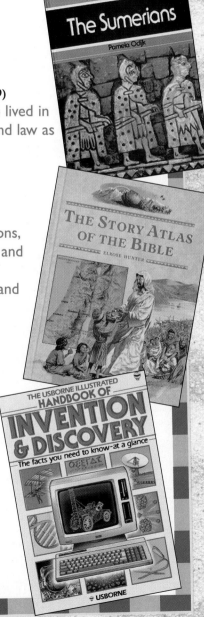

The Sumerians by **Pamela Odijk** (Silver Burdett Press, 1989)
Do you know about the lives of the Sumerians, the people who lived in the land of Mesopotamia? Find out about their land, language, and law as you read about this ancient civilization. (*nonfiction*)

The Story Atlas of the Bible by **Elrose Hunter**
(Silver Burdett Press, 1996)
Journey back in time over 4,000 years, using the maps, illustrations, and dramatic narrations in this book to learn about the people and places of biblical times. Follow Moses as he leads the Israelites from slavery out of Egypt, and witness the struggle to win the land of Canaan. (*nonfiction*)

**The Usborne Illustrated Handbook of Invention &
Discovery** by **Struan Reid** (EDC Publishing, 1987)
Learn more about the inventions and discoveries of the ancient peoples of the Fertile Crescent—writing, numbering systems, weighing instruments, and the oldest known map of the world. You'll also find interesting information about inventions and discoveries—from charcoal to satellites.
(*nonfiction*)

SKILL POWER

Reading Historical Maps

Knowing how to read historical maps helps you learn about the past.

UNDERSTAND IT

Suppose you found a map of your community from, say, 125 years ago. How different your town or city would look! You'd be able to pick out some familiar landmarks —roads, rivers, and buildings. But, in the place of the neighborhoods and business districts of today, the map probably would show forests or open fields. What's more, the old map would show some features— buildings, canals, and streets—that are no longer there.

Look at the map on this page. Which items shown on the map do you think are still there? Which have probably passed into history?

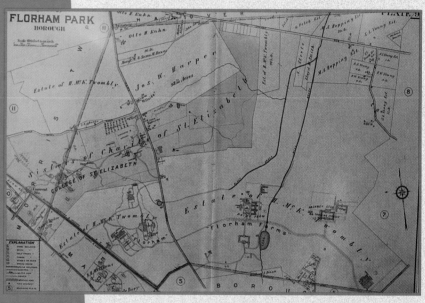

Old maps help us understand things as they were or as they happened in the past.

EXPLORE IT

The earliest known map of the world dates back to Babylonia, an empire you'll read about in this chapter. What could you learn from this map?

Like old maps, historical maps help us understand the past. Modern-day mapmakers create historical maps to show us the nations and empires of long ago. By studying historical maps, we learn where and how people once lived.

If you were to search for an ancient empire on a modern map or globe, you'd never find it. Since the empire no longer exists, it is not on maps of the modern world. To see this ancient civilization, you need to use historical maps.

Look at the map of the Fertile Crescent on page 50. Compare the historical map of the Fertile Crescent with a present-day political map of the same region. Can you find the Mediterranean Sea on both maps? What are some of the present-day countries that now occupy the Fertile Crescent?

The earliest known map of the world was drawn on a clay tablet.

TRY IT

At your school or public library, find historical maps of your town, city, or region. Study the maps to see how your community has changed and how it has stayed the same. Make one list of features shown that still exist today. Make another list of features that have disappeared over time. Finally, make a third list that names some important things that have been added to your community since the time of the historical map.

As a class, make a large copy of your historical map for a bulletin-board display. On the map, place some of the modern roads and buildings that have been built in recent years.

SKILL

POWER SEARCH *Look for other historical maps in this chapter. What do they show you about the past?*

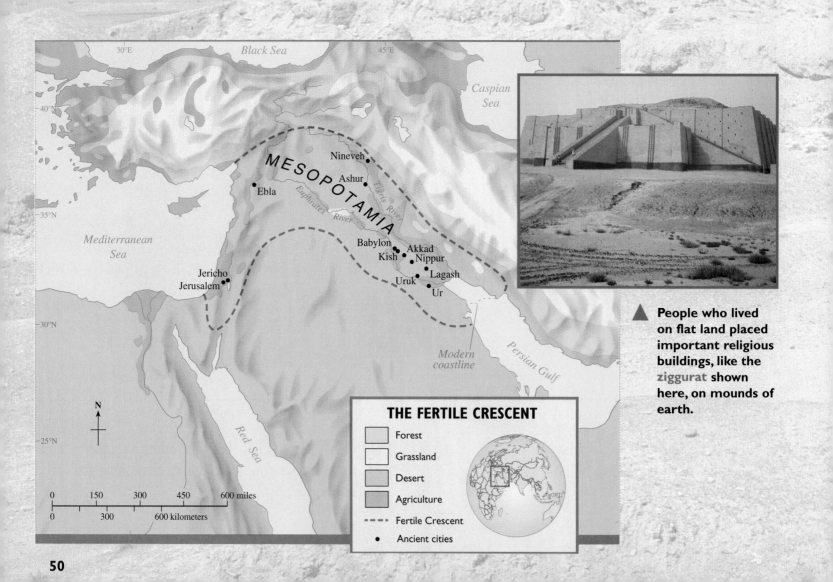

1

Setting the Scene

⭐ **KEY TERMS**

ziggurat
city-state
scribe
caravan
empire
dowry

THE FERTILE CRESCENT

FOCUS This part of the world saw the development of civilization. Today we can still see evidence of the cultural legacy of that civilization.

Black Sea

Caspian Sea

30°E   45°E

40°N

MESOPOTAMIA

Nineveh

Ashur

Ebla

35°N

Euphrates River

Tigris River

Mediterranean Sea

Babylon   Akkad
Kish   Nippur
            Lagash
Jericho   Uruk
Jerusalem   Ur

30°N

Modern coastline

Persian Gulf

▲ People who lived on flat land placed important religious buildings, like the **ziggurat** shown here, on mounds of earth.

N

25°N

Red Sea

| 0 | 150 | 300 | 450 | 600 miles |

| 0 | 300 | 600 kilometers |

THE FERTILE CRESCENT

☐ Forest

☐ Grassland

☐ Desert

☐ Agriculture

– – – Fertile Crescent

• Ancient cities

50

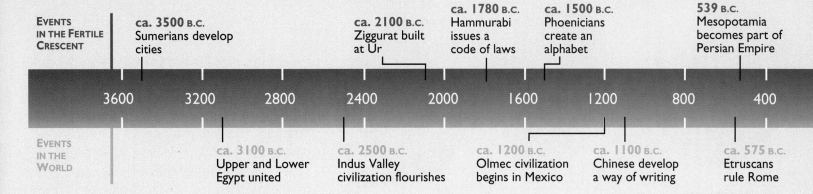

EVENTS
IN THE FERTILE
CRESCENT

ca. 3500 B.C.
Sumerians develop
cities

ca. 2100 B.C.
Ziggurat built
at Ur

ca. 1780 B.C.
Hammurabi
issues a
code of laws

ca. 1500 B.C.
Phoenicians
create an
alphabet

539 B.C.
Mesopotamia
becomes part of
Persian Empire

3600   3200   2800   2400   2000   1600   1200   800   400

EVENTS
IN THE
WORLD

ca. 3100 B.C.
Upper and Lower
Egypt united

ca. 2500 B.C.
Indus Valley
civilization flourishes

ca. 1200 B.C.
Olmec civilization
begins in Mexico

ca. 1100 B.C.
Chinese develop
a way of writing

ca. 575 B.C.
Etruscans
rule Rome

A Cradle of Civilization

As you can see from the map, the Fertile Crescent forms a semicircle from the Persian Gulf to the shore of the Mediterranean Sea. The land is largely mountains and deserts, with marshes and swamps near rivers.

The eastern part of the Fertile Crescent is Mesopotamia (mes uh puh-TAY mee uh), which means "the land between the rivers." People here learned much more than how to stay alive by gathering or catching food. The first known civilization began here, where some of the great discoveries of all time were made.

The Land Between the Rivers

The two main rivers that flow through Mesopotamia are the Tigris and the Euphrates (yoo FRAYT eez). More than 7,000 years ago, people began to farm the land. Little rain fell on the fertile soil of the valley between the rivers. This meant that to keep their seedlings alive, farmers had to dig canals to bring river water to the fields. People began to live in small villages so that they could work together to bring water to their land.

The only tools that farmers had were sharp digging sticks, made of wood or animal horns, that barely broke the hard soil. Around 4000 B.C., Mesopotamians invented the plow. It seems like such a simple idea: Attach a rope to a heavy, sharp piece of wood and drag it on the ground to make a furrow. But no one had thought of it before.

Then about 5,500 years ago, some of the most prosperous villages in the area called Sumer (SOO mur) grew into cities. Each of them was the center of a farming region that became part of a **city-state**. The cities of Sumer varied in size. The largest, the city of Uruk, had over 25,000 people and covered almost 1,000 acres of land. Later other groups moved into Mesopotamia and built the cities of Akkad (AK ad) and Babylon (BAB uh lun).

The People of the City-States

The population of the cities was divided into three main groups. At the top were the nobles and priests. Merchants, **scribes**, craftworkers, and free farmers came next. At the bottom

 ziggurat A temple tower

 city-state A city that governs itself as well as the land and people around it
scribe A person who copies information and keeps records

This headdress was worn by the Sumerian queen Shub-ad. The head is modeled after a female skull from the same time period.

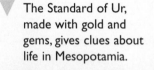
Wealth brought leisure to the Fertile Crescent. Women had the time to design elaborate hairstyles.

The Standard of Ur, made with gold and gems, gives clues about life in Mesopotamia.

bandits or invaders appeared, the farmers fled into the city for safety. In peaceful times they brought crops to marketplaces. The city was divided into districts. There was a special section where potters lived, for example, and other sections for metalworkers or textile makers.

The Heart of City Life

The largest building in each city was the ziggurat. As you see from the picture on page 50, it was a step-shaped structure made of baked mud bricks. At the top was a shrine with a couch and table for the god or goddess who was the city's protector. The outside of the shrine was decorated with bricks glazed in colors, especially bright blue. The Sumerian religion had many gods. The people thought the gods were like humans, able to become angry, sad, or happy.

were enslaved people and farmers who did not own their land. Some of the slaves were captives taken in war. Others were people who sold themselves into slavery to pay debts.

Each city-state had everything its people needed. The farmers who lived in villages surrounding the central city provided enough food for all. Artisans, or craftworkers, within the city made products that farmers and other city-dwellers used, such as decorated clay pots, blankets, rugs, and jewelry.

The Sumerians (soo MIHR ee unz) built walls around their cities. When

Temples were supported by crops grown in special fields outside the city. Sumerians believed that the gods owned the land. Priests who led the worship at the ziggurats were in charge of the irrigation systems. The priests understood the calendar and knew when it was time to release water to the farmers' fields.

The next largest building in a Sumerian city was the palace of the king. The king ruled the city-state. Some kings were so important that they were considered godlike, and legends grew about them. One such king was the hero of another Sumerian first—the epic, a long poem about heroic deeds.

Gilgamesh (GIHL guh mesh), king of Uruk, was the hero of the Sumerians' favorite story. He was a real person, but storytellers over the centuries added their own versions of his deeds. By about 2000 B.C. their tales had been written down.

One story was that Gilgamesh was part god and part human. His human side meant that someday he must die. He could not accept this. He wanted to find the secret of immortality so that he could live forever. At last, after many adventures that included serpents, floods, and battles, Gilgamesh accepted his fate. Someday he too would die.

Epic poems were just one of the many inventions Mesopotamians created. They made contributions to transportation that changed the world.

▲ Gilgamesh

Wheels, Sails, and Caravans

In about 3500 B.C., potters in Mesopotamia learned an easy way to make bowls. They put clay on a table that turned on its base. As it spun, the potter's hands shaped the clay. A few centuries later someone realized that two wheels could be stood on their sides, joined by a log, and attached to a cart. Wheels changed forever how people and things moved from place to place.

Another invention that made transportation easier was the sail. With sails, Sumerian ships could travel faster than ships that were powered by oars. Some ships sailed to the Persian Gulf, even as far away as India.

Other merchants put together caravans that went overland to distant cities. The merchants of Sumer traded farm products for lumber, minerals, and gems that did not exist in the Fertile Crescent. Cities became centers of great riches.

Inventive City Dwellers

To govern a large city-state, it was necessary to keep records. The size of canals, the amount of land to be planted, the products bought and sold by merchants—all had to be measured and calculated. Sumerians started to keep records by making marks with a pointed reed in soft clay. This was the origin of writing. They were also the first people to use arithmetic to add, subtract, multiply, and divide.

★ *caravan* A group of people and goods traveling together

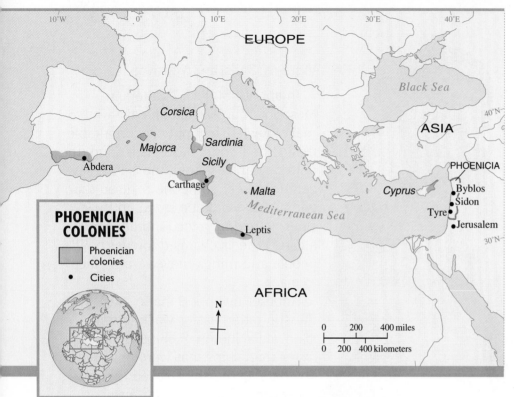

PHOENICIAN COLONIES

- ▨ Phoenician colonies
- • Cities

The most famous Babylonian king was Hammurabi (ham uh RAH bee). A mighty conqueror, he was a wise ruler.

Hammurabi's Code

Sumerians were the first to write laws. Hammurabi combined laws into a code, or organized list, of laws. In about 1780 B.C. he had the laws carved on a stone column for everyone to see.

Punishment reflected the crime. One law read, "If a man breaks the bone of another man, they (the people) shall break his bone." The code treated women relatively well. A woman kept control over her **dowry** and could divorce her husband if he treated her cruelly.

A Trading Empire

As you can see on the map, the cities of Tyre, Byblos, and Sidon were on the shores of the Mediterranean Sea. Here lived the Phoenicians (fuh-NIHSH unz), the greatest sailors of the ancient world. In small wooden boats, they boldly traded and colonized all along the coast of the Mediterranean Sea. They went out into the Atlantic Ocean and down the coast of Africa.

Their most important products were lumber, from the valuable cedars of Lebanon, and purple dye. Only they knew how to make the dye from sea snails. It was so highly prized that it became the color of royalty.

The greatest and most lasting item the Phoenicians spread in their trade

Hammurabi receives the law from the sun god.

Powerful Empires Arise

The wealth of the Sumerian city-states attracted the people living in the deserts and mountains of Mesopotamia. Eventually the high walls that protected the cities were not enough to keep these people out. Sumerian achievements were not lost when their city-states became part of larger **empires**. Others saw the value of writing, mathematics, the wheel, and the plow. Civilization began to spread throughout the Fertile Crescent. You will learn more about specific empires later in this chapter.

A wave of conquerors—the Amorites (AM uh ryts)— came from the west. They made the village of Babylon on the Euphrates River their capital and went on to make it a beautiful city.

⭐ **empire** Many different lands brought under one government

dowry The property a woman brings to a marriage

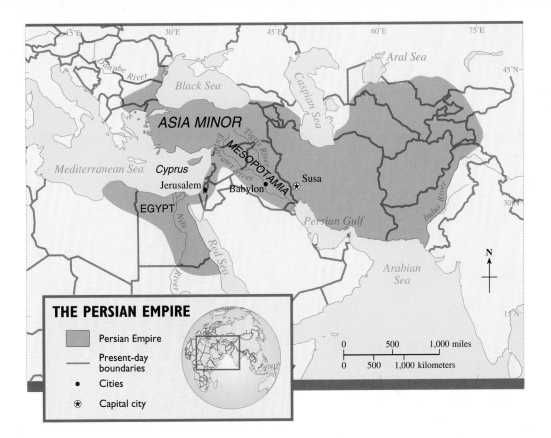

THE PERSIAN EMPIRE

- Persian Empire
- Present-day boundaries
- • Cities
- ✪ Capital city

SHOW WHAT YOU KNOW!

REFOCUS
COMPREHENSION

1. Where was Mesopotamia located?

2. List at least three important discoveries or inventions made by the people who lived in the Fertile Crescent.

THINK ABOUT IT
CRITICAL THINKING

Do you think the Sumerians or the Phoenicians made the more important contribution to the development of writing?

WRITE ABOUT IT
ACTIVITY

Sumerian inventions such as the plow and the wheel made life easier for many people.

Write a description of an invention that could make your life easier.

was an alphabet much like the one we use today. The Phoenicians simplified the Sumerian writing system, which had over 900 symbols, into one that used only 22. They created a system in which each letter stood for a single sound. Fewer marks were needed to express ideas. The Phoenician alphabet had no vowels, but the Greeks added them later. If you're glad you only had to learn a simple alphabet, thank the Phoenicians.

More Conquerors

Persians led by Cyrus the Great conquered the city of Babylon in 539 B.C., and Mesopotamia became part of the vast Persian Empire. The map shows that the empire spread all the way from India to Egypt.

The great days of Mesopotamian civilization were over. Persians were

the first people from outside the Fertile Crescent to conquer Mesopotamia. The Persians maintained much of their own culture. However, the enormous achievements of the Mesopotamian people have not been lost. They are still influencing our world today.

▼ This is the royal seal of Cyrus the Great. It was used on all official documents.

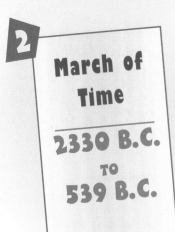

2

EMPIRE BUILDERS

FOCUS *Mesopotamia was the scene of the rise and fall of great empires for nearly 2,000 years.*

SARGON OF AKKAD

Sargon was a great warrior. He was not content to rule just his city of Akkad. About 2330 B.C. he swept down on the city-states of Sumer and captured them. Sargon was tireless in his conquests and brought all of Mesopotamia under his rule. This included the present-day countries of Israel, Lebanon, Syria, Jordan, southern Turkey, Iraq, and much of Iran.

Legend says that he stopped fighting only when he reached the Persian Gulf, where he washed the blood off his weapons. Although he was a fierce warrior, Sargon was the only person who could hold his great empire together.

The kings who followed Sargon were weaker, and the empire lasted only about 200 years. The cities of Sumer regained their independence—but not for long.

THE BABYLONIANS

The Amorites invaded Mesopotamia around 2000 B.C. Along the shore of the Euphrates River, they occupied the village of Babylon, which grew to be a beautiful city with a grand ziggurat.

Hammurabi was the greatest Babylonian ruler. He was an outstanding leader who supported the growth of the arts in his kingdom. Babylon became famous for its wealth and entertainments. People still sometimes refer to a rich and pleasure-loving city as a "Babylon."

Hammurabi is best remembered for his code of laws. This was the first known attempt by an empire to write down all of its laws. Later kings were unable to hold together the lands Hammurabi had conquered. Now the city of Babylon lies in ruins, but the code of law is still important.

| 2330 B.C. | ca. 2000 B.C. | | | 612 B.C. | 539 B.C. |
| Sargon conquers Sumer | Babylon is built on Euphrates River | | | Assyrian empire collapses | Chaldeans conquered by Persians |

| 2500 | 2100 | 1700 | 1300 | 900 | 500 |

THE WARLIKE ASSYRIANS

A people known as the Assyrians (uh-SIHR ee unz) came down the Tigris River from the north about 1,300 B.C. The Assyrians were as skilled at war as other people were at trade or farming. They invented many new tools of war—the short sword, the battering ram, and armor such as shields, helmets, and breastplates. They built fortresses on wheels, which they used to attack the walls of cities. Even in Assyrian art, the people are shown hunting and fighting.

The Assyrians built the greatest empire the world had ever seen. At the height of their power, they controlled not only Mesopotamia but also Syria, Phoenicia, the kingdom of Israel, and parts of Egypt.

However, the Assyrians exhausted themselves through constant fighting. They were cruel rulers and were hated throughout their empire. So when the Chaldeans (kal DEE unz) attacked, the Assyrian empire quickly collapsed. In 612 B.C., the Assyrians disappeared from history.

THE CHALDEANS

The Chaldeans lived in southern Mesopotamia. They made Babylon the capital of their new empire after they defeated the Assyrians. They rebuilt Babylon into the greatest city of its time.

Babylon's hanging gardens were one of the Seven Wonders of the Ancient World. Flowers and trees were planted on a huge platform, watered by hidden pipes. The gardens were built by King Nebuchadnezzar (neb yuh kud NEZ ur) as a gift for his wife. She was born in the mountains and loved the plants that grew there.

The Chaldeans made the first map of the stars. They named constellations after animals. Their empire survived for less than a century. In 539 B.C. they were conquered by the Persians.

REFOCUS
COMPREHENSION

1. Why do we remember Sargon of Akkad?

2. What was the extent of the Assyrian empire?

THINK ABOUT IT
CRITICAL THINKING

Why was the code of Hammurabi such an important contribution to civilization?

WRITE ABOUT IT
ACTIVITY

Explain why you think the hanging gardens of Babylon were regarded as one of the Seven Wonders of the Ancient World.

THE HEBREWS

FOCUS *The belief in one God, which is basic to Judaism, Christianity, and Islam, was born in the Fertile Crescent.*

An Ancient People

You won't ever meet a Phoenician or a Sumerian or an Akkadian. The ancient nations where those people lived have disappeared. Of all the ancient people who lived in the Fertile Crescent, only the Hebrews have kept their identity as a people. Today they are known as Jews, after the kingdom of Judah, where they lived long ago. You can see the kingdom of Judah on the map on page 59.

We know about the customs and beliefs of the Hebrews from what is written in the Bible. The Bible also contains great poetry and stories as well as religious teachings that have influenced the other religions of the world.

Before the Hebrews, the peoples of the Fertile Crescent worshiped many gods. The Hebrews accepted the idea of a belief in one God. This is called monotheism.

The Pierpont Morgan Library, New York. B.34.

Rembrandt was one of many artists who were inspired by the Bible. This etching shows Abraham and Isaac.

The Promised Land

According to the Bible, the story of the Hebrews begins with a man named Abraham. He lived in Ur, part of Mesopotamia, and was a nomad who moved his flocks from place to place in search of pasture land.

The Bible tells that God appeared to Abraham and made a **covenant** with him. God promised to give Abraham and his descendants a land of their own if they would worship Him. According to the Book of Genesis, God promised, "Unto thy seed have I given this land from the river of Egypt unto the great river Euphrates."

Abraham took his family west to the eastern Mediterranean seacoast. They settled in the land of Canaan (KAY nun), which was "flowing with milk and honey." The covenant with God was renewed by Abraham's son Isaac and grandson Jacob, who was also known as Israel.

After several centuries a famine came to Canaan. The Hebrews followed Jacob's son Joseph to Egypt. There the Hebrews remained for many generations.

⭐ *covenant* An agreement

The Exodus

The Bible tells that the Hebrews were enslaved by the pharaoh in Egypt. But another Hebrew leader, Moses, appeared. According to the Bible, God told Moses to lead the Hebrews out of Egypt. When the pharaoh refused to let them go, God punished the Egyptians by sending an angel to kill the firstborn child in every house. The angel passed over the houses of the Hebrews, sparing their children. Every year, on the feast of Passover, Jewish families celebrate that night.

The departure from Egypt is known as the Exodus. Hebrews crossed the Red Sea, entering the Sinai (SEYE neye) Desert. Moses went to the top of Mount Sinai to receive the tablets of the Ten Commandments from God.

The commandments forbid murder, theft, envy, lying, adultery, and the worship of idols. God commands his followers to worship Him alone. Children are taught to always honor their parents. One day of rest and prayer is to follow six days of work. The Ten Commandments have formed the ethical code of both Judaism and Christianity.

After wandering in the desert for 40 years, the Hebrews again settled in Canaan. They worshiped in a tent called the **Tabernacle**. Here was kept the ark of the covenant, a chest containing the actual tablets of the Ten Commandments.

⭐ **tabernacle**   A shrine or place of worship

By this time the Hebrews had divided into 12 tribes. Each tribe was descended from one of the sons of Jacob. Enemies were raiding the Hebrew villages and destroying their crops. They decided that they would be stronger if they united under a king.

Hebrew Kings

King David, the Hebrews' greatest military leader, conquered the land that stretched from Mesopotamia to Egypt. After

▲ Moses receiving the Ten Commandments, as painted by Rembrandt

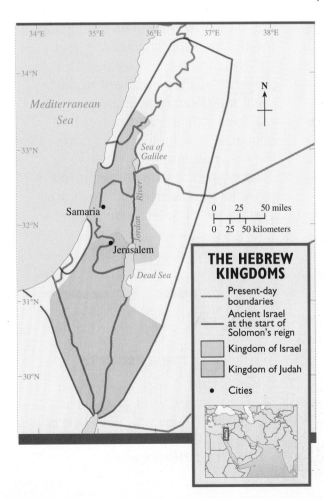

THE HEBREW KINGDOMS

— Present-day boundaries
— Ancient Israel at the start of Solomon's reign

▨ Kingdom of Israel
▨ Kingdom of Judah

• Cities

The Torah is just as important to Jews today as it was in ancient times.

David captured Jerusalem, he made it the capital of his kingdom.

His son Solomon built Jerusalem into a great city. He started work on a magnificent temple. The temple was a permanent home for the ark of the covenant. It showed that the Hebrews had finally become the strong nation that God had promised. Solomon was also a great poet whose love songs make up a small part of the Bible.

Two Kingdoms

Soon after Solomon's death, however, the 12 tribes divided into two kingdoms. Ten tribes formed the Kingdom of Israel in the north, with a new capital at Samaria (suh MAYR ee-uh). Jerusalem remained the capital of the Kingdom of Judah in the south.

Divided, the Hebrews were not as powerful as they had been under David and Solomon. The Assyrians captured Samaria and drove the people of Israel into distant parts of the Assyrian empire.

Later the Babylonians captured Jerusalem and destroyed the temple. The people of Judah were enslaved and sent to Babylon. The Babylonian captivity lasted for 70 years. When the Persians conquered Babylon, the people of Judah were allowed to return to their kingdom. They rebuilt the temple.

After the return to Judah, Hebrew scholars wrote down the first five books of the Bible. These books are also called the Torah, which means "law." The Torah was based on teachings that had been passed on orally since the time of Moses.

The Kingdom of Judah survived for another four centuries. In 63 B.C. the Roman Empire conquered it. About 100 years later, the Jews rebelled. But Roman power was too great. To punish the Jews, the Romans destroyed the temple and exiled the Jews. This began the Diaspora, or dispersal, when Jews lived in many other parts of the world.

Throughout nearly 2,000 years, the Jews have continued to follow the laws and traditions of their ancestors. Despite persecution and attempts to force them to abandon their religion, they have kept the ancient covenant that God made with Abraham.

SHOW WHAT YOU KNOW!

REFOCUS
COMPREHENSION

1. What was the contribution of Abraham to the religion of the Hebrews?

2. What were the contributions of Moses?

THINK ABOUT IT
CRITICAL THINKING

Which king—David or Solomon—made what you would consider to be the greater contribution to the Hebrew people?

WRITE ABOUT IT
ACTIVITY

Pick an episode in the history of the Hebrews and write about it as if you were there.

4

You Are There

LEARNING TO BE A SCRIBE

FOCUS *A rigorous system of education gave scribes the skills that made them valuable members of society.*

Why Be a Scribe?

If you live in Mesopotamia, you might want to become a scribe when you grow up. As a scribe you can always find a high-paying job. The governments of city-states and empires need people who can write. Marriage contracts, legal codes, and lists of taxpayers have to be recorded. Merchants and traders must make lists of their goods as well as calculate profits and losses.

Off to School

You will have to go to school, but only parents who are relatively wealthy can afford the fee. One day your father tells you that you are a lucky boy. You are about to become a "school-son," which is what students are called. That's right—school-*son*! Almost no girls receive an education of this kind.

You have to hurry to be on time, for your "school-father," or teacher, will hit you with a cane if you are late. You sit on a mud-brick bench and begin the hard work of memorizing the hundreds of signs that make up the Sumerian written language.

By the way, even if you are a school-son in the time of the Babylonian or Assyrian empire, you still have to learn to write Sumerian. Even though no one speaks it any more, the Sumerian written language is still used in Mesopotamia. It is as if you spoke English but had to learn to write in Latin.

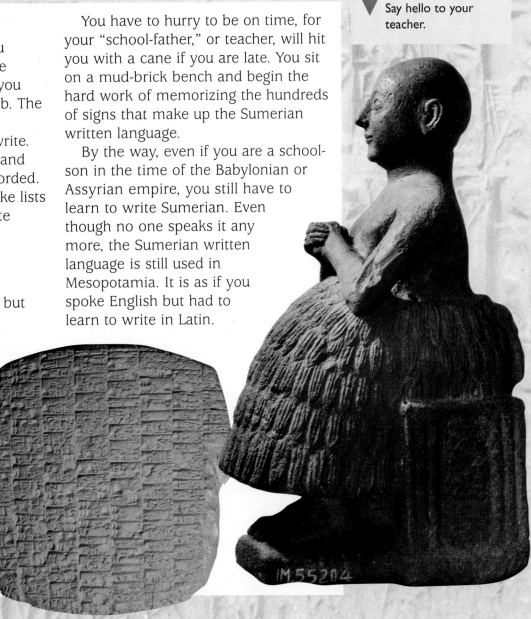

▼ Say hello to your teacher.

A **cuneiform** tablet ▶

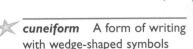

cuneiform A form of writing with wedge-shaped symbols

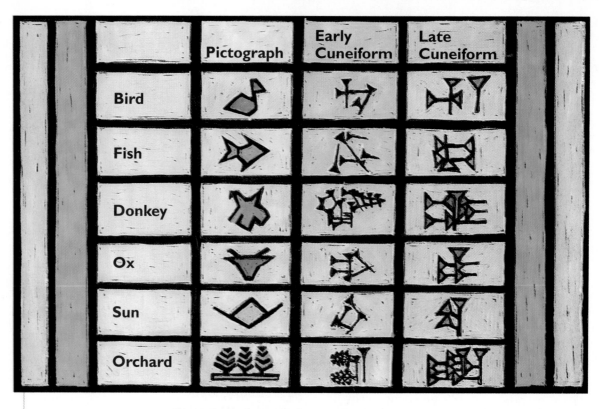

	Pictograph	Early Cuneiform	Late Cuneiform
Bird			
Fish			
Donkey			
Ox			
Sun			
Orchard			

Development of Cuneiform Writing

These clay pieces covered with cuneiform prayers were found in a temple.

The teacher shows you a clay tablet with several different symbols on it. You have to learn what sounds each symbol represents so that you can combine them into words. Once you have the sounds memorized, you begin to study lists of words organized by category.

The list for sciences includes names for animal and human body parts, stones, stars, birds, and fish. Then there are the words of commerce, such as *cargo, weight,* and *merchant.* There are thousands of words of many kinds. You have to memorize all of the words before you will be allowed to copy short sentences.

Don't Act Up!

If the school-father moves on to another boy, you are supposed to continue working. If you get tired of sitting on the bench and start to move around, watch out! The school-father and his assistants have canes ready to punish anyone who misbehaves.

A school-son wrote in an essay:

My school-father read my table, and said: "There is something missing." He caned me.

The fellow in charge of neatness said: "You loitered in the street and did not straighten out your clothes." He caned me.

The fellow in charge of silence said: "Why did you talk without permission?" He caned me.

And the list goes on for another six reasons for caning! So you should pay attention and follow all the rules.

Tablets and Sticks

When you can recognize the symbols and words, the school-father gives you your writing tools. You write on a tablet of wet clay. You use a **stylus** with a small wedge at the tip. As you can see from the picture on page 62, all the words are formed from wedge-shaped marks. The name *cuneiform* comes from a Latin word meaning "wedge."

Your tablet is small, only a few inches wide and long. The marks have

---

stylus A pointed tool used in writing on a soft surface

to be made quickly, before the clay dries, so you have to memorize the words carefully. You won't have much time to think about them. Later you will practice on larger tablets. Experts can use ones that are two or three feet long and weigh as much as 20 pounds.

More Things to Learn

If you want to be a good scribe, you have to learn more than writing. Knowing how to add, subtract, multiply, and divide will help you become a tax collector or a bookkeeper for a merchant. If you show talent, you will learn more advanced mathematics. These are needed for surveying land, building houses and city walls, or making maps like the one below.

Every student is also expected to learn to use the Sumerian water clock and lunar calendar. These are needed to calculate the times for religious rituals, the planting of crops, and the distribution of water to the fields. You may find one additional use for telling time: You can figure out how much longer it will be before you become a scribe!

This Babylonian map is over 2,500 years old.

Mountain

City of Babylon

Assyria

Bitter River

SHOW WHAT YOU KNOW!

REFOCUS
COMPREHENSION

1. What kinds of things did a scribe have to learn?

2. How was cuneiform written?

THINK ABOUT IT
CRITICAL THINKING

Why is it easier to write with symbols than with pictures?

WRITE ABOUT IT
ACTIVITY

Write a letter to a student in the scribe school, contrasting your school day with his.

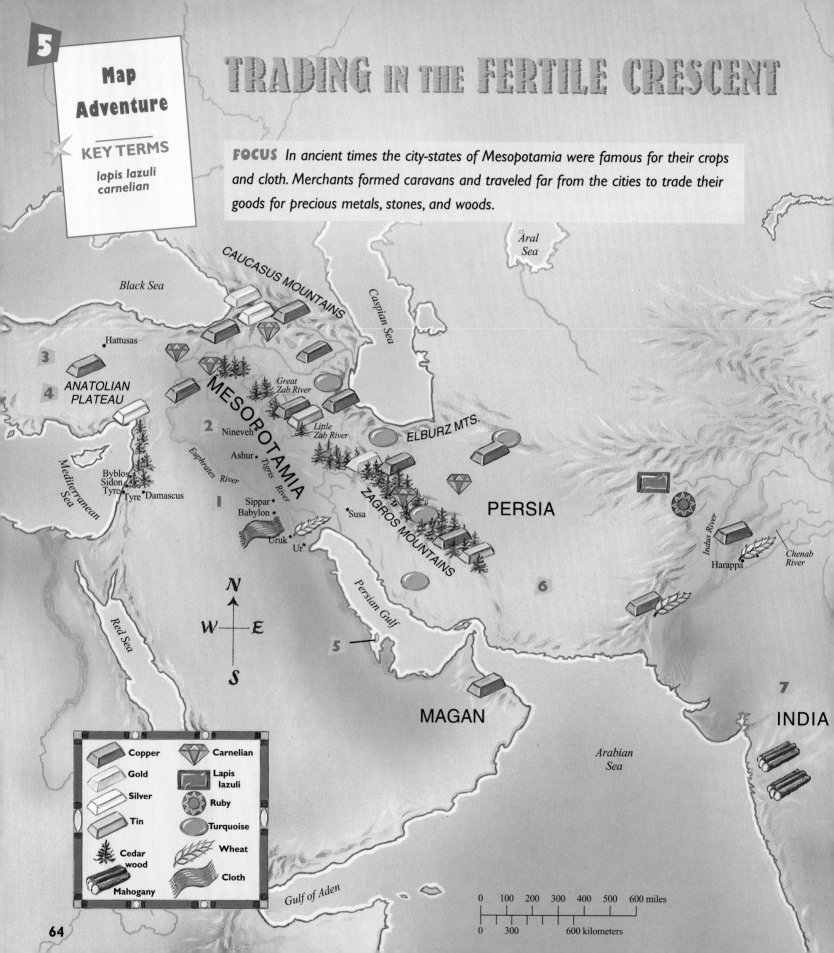

Map Adventure

★ KEY TERMS

lapis lazuli
carnelian

TRADING IN THE FERTILE CRESCENT

FOCUS In ancient times the city-states of Mesopotamia were famous for their crops and cloth. Merchants formed caravans and traveled far from the cities to trade their goods for precious metals, stones, and woods.

Aral Sea

Black Sea

CAUCASUS MOUNTAINS

Caspian Sea

3

· Hattusas

4 ANATOLIAN PLATEAU

MESOPOTAMIA

Great Zab River

Little Zab River

ELBURZ MTS.

2 Nineveh

Ashur · *Tigris River*

· *Euphrates River*

Mediterranean Sea

Byblos ·
Sidon ·
Tyre ·
· Tyre · Damascus

1

Sippar ·
Babylon ·

· Susa

ZAGROS MOUNTAINS

PERSIA

6

Indus River

Harappa ·

Chenab River

Uruk ·
Ur ·

N
W   E
S

Red Sea

Persian Gulf

5

7

MAGAN

INDIA

Arabian Sea

Copper		Carnelian	
Gold		Lapis lazuli	
Silver		Ruby	
Tin		Turquoise	
Cedar wood		Wheat	
Mahogany		Cloth	

Gulf of Aden

0	100	200	300	400	500	600 miles

0	300	600 kilometers

Adventure in the Fertile Crescent

You are a merchant in Babylon. Babylon is located along the Euphrates River, which provides the water and rich soil needed to grow crops. Yet the city does not have many more resources. Look at the list of items the city needs. Where will you find them? Study the map and plot out the routes your caravan will take. Describe these routes in a logbook. Use details such as directions and landforms in your descriptions.

Map Legend

1 Babylon Babylon was one of the largest cities in the ancient world.

2 Tigris and Euphrates rivers These rivers provided natural routes to transport goods, but most merchants preferred to travel overland by caravan. Traders were afraid of the floods, whirlpools, and robbers that made river travel dangerous.

3 Caravans In ancient times, large groups of people transported their goods in caravans of donkeys and wagons. These caravans traveled on land routes that were safe from the dangers of river travel. People also found that when they traveled in large groups, they were more protected from robbers.

4 Anatolia The mountainous region of Anatolia was the source of many products. Many different people lived in Anatolia, including the fierce Hittites who made the city of Hattusas their capital.

5 Dilmun The island of Bahrain was known to Mesopotamians as Dilmun. It was a center of trade, where merchants from the city-states of Mesopotamia could buy goods from Persia, India, and Magan.

6 Persia Merchants found many precious stones in the mountains of Persia. Rubies, turquoise, lapis lazuli, and carnelian were used to make beautiful jewelry.

7 India India, far from Mesopotamia, was the source of many exotic goods. Merchants journeyed there to trade for exotic wood, ivory, and seashells.

⭐ *lapis lazuli* A dark blue gemstone
carnelian A clear red gemstone

MAP IT

1. The people of Babylon know that if you mix copper and tin you get a stronger metal called bronze. Babylon does not have copper or tin. Where can you go to find them?

2. Babylon is a growing city and needs strong wood for building. There are few trees in Mesopotamia, but tall trees grow somewhere in this region. Where will your caravan go to find strong wood?

3. Jewelry fetches a handsome price in the city's markets. Gold and silver are mined somewhere in the area. What city is located near the source?

4. Your jewelry will be more valuable if you add precious stones to your designs. These stones can be found high in the mountains. Locate the cities where you could buy these stones.

EXPLORE IT

Beware! Traveling over land can be dangerous. Nomads have been known to prey upon slow-moving caravans. This time assume that you will be using a boat to carry your goods. Plot new routes using only the waterways that are available.

SUMMING UP

1 DO YOU REMEMBER...
COMPREHENSION

1. Where is the Fertile Crescent located?

2. What common need led people to live in the first small villages in the Fertile Crescent?

3. What led the Sumerians to develop the first system of writing?

4. What was different about the ways the Phoenicians and Assyrians spread their civilizations?

5. What is King Hammurabi of Babylon most remembered for?

6. In what major way was the Hebrew religion different from earlier religions?

7. How did King David and King Solomon make the Hebrew nation strong?

8. What important jobs did scribes do in Mesopotamia?

9. Why was it so difficult to become a scribe?

10. What were some of the items carried by trade caravans?

2 SKILL POWER
READING HISTORICAL MAPS

In this chapter you used historical maps to learn about different civilizations in the Fertile Crescent. Why, do you think, were most of the cities of these civilizations built near rivers or on seacoasts?

3 WHAT DO YOU THINK?
CRITICAL THINKING

1. Which of the inventions or developments in the Fertile Crescent, do you think, was most important? Give your reasons.

2. Explain why the history of the Fertile Crescent often seems like a history of battles.

3. The Sumerians were the first to write down laws and punishments. Do you think this was likely to cut crime? Why?

4. Compare the contributions that Moses and Solomon made to the Hebrew people.

5. How would learning to write in ancient Mesopotamia be very different from learning to write in your school?

4 SAY IT, WRITE IT, USE IT
VOCABULARY

Select pairs of terms from the list below. For each pair of terms, write a sentence that shows you understand what the terms mean. Be sure to use all the terms.

caravan	empire
carnelian	lapis lazuli
city-state	scribe
covenant	stylus
cuneiform	tabernacle
dowry	ziggurat

5 GEOGRAPHY AND YOU

MAP STUDY

The map below shows the boundaries of present-day nations. Study a world map and make a list of the nations that exist today that were once part of King Solomon's empire.

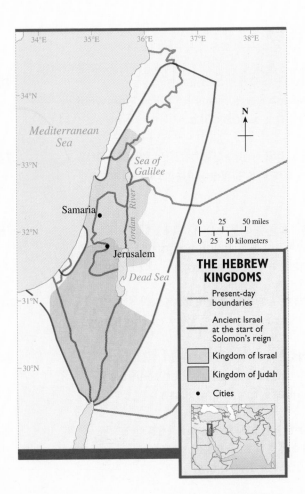

34°E   35°E   36°E   37°E   38°E

34°N

N

Mediterranean Sea

33°N

Sea of Galilee

Samaria •

32°N

Jerusalem •

Jordan River

0   25   50 miles
0   25   50 kilometers

Dead Sea

31°N

30°N

THE HEBREW KINGDOMS

— Present-day boundaries

— Ancient Israel at the start of Solomon's reign

☐ Kingdom of Israel

☐ Kingdom of Judah

• Cities

6 TAKE ACTION

CITIZENSHIP

The first villages in Mesopotamia arose when people worked together to bring water to their farmland. People today still cooperate to strengthen their communities. Think about a problem in your community. Maybe there's a busy corner that needs a traffic light, an abandoned building that should be boarded up, or a playground that needs new equipment. With a group of classmates, discuss the problem and suggest a solution. Then share your ideas by writing to your local newspaper or talking with local officials.

7 GET CREATIVE

LANGUAGE ARTS CONNECTION

This is a Sumerian game board with playing pieces. Think about how the game might have been played. Then create a list of a few basic rules.

LOOKING AHEAD   Get ready to learn about another great civilization that developed around a river.

THE EGYPTIAN

Many of the ideas and the skills that you have learned have their roots in ancient Egypt. Read this chapter to find out how they began and developed.

CONTENTS

◀ Look on page 77 for an artifact that helped people learn about ancient Egypt.

EMPIRE

These books tell about some people, places, and events that make ancient Egypt so captivating. Read one that interests you and fill out a book-review form.

READ AND RESEARCH

The Riddle of the Rosetta Stone **by James Cross Giblin**
(HarperCollins Publishers, 1990)
Discover how the finding of the Rosetta stone in 1799 unlocked the door to learning about ancient Egypt. Read a translation of the hieroglyphics on the stone, which took scholars many years to figure out. (*nonfiction*)

The Tombs of the Pharaohs **illustrated by Sue Clarke**
(Hyperion, 1994)
This pyramid-shaped book tells the story of the pharaohs' tombs in Giza and the Valley of the Kings. Three-dimensional pages help you understand the pharaohs' belief in the afterlife. (*nonfiction*)

The Egypt Game **by Zilpha Keatley Snyder** (Atheneum Publishers, 1967)
Six children, pretending to be Egyptians, play in an empty lot behind an antique shop. They even develop their own secret code. Their Egyptian game is just for fun until mysterious things begin happening to the players. (*fiction*)

Into the Mummy's Tomb **by Nicholas Reeves** (Scholastic, 1992)
Enter the Valley of the Kings and join in the archaeological search for King Tut, the boy king of Egypt, who was buried over 3,000 years ago. You will be amazed when you read about the treasures found in the secret chambers of his burial place. (*nonfiction*)

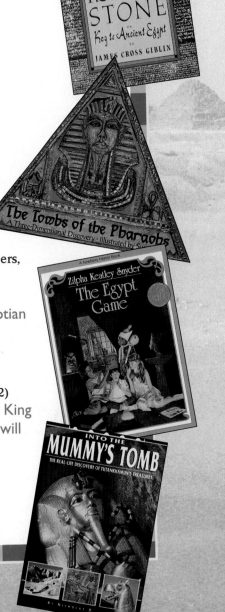

SKILL POWER
Reading a Cross Section

Knowing how to read a cross section can help you understand how the insides of things look or work.

UNDERSTAND IT

Did you ever cut an apple in half to see the star pattern the seeds make? If you did, you were looking at a cross section. With an apple it is easy to make a cross section. However, it is not always possible to cut something open to see what it looks like inside. For example, you cannot cut the earth in half to see its layers, and you cannot split a building in two to see how it is built. However, you can find cross-section drawings that show what the inside of the earth looks like or how a building is made.

EXPLORE IT

A cross section is a useful way to show parts of an object that usually cannot be seen. Zoologists sometimes use cross sections to explain the body structures of animals and show where animals live. Look at the cross section of a prairie-dog town.

- What is the name of the spot where a prairie dog enters the town?

- How do you think the prairie dog uses the turnaround shelf?

- What does this cross section show about methods used by prairie dogs to protect their towns?

▼ A cross section of an apple shows the seeds in a star pattern.

This is part of a large prairie-dog community called a town. ▶

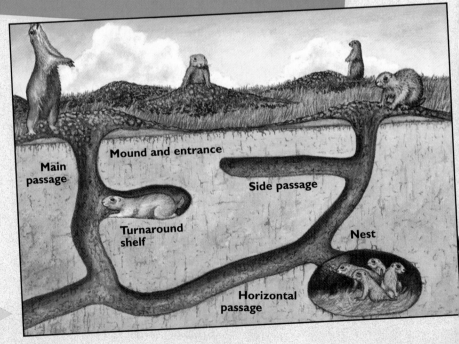

Main passage

Mound and entrance

Side passage

Turnaround shelf

Nest

Horizontal passage

TRY IT

Work with a few of your classmates to make a mobile or a table-top display of cross sections. Whenever you can, include a real cross section, such as a crosswise slice of a small log, a broken floppy disk, or half of a rosebud. If you cannot get a real cross section, make a cross-section drawing. To get ideas, think of things you are curious about. What might the inside of an anthill look like if you could see a cross section? What does a cross section of a sneaker look like?

Label your mobile or display, so that viewers will understand it better.

Sneaker

Log

Ant farm

Prairie dog

SKILL POWER SEARCH Find the cross section in this chapter. What did you learn from it?

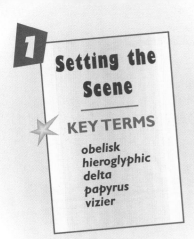

Setting the Scene

⭐ **KEY TERMS**

obelisk
hieroglyphic
delta
papyrus
vizier

AN ANCIENT CIVILIZATION

FOCUS *The Nile was and is Egypt's most important physical feature. Life in ancient Egypt centered around this mighty river.*

The Gift of the Nile

Herodotus (huh RAHD uh tus), a Greek historian who visited Egypt about 2,500 years ago, wrote, "Egypt is the gift of the Nile." He stood in awe of the great achievements of a civilization much older than his own. In Herodotus' time, huge stone pyramids, towering **obelisks**, and images of Egyptian rulers rose high above the sandy soil. Many temple walls were covered with paintings and **hieroglyphics** (hye ur oh GLIHF-ihks).

Without the Nile River, which you can see on the map, these marvels would never have appeared. Located in the northeastern corner of Africa, Egypt is within the Sahara, the world's largest desert, where almost no rain falls. It is the Nile, the world's longest river, that brings the gift of water from which Egyptian civilization sprang. From its sources in the south, the Nile flows northward for more than 4,100 miles until it reaches the Mediterranean Sea.

The Pattern of the Year

The Nile overflowed its banks each summer and deposited fine particles of soil called silt that enriched the land. The farmers came to depend on the regular pattern of the Nile to know when to plant crops. Before the floods came, they built dikes and reservoirs. Villages grew up along the Nile.

Until about 5,000 years ago, Egypt was divided into two parts. The southern part, about 600 miles long, was called Upper Egypt. Here the irrigated river valley was only about 13 miles wide. Farmers had to conserve water throughout the year by using canals and reservoirs.

Lower Egypt was the northern part of the country. There the Nile fanned out into a **delta** of seven main branches. The land there was more fertile than in Upper Egypt, and water was more plentiful.

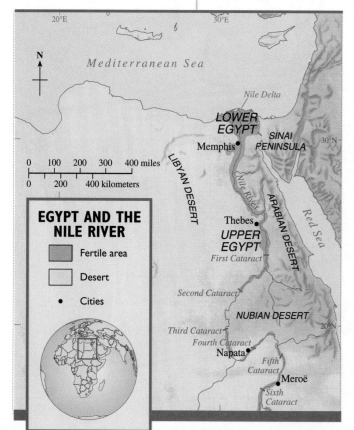

EGYPT AND THE NILE RIVER

▨ Fertile area
☐ Desert
• Cities

Mediterranean Sea
Nile Delta
LOWER EGYPT
Memphis
SINAI PENINSULA
LIBYAN DESERT
Nile River
ARABIAN DESERT
Red Sea
Thebes
UPPER EGYPT
First Cataract
Second Cataract
NUBIAN DESERT
Third Cataract
Fourth Cataract
Napata
Fifth Cataract
Meroë
Sixth Cataract

0 100 200 300 400 miles
0 200 400 kilometers

⭐ **obelisk** A four-sided pillar with a top shaped like a pyramid
hieroglyphic A picture or symbol representing a word, syllable, or sound

⭐ **delta** Land formed by mud and sand in the mouth of a river

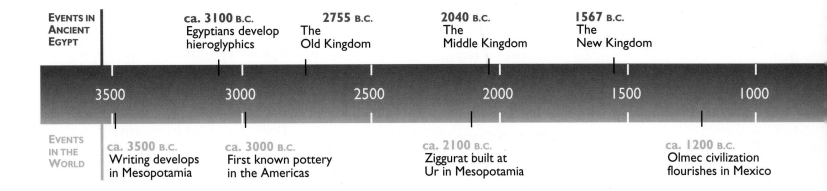

		ca. 3100 B.C. Egyptians develop hieroglyphics	2755 B.C. The Old Kingdom	2040 B.C. The Middle Kingdom	1567 B.C. The New Kingdom

EVENTS IN ANCIENT EGYPT

3500　3000　2500　2000　1500　1000

EVENTS IN THE WORLD

ca. 3500 B.C.
Writing develops
in Mesopotamia

ca. 3000 B.C.
First known pottery
in the Americas

ca. 2100 B.C.
Ziggurat built at
Ur in Mesopotamia

ca. 1200 B.C.
Olmec civilization
flourishes in Mexico

Tracking the Nile's annual pattern helped the Egyptians develop a calendar. It was remarkably accurate, with a year of 365 days divided into 12 months of 30 days each. The five extra days fell at the end of the year.

Trade and Commerce

Thriving agriculture made Egypt virtually self-sufficient. The major crops were wheat, barley, and flax, from which clothing was made. Farmers also grew lentils, onions, dates, figs, cucumbers, and grapes. Farmers kept herds of African cattle, pigs, goats, and sheep.

Egypt's natural resources included stone for building houses and temples, as well as gold and silver, which were used for jewelry. Copper was mined in the Sinai Desert.

Egyptians discovered that a reed called **papyrus** (puh PYE rus), which grew on the banks of the Nile, could be used in many ways. They built boats by binding papyrus reeds in bundles. They also made baskets, mats, sandals, ropes, and paper for writing. See the drawing.

Products were moved in boats. Because the Nile flowed north, the boats could float in that direction, steered by an oar. A gentle trade wind blew from the north, enabling boats with sails to travel south against the current. But easy sailing ended at the first of the Nile's six cataracts, or waterfalls.

Egypt's wealth lured foreign invaders, yet Egypt remained partially protected by the natural barrier of the Sahara. Egyptian merchants often went beyond their borders to trade. Cedar trees from Lebanon were used for buildings and boats. Perfumes, spices, and incense came from Punt, today's Somalia.

 papyrus A tall reed that grows in the Nile valley, the pith (spongy center part) of which was used to make a paperlike substance

Uses of Papyrus

Growing Into a Nation

About 5,000 years ago a warrior-king named Menes (MEE neez) united Upper and Lower Egypt into a nation. He established Memphis, near the modern city of Cairo, as the capital.

This event marked the beginning of a glorious 3,000-year history. During that time, 30 dynasties, or ruling families, occupied the throne of Egypt.

The first hieroglyphic writing also dates from this era.

The Old Kingdom

During the Old Kingdom, Egyptian civilization blossomed. The kings built pyramids and monuments.

Claiming to be god-kings, rulers encouraged religious devotion by building temples to the Egyptian gods.

King Khafre (KAF ray) ordered the construction of the Sphinx, a figure with the head of a human and the body of a lion.

The Middle Kingdom

The ambitious building programs of the Old Kingdom were too costly—in both tax money and workers needed. There was unrest, and the kings' control over Egypt weakened. Parts of Upper Egypt broke away from the government at Memphis.

The time of disunity lasted for about a century. Then a ruler from Upper Egypt again gained control over the whole country. He founded the Middle Kingdom and made Thebes the new capital.

Rulers of the Middle Kingdom still built pyramids, though smaller than before. Irrigation projects along the Nile made more farmland available, but Egyptians did not recover the spirit of confidence that had marked the Old Kingdom. The Middle Kingdom was brought to an abrupt end by a powerful foreign enemy.

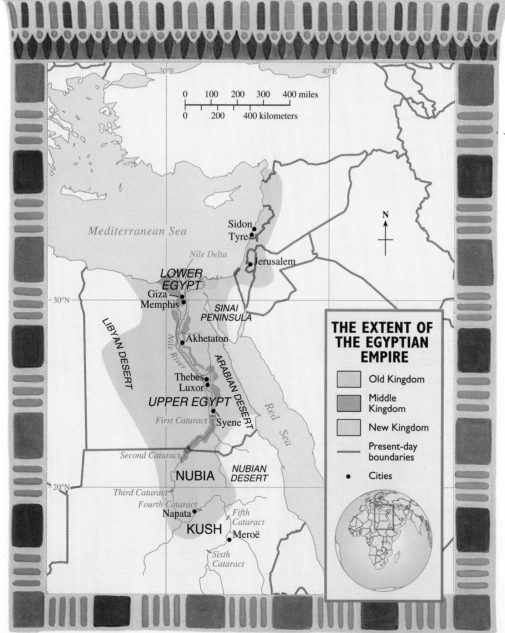

THE EXTENT OF THE EGYPTIAN EMPIRE

- Old Kingdom
- Middle Kingdom
- New Kingdom
- Present-day boundaries
- • Cities

The New Kingdom

The Hyksos (HIK sohs), warriors from the east, invaded northern Egypt. They used war chariots pulled by horses, which were unknown to Egyptians. Though the Hyksos conquered Lower Egypt, they were not able to advance as far as Thebes.

For about 200 years the Hyksos ruled Lower Egypt. Egyptians learned how to use the horse-drawn war chariots, and they drove the Hyksos out of their land. This marked the beginning of a new period in the history of Egypt.

The rulers of the New Kingdom took the title *pharaoh* (FER oh), which means "great house." Having come to power by mastering warfare, they embarked on their own conquests. Great warrior-pharaohs like Thutmose III (thoot MOH-suh) and Ramses II led armies into Asia and conquered the Fertile Crescent. Egypt became an empire.

Pharaohs resumed massive building projects of enormous temples, which had gigantic figures of gods and pharaohs in them. Sometimes these huge figures were carved into the sides of rock cliffs.

The New Kingdom lasted for five centuries, but its grandeur gradually dimmed. More powerful nations arose around Egypt, and control of Egypt passed into foreign hands. Assyrians, Persians, Greeks, and Romans all made Egypt part of their empires in the centuries that

This statue of Ramses II was found at the temple in Luxor, Egypt.

followed. Only the great monuments remained as testimony to the glorious days of one of the world's first great civilizations.

The Ruling Class

Egyptian society was organized like a pyramid. At the top was the pharaoh, who was regarded as a god. He ruled with the help of a **vizier**.

The ruling class was made up of nobles and priests. Most nobles held government positions and owned large estates. The priests paid no taxes and grew wealthy from donations that all Egyptians—from pharaohs to farmers—made to the gods. Because they were responsible for pleasing the gods, priests enjoyed great power. The Egyptians believed that the gods controlled the universe, so it was important to please the gods. A few of these gods are pictured on page 80.

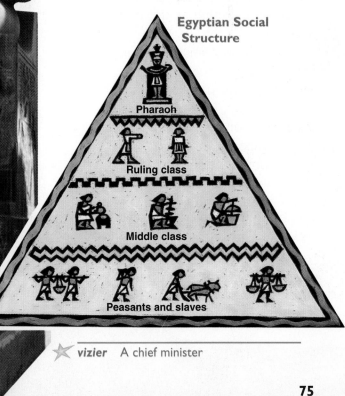

Egyptian Social Structure

Pharaoh

Ruling class

Middle class

Peasants and slaves

★ **vizier** A chief minister

75

The Middle Class

Egypt had a middle class composed of skilled people such as physicians and artisans. Craftworkers made and sold jewelry, pottery, papyrus products, tools, and other useful things.

Women worked as priestesses, weavers, perfume-makers, musicians, and dancers. Soldiers fought in wars but also supervised building projects.

Peasants and Slaves

The vast majority of Egyptians made up a third class, consisting of peasants and enslaved people. Slavery became the fate of prisoners of war. Some slaves were also obtained in trade with other countries.

Peasant farmers tended the fields, raised animals, kept the canals and reservoirs in good order, worked in the stone quarries, and built the royal monuments. Farmers paid taxes that could be as much as three fifths of their yearly crop.

A small number of peasants moved upward in the social structure. Families saved to send their sons to a school to learn a trade. Village schools were run by priests or by artisans who taught their skills.

If a boy learned to read and write, he could find a job as a scribe. Professional scribes were much in demand. The largest employer was the government. It was possible for a young man born on a farm to work his way up to the higher ranks of the government.

Egyptian Accomplishments

Building pyramids was an amazing feat of engineering. Early pyramids were made of mud bricks baked in the sun. When builders tried to make larger pyramids, some fell down.

A vizier named Imhotep (ihm HOH-tep) created the first pyramid made entirely of stone blocks. You can see the picture of this Step Pyramid on this page. Imhotep built a series of platforms, each smaller than the one beneath it.

Later pyramids dwarfed the Step Pyramid in size. Builders followed the same plan but used small stones to fill in the steps to form a smooth slope. The Great Pyramid, tomb of the ruler Khufu (KOO foo), remained the tallest building in the world until the twentieth century.

It would have been impossible to build such structures without a knowledge of mathematics, especially geometry. Here too the gift of the Nile helped the

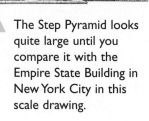

▲ The Step Pyramid looks quite large until you compare it with the Empire State Building in New York City in this scale drawing.

Egyptians develop such skills. Farmers had to measure and calculate the volume of water in building their canals and reservoirs. Also, the flooding washed away stones used to make boundaries. Professional surveyors needed mathematical skills to relocate the dividing lines.

Egyptian doctors were highly skilled. They performed operations on the brain, and X-rays of the skulls of mummies show that the patients survived. Perhaps the oldest known scientific document is an Egyptian papyrus on medical treatment.

The Rosetta Stone

The practical need to keep records probably led the Egyptians to develop hieroglyphics, their system of writing. The meaning of this writing was lost for centuries. Then, in 1799, French soldiers found a slab of black stone buried near the town of Rosetta in the Nile Delta. This stone proved to be the key to the lost language.

Carved on the so-called Rosetta stone was a message in three kinds of writing. Two were in ancient Egyptian languages, and the third was in Greek. After studying the stone for more than 20 years, a French scholar figured out how to translate the Egyptian writing.

HIEROGLYPHICS		
Description	Hieroglyphic Symbol	Sound
vulture		A-AS IN FAT
flowering reed		Y
foot		B
owl		M
loaf		T
mouth		R
twisted flax		H
basket		K
hand		D
snake		S

(*Left*) The early Egyptian writing used hieroglyphics, shown in the middle column.

(*Above*) Decoding the Rosetta stone allowed the secrets of ancient Egypt to be revealed.

SHOW WHAT YOU KNOW!

REFOCUS
COMPREHENSION

1. What are the major divisions of ancient Egyptian history?

2. How was ancient Egyptian society organized?

THINK ABOUT IT
CRITICAL THINKING

How did the regular pattern of the Nile influence what the ancient Egyptians were able to accomplish?

WRITE ABOUT IT
ACTIVITY

Think about what it would be like to be working with the scholar who is trying to break the code of the Rosetta stone.

Write a letter to a friend, telling what difference it will make to the world if you succeed.

PREPARING FOR THE AFTERLIFE

FOCUS *To Egyptians, death was only the beginning of a new life that they prepared for in special ways.*

▲ Three-dimensional images of Winnie were produced by CAT scans.

Belief in an Afterlife

Many people consider **mummies** to be as fascinating a part of Egyptian civilization as the pyramids. The custom of preserving the bodies of the dead came from the belief in an afterlife. The first step in the afterlife was being judged by the god Osiris, shown on page 80. To the Egyptians, death was not the end of life. It was only the beginning of a new and joyous one. They preserved the body so that it could take part in a new life.

As early as 10,000 years ago, Egyptians buried tools and food with their loved ones. These items probably were intended for use in the afterlife.

The Creation of Mummies

The arid climate of Egypt tended to keep bodies from decaying. Egyptian scientists sought to find even better ways of preserving them. Because the internal organs and brain decayed first, most were removed. Each organ was placed in a decorated container. The brain, regarded as having no importance after death, was tossed away. But the heart, which was thought to be the seat of wisdom and conscience, was left in the body.

Then the body was placed in **natron**, which drew the moisture from it. After 40 days the dried corpse was wrapped in hundreds of yards of white linen for final burial. The whole process took about 70 days.

The earliest mummies date from the time when Menes unified Egypt. At first, only kings and their families received such treatment after death. Over time, noble families also adopted the practice.

Eventually anybody who could afford it arranged to have themselves mummified after death. Peasants saved for it the same way people today save for a big wedding. Mummification became so popular that even pets were mummified.

Going to the Next World

Ancient Egyptians did not believe in the modern idea "You can't take it with you." They not only preserved the body but also buried it in tombs that imitated life on earth. Wealthy farmers were buried with their

---

★ **mummy** A body treated for burial with preservatives to keep it from decaying

★ **natron** A mineral salt found in soil from dry lake beds

An Egyptian mummy was wrapped in linen and placed in a decorated mummy case.

Bodies of the dead were taken to a workshop, where the mummification process began.

cattle, carpenters with their tools. The corpse was dressed in his or her favorite jewelry. Finding these artifacts has helped us know what life was like in ancient Egypt.

A Look Inside a Tomb

In the nineteenth and early twentieth centuries, scholars began to open the tombs of ancient Egypt. Mummies were examined and afterward displayed in museums all over the world.

In 1922 one of the few royal tombs that had not been looted by grave robbers was discovered. Inside was the mummy of the boy-king Tutankhamen (toot ahngk AH mun), who ruled Egypt in the fourteenth century B.C. "King Tut" captured the imagination of the world. The fabulous treasure buried with him gave only a glimpse of the wealth of far more important pharaohs.

Modern Technology

Today's technology has helped scholars learn more about ancient Egypt. In 1988 a team of scientists in Indianapolis used the X-ray imaging technology known as the CAT scan to look into the mummy of an upper-class Egyptian woman. Her name was Wenu-hotep. The scientists nicknamed her Winnie.

The scientists did not have to unwrap Winnie's linen bindings. The CAT scan did that without disturbing her body. Layer by layer, the scan made three-dimensional images of her face, skull, and body. You can see a CAT scan of Winnie's head in the image on page 78.

Winnie was a fashion-conscious woman who wore kohl, or black eye makeup. She used perfume, shaved her head, and wore a wig. That too was the fashion among upper-class women—and men—of her time. We can tell even more about Winnie based on the objects that were buried with her.

The CAT scan showed that Winnie's bones had matured, indicating that she was in her 30s or 40s when she died. There were no signs of illness. Most healthy Egyptians of that time may not have lived much longer than she did.

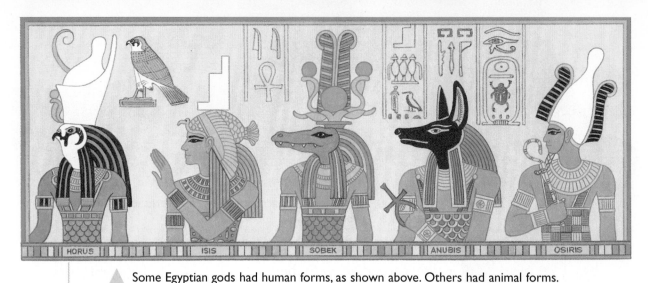

| HORUS | ISIS | SOBEK | ANUBIS | OSIRIS |

Some Egyptian gods had human forms, as shown above. Others had animal forms.

Internal organs of mummies were stored in jars like this one.

The Lady of the House

Lady of the House, written on Winnie's coffin, meant that she was married. Like all Egyptian women of the time, Winnie could own personal property after marriage. She also kept her dowry. Winnie probably prayed to the goddess Isis, shown above, who protected women and their rights.

Women held high status in ancient Egypt. They were allowed to work in some jobs outside their homes. Since Winnie was wealthy, she may not have had to work, and she probably had servants. But she might have run her husband's estate, business, or government office when he was absent.

In all likelihood, Winnie's life was a happy one. If she had not been happy with her husband, she could have gone to court to divorce him. Then she could have married again. In addition, she was entitled to one third of the property she and her husband owned.

If she had time to prepare for death, Winnie would have been confident that she would live again. By paying to have her mummified, her relatives indicated that they probably shared that same belief.

In a way, 2,500 years later, Winnie has come to life again, although not quite in the way ancient Egyptians believed she would. And she has told us much about her life.

SHOW WHAT YOU KNOW!

REFOCUS
COMPREHENSION

1. Why did the Egyptians preserve the bodies of the dead?

2. What rights and responsibilities did Egyptian women have?

THINK ABOUT IT
CRITICAL THINKING

To what social class did Winnie belong? How did scientists figure out what her class was?

WRITE ABOUT IT
ACTIVITY

Suppose that you are a woman of Winnie's class in ancient Egypt. Write a journal entry describing a typical day in your life.

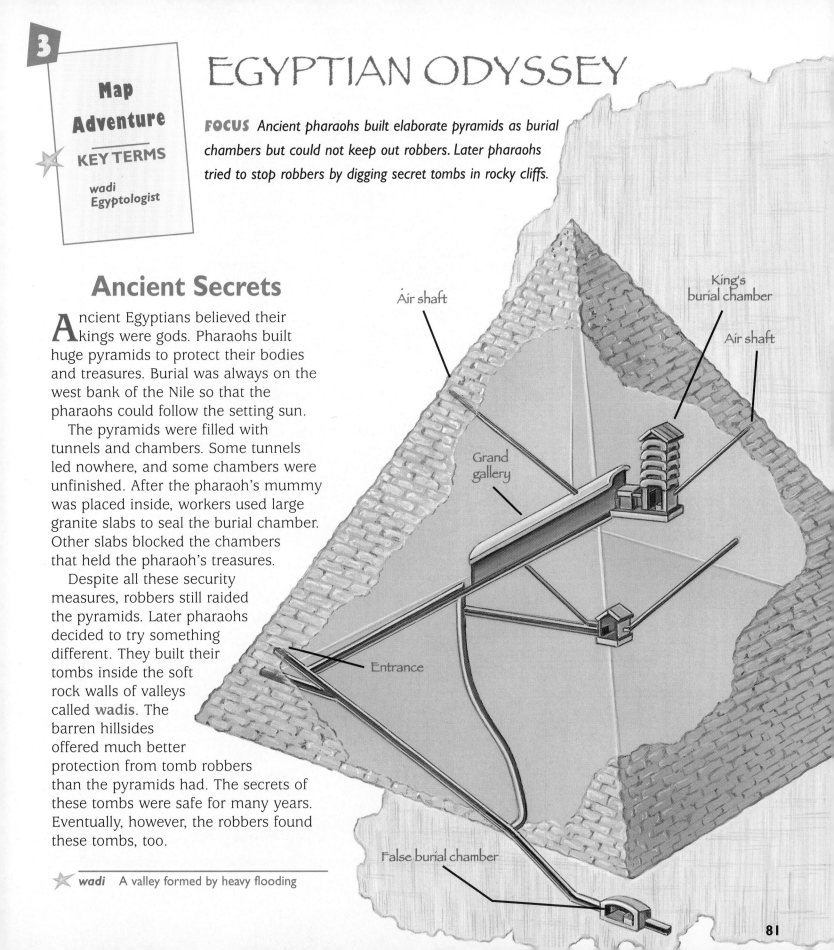

Map Adventure

——

KEY TERMS

★ wadi
  Egyptologist

EGYPTIAN ODYSSEY

FOCUS *Ancient pharaohs built elaborate pyramids as burial chambers but could not keep out robbers. Later pharaohs tried to stop robbers by digging secret tombs in rocky cliffs.*

Ancient Secrets

Ancient Egyptians believed their kings were gods. Pharaohs built huge pyramids to protect their bodies and treasures. Burial was always on the west bank of the Nile so that the pharaohs could follow the setting sun.

The pyramids were filled with tunnels and chambers. Some tunnels led nowhere, and some chambers were unfinished. After the pharaoh's mummy was placed inside, workers used large granite slabs to seal the burial chamber. Other slabs blocked the chambers that held the pharaoh's treasures.

Despite all these security measures, robbers still raided the pyramids. Later pharaohs decided to try something different. They built their tombs inside the soft rock walls of valleys called **wadis**. The barren hillsides offered much better protection from tomb robbers than the pyramids had. The secrets of these tombs were safe for many years. Eventually, however, the robbers found these tombs, too.

★ **wadi**   A valley formed by heavy flooding

Air shaft

King's burial chamber

Air shaft

Grand gallery

Entrance

False burial chamber

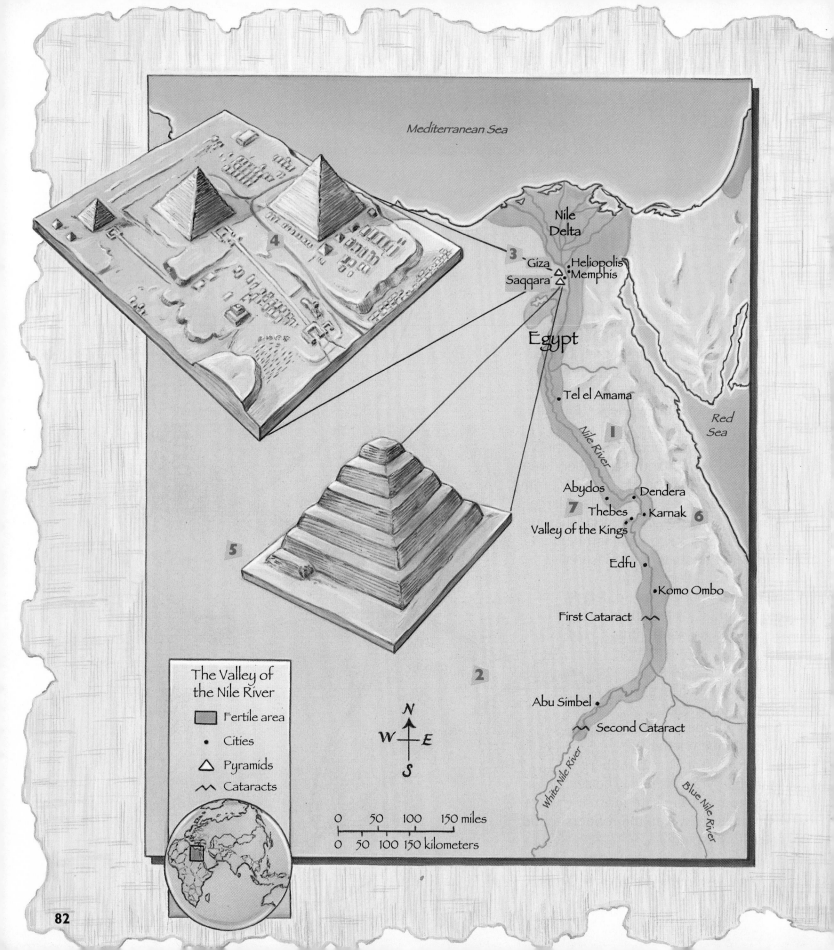

Mediterranean Sea

Nile
Delta

Egypt

4

3

Giza
Saqqara

Heliopolis
Memphis

Tel el Amama

Nile River

1

Red
Sea

Abydos
Thebes
Valley of the Kings

Dendera
Karnak

7

6

5

Edfu

Komo Ombo

First Cataract

2

Abu Simbel

Second Cataract

White Nile River

Blue Nile River

The Valley of
the Nile River

Fertile area

• Cities

△ Pyramids

∿ Cataracts

N
W—E
S

0   50   100   150 miles
0 50 100 150 kilometers

82

An Ancient Adventure!

Y<small>ou</small> are a traveler in ancient Egypt. When you arrive in Giza, you overhear two men discussing the secret burial ground of the pharaohs. Could they be robbers? Their talk excites you, and you decide to locate the tombs before they do. Use what you know about ancient Egypt to help you explore. Watch out for traps!

Map Key

1 Nile River The Nile flows north from central Africa for over 4,000 miles before spilling into the Mediterranean Sea.

2 Sahara Harsh desert conditions across most of northern Africa helped protect Egypt from invaders.

3 Giza Some pharaohs of the Old Kingdom built their pyramids at Giza. Here you will also find the statue of the Great Sphinx.

4 The Great Pyramid It took more than 2 million stone blocks and 100,000 workers over 20 years to build this pyramid for King Khufu. The base of the Great Pyramid covers more than 13 acres.

5 Step Pyramid Egyptologists believe this was the first pyramid ever built. It still stands at the ruins of Memphis.

6 Karnak This ancient city on the east bank of the Nile River is the site of the Temple of Amon-Ra—worshiped as the king of the gods during the New Kingdom.

7 Thebes The ancient city of Thebes was the capital during the New Kingdom.

★ *Egyptologist* A scientist who studies the remains of ancient Egypt

MAP IT

1. You leave the pyramids at Giza to search for the mysterious burial ground. A stranger tells you to sail upstream. In which direction should you sail?

2. You stop near Memphis. A farmer tells you that the secret tombs are located nearby. You follow his directions and arrive at the Step Pyramid. How do you know that the farmer was wrong?

3. As you continue your journey upstream, you hear rumors of a burial site farther south. When you ask for directions, a fisherman tells you to sail to Komo Ombo to find the secret tombs. Should you go? Why or why not?

4. You stop to examine the temples at Dendera. There you meet another Egyptologist, who shares a new clue. He tells you the secret tombs are north of Edfu. Which way do you sail next?

5. You decide to land at Thebes. A hot desert wind blows from the west. The sun bakes the rocky cliffs around you. Do you think you have finally found the secret tombs? Why or why not?

EXPLORE IT

You own a stone quarry below the First Cataract. You just received an order for stone for the Great Pyramid. Prepare sailing instructions for your barge captain.

THE KINGDOM OF KUSH

FOCUS *Conquests and trade between Egypt and the kingdom of Kush lead to an exchange of ideas as well as goods.*

Early Links Between Egypt and Kush

South of Egypt was the kingdom called Kush, today's Sudan. It lay, like Egypt, in the Nile River valley. From the time of the Old Kingdom, Egyptian caravans traveled south, carrying grain for trade. They returned with such items as ivory, incense, hides, and precious stones.

The most important trade with Kush was in gold and enslaved people. Egyptians used slaves from Kush as household servants. Some also served in the pharaoh's army.

During the Middle Kingdom, the Egyptians took steps to protect this trade. They built forts along the Nile to guard the caravans. These links were broken after Egypt was invaded by the Hyksos, warriors from the east.

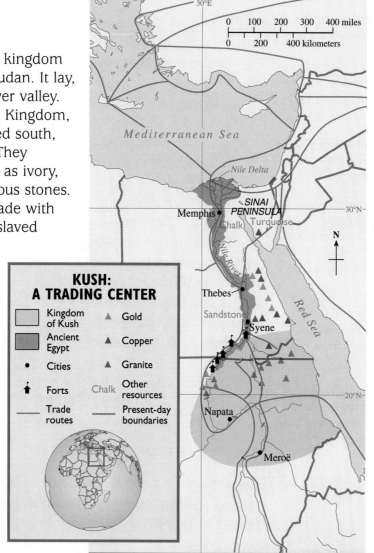

KUSH: A TRADING CENTER

- Kingdom of Kush
- Ancient Egypt
- Cities
- Forts
- Trade routes
- ▲ Gold
- ▲ Copper
- ▲ Granite
- Other resources
- Present-day boundaries

A Part of Egypt

During the New Kingdom, Pharaoh Ahmose I (AHM ohs) conquered Kush and made it a part of Egypt. Then he appointed a governor. The Kushite nobles were forced to deliver gold and slaves as **tribute** to Egypt. Children of the nobles often were sent to the pharaoh's court to serve as pages.

Under Egypt's rule, the people of Kush adopted many elements of Egyptian civilization. They began to worship the same gods and write in hieroglyphics. The upper class of Kush spoke the language of Egypt. At Napata (NAP ut uh), the capital of Kush, Egyptian-style temples were dedicated to the sun god, Amon-Ra. Soon the

---

⭐ **tribute** A payment given by subjects to rulers

Kushites were building their own pyramids, which had flat, not pointed, tops.

Kush Rules Egypt

Egypt's power declined at the end of the New Kingdom, and Kush's power increased. When King Kasha Kush launched invasions against his once-powerful northern neighbor, he was able to conquer Upper Egypt.

His successor, King Piankhi (PYANG-kee), led an army north into Lower Egypt. After capturing Memphis, Piankhi went farther north to the town of Heliopolis, or "city of the sun." It was under the protection of the sun god. Piankhi marched to the temple and demanded to enter the sacred pyramidion-house—the dwelling place of the god. The doors were bolted shut. Only priests and the pharaoh were permitted inside. Realizing that Piankhi was now in control, the priests dressed him in the pharaoh's robes. Piankhi's triumph was described on a pillar he set up.

*He came into the house of Ra and entered into the temple with great praise. . . . He was purified with incense and **libations**; garlands from the pyramidion-house were presented to him. The king himself stood alone: he broke through the bolts, opened the double doors, applied the clay, and sealed them with the king's own seal.*

Piankhi became the new pharaoh. The reign of Kushite pharaohs is counted as the 25th Egyptian dynasty. Kushite rule over Egypt lasted only 52 years. Assyrians invaded Egypt and defeated Taharqa (tuh HAHR kuh), the last Kushite pharaoh, who fled back to Napata.

A Continuing Civilization

Later Egyptian rulers tried to reconquer Kush, and they **sacked** Napata. As a result, the Kushites moved their capital farther south on the Nile, to Meroë (MER oh ee).

There they raised pyramids and monuments, showing that their civilization continued to flourish. Some of these structures remain today. Modern scholars have learned that queens as well as kings ruled Kush.

Gradually the people of Kush developed their own form of writing. Unfortunately, this script has not yet been decoded. Scholars still have much to learn about the civilization of ancient Kush.

This Kushite image of the goddess Hathor shows Egyptian influence.

Museum Expedition, courtesy of Museum Of Fine Arts, Boston

SHOW WHAT YOU KNOW!

REFOCUS
COMPREHENSION

1. What kind of trading relationship existed between Egypt and the kingdom of Kush?

2. What event brought the Kushite rule of Egypt to an abrupt end?

THINK ABOUT IT
CRITICAL THINKING

Why did Piankhi demand to enter the sacred dwelling place of the sun god?

WRITE ABOUT IT
ACTIVITY

You are an officer in Piankhi's army seeking to conquer Egypt. You want to let your family back in Kush know the result of the invasion. Write a message, to be sent by a courier, detailing what happened.

★ **libation**   The ceremony of pouring wine or oil to honor a god

★ **sack**   To rob a captured city

5

March of Time

3100 B.C. TO 30 B.C.

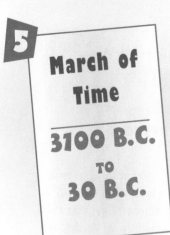

IMPORTANT RULERS

FOCUS *Egypt had many rulers. Some were especially noteworthy for being fair or harsh, silly or serious, or even for being a woman.*

UNITING EGYPT

According to ancient tradition, Menes founded Egypt's first dynasty. Menes came from the town of Thinis in Upper Egypt.

Before Menes, Egypt was divided into two kingdoms. The kings of Lower Egypt wore a red crown, and those of Upper Egypt donned a white crown. As a symbol of the unity of the country, Menes designed a crown that combined both colors.

Menes ruled for 62 years, so he must have been very young when he united Egypt. Even so, he did not die of old age. According to a priest, Menes was killed by a hippopotamus while bathing in the Nile.

THE PHARAOH IS A WOMAN

Hatshepsut (hat SHEP soot) was one of the most remarkable women in Egyptian history. She ruled for her stepson, a child. In time she declared herself pharaoh and wore male clothing and a false beard. Hatshepsut's reign was a time of peace. She encouraged trade and rebuilt temples.

Hatshepsut was proud of her achievements. She decorated the walls of a temple at Deir el Bahri with carvings that show her as a child of the sun god, emphasizing her right to the throne.

After Hatshepsut died, her stepson became the ruler. He erased her name from the monuments she had built and destroyed all the statues of her he could find. Even so, the memory of Hatshepsut has survived.

THEY WORSHIPED ONE GOD

Pharaoh Akhenaton (ah kuh-NAHT un) was known as "the criminal." He declared that there was only one god, Aton, the sun that shone on everyone.

This startling idea aroused the wrath of the priests and nobles. Some of them blamed Akhenaton's wife, Queen Nefertiti (nef ur TEE tee), for influencing her husband.

Akhenaton and Nefertiti left Thebes, the capital, and built a new city 300 miles to the north. They named it Akhetaton, "the horizon of Aton." There they built a temple without a roof so that the god Aton could shine inside.

ca. 3100 B.C.	1472 B.C.	1379 B.C.	ca. 747 B.C.	48 B.C.
Menes unifies Egypt	Hatshepsut becomes ruler	Akhenaton declares there is one god	Piankhi conquers Egypt	Cleopatra meets Julius Caesar

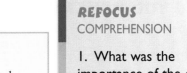

| 3000 | 1500 | 1000 | 500 | B.C. | A.D. |

A MONUMENTAL PHARAOH

The Bible tells how Moses led the Hebrews out of Egypt to escape a cruel pharaoh, who was probably Ramses the Great. Egyptians admired this pharaoh. He built many monuments. The most famous one was at Abu Simbel, on the west bank of the Nile. Two huge temples were carved in the rock. By the entrance were four statues of Ramses, each 65 feet high.

In 1955 the Egyptians began to plan a dam across the Nile. Fifty nations contributed funds to save the statues.

THE WARRIOR WHO BECAME PHARAOH

After Piankhi conquered Egypt, he had the story of his life carved into a stone pillar, which tells us most of what we know about him. Piankhi was born into the royal family of Kush and trained to be a warrior.

Like the Egyptians, the Kushites worshiped Amon-Ra, the sun god. One day Piankhi wrote that he heard Amon-Ra speak to him: "I ordained that you would be ruler of Egypt."

So, when Piankhi became king at the age of 21, he knew his destiny. That was why, when he conquered Egypt, he went to the temple of Amon-Ra to claim his birthright.

HAIL, CAESAR!

Cleopatra's family had ruled Egypt since Alexander the Great conquered it. Queen at age 18, Cleopatra saw a new threat to Egypt: Rome. Julius Caesar, a Roman general, soon arrived to rule Egypt. Cleopatra hid inside a rolled-up rug and had a slave take it to Caesar as a gift. As she had hoped, Caesar let her rule with him.

After Caesar died, Cleopatra and Mark Antony fought against Octavian for control of Egypt. They lost. Cleopatra took her own life when she could not make peace with Octavian.

SHOW WHAT YOU KNOW!

REFOCUS
COMPREHENSION

1. What was the importance of the crown that Menes designed? What did it represent?

2. Which social class was particularly angry with Akhenaton? Why?

THINK ABOUT IT
CRITICAL THINKING

Why was saving Ramses' statues from the rising waters so important to 50 modern nations?

WRITE ABOUT IT
ACTIVITY

Suppose you are a native Egyptian at the time of Julius Caesar and Cleopatra. Write a description of your feelings about being ruled by Rome.

SUMMING UP

1 DO YOU REMEMBER...
COMPREHENSION

1. What did Menes do?

2. For what is the Old Kingdom of ancient Egypt most remembered?

3. Which people were at the top of ancient Egyptian society? Who was in the middle?

4. How did modern scholars learn to read hieroglyphics?

5. Why did the Egyptians bury tools, animals, jewels, and other things with their dead?

6. How did scientists learn so much about Winnie?

7. What was the purpose of the Egyptian pyramids?

8. Why were pharaohs' tombs built near Thebes?

9. During the New Kingdom, how did the relationship between Egypt and Kush change?

10. Who was Cleopatra? What role did she play in ancient Egypt?

2 SKILL POWER
READING A CROSS SECTION

In this chapter you practiced reading a cross section of an ancient pyramid. Can you find examples of cross sections that show objects from modern life? Team up with a partner at the library and set a time limit of one hour. Try to find the most interesting cross section possible. Later share your cross section with the class and vote on which is most interesting.

3 WHAT DO YOU THINK?
CRITICAL THINKING

1. Why has ancient Egypt been described as the gift of the Nile?

2. Ancient Egypt thrived for over 2,000 years. What can you infer about the civilization?

3. Do you think the time and energy spent building the pyramids was worth it? Were there other public works that would have made more sense?

4. Explain how and why the burial of pharaohs would have been different if the sun set in the east instead of in the west.

5. What, do you think, are three main sources of information about life in ancient Egypt?

4 SAY IT, WRITE IT, USE IT
VOCABULARY

Select two terms from the list below, such as *delta* and *Egyptologist*. Put each term in the center of a circle. Then draw spokes out from the center. On each spoke, write one of the other terms in the list and tell how the term on the spoke relates to the term in the center. Use as many terms as you can.

delta	obelisk
Egyptologist	papyrus
hieroglyphic	sack
libation	tribute
mummy	vizier
natron	wadi

5 GEOGRAPHY AND YOU
MAP STUDY

1. The Nile River flows from south to north. When people sailed from the old capital in Memphis to the new capital in Thebes, did they sail with the current or against it?

2. Knowing what you do about the direction in which the Nile flows, explain why Upper Egypt and Lower Egypt are named as they are.

3. What does the shape of the Middle Kingdom tell you about the importance of the Nile River?

4. Which city on the map is closest to the Fourth Cataract?

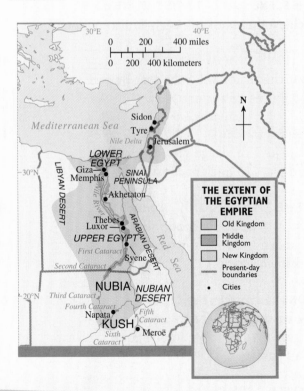

6 TAKE ACTION
CITIZENSHIP

Ancient Egypt had a great impact on the countries around it. With a group of friends, think about some customs and traditions from other countries that Americans have borrowed and made their own. These might include words, holidays, traditions, entertainment, foods—the list could go on and on. Make a chart or give an oral report that tells how these borrowings have made our country a richer place.

7 GET CREATIVE
MATH CONNECTION

Like hieroglyphics, Egyptian numbers were based on pictures.

Lotus	(𓆼)	= one thousand
Rope	(𓏤)	= one hundred
Arch	(∩)	= ten
Stroke	(/)	= one

This is how you would write the number 1,236.

Count like an Egyptian. Do a few three- or four-digit addition or subtraction problems. Ask a classmate to check your work.

LOOKING AHEAD Find out what was going on in India at about the same time that the ancient Egyptian civilization was developing.

EMPIRES OF

How do we know about the early cities of ancient India and the people who built them? Why is ancient India's culture sometimes called a lost civilization? Read this chapter for answers to these questions.

CONTENTS

▼ Do you know the origins of this game? Find out on page 99.

ANCIENT INDIA

These books tell about some people, places, and events that make ancient India such a fascinating country. Read one that interests you and fill out a book-review form.

READ AND RESEARCH

The King's Chessboard **by David Birch, pictures by Devis Grebu** (Penguin USA, 1988)
When a wise man requests a reward as simple as a few grains of rice, the king doesn't think twice about it. That's nothing, right? Watch as the wise man teaches *you* and the king that "nothing" isn't as small as you think. (*folk tale*)

Savitri: A Tale of Ancient India **by Aaron Shepard, illustrated by Vera Rosenberry** (Albert Whitman & Co., 1992)
When Princess Savitri chooses Satyavan to be her husband, she is warned by a seer that Satyavan's life will soon end. Can Savitri devise a clever way to save her husband? (*folk tale*)

The Ganges Delta and Its People **by David Cummings** (Thomson Learning, 1994)
Life on this delta has always been difficult. Even today, survival is a struggle. What do you think living there centuries ago must have been like? (*nonfiction*)

India **by Sylvia McNair** (Childrens Press, 1994)
The first few chapters of this book will give you a view of the geography, history, and culture of India during ancient times. Discover the rich religious history that made India and its early leaders so extraordinary. (*nonfiction*)

SKILL POWER

Reading Special-Purpose Maps

Knowing how to read special-purpose maps can help you learn interesting information about places.

UNDERSTAND IT

Do you ever watch the weather forecast on TV? The weather forecaster uses special-purpose maps to show where weather patterns are expected to develop. Your parents may use a different kind of special-purpose map—a road map—to follow a route when they are driving. There are lots of different kinds of maps and many special kinds of information that they provide.

EXPLORE IT

The special purpose of a map is usually stated in the name of the map. What is the purpose of this map?

Monsoons are winds that have great importance for the people of India. From about June through September, winds blow from the Arabian Sea and the Indian Ocean, bringing hot, wet weather. During the rest of the year, the wind blows from land toward the water, bringing cooler weather.

Use the map legend and the compass rose to help you get information from this map. From which direction does the summer monsoon blow? From which direction does the winter monsoon blow?

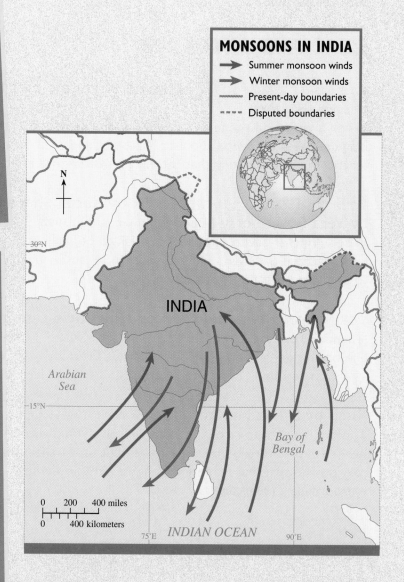

MONSOONS IN INDIA

→ Summer monsoon winds
→ Winter monsoon winds
~~~ Present-day boundaries
---- Disputed boundaries

N

30°N

INDIA

Arabian
Sea

15°N

Bay of
Bengal

0   200   400 miles
0   400 kilometers

75°E   INDIAN OCEAN   90°E

TRY IT

Think of a place you would like to have a special-purpose map of. Perhaps you'd like to share information on a map of your favorite amusement park. Or maybe you'd like to show the route you took on your vacation. You might even want to learn about places on Earth's moon. When you have decided on a special-purpose map, do some research to find a map that either shows the information you want or gives you enough information so that you can draw your own map. Share your map with your classmates.

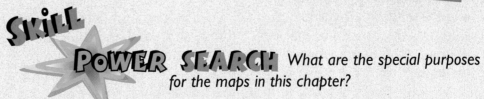

SKILL POWER SEARCH *What are the special purposes for the maps in this chapter?*

Setting the Scene

★ KEY TERMS

subcontinent
caste
untouchable
caste
reign

EARLY TIMES IN INDIA

FOCUS *Cities in the Indus Valley were nearly as old as those in ancient Mesopotamia and Egypt.*

Land of the Monsoon

Kalidasa (kahl ee DAHS uh), India's greatest playwright, wrote, "The wind is an angry fan, and the world a furnace." He was referring to the hot monsoon winds that blow across India every April and May, bringing heat so intense that the air seems to ripple. Land dries, people and animals lose energy, and plants wilt.

Finally the southwest monsoon breaks. Rain begins like an explosion, lasting from June to September. The farmers rejoice, for the rain brings to life the crops they have planted. During the winter monsoons, which are dry, the wind blows from the opposite direction. Crops are planted again in October in preparation for the winter monsoon.

The triangular peninsula known as the Indian **subcontinent** contains the modern nations of India, Pakistan, Nepal, and Bangladesh. This subcontinent is nearly half the size of the United States. Within it are many landforms and extremes of weather.

INDUS VALLEY CIVILIZATION

- Indus Valley
- Present-day boundaries
- Disputed boundary

HINDU KUSH

Brahmaputra River

HIMALAYAS

• Harappa

Indus River

• Mohenjo-Daro

Ganges River

Narbada River

Arabian Sea

DECCAN PLATEAU

Bay of Bengal

N

0   250   500 miles
0   250   500 kilometers

75°E   90°E   30°N   15°N

★ **subcontinent**   A large landmass that is smaller than a continent

Two mountain ranges, the Himalayas (hihm uh LAY uz) and the Hindu Kush, separate the subcontinent from the rest of Asia. The climate is tropical in the southern part of the subcontinent. The central area of the subcontinent is a vast plateau; much of the land is known as the Deccan (DEK un) Plateau.

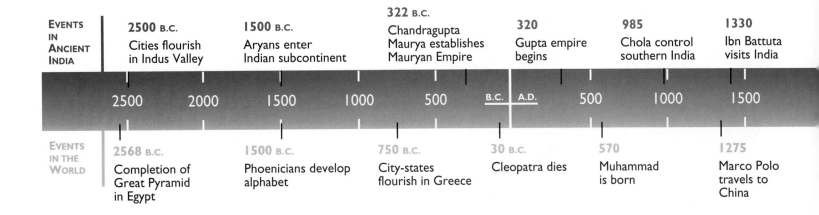

EVENTS IN ANCIENT INDIA	2500 B.C. Cities flourish in Indus Valley	1500 B.C. Aryans enter Indian subcontinent	322 B.C. Chandragupta Maurya establishes Mauryan Empire	320 Gupta empire begins	985 Chola control southern India	1330 Ibn Battuta visits India
	2500 2000	1500 1000	500	B.C. A.D. 500	1000	1500
EVENTS IN THE WORLD	2568 B.C. Completion of Great Pyramid in Egypt	1500 B.C. Phoenicians develop alphabet	750 B.C. City-states flourish in Greece	30 B.C. Cleopatra dies	570 Muhammad is born	1275 Marco Polo travels to China

West of the peninsula is the Arabian Sea; east of it, the Bay of Bengal. Both are part of the Indian Ocean.

Melting snow from the Himalayas is the source of India's three largest rivers. The name *India* comes from the Indus River in the northwest. In the northeast, the Ganges (GAN jeez) and the Brahmaputra (brah muh POO truh) rivers flow into the Bay of Bengal.

A Lost Civilization

The earliest Indian civilization in the Indus Valley flourished 4,500 years ago. As you can see on the map, two of its major cities were Harappa (huh-RAP uh) and Mohenjo-Daro (moh hen-joh DAHR oh). The residents made bronze tools and built their houses with baked mud bricks. These people were among the first to wear cotton clothes. They invented a form of writing, but no one can read it today. Seals with Indus Valley writing have been found in cities of Mesopotamia, which tells us that people of these regions traded with one another.

The Indus Valley people had many things to use for trade. They made jewelry that both men and women wore. Officials wore gold armbands and headbands. Women donned bracelets, anklets, necklaces, beaded belts, and fancy hair combs or pins. Potters made cooking utensils, as well as writing sticks, statues, back scratchers, dice, and game pieces.

The First City Planners

In contrast to the ancient cities of Mesopotamia, which grew in a haphazard fashion, Indus cities had streets laid out in a rectangular grid. All the houses looked alike. Even the size of the bricks was the same. Archaeologists have found no large palaces or temples in the cities.

Homes in the Indus Valley had indoor wells and plumbing. Residents could draw water from the wells, and shower by pouring it over their bodies. Sloped floors took the water to a drain. Sewers and drainpipes ran under the city streets.

The people of Indus Valley cities had a highly developed way of life. They even made clay toys, such as those shown on the next page, for their children. But around 1750 B.C. civilization underwent a series of crises in

In this terra-cotta toy, oxen pull a chariot and rider.

the Indus Valley. The people first crowded into and then abandoned the cities; no one knows why. Scholars now believe that it might have been a natural disaster, such as a flood, or a change in climate.

Newcomers From the Northwest

At about the same time, nomadic peoples came through the mountain passes of the Hindu Kush and into the Indus Valley. They called themselves Aryans (AR ee unz). They spoke Vedic, from which Sanskrit (SAN skriht), an ancient Indian language, and other Indian languages later developed.

The Aryans used horses to pull their fast chariots, giving themselves an advantage in warfare. Soon the Aryans dominated the region. These early tribes built no monuments or cities.

The Aryans valued land, which they needed for cows, sheep, and goats. As time went on, they began to farm. They were among the first people to grow sugar cane.

By about 600 B.C. the Aryans had spread east to the Ganges River

The large painted jar with a border of birds was made in Harappa.

valley and south into the Deccan Plateau. States were formed, and cities appeared once again.

The Aryans held religious beliefs that would influence all of Asia. Their religious poems and hymns were passed on by word of mouth for centuries. After writing developed, the verses were collected into books called Vedas (VAY duz), a name that means "knowledge." The oldest and most important of the Vedas is the Rig-Veda. About one third of its hymns are addressed to Indra, the chief god. Much of what we know of the people of that time comes from what we have learned from the Vedas.

A Priestly Class

Over time, priests became almost as powerful as the rulers because priests knew how to perform long religious ceremonies correctly. The people believed that these ceremonies were necessary to please the gods.

The priests' power was increased by the division of society into four mythical classes. According to the Rig-Veda, these classes came from different parts of a being who sacrificed himself to create the world. *Brahmans,* or priests, came from his mouth. *Kshatriya* (kuh-SHAT ree yuh), or warriors, came from

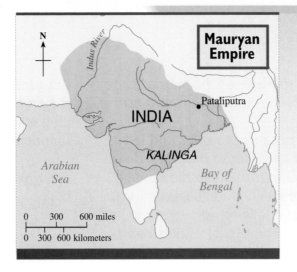

Mauryan Empire

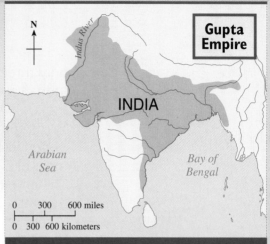

Gupta Empire

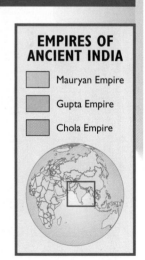

Chola Empire

his shoulders. *Vaishya* (VYS yuh), or traders and landowners, came from his thighs; and *Shudra,* or peasants, came from his feet.

In time, many **castes** appeared. Among them were the **untouchable castes**. People in these castes did the most lowly work in Indian society. Brahmans regarded the untouchable castes as impure and would not perform ceremonies for them.

Some people rejected the Brahmans' claim to be the main spiritual leaders. Such people would often leave their homes and wander from place to place, trying to find the meaning of life. Among them were Siddhartha Gautama (sihd DAHR tuh GOUT uh-muh), who became Buddha, and Mahavira (muh hah VEE ruh), the founder of Jainism (JYN ihz um).

Southern India

Southern India was not invaded by the Aryans. There was a considerable amount of trade with Greece and Rome. Sometimes travelers commented on the wealth of the country's seaports and the power of its women.

⭐ *caste* Any one of the Hindu social classes into which a person was born and which ruled his or her relations with others
untouchable caste A group of families who were considered low in status and were discriminated against

Although the Aryans did not reach that far south, some of their religious ideas did. These ideas were blended with beliefs in other gods and goddesses.

A Mighty Expansion— The Mauryan Empire

Three empires—the Maurya (MOUR yuh), the Gupta (GOOP tuh), and the Chola (CHOH luh)—developed in ancient India. The maps show the sizes of the empires.

When Alexander the Great, whom you will learn about in Chapter 7, entered India in 327 B.C., there were many kingdoms. The most powerful was Magadha (MUG ud uh), on the Ganges River plain.

A young prince, Chandragupta (chun druh GOOP tuh) Maurya, united the Indian kingdoms and founded the Maurya dynasty. Within five years of Alexander's invasion, Chandragupta had conquered the Magadha kingdom. In

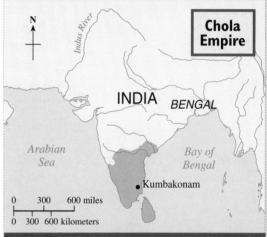

EMPIRES OF ANCIENT INDIA

- Mauryan Empire
- Gupta Empire
- Chola Empire

only three more years, he subdued the Indus Valley and the rest of northern India.

His son became the ruler and led troops into the Deccan Plateau, adding most of southern India to his domain. The empire reached its full extent in the **reign** of Asoka (uh SHOH kuh).

In the Maurya capital, multistoried houses rose high on the riverbanks. The wealthy used golden bowls and wore clothing with golden threads. Perhaps 50 million people with different languages, religions, and customs lived in the empire. Asoka was a wise ruler as well as a conqueror. It wasn't until modern times that so much of India was ruled by one government.

After Asoka's death, his sons fought each other for the throne. In the disorder, areas began to break off from the empire. In 184 B.C. the last Maurya king was assassinated by the commander of his own army.

A High Point—The Gupta Empire

India remained divided into many kingdoms until about A.D. 320. Then a man who called himself Chandra (CHUN druh) Gupta founded a new empire. The Gupta dynasty, which lasted for 200 years, marked a high point in Indian culture.

India's two great Sanskrit epic poems, the *Mahabharata* (muh HAH BAH-ruh tuh) and the *Ramayana* (rah MAH-yuh nuh), probably took their final written form during this period. *Mahabharata*, which means "great story," is among the longest poems ever written. It tells about the struggle between rival families to rule a kingdom in northern India. Artists were inspired by the story and painted scenes from it. A collection of animal fables, the *Panchatantra,* was also written down during the Gupta era.

Gupta artists and sculptors glorified India's religions. As you look through this chapter, you can see examples of the kinds of work they produced.

Indians also excelled in science and medicine. In Gupta universities, mathematicians developed a number system with a decimal point and a zero. The Arabs later learned this system from the Indians. What we call Arabic numerals today are really Indian numerals.

A painting of Krishna, a Hindu god, presenting a lotus to his friend Radha

---

★ *reign*   A period of royal power, authority, or rule

Above, the ancient game of chess played on a computer; *right,* a chess piece from the Chola dynasty

A Dynasty of Tigers—The Chola

Kings of the Chola dynasty ruled parts of southern India, beginning about A.D. 100. According to legend, Karikalan Chola, the first ruler, took the tiger as a symbol of his dynasty.

About 750 years later, the Chola made up one of only three large kingdoms in the south. But a series of Chola warrior-kings conquered the other two. By the reign of Rajaraja (RAHJ uh rahj uh), beginning in 985, the Chola controlled all of southern India. Under his son, Rajendra (ruh JAYN-druh), the kingdom grew even larger. You will learn more about Rajendra later in this chapter.

Chola kings were Hindus who used their wealth to build temples. But there was also time for games. A favorite pastime was chess. Scholars believe the game originated in India during this period. At first, it had four players, and dice were thrown to determine who moved. Today it has two players—one might even be a computer!

Reading and writing were pleasurable pastimes during the Chola period.

SHOW WHAT YOU KNOW!

REFOCUS
COMPREHENSION

1. How do the summer and winter monsoons affect India's climate?

2. Explain the system of four mythical classes.

THINK ABOUT IT
CRITICAL THINKING

Compare and contrast the accomplishments of the Aryans and the Guptas.

WRITE ABOUT IT
ACTIVITY

Suppose you are an archaeologist uncovering the ruins of Mohenjo-Daro and Harappa. Describe what the streets and homes you've found show about the people who built them about 4,500 years ago.

RELIGIONS OF ANCIENT INDIA

FOCUS *The beliefs of three religions of ancient India—Hinduism, Buddhism, and Jainism—helped shape the Indian civilization and are still practiced today.*

The Hindu Religion

Hinduism is the oldest of the major religions of India. It had no single founder. The word *Hindu* means "an inhabitant of India." Over time the religion has developed from the traditions of the many people who live in the Indian subcontinent.

Hinduism began with people who referred to themselves as Aryans. Hindus often say that Hinduism is a way of life, not just a set of religious beliefs.

Hindus worship God in many forms, such as Brahma, the creator; Vishnu, the preserver; and Shiva, the destroyer. The Mother Goddess, wife of Shiva, is known as Parvati, Mahadevi, and other names. The Rig-Veda says: "Truth is one, though the sages (wise people) call it by many different names."

Another basic idea of Hinduism is **reincarnation**. This is the belief that the soul of every person has lived

The god Shiva, with four arms and poised on one foot, is the Lord of the Dance.

from the beginning of time in the bodies of humans or animals. A person is born, dies, and is reborn continuously in different bodies. A person's condition in life is determined by his or her **karma**, or the actions he or she took in this and previous lives. In Hinduism the goal of a religious person is to end the cycle of rebirth, reaching perfection and blending with the soul of the universe.

Usually each village has several gods and goddesses whose statues are in local temples. There also are gods that each family worships. An individual chooses one god to worship, often carrying a picture of him or her.

The Teachings of Buddha

Around 500 B.C. a prince, Siddhartha Gautama, set out to learn why people suffer. For years he wandered as a beggar, practicing self-denial. Siddhartha ate very little. One day he realized that self-denial was not helping him toward his goal.

 reincarnation The continuation of a soul, upon the death of one body, into another body or form

karma All the actions in a person's life that affect the next life

Siddhartha sat down under a tree and stayed there until he found enlightenment. He discovered a way to end people's suffering. From that time on, he was known as Buddha, which means "Enlightened One."

Buddha spent the rest of his life teaching others how to find enlightenment. Through his teachings, he attracted many followers to his beliefs. He taught them: "A man is not learned because he talks much; he who is patient, free from hatred and fear, is called learned." A wise person understands that "the fault of another is easily seen, but the fault of oneself is hard to see."

The Four Noble Truths

Buddha outlined how to end one's suffering by following the Four Noble Truths. The first truth is that everyone suffers. The second truth is that the cause of suffering is desiring things. The third truth is that to end suffering, one should stop desiring things. The fourth truth is that the way to stop suffering is to follow the Eightfold Path.

The Eightfold Path is a series of eight steps that stress good behavior. Some of the steps are right conduct,

These statues of Buddha show him seated in the lotus position, which is part of the practice of **yoga**.

The lotus blossom is a symbol used to represent Buddha.

right speech, right views or opinions, and right effort.

Buddha recommended the following actions: Refrain from taking life, from taking what is not given to you, from speaking untruths, and from thinking or doing things that could cloud the mind.

In time, many people living in India accepted Buddha's teachings. Later, Buddhism spread beyond India to Tibet, China, Japan, Mongolia, Korea, and the other nations of Southeast Asia. Buddhism became more influential in those countries than it is in India today.

 yoga Indian exercises and postures designed to discipline the body and clear the mind

▲ Ornate marble carvings add to the beauty of a Jain temple.

Jainism — A Religion of Nonviolence

Mahavira, the founder of Jainism, lived at the same time as Buddha. Like Buddha, Mahavira came from a wealthy background and grew up in northeastern India. At the age of 30, he also set out to seek truth.

After 12 years of self-denial, he found his own understanding of truth. He taught that right knowledge, right conduct, and purity are essential. He believed people were caught in the cycle of rebirth because their past misdeeds clung to their souls.

Mahavira's death gave the name to his religion. *Jain* means "to conquer." To his followers, Mahavira had conquered the chains that bound his soul to continuing reincarnations.

Above all, Jainism is a religion of nonviolence. Mahavira told his followers that they must not harm people or animals in any way. Animals, birds, insects, and people have souls that must be protected.

The rule against violence to animals kept Jains from farming. They did not want to kill worms or other creatures in the earth. Even today some Jains carry a whisk broom, which they sweep before them to ensure that they will not step on insects. To make a living without farming, many Jains became merchants.

After about A.D. 1000, Jainism began to decline. However, its ideas remained influential. The leader of the Indian independence movement, Mohandas Gandhi (moh hun DAHS GAHN dee), was a Hindu inspired by Jainism. He made its practice of nonviolence a part of his philosophy.

SHOW WHAT YOU KNOW!

REFOCUS
COMPREHENSION

1. What are the main beliefs of the Hindu religion?

2. Why was Siddhartha Gautama called Buddha?

THINK ABOUT IT
CRITICAL THINKING

Do you think nonviolence is a difficult or easy path to follow? Use examples from your own experience to explain your answer.

WRITE ABOUT IT
ACTIVITY

Suppose that you listened to some of Buddha's sermons. Summarize briefly what he taught his followers.

WORSHIP, WORK, AND PLAY

FOCUS *Family worship and work were important parts of life in ancient India. Families also enjoyed various forms of entertainment, including festivals and dramas.*

Your Family

If you live in an Indian village during the Gupta era, your house is full of people. When your parents married, they did not move into a home of their own. They live with your father's parents. Your father's brothers and their wives also live here. Naturally there are many children.

The heads of the family, for as long as they live, are your grandparents. All the money that anyone in the household earns is turned over to them. They give it out as it is needed—to buy food, clothing, or any of the other things that people in the household require.

Your grandmother is highly respected. All the women and girls of the family answer to her. Women have a lot to do. In addition to cooking, they spin cotton fibers into cloth, grind wheat or rice, churn butter, and look after young children.

Living in such a large family means you have little privacy. If you misbehave, any of the men and

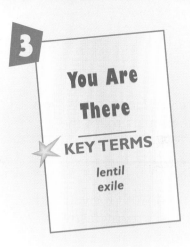

▲ A woman in a temple performs a special dance.

women in the house can scold you. On the other hand, you have many people to comfort and teach you. Even when you were very young, you learned to take part in the chores at home and also in the fields.

Day Begins

The day's work starts early. When the weather is hot, everyone gets up when it is still dark. The men want to do much of the farm work before the sun rises. The first thing you do is to take a quick bath in cold water. That certainly gets the day off to a refreshing start!

Then you can eat breakfast. There really are no strict mealtimes, and family members may eat when they feel like it. Usually your meals consist of buttermilk, wheat bread or rice, lentils, and vegetables. Since your family is Hindu, you never eat beef. The cow has been considered sacred in India for hundreds of years. But you may occasionally have fish, chicken, lamb, or goat.

Ganesh, a god believed to help people overcome obstacles, is shown as part man and part elephant.

⭐ **lentil** A plant, with seeds growing in pods, used as food

A spring festival, where merrymakers use paint to add to the celebration

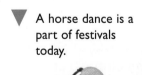

A horse dance is a part of festivals today.

Your Village

Members of your family may go to the village temple to ask a favor from a god or goddess there. The priest, or Brahman, rings a bell at the door of the temple to draw the attention of the god or goddess. People worship the statue that the god or goddess lives in. The priests regularly bathe and dress it.

Villagers bring gifts to the temple. These may be food or flowers. Sometimes the priests carry the statue around the temple while they play music and chant hymns. In some of the largest temples, women perform special dances, as shown in the picture on page 103.

During most of the day, villagers work. They plant and harvest crops. They cut down trees to prepare new farmland, dig irrigation ditches, and keep the roads in good condition. They must also repair the fences that surround the village and the fields. Lions, tigers, and many other wild animals roam the countryside.

Seasonal Festivals

Life is not all hard work for you and your family. There are many festivals and celebrations during the year that provide a break from everyday routine.

On one of these holidays, your family takes a trip to a nearby city. Caste rules are less strict there. The streets are thronged with people who have come for the merrymaking and dancing. Flags and banners decorate the buildings, and people carry colorful parasols for shade from the blazing sun.

In your village you've never seen the countless things that are for sale here. Merchants offer sweet cakes, garlands of flowers, jewelry, silk cloth, and betel leaves for chewing. You can stop at a shop to buy fruit, sugar candy, cooked rice, and chunks of cooked meat.

You go to the courtyard of the temple, where a play is about to start. It begins with a prayer to the gods. This play is from the great epic poem *Ramayana*. Each evening for ten or more days, parts of the story are presented. You already know much of this story, having heard it told by family members in the evenings.

Rama and Sita

Set in ancient times, *Ramayana* tells the story of the hero Rama, heir to the throne of Ayodhya (uh YOHD yuh), in

northern India. He is sent into **exile** by his father, the king, for 14 years because of a second queen's plot to make her son, Bharata (BAH ruh tuh), king. Rama gives away his possessions. His wife, Sita, and Lakshman, his brother, go away with Rama.

When Bharata learns what has happened, he declares that he will never be king. He puts his half-brother Rama's sandals on the throne and promises to rule only in Rama's name until Rama returns.

Then Rama, Sita, and Lakshman wander through the forests. The evil king Ravana seizes Sita and carries her to his island kingdom of Lanka (today Sri Lanka). Rama is wild with grief.

Rama seeks help to rescue Sita, who remains faithful to him. He is aided by Lakshman and a vast army of animals—monkeys, bears, a vulture, and a squirrel.

A Happy Ending

You, like everyone in the audience, hope there will be a happy ending. You are not disappointed. In the battle to free Sita, the wicked Ravana is killed. Rama and his beloved wife, Sita,

▲ The audience suffers with Sita as she is separated from Rama.

are together again. After the 14 years of exile are over, the wanderers return home. Bharata washes Rama's feet and presents the sandals to him. Rama then becomes king.

Hindu theater usually has a spiritual purpose. It is supposed to leave the audience with a feeling of divine justice and peace. You certainly feel that way as you head back to your village.

◄ Both men and women perform the horse dance.

⭐ **exile** A forced living away from one's country

REFOCUS
COMPREHENSION

1. Who were the heads of the family in ancient India?

2. What role did the temple play in village life?

THINK ABOUT IT
CRITICAL THINKING

Write a few paragraphs comparing a holiday in an ancient Indian city with a holiday you celebrate with your family.

WRITE ABOUT IT
ACTIVITY

Suppose you saw a performance of the play from the epic *Ramayana*. Write a letter to a friend in another village, describing the play you had just attended.

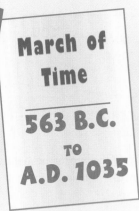

March of Time

563 B.C. TO A.D. 1035

OUTSTANDING LEADERS

FOCUS *Strong rulers and important religious leaders deeply influenced the development of the Indian civilization.*

MAKING A CHOICE

According to an old story, Siddhartha Gautama's mother had a strange dream before his birth, about 563 B.C. An elephant with six tusks, carrying a lotus flower in its trunk, touched her. Brahmans told Siddhartha's father, the king, that the dream meant that his son would be either a great king or a holy man.

To make sure that Siddhartha would choose to be a king, his father showered him with luxuries. Whenever the young man left the palace, the king's guards cleared the streets of all unpleasant sights.

One day, though, Siddhartha saw an old man, a sick man, a corpse, and a peaceful holy man. The sights touched his heart and made him set out on his quest for the meaning of life.

RULING WITH KINDNESS

Asoka became India's most beloved leader about 269 B.C. His life changed after he conquered the empire and saw the suffering that wars caused. Saddened, Asoka found peace in Buddhism. To help others learn Buddha's teachings, Asoka sent teachers to other lands, such as Egypt and China.

Asoka governed with kindness instead of force. He sent "overseers of the law" to make sure that local officials promoted "welfare and happiness . . . among servants and masters, Brahmans and rich, the needy and aged."

563 B.C.
Buddha is born

232 B.C.
Asoka dies

376
Chandra Gupta II
begins rule

1014
Rajendra extends
empire

600   400   200   B.C. | A.D.   200   400   600   800   1000

SHOW WHAT YOU
KNOW!

REFOCUS
COMPREHENSION

1. How did the teachings
of Buddha influence
Asoka?

2. How did Rajendra
help spread the influence
of Indian culture?

THINK ABOUT IT
CRITICAL THINKING

Would you rather have
lived in the kingdom of
Asoka or of Chandra
Gupta II? Explain your
answer.

WRITE ABOUT IT
ACTIVITY

Write an explanation of
the difficult choice that
Siddhartha Gautama
made as a young man.

LEARNING THRIVES

About A.D. 376, Chandra Gupta II, greatest king of the Gupta dynasty, ruled a large empire. He extended it from the Bay of Bengal to the Arabian Sea. During this time, the arts and learning flourished. Chandra brought many talented writers and artists to his courts. One was Kalidasa, India's greatest playwright.

Chandra held tournaments in which the poets competed. Winners often used clever wordplay, riddles, and puns. Sometimes the king would suggest a topic or rhyme scheme, and the poets would try to see who could use it in the most surprising way.

EXTENDING THE EMPIRE

Rajendra was the greatest ruler of the Chola dynasty. In about A.D. 1014 he extended the empire east and north. Rajendra's army overran the Deccan Plateau. Then Rajendra conquered Bengal, far to the north. On this expedition his soldiers reached the Ganges River, which was sacred to Hindus. The soldiers brought back some of its water to their new capital.

Rajendra also built a powerful navy that defeated pirates in the Indian Ocean. Chola ships landed in parts of what are now Malaysia and Indonesia. They created routes that helped spread the influence of Indian cultures to these areas.

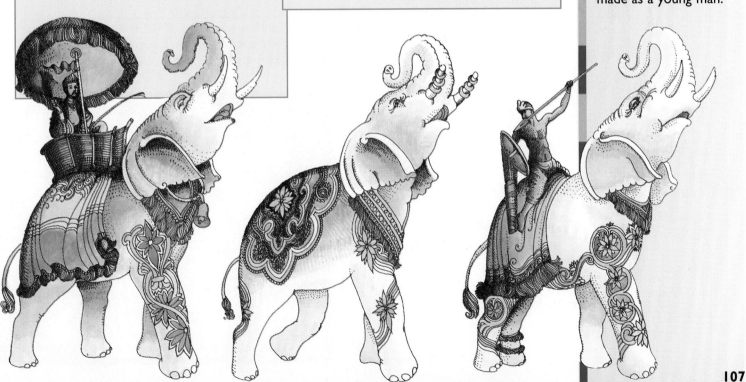

107

Connections

★ KEY TERMS

ambassador
corporal punishment
catapult

▲ Xuan Zang

TALES OF TRAVELERS

FOCUS *Much of what we know about ancient India comes from accounts written by people who traveled to India from other lands.*

A Visitor From Greece

Books written by visitors from other countries give us important information about early India. The map shows routes taken by four travelers to India.

Megasthenes (muh GAS thuh neez) served as a Greek **ambassador** to the court of Chandragupta Maurya. Although Megasthenes' book on India is lost, parts of it were quoted by other ancient writers. They give us a look at life in the Mauryan Empire around 300 B.C. Megasthenes wrote:

Indians lead happy lives, being simple in their manners and frugal. . . . Their . . . food is principally rice. The simplicity of their laws and their contracts appears from the fact that they seldom go to law. Their houses and property are for [the] most part unguarded. These things show their moderation and good sense, but other things they do . . . one cannot approve . . . they always eat alone. . . .

Two Chinese Pilgrims

After Buddhism spread to China, some Chinese Buddhist monks traveled to India to study Buddhism at its source. Fa Xian (fah ZHEE ahn), one of these pilgrims, traveled through India in the fifth century and studied Buddhist writings at the University of Nalanda. He was impressed to find that, although he was a foreigner, people treated him kindly.

Describing central India, Fa Xian wrote, "The kings govern without **corporal punishment**." He found the laws to be less severe in India than those in China. He also noted that Indians ate no meat.

Two centuries later, another Chinese Buddhist, Xuan Zang (zoo ahn chang), spent 16 years in India.

★ **ambassador** An official who represents his or her government in a foreign land
corporal punishment A whipping or beating

This is all that remains of the once great University of Nalanda. ▶

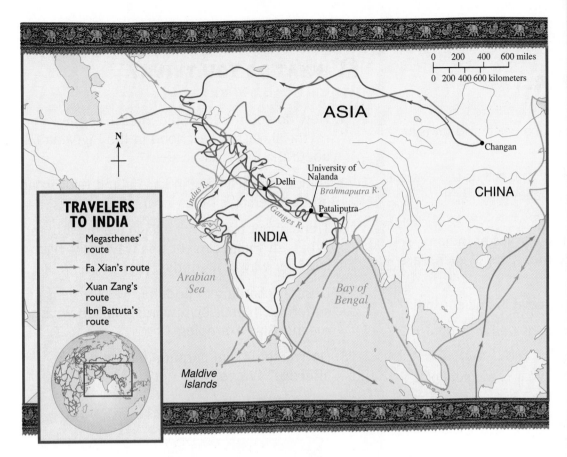

TRAVELERS TO INDIA

→ Megasthenes' route
→ Fa Xian's route
→ Xuan Zang's route
→ Ibn Battuta's route

SHOW WHAT YOU KNOW!

REFOCUS
COMPREHENSION

1. What seems to have surprised Megasthenes most about the lives of people in India?

2. What was Fa Xian studying at the university?

THINK ABOUT IT
CRITICAL THINKING

Why are books about ancient India by travelers from other lands important to us today?

WRITE ABOUT IT
ACTIVITY

Suppose you were in Ibn Battuta's group visiting India. Write a journal entry telling about an event you witnessed or a custom that interests you.

Describing the people, he wrote:

They are very particular in their personal cleanliness. . . . All wash themselves before eating; they never use that [food] which has been left over [from other meals]. . . . After eating they cleanse their teeth with a willow stick, and wash their hands and mouth.

A North African Visitor

After 1330, Ibn Battuta (IHB un bat-TOO tah) set off for India. In Delhi, he described the grand procession in which its ruler entered the city:

On some of the elephants there were mounted small military

catapults, and . . . parcels of gold and silver coins mixed together were thrown from these machines. The men on foot in front of the sultan and the other persons present scrambled for the money.

Ibn Battuta served the ruler of Delhi for eight years as a judge. Even so, he remarked, "The sultan was far too free in shedding blood. . . . Every day there are brought to the audience-hall hundreds of people [to be killed]."

Later, Ibn Battuta traveled to China and visited African kingdoms south of the Sahara. Ibn Battuta's journals give us a rare firsthand account of the world during the fourteenth century.

⭐ **catapult** An ancient weapon used to throw rocks or arrows

SUMMING UP

1 DO YOU REMEMBER...
COMPREHENSION

1. Which four modern nations are found on the Indian subcontinent?

2. What details do we know that tell us the earliest civilization in the Indus Valley was highly developed?

3. What were four mythical classes of Indian society, and what were members of each class supposed to do?

4. What did the Maurya achieve in ancient India?

5. What are the three forms of God in Hinduism? What is the role of each?

6. According to Hinduism, what is the goal of a religious life?

7. What did Buddha teach about the way to a satisfying life?

8. Describe the typical Indian household during the Gupta empire.

9. How did the Maurya leader Asoka rule India?

10. What did the Greek traveler Megasthenes admire about life in early India?

2 SKILL POWER
READING SPECIAL-PURPOSE MAPS

Thumb through this book to find three special-purpose maps. Write two or three sentences about each map, explaining what its special purpose is.

3 WHAT DO YOU THINK?
CRITICAL THINKING

1. How do you think people in each of the mythical classes described in the Rig-Veda felt about the four-class system?

2. How might believing in karma and reincarnation affect a person's behavior in life?

3. Think about traditional village life in early India. What advantages might this way of life have over our way of life today?

4. Desire, according to Buddha, was the cause of suffering. In your own words, explain what this means. Give examples.

5. Do you think that corporal punishment is effective? Why or why not?

4 SAY IT, WRITE IT, USE IT
VOCABULARY

Think about what it must have been like to be one of the traders or officials who visited India long ago. Write an account of the land and people to share with friends. In your account, use as many of these terms as possible.

ambassador	lentil
caste	reign
catapult	reincarnation
corporal punishment	subcontinent
exile	untouchable caste
karma	yoga

5 GEOGRAPHY AND YOU
MAP STUDY

Use the map below to answer these questions.

1. Which travelers made the trip from Changan to Delhi?

2. Only two of the four travelers passed through Pataliputra. Who were they?

3. What color represents the person who traveled the fewest number of miles in India? Who was that person?

4. Which traveler doubled back on several legs of his journey?

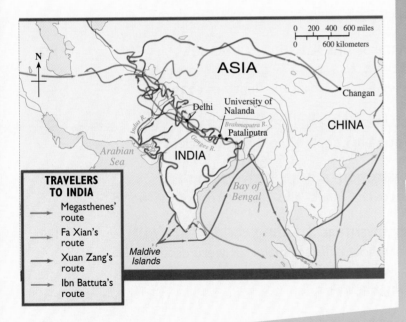

6 TAKE ACTION
CITIZENSHIP

India's beloved Asoka was one of the first rulers to promote welfare and happiness among the elderly and those in need. Our society also tries to help people who are in need. Gather information about a soup kitchen or other nonprofit organization in your area that provides food or clothing for those in need. Make a list of donations, other than money, that the organization accepts. Then use your list to make a poster to encourage donations.

7 GET CREATIVE
LANGUAGE ARTS CONNECTION

Try having a wordplay tournament like the ones Chandra Gupta II organized. Write a topic that interests you on a slip of paper. Put everyone's papers into a basket. Draw a paper and use the topic in a surprising way. You might write comedy routines, funny stories, or clever rhymes about the topic.

LOOKING AHEAD Find out in the next chapter how India's neighbor China developed and what contributions it made to the world.

EXPLORE DYNASTIES OF

Explore ancient China, a civilization of greats: great size, great numbers of people, great ruling families, great thinkers, and great inventions.

CONTENTS

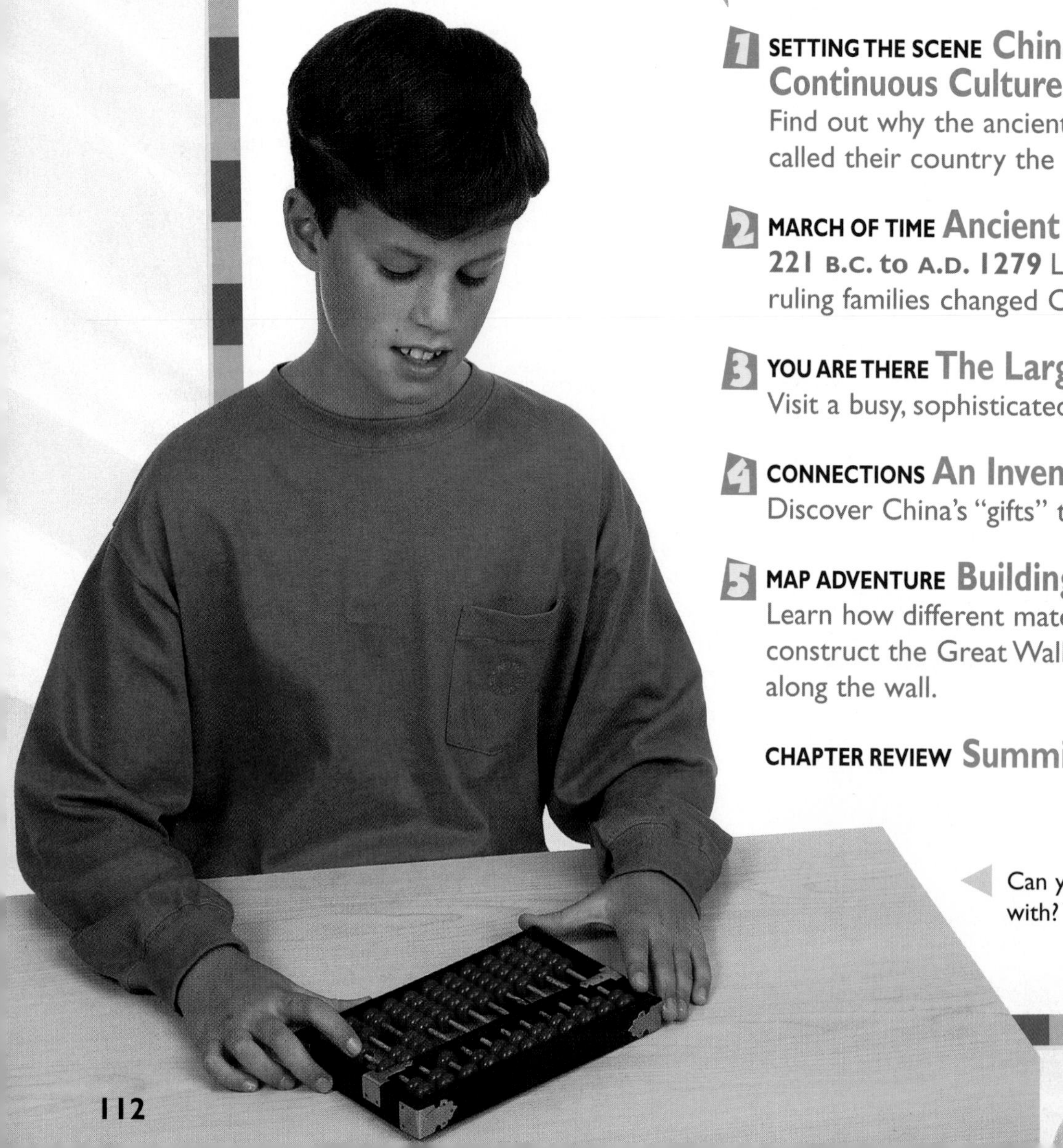

Can you guess what this boy is working with? You can find out on page 129.

ANCIENT CHINA

These books include fascinating facts and fanciful tales about ancient China. Read one that interests you and fill out a book-review form.

READ AND RESEARCH

The Chinese by **Pamela Odijk** (Silver Burdett Press, 1989)
Using photographs, drawings, and maps, you will explore ancient Chinese civilizations. Journey back through history and find out about the daily life, land, law, and legends of the Chinese people. (*nonfiction*)

The Great Wall of China by **Leonard Everett Fisher** (Macmillan Publishing Co., 1986)
If you were the emperor of China 2,200 years ago, you would have to do something to keep out invaders from the north. But what would you do? See how the real emperor and his people solved this problem. (*nonfiction*)

The Terra Cotta Army of Emperor Qin by **Caroline Lazo** (New Discovery Books, 1993)
Read more about the first emperor of China. Find out how building the Great Wall and the emperor's tomb caused great suffering to the workers. (*nonfiction*)

The Ch'i-lin Purse: A Collection of Ancient Chinese Stories
retold by Linda Fang (Farrar Straus & Giroux, 1995)
Meet a man who steals sweet potatoes, a carp-fish spirit who changes herself into a woman, and many other unusual characters in this collection of ancient Chinese tales. (*fiction*)

Skill Power

Reading a Process Diagram

Knowing how to read a process diagram can give you important information about how something works or how something is done.

UNDERSTAND IT

An ancient proverb says, "One picture is worth more than a thousand words." If you have ever tried to put together a bicycle by reading directions without a diagram, you know what the proverb means. It is much easier to understand a process if you have a picture that helps you follow a written description.

EXPLORE IT

According to a Chinese legend, in A.D. 105, Cai Lun pounded the inner bark of a mulberry tree into pulp and used the pulp to make paper as we know it today. Read the steps in papermaking and follow them in the diagram, from left to right. Then make up two questions about the papermaking process and ask a classmate to answer them.

- A *barking drum* removes bark from logs.
- A *chipper* cuts logs into chips. A *chip washer* cleans them.
- A *digester* breaks up wood fibers. A *refiner* makes them flexible.
- *Pulp washers* wash away chemicals. A *screen* removes knots.
- In a *headbox*, wet fibers are spread onto a screen called a *wire*, where water drips off.
- *Press rolls* squeeze out water. *Steam-heated cylinders* help dry the paper.
- A *calendar stack* smooths the dry paper and feeds it onto a *reel*.

▼ Follow the diagram to see how paper is made today.

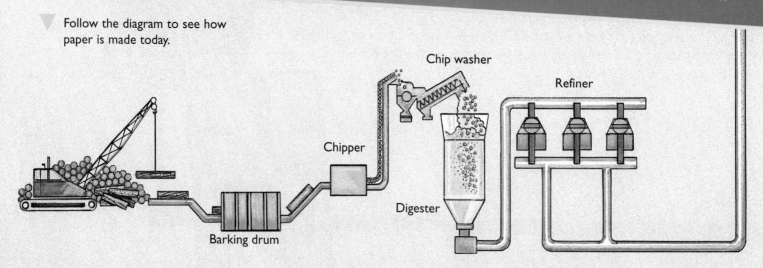

Chip washer

Refiner

Chipper

Digester

Barking drum

Making Lasagna

Prepare Cheeses

Brown Meat

Make Sauce

Cook Noodles

Layer Ingredients

350°

Bake at 350° F for 30 minutes.

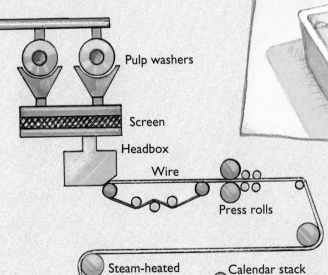

Pulp washers

Screen

Headbox

Wire

Press rolls

Steam-heated cylinders

Calendar stack

Reel

SKILL POWER SEARCH *Find another process diagram in this chapter. What information does it give you?*

1

Setting the Scene

KEY TERMS

dialect
loess
barbarian
cultivate
ideograph
calligraphy

CHINA: THE OLDEST CONTINUOUS CULTURE

FOCUS *Civilization in China has had a very long and glorious history. Keys to its development have been China's great size and population and its people's respect for rules of behavior and the customs of the past.*

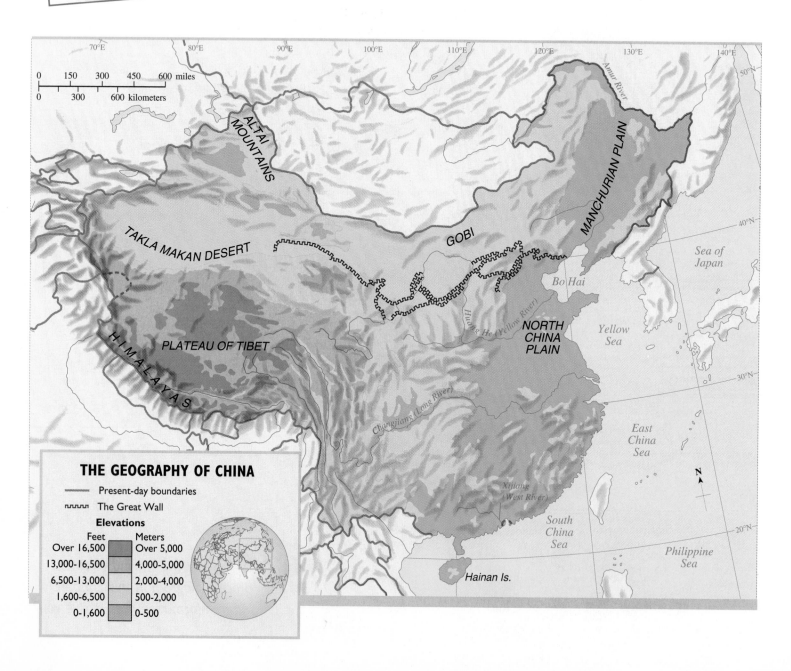

THE GEOGRAPHY OF CHINA

— Present-day boundaries

〜〜〜 The Great Wall

Elevations

Feet	Meters
Over 16,500	Over 5,000
13,000–16,500	4,000–5,000
6,500–13,000	2,000–4,000
1,600–6,500	500–2,000
0–1,600	0–500

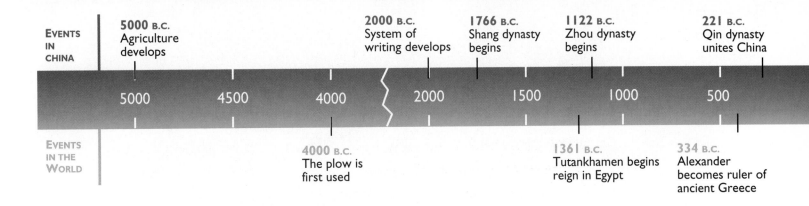

EVENTS IN CHINA	**5000** B.C. Agriculture develops			**2000** B.C. System of writing develops	**1766** B.C. Shang dynasty begins	**1122** B.C. Zhou dynasty begins	**221** B.C. Qin dynasty unites China

| 5000 | 4500 | 4000 | 2000 | 1500 | 1000 | 500 |

| EVENTS IN THE WORLD | | **4000** B.C. The plow is first used | | **1361** B.C. Tutankhamen begins reign in Egypt | **334** B.C. Alexander becomes ruler of ancient Greece |

A Vast Land

As a young man, Christopher Columbus read Marco Polo's account of his overland journey to China. Columbus was inspired by Polo's tales of China's splendor, large population, and wealth. He set out to organize a trip westward across the Atlantic, expecting to reach China on the other side. What he found, of course, were the Americas.

China stretches from Russia in the north to Vietnam in the south, and from India in the southwest to the Pacific Ocean. It is the third largest country in size—only Russia and Canada are larger. This vast territory includes many different regions, each with its own distinctive characteristics. There are mountains, deserts, grasslands and tropical forests. Each region has its own local customs, styles of cooking, dress, and **dialects** (DEYE uh lekts) of spoken Chinese.

China has three major rivers. The Huang He (hwahng huh), or Yellow River, flows through the dry northern plain. When it floods, it deposits soil called **loess** (LOH es). Farther south are the Changjiang (CHAWNG jeeahng), or Long River, and the Xijiang (SHEE-

jeeahng), or West River. As the map on page 116 shows, all three rivers run from west to east. Because of this, communication and transportation between the north and the south have always been difficult.

A Sense of Superiority

The Chinese sense of superiority detected by Polo was well founded. From about 221 B.C. to A.D. 1279, no other country could match China's accomplishments. Despite long periods of political unrest, China is the world's oldest continuous civilization.

China's geography isolated its people from other great civilizations. To the south and east, however, there were neighbors who appreciated Chinese culture and adopted many of its features. Countries such as Korea, Japan, and Vietnam belong to this category.

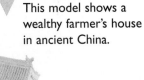

This model shows a wealthy farmer's house in ancient China.

Royal Ontario Museum, Canada

---

 dialect A variety of a language, used only in a certain region or among a certain people
loess A yellowish, fine-grained soil that is very fertile

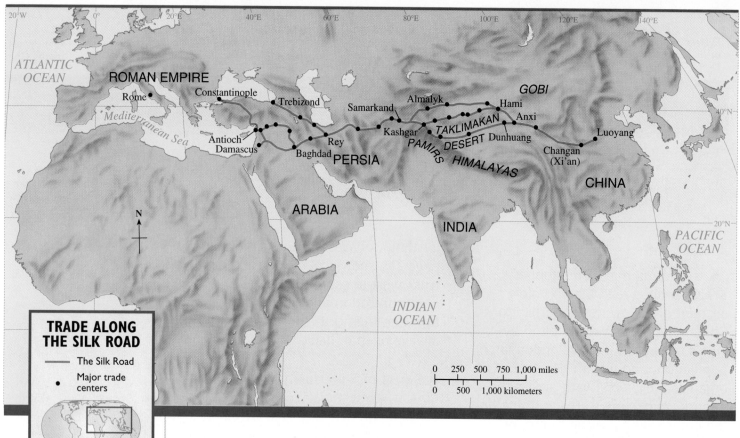

TRADE ALONG THE SILK ROAD

— The Silk Road

• Major trade centers

As a result the Chinese came to believe that they were superior to other peoples. They called their country the Middle Kingdom. In their view, China seemed to be in the center of many rings. The rings closely surrounding China contained loyal subject peoples. The outer rings were filled with everyone else—people the Chinese called **barbarians**.

In spite of geographical barriers and because their goods were in demand by others, the Chinese traded with areas as far away as the Roman Empire, on the Mediterranean Sea. The world outside of China was eager to have the beautiful silk cloth and the bowls and cups crafted of fine porcelain or jade. As the map shows, the main route for the exchange of goods was called the Silk Road.

China's Early Roots

China's roots go back at least 7,000 years to the Huang He, or Yellow River valley. Here, farmers using stone tools first began to cultivate the loess. Over many centuries, these farmers learned to grow crops such as millet and rice. The loess was very fertile, but rainfall was scanty. It took enormous cooperative efforts to build dikes and canals to channel and conserve the precious water.

The farmers cooked their meals in earthen pots. They trained dogs and horses and raised pigs, chickens, cows, and sheep for food. They built houses and village walls out of packed earth and made clothing out of hemp, which is a plant fiber that can be woven, and silk. Their religion was based on ancestor worship.

⭐ **barbarian**   An uncivilized or crude person

In time the farmers increased the area of **cultivated** farmland. The resulting food surplus made it possible for some people to work at other tasks. The Chinese, however, never forgot the importance of agriculture. In their social structure, farmers ranked above craftworkers and merchants.

The Early Dynasties

As farming villages formed larger communities, one family in each community became more powerful. Thus, families—or dynasties— began to rule large areas of China. The earliest records are of the Shang (shahng) dynasty, from about 1766 to 1122 B.C.

During the Shang dynasty, artisans created beautiful bronze vessels to hold food and wine and to use in religious ceremonies. The Shang Chinese also used bronze to make weapons. They used these weapons to conquer land to the south of the Huang He valley.

The Shang kings worshiped many different nature gods. The supreme god was Shang Di (shahng dee), later known as Tian (teeyen), meaning "sky" or "Heaven." For over 3,500 years Chinese rulers paid homage to him in elaborate ceremonies.

The Shang dynasty was overthrown by invaders from the western border

areas of China. The conquerers called their new dynasty the Zhou (joh). This dynasty ruled longer than any other in Chinese history—over 800 years. During this period, trade increased and walled cities began to grow.

The First Emperor

In 221 B.C. the ruler of the state of Qin (cheen) in northwestern China conquered all of China. He then declared himself to be the First

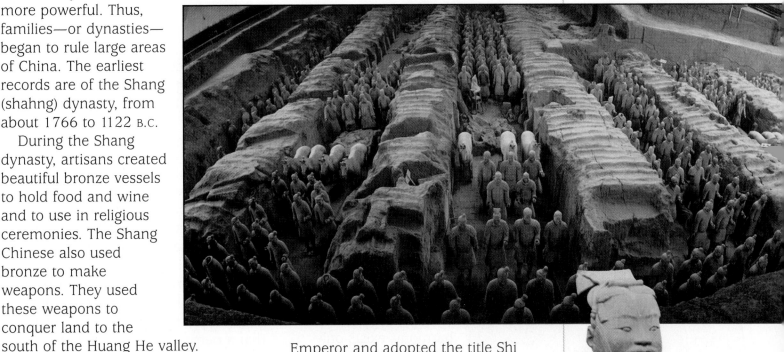

Emperor and adopted the title Shi Huang Di (shur hwahng DEE).

Few people in history have had such large ambitions. He built roads to connect all the portions of his empire with his capital. His army marched south, conquering all the way to the northern part of present-day Vietnam. To keep out the barbarians from the north,

The First Emperor filled his burial tomb with 7,000 life-sized clay soldiers. Each figure had a different face.

cultivate To dig, fertilize, and remove weeds before planting seeds

The symbol of yin and yang is a circle divided by a wavy line. Within each half is a small circle of its opposite color.

Candidates for government service had to pass difficult examinations. This shirt was found with test answers written on it.

Fuji Saiseikai, The Yurinkan Museum, Kyoto

the First Emperor connected existing walls to create the Great Wall of China. Supposedly a million workers lost their lives during the wall's construction. He also built an enormous palace with hundreds of rooms. One of his first acts as emperor was to order workers to begin constructing his tomb, which consisted of a huge mound of earth.

The First Emperor's successors were not as powerful as he was. A revolt overthrew the third ruler of the Qin dynasty. A new dynasty, the Han (hahn), took its place and became the model for future dynasties.

Respect for Harmony

Chinese civilization respected the idea of harmony. This respect is probably related to the ancient Chinese idea of yin and yang—two opposing forces that govern the universe. Yang is strong, light, and superior. Yin is weak, dark, and inferior. But nothing is ever completely yin or completely yang. A proper balance, or harmony, exists only when both are present.

About 2,500 years ago, during a period of unrest, several Chinese philosophers searched for a way to restore harmony to the land. The most important of these philosophers was Confucius (kun FYOO-shus). Confucius taught a very basic ethical lesson: "Do not treat people the way you would not like to be treated." He thought that China's problems could best be solved by emphasizing family loyalty, correct behavior, and social responsibility. He believed that moral education—understanding the difference between right and wrong—would show people how to act correctly. He encouraged the study of poems and histories from China's past. These works became the basis for the Chinese Classics. In later dynasties, people had to pass tests on these writings to become government officials.

The Three Teachings

Confucianism, with its active social philosophy, was considered yang. Its yin counterpart was Daoism (DOU ihz-um), a philosophy developed during the Han dynasty. Its founder was named Laozi (lou dzuh). While Confucianism was mainly concerned with people in society, Daoism dealt with people in nature. Daoists believed that a person should try to escape from society rather than try to manage it. Laozi urged his followers to retreat into nature.

The third major system of thought in China was the religion of Buddhism, which you read about in Chapter 5. Buddhism reached China during the later Han dynasty.

Oracle bones, often made from the shells of tortoises, were heated until they cracked. The shapes and lengths of the cracks were used to answer questions. The questions then were written on these bones.

writing was based on symbols called characters. Originally, characters were pictures of things and were called **ideographs**. Later the Chinese developed a complicated system of combining sounds and ideas without using an alphabet. Today there are nearly 5,000 such characters in common use.

This system of writing has helped to unify Chinese people throughout their history. Though there are many Chinese dialects, the meaning of any written character is always the same.

The characters were also forms of great beauty. **Calligraphy** became an art as important as poetry or painting. So great was the Chinese respect for the four tools used in writing—paper, brush, inkstone, and ink—that they were known as the Four Treasures.

It was a sign of Chinese harmony that eventually most Chinese people came to accept all three philosophies, called the Three Teachings. Each of them fulfilled different needs. Confucianism helped people live together. Daoism helped people find peace within themselves. Buddhism satisfied the need for religion.

The Four Treasures

The earliest examples of Chinese writing exist on 3,500-year-old bones. Used to predict the future, they were called oracle bones. The system of

This thousand-year-old painting includes a poem written in characters.

⭐ **ideograph** A symbol representing a thing or idea
calligraphy The art of fine handwriting

SHOW WHAT YOU KNOW!

REFOCUS
COMPREHENSION

1. What did the Chinese mean when they called their country the Middle Kingdom?

2. How did the Chinese overcome the problem of having many different dialects?

THINK ABOUT IT
CRITICAL THINKING

How might the Chinese have used the idea of yin and yang to explain things that happened to them?

WRITE ABOUT IT
ACTIVITY

If you were required to follow the philosophy of either Confucianism or Daoism, which would you choose? Give reasons for your selection.

ANCIENT DYNASTIES

FOCUS *The Chinese emperors created unity by establishing strong central governments. Each dynasty built upon the economic and cultural growth of the one before.*

THE QIN DYNASTY

The Qin dynasty, which lasted from 221 to 206 B.C., gave its name to the country of China. Its founder, the First Emperor of China, set out to unify his nation. He established standard weights and measures for all of China. His government issued round coins with square holes so that they could be carried on strings. Even the length of cart axles was standardized so that travelers would not have to change carts when they crossed state borders.

The most important change was the standardization of Chinese characters. Even today the characters still have the same basic shapes and meanings as they did so many centuries ago.

The First Emperor also laid the foundations of the Great Wall to protect China from invaders from the north. Though the Qin dynasty fell apart soon after the First Emperor died, many of his changes survived.

THE HAN DYNASTY

Liu Bang (leeow bahng), a peasant, became the first ruler of the Han dynasty in 206 B.C. He surrounded himself with wise counselors. They shaped a strong government in which Confucianism became the official state philosophy. The Han dynasty was so respected that Chinese to this day call themselves "people of Han."

During the Han era, China extended its borders. Its soldiers guarded the oases on the Silk Road. Chinese merchants carried goods such as silk, salt, pottery, iron, and bronze to trade with the Roman Empire. Gold and jade were also carried on the Silk Road. Han artisans created burial suits for their leaders by fastening together thousands of thin pieces of jade.

221 B.C.
Qin dynasty begins

206 B.C
Han dynasty begins a 400-year rule

A.D. 618
Tang dynasty begins

A.D. 960
Song dynasty begins

A.D. 1279
Foreign invaders conquer all of China

300   100 B.C.   A.D. 100   300   500   700   900   1100   1300

SHOW WHAT YOU KNOW!

THE TANG DYNASTY

In 638 a young girl named Wu Zhao (woo jou) was called to serve in the household of the second emperor of the Tang (tahng) dynasty. No one could have guessed that one day she herself would take the throne. She is the only female "Son of Heaven" in Chinese history.

Wu helped establish a competitive testing system for government officials. The few who passed the first round were eligible to take further tests. During the finals, which lasted for days, the people were locked in tiny cells. These exams produced a civil service system in which what you knew was more important than whom you knew.

Two of China's greatest poets—Li Bai (lee bye) and Du Fu (doo foo)—lived during the Tang era. Li Bai was a free spirit who wrote: "Life in the world is but a big dream;/ I will not spoil it by any labor or care." Very different was Du Fu, who wanted to serve in the government but failed the exams.

Both printing and gunpowder, which you will read about later in this chapter, were Tang inventions.

THE SONG DYNASTY

The Song dynasty (960–1279) was a time of great achievement in the arts. Emperor Hui Zong (hway dzawng), who loved to paint flowers and birds, opened the Academy of Painting at his capital. On the palace grounds a factory produced gorgeous porcelain vases and dishes.

The Song era was also a time of growth and economic progress. New strains of rice allowed farmers to harvest two or more crops each year. The resulting food surplus enabled the population to grow to over 100 million.

Unfortunately for the Song, tribes to the north were on the march. In 1115, nomadic invaders drove the Song from their northern capital. Not long after, the most powerful of all the nomadic peoples, the Mongols, overcame the southern capital of the Song dynasty.

REFOCUS
COMPREHENSION

1. Name at least one major change or event from each dynasty that contributed to present-day Chinese culture.

2. Why have government exams been so important to the Chinese people?

THINK ABOUT IT
CRITICAL THINKING

Each of the great dynasties of China had powerful armies. Think of some reasons why the armies were necessary.

WRITE ABOUT IT
ACTIVITY

Design a flag or banner to represent a Chinese dynasty. Write a paragraph explaining its symbols and their meanings.

THE LARGEST CITY

FOCUS *In the 1200s, China's social life, living conditions, culture, and technology made it the most advanced country in the world. Hangzhou, China's largest city, was a good place to experience what the country had to offer.*

▲ Eating out in a big city in ancient China was great fun. On the street level were small stalls where snacks could be bought. In the two- and three-story buildings above the stalls were restaurants where fancy meals were available.

A Visit to the City

Marco Polo has called Hangzhou (HAHNG joh) the most beautiful city in the world. You know you are going to enjoy your visit. You can enter the city through any of its 13 large gates or through one of the five canal gates, if you are approaching by boat. Then you head for the Imperial Way—the straight, wide road that will take you to the heart of the city.

You will be amazed at all the activity. Porters scurry past, carrying baskets attached to poles across their shoulders. Look out for the men carrying a wealthy official in the sedan chair balanced on their shoulders.

Merchants here sell all kinds of products, and you can pay with paper money. Silk, porcelain, teas, and precious metals are all for sale. You might be interested in jewelry, which is a specialty of Hangzhou. Other popular products are artificial flowers, children's toys, and printed books. Merchants from outside the city sell ivory, coral, pearls, crystals, and rare and fragrant woods.

Let's take a look at the south side of the city near the Imperial Palace. This area is where the wealthy live. Their beautiful houses include well-stocked libraries and precious works of art. Many high government officials live on the Hill of Ten Thousand Pines. Notice the upturned and decorated tile roofs on their houses. Only government buildings and the homes of high officials can have this kind of roof.

Eating Out

The food is going to please you. There are so many restaurants to choose from. The table will be set with chopsticks and spoons. Hangzhou's poor eat rice, simple vegetables, and perhaps some pork or dried fish. They wash down the food with tea. If you have a little more money, you can feast on chicken, goose, pigeon, lamb, and shellfish.

Fun for Everyone

Hangzhou has entertainment for everyone. Perhaps the most amazing shows are found on the streets themselves. You can see **martial arts** experts, kite flyers, jugglers, puppeteers, dancers, comedians, and snake charmers. Somebody will show you a bird, fish, or even an insect that they have trained. There is no end to the fun you can have in Hangzhou.

▶ Acrobats were among the street entertainers in Hangzhou. These clay figures capture a trapeze act.

Royal Ontario Museum, Canada

★ **martial arts** Artistic forms of movement related to self-defense or attack

SHOW WHAT YOU KNOW!

REFOCUS
COMPREHENSION

1. Look again at the scroll painting on page 124. Describe the clothing that people wore in a big city in ancient China.

2. How might you recognize the house of a wealthy or important person in Hangzhou?

THINK ABOUT IT
CRITICAL THINKING

What impressed you most about the city of Hangzhou? Explain your answer.

WRITE ABOUT IT
ACTIVITY

Your visit to Hangzhou has moved you to write poetry. Compose a short poem giving your impressions of this great city.

Connections

KEY TERMS

pharmacist
technician
magnet
pilot
seismograph

AN INVENTIVE PEOPLE

FOCUS *Many inventions were used in China hundreds of years before appearing in Europe. Some of these—printing, gunpowder, and the compass—changed the history of Europe.*

Early Inventions

In 1620 the English philosopher and scientist Sir Francis Bacon wrote that three recent inventions—printing, the magnetic compass, and gunpowder—had changed the world. Printing had made it possible for ideas to spread more rapidly. Gunpowder and guns put an end to the era of knights and castles. The compass made possible the European voyages of discovery. What Bacon did not know was that the Chinese had been using these inventions centuries before the rest of the world even knew about them.

Silk and Paper

According to a Chinese legend, the wife of an emperor sat down under a mulberry tree in her garden. As she looked up, she saw caterpillars spinning their cocoons. "If only we could weave their thread into cloth," she said, "how wonderful it would be."

That is the legendary beginning of Chinese silk making. Archaeologists do know for sure that Chinese were weaving the threads of silkworms into cloth as early as 4,000 years ago.

Silk has long been one of China's most prized products. It gave its name

to the Silk Road across Asia, along which it was carried to the west. It was rolled into scrolls and used as the background for painting and calligraphy.

Another legend says that an inspector in the workshops of the Han emperor invented paper. The first paper was made from mulberry bark that had been mashed to pulp. Water

Follow the steps in this chart to learn how a moth makes a material that can be made into cloth.

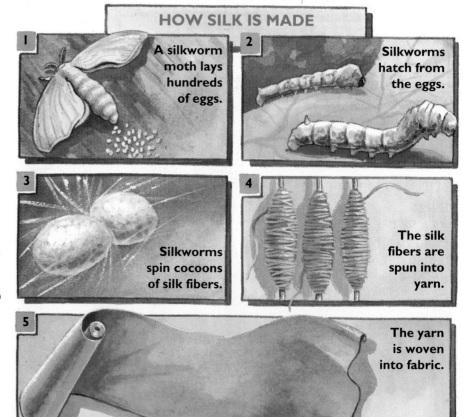

HOW SILK IS MADE

1 A silkworm moth lays hundreds of eggs.

2 Silkworms hatch from the eggs.

3 Silkworms spin cocoons of silk fibers.

4 The silk fibers are spun into yarn.

5 The yarn is woven into fabric.

Special looms allowed silk weavers to make cloth in complicated patterns.

into the wood. A thin coating of ink was spread on the block, and fresh sheets of paper were pressed onto it to produce a printed page. The same technique was used for illustrations and drawings.

As people found more uses for printing, it spread rapidly. The Chinese government encouraged the printing of the Confucian classics, dynastic histories, law codes, and other official documents. It also helped to publish encyclopedias and texts on religion, philosophy, painting, poetry, law, astronomy, agriculture, and warfare.

The final development of printing occurred around 1048, when a scholar developed movable type. He realized that by making individual characters, he could rearrange them in any order instead of having to make new blocks. He molded the type out of clay and hardened it by firing. During the next few centuries, other Chinese began to make type out of wood, and then later from metal.

and plant gums were added to the pulp, and the mixture was strained and spread on a screen to dry.

Paper caught on. It was cheaper than silk, and artists liked the way it held ink. Paper was used to cover window openings and walls. Chinese paper spread to Korea and from there to Japan. Later the paper-making techniques reached India and then the Arab Empire. It was through Muslim Spain that paper reached the rest of Europe around 1150.

Printing Develops

Printing began during the Tang dynasty, hundreds of years after the invention of paper. Chinese Buddhist monks developed the idea of block printing in the seventh century. Someone sketched a manuscript page on a thin piece of paper. This was placed face down on a block of wood. The reversed characters were carved

Paper Money

Another important use for printing was paper money. The Song government began to issue it in the eleventh century, the first time it appeared anywhere. The printing office, located near Hangzhou, employed about 200 printers. Almost as soon as paper money appeared, counterfeiters tried to copy it. So the government printers designed money with complicated designs, just like the ones you see on paper money today.

Uses of Gunpowder

Gunpowder was first invented in the ninth century. It was an accidental discovery that resulted from medical research. A Chinese **pharmacist** combined sulphur and saltpeter with charcoal. Sulphur was used to treat skin diseases, and saltpeter was used to lower fevers. The addition of charcoal produced *huoyao* (HWOH you), or "fire medicine." Huoyao was still used in medical treatments as late as the seventeenth century. However, the fact that it burned rapidly made it useful in other ways.

The first nonmedical use of gunpowder may have been for fireworks. Beautiful fireworks were used at festivals during the Song dynasty. One, called the box lantern, was hung in a high place and set afire. Layer by layer, paper characters appeared as a story unfolded in the midst of whirling sparks.

The Chinese soon found military uses for gunpowder. By the eleventh century, gunpowder was being used in simple bombs and grenades (gruh-NAYDZ), as well as bamboo flame throwers and primitive rockets. By 1221, Chinese **technicians** could produce large bombs that were "shaped like gourds, with small mouths, and cast in iron two inches thick." These weapons, according to a Chinese account, were capable of shattering city walls.

The year 905 saw the invention of a "fire-spurting lance." This weapon, shown on page 123, shot pellets out the end of a long piece of bamboo. This later led to the development of metal-barreled guns and cannons.

Navigation Tools

A written record from the third century B.C. says, "When the people of the State of Zheng go out in search of jade, they carry a south-pointer with them so as not to lose their way in the mountains."

In the eleventh century Chinese **magnets** shaped like fish were placed in bowls of water so that their heads pointed south. Around that time, Chinese ships began to take boxes with floating compass needles on sea journeys. This enabled their **pilots** to navigate at night or when the sky was overcast. During the Song dynasty, Chinese merchant ships traveled to Japan, Southeast Asia, India, and even beyond.

Some parts of China's rivers were blocked by rapids and low waterfalls. Boats had to be carried around them on land. Chinese engineers developed locks to harness the rivers. These locks were like small dams. As a boat entered one part of the river, the lock behind it was closed. Gradually the water would rise, letting the boat float up to the next section of river. The locks greatly improved river transportation.

▼ In time, Spanish and Portuguese explorers adopted the Chinese compass.

★ **pharmacist** A person trained to prepare drugs and medicines
technician A person trained in a certain job or science

★ **magnet** An object that can attract iron or steel
pilot A person who steers a ship

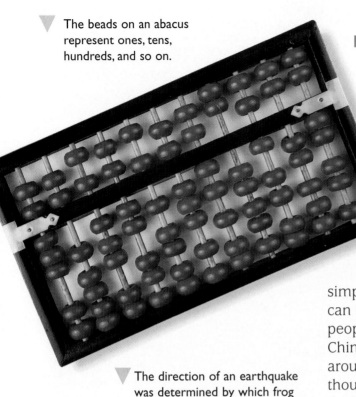

The beads on an abacus represent ones, tens, hundreds, and so on.

The direction of an earthquake was determined by which frog caught a ball dropped from the dragon above it.

Even More Inventions

There are countless other inventions that Chinese people developed. The abacus (AB uh-kus), which originated in the Fertile Crescent, reached China in the sixth century B.C. The Chinese improved it so that it could be used for such complicated calculations as square roots and algebra.

The wheelbarrow seems like a simple idea. Yet a worker using one can carry heavier loads than two people lifting together. The first Chinese wheelbarrows appeared around A.D. 200. It was over a thousand years before Europeans used these labor-saving devices.

A Chinese scientist invented the first **seismograph**, or earthquake detector, in A.D. 132. An example of one of these instruments is shown here.

Chinese textile makers used water power to run machines in the fifth century. Mechanical clocks were being made in China in the eighth century. Kites, suspension bridges, and porcelain technology are also among the many Chinese gifts to the world.

 seismograph An instrument used to measure the strength of earthquakes

SHOW WHAT YOU KNOW!

REFOCUS
COMPREHENSION

1. How was silk production important to the Chinese both inside and outside their country?

2. What two inventions allowed the Chinese to make books?

THINK ABOUT IT
CRITICAL THINKING

Which of the inventions you read about affected the lives of Chinese children the most? Explain your choice.

WRITE ABOUT IT
ACTIVITY

Write an advertisement to help the ancient Chinese sell magnetic compasses to Europeans.

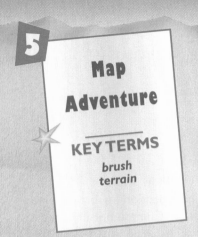

5

Map Adventure

KEY TERMS

brush
terrain

BUILDING THE GREAT WALL

FOCUS Stretching 4,000 miles across China, the Great Wall winds like a serpent through the landscape. Over the centuries it has changed its skin as a serpent does. Several dynasties have rebuilt the Wall. All have left their particular marks along its rambling length.

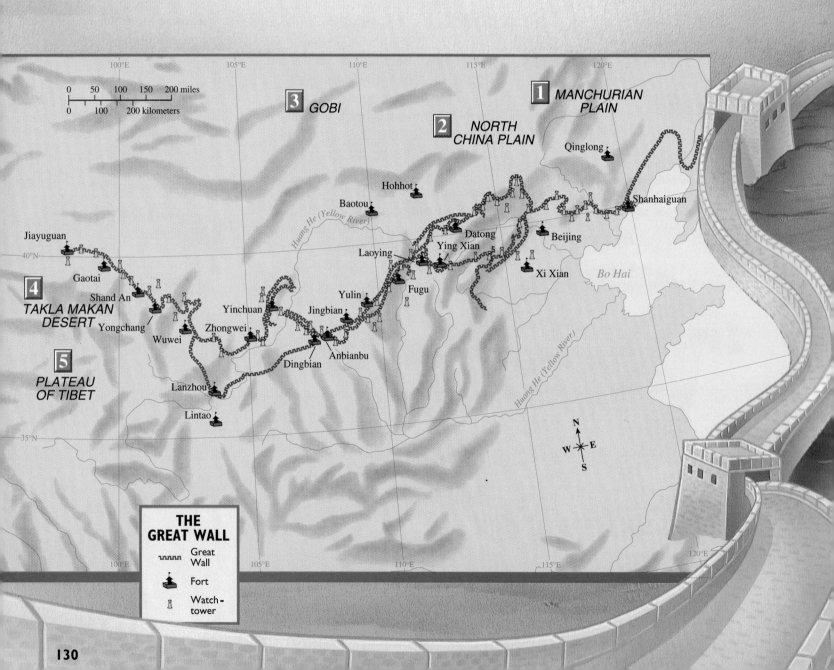

1	MANCHURIAN PLAIN
2	NORTH CHINA PLAIN
3	GOBI
4	TAKLA MAKAN DESERT
5	PLATEAU OF TIBET

Qinglong

Hohhot

Baotou

Shanhaiguan

Huang He (Yellow River)

Jiayuguan

Datong

Beijing

Gaotai

Ying Xian

Laoying

Bo Hai

Shand An

Xi Xian

Yulin

Yinchuan

Fugu

TAKLA MAKAN DESERT

Yongchang

Jingbian

Wuwei

Zhongwei

Anbianbu

Dingbian

PLATEAU OF TIBET

Lanzhou

Huang He (Yellow River)

Lintao

N
W E
S

THE GREAT WALL

Great Wall

Fort

Watch-tower

100°E   105°E   110°E   115°E   120°E

40°N

35°N

0 50 100 150 200 miles
0 100 200 kilometers

Great Walls Take Time

The construction of the Great Wall began during the Qin dynasty, when a series of small existing walls were joined together. Hundreds of years later, during the Ming dynasty, the Wall was reinforced with bricks and made into the Great Wall as it stands today. Originally used for defense, the Wall was equipped with watchtowers, military stations, and fortresses. Gateways, or passes, were also built along the Wall so that travelers could get through it without having to go around it. Eventually the passes were used as avenues of commerce, as traders came through and exchanged silk, wool, and gold.

MAP KEY

1 **Manchurian Plain**

2 **North China Plain**

The Manchurian and North China plains have some of the best farmland in China, with rich, fertile soil.

3 **Gobi**

4 **Takla Makan Desert**

The Gobi and Takla Makan deserts are mostly sand, with some *brush* in the oases.

5 **Plateau of Tibet**

The *terrain* here yields rock and gravel primarily.

⭐ *brush*   Low, shrublike vegetation
terrain   Ground or area of land

MAP IT

It is a time during the Qin dynasty. You have been assigned to supervise construction of three separate portions of the Wall at different locations along its span. You realize that the first walls were built of materials readily available in the area. For example, sections in the desert were built of regional supplies such as sand, pebbles, and twigs layered into wooden molds. In the mountains, stones that had been quarried nearby were used. On a loess flatland, the builders had packed wooden frames with mud from local fields.

Using the coordinates below, you must determine in what geographic regions your sections of the Wall are located. Use the map to see what materials will be readily available in your construction area. Make a list of the raw materials you will need for the three separate projects. Your building assignment includes three portions of the Great Wall at the coordinates given here.

1. *Approximately 38°N/110° E*
2. *Approximately 40°N/120° E*
3. *Approximately 40°N/100° E*

EXPLORE IT

The Great Wall was wide enough to move soldiers and equipment along its top when necessary. Troops stationed at forts and towers would stand guard in case of an attack, and they moved from one station to another to help neighboring troops. You are a general dispatching troops to forts on the Wall at the following coordinates. What are the names of the forts where you will be sending soldiers?

1. *41°N/98°E*
2. *39°N/99°E*
3. *37°N/105°E*
4. *38°N/109°E*
5. *40°N/112°E*
6. *40°N/120°E*

SUMMING UP

1 DO YOU REMEMBER...
COMPREHENSION

1. When and where did Chinese civilization begin?

2. Which of China's neighbors adopted many features of Chinese culture?

3. What were the three teachings that influenced China?

4. In what ways did the Qin dynasty work to unify China?

5. What was the Silk Road?

6. What did Marco Polo say about Hangzhou?

7. Trace how the Chinese invention of paper reached Europe.

8. What invention in 1048 improved Chinese printing?

9. Describe how the Chinese invented gunpowder.

10. What were the reasons for building the Great Wall?

2 SKILL POWER
READING A PROCESS DIAGRAM

The process diagram on pages 114–115 shows how paper is made today. Reread pages 126–127 to recall how the Chinese first made paper during the Han empire. Then draw your own process diagram for this early method of making paper. Label and describe the steps.

3 WHAT DO YOU THINK?
CRITICAL THINKING

1. How might respect for harmony have helped China remain the oldest continuous civilization?

2. Why is competitive testing for government officials a good idea?

3. Why would a westerner visiting Hangzhou in 1270 be very surprised?

4. Which invention—printing, gunpowder, or the compass—probably had the greatest effect on Chinese culture?

5. Are walls a successful way to keep people apart? Explain your answer.

4 SAY IT, WRITE IT, USE IT
VOCABULARY

Write a sentence for each of the terms below to show you understand its meaning.

Then find each term in the glossary to check your understanding.

barbarian	ideograph	pilot
brush	loess	seismograph
calligraphy	magnet	technician
cultivate	martial arts	terrain
dialect	pharmacist	

5 GEOGRAPHY AND YOU
MAP STUDY

Use the map below to answer these questions.

1. What is the name of the mountain range in the southern part of China?

2. What deserts are shown on the map?

3. Approximately how many lines of longitude does China cross?

4. What is the name of the northernmost river in China?

5. What are three seas off the China coast?

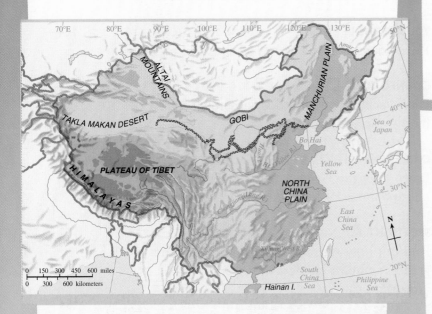

6 TAKE ACTION
CITIZENSHIP

Competitive testing gave ancient China a government of educated and well-qualified officials. Today most careers—including government work—require some education or training. Select a career that interests you and find out what education and training it requires. Share your career information with the class.

7 GET CREATIVE
LANGUAGE ARTS CONNECTION

Try your hand at the Four Treasures. Using a brush or pen and ink, try to create a combination painting-poem, such as the one at the bottom of page 121. Try to write the words in your poem in a calligraphic style. Also make sure that your poem and painting express the same theme.

LOOKING AHEAD
Like ancient China, early Greece contributed greatly to the growth of civilization. You'll learn about Greece in Chapter 7.

CIVILIZATIONS OF

Whenever you watch a school play or admire the columns of a monument, you are enjoying cultural gifts passed down through the ages from the ancient civilization of Greece.

▼ On pages 144–145, you will learn how this athlete is continuing a tradition started in Greece over 2,700 years ago.

CONTENTS

ANCIENT GREECE

These books tell about some legendary heroes of ancient Greece and relate some of the myths that make the Greek culture so fascinating. Read one that interests you and fill out a book-review form.

READ AND RESEARCH

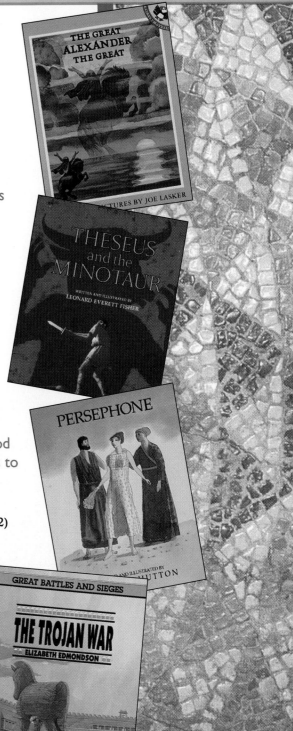

The Great Alexander the Great **by Joe Lasker** (Penguin USA, 1983)
The story of how seven-year-old Alexander acquired his horse, Bucephalus, still amazes readers today. When he became king, Alexander and his soldiers forged one of the greatest empires in history. Let the illustrations help you imagine the courage and creativity of this great leader. (*biography*)
• *You can read a selection from this story on page 154.*

Theseus and the Minotaur **retold by Leonard Everett Fisher** (Holiday House, 1988)
Theseus must defeat the Minotaur, a horrible monster, or else he and 13 other youths from Athens will be doomed! Is Theseus up to the challenge? Read the story and find out. (*folk tale*)

Persephone **retold by Warwick Hutton** (Simon & Schuster Children's Publishing, 1994)
In this famous Greek myth, a beautiful maiden is kidnapped by Hades, the god of the underworld. Find out how Zeus' decree of justice causes the seasons to change. (*mythology*)

The Trojan War **by Elizabeth Edmondson** (New Discovery Books, 1992)
Read about the people who lived in Greece and Troy 3,000 years ago. The author uses the poetry of Homer and the writings of scholars to describe the events of the Trojan War. (*nonfiction*)

SKILL POWER

Using Primary and Secondary Sources

Identifying primary sources and knowing when to use them can give you important information about the past.

UNDERSTAND IT

What is the difference between an interview with an Olympic gold medalist and an entry about the athlete in a sports encyclopedia? The interview is a primary source, while the encyclopedia entry is a secondary source.

When learning about the past, historians prefer to use primary sources. Primary sources are writings and objects that give firsthand descriptions of events and people. Letters, diaries, and news reports can be primary sources. So are photos and recordings of events, as long as they have not been tampered with.

Secondary sources use facts from other books to describe or interpret an event. These sources are not created by people who were actually involved in the events.

EXPLORE IT

How would a historian who wanted to study the Olympian Games in ancient Greece use primary sources? Some ancient Greek writings would tell about the games. For example, one Greek author described Olympian athletes this way: "They seem fine fellows, and strut about, the heroes of the town!"

Ancient Greek vases, statues, and paintings are also primary sources. By studying them, a historian could learn details about the games. The ruins of the stadium at Olympia in Greece—another primary source—would also hold many clues. A historian who had all the details could create a picture of the ancient Olympian Games.

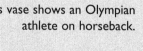
This vase shows an Olympian athlete on horseback.

Suppose some historians from far into the future were trying to find out about athletics in the United States today. Find and bring to class some primary sources to choose from—a score card from a game, a sports schedule, an interview with a professional athlete, or a videotape of a game.

With a group of your classmates, take the roles of future historians. Study the primary sources for athletics that you have collected. Then try to imagine what historians would find most interesting or important about the sources. Make a list of facts and conclusions about each primary source.

LOOKING AT SPORTS

I wore this cap to the Super Bowl!
Rich Hensley

My favorite Baltimore Oriole player.
Paul Faber

Mercy High School
Varsity Field Hockey

My sister's field hockey team and their schedule.
Shelly O'Malley

I hope to follow in the footsteps of Bonnie Blair—Olympic Champ!
Michele Costa

Videotape of the Stanley Cup Champs!
Scott Tang

Souvenirs bought at an Oilers game.
Keisha Jackson

SKILL POWER SEARCH Find other primary sources in this chapter about ancient Greece. What conclusions can you draw from each source?

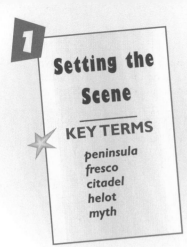

1 Setting the Scene

KEY TERMS

peninsula
fresco
citadel
helot
myth

ANCIENT GREECE

FOCUS *The Greek civilization originated in the eastern part of the Mediterranean Sea. The nature of the land and the presence of the sea influenced the type of civilization that developed.*

The Greek Peninsula

The map below tells you two important things about Greece—the land is hilly and rugged, and you are never far from the sea. The earliest Greeks settled in the southern part of the Balkan **Peninsula** and on the rocky islands in the northeastern part of the Mediterranean Sea. As the map shows, the southernmost part of this peninsula, called the Peloponnesus (pel uh puh NEE sus), is almost an island.

Rugged Land, Rugged People

Wherever they settled, Greeks could see mountains all around them. Mount Olympus, the highest mountain, was thought to be the home of the gods. Nestled in among the mountains and along the coasts were plains suitable for farming. In these areas, small independent communities sprang up, separated from each other by their rugged surroundings.

Making a living was difficult. The growing season tended to be dry, and Greece had no great rivers to provide water for irrigation. Fresh water came from shallow streams and rivers, many of which dried up in the summer.

The main farm crops were wheat, barley, and beans. Citrus trees and grapevines grew on the rocky hillsides. Olive trees, which by legend were a gift from the goddess Athena, provided food and oil for cooking. Small herds of sheep, goats, and cattle provided milk, cheese, and meat.

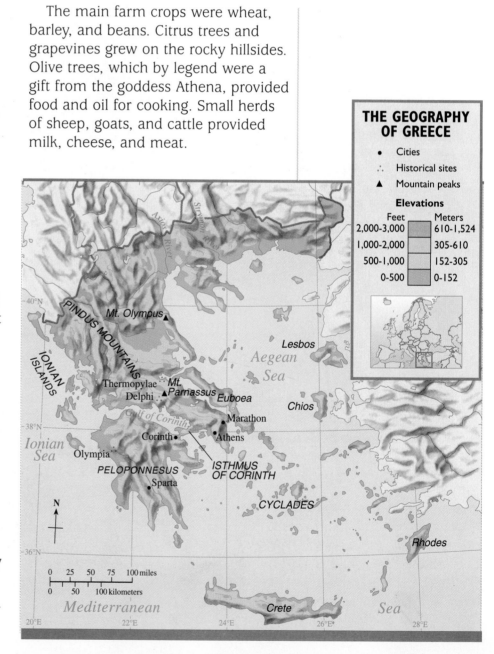

THE GEOGRAPHY OF GREECE

- • Cities
- ∴ Historical sites
- ▲ Mountain peaks

Elevations

Feet		Meters
2,000-3,000		610-1,524
1,000-2,000		305-610
500-1,000		152-305
0-500		0-152

⭐ **peninsula** A piece of land almost surrounded by water and connected to a larger body of land

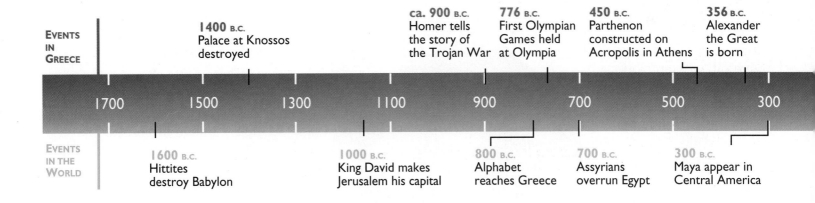

EVENTS IN GREECE		**1400** B.C. Palace at Knossos destroyed			**ca. 900** B.C. Homer tells the story of the Trojan War	**776** B.C. First Olympian Games held at Olympia	**450** B.C. Parthenon constructed on Acropolis in Athens	**356** B.C. Alexander the Great is born

1700	1500	1300	1100	900	700	500	300

EVENTS IN THE WORLD	**1600** B.C. Hittites destroy Babylon	**1000** B.C. King David makes Jerusalem his capital	**800** B.C. Alphabet reaches Greece	**700** B.C. Assyrians overrun Egypt	**300** B.C. Maya appear in Central America

Importance of the Sea

From the beginning the sea played an important role in the lives of Greek people. Because so much of the land was mountainous, travel by sea was easier and faster than overland travel. As the population of the mainland grew, the shortage of fertile land forced people to settle and colonize many of the islands surrounding the mainland peninsula. Over time, Greek merchants established trade routes among the colonies and with many cities along the coasts of the Aegean and Mediterranean seas.

Earliest Settlers

One of the earliest civilizations in the Greek region began about 5,000 years ago. It was on the island of Crete (kreet). The early settlers of this island are called Minoans (mih NOH unz), after their legendary king, Minos.

Many scholars thought that the Minoan culture might not have actually existed. In 1900, however, Sir Arthur Evans, an English archaeologist, discovered the ruins of Knossos (NAHS-us) and the palace of King Minos.

As the ruins were uncovered, Evans was astounded by the splendor of the palace. Much of the artwork consisted of **frescoes**, which covered the walls of the palace, shops, and other buildings. When Evans saw the brightly colored paintings of stylish, beautiful women, he compared them to the people of Paris, the most fashionable and modern city of his time.

The Minoan Era

After the discovery of Knossos, ruins of several other communities were discovered on the island. Unlike early settlements in other parts of the world, Cretan communities were not surrounded by walls. The island of Crete was a natural fortress. Minoan sailors patrolled the sea to keep pirates and invaders away.

Crete's location at the crossroads of the eastern Mediterranean world made the island a natural trading center. Minoan ships sailed to Asia, Africa, and

▼ This vase shows a scene from Greek daily life.

★ *fresco* A painting made with watercolors on wet plaster

Europe, carrying cargoes of olive oil, woolen cloth, perfumes, and metalware. They returned with gold and pearls from Egypt, tin from Persia, and cedar from Lebanon.

Around 1450 B.C. a combination of events brought the Minoan era to an end. Most historians believe that a series of natural disasters, such as volcanic eruptions and earthquakes, weakened the Minoan communities. They were then overrun by Mycenaean (mye suh NEE-un) invaders from the Greek mainland. The Minoan civilization never recovered.

The Mycenaeans Rule

The Mycenaean civilization was named for the town of Mycenae in the Peloponnesus. Unlike Minoans, the Mycenaeans were devoted to warfare. Their palaces were strong-walled fortresses, called **citadels**. Each citadel was the center of a small community ruled by a king. From these citadels the king, with the help of his soldiers, controlled the activities of the surrounding villages and farms.

The era of Mycenaean rule did not last long. Although historians are not sure why, the Mycenaean civilization declined rapidly. By about 1200 B.C. its cities were in ruins. Invasions by other Greeks from the north put an end to the Mycenaean era.

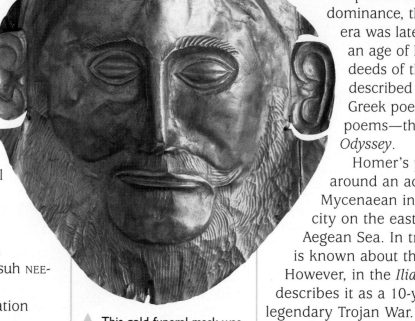

▲ This gold funeral mask was once believed to be a likeness of Agamemnon, the king of Mycenae.

An Age of Heroes

Despite its short period of dominance, the Mycenaean era was later thought of as an age of heroes. The deeds of these heroes are described by Homer, a Greek poet, in two epic poems—the *Iliad* and the *Odyssey*.

Homer's poems center around an actual event—a Mycenaean invasion of Troy, a city on the east coast of the Aegean Sea. In truth, very little is known about this event. However, in the *Iliad*, Homer describes it as a 10-year battle—the legendary Trojan War.

In Homer's account, both sides had brave warriors, such as Achilles (uh-KIHL eez), Hector, and Odysseus (oh-DIHS ee us). On page 156 you can read about how the Trojan War ended when the Mycenaeans tricked their way into Troy and destroyed the city.

Rise of the City-States

With the end of the Mycenaean era, early civilization went into decline. It began to revive about four centuries later. Population increased and villages grew into cities. Over time, many cities became powerful city-states.

The spread of literacy encouraged the development of a more highly organized society. When the Greeks adopted the Phoenician alphabet, they added vowels. It was around this time that Homer's epics were written down.

⭐ *citadel*   A fort built on a high point for defending a town

The most powerful city-states were Sparta, in the Peloponnesus, and Athens, on the Attic plain in the northern peninsula. A third city-state, Corinth, used its position on the narrow strip of land that connects the Peloponnesus to the rest of the Greek mainland to control trade between north and south.

Though Greeks spoke a common language, the country had no single ruler. People thought of themselves as citizens of their city-state, or polis. Citizens of different city-states seldom acted together, except when invasion threatened them all.

The Warrior Spartans

Sparta, one of the two great city-states, was a warrior polis. Through conquest the Spartans had gained control of much of the southern Peloponnesus. The conquered people were forced to farm the land to provide food for the Spartans. These people, called **helots** (HEL uts), greatly outnumbered the Spartans.

To keep themselves dominant over the helots, the Spartans devoted most of their energies to military training. A healthy Spartan boy stayed with his parents only until the age of seven. Then he left home and lived in a barracks. His life of strict military discipline would continue until he

reached the age of 30. At that time he was allowed to marry and live in his own home. Even then, he spent much of his time in military training.

The military nature of Spartan society affected girls as well. They were required to take part in sports and athletic exercises. It was believed that children born to women in good physical condition would be healthy and strong. Such children would be better prepared to carry on the warrior tradition of Sparta.

The Glory of Athens

The polis of Athens made great contributions to modern civilization. Its art, literature, building design, and ideas formed the foundation of Western civilization. Athenian ideals continue to inspire people today.

Like many city-states, Athens developed around an acropolis (uh KRAHP uh-lihs), a citadel built on a high, flat-topped hill. Many temples to the gods were built on the Acropolis of Athens. The most famous of

▲ This ancient plaque depicts the warlike nature of the Spartan people.

◄ A Spartan girl kept in physical shape by running.

⭐ **helot** A person forced to work for another person

141

these is the Parthenon, dedicated to Athena, the goddess of wisdom and the city's namesake. A sacred olive tree that grew here was considered to be Athena's gift to the Greeks.

Three miles from ancient Athens lay the sea. It was not only a source of food but also a highway to other parts of the world. Athens had colonies in Asia, on the eastern shore of the Aegean, and on the Black Sea. Grain grown in these colonies was shipped back to Athens. To protect the sea routes to these colonies, Athens developed a powerful navy.

Victory at Marathon

Athens encouraged citizens to participate in the running of the polis. This personal involvement ensured the loyalty of those citizens who would have to defend the city when it came under attack. This loyalty was put to the test during the battle of Marathon, some 26 miles from Athens. Although greatly outnumbered, the Athenians defeated Persian troops in a famous battle at that site. You will read more about this battle on page 156.

Life in Athens

Life in Athens was much different than in Sparta. In Athens, people followed pleasant, "normal" daily routines. The agora (AG uh ruh), or marketplace, was the center of Athenian life. Men did the shopping. As they shopped, they would stop to gossip and talk over the issues of the day. Under the colonnades, or roofed sidewalks, the philosophers argued with each other and taught young men how to think and reason.

Women spent most of their time at home, weaving and sewing. If they went out, they were usually accompanied by a helot. Helots also did the housework and cooking. Women had no legal rights. The husband had complete authority over everyone who lived in his house.

Girls were educated at home by their mothers. Boys went to school, where they learned to read, write, and do calculations. Afternoons were spent in the gymnasium.

Ruins of the Parthenon in Athens, Greece (*top*); a reproduction of the Parthenon in Nashville, Tennessee (*bottom*)

Scenes on an ancient vase show students in Greek classrooms.

SHOW WHAT YOU
KNOW!

REFOCUS
COMPREHENSION

1. What was the earliest civilization in the Greek region, and where was it located?

2. Why did the development of a city-state start with an acropolis?

THINK ABOUT IT
CRITICAL THINKING

What circumstances led Greece to establish colonies early in its history?

WRITE ABOUT IT
ACTIVITY

Six months ago you and your family moved from Sparta to Athens. Write a letter to your best friend in Sparta describing how your life has changed since you left.

Greeks and Their Gods

Greeks believed in many gods and built temples for some of them. People worshiped outside the temple doors, which could be opened to reveal the statue of the god therein. The origins and activities of the gods were described in stories known as **myths**.

According to Greek mythology, the gods mingled with humans, guiding them and punishing them as they saw fit. Perhaps the best example of people interacting with a god can be found at Delphi.

The temple at Delphi was the home of the god Apollo. People traveled to Delphi from all parts of the Greek world to seek advice before making an important decision. For a fee, visitors were allowed to ask their questions of a priestess, who would receive and relay Apollo's responses. Often the responses were ambiguous, or unclear, and the questioners would have to interpret the answers from Apollo as best as they could.

 The priestess at Delphi

The Golden Age

After their victory over the Persians at Marathon, the citizens of Athens felt a surge of confidence. During the next two centuries, Athenians produced the great plays, art, philosophies, and building designs that have influenced the world ever since.

The leader of Athens during this golden age was Pericles (PER ih-kleez). Though he was only one of ten generals who were elected each year, Pericles had greater influence on the people of Athens than anyone else. His long, stirring speeches encouraged Athenians to see themselves as a special people.

The Golden Age of Athens ended with the Athenian defeat at the hands of the Spartans in the Peloponnesian War. You will read about this war on page 157. The Peloponnesian War would also leave the city-states vulnerable to invasion by Macedonia (mas uh DOH nee uh), a kingdom in northern Greece.

⭐ **myth** A traditional story about the origins and activities of the gods

A DAY AT THE OLYMPICS

FOCUS *The ancient Greeks placed a great emphasis on athletics and physical fitness. The modern Olympic Games are a revival of the ancient athletic contests in which all Greeks participated.*

▼ The finish line at the first Olympian Games (*top*); opening ceremonies at the 1988 Summer Olympics in Seoul, Korea (*bottom*)

A Dream Come True

It's a dream come true! You're in the stadium at Olympia, sitting with boys and men from your city. It's the third day of the five-day Olympian Games, a festival in honor of the gods. On the first two days, you saw several events, including the opening ceremonies and the chariot race. Today you are looking forward to the footraces, especially the **marathon**. You've arrived early, and while you wait for the races to begin, you daydream about the events taking place around you.

★ *marathon*   A footrace of 26 miles, 385 yards

▲ Chariot racing shown on an ancient Greek vase

How It All Started

For hundreds of years the Olympian Games have been held every four years. Athletes have traveled from all corners of the Greek world to take part in the contests.

The festival is a time of peace for all Greeks. No matter what political feuds or city-state wars might be underway, everything is put on hold for the games. All rivalries are transformed into intense athletic competition on the field. Each athlete competes as an individual. There are no team events. But victory in the games brings great honor to an athlete's home city.

Respect in the Stands

As you look around, your attention turns to an old man as he slowly climbs the steps of the stadium, looking for a seat. Just then, the crowd starts to roar. The runners have come out for the start of the 192-meter race called the *stade*. The crowd behind the old man becomes restless. Shouts of "Sit down!" and "Get out of the way!" are directed at him.

After much jeering and insults, the old man reaches the section of seats assigned to the Spartans. As he starts looking for a seat there, all the young boys and several Spartan men stand and offer him their own seat. As people in other sections see what is happening, they stand and applaud. The crowd recognizes this traditional sign of respect for the elderly. The old man gratefully takes a seat and with tears in his eyes, says, "Alas for the evil days. Because all the Greeks know what is right, but only the Spartans do it."

Statue of Athena, the Greek goddess of wisdom and skills ▶

Zeus ruled over all the other Greek gods.

Spoils for the Victors

Now that you and the people around you have been reminded of an important lesson, your attention returns to the games. At the end of the day, you return to the camp that has been set up nearby for people from your city. You know that you will have trouble getting to sleep, looking forward to the next day's events.

The final event is the awarding of prizes—crowns made of sacred olive branches. The victorious athletes will be treated as heroes at home. As you leave the stadium, the old man glances up and catches your eye. His eyes seem to say, "Zeus willing, I'll see you here at the Olympian Games four years from now."

SHOW WHAT YOU KNOW!

REFOCUS
COMPREHENSION

1. How was it possible for athletes from unfriendly city-states to compete against each other in the Olympian Games?

2. What did the Spartan fans' behavior reveal about their feelings for elderly people?

THINK ABOUT IT
CRITICAL THINKING

Compare and contrast the ancient Olympian Games with the modern Olympic Games.

WRITE ABOUT IT
ACTIVITY

Write an entry in your journal describing your trip home with friends from your first Olympian Games.

145

OUR GREEK HERITAGE

FOCUS *Greek achievements in art, drama, science and medicine, building design, and government influence and enrich our lives today.*

Spread of Greek Culture

Greek civilization spread as the city-states established colonies in other areas. As the map shows, colonization brought Greek culture to the northern shores of the Aegean and Black seas and to parts of southern Europe and the coast of northern Africa.

The Greek colonies in Italy had a special significance. When Rome became the most powerful city in the Mediterranean, its people held a high respect for the many contributions of Greek civilization. As the Roman Empire spread beyond Italy, it carried Greek culture far beyond the Mediterranean into northern Europe.

Today, more than 20 centuries after the last great flowering of Greek civilization, the contributions of Greece make up an important part of our

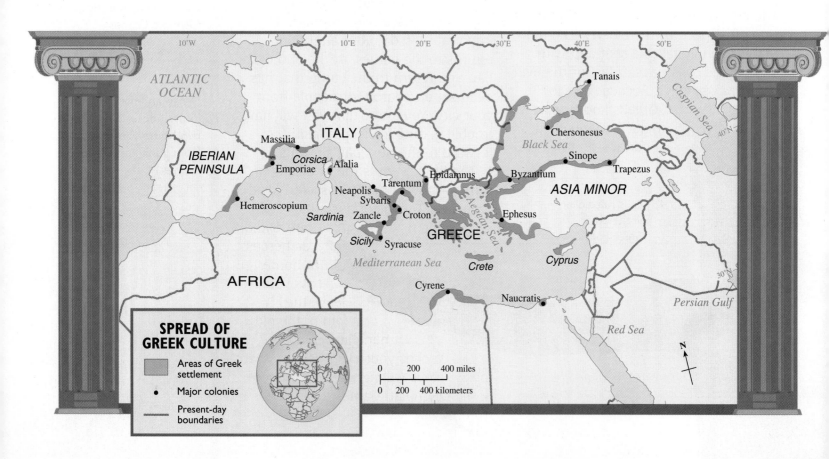

SPREAD OF GREEK CULTURE

- Areas of Greek settlement
- Major colonies
- Present-day boundaries

heritage. The ideas, art, literature, and **architecture** of the Greeks still have power to shape the hearts and minds of human beings.

A Heritage in Marble

The Greek love of beauty found its highest expression in sculpture. The favorite subject of Greek sculptors was the human body. Gods, goddesses, athletes, and heroes were all depicted as perfectly formed human beings.

Greek architects were not the first to use columns to support the roofs of buildings. But the Greeks refined the column into a sophisticated element of architecture. The picture below shows the influence of Greek architecture in the design of a modern building.

Poetry and Music

Greek poetry was usually written for public performances with musical accompaniment. Readers recited the poetry while musicians played a variety of musical instruments.

Among the best-known poets were Homer and Sappho (SAF oh), the most famous female writer of the ancient world. While Homer's works tell of war and the heroic deeds of men, Sappho's poetry describes love, friendship, and joy.

Stories and Legends

The Greeks created myths and stories that still stir people's souls. Many myths tell about the gods and their deeds. Some explain the forces of nature. For example, the story of Persephone (pur SEF uh nee) tells why we have seasons.

Persephone was the beautiful daughter of Demeter, the goddess of agriculture. One day Hades, god of the underworld, carried Persephone off to his domain. While Demeter mourned the loss of her daughter, all the plants stopped growing and famine swept the land. To save the earth, Zeus decided that Persephone would divide her time between her mother and Hades. In spring and summer, she would live with Demeter, and plants would thrive. For the rest of the year, she would live in the underworld with Hades, and plants would wither and die.

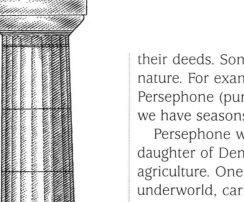

 Types of Greek columns include Doric (*top*), Ionic (*left*), and Corinthian (*right*).

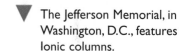 The Jefferson Memorial, in Washington, D.C., features Ionic columns.

⭐ **heritage** A system of ways and beliefs handed down from one generation to another
architecture A style or special way of building

Drama—Acting Out Stories

The earliest record of people acting out a story began in Athens, at a festival held in honor of Dionysius (deye uh NIHSH us), the god of wine and fertility. The merrymaking included dances, songs, and poetry. At some point, acting out ancient legends became part of the festivities. Then playwrights began to create their own stories.

Playwriting soon became a contest. Every year about 20 to 30 new plays were presented at the festival, with judges awarding prizes to the best play. The idea caught on, and soon theaters were built and playwrights and actors became respected members of the community.

The most famous Greek playwrights were Aeschylus (ES kih-lus), Sophocles (SAHF uh kleez), Euripedes (yoo RIHP uh deez), and Aristophanes (ar ih STAHF-uh neez). The first three wrote about serious subjects—war, misfortune, and injustice. Aristophanes may have been the most courageous of the playwrights, since he wrote comedies. He dared to poke fun at politicians and other important people in Greek society.

▲ Socrates, Plato, and Aristotle (*right to left*) were the best-known Greek philosophers.

Modern performances of Greek plays ▶ are often held in ancient theaters such as the one shown here.

Great Philosophers

Philosophy was a vital part of many Athenians' lives. Greek philosophers wanted to learn everything they could. They learned by asking such questions as these: How should people behave? What is truth?

The three most important Greek philosophers all lived in Athens during the fifth and fourth centuries B.C. The first was Socrates (SAHK ruh teez). He was a familiar figure in the agora. Socrates taught by asking questions. Each answer would lead to another question.

Plato, the second great philosopher, described the ideal form of government in his great work *The Republic*. This republic would be ruled by philosophers, for they understood what was best for everyone.

★ *philosophy* The study of what people think about the meaning of life

Aristotle (AR ihs taht ul) was Plato's most famous pupil. In his lifetime, Aristotle wrote dozens of books on many different subjects. For many centuries after his death, Aristotle was regarded as the one man who knew more than anyone else.

Mathematics and Science

The Greeks excelled at mathematics. Euclid (YOO klihd) developed a field of geometry that still bears his name. If you take that subject, you will study the very same things that Euclid discovered 23 centuries ago.

Archimedes (ahr kuh MEE deez) was a scientist and philosopher who made an important discovery while taking a bath. Seeing the water rise as he lowered himself into his bath, Archimedes realized that the change in the volume of water in the tub was equal to the volume of an irregularly shaped object—his body. As the story goes, he jumped from his bath and ran into the street, shouting "Eureka!" or "I have found it."

Greek scientists knew that the earth was a sphere and that the sun appeared to revolve around the earth. Eratosthenes (er uh TAHS thuh neez) used this knowledge and his knowledge of mathematics to calculate the circumference of the earth. The

In this painting Hippocrates, right, is shown talking to Galen, a Greek physician who lived several hundred years later.

results of his calculations were very close to the figure that is accepted by scientists today.

Medicine

Greeks made great advances in medicine. Originally, people believed that disease was sent by the gods. The people prayed to Asclepius (as KLEE-pee us), the god of medicine, to cure them.

Hippocrates (hih PAHK ruh teez) is considered to be the father of modern medicine. Throughout his life he fought superstition about disease. He looked at the ailments of his patients and tried to find cures that worked. He wrote a code of ethics that began by cautioning doctors not to harm their patients. Most doctors today repeat the Hippocratic oath when they graduate from medical school.

SHOW WHAT YOU KNOW!

REFOCUS
COMPREHENSION

1. What features of a building are most closely associated with Greek architecture?

2. If Aristophanes were alive today, would he be more likely to write scripts for TV or study the solar system? Explain.

THINK ABOUT IT
CRITICAL THINKING

Suppose the earliest Greeks had settled in the middle of a continent. How might this fact have affected the spread of Greek culture?

WRITE ABOUT IT
ACTIVITY

Think about some interesting natural event, such as the forming of a rainbow or the changing of the shape of the moon. If you had been living in ancient Greece, how might you have explained the event?

BIRTH OF DEMOCRACY

FOCUS *The idea of a democratic society—one in which ordinary citizens played an active role in making decisions that affected them—was introduced by the Greeks. It was a model for all future democratic systems of government.*

▲ A town meeting is an example of a direct democracy.

Solon, the Father of Democracy

Early Greeks were governed by kings. Later, wealthy landowners became the aristocrats of the city-states. These aristocrats started to choose leaders known as archons. An archon had many functions. He was the chief judge as well as the leader of the city's military forces.

Early in the fifth century B.C., Solon was named archon of Athens. He was a general and a wealthy merchant.

When Solon took office, Athens was in deep financial trouble. Many people were in debt. Some farmers had been forced to sell themselves into slavery to pay their debts.

Solon introduced a series of social and political reforms. He canceled all debts and all mortgages on land. He then freed those people who had been sold into slavery to pay off their debts.

The Right to Vote

Solon drew up a constitution that extended the right to vote to all male citizens. He offered citizenship to skilled foreigners who chose to work in Athens. There was a property requirement for holding public office, but any male citizen, no matter how poor, could participate in the assembly.

The assembly met about 40 times a year. The men brought folding chairs or sat on the ground. Issues were discussed, and people raised their hands when a vote was called for. The assembly also elected the Council of Four Hundred, which took care of day-to-day government business. The city-state of Athens now had a **direct democracy**.

⭐ ***direct democracy*** Participation in government by all citizens directly, not through representatives

▲ Jury members voted guilt or innocence by the token they placed in the jar.

The Age of Pericles

Pericles is considered the greatest statesman in ancient Greek history. He came to power in Athens in the middle of the fifth century B.C. Pericles started a system of payment for public service to bring more people into the political process. The system of laws was improved, and citizens were chosen to serve on **juries**. Jury members were paid so that defendants in trials would be judged by a cross section of citizens.

Pericles made it more difficult for a person to become a citizen of Athens. For a person to become a citizen, both parents had to have been citizens.

Citizens made up only about 10 percent of the Athenian population. Slaves and most foreign-born residents were not allowed to participate in government.

Women were never allowed to vote. Though this seems unfair today, even in the United States women did not gain the right to vote until 1920.

Greek Ideas on Citizenship

The Greeks had a good reason for having citizens play a greater role in their government. Athenian leaders felt that the sense of being involved strengthened the city. The historian Herodotus (huh-RAHD uh tus) believed that democracy enabled the Greeks to defeat the Persians. He pointed out that before Athens was a democracy, it had no better success at war than any other oppressed state. Yet once democracy was in place, Athenians proved to be "the finest fighters in the world."

Herodotus explained that people who are held down by authority deliberately shirk their duty. They do not work willingly for a ruling class. On the other hand, people who have a greater stake in their future serve willingly and enthusiastically to preserve their state and their freedom.

◀ Pericles was a great Athenian statesman.

jury A group of people called into court to give a verdict in a dispute

Spotlight

⭐ **KEY TERM**

infantry

📖 **LITERATURE**

The Great
Alexander the
Great

ALEXANDER THE GREAT

FOCUS *At the pinnacle of his success, Alexander the Great ruled over the greatest empire in history.*

Education of a Prince

Alexander was born to rule. He was the son of Philip II, king of Macedonia (mas uh DOH nee uh), a small rural country in the northern part of the Greek peninsula. Philip was a true warrior-king. His dream was to expand his kingdom to include all of Greece and the Persian Empire.

Alexander was educated by tutors. His first tutor taught him to read and write. He also put Alexander through a program of rigorous physical training to prepare him for his future as a warrior.

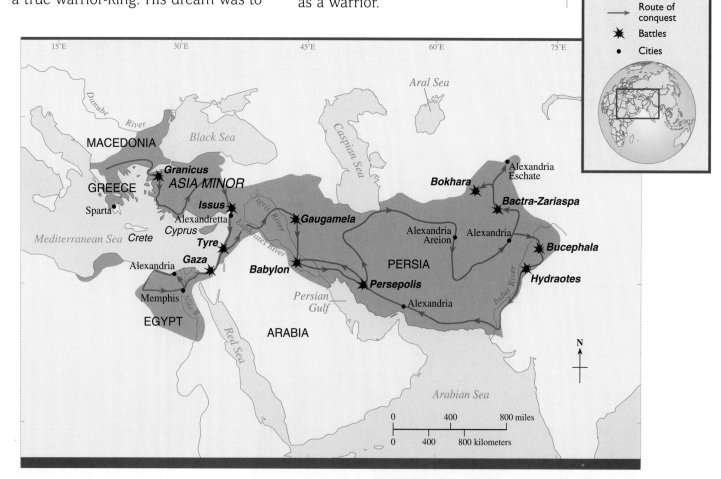

ALEXANDER'S CONQUESTS

Alexander's empire

→ Route of conquest

✴ Battles

• Cities

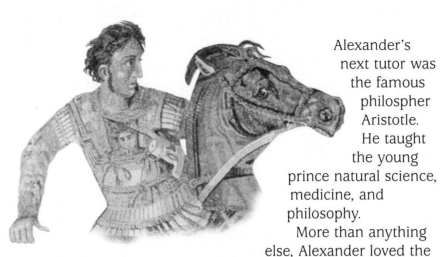

▲ A detail from a mosaic shows Alexander leading his troops to victory over Darius.

Alexander's next tutor was the famous philospher Aristotle. He taught the young prince natural science, medicine, and philosophy.

More than anything else, Alexander loved the tales of Greek heroes, especially the *Iliad*. He wanted to become a bold warrior like Achilles. Throughout his military life, Alexander would keep two things under his pillow at night—a copy of the *Iliad* and a dagger.

Alexander's military training was handled by his father, the best military mind of the day. Some historians consider Philip to have been the first modern military leader. Tactics he developed for his **infantry** were copied and used by other armies for hundreds of years.

A New Ruler Takes Command

At the tender age of 18, Alexander was a general in Philip's army. He had already proved himself as a leader in battle when the Macedonians defeated the combined forces of Athens and Thebes (theebz).

Thus, in 338 B.C., Philip was the most powerful man in Greece. Two years later he was dead, murdered by one of his bodyguards. Alexander of Macedonia, soon to become known throughout the world as Alexander the Great, was now a king.

Alexander Versus Darius

After securing power in Greece, Alexander set out to achieve his father's dream of invading and conquering the Persian Empire. For the next 13 years, Alexander would become a familiar figure on the battlefield. Astride his great horse, Bucephalus (byoo SEF uh lus), he would lead his troops in pursuit of the Persian ruler, Darius (duh REE us) III.

The two rulers would meet in battle several times. Each time, Alexander's army would prevail, but Darius would always escape to fight again. Finally, after suffering several defeats at the hands of the Macedonians, the Persian soldiers took matters into their own hands. With Alexander in hot pursuit, they killed Darius and fled. Alexander could now claim to be ruler of the Persian Empire.

The Most Powerful Man in the World

Having reached their goal, Alexander's troops wanted to go home. But Alexander had other ideas. He now set his sights on India. For several years, his armies kept winning battles and expanding their empire, as shown in the map on page 152.

Even as he planned new conquests, Alexander became ill. Disease proved to be an enemy that even Alexander the Great could not defeat. As word spread that Alexander was dying, his soldiers passed by his bed to see him one last time. Alexander, ruler of the largest empire the world had ever seen, died at age 33.

★ *infantry*   Soldiers who are trained and armed for fighting on foot

The Great Alexander The Great

Story and Pictures by Joe Lasker

Alexander was one of history's legendary figures. He and his great horse, Bucephalus, were inseparable partners throughout Alexander's reign over a great empire. How did this partnership between a man and his horse come to pass? Read about the first meeting of boy and horse and learn how the bond between them was formed.

The shaken stablemaster limped over to the king. "Sire, I beg you not to buy this horse. He is unmanageable." Philip nodded in agreement.

Alexander pushed his way into the circle of men around the king. "No! Don't listen! He's a good horse!" he shouted at his father. The bearded elders were astonished at Alexander's rudeness. Philip, annoyed, glanced down at his son, then went on discussing war.

"Father! Listen!" demanded the boy. "They don't know how to handle him!"

The king's one good eye flashed in anger. "Are you telling me my horseman can't handle horses?"

"No, sir—well, I mean, I think I know how to control him." Everybody laughed at Alexander.

"And after you tame him, will you pay for him?" mocked the king.

Alexander would not back down. "I will somehow."

"All right, by Zeus," growled Philip. "I'll bet you the price of the horse you can't ride him."

Silent and anxious, everybody watched the young prince. Without hesitation he ran toward the horse. As he came closer, Alexander's run changed to a slow walk. The great black stallion loomed larger than when seen from a safe distance.

Alexander's heart pounded with fear, but he could not turn back now. He had been taught that courage and honor counted for more than life itself.

Slowly he reached for the reins. He could see that the animal was as frightened as he was. Pity mingled with Alexander's fear. Perhaps his feelings were sensed by the horse, for he allowed Alexander to turn him around, facing into the sun.

The boy lightly swung himself onto the horse's bare back. The stallion leaped forward, powerful hooves pounding the earth. Alexander bent low, talking softly into the horse's ear while applying just enough pressure to keep him headed into the sun. Gradually the horse grew calmer. Alexander straightened up, laughing joyously. The horse galloped free. Everybody cheered. Then Alexander cantered back to his father.

"Well done, my son!" Philip cried. "What magic did you use?"

"No magic, Father," Alexander answered. "He was frightened by his own shadow. I turned him to face into the sun. When he no longer saw his shadow, he was mine."

This horse and rider cast their shadow across the world. Bucephalus became the most famous horse in history. He never let anyone but Alexander ride him. When Alexander was preparing to mount, the noble horse would lower his body to help him on. In battle Alexander always rode Bucephalus.

Want to read more? You can find out about Alexander's life by checking this book out of your school or public library.

REFOCUS
COMPREHENSION

1. Why did Alexander's father choose to handle his son's military training?

2. What dream of his father did Alexander fulfill?

THINK ABOUT IT
CRITICAL THINKING

How might the story of young Alexander's first encounter with Bucephalus have been different if it had occurred on a cloudy day?

WRITE ABOUT IT
ACTIVITY

You are a private in Alexander's army. Write a letter home describing how you and the rest of the troops feel about your leader.

6

March of Time

1200 B.C. TO 404 B.C.

A WARLIKE PEOPLE

FOCUS *The ancient Greeks were fond of battle. For centuries, war was being waged on some scale somewhere in Greece.*

GREEK GIFT CONQUERS TROY

About 1200 B.C. the Greeks attacked Troy. However, they were not able to crack the city's defenses, nor could the Trojans drive the Greeks back to their ships. The war dragged on for ten years, with neither side gaining an advantage. Only a new strategy would break the deadlock.

Odysseus devised a plan. The Greeks built a huge wooden horse, and a squad of soldiers hid inside it. The horse was then left outside the city gate. The rest of the Greeks boarded their ships and sailed out of sight.

The Trojans, of course, were curious. Despite warnings from the prophetess Cassandra, the Trojans dragged the wooden horse into the city. In the middle of the night, the Greek soldiers emerged and opened the gate. The Greek army, which had returned during the night, entered the city and took the Trojans by surprise. The Greeks slaughtered the people of Troy and set fire to the city.

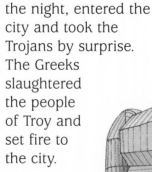

GREECE 2, PERSIA 0

In 490 B.C., Darius I, ruler of the Persian Empire, sent an army to attack Athens. The first great battle was fought at Marathon, about 26 miles north of Athens. The Persians outnumbered the Greeks by more than two to one. But the Greeks drew the Persians into a trap, making them think they were facing only a handful of Greek soldiers. When the Persians attacked, the rest of the Greek force surrounded and soundly defeated them.

A messenger ran from the battlefield to Athens with news of the victory. After shouting "We have won!" he dropped dead from exhaustion. The marathon race that people run today takes its name from this heroic feat.

Ten years later, Darius' son Xerxes (ZURK seez) sought to avenge his father's defeat. Xerxes quickly conquered several cities, including Athens. However, about 300 Greek soldiers from Sparta managed to hold off the Persians at a narrow pass in Thermopylae (thur MAHP uh lee) long enough for the rest of the Greek army to escape. A year later the Greeks defeated the Persians in a major sea battle at Salamis (SAL uh mihs).

1200 B.C.
Start of the
Trojan War

480 B.C.
Spartans hold off
Persians at
Thermopylae

418 B.C.
Spartans defeat
Athenians at
Mantinea

405 B.C.
Spartan navy
conquers Athens

| 1200 | 500 | 450 | 400 |

WAR OF THE CITY-STATES

The two greatest Greek city-states, Athens and Sparta, fought each other in the Peloponnesian War, which lasted from 431 to 404 B.C. One of the most important battles took place in 418 B.C. at Mantinea (man tuh NEE uh).

The two powers were evenly matched. But the Athenians gained the upper hand because of a new tactic they devised. When the Spartans fought in formation, they tended to move slightly to the right. This was because each soldier carried his shield in his left hand. Knowing this, the Athenians attacked the left side of the Spartans' formations.

The Spartan soldiers were forced to retreat. However, instead of following up their advantage, the Athenians stopped attacking and marched off to loot the Spartan baggage train. The disciplined Spartans regrouped and attacked the Athenians. Disorganized and caught by surprise, the Athenians fled from the battlefield. They would never challenge the Spartans in a land battle again.

However, the Athenians still had a powerful navy. In 415 B.C. they sailed across the Mediterranean toward Syracuse, a rich Spartan colony on the island of Sicily. Instead of attacking Syracuse, the Athenians decided to starve the people, forcing surrender. This decision gave Sparta time to send in reinforcements. In 413 B.C., Spartan ships trapped and defeated the Athenian fleet, leaving Athens itself ripe for the taking. In 405 B.C. the Spartan navy besieged Athens. Starved and discouraged, the Athenians surrendered the following year.

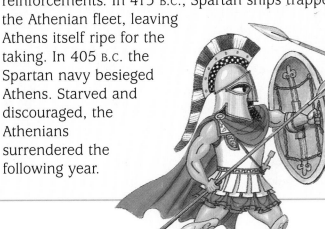

REFOCUS
COMPREHENSION

1. Why did the Trojan War last as long as it did?

2. Briefly describe two mistakes made by the Athenians during their war with Sparta.

THINK ABOUT IT
CRITICAL THINKING

How might the results of the Trojan War have been different if the Trojans had listened to Cassandra?

WRITE ABOUT IT
ACTIVITY

You live in Troy, and you record in your journal each day's events during the war with Greece. Describe in your journal what happens on the day that the Greeks leave a great wooden horse outside your city's gates.

SUMMING UP

1 DO YOU REMEMBER...
COMPREHENSION

1. Why was agriculture difficult in ancient Greece?

2. Why was the sea so important to the ancient Greeks?

3. How did the main interests of the Spartans differ from those of the Athenians?

4. Why did so many Greeks travel to the temple at Delphi?

5. Why did the ancient Greeks hold the Olympian Games?

6. Tell how drama began in ancient Greece.

7. Why is Solon called the Father of Democracy?

8. How did Pericles improve Greek democracy?

9. What important empire did Alexander the Great conquer?

10. How did the Greeks manage to conquer Troy in 1200 B.C.?

2 SKILL POWER
USING PRIMARY AND SECONDARY SOURCES

Choose three illustrations in this chapter that are primary sources. Select pictures that you think are the most interesting or informative. Then study the pictures and list what they tell you about life in ancient Greece. Be creative and try to draw as many conclusions as you can from the illustrations you choose.

3 WHAT DO YOU THINK?
CRITICAL THINKING

1. Why do you think the myths about Greek gods and goddesses still fascinate many people today?

2. Give three or more examples of ways in which the Greek heritage lives on in your town or community.

3. The Olympian Games were always held at Olympia. Do you think the modern Olympics should always be held at the same place every four years? Explain why you feel as you do.

4. Plato thought the ideal government would be run by philosophers who understood what was best for others. Tell whether you agree.

5. Alexander the Great hoped to conquer and rule the world. What do you think of this goal?

4 SAY IT, WRITE IT, USE IT
VOCABULARY

You're about to take a vacation in Greece. Your plan is to learn as much as you can about life in ancient times there. Write a few paragraphs that tell what you would try to do and see during your visit. In your writing, use as many of the vocabulary terms as you can.

architecture	infantry
citadel	jury
direct democracy	marathon
fresco	myth
helot	peninsula
heritage	philosophy

5 GEOGRAPHY AND YOU

MAP STUDY

To complete this exercise, compare the map on page 146 with an atlas map that shows the same area.

In what present-day countries might you find remains of the following Greek colonies?

1. Byzantium
2. Syracuse
3. Cyrene
4. Massilia

6 GET CREATIVE

LANGUAGE ARTS CONNECTION

Many English words come from Greek roots. You probably can list some words made from the roots below.

auto- self	**-cracy** rule
bio- life	**-graphy** writing
demo- people	**-logy** the study of
geo- earth	**-phobia** fear
philo- love	**-sophic** wisdom

Using the roots, make up some original words and draw cartoons to illustrate them.

7 TAKE ACTION

CITIZENSHIP

The leaders of Athens wanted citizens to be involved in their community. They believed that this would strengthen their city.

You can help your community by planning a project such as picking up trash in a park, playground, or community garden. Find out how your community recycles glass, cans, newspapers, magazines, and plastic. As you clean up, separate the recyclable materials.

LOOKING AHEAD

In Chapter 8 you will see how the culture of ancient Rome differs from the culture of Greece.

EXPLORE

THE HERITAGE

How is our government like that of the Roman Republic? What event ended Rome's early form of government? Why did Roman senators assassinate Julius Caesar? Read this chapter to find answers to these questions.

This girl is holding a groma. Look on page 178 to learn what it was used for.

CONTENTS

OF ROME

These books tell about some people, places, and events that make Rome so interesting. Read one that interests you and fill out a book-review form.

READ AND RESEARCH

Detectives in Togas by **Henry Winterfeld** (Harcourt Brace Jovanovich, 1990)
Think about what it would be like to find strange writing on a temple wall or your teacher stuffed in a closet. A bunch of Roman friends find themselves in the middle of this mystery after Rufus, their friend, is blamed for their misdeeds. Will they find out who really did it before it's too late? (*historical fiction*)

Constantine by **Nancy Zinsser Walworth** (Chelsea House Publishers, 1989)
Learn all about Constantine, one of the most influential leaders in the Roman Empire. Follow him from his childhood to his last days as emperor. You will see how one man inspired the rise of Christianity. (*biography*)

City: A Story of Roman Planning and Construction by **David Macaulay** (Houghton Mifflin Co., 1974)
After a flood destroyed many small villages in northern Italy, the emperor ordered that a new city be built. Witness how Roman cities were built long ago. (*nonfiction*)

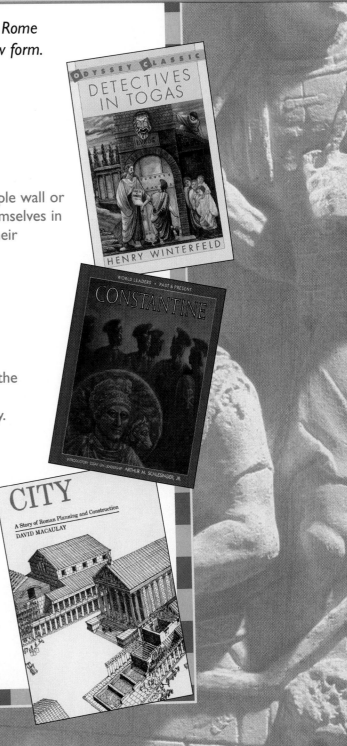

Comparing Maps

Comparing maps from different times in history can help you understand how events sometimes change geography.

UNDERSTAND IT

Have you ever gone back to a place after you have been away for a while and noticed changes in the way it looks? Maybe a sandy beach is smaller than it used to be. Perhaps new houses are being built on farmland. Changes like these happen when wind erodes a beach or a farmer's land becomes worth more for development than for growing crops. Both of these events can change the way a map of the area looks. Events such as wars, treaties, and natural disasters also can change the geography of an area.

EXPLORE IT

To see how political geography changes over time, look at the two maps of Italy on the next page. See if you can find the answers to these questions by comparing the maps.

- Around 1200, what were the main parts of Italy?

- What are the names of three of the places that replaced the Holy Roman Empire in northern Italy by 1500?

- Do the Papal States appear to have changed between 1200 and 1500?

- Many cities such as Florence became city-states by 1500. Why might they have been more likely to be invaded by other countries than the empires of 1200 were?

- What other differences do you notice between the two maps?

Farmland is often sold to developers, who then build houses on it.

HOLY ROMAN EMPIRE

Italy in 1200

Venice
VENICE
Genoa
PAPAL STATES

N

Corsica
Rome
Naples
Sardinia
KINGDOM OF THE TWO SICILIES

Adriatic Sea
Tyrrhenian Sea
Ionian Sea
Mediterranean Sea
Sicily

45°N
40°N
10°E   15°E

0   75   150 miles
0 75 150 kilometers

Italy in 1500

MONTFERRAT   MANTUA
SAVOY   MILAN   VENETIAN REPUBLIC
ASTI   Venice   FERRARA
Genoa
MODENA
SALUZZO   LUCCA
FLORENCE   PAPAL STATES
GENOA   SIENA
Corsica
Rome
SARDINIA
PAPAL STATES
Naples
KINGDOM OF THE TWO SICILIES

Adriatic Sea
Tyrrhenian Sea
Ionian Sea
Mediterranean Sea
Sicily

45°N
40°N
10°E   15°E

POLITICAL DIVISIONS IN ITALY

Present-day Italy

Boundaries

• Cities

TRY IT

Think about how your state, city, or town may have changed over the last 10 to 25 years. Work with your classmates to do research about the changes. Find or draw maps of then and now. Try to get photographs that show how things have changed. Ask adults to tell you what things were like at the time you are comparing to the present. Write articles about the information you gather. Then put your maps, photographs, and articles together to publish a class newsletter.

SKILL

POWER SEARCH Take a tour of Rome by comparing maps of republican Rome and imperial Rome on pages 172–173.

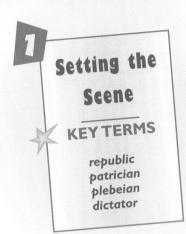

1

Setting the Scene

KEY TERMS

republic
patrician
plebeian
dictator

AN IMMENSE EMPIRE

FOCUS *Many achievements of the Romans still influence our lives today. Among the most important are language, laws, and engineering.*

The Boot

The ancient saying "All roads lead to Rome" gives an idea of the power of the Roman Empire. Within the territories they conquered, Roman soldiers built a vast network of roads, some of which still exist today. Traders could travel along the roads in safety, carrying goods and spreading Roman culture, power, and wealth. The story of this empire, the largest of the ancient world, begins with seven villages that became the city of Rome.

As you can see on the map, Rome is near the western coast of the Italian peninsula. Today this peninsula, shaped like a boot, is the country of Italy. About 760 miles long, the boot juts into the Mediterranean Sea. At the tip of the boot is the island of Sicily.

North of the peninsula are the Alps, a range of high, rugged mountains. Running like a spine down the Italian peninsula are the Apennine (AP uh-nyn) Mountains. On either side of the mountains are fertile river valleys.

South of the Po River, Italy has a warm climate. Since ancient times, farmers here have grown grain, olives, grapes, and vegetables.

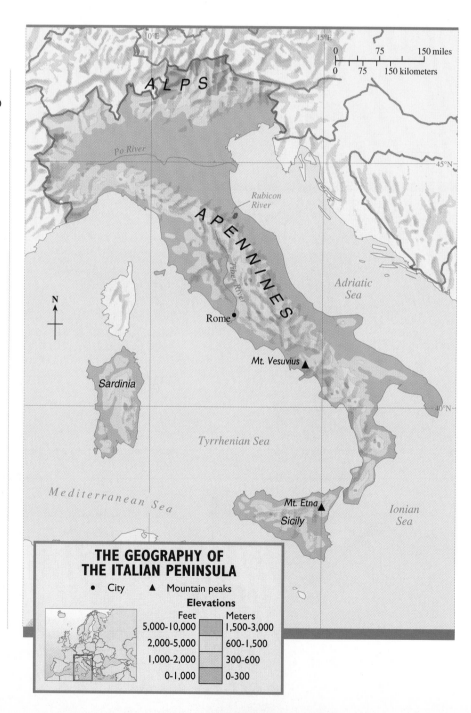

THE GEOGRAPHY OF THE ITALIAN PENINSULA

- City ▲ Mountain peaks

Elevations

Feet	Meters
5,000–10,000	1,500–3,000
2,000–5,000	600–1,500
1,000–2,000	300–600
0–1,000	0–300

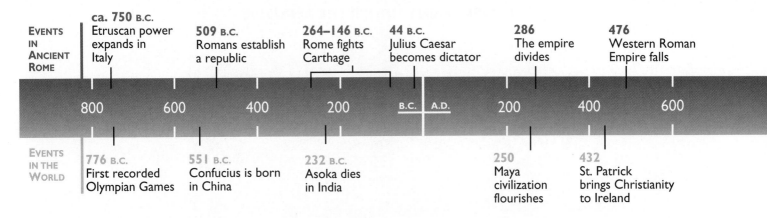

EVENTS IN ANCIENT ROME							
ca. 750 B.C. Etruscan power expands in Italy	**509** B.C. Romans establish a republic	**264–146** B.C. Rome fights Carthage	**44** B.C. Julius Caesar becomes dictator	**286** The empire divides	**476** Western Roman Empire falls		

800   600   400   200   B.C. A.D.   200   400   600

EVENTS IN THE WORLD					
776 B.C. First recorded Olympian Games	**551** B.C. Confucius is born in China	**232** B.C. Asoka dies in India	**250** Maya civilization flourishes	**432** St. Patrick brings Christianity to Ireland

The First Italian Civilization

In ancient times, many groups of people lived within the boot. Each group had its own language and culture. People who settled on the plain of Latium, in central Italy,

▼ An Etruscan bronze shows a mythical chimera, which had parts of a lion, a goat, and a serpent.

spoke a language that became known as Latin.

The most powerful group, the Etruscans, were in northern Italy. We know much about the Etruscans from their huge tombs, which were sometimes shaped like beehives. Carved from rock, the tombs imitated Etruscan homes. The walls of the tombs are adorned with frescoes showing lavish banquets.

By 600 B.C. the Etruscans conquered most of northern and central Italy, including Rome. The Romans first learned writing, engineering, and road building from the Etruscans.

The Roman Republic

In 509 B.C. the Roman hero Junius Brutus chased the last Etruscan king out of the city. The Romans resolved never to have another king. Instead they established a **republic**. Rome was led by two top officials called consuls; they were elected from the Senate, a council of elders. Each consul served for a year.

The citizens of the Roman Republic were divided into two social classes. The more

★ **republic** A form of government that allows citizens to choose representatives to rule

GOVERNMENT UNDER THE REPUBLIC

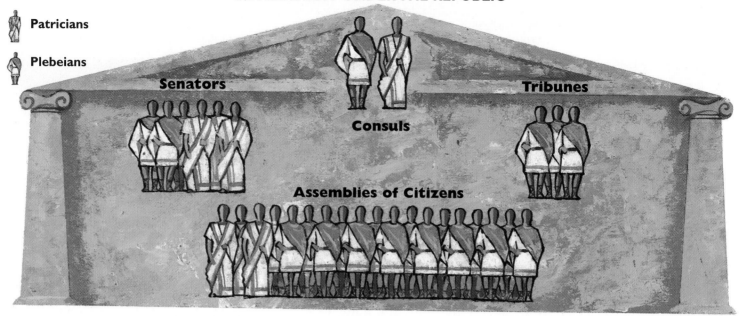

Patricians

Plebeians

Senators

Consuls

Tribunes

Assemblies of Citizens

powerful and wealthy were called **patricians**, who were allowed to serve in the Senate. The majority of the citizens were **plebeians**. These included the merchants, craftworkers, laborers, soldiers, and farmers. They could not hold public office and had almost no voice in government.

Even though plebeians did not have the same rights as patricians, they had to pay taxes and serve in the military. Plebeians were so angry about this injustice that they left Rome. This meant that patricians did not have enough people to do work for them or to help defend Rome in the event of an attack. Plebeians refused to return unless they were given more say about how things were run. Finally, patricians gave in. They let plebeians elect their own officials, called tribunes.

At first, patricians only allowed the tribunes to make laws for plebeians, while patricians in the Senate made

▲ Former slaves could become citizens of Rome.

laws for all citizens. Plebeians protested against this, too. Finally a democratic form of government emerged, with both patricians and plebeians making laws for all citizens.

Conquest and Expansion

When Rome became a republic, it was a city-state of only 350 square miles. Rome started to expand by conquering the Etruscans.

Then Romans turned to the Greek colonies in southern Italy. The army of King Pyrrhus (PIHR us) of Greece defeated the Romans several times but was forced to go home when the Romans brought in reinforcements. By 275 B.C., Rome controlled all of Italy.

War With Carthage

Across the Mediterranean Sea on the coast of Africa was the city of Carthage. Romans felt threatened when Carthaginians took over Greek cities in Sicily. The two powers clashed in three wars called the Punic Wars.

⭐ **patrician**   A member of the upper class
plebeian   One of the common people

The First Punic War ended with the Carthaginians giving up Sicily, which became the first Roman province. Soon, however, Carthage tried to avenge the defeat.

In the Second Punic War, the Romans faced Hannibal, one of the great generals of ancient times. Hannibal handed the Roman army the worst loss in its history at the battle of Cannae. The Romans later invaded Carthage. Hannibal was defeated at the battle of Zama and lost the war.

In the Third Punic War, Rome set out to utterly destroy its longtime rival. Roman legions not only leveled the city of Carthage and enslaved its people but they also spread salt on the ground so that nothing would grow. After defeating Carthage, Rome controlled the Mediterranean world.

Wealth from the conquered territories poured into Rome. Even so, it was not shared equally, and the gap between rich and poor grew wider. Roman armies enslaved many prisoners of war, creating another source of unrest within Rome. A great slave rebellion resulted.

Caesar Seizes Power

As Rome grew more dependent on the army to keep order, the power of Roman generals increased. The most famous general was Julius Caesar.

When the Senate ordered Caesar home, he brought his army with him. His action led to a brief civil war. After Caesar triumphed, he became **dictator** of Rome in 44 B.C.

▲ Trajan's column (*below*) shows Roman war scenes. A detail (*above*) shows workers building a wall.

Many Romans gladly accepted Caesar's rule. They hoped that a strong leader would bring peace. Caesar carried out many reforms. He tried to help poor Romans by offering them free land in unsettled parts of the empire. Caesar even changed the calendar by using the more accurate Egyptian one.

Caesar's power frightened some members of the Senate. A group of patricians plotted to murder him. On March 15 in 44 B.C., Caesar was stabbed to death in front of the Senate. His assassins believed that they were acting to restore the Roman Republic. But that did not happen.

The First Emperor

In his will, Caesar named his 18-year-old great-nephew Octavian as his legal son and heir. Octavian formed an alliance with Mark Antony, one of Caesar's officers, and took over the government.

However, neither Octavian nor Antony was content to share power. During the sea battle of Actium, Octavian defeated Antony's fleet. He became master of the Roman world.

Octavian is recognized as the first Roman emperor, although he never took that title. He allowed the Senate to continue to meet, and he followed the forms of republican rule. The Senate gave him the title *Augustus*, meaning "worthy of honor."

★ *dictator* A person who takes complete charge of a government

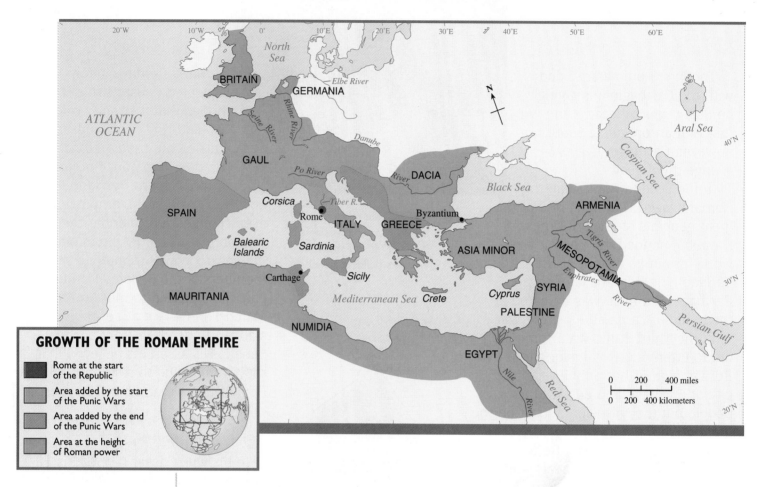

GROWTH OF THE ROMAN EMPIRE

- Rome at the start of the Republic
- Area added by the start of the Punic Wars
- Area added by the end of the Punic Wars
- Area at the height of Roman power

Augustus' reign, which lasted until his death in A.D. 14, was a golden era of Roman civilization. Augustus improved the city by adding new temples, a water system, and roads. He encouraged the work of poets and artists. Great writers of his time included Horace, Virgil, and Livy. His rule is known as the Augustan Age.

Pax Romana

The Augustan Age began two centuries of general peace, known as the Pax Romana, or Roman peace. More than 50 million people lived in the Roman Empire. As the map shows, it spread from the Caspian Sea in the east to Spain's Atlantic coast in the west, and from Britain in the north to Egypt in the south.

Roman civilization had an influence that continues today. Roman law spread throughout the Roman Empire. The languages of some of the modern European nations, such as France, Italy, and Spain, came from Latin.

The Empire Declines

By the time Emperor Marcus Aurelius (uh REE lee us) died in A.D. 180, the empire was showing signs of weakness. Although the first emperors had been relatives of Augustus, the army had chosen the later ones. Many were not capable rulers. As central authority declined, so did the empire. The roads were no longer kept in good condition, and some of the distant provinces began to break away from the empire.

Two emperors tried to stop the decline of the empire—Diocletian (dye uh KLEE shun) and Constantine. Diocletian was made emperor by his troops. He tried to restore imperial authority. All who came into his presence had to kneel and kiss the hem of his robe. To improve the administration of the empire, he divided it into two parts.

After Diocletian's death, there was a struggle for power. The winner was Constantine. He ruled both halves of the empire. Constantine built a new capital in the ancient Greek city of Byzantium. It was named Constantinople in his honor.

After Constantine died, the empire was divided again. Each part was ruled by an emperor, one in Rome and one in Constantinople. The western empire faced the threat of warlike tribes whom the Romans called barbarians.

The Fall of Rome

Most of the barbarians who invaded the Roman Empire were Germanic-speaking peoples from central and northern Europe. Their way of life was based on farming, hunting, herding, and war. As their numbers grew, they needed more pasture land, and they crossed the borders of the empire.

These Germanic people waged war with the Romans and gradually carved off portions of the empire. Finally several groups of Germanic people invaded Italy. In 476 they forced the last Roman emperor in the west, Romulus Augustulus, to resign. The glory of the Western Roman Empire was over.

▼ Emperor Hadrian of Rome ordered the building of Hadrian's Wall to keep northern tribes from invading settlements in Britain.

SHOW WHAT YOU KNOW!

REFOCUS
COMPREHENSION

1. After conquering the Etruscans, the Romans didn't want another king. What kind of government did they set up?

2. What was the Pax Romana?

THINK ABOUT IT
CRITICAL THINKING

Why was Julius Caesar able to seize power and become dictator?

WRITE ABOUT IT
ACTIVITY

Few governments have lasted as long as the Roman Empire, but the western part fell in 476. Write an explanation telling what you believe led to Rome's decline.

Spotlight

KEY TERMS

parable
disciple
epistle
persecute

THE SPREAD OF CHRISTIANITY

FOCUS *Although early Christians were treated cruelly, the new religion of Christianity deeply influenced events and people around the world.*

A New Religion

Christianity began in the land of the Jews under the rule of the second Roman emperor. Over the next three centuries, this religion that started with a small group of Jewish people would become the official religion of the Roman Empire.

You learned in Chapter 3 that Jewish people lived for centuries under foreign rule, including that of Rome.

During this time, their prophets told the people of Israel that one day God would send a savior to free them.

Jesus of Nazareth

Jesus of Nazareth was born into this world of Roman occupation. As a young man, Jesus began to teach love of God and love of one another. He

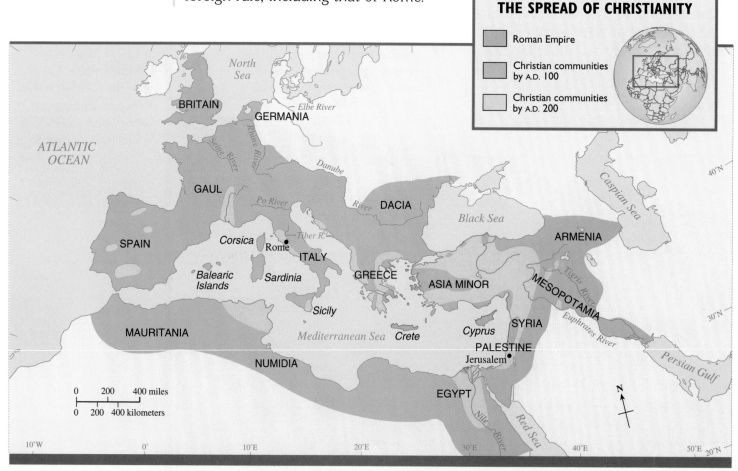

THE SPREAD OF CHRISTIANITY

- Roman Empire
- Christian communities by A.D. 100
- Christian communities by A.D. 200

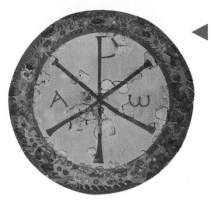

The Chi-Rho was an early Christian symbol made of two Greek letters, chi (X) and rho (P).

▲ This portrait shows Emperor Constantine and his mother, St. Helena.

often used simple **parables** to make his point, and he promised salvation for those who followed his teachings.

Jesus chose a special group of followers called **disciples** to help spread his teachings. These teachings were later written down. The collected writings, called the Gospels, make up the first section of the New Testament, which is part of the Christian Bible.

Followers of Jesus came to believe him to be Christ the Lord, son of God, and the savior spoken of by the Jewish prophets. As his influence grew, some Romans came to fear him. Jesus was accused of planning a revolt against Rome. For this supposed crime, he was arrested, tried, and executed.

Spreading the Word

According to the Gospels, Jesus rose from the dead three days after his execution. He told his disciples to carry his message to all the world. Followers of his teachings became known as Christians. *Christ* is a Greek word meaning "Messiah."

Jesus' disciples preached Christianity in many parts of the Roman world. Paul of Tarsus, a Jew who at first opposed Christianity, spread the religion to many people. He traveled widely and kept in touch with Christians in other cities by writing **epistles**. Some of his epistles are included in the New Testament.

A State Religion

People who lived in the Roman Empire were allowed to worship their own gods. They were also required to worship and make offerings to the emperor. People who refused were regarded as traitors. Christians refused to worship the emperors, and they were **persecuted**, but the persecutions did not stop the spread of Christianity.

In 313, Emperor Constantine declared religious freedom for Christians. In fact, he himself became a Christian. In about 392, Emperor Theodosius made Christianity the official religion of the empire.

★ **parable** A brief story that teaches a moral lesson
disciple A follower of a teacher or leader

★ **epistle** A letter
persecute To treat cruelly and unfairly

ROME: A CHANGING CITY

FOCUS *As the Roman Empire grew, so did the capital city of Rome. The city of the republic changed. Emperors boasted of their wealth and power by constructing impressive monuments and public buildings.*

Adventure in Imperial Rome!

Republican Rome was a simple city centered on the Forum. Imperial Rome was a city of over 1 million people. Busy shops and warehouses lined the streets. Citizens crowded into theaters, parks, baths, and markets. Emperors hired architects, engineers, and craftworkers to create magnificent buildings.

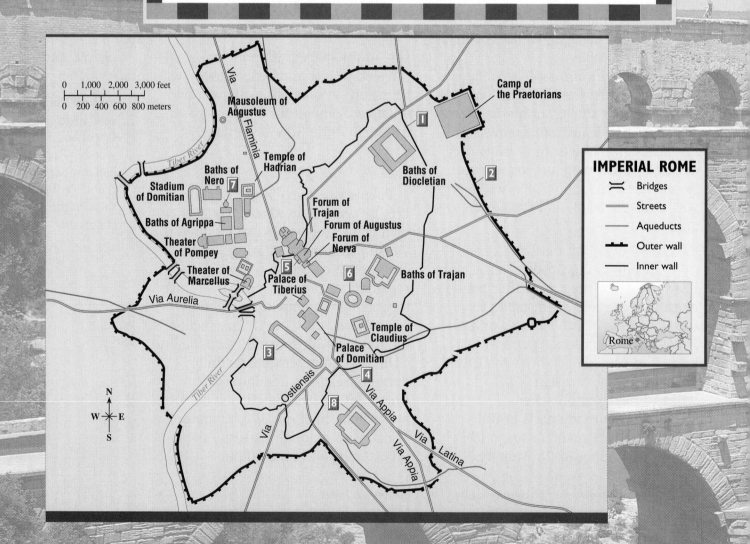

0   1,000 2,000 3,000 feet
0   200 400 600 800 meters

Camp of the Praetorians

Mausoleum of Augustus

Temple of Hadrian

Baths of Nero 7

Baths of Diocletian

Stadium of Domitian

Baths of Agrippa

Forum of Trajan

Forum of Augustus

Forum of Nerva

Theater of Pompey

Theater of Marcellus

Palace of Tiberius 5

6 **Baths of Trajan**

Via Aurelia

Temple of Claudius

3 **Palace of Domitian**

Via Ostiensis

Via Appia

8

Via Latina

Via Appia

Via Flaminia

Tiber River

N
W — E
S

IMPERIAL ROME

⚍ Bridges
— Streets
— Aqueducts
•▪•▪• Outer wall
— Inner wall

Rome

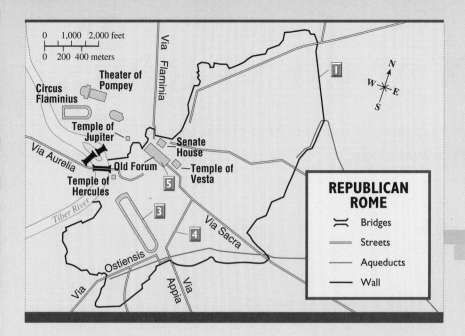

Map Key

1 Servian Wall Built around 380 B.C., this was the first stone wall to protect the city. It surrounded almost 700 acres of land.

2 Aurelian Wall Finished around A.D. 274, this long stone wall served as the city's limits into the twentieth century.

3 Circus Maximus After a few additions were built, this vast stadium could hold over 250,000 spectators. Romans cheered as chariots raced around the dangerous track.

4 Via Appia The via, or road, was built in 312 B.C. for military transportation, but became the main trading route between Rome and southern Italy. It was almost 400 miles long.

5 Roman Forum This was always the center of political, social, and religious life in Rome. Many emperors and nobles built palaces overlooking the square. Some emperors even added their own buildings to the Roman Forum.

6 Colosseum Romans came to this amphitheater to watch gladiators and wild beasts fight. The arena of the Colosseum was sometimes flooded for mock sea battles.

7 Pantheon This temple was built about A.D. 126 by the Emperor Hadrian to honor all the Roman gods. The bronze on its dome could be seen from miles away.

8 Baths of Caracalla This huge complex included a steam room, a gym, a sports stadium, shops, and a library. The water was supplied by one of Rome's aqueducts. Almost 2,000 Romans visited these baths every day.

⭐ **aqueduct** A structure made for bringing water from one place to another

MAP IT

1. Picture yourself working as a city guide in imperial Rome. A customer wants to visit a bath. Where can you take him? What can you tell him about the place?
2. The next day, you meet a customer at the Pantheon. He tells you he has urgent business at the Forum. What main road will take him there? In which direction should he travel?
3. The emperor announces that tomorrow will be a holiday, with chariot races and gladiator battles. You suggest to a customer that she attend the events. Where should she go for each one?
4. A customer asks you what road she should take to southern Italy. What do you tell her? What buildings will she pass on this road before leaving the city?

EXPLORE IT

A newcomer to imperial Rome wants to visit the Theater of Pompey, which is between the Via Aurelia and the Via Flaminia. What places around the theater did not exist in republican Rome?

4

LIFE IN ANCIENT ROME

FOCUS *Life in Rome was full of color and excitement for its citizens. Some artifacts, ideas, and customs of ancient Rome remain today.*

Fashion, Food, and Fun

If you live in ancient Rome, you are in the capital of the largest and most powerful empire in the world. The heart of the city is the Forum, at the foot of Palatine Hill. Here you can see the Golden Milestone, from which all distances to other parts of the empire are measured.

The Curia, the meeting place of the Senate, is in the Forum. You can see the senators standing on the steps in their **togas**. Only citizens are allowed to wear togas, which are usually saved for public ceremonies because they are so bulky.

No chariots are permitted in the Forum, so you can walk about freely. Romans gather to discuss the latest news that messengers bring from all parts of the empire. There are no newspapers, so the best way to learn what is going on in Rome or the rest of the world is to keep your ears open when you are in the Forum.

There are shops in the Forum, where you can buy goods of all kinds. You will see merchants from places as distant as Spain and Egypt. You can buy grilled lamb sausages at food

▲ A typical street corner in Rome, showing the wall of a building cut away so you can see inside

✦ **toga** A loose garment worn in public

Some Roman dogs wore identity tags in case they got lost. This bronze tag says "You have trained me to respond to your voice only."

Some Roman toys— a chariot and horse and a doll with movable joints

stalls. Street performers and snake charmers entertain you, hoping to earn coins.

The Adventure of City Life

Rome is not an easy place in which to find your way around. Your street has no name and your house has no number. There are few sidewalks, so you have to watch out for passing chariots.

You may also have to dodge garbage thrown from the windows of the multistory apartment buildings. Some of these apartments are so poorly built that they occasionally fall down. Most are built of wood, and fire is an ever-present danger, since people cook their food in open fireplaces. The emperor Augustus started the city's first fire department, but a great fire still managed to spread through 10 of the city's 14 districts.

Wealthy Romans, of course, do not live in crowded apartments on streets smelling of garbage. They have mansions on the more fashionable hills, such as Palatine Hill. Their comfortable homes have indoor plumbing that is connected to the huge sewer system called the Cloaca Maxima (kloh AY kuh MAKS ih muh).

Aqueducts, such as the one shown on page 176, bring fresh water into the city. The city has many fountains where those who cannot afford indoor plumbing can draw water.

Anyone can visit the public baths, which are popular Roman gathering places. You can start with vigorous exercise. After exercise, you might move into a hot tub and then into a cold bath. But the baths have far more to offer. You can visit a library or even attend lectures or concerts in the larger establishments.

Father Knows Best

The center of Roman life is the family. A Roman family includes more than just parents and children. Under the same roof live grandparents, other relatives, and married sons with their wives and children. The Roman home is a small world in itself.

A marble relief on a boy's tombstone shows some of the events in the boy's daily life.

The Pont du Gard in Nimes, France, was constructed by Romans as part of an aqueduct to bring water to the city.

Cicero was a brilliant orator, politician, and writer.

Your father is the absolute head of the family. Legally he can condemn to death any member of the household—though this rarely occurs. Your newborn brother or sister is brought to him for approval. If he picks the child up, he shows that he accepts it.

What's in a Name?

On the ninth day after birth, a new baby is named in a special ceremony. A boy has three names—a first name chosen by his parents, a middle name showing his father's clan, and a third for the particular branch of the clan to which his father belongs. For example, a famous orator of Caesar's time was Marcus Tullius Cicero.

A girl has only two names. Her first name is the feminine form of her father's clan. A second name indicates her birth order among the daughters. Cicero's second daughter would be Tullia Secunda. When a girl marries, she adds her husband's family name.

At the naming ceremony, the child receives a **bulla**. A girl wears it until she marries, and a boy wears it until his coming-of-age ceremony when he is about 16.

Teenagers Become Adults

If you are a boy born into a citizen's family, your father and family friends take you to the Forum. There you exchange your boyhood clothing, a purple-bordered toga, for the plain white adult toga. You are given a man's haircut and your first shave. A banquet follows, at which you are formally made a member of your clan and become a citizen.

If you are a girl, when you are about 14, you take your childhood clothes and toys and present them to the household gods. You begin wearing a

 bulla   A charm worn for protection

Help From the Gods

In your household there are religious shrines that honor the spirits of dead ancestors as well as household gods. Each day your family gathers to ask these gods for protection from harm. There are numerous such gods, but your family has chosen a certain one to honor at its shrine. There is even a god of doors, named Janus, with two faces looking in opposite directions. The month of January is named after Janus.

School Days

If you are an upper-class Roman child, you go to school. Boys and girls attend school to learn reading, writing, and arithmetic. When girls are 12 or 13 they leave school, but most of them continue their education at home with private tutors. Some Roman writers believe that girls receive a better education than boys because they spend longer hours studying.

Roman boys continue their schooling with classes in Greek and Latin grammar, history, geography, and astronomy. After his coming-of-age ceremony, a boy may study writing and speaking to prepare for his adult role as a citizen active in politics.

Bread and Circuses

To maintain their popularity, Roman emperors distribute free food, usually bread and meat, to the poor. They also sponsor the free entertainment at the

▲ A girl from Pompeii holds a stylus and a book.

flowing garment called a *stola*. Soon afterward, your father finds a suitable man to be your husband.

At your engagement you receive a ring from your future husband. The wedding takes place at your parents' home. Your bridal veil is bright orange. You and your husband seal your vows by clasping hands. After the ceremony you and your groom travel to his house, where he carries you through the doorway of your new home.

Although Roman women have a great deal more freedom than the women of Greece, your mother's chief duty is to run the household. Even middle-class families have a few slaves to help, and wealthy families may have hundreds of slaves.

Women have few legal rights. They are not allowed to vote or hold public office. As a wife and mother, the Roman woman is expected to set an example of virtue and duty. This family structure is seen as the source of Rome's strength.

The Colosseum was built in Rome with about 200,000 tons of stone.

Colosseum and the Circus Maximus, where there is a huge racetrack. More than 150,000 people can gather to watch horse and chariot races.

Domes and Gromas

You can be justly proud of the outstanding engineering skills of Rome's builders. They have made the city a wonderful place for you to live. You can enjoy the grand buildings, baths, aqueducts, and roads they have constructed.

In addition to the Colosseum, which covers 6 acres, you can marvel at the Pantheon (PAN thee ahn). This temple

A Roman road builder uses a groma.

has perhaps the most famous dome in the world. Roman builders are said to have invented the dome and then discovered how to keep it from breaking and falling in.

Some of the builders' methods were learned from the Etruscans. Others were learned from the Greeks. But the Romans discovered much on their own. One of the tools they use is the groma, which you can see at left. It helps builders survey land. The groma helps Romans create a livable city.

On the Road Again

You find travel in Rome is surprisingly easy. Roman engineers have used highly developed methods to construct paved roads and arched stone bridges. The Appian Way is the chief highway. It connects Rome with southern Italy. The well-maintained network of roads makes it easy to move troops, goods, and messages throughout the empire.

SHOW WHAT YOU KNOW!

REFOCUS
COMPREHENSION

1. Why was travel in Rome easy?

2. What role did engineers play in Rome?

THINK ABOUT IT
CRITICAL THINKING

Select a word, such as *exciting* or *dull*, that tells what you think about life in ancient Rome. Then list as many examples as you can that fit your word.

WRITE ABOUT IT
ACTIVITY

Write a few paragraphs comparing the life of a woman in ancient Rome with that of a woman you know today.

Citizenship

KEY TERMS

plaintiff
defendant

CITIZENS OF ROME

FOCUS *The Romans established a practical framework for citizenship and a government of laws. Many modern countries continue to be influenced by these Roman traditions.*

Plebeian Unrest

About 450 B.C., invaders began to raid Roman lands. The patricians of Rome, who controlled the government, sought to raise an army to defend Rome's territory. But they needed recruits from the more numerous plebeians.

The plebeians had long resented the dominance of the patricians. Now they saw their chance to win more rights. Plebeians refused to serve in the army unless the patricians granted some of their demands.

The Twelve Tables

The plebeians wanted a written code of laws. Previously, judges had decided legal disputes. The plebeians argued that a written code would make the laws clear to all.

The result was the Twelve Tables, the first written laws of the Roman Republic. They had a great influence on later Roman law as well as on the laws of many modern countries.

Table One set down the rules for a trial. The first rule stated that a **plaintiff** must summon the **defendant** to court. This rule is the basis for the

present-day right to be notified in writing with a summons if you are going to be sued.

Some of the tables reflected Roman customs that we would not regard as just. Table Eleven, for example, forbade marriage between plebeians and patricians.

Even so, having a written code of laws was a great step forward. Knowing the law is a form of protection for a citizen. Without

The ruins of the Roman Forum only hint at its early grandeur, shown in the artist's drawing below.

---

plaintiff A person making a complaint against another in a court
defendant A person who is being accused

written laws, you would not know if you were breaking the law. Also, written law makes it clear that the same laws apply to everyone of equal status. Every Roman schoolboy had to memorize the Twelve Tables. They were also posted in public places.

The letters on this manhole cover on a modern Roman street are a legacy of ancient Rome.

Roman Law

Roman law continued to develop as Rome changed from a city-state into an empire. The law applied in different ways to male citizens, women, non-Romans within the empire, and enslaved people.

A code called the law of citizens applied to Roman citizens. Citizens were not just people who were Roman by birth. Unlike ancient Greece, Rome allowed foreigners to become citizens.

Roman women did not have the same rights as men, but the law of citizens protected them. They could not vote or hold office. When a female was born, her father was her guardian; when she married, her husband became her guardian. The law specified how the guardian should treat her. A woman could own property, but her guardian took care of it.

Rights of Non-Romans

Non-Romans within the empire were governed by a code called the law of peoples. Governors of Roman provinces used this code of law to administer their territory. A non-Roman could sue a Roman citizen under the law of peoples.

Roman governors were also instructed to follow local laws whenever possible. Pontius Pilate, the Roman governor of Judah, faced such a problem when Jesus was brought before him by the Jewish high priests. Pilate told the high priests to judge him according to their own laws. When they refused to do that, Pilate himself condemned Jesus.

Enslaved people had few rights. They were treated as property. However, they could be freed by their masters and later become citizens.

Pride in the Republic

The staffs of the Roman legions and many public buildings bore the initials SPQR. These stood for *S(enatus) P(opulus)q(ue) R(omanus)*—"the Senate and the People of Rome."

This phrase summarized what Romans were proudest of—their republican form of government. There was no king. The government rested on the will of the people and their representatives in the Senate. Only men could be members of the Senate. Roman law remained in force throughout Rome's history.

Today, in order to gain favor with voters, some people criticize elected officials. They believe that this will convince people to agree with their point of view. Things were the same in Rome. When Senator Marcus Tullius Cicero ran for consul, his brother wrote him this advice:

Barbara Mikulski

Dianne Feinstein

Olympia Snowe

Barbara Boxer

Carol Moseley-Braun

Nancy Kassebaum

Patty Murray

Kay Bailey Hutchison

▲ Unlike the all-male Roman Senate, there are women in the United States Senate.

SHOW WHAT YOU KNOW!

REFOCUS
COMPREHENSION

1. Why were the Twelve Tables important?

2. What rights did women have?

THINK ABOUT IT
CRITICAL THINKING

Why was Cincinnatus thought of as a model citizen?

WRITE ABOUT IT
ACTIVITY

The founders of the United States used the Roman Republic as a model. Write a comparison showing how the government of the United States is like that of Rome.

Let the voters say and think that you know them well, that you greet them by name, that you are generous and open-handed. . . . If possible accuse your competitors of having a bad reputation for crime, vice or bribery.

Roman Heritage

The Roman Republic had a great influence on later governments and laws. Some Roman law is still part of the laws of many countries today. The English words *government, legal, constitution, court, judge, senate, president, council,* and *citizen* all come to us from the Latin language of Rome.

A Model for Today

The founders of the United States used Rome's republic as a model when they wrote the Constitution. They gave the name *Senate* to the upper house of Congress. They made sure that the President would not have absolute power. Laws had to be passed by representatives of the people.

Veterans of the American Revolution formed the Society of the Cincinnati to keep republican ideals alive. It was named after Cincinnatus, a Roman farmer who went to war when Rome was threatened by invaders. For a time, he became dictator to keep order in Rome. But he believed in the republic and did not want to remain a dictator. So he retired to his farm. To Americans who fought for liberty, Cincinnatus represented the Roman ideal. He was a citizen who served his country in time of need and then gave his power back to the people.

IMPORTANT EVENTS

FOCUS *A variety of events—factual and legendary—add interest to the culture and history of ancient Rome.*

THE FOUNDING OF ROME

According to legend, Romulus (RAHM yoo-lus) and Remus (REE mus), twin sons of the god Mars, founded Rome. They were abandoned as infants and were tossed into the Tiber River. They floated to shore, and a she-wolf carried the infants to her cave. Sculptors depicted her feeding the boys with her own milk.

Years later, as young men, the twins set off to found a city. The brothers argued about which one should be king. They asked the gods for a sign to decide the matter. After Romulus was chosen, the brothers fought, and Remus was killed. Romulus then named the city after himself and ruled it.

HANNIBAL

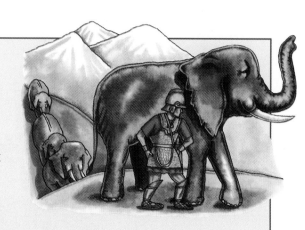

Hannibal, the great general of Carthage, spent most of his life preparing to fight the Romans. His father, Hamilcar Barca, had been a general in the First Punic War. Hamilcar made his son promise to avenge Carthage's defeat.

When Hannibal was 9, he accompanied his father on an invasion of Spain. After Hamilcar died, Hannibal, at age 26, took command of Carthage's military forces.

Hannibal set out to fight the Romans with an army of 46,000 men with horses and about 60 elephants. In an awe-inspiring march, Hannibal led his forces over the Alps from Spain to enter Italy in 218 B.C. His men built roads through the snow-covered mountain passes to allow the elephants to walk through. To get the animals across rivers, Hannibal's troops built floating platforms with earthen sides so that the elephants would think they were on land.

Hannibal failed to conquer Rome. He returned to protect Carthage but was defeated. However, the clever tactics he used to fight Roman armies have been studied in military schools for more than 2,000 years.

ca. 750 B.C.
Legendary
founding of Rome

218 B.C.
Hannibal crosses
the Alps

50 B.C.
Julius Caesar
returns to Rome

79
Mount Vesuvius
erupts

750   450   150   B.C. | A.D.   150

JULIUS CAESAR

Julius Caesar's fame as a leader is so great that his name came to mean "ruler." He wrote classic accounts of his military victories. The best-known saying contains only three words: *Veni, vidi, vici*— "I came, I saw, I conquered."

Caesar won fame for his military successes in Gaul, part of western Europe north of the Alps. He made sure that news of his victories reached Rome, giving him the reputation as a powerful leader.

In 50 B.C. the Senate ordered Caesar to return to Rome. Roman law forbade a general to lead his troops across the Rubicon River into Italy. However, Caesar defied the law and crossed the Rubicon with his army. The phrase *crossing the Rubicon* still means "to pass the point of no return."

ERUPTION OF VESUVIUS

Pliny the Elder, a Roman scientist and writer, lived by the Bay of Naples. On August 24, A.D. 79, he dined with his sister. Her son, Pliny the Younger, wrote that his mother saw "a cloud of unusual size. . . . At first it was white, then murky and spotted, as if it had carried up earth and cinders." What they saw was the eruption of a volcano, Mount Vesuvius (vuh SOO vee us).

The ashes and rocks thrown up by Vesuvius buried the city of Pompeii (pom PAY ee). A layer of rock and ashes covered what had once been a city of 20,000 people. The disaster was so great that the emperor Titus personally comforted the victims and used his own money to help them.

The disaster preserved the ancient Roman city. In 1748, treasure hunters dug tunnels into the mound where Pompeii had once stood. They found marble statues and other objects, which they sold. Archaeologists began to excavate the site about 1860. The ruins of Pompeii have revealed much about how Romans lived more than 19 centuries ago.

SHOW WHAT YOU KNOW!

REFOCUS
COMPREHENSION

1. Why do we remember Hannibal?

2. What can we learn from the ruins of Pompeii?

THINK ABOUT IT
CRITICAL THINKING

What did it mean for Julius Caesar to cross the Rubicon?

WRITE ABOUT IT
ACTIVITY

Write a skit about the quarrel between the twins Romulus and Remus after they founded Rome.

SUMMING UP

1 DO YOU REMEMBER...
COMPREHENSION

1. Who were the Etruscans?

2. Why is the form of government of the early Romans so important?

3. Why was it important to the Romans to defeat Carthage?

4. How did the Western Roman Empire finally fall?

5. How were the first Christians treated by the Romans?

6. How did the Forum change when Rome became the capital of the empire?

7. Why was the Forum important?

8. How did the roles of men and women differ in ancient Rome?

9. Why was the Augustan Age known as a golden era of Roman civilization?

10. What do the initials *SPQR* stand for?

2 SKILL POWER
COMPARING MAPS

Look at the map of the ancient Roman Empire on page 168. Compare this historical map with modern maps of Europe, Africa, and Asia in the Atlas section of this book. Then, on a sheet of paper, list the names of all the modern-day countries that lie at least partly within the old Roman boundaries.

3 WHAT DO YOU THINK?
CRITICAL THINKING

1. What do you think were the two longest-lasting achievements of the Roman Empire?

2. Think about how Roman officials changed their attitude toward Christianity during the 300s. What might account for this change?

3. How can a river influence the growth of a city?

4. Explain whether you agree with this statement: Rome had a republic but not a democracy.

5. What would be the advantages of living in Rome when it was the capital of a large empire? What were the disadvantages?

4 SAY IT, WRITE IT, USE IT
VOCABULARY

Take the role of a modern lawyer in ancient Rome. Choose one of these cases: The Case of the Torn Toga or The Case of the Broken Bulla. Using at least 10 of the terms below, write the argument you would use to defend your client.

aqueduct	patrician
bulla	persecute
defendant	plaintiff
dictator	plebeian
disciple	republic
epistle	toga
parable	

5 GEOGRAPHY AND YOU

MAP STUDY

Write five true or false statements such as those given below about the information shown on this map of the Roman Empire.

- Spain was not part of the Roman Empire.
- The Caspian Sea is east of the Black Sea.

Exchange your statements with a classmate.

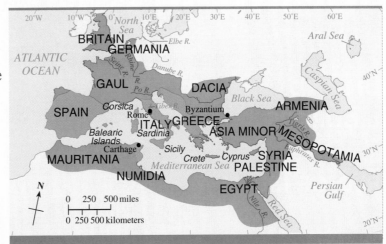

6 TAKE ACTION

CITIZENSHIP

Knowing the law protects a citizen. That's why the Twelve Tables were posted in public places in ancient Rome. With a group of classmates, find out about the rules that are broken most often in your school. To do so, talk with the school's superintendent, principal, and teachers. On pieces of posterboard, name and describe the rules. List the penalties for breaking them, too. Use your posters for a bulletin-board display.

Rule	Penalty
1. Walk in the halls.	Stay at the end of the line for a week.
2. Put litter in baskets.	Clean up litter.
3. Play by the rules in gym.	Sit on the sidelines for a day.
4. Take care of the property of others.	Write a paragraph about proper care.

7 GET CREATIVE

LANGUAGE ARTS CONNECTION

The Romans didn't have newspapers, but you can give them one. Choose one news event from ancient Rome that people would have wanted to know about. Write an eye-catching headline and a short account of the event. Later you can combine your news stories with those of your classmates to create a Roman newspaper.

LOOKING AHEAD
In the next chapter you'll see how cultures in Byzantium and Europe built upon the foundations of ancient civilizations.

THE Middle Centuries

How Did People Start to Reach Out?

The middle centuries were a time of great change. Learn how people came to exchange ideas and develop new cultures and how civilizations grew and became strong.

DISCOVER

CHAPTER 9

BYZANTIUM

The fall of the Roman Empire in the fifth century brought about great changes. Read this chapter to find out what happened in the centuries that followed.

On page 208 you can find out how this boy is acting like a squire.

CONTENTS

AND MEDIEVAL EUROPE

These books tell about some people, places, and events of interest during the Middle Ages. Read one that interests you and fill out a book-review form.

READ AND RESEARCH

Catherine, Called Birdy **by Karen Cushman** (Harper Collins Publishing, 1995)

Through her diary, 14-year-old Catherine will draw you into her life and thoughts in medieval England. You will cheer each time she cleverly drives away an unfit suitor chosen by her father. (*historical fiction*)

•*You can read a selection from this story on page 210.*

Cities Then and Now **by Jim Antoniou** (Macmillan Publishing Co., 1994)

Learn all about the great city of Istanbul in the time it was known as Constantinople. Elaborate drawings of the city will help you find out about people and places in the Byzantine Empire. (*nonfiction*)

Adam of the Road **by Elizabeth Janet Gray** (Penguin USA, 1987)

Eleven-year-old Adam travels the roads of England with his father, a wandering minstrel, and his dog, Nick. But when his father and his dog disappear, Adam is on his own. Will he find them again? (*historical fiction*)

Castles **by Philip Steele** (Kingfisher Books, 1995)

Find out about the castles of the Middle Ages—from how they were built to the people who lived there. Detailed drawings will help you see what castle life was like. (*nonfiction*)

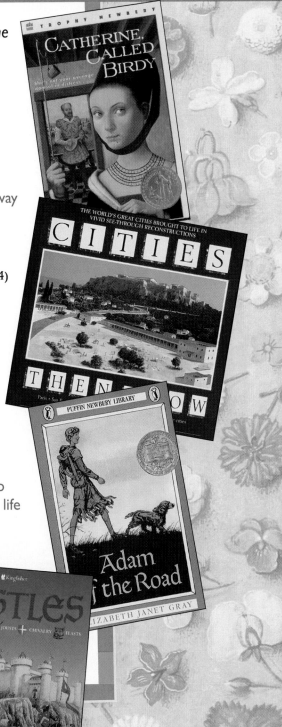

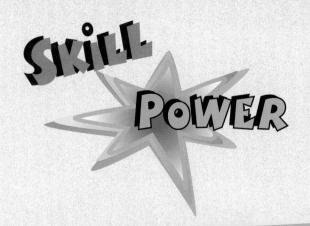

SKILL POWER

Making Inferences

Knowing how to make inferences will help you better understand information that is not directly stated in the material that you are reading.

UNDERSTAND IT

Writers do not always explain everything directly in a story or article. To understand what is not stated directly, you need to make inferences by "reading between the lines." To do this you use clues from the text—word clues—and what you know from your own experience to figure out what a writer is trying to convey.

How do you make an inference? Read this short passage and find out.

From his window, Chaucer could see garden, orchard, and meadow. Within easy walking distance, he could roam through hills and forest.

The writer doesn't say directly whether Chaucer lived in city or country surroundings. However, you can use the places mentioned—orchard, meadow, and so on—and your own knowledge about city and country surroundings to make an inference that Chaucer lived in country surroundings.

EXPLORE IT

You may be surprised to learn that there are different types of inferences you can make. Here are some examples.

- People or Animals *Arthur put on his armor and attended to his horse. Now they were ready for battle.* Who or what is Arthur?

- Location *The lord lived in a huge stone dwelling with great outer walls, high towers, and large courtyards. There was even a dungeon.* In what kind of a building does the lord live?

- Object *The large cloth with three crowns began to wave wildly in the wind as it was hoisted on a pole.* What is the large cloth?

- Time *Even though the sun had set an hour ago, the peasants kept on working. They could barely see the ground they were plowing.* What time of day is it?

Did you figure out that Arthur is a knight, the lord lived in a castle, the object is a flag, and the time is nighttime? Congratulations! You know how to make inferences!

Geoffrey Chaucer is considered one of the greatest English poets. The country setting described above actually refers to London, which had a lot of open land at the time.

TRY IT

Spend some time with family members reading a newspaper or news magazine. Select an article or feature story or a few advertisements and study the material carefully to see what the writer has not directly stated but has implied.

Write down any inferences you can make from the material and circle the word clues that helped you make those inferences. Share your reading material and inferences with classmates and show them the clues that you used.

Collect into a booklet the reading material and inferences that you and your classmates have shared. Prepare a cover for the booklet with the title "Searching for the Whole Story," or make up a title of your own. Share the booklet with other classes on your grade level.

SKILL POWER SEARCH As you read this chapter, look for places where the writer is implying something rather than stating it directly.

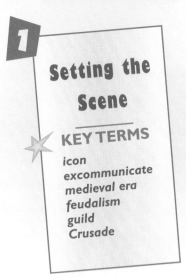

Setting the Scene

KEY TERMS

icon
excommunicate
medieval era
feudalism
guild
Crusade

BYZANTINE EMPIRE AND MEDIEVAL EUROPE

FOCUS *The cultural traditions of modern Europe were planted during the Middle Ages. They took root in the Byzantine Empire in eastern Europe and in medieval society in western Europe.*

The Roman Empire in the East

By the end of the fifth century, after nearly two centuries of decline, the Western Roman Empire—the part governed by Rome—could no longer survive. By contrast, the eastern part of the Roman Empire continued to thrive. The Eastern Roman Empire became known as the Byzantine (BIHZ-un teen) Empire.

The name *Byzantine* comes from Byzantium (bihz AN tee um), a Greek city that once stood on the site of Constantinople (kahn stan tuh NOH-pul), the capital city of the Byzantine Empire. Although the people of Constantinople spoke Greek, they considered themselves Romans.

The Byzantine Empire lasted another thousand years after the decline of the empire in the west.

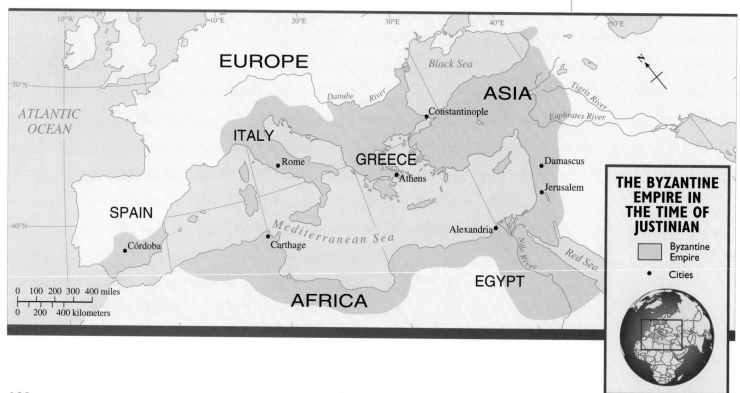

THE BYZANTINE EMPIRE IN THE TIME OF JUSTINIAN

Byzantine Empire

• Cities

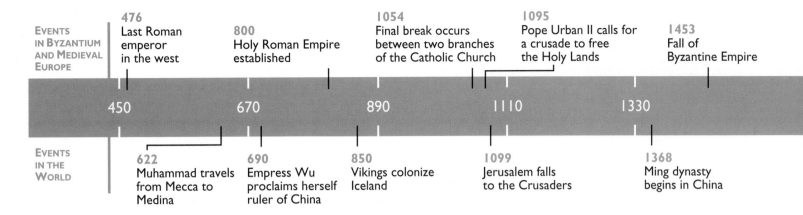

EVENTS IN BYZANTIUM AND MEDIEVAL EUROPE

476 Last Roman emperor in the west

800 Holy Roman Empire established

1054 Final break occurs between two branches of the Catholic Church

1095 Pope Urban II calls for a crusade to free the Holy Lands

1453 Fall of Byzantine Empire

450　　　670　　　890　　　1110　　　1330

EVENTS IN THE WORLD

622 Muhammad travels from Mecca to Medina

690 Empress Wu proclaims herself ruler of China

850 Vikings colonize Iceland

1099 Jerusalem falls to the Crusaders

1368 Ming dynasty begins in China

As the map shows, the Byzantine Empire extended from Asia Minor and Egypt to include most of the land washed by the Mediterranean Sea.

Emperor Justinian

From time to time the Byzantine Empire was blessed with gifted rulers. One was Emperor Justinian (jus TIHN-ee un), who ruled in the sixth century for almost 40 years. Justinian often sought, and followed, the advice of his dynamic wife, Theodora. In fact, Theodora played such an important decision-making role that some citizens whispered that she, not her husband, ruled Byzantium.

During Justinian's reign, his armies fought several successful battles, and roads, aqueducts, and other public works were completed. His most spectacular project was the church of Hagia Sophia (HAY jee uh sah FEE uh), which means "holy wisdom." The huge dome of this great church towers 179 feet above the ground.

Artists decorated the ceiling of this church with mosaics. They used pieces of colored glass and stone to create lovely designs. Artists also created **icons** to hang on the walls.

A Heritage Preserved

Justinian's most far-reaching achievement was the preservation of ancient Roman laws. He had these laws reviewed, made easier to understand, and written down. The result was the Justinian Code, which became the legal foundation for nearly every modern European nation.

The modern world can also thank scholars from the Byzantine Empire for saving and preserving classic Greek literature. Byzantine rulers who came after Justinian supported and encouraged the work of these scholars. If it hadn't been for the Byzantine scholars and the Muslims, whom you will learn about in Chapter 10, the science and philosophies of ancient Greece might have been lost forever.

The Byzantine style of building was copied in this Italian lamp.

⭐ *icon*　A sacred image or picture

In an age when most people could not read, pictures like this icon of Jesus taught them about their religion.

Split in the Christian World

Like the Roman Empire, the Christian world also developed two major religious centers—Rome and Constantinople. Many differences flared up between the Western and Eastern Churches. In 381, for example, the church in Constantinople rejected the idea that the pope in Rome was the higher spiritual authority.

And there were other issues. The Western Church didn't allow divorce; the Eastern Church did. Services of the Western Church were conducted in Latin; those of the Eastern Church were conducted in languages spoken by the people attending the masses.

Both the Eastern and Western Churches claimed their beliefs to be true and those of the other church false. Over time the two churches drifted further and further apart.

The final break between the two branches of the church came in 1054. In that year Pope Leo IX in Rome **excommunicated** the patriarch (PAY-tree ahrk), or head, of the Eastern Church. Patriarch Michael Cerularius (sur yuh LAR ee us) returned the favor by excommunicating the pope.

The Orthodox Church

The split in the Christian church has never healed. Today the Western Church is called the Roman Catholic Church, while the Eastern Church is called the Orthodox Church.

Both the Roman Catholic Church and the Orthodox Church sent missionaries to foreign lands to spread the gospel. Missionaries from the

excommunicate To punish by revoking the right to take part in church rituals

Today the Hagia Sophia is a museum.

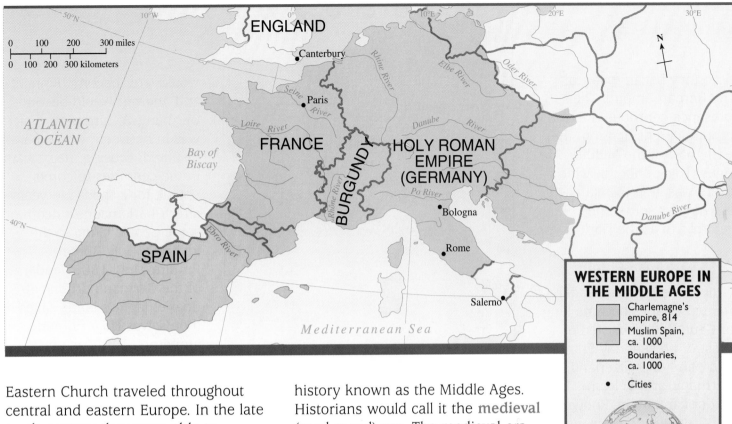

WESTERN EUROPE IN THE MIDDLE AGES

- Charlemagne's empire, 814
- Muslim Spain, ca. 1000
- Boundaries, ca. 1000
- • Cities

Eastern Church traveled throughout central and eastern Europe. In the late tenth century they were able to convert the Russians. It seemed that the Russian leader Vladimir wasn't happy with his country's "god of thunder" and "forest and water spirits." So, the story goes, Vladimir looked for a better religion. He talked to Muslim, Jewish, and Christian teachers, finally settling on Christianity. That's why today most Russians are members of the Orthodox Church.

Changes in Western Europe

While the Byzantine Empire was prospering, the people in western Europe were going through troubled times. The region was about to enter a period of history known as the Middle Ages. Historians would call it the **medieval** (med EE vul) **era**. The medieval era began with the collapse of the Roman Empire. It would last about a thousand years, and it would change a great deal during that time.

During the decline of the Roman Empire, Germanic groups had moved into the area from the north. The Romans called them barbarians because they had such different cultures. They weren't organized into large governments. They were tribes united by family ties. The chief of the tribe was usually the strongest and most successful warrior.

These barbarians, and other groups from northern and central Europe, ventured into the empire in search of the benefits offered by Roman life. Many of them remained, and little by

---

⭐ **medieval era** The time period between A.D. 500 and 1500

little they became part of the Roman Empire. Their presence contributed to the empire's transition into the early part of the Middle Ages. This period, in which there was little formal learning, is sometimes referred to as the Dark Ages.

A New Roman Empire

In 768 a German leader named Charles became king of Gaul. Gaul consisted of most of present-day France and parts of Switzerland, Germany, and Belgium. This leader came to be known as Charles the Great, or Charlemagne (SHAHR luh-mayn). As the map on page 195 shows, Charlemagne conquered a lot of territory during his 43-year reign. As a result, his kingdom included all of France, Switzerland, Belgium, and the Netherlands. It also included parts of Italy, Germany, and Spain.

In 800, Pope Leo III crowned Charlemagne emperor of the Holy Roman Empire. Thus the idea of the old Roman Empire was kept alive. The crowning of Charlemagne gave the impression that the pope had more power than the emperor. This set up a power struggle between popes and emperors that would last throughout the Middle Ages.

The "Empire" That Wasn't

Charlemagne's empire did not last long after his death. His grandsons divided it into three parts. One part

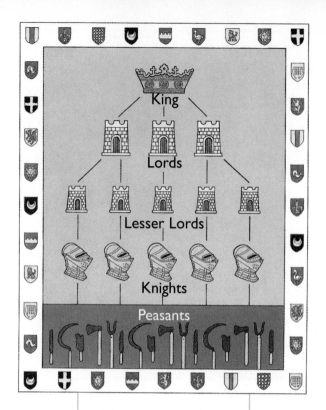

The Feudal System

would later become France, and another would become Germany. A third part, which was in between, would be disputed, causing many wars in the centuries to come.

Still, for a thousand years after Charlemagne's death, some people clung to the idea of a Holy Roman Empire. Until 1806, leaders of the German portions of Charlemagne's lands called themselves Holy Roman emperors. This was mostly just a title. And even that was wrong! As the French philosopher Voltaire (vahl-TER) would observe, the Holy Roman Empire wasn't particularly holy, it wasn't Roman, and it wasn't a true empire. Europe during the Middle Ages was a land of small kingdoms and little political unity.

Feudalism—Many Little "Kingdoms"

Even before Charlemagne's reign, western Europe had come under attack by the Vikings. You will learn more about these northern invaders on page 201. With the death of Charlemagne, the possibility of a strong central government was lost. People became frightened and wondered who would protect them from the Viking invaders and other enemies.

Most minor noblemen felt they had no choice but to turn to any strong

person who promised protection. Such a person—called a lord—might be a king, a leader in the Church, or a more powerful noble.

These lords needed fighters, or knights, to help them stay strong. To keep the loyalty of his knights, each lord promised them protection and financial security.

Knights were given special privileges or pieces of land, called fiefs (feefs). In return, each knight promised loyalty and military service to his lord. Upon swearing his loyalty, a knight became known as a vassal.

This complex system, known as **feudalism** (FYOOD ul ihz um), meant that one noble could be a lord over a lesser noble and, at the same time, be a vassal to a higher noble. Over time, feudalism developed into a form of government and protection for an economic way of life. The chart on page 196 shows the organization of a typical feudal system.

Manorialism

The land that a vassal received was called a manor. It usually included a manor house, farmland, and a group of peasants. Most of these peasants were serfs. Serfs were not slaves, but they weren't free, either. Serfs were bound by law to work on the manor where they were born. Their efforts supported the lord of the manor and his family.

Each manor was self-sufficient. The peasants raised most of what they needed to live. They grew all their own food. They raised farm animals for food and wool. And they managed the trees in the forest for fuel and lumber. For several centuries, the practice of manorialism was the economic heartbeat of medieval Europe.

Revival of Towns and Trade

After the decline of the Western Roman Empire, towns all but disappeared from Europe. During the Dark Ages, even the large cities suffered. By the end of the ninth century, the population of Rome—the largest city in Europe—fell from about 1 million to only a few thousand. European trade was all but abandoned during this period.

Early in the tenth century, things began to improve and towns began to revive. Many people found that they

⭐ *feudalism* A political and economic system prevalent in Europe in the Middle Ages

▼ A typical manor could resemble a small village.

▲ This painting shows a medieval apothecary, or drugstore.

were not suited to life on a feudal manor. Peasants, lesser nobles, and scholars were among those who chose to live in the towns that now dotted the countrysides.

Medieval towns consisted of rough wooden houses crammed together along narrow streets. Stone walls encircled the towns, providing protection from the outside world. As uncomfortable as they were, medieval towns became centers of learning, art, and commerce.

European trade began to pick up, helping to make the towns interesting places. Woven goods, leather goods, and other products were made and traded in towns in Europe and in countries outside Europe as well.

Craftworkers and Guilds

As trade increased, the craftworkers who made products for trade became more prosperous, and their skills were more in demand. In response to this demand, craftworkers formed **guilds** to help them take advantage of their favorable situation.

The guild for a particular trade limited the number of people who could practice that trade. Only a master craftworker could become a member of a guild.

A young person who wanted to learn a trade would work for a guild member for several years. These trainees usually lived in the home or shop of the guild member, and they did not receive wages.

After several years of learning and practicing the basic skills of the trade, the trainee became a journeyman. Journeymen received pay for their work, and those that became skilled enough could apply for membership as masters in the guild.

Women at Work

Guilds served several purposes. They helped to control the number of people who worked in each trade. They also helped to ensure the quality of the products created by the craftworkers. Perhaps one of the most significant contributions of the guilds was recognition of the role of women in the work force. Wives commonly worked alongside their husbands in some trades. And a father would have daughters and sons alike train in his trade. In this way the business would become a family affair.

In many cases a woman carried on the family business after the death of her husband. So women became recognized as master craftworkers and guild members. In time, some working women became valued and respected members of a community of craftworkers that had previously been reserved for men.

★ **guild** An organization of people in a craft or trade

The Decline of Feudalism

The development and growth of towns gradually led to the end of feudalism. As towns became centers of trade, more and more people left the farms and manors and moved to the towns.

Councils were set up to help govern the new towns. Modern urban life as we know it today was beginning to develop. As this development continued, the feudal way of life began its final decline.

Religion in the Middle Ages

The Middle Ages are sometimes called the Age of Faith. Many people, especially those in the larger cities, became angered and frustrated by the vice and corruption they saw, both in local governments and in the Church.

Some of these people gave up everything they owned and joined religious communities. They spent their days praying, studying the Bible, and doing physical labor. Men who did this were called monks, and their communities were called monasteries. Women in religious orders were called nuns, and they lived in convents.

Some people fulfilled their calling by traveling to religious shrines. Such people were known as pilgrims, and their journeys were called pilgrimages. Other Christians showed their faith by answering the call of Pope Urban II. In 1095 he called for a **crusade** to free the Holy Land in the Middle East from the Muslims. Over the next 150 years, a number of crusades were carried out, which met with mixed success. You will read about one of these Crusades on page 207.

▲ These are pilgrim badges from Canterbury.

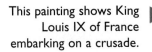
This painting shows King Louis IX of France embarking on a crusade. ▶

Crusade Any of the wars fought during three centuries by the Christians of Europe against the Muslims

You will read about one of these Crusades on page 207.

SHOW WHAT YOU KNOW!

REFOCUS
COMPREHENSION

1. How did the Eastern Roman Empire come to be called the Byzantine Empire?

2. Why did feudalism develop as a form of government?

THINK ABOUT IT
CRITICAL THINKING

What were some of the important legacies of the Byzantine Empire?

WRITE ABOUT IT
ACTIVITY

Use the illustration on pages 196–197 and the information in the text as sources and write a description of a day in the life of a serf.

PEOPLE AND EVENTS

FOCUS *The Middle Ages was a time of great individual achievement as well as incredible suffering and misery.*

SAINT BENEDICT

Benedict of Nursia was a young Italian aristocrat who became angered and disappointed by the vice he encountered in Rome. Around 520 he left the city and fled to the wilderness. He wanted to be alone to think about the glory of God.

Benedict set such a powerful example of holiness that other men flocked to his side. He organized his followers and they built a monastery at Monte Cassino. Benedict drew up a strict set of rules to be followed by members of his monastery.

According to the Benedictine rule, the leader had complete authority over all activities of the monks in his monastery. The monks vowed to live in poverty, engage in manual labor, attend eight religious services a day, and study hard. These rules proved to be so popular that other Benedictine monasteries and convents were formed all over Europe. The rules were also adopted by many other religious orders.

JUSTINIAN CODE

In 528, Emperor Justinian appointed a group of lawyers to collect and update old Roman laws. The resulting Justinian Code included the Digest, a summary of opinions by great judges; the Institutes, a list of legal principles; and the Novels, a set of "novel," or new, laws drawn up by Justinian himself.

Justinian's code had a big impact on Europe. Some rulers used it to support their claim that they were free to do whatever they wished. They pointed to the part of the code that stated "What pleases the prince has the force of law." On the other hand, the code also said that a ruler's power came from the people, not from God. Some people said that this supported the idea of constitutional rule and limited power for rulers.

CHARLEMAGNE

In 800, Pope Leo III crowned Charlemagne as emperor of the Holy Roman Empire. This was a smart move for Pope Leo, because he needed Charlemagne's military might.

For Charlemagne, the pope's action gave him a new title, but little else. Still, the coronation was an important event in history. It symbolized the formation of a new society that was separate from the Byzantine and Muslim civilizations. It also set the stage for centuries of conflicts over who was more powerful—the pope or the emperor.

VIKING RAIDS

The Vikings, or Norsemen, were not your stay-at-home types. They were constantly sailing from their native Scandinavia to explore new lands. In about 986, Erik the Red discovered Greenland and started a settlement there. His son, Leif Eriksson, was one of the first Europeans to reach North America.

The Vikings were considered barbarians who lived largely by piracy. For reasons that are not clear, around 800 the Vikings launched a series of raids on Europe. They attacked Charlemagne's empire as far south as Spain and Italy. They attacked England and named one of their own, Canute (kuh NOOT), as king of England. But like the German invaders before them, the Vikings slowly settled down and learned to live by trade rather than by plunder.

WILLIAM THE CONQUEROR

England's Anglo-Saxon king, Edward—a weak and ineffective leader—died without leaving an heir. In France, William, the duke of Normandy, saw England as a ripe apple ready to be picked.

Back in England, Harold, the newly crowned king, fought off an attack by the Vikings. But the victory left his forces very weak. William and his Norman soldiers took advantage of the situation. They crushed Harold's army at the battle of Hastings in October 1066.

William thus became King William I of England. Throughout the ages, however, he will be remembered simply as William the Conqueror.

ELEANOR OF AQUITAINE

Eleanor of Aquitaine may have been the most powerful woman of her time. By age 32 she had already been queen of France and was the queen of England. In 1137 she married King Louis VII of France. It turned out that Louis had married Eleanor for her family fortune and influence. The marriage ended in divorce, and Eleanor married Duke Henry of Normandy. In 1154 when the duke was crowned King Henry II, Eleanor became queen of England.

Henry refused to share power with Eleanor or their sons. When Eleanor and her sons rebelled, Henry put down the rebellion and tossed Eleanor in prison. When Henry died, Richard I inherited the throne. One of Richard's first acts was to free Eleanor, his mother. A woman of great heart and determination, Eleanor outlived both her husbands and eight of her ten children.

KING JOHN AND THE MAGNA CARTA

On June 15, 1215, a group of powerful nobles forced King John of England to sign the Magna Carta. This document listed the nobles' demands for reform, and it also required that the king obey the laws of the land.

The Magna Carta set down legal principles that are still with us. It stated, for example, "A free man shall not be forced to pay a large fine for a minor offense." In other words, the punishment should fit the crime. The Magna Carta also made it clear that free people could not be put in jail without a fair trial.

The Magna Carta also stated that no new taxes could be levied without the approval of the "common council," which included nobles, church leaders, and townspeople. As you can see, the Magna Carta was an early effort to establish certain rights and liberties that we enjoy today.

MICHAEL VIII PALAEOLOGUS

In 1204, Christian soldiers on the Fourth Crusade sacked Constantinople. After three days of looting and bloodshed, the beautiful city was in ruins. This incident was an ugly event in Europe's history.

In the face of this outrage, some Byzantine forces refused to quit. In Asia Minor, Emperor Michael VIII Palaeologus (pay lee AHL uh gus) of Nicaea (neye SEE uh) took back Constantinople on July 25, 1261. He rebuilt the city, reopened the University of Constantinople, and set up a dynasty that ruled the Byzantine Empire until its end in 1453.

The Byzantines carefully prepared their capital city against future attacks from western Europe. But in the process they neglected their eastern frontiers. This turned out to be a mistake. The final invasion of the Byzantines was by Turks from the east.

1154	1215	1261	1347	1431
Eleanor of Aquitaine becomes Queen of England	King John signs the Magna Carta	Byzantine army recaptures Constantinople	Black Death introduced into Europe	Joan of Arc burned at the stake

1200   1300   1400   1500

THE BLACK DEATH

In 1347 an Italian ship returned from Asia. No one knew it, but the ship carried rats infected with a deadly disease called the bubonic (byoo BAHN ihk) plague. The plague spread quickly from rats to fleas, and then from fleas to humans. Over the next three years, it attacked people all across Europe. Because dark blotches appeared on victims' skin, the plague was nicknamed the Black Death. Once infected, most of its victims died in one to three days.

No one knows for sure how many people died from the Black Death. The best guess is somewhere between one quarter and one third of Europe's population. Crowded cities were hardest hit. In Florence, Italy, two thirds of its 100,000 inhabitants died in 1348 alone. In Paris, 800 people a day died! The Black Death ended in 1350. But for decades afterward, occasional outbreaks of the plague continued to terrify the people of Europe.

JOAN OF ARC

One of the most heroic women of the Middle Ages was a simple peasant, Joan of Arc. In 1425, when Joan was a young girl, she began hearing "voices." They told her to free France from English control.

Joan went to see Charles VII, the future king of France. Most people thought she was crazy, but Charles decided she was telling the truth. In 1429 he sent her to save Orleans, a French city surrounded by an English army. Clad in white armor, Joan led the French forces to victory.

The victory at Orleans turned the tide of the war. By 1437 the French had driven the English from France. Joan was not so lucky. Captured and found guilty of witchcraft by the English, Joan of Arc was burned at the stake on May 30, 1431.

SHOW WHAT YOU KNOW!

REFOCUS
COMPREHENSION

1. Tell why the rules of Saint Benedict, the Justinian Code, and the crowning of Charlemagne were important.

2. Which events show that conflict and warfare were common in the Middle Ages?

THINK ABOUT IT
CRITICAL THINKING

What one event discussed on pages 200–203 had the greatest effect at the time it happened? Did it also have the longest-lasting effect? Why do you think this is so?

WRITE ABOUT IT
ACTIVITY

Make a list of questions you would like to ask one of the people mentioned in this lesson.

THE FLOURISHING OF CULTURE

FOCUS *The changes in political and religious life during the Middle Ages were accompanied by equally dramatic changes in education, art, architecture, and literature.*

Education in the Middle Ages

The Crusades opened people's eyes to the magnificent Muslim culture. Many Europeans realized that in order to duplicate such achievements, more educated people were needed.

To meet this need for education, an institution new to Europe arose—the university. Each university was usually devoted to one special area of study. For example, medicine was studied at the University of Salerno, law at Bologna, and philosophy and theology at Paris.

When universities were first established, books were hand-printed and very expensive. Most students could not afford to buy their own books, so they simply took notes as the teacher read from his book. In 1455, Johannes Gutenberg used his new invention, a printing press with movable type, to publish a copy of the Bible. Fifty years later, presses with movable type were available in more than 250 European cities. Now textbooks and other printed materials could be produced cheaply enough for students and the general public to afford them.

Medieval Art and Architecture

Visual arts flourished during the Middle Ages, mostly centering around religious themes. One great art form was the stained-glass window, which often depicted Biblical scenes. Since only a handful of people could read or write,

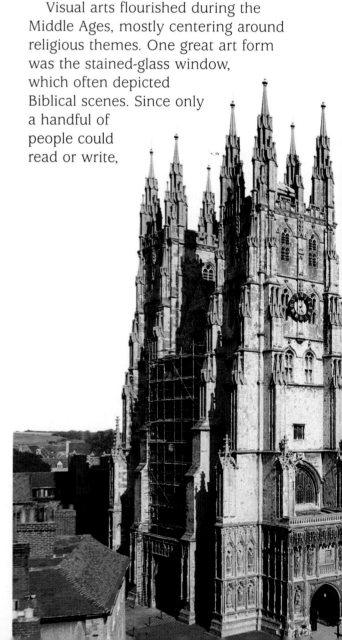

Panels from the Bayeux Tapestry

Canterbury Cathedral

such windows served as a "school for the illiterate." People could "read" the Bible by studying the windows.

Paintings and **tapestries** served a similar purpose. The pictures at the top of the page show some panels from the Bayeux (BAY yoo) tapestries in France. These famous tapestries show 72 scenes from the Norman conquest of England in 1066.

The most spectacular example of medieval architecture was the cathedral. These huge churches, built by Christians to honor God, towered over all other buildings in medieval Europe. Other art forms, such as sculpture and glasswork, were used to decorate and enhance cathedrals.

The Gothic style of architecture became popular about 1150. Tall and airy, Gothic churches have thin walls and huge stained glass windows. Two of the most famous Gothic cathedrals are Canterbury Cathedral in Canterbury, England, and Notre Dame Cathedral in Paris, France.

Literature in the Middle Ages

Writers in the Middle Ages produced many fine works of literature. Most were written in Latin, but they did not all have religious themes. University students often gathered to write clever poems celebrating good wine, true love, and loyal friends.

Among the most popular writers of the Middle Ages were Dante Alighieri (ahl eeg YE ree) and Geoffrey Chaucer. Both of them wrote in the vernacular (vur NAK yuh lur), or the everyday language of the people where they lived. This writing style enabled more people to read their works.

⭐ *tapestry* A rich, heavy cloth with designs and scenes woven into it

◀ This window tells the Biblical story of Abraham and Isaac.

This painting shows the artist's concept of the pilgrims in *Canterbury Tales*.

Dante completed his masterpiece, *The Divine Comedy*, shortly before his death in 1321. This poem tells of his imaginary journey through hell, purgatory, and heaven.

Chaucer's *Canterbury Tales* recounts the story of 30 pilgrims traveling to Canterbury Cathedral. The travelers came from many levels of society. To pass the time during their journey, each pilgrim has to tell a story. Using humor and wit, Chaucer used these tales to expose the social and moral evils of his day.

Chaucer's works also had a telling influence on the language of his people. The dialect he used eventually became the basis for modern English.

Contributions of Women

Women were also major contributors to medieval literature. More than 300 years before Joan of Arc heard voices, Hildegard of Bingen experienced visions. These visions were recorded by a monk named

This is an illumination from Hildegard's book of visions.

Volmar. The result was *Scivias*, a book of prophetic visions that tell of the relationship between God and people.

Hildegard founded a community of Benedictine nuns. She wrote music for the nuns to sing and a medical book of herbal cures. She also corresponded with popes and emperors. A modest woman, Hildegard once described herself as "a feather on the breath of God."

SHOW WHAT YOU KNOW!

REFOCUS
COMPREHENSION

1. How did Gutenberg's invention contribute to the advancement of education?

2. How did stained-glass windows serve as a "school for the illiterate"?

THINK ABOUT IT
CRITICAL THINKING

Why did the fact that Dante and Chaucer wrote in the vernacular help make their works so popular?

WRITE ABOUT IT
ACTIVITY

Think about a special building you would like to visit. Write a description of what you will see.

CHILDREN'S LIVES

FOCUS *Childhood didn't last long in the Middle Ages. Often children married or began learning trades even before their teenage years. Still, like children everywhere, they found time to have fun.*

Going on a Tragic Crusade

At first you were too excited to notice the sharp rocks cutting into your feet. But as you climbed higher into the mountains, it became almost impossible to ignore the frostbite eating into your toes. Having no food to eat, you felt dizzy and weak. Every night, dozens of your fellow travelers froze to death by the side of the road.

You wondered how you got yourself into this mess. But the answer, you knew, was simple: You believed you were on a holy mission.

The mission, called the Children's Crusade, began in the spring of 1212. A French boy named Stephen announced that God had called him to lead a crusade of children. In Germany a boy named Nicholas made the same claim. Both boys said they would lead their followers to the Mediterranean Sea. There, they promised, God would part the waters and allow them to walk into Jerusalem, capturing the Holy Land for all Christians.

You were just one of thousands of French and German children who believed the boys and rushed to join their crusade. You followed Nicholas, and you spent weeks struggling to cross the Alps. That's how you came to be half-starved and half-frozen, stumbling along a mountain pass. Two out of every three children on this journey died.

If you had gone with Stephen, the trip would have been easier. But you'd have been disappointed in the end. You'd have reached the shores of the Mediterranean only to find the sea would *not* open up.

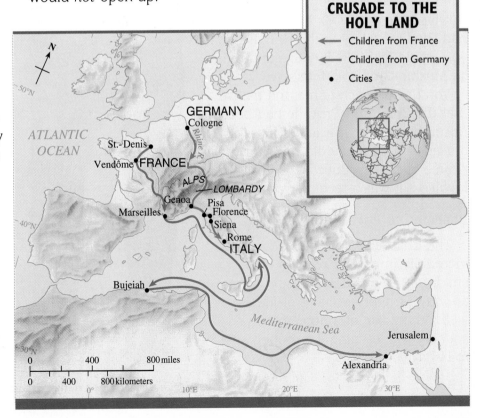

THE CHILDREN'S CRUSADE TO THE HOLY LAND

← Children from France
← Children from Germany
• Cities

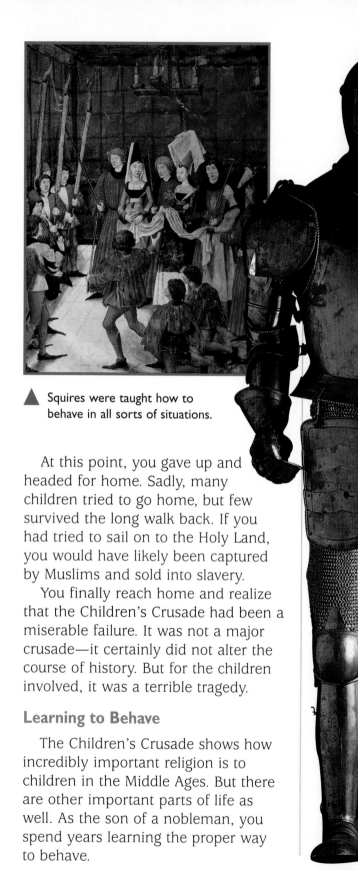

Squires were taught how to behave in all sorts of situations.

At this point, you gave up and headed for home. Sadly, many children tried to go home, but few survived the long walk back. If you had tried to sail on to the Holy Land, you would have likely been captured by Muslims and sold into slavery.

You finally reach home and realize that the Children's Crusade had been a miserable failure. It was not a major crusade—it certainly did not alter the course of history. But for the children involved, it was a terrible tragedy.

Learning to Behave

The Children's Crusade shows how incredibly important religion is to children in the Middle Ages. But there are other important parts of life as well. As the son of a nobleman, you spend years learning the proper way to behave.

One of a squire's duties was to help a knight put on his armor.

In your early years this training is done at home. You and your brothers and sisters learn lots of things just by watching what goes on around you. You live in a castle complete with servants, gardens, and stables. Here you learn to make beds and serve meals. You and your brothers may even learn Latin.

Castle to Castle

When each child reaches the age of eight or nine, he or she is sent to live in the castle of another family. The boys serve as squires in their new surroundings. As a squire you learn your duties as a nobleman. You practice using a sword and handling armor. You learn to dance, play chess, and carve meat.

The girls are sent off to other castles to learn about their future duties. Someday they'll have their own castles to run, so they need to know how to manage money, supervise servants, and plan feasts. They also have to know how to make wine, tend gardens, and nurse the sick.

The girls have to learn these lessons pretty quickly, because they might be married by the time they're 12 years old! You and your brothers will also marry young—probably around age 14.

Making shoes was a good trade for an apprentice to learn.

A Hard Day's Work

You have friends whose parents are not of the nobility. The lessons these children learn are somewhat different from yours. They are not interested in the proper way to serve wine; they're more concerned with how they will earn a living.

Children of working-class parents are often sent to serve as **apprentices**. Boys are usually apprenticed to a master craftworker, while girls are more commonly apprenticed to the master's wife. In either case the children live with the master's family. They soak up every bit of knowledge they can about shoemaking or weaving silk or whatever trade or craft they are learning. With luck, they might someday become master craftworkers themselves.

Fun and Games

Even though medieval children have a lot to learn, they also have time for fun and games. As the child of a nobleman, you play hiding games in your castle. You also frolic with small dogs, tame squirrels, and other castle pets. You sometimes play horseshoes, marbles, or even early forms of tennis or football.

Children of working-class parents also have plenty of games and hobbies. They can dance, wrestle, or play dice games. In the winter they might have a snowball fight or go ice-skating, using animal shinbones as runners. Every now and then, the children might see jugglers, acrobats, animal trainers, or puppeteers perform as they pass through town.

Kites and tops are still popular toys today.

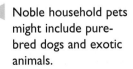

Noble household pets might include pure-bred dogs and exotic animals.

 apprentice A person learning a trade by working with a master skilled in that trade

Catherine, Called Birdy

by Karen Cushman

Catherine, a young girl who lives on a small English manor, visits a friend who lives in a castle. Read about Catherine's impressions of castle life as she recorded them in her diary.

18TH DAY OF FEBRUARY

Just before dinner, Morwenna and I and our escorts arrived at Aelis's castle. Clattering over the moat bridge, we passed through the main gate into the castle yard. The castle seemed like a small stone city. Huddled against the great curtain wall with its stone towers were buildings of all sizes—a slope-roofed storage shed, a kitchen with a chimney like a church steeple, the great hall, a brewhouse, thatched barns and stables, a piggery, a smithy, and the chapel.

The yard teemed with sights and sounds. Great snorting horses coming or going or just milling around stirred the rain and snow and dirt into a great muddy slope. Peasants held wiggling, squawking ducks and chickens by the feet, shaking them in the face of anyone who might buy. Laundresses stirred great vats of dirty clothes in soapy water like cooks brewing up some gown-and-breeches stew. Bakers ran back and forth from the ovens at the side of the yard to the kitchen with great baskets of steamy fresh bread. Masons chipped stones and mixed mortar as they continued their everlasting

CATHERINE, CALLED BIRDY

She's not your average damsel in distress . . .

KAREN CUSHMAN

repairs. Everywhere children tumbled over each other and everyone else, stealing bread, chasing dogs, splashing and slopping through the mud.

As we drew near to the great hall, the smells overpowered even the noise—the sour smell of the sick, the poor, and the old who crowded about the door, waiting for scraps of food or linen, the rotten sweet smell of the garbage and soiled rushes piled outside the kitchen door, and above all the smell of crisping fat and boiling meat and the hundreds of spices and herbs and honeys and wines that together made a castle dinner.

The great hall seemed larger than our whole manor at Stonebridge, and the tables were laid with enough golden plate to make my father die of greed were he but to see it. Dinner was festive, with wine and musicians and minstrels and much laughter. And food such as we see at home only for a feast, and never in winter—eels in quince jelly, hedgehog in raisins and cream, porpoise and peas, spun sugar castles, boats, and dragons—but I noticed that many of the dishes had snow on them, for the kitchens are outside in the yard and food must be carried through the snow to the hall.

After dinner Aelis and I walked about the castle yard for a few minutes, but it was too cold, so we ducked into the kennels to see her new hounds. A stable boy not more than ten years old sleeps there to see to their needs—how thin and cold he looked. The dogs were cleaner and better fed. I gave him some cheese and bread I had concealed in my sleeve for later, for I did not relish crossing the yard in the middle of the night to steal food from the kitchens the way I do at home.

Want to learn more about the life of a young girl in medieval England? Check this book out of your school or public library.

SHOW WHAT YOU KNOW!

REFOCUS
COMPREHENSION

1. What was the Children's Crusade?

2. Why were noble children sent to live with other families?

THINK ABOUT IT
CRITICAL THINKING

Both children of nobility and children of working-class families had to learn trades. What were the differences?

WRITE ABOUT IT
ACTIVITY

List five things Birdy noticed during her visit to the castle. What would have made the biggest impression on you?

Map Adventure

KEY TERMS

portcullis
armorer
castellan

YOUR PLACE IN THE CASTLE

FOCUS In medieval Europe, nobles built huge elaborate houses called castles. A castle was more than just a home—it was a high, walled town. Hundreds of people, including the noble family, called these fortresses home.

Explore a Castle

You cross the drawbridge and enter through the **portcullis**. Soldiers pace the wall-walk, while children play in the inner ward below. Clanging fills the air as the **armorer** hammers out the lord's new suit of armor. The blacksmith and a stableboy prepare horses for the knights, who will hunt game. Food and firewood are brought in by local peasants, while cooks, butchers, and bakers scurry around the kitchen, preparing tonight's banquet. Everyone pitches in to keep the castle running!

Map Key

1 Moat

2 Drawbridge and portcullis

3 Outer gatehouse

4 Sentry room

5 Castellan's quarters

6 Guardroom

7 Latrine

8 Armory and storeroom

9 Outer ward

10 Soldiers' quarters

11 Kitchen garden

12 Workshops, stables, and servants' quarters

13 Storerooms and servants' quarters

14 Water storage

15 Kitchen

16 Great hall

17 Chapel and strong room

18 Lord's quarters

19 Tower stairs

20 Inner ward

MAP IT

1. After entering the castle, you realize that your horse has lost a shoe. Where would you take the horse? Who could make a new shoe?

2. You notice that there are large towers located at each corner of the castle. What advantage do these towers provide? Why are they located near the castle entrance?

3. You speak to the castellan and he hires you as a castle guard. Where might you be stationed? What would your assignment be? Where will you sleep at night?

4. That evening the lord hosts a huge banquet. When the meal and the musicians are done, the lord decides to retire for the evening. Trace the route he will take from the great hall to his quarters.

EXPLORE IT

Design a castle of your own. Where will you put your great hall and your kitchen? Remember to include towers, a portcullis, and a stable in your design. Explain the importance of each part of your castle.

⭐ **portcullis** An iron and hardwood gate that can be quickly lowered during an attack
armorer A person who makes armor for a lord and his knights
castellan The governor of a castle

SUMMING UP

1 DO YOU REMEMBER...
COMPREHENSION

1. About how long did the Byzantine Empire last after the fall of the Roman Empire in the west?

2. Into what two religions did the Christian Church divide in 1054?

3. How did the Crusades lead to the development of universities?

4. What forms of art flourished in the Middle Ages?

5. Who was William the Conqueror and what did he conquer?

6. What legal principles did the Magna Carta establish?

7. What did Joan of Arc accomplish in 1429?

8. Of what countries was Eleanor of Aquitaine the queen?

9. What sorts of lessons did a squire need to learn?

10. How is a castle protected?

2 SKILL POWER
MAKING INFERENCES

In this chapter you read about making inferences. Look again at the people described in the March of Time on pages 200–203. Choose three of these people and make an inference about each. Base your inferences on the details on the page as well as what you may know already.

3 WHAT DO YOU THINK?
CRITICAL THINKING

1. Would you agree that feudalism was a poor substitute for a strong central government? Why?

2. Both Dante and Chaucer wrote in the vernacular. What does this tell you about how Europe was changing in the late Middle Ages?

3. How did Theodora and Eleanor of Aquitaine exercise their power?

4. How does the Children's Crusade show the importance of religion in daily life in the Middle Ages?

5. What, do you think, would be the advantages and disadvantages of living in a castle?

4 SAY IT, WRITE IT, USE IT
VOCABULARY

Tell whether you would rather be a squire or an apprentice during the Middle Ages. In a paragraph, explain your choice. Use four or more of the vocabulary terms below as you explain your choice.

apprentice	guild
armorer	icon
castellan	medieval era
Crusade	portcullis
excommunicate	tapestry
feudalism	

5 GEOGRAPHY AND YOU
MAP STUDY

Compare the maps on pages 192 and 195. Write a paragraph describing the territory that was no longer a part of the Byzantine Empire by the time of Charlemagne.

6 TAKE ACTION
CITIZENSHIP

Although the tragedy of the Children's Crusade seems unbelievable today, many of our nation's children face serious dangers in their homes and neighborhoods. Research the most common causes for childhood injuries and death. Then make up a list of safety tips to help baby sitters and parents avoid these accidents.

7 GET CREATIVE
PHYSICAL EDUCATION CONNECTION

During the Middle Ages, people were entertained by traveling jugglers, acrobats, puppeteers, jesters, and singers. With your classmates, find out about forms of entertainment in the Middle Ages. Then, in your gym or schoolyard, stage a medieval fair for some other classes in your school.

LOOKING AHEAD
Read about another great change that took place in the Mediterranean area.

EXPLORE THE WORLD

The religion of Islam created a powerful empire and civilization. Both the religion and the Muslim culture spread from Arabia to Europe, Africa, and the rest of Asia.

CONTENTS

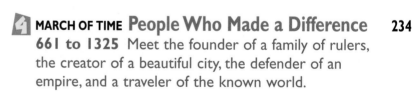

This girl is holding a sextant. Look on page 230 to find what it was used for.

OF ISLAM

These books tell you about the rich heritage of Islam and the Muslim empire. Read one that interests you and fill out a book-review form.

READ AND RESEARCH

The Arabs in the Golden Age **by Mokhtar and Véronique Ageorges** (Millbrook Press, 1992)
Learn how knowledge of the great achievements of the Arab people spread all over the Middle East and northern Africa during the period of the golden age. (*nonfiction*)

Science in Early Islamic Culture **by George Beshore** (Franklin Watts, 1988)
In this book you will read about the early Muslim scholars who used experimentation and observation to gain knowledge that became important to modern scientists and mathematicians. (*nonfiction*)

A 16th Century Mosque **by Fiona MacDonald** (Peter Bedrick Books, 1994)
The art and architecture of the elaborately built Muslim mosques of the 1500s are among the finest ever created. Read about the Muslim leaders and builders and about the lives of the ordinary people who lived during this period of history. (*nonfiction*)

Mecca **by Shahrukh Husain** (Dillon Press, 1993)
Muhammad, the great prophet, proclaimed the Islamic religion that thrives to this day. Trace this holy man's life from Mecca to Medina as he struggled to unify the Arab world. (*nonfiction*)

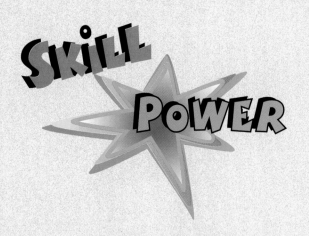

SKILL POWER

Understanding Cause and Effect

Knowing how one event causes another to happen helps you understand what you read.

UNDERSTAND IT

Every day you're surrounded by causes and effects. If you skip breakfast (cause), you will be hungry (effect). If you tease your sister (cause), she will get annoyed (effect). If you study hard (cause), your grades will improve (effect). It's important to understand that your actions cause consequences, or effects. Recognizing causes and their effects when you read history can help you better understand why events happened.

EXPLORE IT

History is full of causes and effects. For example, disagreements between countries (causes) sometimes lead to wars (effects). To understand cause and effect, ask yourself what happened and why it happened. *What* happened is the effect, and *why* it happened is the cause.

These words are clues that there might be a cause and an effect: *because, so, therefore, caused,* or *as a result.* Read this paragraph and think about causes and effects.

In about 610, Muhammad started preaching in Mecca, a city on the Red Sea in what is now Saudi Arabia. His preaching angered many of the rich and powerful people of Mecca. Some people of Mecca made plans to kill Muhammad, so he went in 622 to the city that is now called Medina. There Muhammad found a group of people who helped him. Because he had these followers, he was able to return to Mecca as a conqueror in 630 and turn a religious symbol into a Muslim place of worship.

- Find two words in the paragraph that are clues for cause and effect.

- What are the cause and effect for each place where you found a clue word?

Studying can be a cause that leads to the effect of getting better grades.

TRY IT

Get together with your classmates and think of situations in which one event caused a change in another event. For example, injuries to in-line skaters caused laws to be passed requiring protective helmets, knee pads, and elbow pads. For each situation, draw a cartoon that explains the cause and the effect.

SKILL POWER SEARCH This chapter has many examples of cause and effect. Keep your eyes open and your brain alert for clues.

1

Setting the Scene

★ **KEY TERMS**

Bedouin
oasis
Kaaba
Hijrah
caliph

THE RISE OF ISLAM

FOCUS *Islam, based on the teachings of Muhammad, became a world religion out of which emerged a civilization.*

The Arabian Peninsula

As you can see from the map, Arabia (uh RAY bee uh) is a peninsula surrounded by the Red Sea to the west, the Arabian Sea to the south, and the Persian Gulf to the east. North of Arabia are the lands of the Fertile Crescent, which you read about in Chapter 3.

Until the seventh century B.C., Arabia itself was not so important in the culture of the Middle East. The reason for this is that much of Arabia is a desert. Some Arabs were **Bedouins** (BED oo ihnz) who moved with their flocks. Other Arabs settled in the few **oases** (oh AY seez), where they grew crops and raised sheep, goats, and camels. Arabs also raised the finest horses in the world. Towns arose at some oases. Because of Arabia's location in the center of the Middle East, these towns became part of trade routes. For centuries, camel caravans traveled along these routes.

Arabia's importance increased in the sixth and seventh centuries because the Persian and Byzantine empires were at war. The fighting

disrupted the trade routes to the north, and more merchants started to send their wares through Arabia. One trading center in particular benefited from the shift. This was Mecca. The cities of Mecca and Medina (me DEE-nuh) are central to the story of Islam and Muhammad (muh HAM ud).

THE ARABIAN PENINSULA AT THE TIME OF MUHAMMAD

▢ Arabian Desert
• Cities

★ **Bedouin** An Arab who lives in the desert and moves between established grazing areas

★ **oasis** A fertile area in the desert

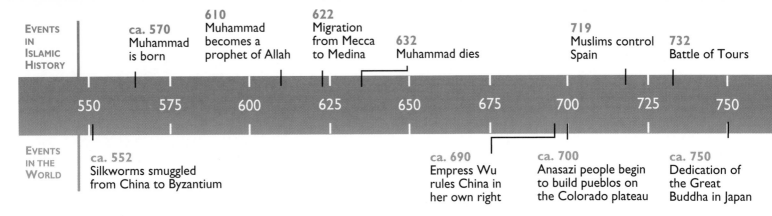

EVENTS IN ISLAMIC HISTORY			**610** Muhammad becomes a prophet of Allah	**622** Migration from Mecca to Medina				**719** Muslims control Spain	**732** Battle of Tours
		ca. 570 Muhammad is born			**632** Muhammad dies				

550 575 600 625 650 675 700 725 750

EVENTS IN THE WORLD	**ca. 552** Silkworms smuggled from China to Byzantium		**ca. 690** Empress Wu rules China in her own right	**ca. 700** Anasazi people begin to build pueblos on the Colorado plateau	**ca. 750** Dedication of the Great Buddha in Japan

▲ Devout Muslims surround the Kaaba in Mecca.

Muhammad's Arabia

The prophet Muhammad was born around A.D. 570 in the city of Mecca, not far from the Red Sea. Even then, Mecca was a holy city for many Arabs because of its place of worship called the **Kaaba** (KAH buh). It contained the Black Stone, an important religious symbol, and idols of many gods.

As Muhammad was growing up, the shift in trade routes brought great wealth to a few Meccans. This wealth put a strain on the traditional values of Arabia. Up until this time, Arabian society was based on the idea that generosity, courage, and wisdom were more important than individual wealth. Those who were prosperous were expected to share their wealth with others less fortunate. Now, however, the desire for riches caused some wealthy traders to forget their responsibility to others.

From a very early age, Muhammad thought about the problems he observed around him. As a young man, Muhammad sometimes went to a cave in the mountains near Mecca, where he would pray for guidance. On one such occasion, around the year 610, Muhammad had a vision. The archangel Gabriel appeared and called Muhammad a prophet of Allah, the Arabic name for God.

Muhammad Begins to Preach

At first, Muhammad was alarmed by the vision, but his wife Khadija (ka-DEE jah) encouraged him. After telling his family and friends about the angel's messages, Muhammad began to preach in public. God through Gabriel had told him to condemn the injustices that wealth had brought to Mecca. Muhammad also opposed the worship of many gods. There was, he said, only one God—Allah.

The important merchants of the city were angered by Muhammad's preaching. They profited from the many pilgrims who came to Mecca to worship at the Kaaba. And, of course, they resented Muhammad's criticism of the pursuit of wealth for its own sake.

Persecuted for his beliefs, Muhammad left Mecca with a few followers in 622. He went to Medina, about 200 miles north. Muhammad's migration from Mecca is called the

---

⭐ **Kaaba** The central holy place of Islam

221

Hijrah (hihzh RAH). It marks the beginning of the Islamic calendar. The year of the Hijrah is the year 1 in this calendar.

In Medina, the townspeople accepted Islam, and Muhammad assumed the leadership of the community. Eight years later, after a military victory, Muhammad also returned to Mecca in triumph.

His message of a single God, with a promise of paradise in the afterlife for believers, swept through the region. Islam offered membership in the community of believers. Anyone who became a Muslim, regardless of class or race, became equal in the eyes of Allah to all other Muslims. Such a message of fairness helped to dissolve the differences that once had split the Arabs into warring communities.

After Muhammad's sudden death in 632, some of the old divisions among the Arab tribes began to reappear. The Islamic community in Medina chose Abu-Bakr, Muhammad's closest advisor, as the first **caliph** (KAY lihf), or successor to Muhammad. Abu-Bakr declared, "If you believed in Muhammad he is dead, but if you believed in Allah he is alive." He managed to subdue the quarreling tribes.

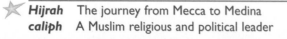

The Arab soldiers were wonderful horseback riders.

Arab Conquerors

The Arab believers in Islam, mounted on horses and camels and armed with lances, bows, and swords, embarked on one of the most remarkable series of conquests in all of world history. As the map shows, the Arab warriors swept everything before them. They believed that they had been chosen to spread God's word. Muslims went into battle with the belief that death would carry them to paradise.

THE SPREAD OF ISLAM

Tours ✳

Bay of Biscay

ATLANTIC OCEAN

SPAIN

Córdoba

Strait of Gibraltar

Tangier

☐ Islam at the death of Muhammad

☐ Islam by about 750

→ Major trade routes

— Present-day boundaries

• Cities

✳ Battle sites

⭐ **Hijrah**   The journey from Mecca to Medina
     caliph   A Muslim religious and political leader

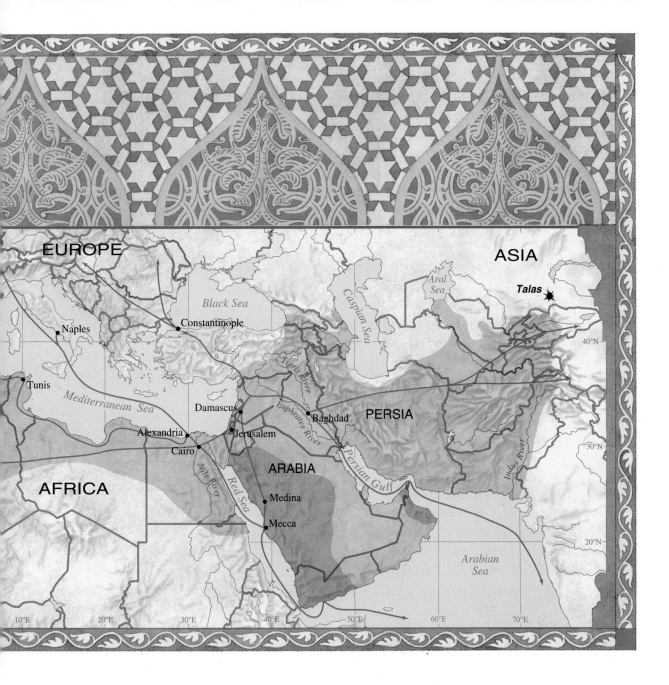

The Arabs seized the Persian capital and over time the whole empire. They spread farther east, reaching the Indus River. Egypt was the next to fall, and from there the Muslims controlled most of northern Africa by 711. In that year they crossed into Spain under the leadership of Al-Tariq. The great rock that dominates the strait that separates Africa and Europe was given the name *Jabal Tariq* ("Tariq's mountain") in his honor.

Important Battles

In 719 the Arabs crossed the Pyrenees (PIHR uh neez) into France.

But in 732, at a daylong battle near the city of Tours (toor), they were defeated by an army led by Charles Martel. This was a very important battle in world history. Martel's victory meant that most of Europe would remain Christian. The Muslims kept their hold on parts of Spain for nearly eight centuries.

Far to the east, the Arabs defeated the Chinese in 751 at the battle of Talas, in central Asia. This too was a decisive battle. The Chinese empire would never again reach that far west, and Islam replaced Buddhism as the major religion of central Asia.

From Community to Empire

In less than 100 years after the death of Muhammad, the Arab empire had spread from the Indus River to the Pyrenees. The Arab Muslims had conquered many non-Arab peoples. Many accepted the religion of Islam.

During this period a new dynasty of caliphs appeared. The Umayyads (oo-MEYE adz) moved the capital of the Muslim empire to Damascus, in Syria. Though they made many positive changes, the caliphs faced rebellions by conquered peoples who resented Umayyad taxes. Many non-Arabs who had become Muslims wanted a greater voice in the government.

In addition, there were some Muslims who criticized the Umayyad rulers for drinking wine,

The American Numismatic Society, New York

▲ You will learn later in this chapter why there are no heads or figures on Muslim coins.

which Islamic teaching forbade. Others believed that only descendants of Ali, the cousin and son-in-law of Muhammad, should be caliphs. In 750 there was a revolt.

New Rulers Make Changes

The new rulers, the Abbassids (uh BAS ihdz), would change the character of the Muslim empire. Under the Abbassids, Muslim civilization became more splendid. The second Abbassid caliph, Al-Mansur (al man-SOOR), built a new capital on the western banks of the Tigris River. Baghdad (BAG dad), the capital, grew into a sprawling city of 1 million people. By the ninth century, only some Chinese cities were larger.

The early years of the Abbassid dynasty were very prosperous. New food crops were brought from India and planted in the Middle East. This brought about a great change in agriculture. Tropical crops such as rice, sugar cane, lemons, limes, bananas, coconut palms, spinach, and eggplant

▼ Gold was fashioned into beautiful jewelry by Muslim artisans.

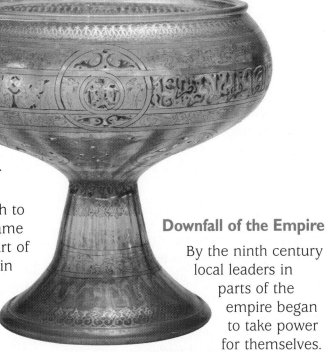

The Metropolitan Museum of Art, Edward C. Moore Collection, Bequest of Edward C. Moore. 1891. (91.1.1538)

allowed the growing season to be expanded into the summer months, when other crops could not grow.

Trade also brought great wealth to the empire. Hundreds of ships came loaded with goods from every part of the empire and beyond—porcelain from China, ivory and gold from Africa, and furs from northern Europe. Shops sold spices, gems, dyes, perfumes, linen and silk, furs, ivory, and beautiful glassware, such as that shown here.

By the ninth century the Abbassid caliphs had become remote from the community and were known as Allah's "shadow on earth." The palace had become a showplace for power and glory. A Muslim historian described the Room of the Tree, one of the many halls in the caliph's palace.

A tree, standing in the midst of a great circular tank filled with clear water. The tree had eighteen branches, every branch having numerous twigs, on which sit all sorts of gold and silver birds, both large and small. Most of the branches of the tree are of silver, but some are of gold, and they spread into the air carrying leaves of different colors. The leaves of the tree move as the wind blows, while the birds pipe and sing.

Downfall of the Empire

By the ninth century local leaders in parts of the empire began to take power for themselves. Many became virtually independent rulers, and paid little attention to the caliph.

Muslim Spain had never recognized the authority of Baghdad. By about 1000, Islamic Spain broke apart into small kingdoms. Christian Spain began to revive and reconquer territory. Finally only the kingdom of Granada was left, and it fell in 1492.

In the east, Turkish nomads began to settle in Islamic territories, sometimes serving as soldiers of the caliph. By about 1037 a group of them, known as Seljuks (SEL jooks), took over some of the empire's lands.

The Crusades further weakened the Muslim empire. But it was Mongol invaders, whom you will read about in Chapter 12, who would destroy Baghdad in 1258. The unity of the Muslim empire was never recovered. The civilization of Islam, however, continued to flourish, perhaps because of the diversity of the Muslim peoples.

SHOW WHAT YOU KNOW!

REFOCUS
COMPREHENSION

1. Describe what Arabia was like at the time of Muhammad.

2. Describe the Muslim empire as it was about 100 years after the death of Muhammad.

THINK ABOUT IT
CRITICAL THINKING

Give reasons why you agree or disagree with this statement: It is very difficult to successfully govern a large empire.

WRITE ABOUT IT
ACTIVITY

Make a list of the goods you would have liked to buy if you had lived in Baghdad.

225

Spotlight

★ **KEY TERMS**

mosque
minaret
alms
fast
hajj

REVELATIONS OF THE PROPHET

FOCUS *The religion revealed through Muhammad has been adopted by hundreds of millions as a way of life.*

▼ This tile shows the location of the Kaaba, Islam's holiest place.

The Role of Muhammad

Muhammad's role is central to Islam. He is considered both the greatest of prophets and the revealer of the truth of Islam. His revelations formed the basis of the religion.

Muhammad knew something of both Judaism and Christianity and also believed with them that there is only one God. Although Muslims respect the prophets of the other two religions, they believe that Muhammad was the last of the prophets.

When Muhammad preached in Medina, some of his followers wrote down the messages. They were gathered in a book known as the Qur'an (koo RAHN), which is the holy book of Islam. It also includes laws on how people ought to live.

Pillars of Islam

The basic duties of all Muslims are known as the Five Pillars of Islam. The first pillar is the statement of faith. With the words "I attest there is no god but Allah, and that Muhammad is the messenger of Allah," Muslims state their faith.

The second pillar is the duty to pray five times a day at set times. Faithful Muslims, wherever they may be, face in the direction of Mecca as they pray. **Mosques** (mahsks) have **minarets** (mihn uh RETS). From these high towers, the people are called to prayer each Friday, the Muslim Sabbath.

The third pillar is the duty of giving **alms**. This is not considered charity. It is, in effect, a religious tax that Muslims pay at a specified time each year. The money is used to help people in need.

The fourth pillar is the **fast**. During Ramadan (ram uh DAHN), the ninth month of the Islamic calendar, Muslims do not eat or drink between dawn and sunset. Young children, the elderly, and anyone whose health would be threatened do not fast.

The fifth pillar is the pilgrimage to Mecca—the **hajj** (haj). Muslims are strongly encouraged to make the hajj at some point in their lifetime. In Mecca, Muslims from all over the world go to the Kaaba, the central point for Muslim worship. Here the pilgrims perform the rituals that emphasize their unity as Muslims.

★ **mosque** Muslim house of worship
minaret A high tower on a mosque
alms A donation to the poor

★ **fast** Going without food or drink
hajj A Muslim pilgrimage

Divisions Within Islam

The unity of Islam was broken in its early years. The first and most fundamental split came about over the leadership of the caliphs. The Sunnite Muslims, who form the majority of Muslims in the world today, accepted the leadership of Abu-Bakr and the caliphs who came after him.

The Shi'i (SHEE uh) Muslims did not. They believed that Muhammad wished his cousin and son-in-law, Ali, to take over the leadership of the community. After Ali's death, the Shi'i Muslims followed one of Ali's sons and later, other descendants of Ali.

▲ This Qur'an is also a work of art.

Some Muslims sought a more personal relationship with God. Many of these people practiced meditation and fasting for long periods of time and gave away all they had. By doing so, they hoped to purify their souls so that they could get closer to God. This movement, known as Sufism (SOO fihz-uhm), always attracted many women. One of the most famous of the early Sufis was Rabi'a (ruh BEE uh). She wrote poetry in which she told of her feelings for Allah.

The Dome of the Rock is another holy place. ▶

SHOW WHAT YOU KNOW!

REFOCUS
COMPREHENSION

1. What are the Five Pillars of Islam?

2. Who are the Sufis?

THINK ABOUT IT
CRITICAL THINKING

How do the ancient divisions within Islam affect the world today?

WRITE ABOUT IT
ACTIVITY

Using figurative language, write a description of the Dome of the Rock.

A RICH CULTURE

FOCUS *Learning, scientific inquiry, the arts, and literature were highlights of Islam's golden age.*

Centers of Learning

The wealth of the Muslim empire helped to bring about an era of scientific discovery and artistic achievement. The caliphs were important patrons of learning and the arts. They invited poets, astronomers, mathematicians, and physicians to their courts.

When royal invitations and offers of high salaries were not enough, some rulers resorted to force. Sultan Mahmud (MAHK mood) of Afghanistan (af GAN ih stan) for example, sent his soldiers to bring Persian poets to his capital. He wanted them to write stories in which he was the hero—and they did.

But most rulers were genuinely interested in the sciences and arts. In 823 an Abbassid caliph built the House of Wisdom in Baghdad. It became a center for scientific study that attracted scholars from all over the Muslim empire. Its library held almost a million manuscripts before the Mongols destroyed Baghdad. The scholars of the Muslim world built on the achievements of Greece, Persia, and India. After the Muslims absorbed Indian and Persian mathematics and science, they developed them further. Among the Muslim contributions were advances in **algebra**. The word *algebra* comes from Arabic *al jabr*. Muslims were also skilled in chemistry, astronomy, physics, and optics, the science of making lenses.

The Muslims were particularly interested in Greek thought and knowledge. In the House of Wisdom, language experts made Arabic translations of Greek manuscripts. These circulated throughout the Muslim world. It was through Muslim Spain that many of the works of Greek philosophers, such as Plato and Aristotle, came to Europe.

Córdoba (KOR duh buh), which was then the largest city in Europe, had a library with 400,000 books. At a time when Christian priests were among the few people in Europe who could read, everybody in Muslim Spain was encouraged to read and write.

The Practice of Medicine

Sickness and disease were a part of life in the ancient world. But people who lived in the Muslim empire were luckier than most who lived in other

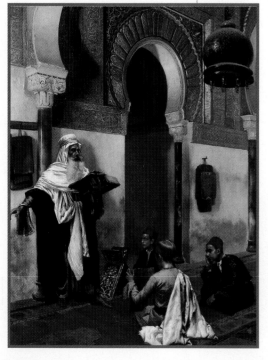

▼ It was important for Muslims to learn to read the Qur'an.

⭐ *algebra* A form of mathematics that uses letters and numbers to solve problems

CONTRIBUTIONS TO MATHEMATICS, SCIENCE, AND MEDICINE

Scientist	Fields of Study	Contributions
Al-Kwarizmi	Astronomy and mathematics	At Baghdad **Observatory** he made astronomical tables to show the movements of stars and planets. In mathematics he was the first to use the expression *al jabr* and to introduce Arabic numerals to the Western world.
Al-Battani	Astronomy	Observing the movements of the stars in Syria for 40 years, he was able to correct the mistakes made by an early Greek astronomer.
Al-Biruni	Astronomy, geography, mathematics, mechanics, medicine, and **mineralogy**	He wrote books on many areas of science. His realization that the earth was a sphere led him to calculate its longitude and latitude.
Ibn Sina (known as Avicenna in the West)	Medicine	His book *The Canon of Medicine* classified all healing drugs and medical practices of the time and was used for centuries as a textbook in the Middle East and Europe.
Al-Razi	Medicine	He was the first to write a description of smallpox and its treatment.

parts of the world. Serious illness was taken care of in clean hospitals that were free to the public. Muslim doctors were highly skilled. They had to pass examinations before they could practice medicine. The city of Baghdad had over 800 doctors.

Some doctors became very famous. They studied Greek, Persian, and Hindu medical arts. Then they wrote books that contained the best information from other cultures and added their own observations about diseases and their treatments.

observatory   A building equipped with instruments to study the stars

mineralogy   The science of minerals

They also gave practical advice. One doctor was asked to choose a site for a new hospital. He hung pieces of meat at various places. A few days later, he chose the spot for the hospital where the meat had spoiled most slowly.

The first pharmacies, or drugstores, opened in Baghdad during the ninth century. Pharmacists, skilled at making medicines, became recognized as different from doctors. But they too had to pass a test to obtain a license from the government. In the pharmacies, ordinary people as well as doctors could buy medicinal herbs, tonics, and ointments from all over the Muslim world. Just as bitter-tasting medicines are sugar-coated today, the prescriptions of the Muslim druggists were blended with rose water and perfumes to make them taste better.

It may have been a pharmacist experimenting with sugar cane from India who made an interesting discovery. The sugar cane produced a kind of brown sugar. The Arabs called it *qand*. This word is the root for our word *candy*.

Mapmakers and Navigators

Muslim scholars also excelled in **applied sciences** and **technology**. They were great mapmakers. Al-Idrisi, who lived in the twelfth century, was the author of the greatest geographic work of his time. He made a map of

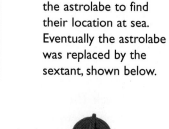

▲ Muslim navigators used the astrolabe to find their location at sea. Eventually the astrolabe was replaced by the sextant, shown below.

the world in which he divided the world into sections. He used knowledge gained from older sources, his own travels, and the accounts of other travelers.

Earlier you learned about the trade that brought so many wonderful goods and exotic products to Baghdad and the other cities in the empire. Today the idea of travel across oceans to faraway places is taken for granted. But think how difficult it would have been to sail out of sight of land without instruments that gave the ship's location.

Instruments of navigation already existed. The Chinese had developed a compass. The astrolabe was an instrument that measured the angle between the sun or a particular star and the horizon. Muslims perfected the compass and astrolabe. These instruments were used by Arabs to cross the Indian Ocean to China. Arab ship pilots also collected books of navigational information that gave the times of tides and courses of winds along the eastern coast of Africa.

Art Based on Nature

Most Muslims believed that the Qur'an teaches that art shouldn't show human or animal figures. Mosques have no paintings or statues of Muhammad.

So Muslim artists often painted flowers and other objects from nature and used geometric patterns. Artisans decorated ceramic and metal bowls,

applied science Science put to practical use
technology A method for dealing with technical problems

Everyday objects like this writing box were also very decorative.

plates, and vases with complicated designs and elaborate lines. This distinctive style is known as arabesque.

Some Muslim Persian and Turkish books contain exceptions to the religious ban on showing human figures. They have magnificently colored prints of figures arranged in elaborate designs. Even in the Persian works, however, the face of Muhammad is nearly always hidden.

Beautiful Calligraphy

Much artistic effort went into calligraphy, or beautiful handwriting. Writing was considered the creation of Allah, and those who used it tried to be worthy of the gift. The ability to write well was a highly respected talent. The Arabic script could be elaborated into endless designs. Such designs were used in mosques and were also often used to decorate the walls of palaces.

Muslims regarded the creation of decorative pages in the Qur'an as the highest form of art. These are similar to the illuminated manuscripts Christian monks made in the Middle Ages.

Grand Buildings

Muslim architecture became a symbol of great artistic talent. The Muslims originally used many of the architectural styles of the Byzantine and Persian empires that they had conquered. They combined these with other influences in a way that became their own.

The caliphs had lavish palaces built for themselves. The Umayyads built theirs at the edges of deserts, as reminders of Arabia, which they came from. The Abbassids, who built palaces in cities, included courtyards with

Calligraphy was an important skill in Muslim culture.

The Alhambra is set in a garden. Inside the building a visitor can look up to see the dome.

Other great Muslim buildings can be found in Iran and Spain. The great mosque of Córdoba was a university as well as a place of worship. It was one of the largest mosques in the Muslim world.

Another Spanish Muslim architectural gem is the Alhambra, in the Spanish city of Granada. This is a palace built by the last Muslim dynasty to rule parts of Spain. The name *Alhambra* means "red," for the exterior walls are made of pinkish stone. Inside, all the surfaces—pillars, ceilings, and walls—are covered with plaster flowers and fantastic colored designs that include Arabic calligraphy. Plaster decorations hang like multi-colored icicles from the Alhambra's domed chambers. It is one of the masterpieces of world architecture.

pools, gardens, and fountains. A distinctive feature of Muslim government buildings was the elaborate decoration. Virtually every surface, inside and out, was covered with geometric patterns and designs.

Some of the greatest achievements were the grand mosques that were built throughout the Muslim world. The first of these masterpieces was the Dome of the Rock, in Jerusalem. This mosque, which is pictured on page 227, was built over the place from which, according to tradition, Muhammad ascended to heaven.

A Poetic People

Just as devout Jews learned Hebrew to read the Bible, Muslims throughout the world studied Arabic, the language of the Qur'an. It was forbidden to translate the Qur'an into other languages. Thus, Arabic became the common language, or **lingua franca**, of the Muslim lands. As the empire expanded, educated people in different countries used Arabic to communicate with each other. Most Muslim scholarly works, such as those

⭐ *lingua franca*   A Latin term used to describe a language used by people whose first languages are different

232

dealing with mathematics, science and medicine, and literature, were written in Arabic.

Poetry had long been an important part of Arab culture. Those who wrote good poetry were renowned. Quite a number of these poets were women. Some were Sufis who wrote deeply religious poems. The poet the Western world knows best is Omar Khayyám (OH mahr keye YAHM). His collection of nature and love poetry is called *The Rubaiyat* (roo beye YAHT). Caliphs enjoyed listening to poetry that described the heroic deeds of the conquering warriors who had won an empire for Islam.

Stories and Legends

Kalila wa Dimna (kah LEE lah wah DIM nah) is a collection of animal stories or fables. It is thought that they were originally written to show kings and princes how to behave. Kalila and Dimna are jackals. Kalila is a trickster. Dimna tries to give good advice. These very old fables came to Muslim literature from India by way of Persia.

During the Muslim era, many great works of prose began to be written as well. Al-Jahiz, who lived in the ninth century, wrote essays about human nature. He wrote, "A man who is noble does not pretend to be noble. . . . When a man exaggerates his qualities it is because of something lacking in himself."

The work of Arabic literature that most people recognize is the book known as *The Thousand and One Nights* or *The Arabian Nights*. It contains stories, many of which came from all over the Muslim empire. You may have read these stories or seen films that were based on them.

Some of the stories are probably not Muslim in origin. They may have been added when these tales were translated into European languages. Most Muslims today do not read these stories.

▼ The regal lion in this Persian illustration is no match for Kalila, the wily jackal.

REFOCUS
COMPREHENSION

1. Why was the House of Wisdom an important center of learning?

2. How did the Qur'an affect Muslim art?

THINK ABOUT IT
CRITICAL THINKING

What was the most important Muslim contribution to learning?

WRITE ABOUT IT
ACTIVITY

Write a description of a House of Wisdom that you would like to see created in your community.

PEOPLE WHO MADE A DIFFERENCE

FOCUS *Rulers, soldiers, and travelers are among the important figures that can be found in Muslim history.*

THE BUILDER OF BAGHDAD

Al-Mansur is best known for building a new Muslim capital, Baghdad. He chose a site with good transportation, natural defenses, cool nights, and no mosquitoes.

"By God I shall build it," Al-Mansur declared. "Then I shall dwell in it as long as I live and my descendants after me. It will surely be the most flourishing city in the world." Baghdad was completed in 766.

The city was built in the form of a circle. It was surrounded by a deep moat and three walls; the largest was 112 feet high. In the very center of the city stood the palace. It was capped by a green dome with the figure of a mounted rider carrying a lance. Supposedly the rider pointed his lance toward any part of the empire where danger threatened.

FOUNDER OF A DYNASTY

In 661, less than 30 years after the death of the Prophet, Muawiya (muh AH wih ya) became the first Umayyad caliph. He was also the first leader of Islam who was not related to Muhammad by blood or marriage. This was a great change for Islam.

Muawiya ruled from his capital in Damascus in Syria, rather than from the religious centers in Mecca and Medina, in Arabia. Not everyone was pleased with his rise to power, but Muawiya was a wise leader. He said, "Let a single hair bind me to my people, and I will not let it snap. When they pull, I loosen, and if they loosen, I pull."

For the next 90 years, the Umayyad dynasty, with the power passing from within the family to sons, brothers, or nephews, extended and ruled the Muslim empire.

661
Umayyad
dynasty founded

766
Building of Baghdad
completed

1191
Saladin defends
Jerusalem

1325
Ibn Battuta
begins his travels

600   700   800   900   1000   1100   1200   1300   1400

DEFENDER OF JERUSALEM

The family of Salah al-Din, or Saladin, were non-Arab Muslims who served the governor of Syria. When Saladin was 14, he joined the army. The era in which he lived was a troubled time. Muslims fought each other for parts of the empire.

After receiving command of the Syrian army at the age of 31, Saladin defeated his Muslim rivals. When the ruler of Syria died, Saladin took control. He united the Muslim armies to capture Jerusalem, which was then under Christian rule.

In 1189, Europeans launched the Third Crusade to take back the holy city. Among the crusaders was Richard the Lionhearted, king of England. He was wounded in the fighting. Saladin, in a gesture that won praise from both Christians and Muslims, sent his own doctor to treat Richard's wounds.

Saladin successfully defended Jerusalem and negotiated a peace with the crusaders in 1192. He died the following year.

TRAVELER OF THE WORLD

In 1325, when he was 21, Ibn Battuta decided to make the hajj to Mecca. Traveling in a camel caravan, he crossed North Africa to Egypt. Because the passage across the Red Sea to Mecca was blocked, he went to Syria and then overland to Mecca.

The journey changed his life. Having met pilgrims in Mecca who came from all parts of the Muslim world, he decided to continue his travels. He went to Persia and then south down the east coast of Africa. Muslim rulers welcomed him everywhere he went.

As you read in Chapter 5, he later went to India and China. He also traveled to the Muslim states of Africa below the Sahara. He found people who spoke Arabic as far away as China. In all he traveled more than 75,000 miles during his lifetime.

SUMMING UP

1 DO YOU REMEMBER...
COMPREHENSION

1. What role did Mecca and Medina play in Muhammad's life?

2. How did Muhammad want to change Arabic worship?

3. What was one way that the early Muslims spread their religion?

4. Why was the battle at Tours in 732 important?

5. Who were the Abbassids?

6. What book contains the messages preached by Muhammad?

7. Into what two main branches did Islam divide?

8. What were some advances made by Muslim navigators?

9. Why was calligraphy an important art form?

10. What role did Saladin play during the Crusades?

2 SKILL POWER
UNDERSTANDING CAUSE AND EFFECT

In this chapter, you read about cause and effect. For each historical development listed below, write a cause.

- Wealthy merchants of Mecca were angered by Muhammad's teachings.

- One hundred years after Muhammad's death, the Arab empire reached from India to Spain.

- The spread of Islam into Europe stopped in 732 near Tours in France.

- By 1492, Spain was no longer Muslim.

3 WHAT DO YOU THINK?
CRITICAL THINKING

1. In what ways did Muhammad try to return Arabian society to traditional values?

2. The Five Pillars of Islam are the basic duties of all Muslims. Which do you think is the most important? Explain your reasons.

3. In what way is a modern college or university like the House of Wisdom in Baghdad?

4. How did the ban on showing human or animal figures affect the decor of mosques?

5. What did the caliph Muawiya mean when he said, "Let a single hair bind me to my people, and I will not let it snap. When they pull, I loosen, and if they loosen, I pull"?

4 SAY IT, WRITE IT, USE IT
VOCABULARY

Use all the terms below to make a crossword puzzle. Every word has to cross at least one other word, and there should be no breaks in the puzzle. Number each word across or down, and write a clue for each word. Trade puzzles with a friend.

algebra	Kaaba
alms	lingua franca
applied science	minaret
Bedouin	mineralogy
caliph	mosque
fast	oasis
hajj	observatory
Hijrah	technology

5 GEOGRAPHY AND YOU
MAP STUDY

The red line shows the travels of Ibn Battuta. List the countries to which he would travel if he were to make his journeys today.

Key to map abbreviations:

Den.	Denmark
Ger.	Germany
Rom.	Romania
Syr.	Syria
Turkm.	Turkmenistan
Afgh.	Afghanistan
Bang.	Bangladesh
Myan.	Myanmar
Thai.	Thailand
Maur.	Mauritania
U.K.	United Kingdom
Kyrg.	Kyrgyzstan

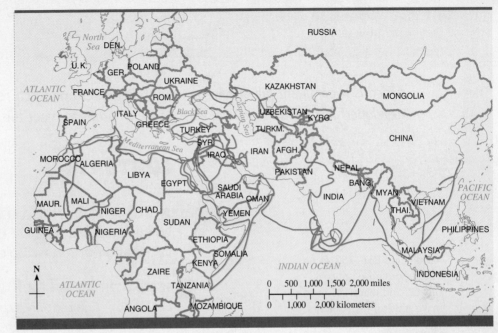

6 TAKE ACTION
CITIZENSHIP

Sharing one's wealth with others who are less fortunate is one of the duties of all Muslims. Most non-Islamic people also have a rich tradition of helping the needy. Giving money is not the only way to help others. You can also give your time and talents. Make a class talent list that tells what talents, abilities, and interests each person has that he or she would be willing to share with others.

7 GET CREATIVE
LANGUAGE ARTS CONNECTION

Muslim writers worked their flowing script into endless decorative designs, often including pictures within and around the words. Try imitating this style as you write the words to a favorite poem or song. Make your script as beautiful as possible.

O beautiful for spacious skies

LOOKING AHEAD Now you will move ahead to the wonders of nearby Africa.

DISCOVER AFRICA SOUTH

Africa is a continent full of environmental differences and rich resources. African societies developed flexible and creative ways of life in order to meet the challenge of living there.

CONTENTS

Read pages 256–257 to find out about some unusual objects and materials used to make musical instruments.

OF THE SAHARA

These books tell about the kingdoms of ancient Africa and what it was like to live in them. Read one that interests you and fill out a book-review form.

READ AND RESEARCH

Ancient Ghana: The Land of Gold **by Philip Koslow** (Chelsea House Publishers, 1995)
Explore the land of ancient Ghana, the first great kingdom of West Africa. Learn about the sources of wealth and power in this "land of gold." (*nonfiction*)

The Royal Kingdoms of Ghana, Mali, and Songhay: Life in Medieval Africa **by Patricia and Frederick McKissack** (Henry Holt & Co., 1994)
Take a journey through three ancient kingdoms of Africa and discover what life was like in these civilizations. Maps and photographs will help you understand the people, places, and traditions of these ancient lands. (*nonfiction*)

Sundiata: Lion King of Mali **by David Wisniewski** (Clarion Books, 1992)
This 800-year-old African tale about a young boy who overcomes physical handicaps and becomes a great ruler of an ancient kingdom will amaze you. Notice how carefully the artist portrays thirteenth-century Africa. (*folk tale*)

SKILL POWER — Using a World Atlas

Knowing how to use a world atlas will help you locate specific information about the world on a variety of maps.

UNDERSTAND IT

When the geographer and map-maker Gerardus Mercator published a book of maps, he named the book after a mythical bearded giant named Atlas. According to an old Greek myth, Atlas had disobeyed the gods, and as punishment he was made to stand and hold up the heavens. Mercator's *Atlas* became so well known that people came to call any collection of maps an atlas.

Next to a dictionary and an encyclopedia, an atlas is the most frequently used reference book. People turn to an atlas to locate unfamiliar places, to plan vacations, to study various features of the earth, or to daydream about faraway places.

EXPLORE IT

In a world atlas you will find political maps, physical maps, weather maps, population-density maps, vegetation maps, and more. Most of the maps have legends to help you read the maps correctly.

Look at the map on the next page, which shows the oceans and continents of the world. By looking at this map, you can quickly get facts about how many oceans and continents there are and where they are located.

Now look through the Atlas in this book on pages 608–628 to discover the kinds of maps it contains. Maybe Mercator was correct in thinking that holding a book of maps is like having the universe in your hands!

This statue of Atlas stands in Rockefeller Center in New York City.

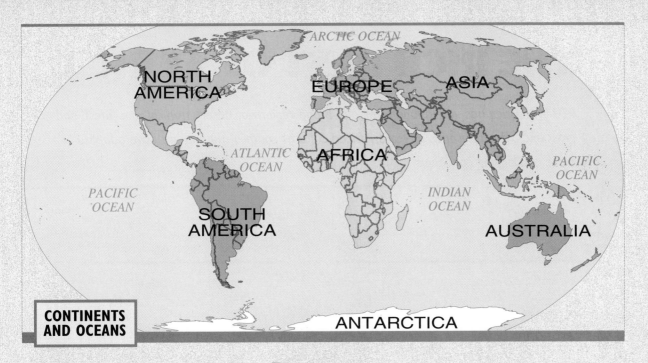

NORTH AMERICA

EUROPE

ASIA

AFRICA

SOUTH AMERICA

AUSTRALIA

ARCTIC OCEAN

ATLANTIC OCEAN

PACIFIC OCEAN

PACIFIC OCEAN

INDIAN OCEAN

ANTARCTICA

CONTINENTS AND OCEANS

How many oceans and continents are there? What ocean separates the Americas from Africa and Europe?

TRY IT

With a group of classmates, plan a travel bulletin-board display. Look through a world atlas to decide on four places to include in your display. Make photocopies of political maps to show cities you would visit, of physical maps to show mountainous areas, and of climate maps to determine what kind of clothing to bring. Select a title for the display, such as "The World at Our Fingertips" or "A Vacation in _____."

SKILL POWER SEARCH *Look carefully at the maps of Africa on pages 620–621 in the Atlas. What facts can be learned from them?*

241

Setting the Scene

⭐ **KEY TERMS**

griot
counselor
contiguous
savanna
till
shifting cultivation

THE RICH PAST OF AFRICA

FOCUS *Africa has varied landforms and broad regions of desert, tropical rain forest, and grasslands. For thousands of years, African cultures south of the Sahara have adapted to these challenging conditions.*

A Spoken Tradition

Through many generations, the history of Africa was carried in the memories of **griots** (gree OHZ). These people had a place of honor in African society. Griots memorized the customs, traditions, and laws of their people. Each ruling family employed a griot to serve as a **counselor** to the ruler and to teach young princes.

A twentieth-century griot in the nation of Guinea (GIHN ee) declared, "I teach kings the history of their ancestors so that the lives of the ancients might serve them as an example, for the world is old but the future springs from the past." Much of what we know about Africa's rich past comes from these sources.

A Varied Landscape

Africa is the second largest continent, three times the size of the **contiguous**, or continental, United States. As the map shows, Africa stretches for about 5,000 miles from the Atlantic Ocean to the Indian Ocean and somewhat more than the same distance north and south.

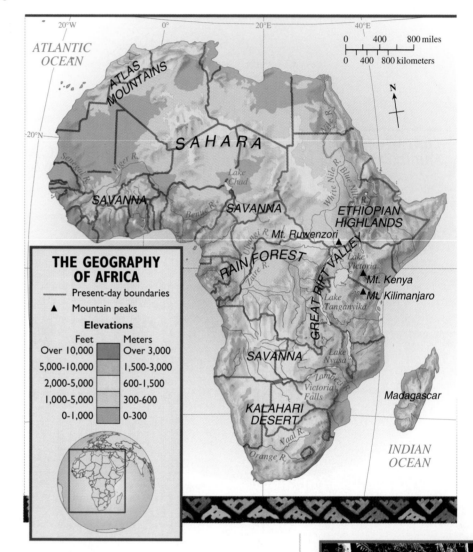

THE GEOGRAPHY OF AFRICA

— Present-day boundaries
▲ Mountain peaks

Elevations

Feet	Meters
Over 10,000	Over 3,000
5,000-10,000	1,500-3,000
2,000-5,000	600-1,500
1,000-5,000	300-600
0-1,000	0-300

The African continent is a vast high plateau that drops off to narrow coastal plains. Within its boundaries are great mountain ranges, turbulent rivers, tropical rain forests, and the largest desert in the world.

⭐ **griot** A person who memorizes and tells the oral history of the people
counselor A person who advises

⭐ **contiguous** Sharing an edge or boundary

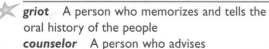

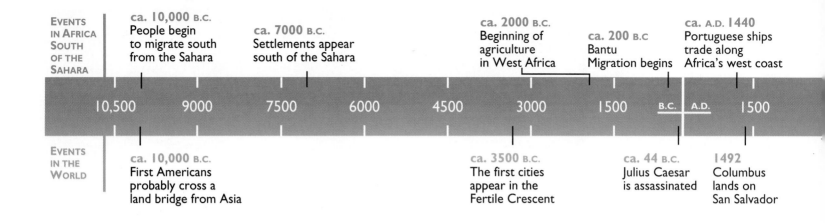

EVENTS IN AFRICA SOUTH OF THE SAHARA	**ca. 10,000 B.C.** People begin to migrate south from the Sahara	**ca. 7000 B.C.** Settlements appear south of the Sahara		**ca. 2000 B.C.** Beginning of agriculture in West Africa	**ca. 200 B.C** Bantu Migration begins	**ca. A.D. 1440** Portuguese ships trade along Africa's west coast	

| 10,500 | 9000 | 7500 | 6000 | 4500 | 3000 | 1500 | B.C. | A.D. | 1500 |

EVENTS IN THE WORLD

ca. 10,000 B.C. First Americans probably cross a land bridge from Asia

ca. 3500 B.C. The first cities appear in the Fertile Crescent

ca. 44 B.C. Julius Caesar is assassinated

1492 Columbus lands on San Salvador

The equator cuts through the center of Africa. Tropical rain forests grow in most of this part of the continent. Air rises from the hot land to form clouds that produce almost constant rainfall.

To the east of the rain forest region is Africa's largest lake, Lake Victoria. It is the source of the Nile River, which flows north into Egypt. Around the lake are rolling plateaus and steep mountains. From Lake Victoria you can see Africa's three highest mountains—Mount Kenya (KEN yuh), Mount Kilimanjaro (kihl uh-mahn JAHR oh), and Mount Ruwenzori (roo wen ZOHR ee).

North and south of the rain forests are two large **savannas**. Beyond the savanna in the north is the Sahara (suh HAR uh), the world's largest desert. It would be wrong, however, to think of it as a barren, sandy wasteland. Drought-resistant shrubs and grasses still grow in the Sahara and in the Kalahari (kah lah HAH ree) Desert, below the southern savanna.

The Challenge of Climate

Africa's northern coast is a fertile region with a mild Mediterranean climate. As you learned in earlier chapters, the Muslim empire and the civilizations of ancient Egypt and Carthage all thrived in this area. At the southern tip of Africa is another region with a similar climate.

(Left) Tropical rain forests are very wet, allowing trees to grow close together to form a dense canopy.

(Middle) Savannas are home to such wildlife as antelope, zebras, and lions.

(Right) The Sahara is difficult but not impossible to cross.

⭐ *savanna*   A flat, dry grassland of the tropics, dotted with shrubs and trees

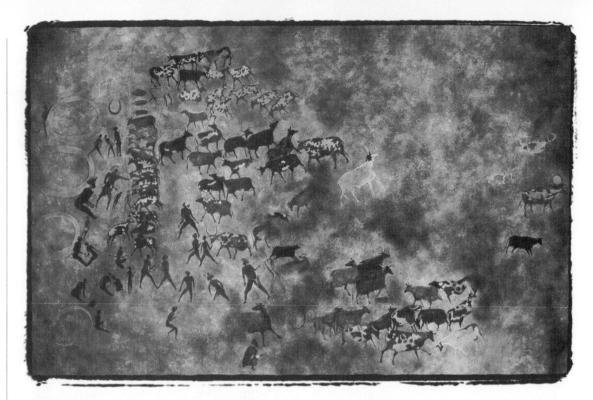

This cave painting was made in prehistoric times, when the Sahara had plenty of water.

In the forest and savanna regions, seasons are determined by rainfall rather than by temperature. Instead of summer and winter, these regions have rainy seasons and dry seasons. All crops must be planted, tended, and harvested during the wet season because there is no rain at all during the dry season.

The quality of the soil has also affected the cultures of Africa. In most parts of the continent, the soil is shallow and lacking in minerals. If used too frequently or **tilled** too deeply, the soil can lose its fertility. For this reason, Africans never used plows. They used digging sticks to punch holes in the soil for the seeds. In addition, they used a method of farming called **shifting cultivation**, in which they would farm a piece of land for only two consecutive years.

The African climate also affects the spread of diseases. Because Africa has no real winter, insects can breed throughout the year. Tsetse (TSET see) flies spread a deadly sleeping sickness in humans and large animals, making it impractical to use horses or oxen.

Besides sleeping sickness, mosquito-carried diseases, such as malaria (muh LER ee uh), are found nearly everywhere in sub-Saharan Africa—that is Africa below the Sahara. People who survive the diseases are left weakened for life.

Flight From the Desert

For many thousands of years, the Sahara was a vast grassy plain, with many rivers and lakes. When the last ice age ended about 12,000 years ago, the rainfall started to decline. Grasses and trees began to die out, and lakes

---

 till To plow and plant land

shifting cultivation To clear and farm land for a short period and then move on to another plot

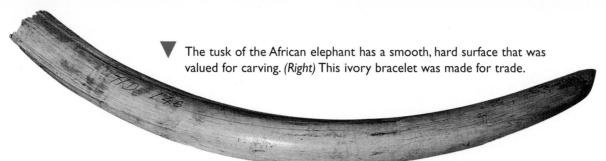

The tusk of the African elephant has a smooth, hard surface that was valued for carving. *(Right)* This ivory bracelet was made for trade.

and rivers dried up. These processes continue to plague the Sahara region at the present time.

The people of the Sahara began to migrate south in search of enough wildlife and water to support hunting, gathering, and fishing. About 9,000 years ago, settlements began to appear in the sub-Saharan region.

Other African hunters and gatherers in the open savannas and the forests moved from place to place in groups of about 50 people. Women gathered roots, seeds, nuts, and berries. Men hunted with spears and bows. Using a large variety of tools, the people made baskets and temporary shelters.

Around 4,000 years ago, Africans in the Niger River valley developed agriculture. They planted rice, sorghum (SOR gum), and millet and raised small herds of sheep, goats, and cattle. With more than enough food and additional migrations of people from the north, the population increased.

The Bantu Migration

Beginning around 200 B.C., Africans from the mountains near Cameroon (kam uh ROON) began to move into other parts of the continent. This is called the Bantu (BAN too) Migration, named after the language they spoke. Today, hundreds of different languages are spoken in the parts of Africa where these people migrated. But scholars have found that the word *Bantu*, meaning "people," occurs in nearly all of these languages.

Trading towns began to grow on Africa's east coast. Indian and Arab merchants brought their goods to trade with Africans from the interior. The Africans of the east coast had their own traditions and language, called Swahili (swah HEE lee), from the Arabic word for "coast."

Through the eastern ports, new crops from Asia—yams, sweet potatoes, and taro—were introduced to Africa. Over time these crops spread to the Bantu-speaking regions. So did techniques for making iron tools, which made it possible to clear the forested land for farming.

Gold was the source of wealth of the ancient West African kingdoms.

An African marketplace today holds hints of traditional cultures.

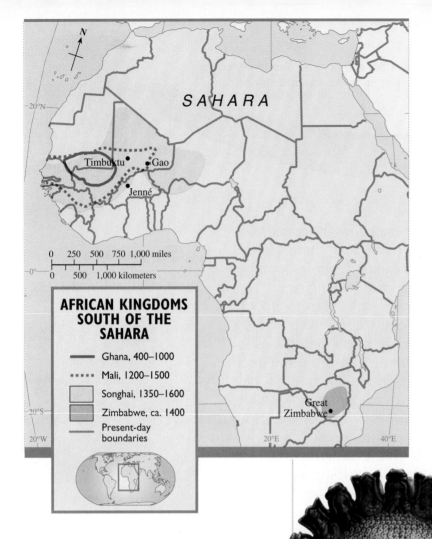

AFRICAN KINGDOMS SOUTH OF THE SAHARA

- Ghana, 400–1000
- Mali, 1200–1500
- Songhai, 1350–1600
- Zimbabwe, ca. 1400
- Present-day boundaries

Because sub-Saharan Africa is so large and geographically diverse, it has never come under the rule of a single empire. Instead, different parts of this vast region have had their own political histories. No single society identified itself as African. People identified themselves as members of a family, a clan, or a chiefdom.

The Desert Highway

From the time of the Roman Empire, trading caravans crossed the Sahara. The Bantu-speaking people had valuable resources to use in trade, such as gold, ivory, and kola nuts, which were used in medicine. In return the Mediterranean traders offered cloth, iron, horses, and salt, which was used in preserving food.

Strong African leaders and groups arose to control the Saharan trade. The first sub-Saharan African kingdom had its beginnings in this way. It was called Ghana, and its location is shown on the map. You will read more about the kingdom of Ghana and other kingdoms on pages 254–255.

After about A.D. 700 the Muslim empire had spread along the north African coast. Camels from Arabia made the trip across the Sahara easier. And Muslim traders brought more than goods—they introduced the religion of Islam to West Africa.

◀ This ivory mask of the queen mother was carved for the king. Her crown and necklace portray Portuguese traders.

Over time the Bantu encountered other peoples—the Mbuti (um BOO-tee) and the Khoisan (KOI sahn). However, the Bantu outnumbered the other groups and had superior technology. The Mbuti and Khoisan could not overpower the Bantu. So these groups of people simply moved to parts of Africa that the Bantu did not want, such as the densest part of the rain forest and the Kalahari Desert of the south.

The Influence of Islam

In Ghana and in later kingdoms, Islam was an important influence. Muslim schools and universities were established in such African cities as Jenné, Gao (GAH oh), and Timbuktu (tihm buk TOO). Most of the people of West Africa are Muslims today.

In 1324, Mansa Musa (MAHN suh MOO suh), ruler of the West African kingdom of Mali, made a pilgrimage to Mecca. He took with him 60,000 people and 80 camel loads of gold dust. Throughout his journey he gave much of the gold dust away. When Mansa Musa returned to Mali, he brought many Muslim scholars and scientists.

European Contact

Starting around 1440, ships from Portugal began to venture south along the west coast of Africa. They were searching for a route around the African continent to Asia. Soon the Portuguese were trading with the Africans along the coast.

Before long, ships from other European countries were visiting West African ports. As you will read in later chapters, Europeans would eventually establish colonies in most of Africa. At first, however, they came to trade. And one item high on everyone's shopping list was enslaved people.

Traditionally, Africans had made slaves of prisoners taken in warfare. These people became part of the communities in which they lived, and they could work to buy their freedom. Now, however, they became another commodity to be traded.

▼ The fame of Mansa Musa, a West African ruler, spread to Europe. His picture appeared on a map from the 1300s.

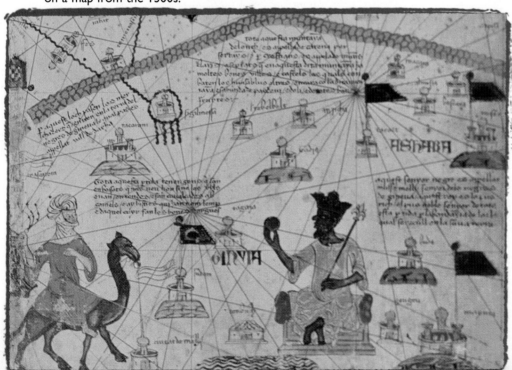

SHOW WHAT YOU KNOW!

REFOCUS
COMPREHENSION

1. If you could fold Africa in half along the equator, in what ways would the two halves be similar?

2. How did ancient African societies respond to changes in climate and increases in population?

THINK ABOUT IT
CRITICAL THINKING

How did a change in climate affect the region of the Sahara and influence the development of sub-Saharan Africa?

WRITE ABOUT IT
ACTIVITY

You want to become a griot for your community. How would you begin to collect stories about the history of your community?

Write a plan to organize your ideas. Tell where you would look, what you would collect, and to whom you would speak.

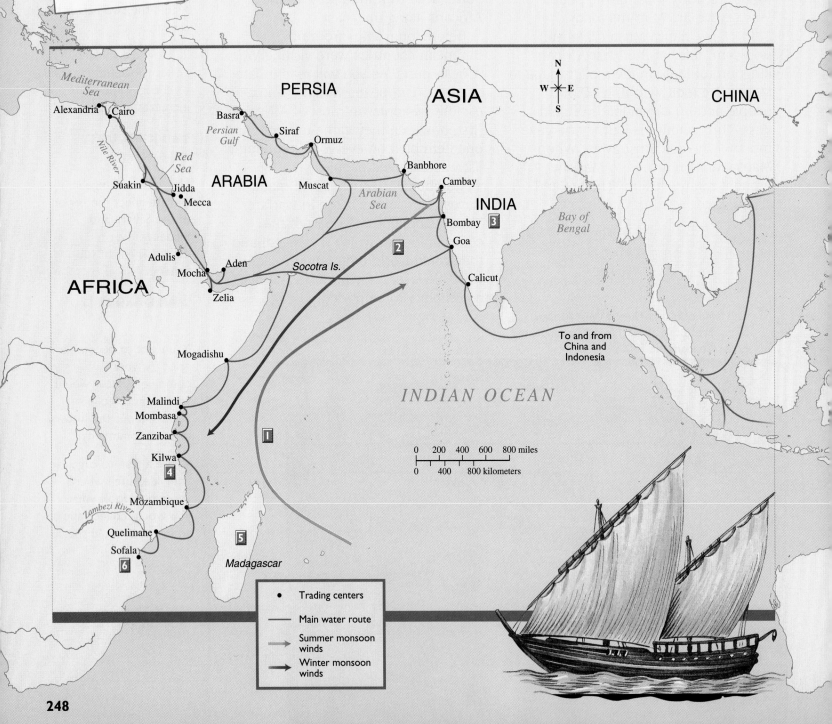

Map Adventure

KEY TERM

dhow

A WEALTH OF TRADE

FOCUS From the 1250s to the late 1400s, the coastal city-states of East Africa prospered from Indian Ocean trading. Predictable seasonal winds made transport across the Indian Ocean dependable and linked East Africa with Arabia, India, Persia, and China.

Mediterranean Sea

Alexandria Cairo

PERSIA

ASIA

CHINA

N
W · E
S

Basra

Persian Gulf

Siraf

Ormuz

Nile River

Red Sea

Suakin Jidda

ARABIA

Muscat

Banbhore

Arabian Sea

Cambay

INDIA

Bay of Bengal

Mecca

Bombay 3

2

Goa

Adulis Aden

Socotra Is.

Mocha

AFRICA

Zelia

Calicut

To and from China and Indonesia

Mogadishu

INDIAN OCEAN

Malindi

Mombasa

1

Zanzibar

0 200 400 600 800 miles

Kilwa

0 400 800 kilometers

4

Mozambique

Zambezi River

Quelimane

5

Sofala

6

Madagascar

- Trading centers
— Main water route
→ Summer monsoon winds
→ Winter monsoon winds

Adventure on the Indian Ocean!

The Indian Ocean is the third largest ocean in the world. Almost completely surrounded by land, its waters touch the coast of Africa in the west and the shores of Australia and Indonesia in the east. With its dependable seasonal winds, the Indian Ocean has been crisscrossed by trade routes for centuries.

Map Key

1 Summer monsoons From June to October, monsoon winds swept up the east coast of Africa and across the Indian Ocean to the western shores of India.

2 Winter monsoons During the winter months of November through April, strong monsoon winds from the northeast traveled southwest across the Indian Ocean to Africa.

3 India Every winter, merchants in India loaded their **dhows** with luxurious silks, cotton, carpets, Persian pottery, and Chinese jewels and spices to trade in East Africa. In the summer the dhows returned from Africa with ivory, gold, timber, copper, feathers, and animal hides.

4 Kilwa This city-state prospered as the base for trade with Sofala and Madagascar. South of Kilwa the monsoon winds weakened. Dhows that continued south risked missing the monsoon winds that would carry them home. So merchants in this area brought their goods to Kilwa to meet the dhows.

5 Madagascar Rice grown on this island was shipped to Kilwa and the city-states of the north.

6 Sofala Copper and gold from this area fetched a high price in India and China. They would be shipped up the coast to Kilwa and then across the Indian Ocean.

MAP IT

1. Suppose you are an Arab merchant living in Mombasa in the year 1350. In January a caravan arrives. You buy a large amount of ivory and timber, intending to trade them in the cities of India. How long will you have to wait before you can set sail? Why?

2. You finally head for India. How many miles will you travel before you land at Calicut?

3. When you arrive at the port of Calicut, a trader greets you warmly. He wants to show you the goods he has to exchange. What goods might you expect to see?

4. Although you have enjoyed your stay in India, you must return home with your new cargo. You intend to sell your foreign goods along the east African coast. When would be a good time to leave Calicut? What stops might you make before you reach Mombasa?

EXPLORE IT

You have prospered as a merchant and decide to retire in the year 1365. Realizing that other merchants could benefit from your experiences, you decide to write a guide for them. Write down some helpful hints, such as when to travel, where to go, what goods to look for, and how far important trading centers are from Mombasa.

★ **dhow** A small wooden ship used by traders

You Are There

★ **KEY TERMS**

lineage
polygamy
forge
initiation rite
status

HOW PEOPLE LIVE

FOCUS *Many values, customs, and beliefs are common to all African cultures south of the Sahara. All place great value on the family and other relationships between people.*

▼ Many traditions of the past are practiced by Africans today.

Your Big Family

As a young person living in Africa, you have been told that your village is part of the kingdom of Mali. However, this fact has little effect on your everyday life. Your place in the world is determined by the family you belong to. Your family is not only parents, brothers, and sisters but also an extended family of aunts, uncles, cousins, and grandparents.

In addition to your extended family, you are part of a **lineage** (LIHN ee ihj). For example, you feel a kinship and a closeness to more distant relatives, such as someone whose great-great-grandmother is the same as yours.

An even greater number of relationships exists within your clan. A clan is made up of several lineages that claim descent from a person who lived a very long time ago. The name of this person may not even be known. But you have been taught the name of your clan so that you can recognize others who belong to it.

▲ This brass palace decoration gives a glimpse of life in an early West African kingdom.

Since the person who founded your clan was a man, your family is traced back through your father. If the clan had been founded by a woman, your family identity would have come through your mother. In that case, your mother's brother would be head of your family.

These things are important, because families, lineages, and clans stick together. Their customs are similar, and they may call on

★ **lineage** All the people who share a common known ancestor

A family lives in a circle of huts. Some huts are for sleeping. Others are used for storing grain and supplies.

each other in times of need. On important occasions, families and lineages meet to celebrate and exchange gifts.

Your Parents

When your parents married, it was an important event. Their marriage joined both of their families together. Your father gave a gift, such as cattle, to your mother's family. This was to make up for the fact that they would be losing a worker.

Your father is not wealthy. He has only one wife—your mother. If he had been wealthy, he would probably have married other women, in addition to your mother.

Polygamy (puh LIHG uh mee) is accepted in most parts of Africa. Husbands are expected to treat all their wives equally well. Ideally the wives don't resent each other. Polygamy gives them someone to share the household chores with. The women can feel as close as sisters.

Your Village

Your village is a busy place. During the growing season, everyone works in the nearby fields. Men prepare new fields by cutting down trees and uprooting grass or other plants. Women plant the seeds, weed, and cultivate. When the harvest time comes, everybody shares the work.

Women do more than just harvest the crops. They carry water from a nearby river or stream, collect firewood, and prepare meals for their families. You can see why wives like more women to share the work!

Meals vary, depending on what is grown in your area. A big pot is used to make stews. Vegetables, such as yams, cassava (kuh SAH vuh) and manioc (MAN ee ahk) roots, and peanuts, are mixed with rice and sometimes chicken. In East Africa, people enjoy bananas, plantains, mangoes, and cucumbers. People along the coast have fish from the sea.

After crops have been harvested, there is time for people in your village to do other things. Skilled people weave cloth, make pottery, and **forge** iron farm tools and weapons. These manufactured goods are not only useful for the community. Along with any extra food, they can be traded for things your village does not have.

 polygamy The practice of having two or more spouses at the same time

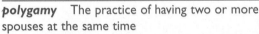 **forge** To shape metal by heating and pounding

251

The women take the trade goods to a marketplace in a larger town or city. Such marketplaces have a chief woman in charge. She regulates the trade and settles any disputes. The women will return to your village with salt, beads, and different foods.

Such a trip is a reminder of the larger world around you. Your village is part of a kingdom. One advantage of this is that your village will receive protection from robbers or invaders. The king or his counselors enforce laws and they judge disputes between villages.

Your people take pride in being part of a kingdom. You feel that if your king is healthy and strong, the kingdom will be, too. The king carries out ceremonies to honor the gods and the ancestors of the clans. You may learn of the kingdom's history by listening to griots.

Your Religion

In a traditional African society, religion is an important part of everyone's life. The central idea of your religion is that people should seek harmony among themselves and with the world around them. The life force that makes plants grow and birds sing is the same force that gives you life.

You believe that one god created the universe. Yet many lesser gods exist who can give help when you need it. Asking for rain when there is drought, asking for a good harvest, asking for protection in time of war—all these are messages you may send through the lesser gods.

One belief of your religion is that your community is more than just the

This Muslim mosque, built around 1200, was part of the kingdom of Mali.

These male teenagers have completed their initation rites into adulthood in a present-day African culture.

In many African cultures today, when girls become women they are allowed to wear elaborate necklaces and earrings.

people who live in it. Your ancestors are also part of it. At a shrine in or near your home, you carry out rituals of respect and leave gifts for them.

You Become an Adult

Certain times in your life are regarded as very important to your community. One of these is your change from a child to an adult.

To become an adult, you must know the proper forms of politeness and the values and laws of your community. Some of these you have learned growing up. Now, you will also take part in special **initiation rites**.

There are separate rites for boys and girls. For a few days or even as long as a month, you will be isolated in your own hut. There, an adult man or woman will teach you secret rituals and tell you about the special roles of men and women.

Part of the initiation may involve having cuts made in your skin. When they heal, raised scars are left behind. The pattern of the scars is a mark of your membership in the community.

During the initiation your hair is re-styled as an adult's. You may also receive new clothing and jewelry. These are outward signs of your new **status**. They are also signals that you are now eligible to marry.

Afterward, you stride proudly through the village. You are now a full-fledged adult member of the community. Your childhood is behind you, and you will now take part in farming, hunting, politics, and trade.

★ *initiation rite* The period of instruction and the ceremony with which a person is admitted into a group
status Position, rank, or standing in a group

SHOW WHAT YOU KNOW!

REFOCUS
COMPREHENSION

1. Draw a diagram of circles to show the important relationships among African people. Label your diagram.

2. How do the roles of men and women differ in African villages?

THINK ABOUT IT
CRITICAL THINKING

Initiation rites help African children become adults. How does this compare with the way children become adults in American society today?

WRITE ABOUT IT
ACTIVITY

An old African proverb says: "Kingdoms may come and go, but the family endures." Write a description of a favorite member of your family or extended family. Give reasons why this person is special to you.

March of Time
———
100
TO
1600

GREAT KINGDOMS

FOCUS *The kingdoms of sub-Saharan Africa used the wealth and knowledge gained from trading with countries to the north and developed great cities, architecture, and works of art.*

THE GREAT ZIMBABWE

The first European explorers to find the Great Zimbabwe (zihm BAH bway), or "stone house," arrived in Africa in 1868. The Europeans were awe-struck by this vast complex of stone walls and buildings.

At the time of the Europeans' arrival, the civilization that built the Great Zimbabwe had thrived for at least 1,000 years. Kings of the region were called Mwene Mutapa and the kingdom took its name from them.

Scientists have found about 400 other stone structures like the Great Zimbabwe in southeastern Africa. They were all built with granite stones chiseled so precisely that no mortar was needed to hold them together.

The Great Zimbabwe itself is the largest. It served as a royal court, a temple, a fortress, and a craft center.

GHANA

Called the Land of Gold by Muslim scholars, Ghana was the first of the great kingdoms of West Africa. Ghana lasted from about A.D. 300 to the 1200s. At the peak of its power, around 1000, the kingdom extended over an area of about 250,000 square miles.

The source of Ghana's wealth was its position on two main trading routes. One led north across the Sahara to the Muslim nations of North Africa. The other extended east to the African state of Bornu (BAWR noo). Goods flowed through Bornu from as far away as the Nile River valley.

Ghana's trade secret was the source of the gold that Muslim traders wanted. It came from mines in the forest kingdoms to the south. The ruler of Ghana profited by levying import and export taxes on the traders in the capital. His power rested on an army of 240,000 men. A Spanish Muslim reported that the king of Ghana "sits in a pavilion around which stand ten horses with gold-embroidered trappings. . . . The door of the pavilion is guarded by dogs . . . who wear collars of gold and silver."

Though Ghana allowed Muslims to freely practice their religion, Moroccan warriors invaded the empire in 1076. They were eventually turned back, but the weakened empire broke up into smaller states.

ca. 100
Work begins on the Great Zimbabwe

ca. 300
The kingdom of Ghana emerges

1230
Sundiata rules Mali

1492
Songhai control Timbuktu

1591
War destroys the Songhai empire

100   300   1200   1500

SONGHAI

After Mansa Musa's death, the Mali kingdom began to decline. By 1492 the Songhai (sawng gye) people had captured Timbuktu and conquered most of Mali.

The most brilliant emperor of the Songhai was Askia Muhammad. He built schools and universities. Like Mansa Musa, Askia also made a hajj to Mecca. He based his administration of the kingdom on Muslim law and government. He divided the empire into provinces under local governors. The governors reported to four viceroys, and a chief lieutenant supervised the viceroys. Everyone was responsible to the emperor.

In 1591 a Moroccan army invaded the Songhai empire. Years of warfare destroyed the trade network, and the empire gradually broke up into independent city-states. The great era of West African kingdoms was over.

CHIEF LIEUTENANT

VICEROYS

GOVERNORS

MALI

In the early 1200s a powerful warrior named Sundiata established a new kingdom in West Africa. Called Mali, this kingdom eventually grew to be twice the size of Ghana.

As Mali grew in strength, North African countries began to reestablish the Saharan trade routes that had once led to Ghana. The kingdom of Mali became wealthy by controlling the trade between the north and the south. Sundiata also encouraged his people to plant crops of millet, rice, and cotton so that they would not be dependent on trade alone.

The greatest king of Mali was Mansa Musa, whom you read about earlier. The scholars he brought back from Mecca established schools and mosques.

Timbuktu became the center of trade in Mali. It was a city of learning, with its own university. Caravans criss-crossed the Sahara, carrying dyes, cloth, weavings, crops, and gold, copper, and silver artifacts.

TIMBUKTU OR BUST

REFOCUS
COMPREHENSION

1. How did the West African kingdoms profit from keeping the source of their gold a secret?

2. How was the Sahara of long ago like a highway?

THINK ABOUT IT
CRITICAL THINKING

How did Askia Muhammad's methods of governing help him to rule over the large empire of Songhai?

WRITE ABOUT IT
ACTIVITY

You are a member of one of the first European groups to visit a kingdom of West Africa. Write a letter home that will convince the rest of your family to join you there.

5

★ **Connections**

KEY TERMS

work song
spiritual

AFRICA: THE MUSIC MAKER

FOCUS *One of the greatest impacts of African cultures on the world has been in music. African and European musical ideas blended to create jazz, the blues, gospel, and rock.*

A Gift of Music

The European slave trade greatly affected Africa, but it also had far-reaching effects on the Americas as well. As Africans were forcibly brought to the Americas, they carried their culture with them.

Music is one of the outstanding examples of the influence of African culture. The chart on page 257 traces the changes in African music in the United States from the 1600s to the present. African music has four major elements that can be found in modern American music styles.

The first major element of African music is call-and-response, in which a leader sings a line to which the audience responds. In the United States, this kind of music was first sung by enslaved people in **work songs**. Later it was adopted for **spirituals**. In the late 1800s, black choral groups popularized spirituals throughout the United States.

The second major element is improvisation, in which musicians create variations on the music as they play. Jazz, which makes frequent use of improvisation, developed among black musicians in New Orleans around 1900. As African Americans migrated north, they brought jazz to urban areas.

The third element is a focus on complex bass rhythms. In Africa, drums carried the bass rhythm. This tradition of drumming has continued

▼ The singers in the group Sweet Honey in the Rock are musical storytellers. They perform using traditional African instruments.

★ **work song** A song sung to match the rhythm of the work
spiritual A religious folk song

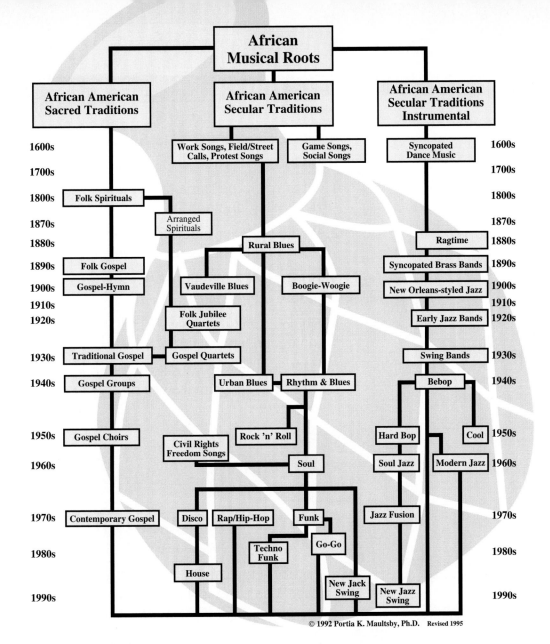

African Musical Roots				
African American Sacred Traditions	**African American Secular Traditions**		**African American Secular Traditions Instrumental**	
1600s	Work Songs, Field/Street Calls, Protest Songs	Game Songs, Social Songs	Syncopated Dance Music	1600s
1700s				1700s
1800s — Folk Spirituals				1800s
1870s	Arranged Spirituals			1870s
1880s	Rural Blues		Ragtime	1880s
1890s — Folk Gospel			Syncopated Brass Bands	1890s
1900s — Gospel-Hymn	Vaudeville Blues	Boogie-Woogie	New Orleans-styled Jazz	1900s
1910s				1910s
1920s	Folk Jubilee Quartets		Early Jazz Bands	1920s
1930s — Traditional Gospel	Gospel Quartets		Swing Bands	1930s
1940s — Gospel Groups	Urban Blues	Rhythm & Blues	Bebop	1940s
1950s — Gospel Choirs	Rock 'n' Roll	Hard Bop	Cool	1950s
1960s	Civil Rights Freedom Songs	Soul	Soul Jazz	Modern Jazz	1960s
1970s — Contemporary Gospel	Disco	Rap/Hip-Hop	Funk	Jazz Fusion	1970s
1980s	House	Techno Funk	Go-Go		1980s
1990s		New Jack Swing	New Jazz Swing	1990s

© 1992 Portia K. Maultsby, Ph.D.   Revised 1995

in many forms of music. But today's rock-and-roll musicians also use electric guitars and keyboards to create the pounding bass beat.

The fourth element is the use of vocal sounds, such as grunts and squeals, to imitate the sounds of nature. Vocalization is an important part of blues music, which developed among nineteenth-century African Americans in rural areas. You can hear it in the songs of modern rhythm-and-blues singers, such as the legendary James Brown and Aretha Franklin. Jazz and rock musicians also use brass and percussion instruments to imitate vocal sounds.

Africans brought their musical traditions to the Caribbean islands, where they influenced such musical forms as reggae (REG ay), rumba, and ska. In recent years, rap and hip-hop music developed among youth in urban areas. They make use of the same African roots that inspired so many other forms of American music.

SUMMING UP

1 DO YOU REMEMBER...
COMPREHENSION

1. What landforms are north and south of the African rain forests?

2. What determines the seasons in Africa?

3. How has the Sahara region been changing for thousands of years?

4. For what purpose did the first strong leaders and groups arise in sub-Saharan Africa?

5. When did Europeans begin to venture down the African coast to trade?

6. What goods were carried to India from Africa?

7. How did the status of a young African change after undergoing initiation rites?

8. What was the main source of wealth of the empire of Ghana?

9. What were the original purposes of the Great Zimbabwe?

10. What are four major elements of African music found in modern American musical styles?

2 SKILL POWER
USING A WORLD ATLAS

Use the Atlas on pages 608–628 to list the modern-day countries in Africa that the equator crosses. Also list the modern-day countries that are along Africa's Atlantic, or western, coast.

3 WHAT DO YOU THINK?
CRITICAL THINKING

1. What might be some disadvantages of depending on griots?

2. Would trade have developed between Africa and Asia without the monsoon winds?

3. How might a traditional African describe the phrase *family values*?

4. Do you think the great African kingdoms were too dependent on trade? Explain.

5. Tell how some of your favorite modern American songs make use of African musical elements.

4 SAY IT, WRITE IT, USE IT
VOCABULARY

Describe a typical day in a traditional sub-Saharan village. Use at least six of the vocabulary terms in your description of what the villagers do and see.

contiguous

counselor

dhow

forge

griot

initiation rite

lineage

monsoon

polygamy

savanna

shifting cultivation

spiritual

status

till

work song

5 GEOGRAPHY AND YOU
MAP STUDY

Find the Great Rift Valley on the map of Africa on page 242. Notice that three mountains are labeled in this area. Read about geographic rifts in an encyclopedia. What effect do rifts have on the areas around them? Does this explain why Africa's highest mountains are near the Great Rift Valley?

6 TAKE ACTION
CITIZENSHIP

One of the purposes of traditional African initiation rites was to teach young people the proper forms of politeness. Being polite to our fellow citizens—even if we don't know them—makes life much more pleasant for everyone. With a group of classmates, talk about instances in which strangers have been polite or impolite to you in public places. Use your discussion to come up with a list of public politeness guidelines that you think all people should follow.

7 GET CREATIVE
MUSIC CONNECTION

With a group of classmates, sing and perform a series of musical numbers that show the influences of African traditions. Using instruments and voices, try to perform examples of spirituals, blues, jazz, and rock that illustrate the four elements described in "Africa: The Music Maker" on pages 256–257. If possible, include the original music of some group members. Before each piece, one member of the group should describe the African influences that the audience will hear.

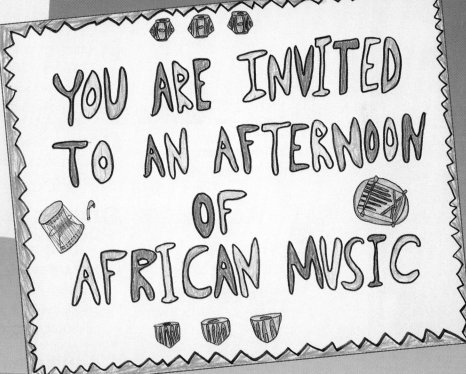

YOU ARE INVITED TO AN AFTERNOON OF AFRICAN MUSIC

LOOKING AHEAD In Chapter 12, learn about the similarities and differences between the empires of China and India.

EXAMINE

THE NEW EMPIRES

You have learned about the great civilizations of ancient China and India. Now you are going to learn how invaders changed these civilizations and were changed by them.

Can you guess what tradition this girl is continuing? Look at page 274 to find the answer.

CONTENTS

OF CHINA AND INDIA

These books tell about some people, places, and events that make China and India so interesting. Read one that interests you and fill out a book-review form.

READ AND RESEARCH

The People Who Hugged the Trees **adapted by Deborah Lee Rose** (Roberts Rinehart Publishers, 1990)
Long ago in India, Amrita and others in her village knew that the trees protected them and gave them shade. What happened when Prince Maharajah ordered that the trees be chopped down? (*folk tale*)

Exploration Into China **by Wang Tao** (New Discovery Books, 1995)
The Chinese invention of the compass allowed navigation by early Chinese and European explorers. In this book you can read about Zheng He, who sailed with a fleet of treasure ships in the name of the emperor. (*nonfiction*)

Kublai Khan **by Kim Dramer** (Chelsea House Publishers, 1990)
Cunning tactics and fierce fighting skills made the Mongols a nightmare for all of Asia. Kublai Khan, a descendant of the ruthless Genghis Khan, crushed all in his path and obtained such wealth that descriptions of it by Marco Polo were barely believed by Europeans. (*nonfiction*)

Sold! The Origins of Money and Trade **by the Geography Department of Runestone Press** (Runestone Press, 1994)
Early coins reflect the history of ancient times. The Chinese used tiny tools as coins, and they were the first to use paper money. You'll find more exciting facts about money in this book. (*nonfiction*)

SKILL POWER

Using Scale to Compute Travel Time

Finding the distance between places on a map will help you figure out the travel time from one place to another.

UNDERSTAND IT

"How long until we get there?" is a question that you probably ask many times when you are traveling by car. If the people you are with have taken the trip before, they probably can answer your question by using what they know from earlier trips. If they have not taken the trip before, the answer may be based on their ability to use maps to compute time and distance.

EXPLORE IT

You can use a map and a ruler or piece of string to figure out the distance between two places. If the route is straight, just measure the distance with a ruler and compare it with the map scale. If the route twists and turns, use a piece of string. For example, to find the distance along the Ganges River between Kanpur and Patna, place a piece of string so that it begins in the city of Kanpur and follows the Ganges River to Patna. Before you lift the string, put a mark on it next to Patna.

Next, place the string on the map scale and find where the mark for Patna meets the map scale. You will see that the distance between Kanpur and Patna along the Ganges River is about 400 miles.

To figure out how long it would take a traveler to walk along the Ganges River from Kanpur to Patna, you need to know how far the traveler can walk each day. If the traveler can walk 20 miles in a day, divide 400 by 20. The trip will take 20 days. How long would it take if the traveler can walk 15 miles each day?

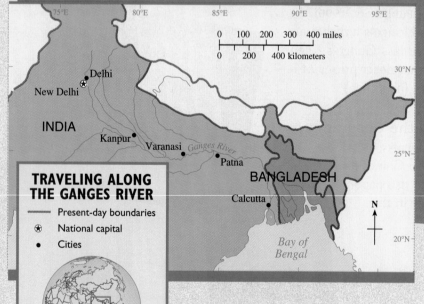

TRAVELING ALONG THE GANGES RIVER

— Present-day boundaries
⊛ National capital
• Cities

TRY IT

Sit back and think about the trip of your dreams. Find maps of places you would like to go to, and figure out what your travel time will be. If your trip takes you on major highways, figure the rate of travel at 65 miles per hour. If you are taking scenic back roads, use 35 miles per hour. Combine your plans with those of your classmates to make a class travel catalog.

SKILL POWER SEARCH

In this chapter you will see maps of ancient China and India. Use what you know about computing travel time to help you understand the difficulties of traveling great distances.

CHINA AND INDIA IN THE MIDDLE CENTURIES

FOCUS *Mongol conquerors brought changes to the traditional cultures of China and India.*

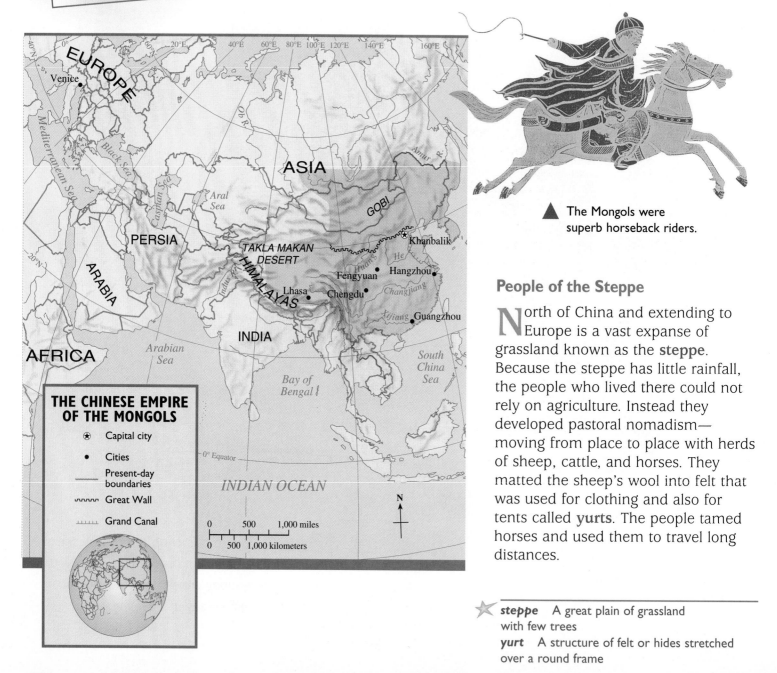

▲ The Mongols were superb horseback riders.

THE CHINESE EMPIRE OF THE MONGOLS

⬥ Capital city

• Cities

— Present-day boundaries

〰 Great Wall

⋯ Grand Canal

0   500   1,000 miles
0   500 1,000 kilometers

People of the Steppe

North of China and extending to Europe is a vast expanse of grassland known as the **steppe**. Because the steppe has little rainfall, the people who lived there could not rely on agriculture. Instead they developed pastoral nomadism—moving from place to place with herds of sheep, cattle, and horses. They matted the sheep's wool into felt that was used for clothing and also for tents called **yurts**. The people tamed horses and used them to travel long distances.

⭐ **steppe** A great plain of grassland with few trees

yurt A structure of felt or hides stretched over a round frame

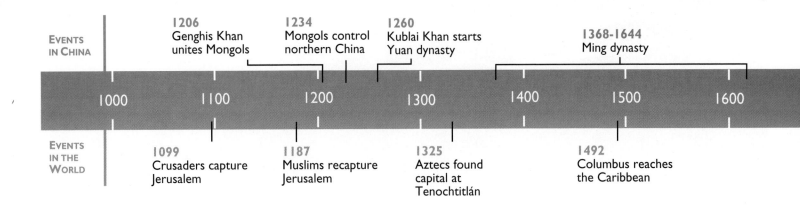

EVENTS IN CHINA

1206 Genghis Khan unites Mongols

1234 Mongols control northern China

1260 Kublai Khan starts Yuan dynasty

1368-1644 Ming dynasty

1000 1100 1200 1300 1400 1500 1600

EVENTS IN THE WORLD

1099 Crusaders capture Jerusalem

1187 Muslims recapture Jerusalem

1325 Aztecs found capital at Tenochtitlán

1492 Columbus reaches the Caribbean

Pastoral nomadism was not a primitive way of life. Nomads lived in close harmony with the very fragile land they inhabited. They had to figure out a way to make a living from the land without destroying it. Their solution was to establish a pattern of **seasonal migration**. Nomadic peoples moved regularly, occupying an area for a short time, when its productivity was high. When the seasons changed, the nomads moved to another site.

Genghis Khan

Nomadic society was organized around the tribe, which was based on kinship. In 1206 a nomadic group called the Mongols united around a tribal prince named Temujin (TEM yuh-jun). He took the name *Genghis* (GENG-gihs) *Khan,* which means "universal ruler." That name definitely described his goal. As the leader of the Mongols, Genghis Khan commanded the most powerful military force of his time and was known for his brutality.

Under Genghis's command, the Mongols fought in China, Korea,

▼ Genghis Khan and his heirs made brutal conquests that gave them control of vast Asian lands.

central Asia, Persia, Russia, and the Middle East. At his death in 1227, the campaigns for control of Persia and northern China were only beginning. His sons continued the fight.

The Mongols brought northern China under their control in 1234. The devastation caused by the Mongol invasion was enormous. In parts of China, as much as 90 percent of the population disappeared. Some fled, but many were killed in the fighting or died in the famines or plagues. Many areas did not recover for centuries.

Kublai Khan

The conquest of southern China was led by Kublai (KOO bleye) Khan, the grandson of Genghis. Kublai had received a Chinese education and was surrounded by advisors who admired Chinese civilization. In 1260, while planning the southern campaign, Kublai proclaimed himself emperor of the Yuan or "original" dynasty, which would rule China until 1368. The map shows the wide extent of the Mongol Empire.

★ **seasonal migration** The moving of herds of animals from pasture to pasture according to the seasons of the year

Kublai and his successors never really became Chinese. The Mongols remained foreign occupiers, and neither they nor the Chinese ever forgot it. Few Chinese people served in the Yuan government. Instead Yuan rulers found their advisors in central Asia and even in Europe. In addition, different systems of taxation and laws were applied to the Mongols and the Chinese.

The Mongols organized a massive restoration of the Grand Canal, the link between cities on the Huang and Chang rivers. Thousands of Chinese were forced to work on the project. Soon after the work was completed, peasants throughout the south rebelled. In 1368 a Chinese peasant named Zhu Yuanzhang (joo yooen-JAHNG) overthrew the Mongols and established the Ming dynasty.

The Ming Dynasty

The third Ming ruler built a new capital at Beijing, much larger than the Yuan capital had been. In the northern part of the city was the Forbidden City. It contained the homes of the emperors and their families. Only members of the royal household and government were permitted inside its walls.

During the Ming dynasty, great economic and cultural strides were made. New forms of literature such as the novel became popular. Ming rulers made extraordinary efforts to improve the country's agriculture, build and repair reservoirs, plant forests, and establish an efficient way of governing. However, following a series of bad harvests and weak rulers, Ming rule collapsed in 1644.

▲ Today the Forbidden City and its treasures are no longer closed to outsiders.

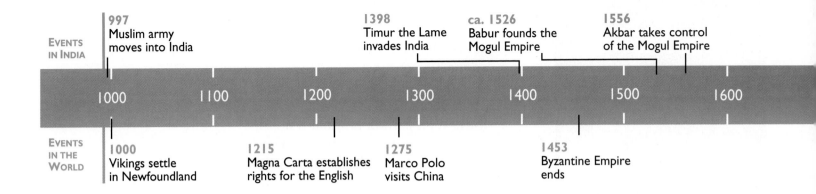

EVENTS
IN INDIA

997
Muslim army
moves into India

1398
Timur the Lame
invades India

ca. 1526
Babur founds the
Mogul Empire

1556
Akbar takes control
of the Mogul Empire

1000   1100   1200   1300   1400   1500   1600

EVENTS
IN THE
WORLD

1000
Vikings settle
in Newfoundland

1215
Magna Carta establishes
rights for the English

1275
Marco Polo
visits China

1453
Byzantine Empire
ends

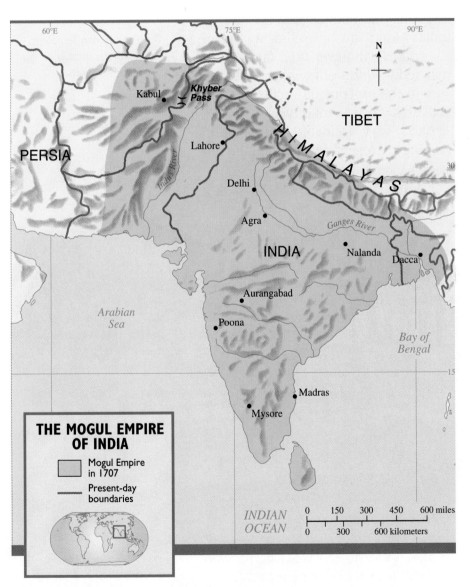

**THE MOGUL EMPIRE
OF INDIA**

Mogul Empire
in 1707

Present-day
boundaries

Change Comes to India

The rise of Islam in the Middle East led to great changes in India. Muslim invasions into the heartland of India began at the end of the tenth century. In 997, Sultan Mahmud (MAHK mood) of Ghazni (GAHZ nee), a Muslim Turk, sent an army through the Khyber (KEYE bur) Pass, which you can find on the map.

At the time, India was divided into many Hindu states. There was little organized resistance. The Muslim invaders swept aside the native rulers in the north and set up a Muslim state. Hindus did not regain control of the Ganges Valley until 1947. They never recovered the Indus Valley, which is today part of Pakistan.

The Muslims in India were intolerant of other religions. They destroyed Nalanda, the center of Buddhist learning in India. Hinduism, with its many gods and religious sculptures, offended the monotheistic Muslims. Muslim warriors destroyed thousands of Hindu temples. Over time, the Muslim persecutions became less severe. Hindus and Muslims in northern India learned to coexist.

Babur, the founder of the Mogul dynasty, is shown in a garden.

This temporary peace collapsed when Timur the Lame, also known as Tamerlane, invaded India in 1398. You will learn more about Timur later in this chapter. Although Timur withdrew the following year, the devastation he caused weakened India. Once more, northern India was broken up into many small states.

Mogul Empire

Early in the sixteenth century, a new power arose in central Asia. This was a **confederation** led by Babur (BAH bur), a descendant of both Genghis Khan and Timur. In 1526 a Muslim chief in northwestern India unwisely asked Babur to help put down a Hindu rebellion. Babur conquered not only the rebels but also the chief who asked him for help. Babur, nicknamed the Tiger, founded what is considered

to be the greatest of the Muslim dynasties of India—the Mogul dynasty.

The most important Mogul ruler was Babur's grandson Akbar (AK bahr), who took control of the empire in 1556, when he was only 13. During his 50 years of rule, the Mogul Empire spread across northern and central India, extending into Afghanistan.

Akbar reached out to the Hindu community, ending the cultural divisions that had plagued northern India. Akbar saw himself as a ruler of all Indians, whatever their faith. He married a Hindu princess and put a stop to the practice of forcibly converting prisoners of war.

Akbar was fascinated by religion, inviting representatives of all faiths to

The Golden Temple in northern India is a holy place for Sikhs.

confederation Groups joined together for a specific purpose; a league or alliance

his court. He even let Jesuits come from Europe to defend Christianity.

The Religion of the Sikhs

A new religion arose in India at this time. In the fifteenth century, Guru Nanak (GOO roo NAHN uk), a wandering holy man, preached that all people were brothers and sisters. He denounced all forms of inequality, including the caste system. He stated, "There is no Hindu, no Muslim," and he tried to combine the best features of both religions. Guru Nanak asked his followers—known as Sikhs (seeks), or "disciples"—to find the truth within themselves.

At first the Sikh religion was a peaceful one. Later, however, Mogul rulers began to torture and kill Sikhs. To defend

Akbar met with people of his empire in formal meetings called audiences.

themselves, Sikhs became more **militant**. They took the name *Singh* which means "lion."

Decline of Mogul Rule

Akbar's successors failed to understand the importance of Hindu and Muslim harmony. They went back to the policy of persecution. Aurangzeb (OR eng zeb) made discriminatory laws against Hindus. You will read more about him later in this chapter.

Later Mogul rulers increased the size of their empire. At the height of Mogul power, the emperor controlled a very large area, which was costly even in times of peace. But attacks against Hindus brought on rebellions and cost an enormous amount of money.

At the same time, Europeans became a growing presence. The British gradually replaced the Moguls as rulers of India after 1707.

 militant   Ready and willing to fight in support of a cause

SHOW WHAT YOU KNOW!

REFOCUS
COMPREHENSION

1. How did the fragile land of the steppes affect the way in which people lived there?

2. How did Akbar's fascination with religion help the people of northern India?

THINK ABOUT IT
CRITICAL THINKING

Compare life in China under Kublai Khan and his successors with life in India during the rule of Akbar.

WRITE ABOUT IT
ACTIVITY

You are a Sikh follower of Guru Nanak. Write a letter to a friend, describing how your beliefs help you get along with people.

269

WHO SITS ON THE THRONE?

FOCUS *Rulers of the Chinese and Indian civilizations came to power in a variety of ways.*

EMPEROR ZHU YUANZHANG

Zhu Yuanzhang, the founder of the Ming dynasty, was nicknamed the Beggar King because he came from a humble background. Orphaned as a child, Zhu had to beg for a living.

China was in a perilous condition, and revolution was in the air. Zhu organized his own band of rebels. They joined the Red Turbans, a group that was trying to overthrow the Mongols.

Zhu and his followers captured Nanjing in 1356, making Zhu one of the most powerful leaders in central China. It took him 12 more years to put down all opposition to his rule. He took the title of emperor in 1368.

For his dynasty he chose the name *Ming,* which means "bright" or "brilliant." Remembering his own years of poverty, he set out to help the poorest Chinese. He established elementary schools in villages all over the country. His government took land from the wealthy and distributed it to landless peasants, along with seeds, tools, and farm animals.

Zhu ruled for 30 years. As he grew older, he became very suspicious. He executed many of his faithful followers, and took virtually all power for himself alone.

TIMUR THE LAME

Timur the Lame was born about 50 miles south of Samarkand, a city along the Silk Road. He began as a sheep rustler. On one of his forays, he ran into trouble and received the injury that gave him his nickname.

Timur organized a band of rustlers into a military force. He called himself the Scourge of God. Those who were in his path probably would have agreed.

Everywhere he went, he left destruction and death in his wake. His most famous calling card was the pyramid of human skulls he left in front of destroyed cities. He spared only artists and craftworkers, who were carried off to beautify his capital, Samarkand.

In 1398, Timur swooped down on India. Leading a cavalry of almost 100,000 men, he seized Delhi. He slaughtered almost all the inhabitants. "Towers were built high with the heads [of the dead] and their bodies were left to the beasts and birds of prey." Timur died in 1405 on his way to conquer China.

1368
Zhu Yuanzhang
becomes emperor
of Ming dynasty

1398
Timur the Lame
invades India

1605–1627
Jahangir rules
India

1658
Aurangzeb crowned
emperor of
Mogul Empire

1350   1400   1450   1500   1550   1600   1650

NUR JAHAN

A beautiful widow named Mehrunissa married Jahangir (juh HAHN geer), who ruled India from 1605 to 1627. He called her *Nur Jahan*, which means "Light of the World." A Persian, she had come to India as a baby with her parents. Her father was an official in Akbar's government, eventually becoming the prime minister. Nur Jahan's niece, Mumtaz Mahal, for whom the Taj Mahal was built, married Jahangir's son. The family brought the best of Persian culture to the court.

As time went on, Jahangir himself lost interest in governing. He preferred hunting and collecting miniature paintings, which are among the cultural glories of Mogul India. Gradually, Nur Jahan assumed his duties and became the power behind the throne. According to a contemporary, "Her authority reached such a peak that the king was such in name only."

AURANGZEB

Aurangzeb, the great-grandson of Akbar, ruled the Mogul Empire from 1658 to 1707. When he was a young man, Aurangzeb served as a provincial governor. During this time, he proved himself a skilled military leader as well. When his father, Shah Jahan, became ill, Aurangzeb won out over his brothers in the fight to take over his father's throne.

In 1658, Aurangzeb crowned himself emperor. He took the title *Alamgir* (AHL um geer), which means "conqueror of the world." It was not a vain boast. Under his leadership the Mogul Empire expanded to its greatest extent. But the wars shrank the treasury and destroyed the Indian lands on which the battles were fought.

Unfortunately, Aurangzeb was a religious fanatic. He persecuted the Hindu population. He levied special taxes on them and restricted their religious festivals. In some places, Hindu temples and shrines were destroyed. These policies sowed the seeds of the hatred that can still divide Muslims and Hindus in India today.

REFOCUS
COMPREHENSION

1. How did Zhu Yuanzhang help the poorest Chinese?

2. What did people mean when they called Nur Jahan "the power behind the throne"?

THINK ABOUT IT
CRITICAL THINKING

Why did Timur the Lame leave human skulls in front of destroyed cities?

WRITE ABOUT IT
ACTIVITY

Make a list with two columns, one labeled *Good Policies* and the other labeled *Bad Policies*. Fill in what you think are the good things and the bad things about Aurangzeb and his rule of the Mogul Empire.

Connections

KEY TERMS

yamb
water clock

MARCO POLO IN CHINA

FOCUS *Marco Polo described a way of life so different from that of the Europeans that they couldn't believe his stories.*

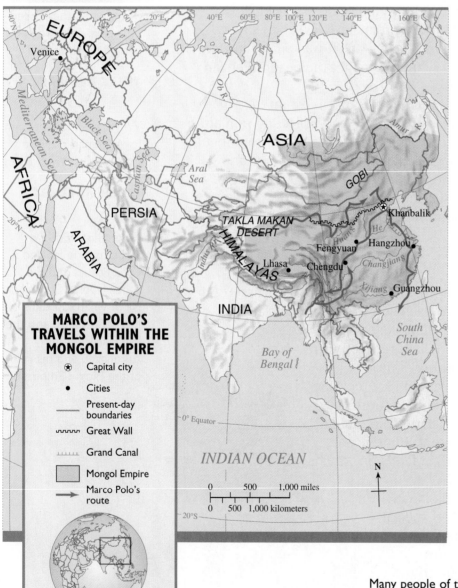

MARCO POLO'S TRAVELS WITHIN THE MONGOL EMPIRE

⊛ Capital city
• Cities
— Present-day boundaries
〜〜 Great Wall
⋯⋯ Grand Canal
▭ Mongol Empire
➝ Marco Polo's route

Marco Polo's Journey

In the year 1298, Marco Polo was taken prisoner during a war between the Italian cities of Venice and Genoa. While in prison, Polo met another captive who was a writer. Polo began to relate a fabulous story—so good that the writer eagerly began to copy it down.

The story that Marco Polo dictated seemed almost impossible to believe. He described his journey across Asia to the court of the emperor Kublai Khan. Polo claimed to have spent 25 years traveling through China and neighboring countries with his father and uncle.

Among other things, Polo reported that the Chinese used paper money and burned black stones for fuel. He said he had eaten nuts as big as a man's head. Europeans,

Many people of the time believed that Marco Polo's book told fanciful—not real—stories. ▶

who used only coins and didn't know about coal or coconuts, thought that the stories must have been made up.

Kublai Khan's Court

Marco Polo departed on his epic journey to the court of Kublai Khan in 1272, when he was 17 years old. After a journey of three years, Polo arrived at Kublai's summer palace at Shangdu. The map on page 272 shows Marco Polo's travels in China.

Polo quickly learned the Mongol language, and Kublai Khan took a liking to him. In the winter, when the court moved to Khanbalik (which is now Beijing), Polo went along. He described Kublai Khan's palace as "the most extensive that has ever yet been known." It covered an area of four square miles.

Kublai Khan was often bored by the details of governing. Among his amusements was hunting. Polo said he used lions to capture game.

It is an admirable sight, when the lion is let loose in pursuit of the animal, to observe the savage eagerness and speed with which he overtakes it. His Majesty has them conveyed for this purpose, in cages placed upon cars [wagons], and along with them is confined a little dog, with which they become familiar. The reason for thus shutting them up is that they would otherwise be so keen and furious at the sight of the game that it would be impossible to keep them under the necessary constraint.

A bank note is evidence that there was paper money in ancient China.

A water clock

Polo learned how Kublai Khan was able to keep informed of matters within his vast empire. "From the city of Khanbalik there are many roads leading to the different provinces," he reported. Every 25 to 30 miles along these roads was a **yamb**. The yambs were large and splendidly furnished. "Even kings may be lodged at these stations in a becoming manner," Polo said. He continued:

At each station 400 good horses are kept in constant readiness, in order that all messengers going and coming on the business of the Great Khan, and all ambassadors, may have relays, and, leaving their tired horses, be supplied with fresh ones.

The Wonders of China

Polo filled notebooks with the wonders he saw and the places he traveled. He marveled at the **water clocks** that were more accurate than the sundials he knew at home. He appreciated the beauty of the silken kites flown for pleasure by the ladies of the court.

Kublai Khan gave Polo a job that let him

yamb An inn and government station house along a busy road
water clock A device for measuring time by the flow of water

273

The fine workmanship of an ancient Chinese tapestry shows women flying kites.

travel through the empire. Polo visited Hangzhou, a magnificent city. Polo said that "its abundant delights . . . might lead an inhabitant to imagine himself in paradise."

Polo was overwhelmed by the variety of goods on sale in Hangzhou.

At all seasons there is in the markets a great variety of herbs and fruits, and especially pears of an extra-ordinary size, weighing ten pounds each, that are white in the inside, like paste, and have a very fragrant smell.

He said that the quantity of pepper on sale was a good indication of how much food was available. Each day, 43 loads of pepper were carried into the city. Each load weighed 243 pounds.

"In other streets," Polo said, "are the dwellings of the physicians and the astrologers, who also give instructions in reading and writing, as well as in many other arts."

Polo noticed that the streets of Hangzhou were paved with stone and bricks, as were all the major roads of the province. However, because the royal messengers used horses, which disliked traveling on brick roads, part of each road was left unpaved.

Carriages continually pass and repass. They are of a long shape, covered at the top, have curtains and cushions of silk, and are capable of holding six persons. Both men and women . . . are in the daily practice of hiring them, . . . and accordingly at every hour you may see vast numbers of them driven along the middle part of the street.

The Khan's Rules and Regulations

Kublai Khan's soldiers patrolled the streets of Hangzhou day and night. At a certain time of night, all fires and lights were supposed to be put out. If a

▲ Kublai Khan and his party of hunters

patroller saw a light, he would put a mark on the door of the house. In the morning the owner would be brought before a judge for punishment.

The people of Hangzhou resented such treatment, for it was a reminder that the Chinese had lost control of their country to the Mongols. Polo reported that the Mongol government kept careful track of each citizen.

Every father of a family, or housekeeper, is required to affix a writing to the door of his house, specifying the name of each individual of his family, whether male or female, as well as the number of his horses. When any person dies, or leaves the dwelling, the name is struck out, and upon the occasion of a birth, [that name] is added to the list.

Kubla Khan

In Xanadu did Kubla Khan
A stately pleasure-dome decree:
Where Alph, the sacred river, ran
Through caverns measureless to man
Down to a sunless sea.
So twice five miles of fertile ground
With walls and towers were girdled round . . .

Samuel Taylor Coleridge

▲ Part of a poem written in 1798

Polo's Story Lives On

Slowly, Europeans began to realize that Polo had told the truth. A 1375 atlas of the world used some of his information about Asia. Christopher Columbus read Polo's book before trying to reach China by sailing west.

The wonders of Kublai Khan's court have inspired poets and storytellers ever since. Today, historians regard Polo's book as one of the best sources of information on China 700 years ago. The story remains as fascinating as it seemed to Polo's prison companion.

SHOW WHAT YOU KNOW!

REFOCUS
COMPREHENSION

1. Why didn't people in Europe at first believe a prisoner's book about Marco Polo's adventures?

2. What are five things Marco Polo found in China that were new to Europeans?

THINK ABOUT IT
CRITICAL THINKING

What might have been Kublai Khan's reason for requiring that each house have a sign on the door naming the people who lived there?

WRITE ABOUT IT
ACTIVITY

Picture in your mind what it would be like to be a European visitor to China in the time of Marco Polo. Write a description of how you felt when you first saw something you had never seen before.

Spotlight

THE TAJ MAHAL

FOCUS *The Taj Mahal—a monument of love—is considered a masterpiece of the culture of Muslim India.*

▲ The Taj Mahal is a major tourist attraction in the city of Agra.

As you can see from this diagram, the Taj Mahal is actually four buildings. ▶

The Emperor's Grief

In 1631, Shah Jahan, the emperor of India, received tragic news. His beloved wife, Mumtaz Mahal, had died. Shah Jahan shut himself in his private chambers and refused to see anyone.

After eight days, Jahan emerged, determined to build a monument to Mumtaz that was "as beautiful as she was beautiful."

Jahan called for **architects** to submit designs for Mumtaz's **mausoleum** (maw suh LEE um). He rejected dozens of plans until he found one he liked. Shah Jahan thought the final plans were so beautiful that he honored the chief architect with the title *Nadir ul Asar*, which means "outstanding."

Building a Wonder

Artisans came to Agra from other cities in India, as well as Burma, Egypt, Ceylon, Persia, and even Europe. More than 20,000 men and women worked on the construction of the building.

A ramp of earth 10 miles long had to be built through Agra as a road for the construction materials. The 70-foot-high walls surrounding the building were made of red sandstone from nearby quarries. The white marble blocks for the tomb itself came from more than 200 miles away.

Once the marble blocks reached the work site on the banks of the Jumna (JUM nuh) River, they were hoisted into place by a pulley system powered by teams of mules and hundreds of human workers. Slowly the Taj Mahal started to rise: first the tomb, then the mosques that stand on either side, and finally the minarets that anchor the four corners. A huge garden with a reflecting pool stands in front of the buildings. The garden alone is longer than three football fields; the top of the dome is 243 feet above the garden. The distance around the entire complex is more than a mile.

Inside and out, the walls were elaborately decorated with inlaid jewels, beautiful calligraphy, and carved flowers. Caravans traveled there from China with jade, from Afghanistan with lapis lazuli, and from Tibet with turquoise. The Indian Ocean supplied the coral and the mother-of-pearl.

Shah Jahan must have watched the work with eager anticipation. After 22 years the mausoleum finally was completed.

The sight of the Taj Mahal has delighted visitors ever since. The marble casts a different spell at dawn, at noon, at dusk, and in the moonlight. Light filters into the dim interior where Mumtaz Mahal rests.

▲ Mumtaz Mahal and Shah Jahan

⭐ **architect**　A person who designs buildings and is in charge of their construction
mausoleum　A large tomb

SHOW WHAT YOU KNOW!

REFOCUS
COMPREHENSION

1. What was the job of the architect of the Taj Mahal?

2. What are the main parts of the Taj Mahal?

THINK ABOUT IT
CRITICAL THINKING

What purpose—other than being a monument showing his love for Mumtaz Mahal—might the building of the Taj Mahal have served for Shah Jahan?

WRITE ABOUT IT
ACTIVITY

Think of a person you love or admire. Write a description of a building, statue, painting, poem, or other memorial you would like to create for that person.

THE SEVEN VOYAGES OF ZHENG HE

FOCUS In the early 1400s the Chinese admiral Zheng He led seven trading voyages throughout Asia. Zheng He's ships sailed thousands of miles, displaying the wealth of China.

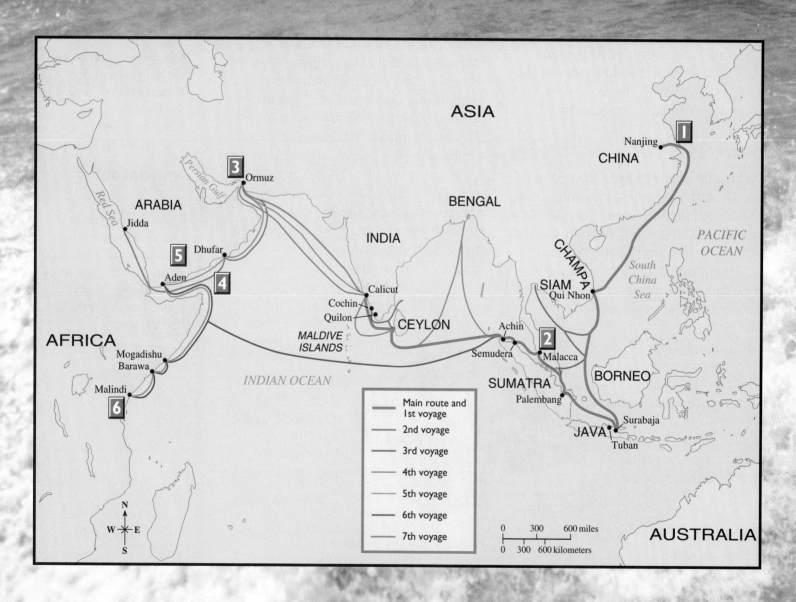

Adventure on a Chinese Treasure Ship

The treasure ships of Zheng He were some of the largest wooden vessels ever afloat. Scholars believe that they measured over 400 feet long and 160 feet wide, with square sails made from red silk. If the winds were favorable, they traveled 200 miles a day. The ships were brightly painted and had designs carved into the wood.

Map Key

1 **First Voyage** Zheng He's first fleet left Nanjing with 317 ships and over 27,000 people. His treasure ships carried Chinese porcelain, silk, and horses to trade. Most of the ships held food, water, and medicine for the long journey to India.

2 **Malacca** This city-state was located along the narrow Strait of Malacca (muh LAK uh). Zheng He built a fort here to store food and goods. Chinese fleets stopped at Malacca for supplies before sailing across the Indian Ocean.

3 **Fourth Voyage** On this voyage, Zheng He led 63 vessels and over 28,000 people. The fleet sailed as far as Ormuz. Here Zheng He met merchants from Africa and invited them to visit the Chinese emperor.

4 **Fifth Voyage** During this voyage the fleet visited Aden and the city-states of East Africa. The sultan of Aden gave the Chinese emperor lions, leopards, zebras, ostriches, white pigeons, and a giraffe.

5 **Seventh Voyage** This was the last voyage of China's treasure fleet. During this mission, the fleet visited the Arabian ports of Jidda and Dhufar and the East African city-states. Zheng He died on the return trip to China in 1433.

6 **Malindi** When the Portuguese explorer Vasco da Gama visited this city-state 66 years later in 1498, he heard rumors of strangers who wore silk and traveled in large ships.

MAP IT

1. You are a navigator on Zheng He's fifth voyage. You must keep track of the fleet's location and the distance it has traveled. Begin by locating Nanjing on the map.

2. Your first stop is at the port of Qui Nhon (kwee NYAWN) in Champa. While Zheng He is trading for ebony, you must write a status report. Through what sea did you pass? How far are you from Nanjing?

3. After leaving Champa, the fleet travels to Surabaja, Palembang, Semudera, and Achin. Where are these cities? How far from Nanjing are you?

4. After stopping in India and Ormuz, the fleet arrives in Aden. Zheng He has gone ashore to trade for pearls and you must update your report. Where did the fleet stop? How far have you traveled now?

5. From Aden the fleet turns southeast toward the cities of Mogadishu (moh guh DEE shoo), Barawa, and Malindi. Complete your report to Zheng He. How many miles have you covered? How many miles is it back to Nanjing? How far is the whole trip?

EXPLORE IT

It is 1433, and the seventh treasure fleet has just returned. Since Zheng He has died, the emperor has asked you to detail all of his voyages for the royal archives. Trace the route of each voyage. Where did each fleet stop? How far did each one travel?

★ **ebony** A dark, hard wood found in Asia

SUMMING UP

1 DO YOU REMEMBER...
COMPREHENSION

1. What was pastoral nomadism?

2. What was the goal of Genghis Khan?

3. Why wasn't India able to defend itself against Muslim invasions?

4. What was the Mogul Empire?

5. What did Kublai Khan accomplish?

6. What did Zhu Yuanzhang accomplish in China?

7. When did Marco Polo leave Europe for China?

8. According to Polo, how did Kublai Khan keep track of his vast empire?

9. Why was the Taj Mahal built?

10. What did Zheng He bring back to China on his fifth voyage?

2 SKILL POWER
USING SCALE TO COMPUTE TRAVEL TIME

Marco Polo traveled from Khanbalik to the city of Hangzhou. Find these two locations on the map on page 272, and use the scale of miles to figure out the distance between them. If Marco Polo covered 20 miles a day, how long would the trip have taken?

3 WHAT DO YOU THINK?
CRITICAL THINKING

1. How might the traditional lifestyle of the Mongols have helped them become skilled raiders and warriors?

2. How did the policies of some Mongol and Mogul rulers cause unrest in their empires?

3. Look at the water clock on page 273. Explain how people probably used it to keep track of time.

4. Do you think that building the Taj Mahal was a sensible decision? Explain your reasoning.

5. Which do you think made the greater impression—the Chinese goods that Zheng He carried on his ships or the ships themselves? Explain your answer.

4 SAY IT, WRITE IT, USE IT
VOCABULARY

Write answers to these questions. Your answers should show you know the meanings of the terms.

1. Would you rather live in a yamb or a yurt?
2. Would you need an architect to build a mausoleum?
3. Why was seasonal migration necessary on the steppe?
4. What might a militant confederation of countries do?
5. Is ebony or a water clock more useful today?

architect	seasonal migration
confederation	steppe
ebony	water clock
mausoleum	yamb
militant	yurt

5 GEOGRAPHY AND YOU

MAP STUDY

Marco Polo and his father and uncle left China in 1291. Use the map scale to answer these questions.

1. How many miles of their journey home were by water?

2. How many miles did they travel over land?

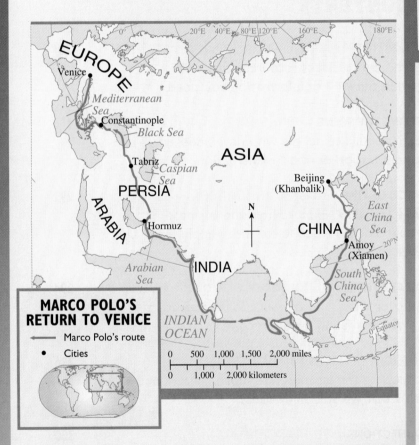

MARCO POLO'S RETURN TO VENICE

→ Marco Polo's route

• Cities

0   500   1,000 1,500   2,000 miles

0   1,000   2,000 kilometers

6 TAKE ACTION

CITIZENSHIP

Few people today would have a nickname like that of Timur the Lame. In our society, people try to be sensitive toward fellow citizens with disabilities. With a group of friends, find out about some of the special problems that Americans with disabilities face. Then research some of the ways in which your state and community are trying to help solve these problems.

7 GET CREATIVE

LANGUAGE ARTS CONNECTION

Beautiful buildings, like this Bahai temple in Illinois, inspire us all. Yet beautiful buildings don't have to be extremely large or expensive. Sketch or photograph a structure in your community that you think is beautiful. It might be a house, a church, a barn, or a public building. List some facts about the building's style of architecture and construction. Then tell why you like the building.

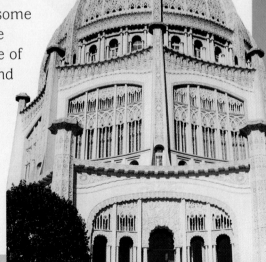

LOOKING AHEAD   **Did the isolation of being an island nation help or hurt Japan? You'll find out in Chapter 13.**

CHAPTER 13

LEARN ABOUT

THE LAND OF

Have you ever written a poem in the haiku form? Do you practice a martial art? Read in this chapter about the country where these arts began.

▼ On page 300, you can find out more about ancient martial arts similar to the one this boy is practicing.

CONTENTS

282

THE RISING SUN

These books tell about some people, places, and events that make Japan so fascinating. Read one that interests you and fill out a book-review form.

READ AND RESEARCH

Exploration Into Japan **by Richard Tames** (New Discovery Books, 1995)
Learn about Japan through the ages, from the earliest settlers to the people of today. Your exploration into Japan will teach you about the history and culture of an island nation. (*nonfiction*)

The Japanese **by Pamela Odijk** (Silver Burdett Press, 1989)
Travel back in time and see the first civilizations of Japan. Through photographs and drawings you will find out about the land, people, religion, and legends of this ancient nation. (*nonfiction*)

Lily and the Wooden Bowl **by Alan Schroeder, illustrated by Yoriko Ito** (Delacorte Press, 1994)
Long ago in Japan, Lily's grandmother placed a wooden bowl on her head to protect her from the outside world. Can the bowl keep Lily safe from the evils of the world? (*historical fiction*)

Judo **by Kevin K. Casey, illustrated by Jean Dixon** (The Rourke Corp., 1994)
Students of judo learn to concentrate because in this martial art the force of opponents is used against them. Photographs and illustrations in this book show the techniques that are important for the powerful throws used in judo. (*nonfiction*)

Skill Power

Gathering and Evaluating Information

UNDERSTAND IT

Do you believe everything your best friend tells you? What about things you read in an encyclopedia? Or stories your grandparents tell about their childhoods? You need to know how to evaluate information to decide what is true. Your friend may be a whiz when it comes to the rules of hopscotch, but probably doesn't know how people live in Japan. Encyclopedias have accurate information about many topics, but they probably do not have the latest information on space flights. And your grandparents' stories may be true, but they might be a little exaggerated.

Reference books are sources that can help you gather and evaluate information.

Knowing how to gather and evaluate information helps historians—and you—understand what really happened in the past.

EXPLORE IT

When you need information, ask yourself questions that help you evaluate, or judge, your sources.

- *When was the material written?* Check the copyright date. If a book was written in 1976, it will not tell about the 1996 Summer Olympics, but it may be a good source for information about life in the 1970s.

- *Is the author qualified?* Does the author have the training and experience to write about the subject? If you are reading a medical book, you should expect it to be written by a physician or other qualified person.

- *How does the new information fit what I know?* If you find a shirt marked "One size fits all," you know enough about the sizes of people to know it cannot be true. Use what you know to check information.

- *Is information based upon facts or opinions?* A fact is a statement that can be proved. It usually can be checked in several sources. Words such as *think, imagine,* and *feel* may show that an author is expressing an opinion—a statement of personal belief.

- *Is information accurate?* If information is current, written by a qualified person, fits what you know, and is found in several sources, it probably is accurate.

TRY IT

With a partner, collect as much information as you can about a subject that interests you. You might consider topics such as these.

- Should people keep unusual animals as pets?

- Should Puerto Rico become the fifty-first state?

- Is pizza junk food?

Try to include both facts and opinions. Ask yourselves the questions listed in Explore It. Then plan a debate where one of you takes one side of the argument and the other takes the opposite side. Have your class evaluate the information you present.

SKILL POWER SEARCH *As you read this chapter, make a list of ten facts you learn.*

Setting the Scene

KEY TERMS

archipelago
constitution
province
shogun

DEVELOPING A CIVILIZATION

FOCUS *The Japanese have taken some of their culture from other Asian countries. But they have developed these borrowings into a culture distinctly their own.*

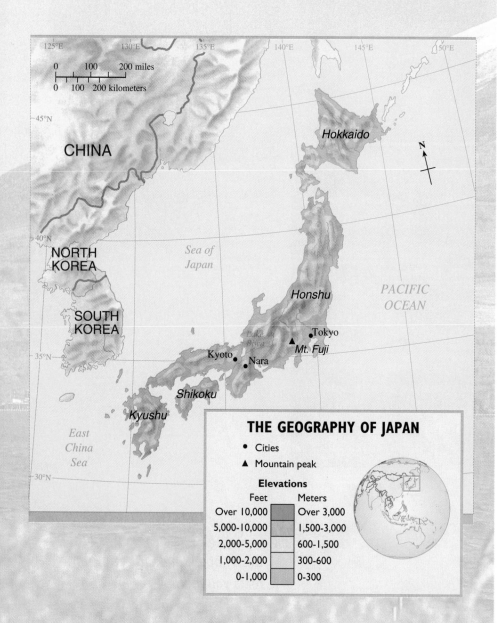

THE GEOGRAPHY OF JAPAN

- • Cities
- ▲ Mountain peak

Elevations

Feet		Meters
Over 10,000		Over 3,000
5,000–10,000		1,500–3,000
2,000–5,000		600–1,500
1,000–2,000		300–600
0–1,000		0–300

An Island Nation

In the year 552, Korean ambassadors brought the Japanese emperor a gift from their king. It was a golden image of Buddha, and with it was a letter praising Buddhism.

In time the Japanese people would adopt Buddhism and develop their own forms of it. Throughout their history the Japanese have absorbed parts of the cultures of their neighbors on the Asian mainland. Yet, as an island nation, Japan has been protected from invaders.

The map shows that Japan consists of four large and thousands of smaller islands in an **archipelago** (ahr kuh PEL-uh goh) off the east coast of Asia. Most of the people live on the four main islands: Hokkaido (hoh KYE doh), Honshu (hahn shoo), Shikoku (SHEE koh-koo), and Kyushu (KYOO shoo).

At its closest, Japan is 125 miles from the Korean peninsula. China is 450 miles away. Their geographical isolation has helped the Japanese develop a unique culture and a sense of themselves as a special people.

The Japanese once thought their country was a poor one. Roughly 85 percent of its land is too mountainous

---

⭐ *archipelago* A chain of islands in a sea

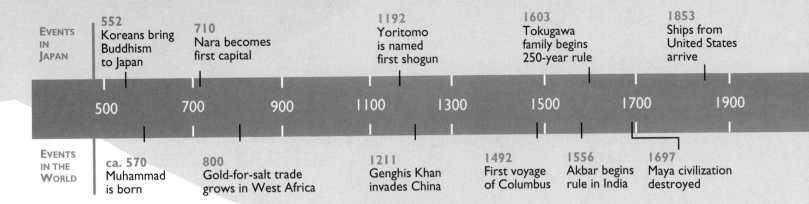

| EVENTS IN JAPAN | 552 Koreans bring Buddhism to Japan | 710 Nara becomes first capital | | 1192 Yoritomo is named first shogun | | 1603 Tokugawa family begins 250-year rule | | 1853 Ships from United States arrive | |

| 500 | 700 | 900 | 1100 | 1300 | 1500 | 1700 | 1900 |

| EVENTS IN THE WORLD | ca. 570 Muhammad is born | 800 Gold-for-salt trade grows in West Africa | | 1211 Genghis Khan invades China | 1492 First voyage of Columbus | 1556 Akbar begins rule in India | 1697 Maya civilization destroyed |

to grow crops. Few raw materials are found under or above ground. Yet Japan's heavy rainfall and relatively warm climate allow its farmers to grow abundant crops of rice.

The Japanese also considered their country to be a small one. But look at the map on this page. If Japan is placed over the east coast of the United States, it stretches almost from Maine to Florida. Japan's 125 million people today make it the ninth largest nation in the world.

Early Peoples

Hunters and gatherers settled in southern Japan as early as 8000 B.C. Archaeologists have found pottery of these people. It was made with a particular rope pattern called *jomon* (JOH mohn). By the third century B.C., rice growing had been introduced.

Seven hundred years later, Japanese rulers built massive tombs shaped like keyholes. The largest of these had a base greater in size than that of the Great Pyramid at Giza, in Egypt. At this time, the important Yamato family began its long reign. The family that rules Japan today traces its ancestry to this ancient family.

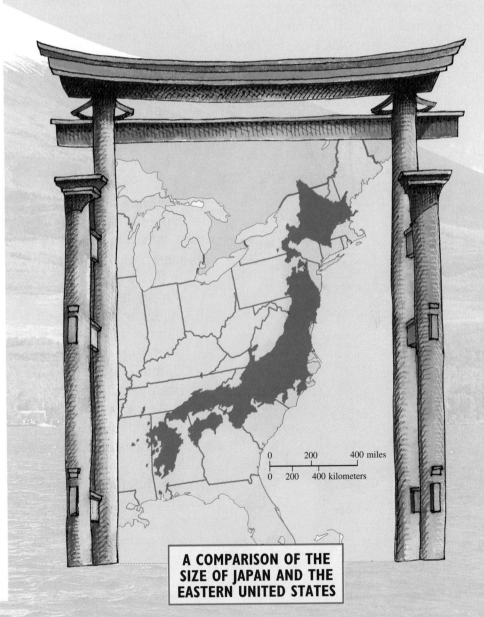

0   200   400 miles
0   200   400 kilometers

A COMPARISON OF THE SIZE OF JAPAN AND THE EASTERN UNITED STATES

287

Knowledge from abroad influenced the development of Japanese culture. The Japanese adopted the Chinese writing system, which used ideographs, even though Japanese is a different spoken language from Chinese.

Inspired by what it had learned, Japan set out to build a strong nation. Near the end of the sixth century A.D., Prince Shotoku (shoh toh KOO) wrote a **constitution**, which outlined what he felt were the principles of government. Shotoku also sent a mission to China to learn more about its achievements. More missions followed for about 200 years.

The Japanese built their first capital city at Nara. It was laid out as a smaller model of the capital of China. Buddhist monasteries and temples dotted the city.

A World of Beauty

In 794 the Japanese moved their capital to Heian-kyo (hay ahn KYOH), later called Kyoto (kee OHT oh). The emperors would continue to live there for more than 1,000 years.

Around that time, missions to China stopped. The Japanese began to develop a culture of their own. At the imperial court at Heian-kyo, a culture based on appreciation of beauty arose.

People were judged by the quality of their handwriting and skill at writing poetry. The noble class enjoyed participating in elaborate ceremonies and poetry contests. The nobles loved to view the gardens during the changes in seasons—the foliage in autumn and the cherry-tree blossoms in spring. Men and women took pride in the elegance of their clothing. But this isolated world of beauty could not last.

As the power of the emperors declined, clans of warriors in the **provinces** began to fight with one another. The two most powerful were the Minamoto (mihn uh MOHT oh) and the Taira (TEYE rah), which briefly controlled the country. But, in a war that ended in 1185, the Minamoto clan won the final victory.

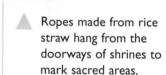

▲ Ropes made from rice straw hang from the doorways of shrines to mark sacred areas.

▲ The horseman in this painting is Minamoto Yoritomo.

★ **constitution** A document that contains the laws or rules of government

province A region of a country, usually having a local government

A Warrior Society

In 1185, Minamoto Yoritomo (yoh-ree TOH moh) was the most powerful man in Japan. He had planned the strategy for his clan's military success.

Seven years later, Yoritomo had the emperor name him **shogun**. His military government ruled Japan.

Yoritomo made no attempt to overthrow the emperor, who continued to perform religious rituals for the good of the country. But the shogun held the real power.

Japan developed a feudal system, similar to that of Europe in the Middle Ages. As you can see on the chart, society was divided into classes, with the emperor, shogun, and daimyo (DEYE myoh) at the top. Then came the samurai (SAM uh-rye), peasants, and craftspeople. The burakumin (BOOR uh koo mihn) were outcasts whose work, such as burying the dead, was considered unclean.

Daimyo, or lords, controlled rural areas of various sizes. They were served by warriors called samurai. The code of the samurai, Bushido (BOO-shee doh), was a simple one. It demanded that samurai be loyal and brave, ready to die for their lord. Samurai wives were expected to be strong, too, and they often shared their husbands' fate.

The Japanese samurai developed artistic skills as part of their training. Talent with the paintbrush was almost as important as skill with the sword. The values that were established at this time would remain important in Japan for centuries.

Civil wars continually plagued Japan, as the powerful daimyo sought to increase their landholdings. From about 1300 to 1600, the history of Japan was the history of the rise and fall of powerful daimyo. It was during this difficult period that westerners made their first appearance in Japan.

⭐ *shogun* A military leader

JAPAN'S FEUDAL SOCIETY

Papers with requests to the kami are folded and hung on a Shinto prayer tree.

They brought firearms, which the Japanese had not seen before. Christian missionaries from Europe began to spread their religion.

A Unified Nation

Three powerful military leaders fought a series of wars that eventually united Japan. The first was Oda Nobunaga (OHD ah noh boo NAH gah). He used firearms to seize power in 1573. After he was assassinated, one of his generals, Toyotomi Hideyoshi (toh yoh TOH mee hee de YOH shee), took control. To maintain control of the people, Hideyoshi forced the peasants to give up their weapons. After that, only samurai were permitted to carry swords.

Hideyoshi next made plans to conquer Korea. He launched two invasions of Korea, hoping to secure a foothold on the mainland. These invasions set the scene for centuries of ill will between the two countries. The Koreans resisted fiercely and, when Hideyoshi died, his soldiers returned home.

Then Tokugawa Ieyasu (toh koo GAH-wah ee e YAHS oo) took control. In 1603 he became shogun and made the position a powerful one again. From then until 1868, the Tokugawa shoguns ruled the country peacefully from the city of Edo, which is now Tokyo. The emperors continued to be powerless in Kyoto.

The Role of Religion

From early times, the Japanese believed that their islands were created by the gods. The emperor claimed to be a direct descendant of Amaterasu (ah mah te RAH soo), the sun goddess.

Shinto is Japan's oldest religion. The word means "the way of the kami," or spirits. The Japanese believe that kami created Japan and are found throughout nature. Shinto shrines, each marked by a wooden gateway called a torii, honor the gods. Shinto stresses the importance of purity and cleanliness. Making offerings to ancestors is also part of Shinto, for kami of ancestors give help to their descendants.

The Japanese added Buddhism and Confucianism to their traditional Shinto beliefs. For the Japanese people, each religion contains its own valuable truths.

Over time, different forms of Buddhism, which you learned about in Chapter 5, became popular. An important one was Zen, which means "meditation," or focusing the mind.

Zen Buddhists look within themselves to find Buddha's nature. Zen teaches that people have to go beyond book learning to discipline themselves. This emphasis on self-discipline made Zen Buddhism popular with the samurai. It also influenced the arts, for poetry and painting are regarded as aids to meditation. Buddhist temples, paintings, and statues are among the greatest works of Japanese architecture and art.

Confucianism, which is based on the teachings of the Chinese philosopher Confucius, strongly influenced Japanese society. Its stress on loyalty to the family and the state appealed to the Japanese love for order. Even today, children are often called by their position in the family, such as elder sister or younger brother, rather than by their given names.

A Closed Country

By the Tokugawa period, feudalism had changed. The Tokugawa shoguns controlled much of Japanese life. Under their rule, Japan enjoyed about 250 years of peace and prosperity.

During this time, Japan was not greatly influenced by the outside world. While Europe was making scientific and technological progress, Japan changed little. But in 1853, ships from the United States appeared off Japanese shores, sailing on the winds of change that led to the downfall of the Tokugawa shogunate.

▼ A 53-foot statue of Buddha sits in a temple at Nara.

REFOCUS
COMPREHENSION

1. What did Japan borrow from other countries?

2. What are the major religions of Japan?

THINK ABOUT IT
CRITICAL THINKING

What are the advantages and disadvantages of living on a chain of islands?

WRITE ABOUT IT
ACTIVITY

Suppose you visited the emperor's court at Heian-kyo. Write a journal entry explaining why you would or would not have liked this society.

291

OUTSIDE INFLUENCES

FOCUS *Because Japan is an island country, the people have developed a high sense of being a special nation. Their history is marked by their reactions to outsiders.*

PROTECTION BY THE DIVINE WIND

In 1281 the people of Japan were awaiting an invasion by the Mongols, who had conquered China and Korea. The Japanese built a huge sea wall for protection. Then the people prayed for victory. The emperor asked the sun goddess to save the islands.

The prayers were answered dramatically. As the Mongol invaders landed, a typhoon—a violent storm—swept in from the sea and destroyed the Mongol fleet in the harbor. Samurai hunted down and killed the invaders who had landed.

The Japanese called the typhoon *kamikaze* (kah muh KAH zee), or "divine wind." They believed that it showed that their land truly was protected by the gods.

ARRIVAL OF MISSIONARY FRANCIS XAVIER

Francis Xavier (ZAY vee ur), a Roman Catholic priest, was the first Christian missionary in Japan, arriving in 1549. During his first two years in Japan, Xavier preached his religion and debated its teachings with Buddhist monks. He baptized about 100 Japanese and trained them to teach Christianity to others.

Xavier said the following of the Japanese.

Judging by the people we have so far met, I would say that the Japanese are the best race yet discovered, and I do not think you will find their match. . . . They are very sociable, usually good and not malicious, and much concerned with their honor, which they prize above everything else.

Xavier left Japan in 1551, but other missionaries continued his work. Some Japanese did not like it when missionaries criticized their religions, but they admired the Christians' charity, dedication, and self-discipline. Thousands of people, including some daimyo and samurai, converted to Christianity.

1281
The divine wind destroys Mongol invaders

1549
Francis Xavier arrives in Japan

1582
Toyotomi Hideyoshi's rule begins

1639
Japan closes its ports to most foreigners

1300   1550   1575   1600   1625   1650

SHOW WHAT YOU **KNOW!**

REFOCUS
COMPREHENSION

1. What did the Japanese call the typhoon? Why?

2. How did the Japanese react to missionaries?

THINK ABOUT IT
CRITICAL THINKING

Why is it generally not wise to close a country to ideas and technology from other lands?

WRITE ABOUT IT
ACTIVITY

What if you lived in Japan and a member of your family was on a trade mission abroad at the time Japan closed? Write a letter to your relative, explaining the new law that prevents him or her from returning home.

FEAR OF BEING CONQUERED

Toyotomi Hideyoshi became the military leader of Japan in 1582. At first, he was friendly with the missionaries. But soon he became suspicious. A shipwrecked Spanish sailor boasted that European soldiers would follow the missionaries to Japan. Because it had so many islands, Japan was not easy to defend. So fear of invasion led Hideyoshi to kill some Christians.

In 1614, Hideyoshi's successor banned Christianity. Christians were even tortured to get them to give up their religion.

THE COUNTRY CLOSES

Though Tokugawa Ieyasu at first encouraged foreign trade, he and his successors came to distrust Europeans and their ideas. Step by step, Japan shut itself off from the outside world.

In 1624 the Tokugawa government expelled all Spaniards. Some years later, it forbade Japanese citizens to travel overseas. Japanese citizens already abroad were not allowed to return home. The government also prohibited the building of large passenger ships.

In 1639, Japan closed its ports to most foreigners except Koreans and Chinese. When the Portuguese sent diplomats the next year, the Japanese beheaded them. The only Europeans allowed to trade with Japan were the Dutch. They alone were allowed to trade because they had not tried to spread Christianity. Though this policy resulted in a closed society, it helped keep the Tokugawas in power and Japan from being colonized.

You Are There

★ **KEY TERMS**

rote learning
meditate

A DAUGHTER OF THE SAMURAI

FOCUS *Traditional education stressed memorizing and much effort. It taught the young to endure hardships to prepare them for life.*

▲ A Japanese woman plays music on a koto.

Bow to the Teacher

As the daughter in a samurai family, you are receiving a good education. Like your brothers, you are expected to carry on the samurai traditions.

Your mother and grandmother are in charge of the house. They began your training at an early age by reading aloud ancient myths as well as the biographies of Japan's great people of the past.

After your sixth birthday, your parents hired a teacher to tutor you at home. Your tutor is a Buddhist priest, a very scholarly man. Today he will begin by teaching you the works of Confucius.

Your classroom is a specially prepared room in your house. You open the sliding doors made of paper framed in wood. Inside are black-bordered straw mats to sit on. There are books and a writing desk. A picture of Confucius hangs in an alcove, and sticks of fragrant incense burn in front of the picture.

You bow to your teacher when you enter the room, and you sit down opposite him. He is seated on a cushion to indicate his superior status. His flowing gray robes are gathered around his knees.

Special Studies

The teacher starts by reading from books that tell about the teachings of Confucius. One teaches that right action comes from the wise use of knowledge. A second book tells about the laws that everyone should follow. Two other books contain the story of Confucius' life and the sayings that his followers wrote down.

Through repetition you begin to memorize these books. The words are like poetry and are not difficult to remember. But today you timidly point out that you don't understand most of what he has read. Your tutor tells you that you are too young to understand Confucius' deep thoughts. You must read them a hundred times to understand them.

So why must you memorize them? Memorizing is good mental discipline. You will store this knowledge in your head. Later on, when you face decisions, Confucius' words will guide you. This is the great benefit of **rote learning**.

In a while you become fidgety and shift your position. The teacher notices this at once. He closes his book

This bonsai tree, only a few inches tall, is kept small by clipping back its limbs and roots.

and tells you that your attitude is not suited for study. He orders you to go to your room and **meditate**.

Ashamed, you bow to the teacher and the picture of Confucius. You back out of the room. It is disrespectful to turn your back on a teacher.

Obedience Is the Rule

The most difficult lessons are taught in the coldest time of year to help you build discipline and character. This is when you learn to write with a brush and inkstone. You gather snow from trees outside. There is no fire in the classroom, and your fingers are freezing as you put some of the melting snow on the inkstone. Reverently you take the brush in your hand. Writing is so important that its tools are almost sacred objects. Though your hands are turning blue, you work slowly. It is important to form each character perfectly.

Because you are a girl, you will also learn to sew, weave, embroider, and cook. You will learn the art of flower arranging and the complex tea ceremony. Though your education is often difficult, you know that a samurai never complains.

SHOW WHAT YOU KNOW!

REFOCUS
COMPREHENSION

1. What subjects did samurai girls study?

2. What happened if a student moved during a lesson?

THINK ABOUT IT
CRITICAL THINKING

What are the drawbacks of rote learning?

WRITE ABOUT IT
ACTIVITY

Write a description of a typical day in the life of a young samurai girl.

★ **rote learning**   Learning by heart, often without understanding

★ **meditate**   To spend time thinking quietly

Spotlight

★ **KEY TERMS**

haiku
novel
samisen
nonconformist

A LIVING CULTURE

FOCUS *Because they are created using ancient techniques, many of the Japanese arts suggest more than they say or show.*

▲ This Japanese work of art depicts a painting and calligraphy party.

Exploring Haiku

Throughout their history the Japanese have enjoyed writing poetry. The most popular form today is **haiku** (HYE koo), a three-line poem that has 17 syllables. The first line has five syllables, the second has seven, and the third has five.

It takes great skill to capture an image or record a moment in just these few words. Many of the finest haiku are carefully constructed spiritual exercises. They help the reader to meditate on nature and its meaning.

Here is a famous haiku, written by Basho (BAH shoh), the master of the form.

An old silent pond!
A frog leaping into it . . .
The sound of water.

Although Basho was the son of a samurai, he preferred to give up his high status for a life of travel and writing. Haiku, his favorite form, remains popular today in Japan.

Women's Writing

Lady Murasaki Shikibu (moor ah-SAHK ee SHEE kee boo) described her father's feelings about having a bright daughter. "Father, a most learned man, was always regretting the fact: 'Just my luck!' he would say. 'What pity she was not born a man!'"

Her words show that there were disadvantages in being a woman in the Japan of about 1,000 years ago. But had Lady Murasaki not been a woman, the course of Japanese literature would be completely different. It was women of this time who created the finest literature.

★ *haiku*   A three-line poem that has 17 syllables

Earlier Japanese literature had been written using Chinese characters. Around the ninth century, an easier system of Japanese writing, called kana (KAH nuh), was developed. However, it lacked the prestige of the Chinese characters, and the male scholars of the time looked down on kana. Thus, it came to be used by women and was sometimes called "women's writing." Today the works of male novelists are virtually forgotten, while the works of the women have become classics in Japanese literature.

The First Novel

The greatest of the women writers was Lady Murasaki. She created *The Tale of Genji* (JEN jee), the world's first **novel** and one of the masterpieces of world literature. Lady Murasaki learned to write when she was a child. She went to serve at the court around the year 1000. Since she was shy, Lady Murasaki disliked the frivolity of the court activities. But from observing what happened there, she was able to draw inspiration for her novel.

The hero of Lady Murasaki's book is Prince Genji, a man of great charm and abilities who has all the characteristics that people at that time valued. He is sensitive to beauty in his surroundings and to the feelings of others. His skill in dance, art, and calligraphy is unmatched.

Yet, even in the happiest moments, there is a ray of sadness in the knowledge that nothing lasts. Lady Murasaki described the effect of Genji's dancing before the court.

Moved beyond words by the beauty of the performance, the Emperor burst into tears, and the High Court Nobles and the princes in his suite also wept. When the song finished, Genji adjusted the sleeves of his robe and waited for the music to start again. Then he resumed his dance to the lovely strains of the next movement. Excited by the rhythm of the steps, he glowed with warm color, and the name 'Genji the Shining One' seemed even more fitting than usual.

Japanese Theater

More than 500 years ago, the Japanese developed a form of drama called noh, which means "talent" or "ability." Noh drama combines old forms of court music and dance with popular entertainment and mime. The plays usually deal with historical subjects, but fictional stories are also popular.

The actors, all male, use slow and graceful body movements to express mood and emotion. Japanese noh, like Greek drama, has a chorus. The actors wear elaborate costumes and masks. The music of flutes and drums accompanies the

▼ Masks used in noh drama

---

novel A long story with a plot that has a beginning, a middle, and an end

performance. The stage is bare and open to the audience on three sides. The actors come on stage by a ramp from their dressing room. By tradition, three small pine trees mark the entrance to the ramp, and pebbles lie on the stage. These are reminders that early noh dramas were presented outdoors.

During the Tokugawa era, wealthy people found two new kinds of drama enjoyable. The first was bunraku (bun-RAH koo), or puppet theater. The Japanese puppets are large wooden figures that take three people to manage. Even so, the puppeteers' remarkable skill enabled the puppets to perform gymnastic feats and stunts that appeared unbelievable.

Bunraku has three elements—the puppets, the chanters, and the story. The chanters tell the story of the play to the accompaniment of the three-stringed **samisen**. Some of Japan's greatest playwrights created bunraku plays. These works include historical dramas and family legends.

Kabuki Drama

Kabuki (kah BOO kee) was the most exaggerated form of Japanese drama during the Tokugawa era. It began as a female art. A young woman named Okuni (oh KOO nee) was the founder. She and her troupe entertained in public places by performing skits and music. The women often dressed like men and they poked fun at well-known, powerful people. Their clever entertainment attracted the *kabukimono* (kah boo kih MOH noh), or **nonconformists** of the time. The form of drama took its name from them.

As kabuki performances became more popular with the people, the government tried to stop the drama by banning women from performing in them. But the plays were too popular to stop. All-male casts then put on lavish performances of kabuki. The actors wore gorgeous costumes, and the stage had elaborate scenery.

Kabuki plays often made comments on events of the day. One very popular story, based on fact, was the tale of the 47 ronin (ROH nihn). A ronin was a samurai without a master. The lord of the 47 ronin had been forced to commit suicide after he struck another lord in the presence of the shogun. His samurai followers, now masterless ronin, plotted illegal revenge. After they killed the lord who had caused their master's death, they also committed suicide. The ronin were immortalized in kabuki dramas that are still a vital part of Japanese culture.

Even today, kabuki dramas include elaborate costumes and scenery.

---

 samisen A musical instrument, somewhat like a guitar, that has a long neck and three strings

 nonconformist A person who does not follow the beliefs and practices of society

A complete tea ceremony can take four hours, which gives guests time to enjoy the beauty of their surroundings.

SHOW WHAT YOU
KNOW!

REFOCUS
COMPREHENSION

1. What are the three major types of Japanese plays?

2. Why is Lady Murasaki Shikibu important?

THINK ABOUT IT
CRITICAL THINKING

Why was meditation important to the Japanese?

WRITE ABOUT IT
ACTIVITY

Write an explanation of why you think haiku is so popular today. Or try your hand at writing a haiku.

Painting

Japanese-style landscape paintings first appeared on paper doors in the homes of the nobility. Soon painters created scrolls that told stories. The most famous is the Genji Scroll, which has passages from the great novel between the pictures.

Later the writing was dropped, and scroll painters told stories through vivid pictures alone. Some presented Buddhist parables; others told animal stories. When the samurai became the ideal in society, tales of battles and daring action became the theme.

A completely different type of art was ink painting. The artist carefully rubbed a hard ink stick in a tray of water until the color of the mixture was just right. Then, with a few quick strokes, the artist brushed the black ink onto the paper to create a picture.

Once on the paper, the ink could not be painted over. The painters had to get it right the first time. The lack of color was not important to them. Nor was it necessary to fill the entire sheet of paper, as a European painter would have done. Like haiku, the art of ink painting suggests a scene with a few careful lines.

The Way of Tea

The tea ceremony began among Zen Buddhist monks as an aid to meditation. The ceremony is held in a carefully prepared room decorated with flowers and a scroll painting.

After the guests are seated, the host or hostess carefully scrapes tea from a hard block, mixes it with boiling water and pours it for the guests in an elaborate manner. The Japanese spend a long time learning how to do each part of the ceremony properly. They believe that the tea ceremony helps them find peace within themselves and beauty in simple things.

All the objects used in the ceremony are articles of beauty. Artisans made lovely iron kettles, porcelain bowls, and silk or cotton containers for tea cakes. The object of the ceremony is to create an atmosphere of peace.

THE MARTIAL ARTS

FOCUS *The real purpose of the martial arts was for self-defense without using unnecessary violence.*

The Art of Defense

Japanese samurai developed many martial arts, or fighting techniques. Several of them involved unarmed combat. To foreigners, the best known of these may be **jujitsu** (joo JIHT SOO). It consists of a variety of handholds that can be used to throw an opponent off balance. Jujitsu could be used in combat or in situations when a samurai was unarmed.

A Japanese artist's version of a samurai swordsman

Speed is important in jujitsu, but its main idea is to use an opponent's strength against himself. Sekiguchi Jushin (say kee GOO chee JOO sheen), a renowned master of the art, was hired to teach a young daimyo. The noble pupil tried to push Sekiguchi off a bridge to test his skill. Grasping his hand, Sekiguchi turned the tables on the daimyo. The young man found himself dangling in midair, with a dagger thrust through his sleeve as a friendly reminder of what would have happened in actual combat.

Many jujitsu masters developed and taught their own styles. Because these methods were kept secret and seldom recorded, most have been lost. One form, judo, has become a popular sport, however.

Kendo, another modern sport, originally was a way of practicing sword fighting. It uses bamboo sticks in place of real swords. Even so,

---

jujitsu   A Japanese system of unarmed combat

kendo   A Japanese form of fencing

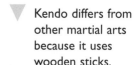

Kendo differs from other martial arts because it uses wooden sticks.

opponents usually wear padded clothing and masks, for the kendo sticks can injure the competitors.

Code of the Samurai

Martial arts were spiritual exercises designed to make a samurai into a better person. They were designed to eliminate violence or selfish bullying. Tsukahara (tsoo kah HAHR ah) Bokuden was a famous Japanese swordsman who fought his first duel at the age of 17 and took part in many wars. By the time he was 50, Tsukahara felt no further need to prove himself. One day Tsukahara was traveling on a ferryboat across a lake. Another samurai on

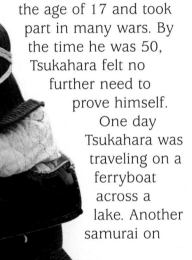

▲ Many children around the world still learn martial arts today.

board began to boast of his skill with a sword. Tsukahara quietly ignored him.

Finally the other samurai asked Tsukahara if he knew anything about swordsmanship. Tsukahara replied that he was skilled at the "no-sword" method. "My method consists not in defeating others," he said, "but in not being defeated."

The other samurai insisted that the boatman stop at an island so that Tsukahara could demonstrate his skill. When the boat reached land, the braggart hopped ashore and drew his sword. Tsukahara took the boatman's pole and shoved the boat away from the land, leaving the other man on the beach. Tsukahara called to him, "Here is my no-sword school. I have just defeated you without a sword."

SHOW WHAT YOU KNOW!

REFOCUS
COMPREHENSION

1. What are the martial arts?

2. Compare jujitsu and kendo.

THINK ABOUT IT
CRITICAL THINKING

What is the advantage of turning your opponent's strength against himself or herself?

WRITE ABOUT IT
ACTIVITY

Write a character sketch of Tsukahara Bokuden, a true master of the martial arts.

SUMMING UP

1 DO YOU REMEMBER...
COMPREHENSION

1. Why did the Japanese once think their country was poor?

2. Describe the roles of the emperor and the shogun in feudal Japan.

3. Why were the samurai respected by the people of Japan?

4. How did Japan under the Tokugawa government respond to Europeans?

5. What did a student in a samurai family have to memorize?

6. What was kana?

7. How were haiku and Japanese ink paintings similar?

8. What was the object of the Japanese tea ceremony?

9. What was the main idea of jujitsu?

10. How did a true master use the martial arts?

3 WHAT DO YOU THINK?
CRITICAL THINKING

1. How were the samurai similar to knights in Europe? How were they different?

2. In general, would you say that Japan's deliberate isolation after 1624 strengthened or weakened the nation?

3. What do you think of the samurai principle of never complaining? In what way might it strengthen an individual?

4. In what ways are kabuki and noh dramas a window into Japan's past?

5. Most of the styles and methods of jujitsu masters have been lost. Why were they never written down?

2 SKILL POWER
GATHERING AND EVALUATING INFORMATION

An important part of evaluating information is checking it for accuracy. Look at a nonfiction book you have read, and list four facts that are given there. Then go to different sources—encyclopedias, almanacs, other library books—to check those facts. Next to each fact you check, list the source you used and whether it agrees with the fact in your book.

4 SAY IT, WRITE IT, USE IT
VOCABULARY

Write a few paragraphs about what you learned about life in ancient Japan. Try to use as many of the vocabulary terms as possible.

archipelago	nonconformist
constitution	novel
haiku	province
jujitsu	rote learning
kendo	samisen
meditate	shogun

5 GEOGRAPHY AND YOU
MAP STUDY

The map below shows that Japan is an archipelago. Look in the Atlas of this book to answer these questions.

1. Can you find three other nations that are archipelagos?

2. Which one of the states in the United States could also be called an archipelago?

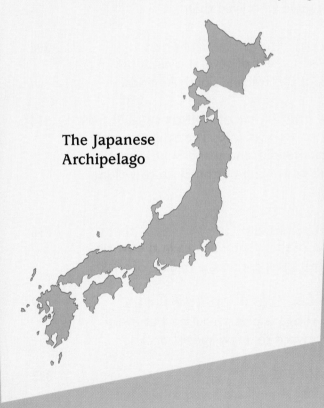

The Japanese Archipelago

6 TAKE ACTION
CITIZENSHIP

In medieval Japan, a true master of the martial arts used them to avoid unnecessary violence and bloodshed. In our modern society, good citizens look for peaceful ways to resolve conflicts, too. With a group of classmates, describe some arguments that have taken place in your school. Then discuss how these conflicts might have been avoided or resolved peacefully. Use your discussion to create a list of guidelines titled Conflict Resolution.

7 GET CREATIVE
LANGUAGE ARTS CONNECTION

Look again at the haiku on page 296. Then try writing your own haiku about some aspect of nature. Your poem should have 17 syllables in all—five syllables in the first line, seven syllables in the second line, and five syllables in the third line.

Leaves, yellow and red,
A swirling autumn carpet
To welcome winter!

LOOKING AHEAD
In the next chapter you will learn about people who built magnificent cities in Central and South America.

DISCOVER

CHAPTER 14

CENTRAL AND

Did you know that in the 1500s one of the largest cities in the world was in Central America? In this chapter you will learn about the civilizations that discovered corn and built great cities.

CONTENTS

Find out on page 312 what this girl is holding and how it is used.

SOUTH AMERICAN EMPIRES

Through factual accounts and fictional stories, these books tell about life in the great early civilizations of Central and South America. Read one that interests you and fill out a book-review form.

READ AND RESEARCH

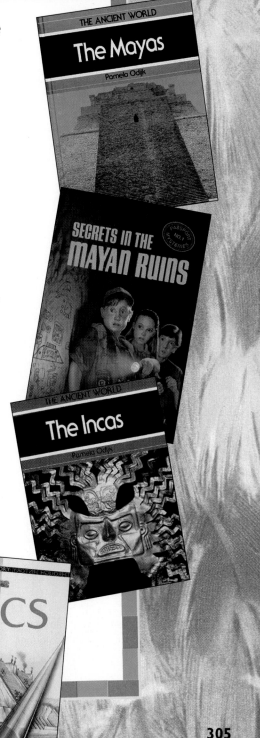

The Mayas **by Pamela Odijk** (Silver Burdett Press, 1989)
Travel back to a time when Maya civilization flourished. Find out about the places in which the Maya lived, the food they ate, the legends they shared, and more. (*nonfiction*)

Secrets in the Mayan Ruins **by P. J. Stray** (Silver Burdett Press, 1995)
Ray and Rachel are exploring the ruins with Andrew, a boy Ray's age, when they discover that criminals are stealing ancient artifacts. Can the children stop them before they get away? (*fiction*)

The Incas **by Pamela Odijk** (Silver Burdett Press, 1989)
Did you ever wonder who the Incas were or what their civilization was like? Examine the history and culture of these South American Indians through maps, drawings, and photographs. (*nonfiction*)

The Aztecs **by Tim Wood** (Penguin Books USA, 1992)
Learn about the history, customs, and everyday lives of these remarkable people through well-written text, brilliant illustrations, and a series of see-through cutaways. (*nonfiction*)

SKILL POWER

Developing Visual Literacy

By looking at art from the past, you can learn a lot about the daily lives of people who lived then.

UNDERSTAND IT

When you look at art that was done 1,000 years ago, it may be hard to understand. However, you can usually learn something about the time by looking carefully at details. Try to answer these questions by looking at the Inca statue.

- What is shown here?
- How would you describe what he is wearing?
- What does this statue tell you about Inca culture?

▲ This clay statue was made nearly 1,600 years ago.

EXPLORE IT

You can learn a lot about life in the past by looking at art. Study the painting shown here, which is titled *The Cottage Home*. What clues does the painting contain to help you learn about the people and their surroundings?

When you look at pictures from the past, ask yourself these questions.

- What is the subject of the art?
- What time in history does the art show?
- What does the art show about life in the past?

What can you learn about life in the past by studying this painting? ▶

TRY IT

Try your hand at creating art that shows what your life is like today. You might draw a picture or make a model of a room in your home. Consider creating a sculpted figure with clay, wood, or papier mâché. Show what the clothing, jewelry, and footwear of today look like. Paint a scene showing activities you and your friends enjoy. Be creative, but remember to use your art to tell a story about life today.

SKILL POWER SEARCH

See what you can learn about the way people lived from the art shown in this chapter.

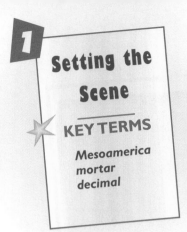
THE GREAT EMPIRES

FOCUS *Over several centuries, different civilizations developed in Central and South America. Each civilization benefited from the cultures of the ones that came before it.*

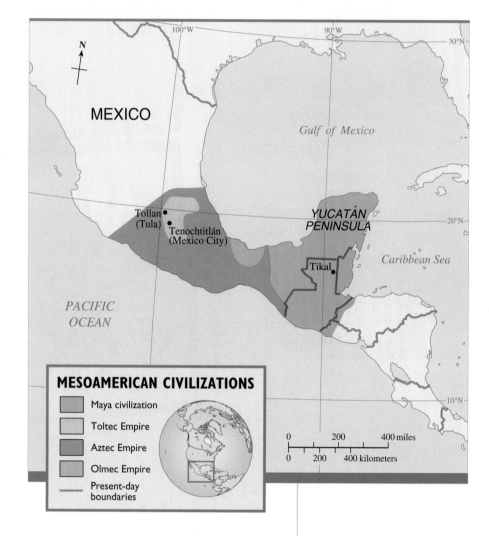

MESOAMERICAN CIVILIZATIONS

- Maya civilization
- Toltec Empire
- Aztec Empire
- Olmec Empire
- Present-day boundaries

The First Americans

Scientists are not sure just when the first people arrived in the Americas. Once they arrived, many of them migrated southward, attracted by warmer climates and more abundant wildlife. In time their descendants reached South America's southern tip.

The first Americans hunted animals and gathered edible plants and berries. As the seasons changed, these people followed their food supply of herd animals and food-bearing plants.

About 6500 B.C. someone discovered that plants could be cultivated. The first foods to be cultivated were squash, peppers, tomatoes, beans, and possibly maize, or corn. Cotton was also grown and woven into cloth.

Planting crops changed peoples' lifestyles. They became farmers, settling in one place to wait for the harvest. As the map shows, some of the earliest settlements were in Mesoamerica (mez oh uh MER ih kuh).

The type of culture that developed in a particular region depended, in large part, on geography. Two mountain chains run north and south through Mesoamerica, one near each coast. The region lying between the two mountain chains is a dry plateau. The coastal areas are forested lowlands where rain is plentiful.

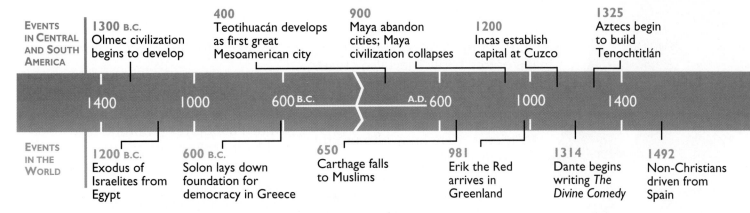

| EVENTS IN CENTRAL AND SOUTH AMERICA | | | | | | |

EVENTS IN CENTRAL AND SOUTH AMERICA

1300 B.C. Olmec civilization begins to develop

400 Teotihuacán develops as first great Mesoamerican city

900 Maya abandon cities; Maya civilization collapses

1200 Incas establish capital at Cuzco

1325 Aztecs begin to build Tenochtitlán

1400 1000 600 B.C. A.D. 600 1000 1400

EVENTS IN THE WORLD

1200 B.C. Exodus of Israelites from Egypt

600 B.C. Solon lays down foundation for democracy in Greece

650 Carthage falls to Muslims

981 Erik the Red arrives in Greenland

1314 Dante begins writing *The Divine Comedy*

1492 Non-Christians driven from Spain

◄ This stone head was carved by Olmecs more than 2,000 years ago.

▼ This statue shows a Maya woman writing on tree-bark paper.

Olmecs: Great Stone Heads

The first significant civilization in Mesoamerica arose in the coastal forests along the southern tip of the Gulf of Mexico. The people who lived here were called Olmecs (AHL meks).

The Olmecs are best known for the huge stone heads they created, some weighing as much as 20 tons. Thought to depict chiefs or ball-players, the heads show men wearing helmets.

The Olmecs had no cities in the modern sense. They created religious centers, where priests, nobles, and artisans lived. They built huge temple-pyramids of earth and wood, where the priests made sacrifices to their gods. The chief Olmec god was part human and part jaguar and was able to take either shape.

The Olmecs thrived for about 800 years. This civilization went into decline and vanished around 400 B.C. At that time the last of their great religious centers was destroyed, either by invaders or by rebellious Olmec subjects.

Maya: The First Great Civilization

As the Olmec civilization declined, another—the Maya—arose along the coastal lowlands. The Maya people clearly benefited from the Olmec culture. They built large pyramids and temples, worshiped a jaguar god, and adopted the Olmec calendar.

The Maya carried Mesoamerican civilization to new levels of achievement. They developed an advanced

system of writing and used paper made of tree bark. They also created a system of mathematics that included a zero. Only two other ancient civilizations, in India and Babylonia, were known to use the zero to calculate.

Unlike the Olmecs, the Maya built cities, some of which had as many as 75,000 people. Although the Maya civilization spread over a wide area, it did not develop into an empire in the familiar sense. There was no central government with a single ruler. Each city and the surrounding region had its own ruler.

A Network of Traders

A network of trade routes linked the Maya regions. People in the highlands had stone, such as obsidian (ub SID ee-un) and jade, which could be used to make knives and jewelry. The high-landers used their stone to trade with lowlanders for colorful pottery, cotton, chocolate, herbs, and feathers. Maya along the seacoast traded their special products, such as salt and cotton cloth.

Maya civilization reached its peak between A.D. 200 and 800. Then its great cities were abandoned. The palaces and temples were left to crumble, and forests gradually grew over them. Scientists are still trying to determine why this great civilization declined and vanished. Perhaps the soil became overfarmed, or drought or disease wiped out most of the population. No one is sure.

▲ Quetzalcoatl, the Toltec feathered serpent, was depicted in different forms.

Toltecs: The Shadowy Empire

The next great civilization to arise in Mesoamerica was that of the Toltecs (TAHL teks). Historians do not know much about this civilization. Legends of later civilizations say that the early Toltecs took over a small settlement called Teotihuacán (tay uh tee wah-KAHN). Using their great skills as builders and organizers, the Toltecs turned Teotihuacán into the greatest city of its time.

Teotihuacán was a holy city, dominated by two mighty pyramids—the Pyramid of the Sun and the Pyramid of the Moon. From the tops of these pyramids, priests worshiped these heavenly bodies. For unknown reasons the Toltecs sacked and burned Teotihuacán around A.D. 900 and settled in Tollan, which is near present-day Tula. Tollan became the capital of the Toltec Empire until its final decline around 1200.

The chief Toltec god was Quetzal-coatl (ket sahl koh AHT ul), the

▼ Feathers decorate this Aztec shield.

feathered serpent god. A priest-king of the same name ruled the Toltecs for many years. According to legend, King Quetzalcoatl was driven out of Mexico by invaders but said he would one day return to reclaim his kingdom.

Aztecs: The Greatest Mesoamerican Empire

Archaeologists do not really know much about the Toltec Empire. However, they do know it was an important part of the legendary history of the next great civilization to arise in Mesoamerica—the Aztecs. One thing is certain—the Aztec Empire represents the greatest success story in early Mesoamerica.

Originally the Aztecs were a wandering group of hunters and farmers who called themselves the Mexica (me CHEE kah). Following the instructions of one of their gods, the Aztecs left their home in the north in search of a new land. After years of wandering, they arrived in the Valley of Mexico. Several other groups had settled the choicest areas of the valley, and they fought to keep the Aztecs from settling there.

Eventually the Aztecs settled on a swampy island in the middle of Lake Texcoco (tay SHOH koh). They met with little resistance because the island had poor soil and no other groups wanted to settle there.

Protected by the waters of the lake, the Aztecs proceeded to construct Tenochtitlán (te nawch tee TLAHN). You will read more about this great city on pages 316–318.

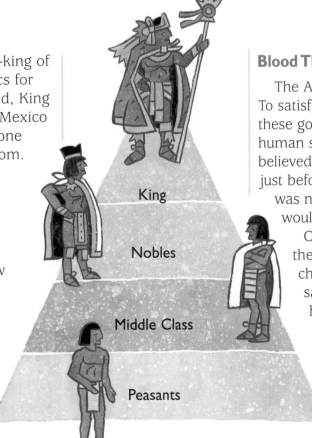

King

Nobles

Middle Class

Peasants

Aztec Society

Blood That Makes the Sun Rise

The Aztecs worshiped many gods. To satisfy the demands of some of these gods, the Aztecs carried out human sacrifices. For example, Aztecs believed that the red color of the sky just before sunrise was blood. If blood was not offered to the gods, the sun would fail to rise.

On certain occasions, Aztecs themselves—men, women, and children—were used for sacrifice. In most cases, however, prisoners of war were sacrificed. Driven by the need for a constant supply of victims, the Aztecs fought an endless series of wars. By the early 1500s they ruled an empire that stretched from the Pacific Ocean to the Gulf of Mexico. At its greatest extent, the Aztec Empire included more than 5 million people.

The 52-Year Cycle

Like earlier Mesoamericans, the Aztecs believed that events occurred in 52-year cycles. The first year of each new cycle was called 1 Reed.

The 1 Reed year had a particular importance for the Aztecs. They believed that they were descended from the Toltecs, whose god-king Quetzalcoatl had long ago disappeared across the sea to the east. According to a Toltec legend, Quetzalcoatl, who was said to have white skin and a beard, would return to his kingdom in a 1 Reed year.

The year 1519 of our present-day calendar was also a 1 Reed year. By

coincidence, it was in that year that the Aztecs had their first contact with people from Europe. The Europeans that arrived in their midst resembled the description of Quetzalcoatl. Moctezuma (mawk tay soo-mah), the Aztec ruler, assumed that their god-king had returned to reclaim his kingdom.

Inca: Empire in the Clouds

About the time that the Aztecs were building Tenochtitlán, a group of tribes was coming together in South America. They called themselves the Incas. After conquering a powerful enemy in 1438, the Incas started a period of expansion that created a mighty empire. This empire would eventually extend more than 3,000 miles along the western side of South America.

As the Inca Empire grew, so did its capital, Cuzco (kooz koh). It was perched high in the Andes Mountains, as you can see on the map. The Incas managed their empire with great skill. Following a victory they would place a colony of loyal Incas among the conquered peoples. The Incas would become part of the community, teaching the conquered peoples about the Inca religion and way of life.

Inca Achievements

Like the Toltecs and Aztecs, the Incas were master builders. They built castles, temples, and other structures, whose impressive ruins can still be seen. They developed a construction technique of fitting large stones together without using **mortar**.

Unlike Mesoamerican civilizations, the Incas had no system of writing.

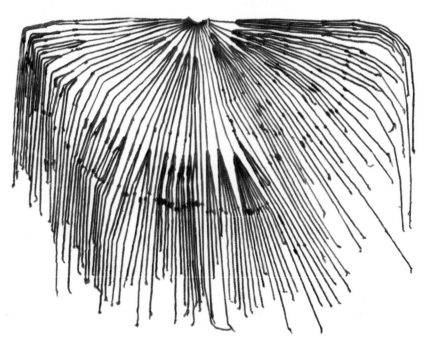

▼ Quipus, like the one shown here, were used by Incas for keeping records.

★ **mortar** A mixture of lime, sand, and water used to cement, or hold, bricks or stones together

However, they did have a **decimal** system of numbers. The Incas carried out their calculations on a quipu (KEE-poo), which was an array of colored strings. By tying knots in the strings in varying patterns, the Incas could add and subtract. This allowed them to keep track of food supplies, trading goods, and events.

The Incas built a fine system of roads to enable the leaders to keep in touch with all parts of their far-flung empire. At regular intervals along the roads, runners waited at way stations. Using a relay system, the runners would carry messages from one end of the empire to the other.

Care for the Living and the Dead

Inca priests were also doctors. They were skilled enough to perform brain surgery by cutting away part of the skull. We know from studying mummified remains that many patients survived these operations.

The Incas had great respect for their rulers. When a ruler died, his body was mummified and placed in a "house of the dead." At religious ceremonies, these remains were removed from their resting places and carried in parades so that the people could honor their rulers once again.

Copper, Tin, and Potatoes

In addition to their engineering skills, the Incas were also excellent metalworkers and farmers. Even before the Incas came to power, Andean people knew how to make bronze from tin and copper. Thus, sturdy bronze tools were available to Inca farmers and artisans.

One of the most important foods cultivated by the Incas was the potato. In the wild the original potato was

▲ This drawing shows Inca farmers cultivating crops.

only as big as a nut. Over time the potato was developed into hundreds of varieties suitable to different growing conditions.

Inca farmers used a digging stick, or foot plow. A row of men would line up in a field and turn the soil. Women would come along to break the clods of earth and plant the seeds.

SHOW WHAT YOU KNOW!

REFOCUS
COMPREHENSION

1. How did the cultivation of plants change the lifestyles of early Mesoamericans?

2. How did the Inca people, who had no system of writing, keep track of supplies and events?

THINK ABOUT IT
CRITICAL THINKING

Why don't archaeologists consider the Maya civilization to have been a true empire?

WRITE ABOUT IT
ACTIVITY

The Inca army has just won another victory, and your family is chosen to be part of a small colony of Incas to move into the conquered area. Write a letter to a friend, telling about your new life.

★ *decimal* Based on the number 10

THE WORK OF HANDS AND MINDS

FOCUS *The early civilizations of Mesoamerica and South America developed ideas and techniques that were advanced for the standards of the times.*

COTTON IS KING

Long before the Incas arrived, people in what is now Peru were making cotton cloth. It was more than 5,000 years ago when Peruvians first spun fibers of wild cotton plants into thread.

Over many centuries the Peruvians developed the art of weaving on a loom. Cloth making became one of their great arts. Because the climate was so dry, some of the textiles they made have survived to the present day.

Three-dimensional birds and flowers decorated headbands and belts. The many bright colors used in these decorations reflect the Peruvians' joyous outlook on life.

THE MAYA CALENDAR

The Olmecs were the first in the Americas to develop an accurate calendar. This calendar was later revised by the Maya.

The Maya knew that the year was slightly longer than 365 days. Their calendar was divided into 18 months of 20 days each. The extra five days were added on to the end of the year. These days were considered unlucky because they didn't belong to a specific month.

Maya priests knew a great deal about the movements of the sun, moon, and planets. This knowledge made it possible for them to accurately measure time and predict certain events, such as eclipses. The priests were also able to tell farmers when to plant their crops and when to prepare for harvest.

"A-MAIZE-ING!"

Maize, the plant we call corn, has never been found growing wild. Scientists know that the first cultivated corn plants grew in the Tehuacán (tay wuh KAHN) valley of present-day Mexico about 5,000 years ago. The cobs were only about two inches long with eight rows of kernels.

The mystery of how corn first developed is still unsolved. It may be that some ancient farmer accidentally crossbred two different kinds of grasses to produce corn. In any case, maize became and continues to be the most important crop in Central and South America.

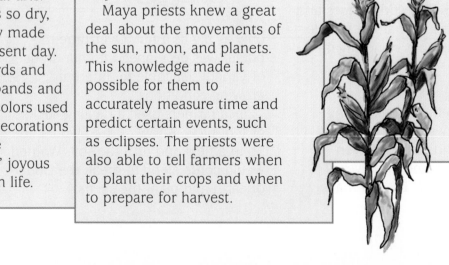

314

| ca. 3600 B.C. | | ca. 1000 B.C. | ca. 100 | ca. 600 |
| Cotton weaving developed | ca. 1000 B.C. Olmec calendar developed | Maize agriculture spreads through Mesoamerica | Advanced metalworking developed in Andes | Maya develop complex system of writing |

3600   3000   2400   1800   1200   600   B.C. A.D.   600

WORKING WITH METAL

The people of the Andes began working with metals about 2,500 years ago. They developed remarkable methods for turning gold, silver, and copper into crowns, masks, plates, statues, and jewelry.

The remarkable thing about the metalwork is that it was accomplished with very simple tools. Stone hammers were used to beat the metal into sheets. Then an artisan used small knives and pointed tools, or awls, to make a design on the metal. Statues were made by joining several pieces of metal together.

Metalsmiths also combined different metals to make alloys. Alloys were harder and stronger than pure metals. One especially hard alloy of gold and copper was used to make a wide variety of objects, including fishhooks.

THE "WRITE" STUFF

The first American writing was part of the Olmec calendar. This writing consisted of symbols for the months. The Olmecs used other symbols as well. However, because they wrote on wood, there are almost no examples of these writings left.

The Maya began using symbols to mark important dates. The Maya, like the ancient Egyptians, used glyphs, or pictures, to stand for a word or idea. There are about 350 such glyphs found on the pillars and walls of Maya ruins, as well as hundreds of combinations of glyphs. The Maya also wrote on paper made from bark, but few of these writings still exist.

As the Maya civilization declined, the people lost the ability to read the glyphs. Today, archaeologists are working to translate Maya writings. Someday they may tell us much more about one of the great civilizations of the Americas.

SHOW WHAT YOU KNOW!

REFOCUS
COMPREHENSION

1. What fact enabled people in what is now Peru to become expert in the art of weaving cloth?

2. How was the knowledge of the Maya priests helpful to the Maya farmers?

THINK ABOUT IT
CRITICAL THINKING

Suppose the Maya had divided their calendar into 15 months of equal length. How many days would each month have? Would there be any "unlucky" days and, if so, how many?

WRITE ABOUT IT
ACTIVITY

You are a member of a team of archaeologists that has just discovered a Maya ruin. In your journal, tell about the writing you find on the walls of a temple.

TENOCHTITLÁN: CITY OF THE AZTECS

FOCUS *An Aztec god led a group of people to a swampy island in the middle of a lake. By the end of the Aztec Empire, the island had become one of the greatest cities in the world.*

The Legend Comes True

The Aztecs' original homeland was in Aztlán, an island somewhere in the north. According to legend one of the Aztecs' gods told them to travel to a new land where the god would make them "lords of all that is in the world."

After two centuries of wandering, the Aztecs arrived in the Valley of Mexico. This valley was surrounded by volcanoes and had an elevation of more than 7,000 feet. A lake, Lake Texcoco, covered much of the valley floor.

All the best land in the valley was already occupied by other settlers, who fought to keep the Aztecs from settling there. Now the Aztec god told them to look for a large cactus with an eagle perched on it. The eagle would be holding a snake in its beak. That was where they would settle.

The next day the Aztecs found the cactus on an island in the middle of Lake Texcoco. Here the Aztecs founded their new home. They called it *Tenochtitlán*, which means "the place of the cactus."

▲ This painting shows the early development of Tenochtitlán, the Aztec capital.

The Floating Gardens

The Aztecs soon discovered why no other people had settled on their island. The land was not fertile, and few crops would grow there. So the Aztecs had to come up with a way to grow enough food to feed everyone.

The Aztec solution to the problem was to create "floating gardens" called *chinampas* (chee NAHM pus). First, they built large rafts made of reeds. Next, they used long poles to anchor the rafts to the lake bottom. Finally, they covered the rafts with thick layers of mud. The mud was very fertile and helped produce large harvests.

Once the chinampas were in place, the Aztecs filled in the spaces between the gardens. They built houses on these filled-in areas, and soon they had a thriving community.

As their settlement grew, the Aztecs began to spread out to other small islands on the lake. They repeated the process by which the original island had been developed. Eventually all of these smaller settlements grew together to produce one large island. On this island the Aztecs built their capital city, Tenochtitlán.

The Great Temple of Tenochtitlán

The centerpiece of the completed city was the Great Temple, the main religious building in Tenochtitlán. Find its location on the map. It was here that the Aztecs, in an effort to please their many gods, carried out most of their human sacrifices.

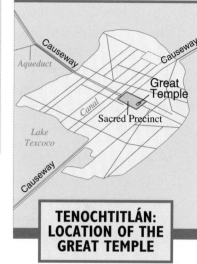

TENOCHTITLÁN: LOCATION OF THE GREAT TEMPLE

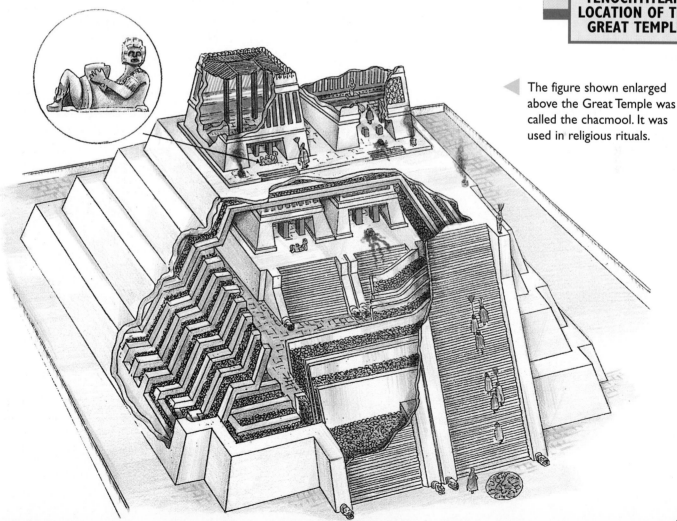

◀ The figure shown enlarged above the Great Temple was called the chacmool. It was used in religious rituals.

317

The Great Temple towered over the rest of the city. At the top of this huge pyramid stood twin shrines. One was dedicated to the god of rain and fertility. The other was dedicated to the god of the sun and war.

These gods represented the two main concerns of the Aztecs. Rain was needed for good harvests, and war supplied prisoners for human sacrifices.

A Magnificent Capital

Tenochtitlán was connected to the rest of the valley by causeways, along which people could travel to and from the mainland. Part of each causeway was a removable wooden bridge. This feature made it possible for troops to defend the city against invaders.

The city was laid out in a pattern of grids. Broad paved avenues led from the causeways into the area of the Great Temple. Many of the smaller roads were actually canals. These

The Aztec calendar stone from the Great Temple at Tenochtitlán

narrow waterways made it easy to travel about the city by canoe.

Aqueducts were built to carry fresh water into the city. The water went to public fountains and to reservoirs throughout the city.

The heart of Tenochtitlán was the Sacred Precinct. Here was located the Great Temple, the ruler's palace, and the main market. On market day, people came from miles around to buy and sell goods and to exchange news.

At the peak of the Aztec Empire's power, at least 100,000 people lived in Tenochtitlán. This was more than twice the population of any city in Europe at that time. Another 300,000 people lived in the suburbs—smaller settlements along the shore.

Upon seeing Tenochtitlán for the first time, one eyewitness exclaimed, "These great towns and buildings rising from the water, all made of stone, seem like an enchanted vision."

causeway   A raised roadway above a body of water

reservoir   A place where water is collected and stored for use

SHOW WHAT YOU KNOW!

REFOCUS
COMPREHENSION

1. Why hadn't any other groups settled on the island that the Aztecs selected as their home?

2. What were two important functions of the causeways of Tenochtitlán?

THINK ABOUT IT
CRITICAL THINKING

The Aztecs were known as a warlike nation of fierce warriors. Why was war an important part of Aztec culture?

WRITE ABOUT IT
ACTIVITY

You have just come from Europe with the first group of explorers to arrive at Tenochtitlán. Write in your diary your impressions of the city.

4

THE LIFE OF AN INCA GIRL

FOCUS *Most Inca people live their entire lives in small farming communities. The routine life of an Inca girl is marked by a number of special occasions.*

Life as "Gentle Breeze"

The first light of day shines over the mountaintops and into your eyes. You sit up and shake your head, trying to wake up. You know it's a special day, but for a few seconds you can't remember why. Then it comes to you. Today is the fourth day of your *quicochico* (kee koh CHEE koh)—your coming-of-age celebration. Today you will become a woman.

Soon you will have to get up from your sleeping place on the floor and prepare for the festivities. But for a few minutes, you lie wrapped in your heavy blanket, thinking about your life.

You were born about 12 years ago in the same house in which you now live. Because there was a light wind blowing, your parents called you Gentle Breeze. You were known by this name until you were given a proper name when you were six years old.

Though you don't remember it, you know that your date of birth was recorded on a quipu by the village keeper of the knotted strings. You also know that your parents weren't allowed to pick you up and hold you in their arms. According to Inca tradition, holding a child is thought to spoil the child and make it weak.

Since your birth you have lived with your family in an *ayllu* (EYE zhoo), a small group of families who share land and farmwork. Most Inca people spend their entire lives in the same ayllu.

The remains of Machu Picchu, an Inca settlement high in the Andes Mountains

No one in your ayllu goes to school. Inca law says: "Knowledge is not for the people, but for those of noble blood." Your father and mother are teaching you everything you need to know to live a normal life in the ayllu.

Family Responsibilities

There is plenty of work for every family in your ayllu, and every person does his or her share. The men and boys work in the fields and tend the animals. Most of the time, women work in the home, spinning thread, weaving cloth, and cooking. However, at times of planting and harvesting, everyone works in the fields.

Sometimes the men have to work outside the ayllu, helping to build towns or roads. The Inca people are proud of their excellent system of roads and are always working to improve it. When workers are needed, they are recruited from nearby towns and villages.

You think about your father and older brother, who just got home yesterday. They were gone for more than a month, helping to build a new section of road. While they were

away, everyone else in your ayllu took on extra responsibilities to make sure all the work was done.

Coming of Age

Suddenly you come out of your daydream with a start. You're still lying on the floor, wrapped in your blanket. It's time to get up and get ready for today's festivities.

For the first three days of the celebration, you have had to fast. Today you will get plenty to eat. But now you have to get ready. After you have a bath, your mother gives you some new clothes to put on.

These are the clothes of a woman. They include a hat and a long dress of **llama** wool with a multicolored belt at the waist. You are given a shawl to wear in cooler weather. You also receive your first piece of jewelry, a pin with a large head. You will use the pin to fasten your shawl.

★ *llama*   A South American animal used for work and for its wool

▼ This Inca road is part of the original system of roads that connected all parts of the Inca Empire.

Colorful festivals, like the Sun Festival, provide occasional breaks in the daily routines of the Inca people today.

REFOCUS
COMPREHENSION

1. Why are males more likely to leave the ayllu from time to time than are females?

2. What are some of the changes a young woman undergoes on the final day of her coming-of-age celebration?

THINK ABOUT IT
CRITICAL THINKING

Would you rather be male or female growing up in an ayllu? Explain.

WRITE ABOUT IT
ACTIVITY

How do you feel about the law requiring ordinary people to be married by age 22? Write a brief paragraph giving your answer and explaining why you feel as you do.

Finally your mother fixes your hair. Until today you have worn your hair loose. It was always falling over your forehead and into your eyes. From now on, your hair will be worn in **plaits** (playts).

At last you are ready. You join the friends and family members who have gathered for your quicochico. The formal part of the celebration ends when you are given a new name— your woman's name. Then you join in the dancing and singing. The festivities last for the rest of the day and well into the night.

Looking Ahead

When you awake the next day, you think about your future. For the next few years, you will work at home. You will learn how to dye cloth and weave it into beautiful patterns. You will also cook meals, clean the house, and work in the fields.

It will be a few years until your next special day—the day you get married. But it doesn't hurt to start thinking about it now. You know that you'll have to act quickly if you want to marry a man of your own choice. If you're not married by age 22, you will be forced to marry—maybe a man you don't even like.

Inca law does not permit ordinary people to remain single. The Inca government wants the population to increase and produce more wealth. So once each year, an Inca marriage inspector arrives in your ayllu. He lines up all the unmarried young men and women, facing each other. If you should end up in such a line, you might be required to marry the man facing you.

But for now you don't have to worry. You still have a few years to wait before you must marry. Until then it's only a daydream.

⭐ *plait* A braid of hair

5

Connections

PLAY BALL!

FOCUS *A ritual ballgame was an important part of the culture in most Mesoamerican and South American civilizations. Although the rules varied from place to place, the incentive to win was the same everywhere—to live to play another day.*

A Popular Pastime

In both the Maya and Aztec civilizations, a ballgame was part of the ritual of religious ceremonies. Every Maya city had a ball court, and the temple complex at Tenochtitlán had one, too. The Aztecs called the game *tlachtli* (TLACK tlee). The origins of the game are unclear, and the rules of the game varied from place to place. However, carvings on walls reveal something about how it was played.

In one version of the game, two teams assembled on a ball court shaped like a capital *I*. Points could be scored by knocking the ball into the section across the far end of the opponents' court.

The ball, made of solid rubber, was about eight inches in diameter—a little smaller and much heavier and harder than a present-day basketball.

▲ Statue of a Maya ballplayer

Players could not use their hands or feet to hit the ball. They knocked it back and forth with knees, elbows, shoulders, and hips. Hitting the ball with your head was unwise, for it could knock you unconscious.

As the stone figure on this page shows, players wore protective padding. Even so, injuries were common since one object of the game was to keep the ball from hitting the

▼ Many ball courts were *I*-shaped and had stone rings, like the one shown, attached to their walls.

Many modern games have certain rules or features that were also found in early ritual ballgames.

SHOW WHAT YOU
KNOW!

REFOCUS
COMPREHENSION

1. How do we know the rules of a game that was played hundreds of years ago?

2. What were two different ways to win a ritual ballgame?

THINK ABOUT IT
CRITICAL THINKING

Which modern-day games have a rule or rules similar to the rules of a ritual ballgame?

WRITE ABOUT IT
ACTIVITY

You're a sportswriter for the Maya *Daily Journal.* You've just watched a game between nobles and prisoners. A member of the nobles' team won the game by putting the ball through a ring. Write about what could happen next.

ground. Players would dive onto the stone floor to keep the ball in play.

Some ball courts had stone rings attached high up on the walls of the court. If a player knocked the ball through one of these rings, his team won immediately. This was a difficult feat, however, for the rings were not much larger than the ball itself.

Some stories about the game say that when a player won the game in this way, he was entitled to take the possessions of all the spectators. Even so, the games drew sizable crowds.

Losers Really Lose

In games played by the Maya, players on the losing team were often sacrificed to the gods. Wall carvings show players kneeling on the court, waiting to have their heads cut off.

This kind of deadly ending to the game was used when one team was made up of prisoners of war. Members of nobility formed the opposing team, and they were bound to win because of the skills they had developed through practice.

Ballgames often had a religious purpose. In some cases the ball court may have represented the sky, in which gods played with the sun and moon. The games may have been meant to celebrate the workings of the universe.

One Maya legend tells of hero-twins who descend into the underworld to play against the Lords of Death. The gods put the twins through a series of tests. For example, one twin has his head cut off to be used as a ball. His brother puts a **gourd** in its place and reattaches the head. In the end the twins cheat death by winning the game and returning home.

---

 gourd A family of plants that includes squash and pumpkin

SUMMING UP

1 DO YOU REMEMBER...
COMPREHENSION

1. For what creations are the Olmec people best remembered?

2. What role did geography play in the trade routes established by the Maya?

3. What were some important achievements of the Maya?

4. What religious practices led the Aztecs to wage frequent wars?

5. How did the arrival of the first Europeans seem to fulfill an old Aztec legend?

6. Why did the Aztecs have to build floating gardens?

7. Why was the Sacred Precinct considered the heart of Tenochtitlán?

8. Where was the Inca Empire located?

9. What was the ayllu in Inca society?

10. What religious significance might the ritual ballgame have had?

2 SKILL POWER
DEVELOPING VISUAL LITERACY

In this chapter you learned how to look at art to learn about the daily lives of people. Now practice your skills. List as many details as you can about Aztec life based on the piece of art on page 316.

3 WHAT DO YOU THINK?
CRITICAL THINKING

1. Why might the Aztec Empire be thought of as the greatest success story in Mesoamerica?

2. What does the way the Maya used math and writing tell you about their civilization?

3. Tell whether you agree with this statement: Religion was extremely important in Aztec life. Use details from the chapter to support your opinion.

4. Think about how the Incas forced people to marry by age 22. Can you suggest a better way by which the government could have encouraged marriage?

5. How was the game of tlachtli like basketball and soccer? How was it different?

4 SAY IT, WRITE IT, USE IT
VOCABULARY

Write a paragraph that compares and contrasts the way of life of the Aztecs and Incas. Use as many of the vocabulary words as possible in your comparison.

causeway	Mesoamerica
decimal	mortar
elevation	plait
gourd	reservoir
llama	

5 GEOGRAPHY AND YOU
MAP STUDY

The map below shows you where the Great Temple was located in Tenochtitlán. Draw a similar map that shows the location of your school. Include major streets and any other important landmarks.

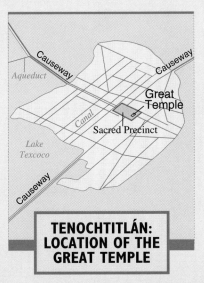

TENOCHTITLÁN: LOCATION OF THE GREAT TEMPLE

7 GET CREATIVE
PHYSICAL EDUCATION CONNECTION

Find out as much as you can about the game of tlachtli. Then try playing the game with a group of classmates, using a soccer ball. (You can make rings from cardboard.) Make up rules as you play. Afterward, try to sum up why you think the game was so popular in Mesoamerica.

6 TAKE ACTION
CITIZENSHIP

Inca leaders believed that "knowledge is not for the people, but for those of noble blood." Today we know that the ability to read and write is vitally important for everyone. You can volunteer to help young students practice reading and writing. You can also read aloud to help them get hooked on books.

LOOKING AHEAD In the next chapter you will learn about an era of dramatic and exciting changes in Europe.

GLOBAL
Expansion

What Made People Look for New Ideas and New Lands?

This was a time of discovery. Europeans have learned from other cultures and developed new ideas. Examine the effects on other parts of the world.

DISCOVER

CHAPTER 15

THE RISE OF

In the centuries following the Black Death, Europe passed from a period of great despair to one of tremendous change, growth, and accomplishment.

Look on page 335 to find the origins of the modern Spanish guitar shown here.

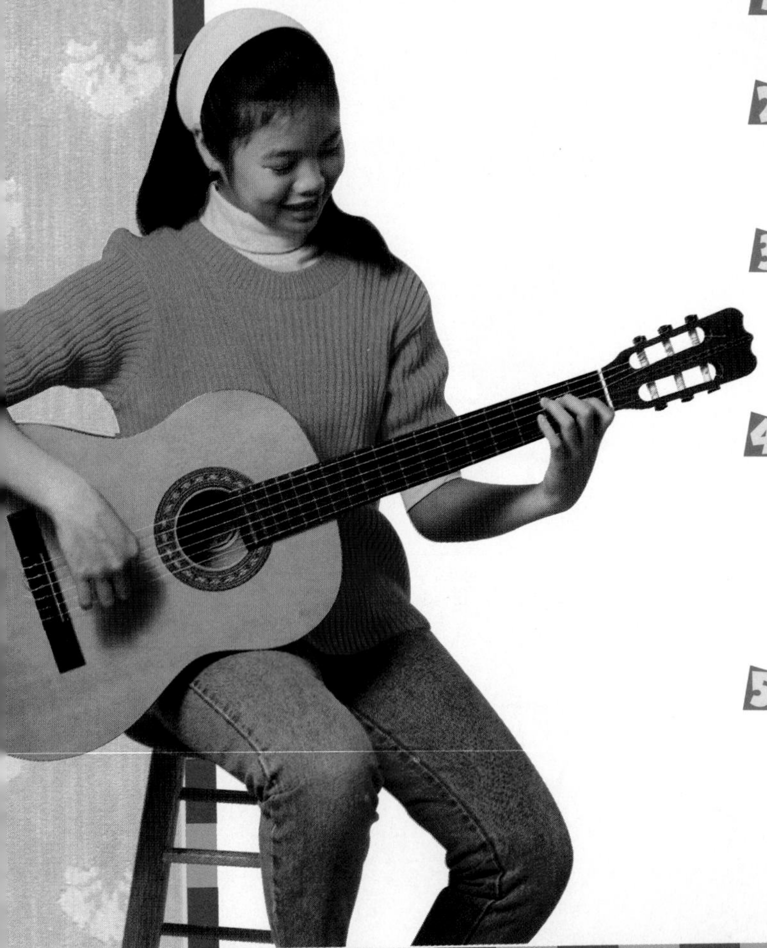

CONTENTS

MODERN EUROPE

These books tell about the Renaissance and about Europe during and immediately after the Renaissance. Read one that interests you and fill out a book-review form.

READ AND RESEARCH

Bard of Avon: The Story of William Shakespeare **by Diane Stanley and Peter Vennema, illustrated by Diane Stanley** (William Morrow & Co., 1992)
Even as a child, William loved the theater. The ideas for many of his plays came from the history of England. As you read about these productions, you will see why people flocked to attend Shakespeare's plays. (*biography*)
•*You can read a selection from this book on page 348.*

The Silk and Spice Routes: Exploration by Sea **by Struan Reid** (New Discovery Books, 1993)
Even before written records were kept, people traveled the spice routes over land. Find out about journeys of adventure on the sea routes that link the East and the West. (*nonfiction*)

Science Discoveries: Isaac Newton and Gravity **by Steve Parker** (Chelsea House, 1995)
Follow the story of Isaac Newton, from his early years to his great discoveries. You will see why his studies of color, light, gravity, and motion changed the world of science. (*biography*)

The Apprentice **by Pilar Molina Llorente, pictures by Juan Ramón Alonso** (Farrar, Straus & Giroux, 1993)
This delightful novel about an aspiring artist will give you a good idea about life in Italy during the Renaissance. (*historical fiction*)

Skill Power

Formulating Generalizations

Knowing how to make and recognize generalizations can help you evaluate statements.

UNDERSTAND IT

You probably make generalizations every day. If you say, "Everyone in my family likes spaghetti," you are making a generalization. It can be supported by interviews in which each family member confirms that he or she likes spaghetti.

Sometimes you may feel yourself getting angry when you hear someone say, "You just can't trust kids to be responsible today." If so, you probably feel angry because you know that the statement is a false generalization. It can be proved to be false by examples that show young people helping other people, doing well in school, and handling their responsibilities well.

EXPLORE IT

A generalization is a statement that draws a conclusion or makes an inference that is based upon specific details. Some generalizations are true, and some are false.

This true generalization—*The Netherlands is a low-lying country that has both suffered and benefited from the sea*—can be supported by specific details.

- Throughout history, floods have damaged property and cost lives.
- By draining coastal areas and building dikes, the Dutch people have reclaimed rich land for agriculture.
- The Dutch must always be watchful that the sea does not encroach on their land.

This false generalization—*The Netherlands is best known for wooden shoes*—can be proved false by specific details that suggest other possibilities.

- The growing and exporting of flowers and bulbs has become a major business.
- Rotterdam is one of the world's busiest trading ports.
- Wooden shoes are used mostly for ceremonial events.

Growing and exporting flowers and bulbs is a major business in the Netherlands.

TRY IT

Decide on a topic that interests you. It could be teenagers in America, your favorite sport, baby sitting, discrimination, or your favorite kind of book or TV show. Then find as many articles as you can about that topic. Read the articles to find where the author uses generalizations and what specific details support them.

With your classmates, make an exhibit of generalizations that you believe to be accurate. For each generalization, write a fact or two that supports the generalization.

Baby-sitting requires a sense of responsibility.

Small children need to be carefully supervised.

Knowing what to do in an emergency is an important skill for a baby-sitter.

Teenagers are interesting people

A group of teenagers in our town is entertaining at the children's hospital.

Two teenagers started a business of designing and painting T-shirts.

SKILL POWER SEARCH As you read this chapter, notice the generalizations and watch for the details that support them.

Setting the Scene

★ KEY TERMS

Renaissance
Reformation
thesis
nationalism
middle class

A CHANGING EUROPE

FOCUS Between 1400 and 1750, Europe underwent profound—and sometimes violent—changes. These changes affected all aspects of life: religion, art, economics, education, science, politics, and warfare.

125,001 and over
Naples

100,001 to 125,000
Venice   Milan   Paris

50,001 to 100,000
Palermo   Bologna   Seville
Rome   Genoa   Granada
Florence   Lyons

25,000 to 50,000
Verona   Rouen   London
Cremona   Antwerp
Brescia   Ghent

LARGEST CITIES IN EUROPE, ca. 1500

NORWAY   SWEDEN
SCOTLAND
IRELAND
North Sea
DENMARK
Baltic Sea
ENGLAND
ATLANTIC OCEAN
London
Antwerp
Ghent
POLAND
Rouen
HOLY ROMAN EMPIRE
BOHEMIA
Paris
FRANCE
Brescia   AUSTRIA
Verona   HUNGARY
Lyons
Milan
Cremona   Venice
Genoa   Bologna
Florence
PAPAL STATES
PORTUGAL
NAVARRE
Corsica
Rome
SPAIN
Sardinia
Naples
Seville
Granada
Mediterranean Sea
NAPLES
Palermo
Sicily

N

0   200   400 miles
0   200   400 kilometers

Troubled Times

As the fifteenth century began, Europe was about to embark on a period of dramatic change. It would emerge from the medieval period of history and enter the modern period.

The transition from middle age to modern age was not an easy one. At the outset, Europe was beset with problems ranging from disease and famine to peasants' unrest and war. At the time, no one could have predicted the vigorous society that would develop over the next 350 years.

Life and Death

The effects of the plague lasted for many years. Every once in a while, the plague would strike again. No one knew when or where it would hit next. Only one

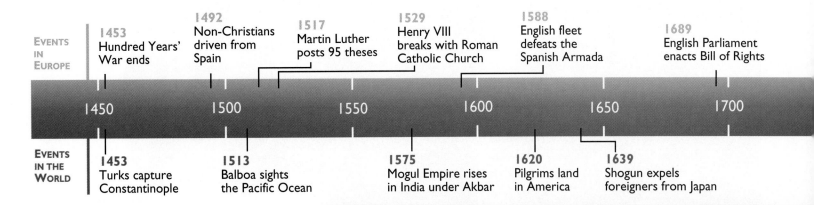

EVENTS IN EUROPE

1453	1492	1517	1529	1588	1689
Hundred Years' War ends	Non-Christians driven from Spain	Martin Luther posts 95 theses	Henry VIII breaks with Roman Catholic Church	English fleet defeats the Spanish Armada	English Parliament enacts Bill of Rights

1450   1500   1550   1600   1650   1700

EVENTS IN THE WORLD

1453	1513	1575	1620	1639
Turks capture Constantinople	Balboa sights the Pacific Ocean	Mogul Empire rises in India under Akbar	Pilgrims land in America	Shogun expels foreigners from Japan

thing was certain—everyday life would never again be the same.

Today when we talk about a population crisis, we mean there are too many people. In the 1400s, however, there were too few people! The map on page 332 shows just how few people were living in the largest cities in Europe. The sudden death of so many people forced Europeans to think long and hard about their future.

Because there were fewer workers, people had to invent better ways of doing things. The population crisis taught people to work more efficiently and to invest in labor-saving devices. In the long run, this made Europeans richer and more productive.

Peasant Revolts

The population crisis caused other changes. Suddenly there were fewer peasants clamoring for land. There-fore, landlords could no longer get high rents. They tried to make up the difference by collecting old feudal dues. Earlier, when rents had been high, landlords hadn't bothered with

▲ In his painting titled *Rent Day*, Bruegel shows the hardships suffered by peasants in paying their landlords.

these dues. Now the landlords needed this money.

Peasants became even more upset when royal governments raised taxes. Between 1350 and 1450, peasants in England, France, and Germany angrily staged a series of revolts. These uprisings, such as the Peasants' Revolt of 1381 in England, produced lots of violence but little change. The ruling classes were better organized and had better weapons.

The Hundred Years' War

Peasants were not the only ones taking up arms. For generations, France and England had been fighting. The conflict began when the English king Edward III also claimed title to the throne of France.

The fighting, known as the Hundred Years' War, took place entirely on French soil. The English won most of the early battles. Then the French rallied around their new leader—Joan of Arc. Under her inspired direction, the French won several victories. By the time Joan was captured and killed by the English, she had helped turn the tide of the war. In 1453, France emerged as the victor.

Non-Christians Driven Out of Spain

In 711 a group of Muslims known as Moors had captured most of the Iberian Peninsula. Some 300 years later, Christian forces began the *Reconquista* (ray kahn KEES tuh), or "reconquest," of the peninsula.

In 1212 the Christians won a major victory, leaving only Granada in Muslim hands. The next major victory came under the leadership of Ferdinand and Isabella, the king and queen of Spain. In 1492 Spanish forces managed to take Granada and drive the Moors from Spain. Then, believing that God wanted Spain to be exclusively Christian, Ferdinand and Isabella expelled the other large non-Christian group in Spain—the Jews.

A New Beginning

Not everyone agrees on when modern history began. Some people put the date at 1453 when Constantinople fell to the Turks. Others fix the date at about 1455, when Johann Gutenberg developed his printing press and movable type. Still others say it was 1492, when Columbus reached the Americas.

But the actual date isn't important. What is important is that Europeans slowly started to change their old ways of thinking. They began replacing medieval ideas with modern ideas.

Many key changes in thinking led to the creation of a modern world. One

▲ Under the leadership of Ferdinand and Isabella, Spanish troops finally conquered the Moors.

Raphael's *School of Athens* illustrates how the philosophers of ancient Greece influenced this Renaissance artist.

Beautiful instruments like this 1640 Venetian guitar were developed during the Renaissance.

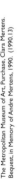

dramatic change known as the **Renaissance** (ren uh SAHNS), or "rebirth," began in Italy in the mid-1300s.

The Renaissance was an exciting time of change in art, music, literature, science, and politics. It began with a desire by many people for a return to the elegance of ancient Greece and Rome. In recalling the cultural heritage of these civilizations, those who introduced the ideas of the Renaissance felt they were bringing about the rebirth of civilization.

Italy was a natural place for the Renaissance to begin. For one thing, Italy was the major population center of Europe. As the map on page 332 shows, it had more large cities than any other region.

Italy had once been the center of the great Roman Empire. Italy had also kept ties with ancient Greek culture.

Some Greek scholars had fled to Italy to avoid an invasion from Turkey. These scholars contributed their knowledge of classical Greece. The new spirit affected artists and writers. They too began to look to ancient Greece and Rome for their inspiration.

Spreading the Word

News of the great things happening in Italy was carried to other countries by visiting scholars. Just as important to the spread of knowledge was the printing press. Before Gutenberg's revolutionary invention, the only book most people had seen was the Bible in their church. Now people could have books of their own, and they could read for themselves what was happening in Italy.

As the Renaissance spread to the rest of Europe, its emphasis changed.

⭐ **Renaissance**   Refers to the great revival of art and learning in Europe in the 1300s, 1400s, and 1500s

The reign of Queen Elizabeth I of England was a period of great achievement in art and literature.

In northern Europe there was less interest in the heritage of ancient Greece and Rome and more in the role of religion in daily life. A movement was started to make religion more relevant to the needs of ordinary people.

In Holland the concept of humanism was introduced by Desiderius Erasmus (des uh DIHR ee us ih RAZ mus). In his book titled *The Praise of Folly*, Erasmus attacked vice, stupidity, and meaningless church ceremony. Erasmus was a loyal Catholic priest. He was also a humanist, a person who wants to deal with the problems people face in this life rather than in the next one.

The Renaissance and the Arts

The new attitudes of the Renaissance were reflected in the arts and in literature. The demand for art was great, especially in urban areas. Many new public buildings were constructed, and these had to be decorated with paintings and sculptures. And many wealthy people had artists create paintings or sculptures for them.

The Renaissance spirit was also evident in literature. In the tradition of the medieval poets Dante and Chaucer, many Renaissance authors wrote in the vernacular, or everyday language of their readers.

William Shakespeare was perhaps the greatest English writer of all time. Not only did Shakespeare write in the vernacular, but he was also a great inventor of words and phrases. You will learn more about this Renaissance genius and his influence on the English language on page 347.

Martin Luther and the Reformation

The Renaissance laid the basis for another movement. The **Reformation** began as an attempt to make changes in the Catholic Church. But it caused fierce religious wars and led to a split in Christianity.

Title page of the first Lutheran Bible ▶

★ **Reformation** Sixteenth-century religious movement aimed at reforming the Catholic Church

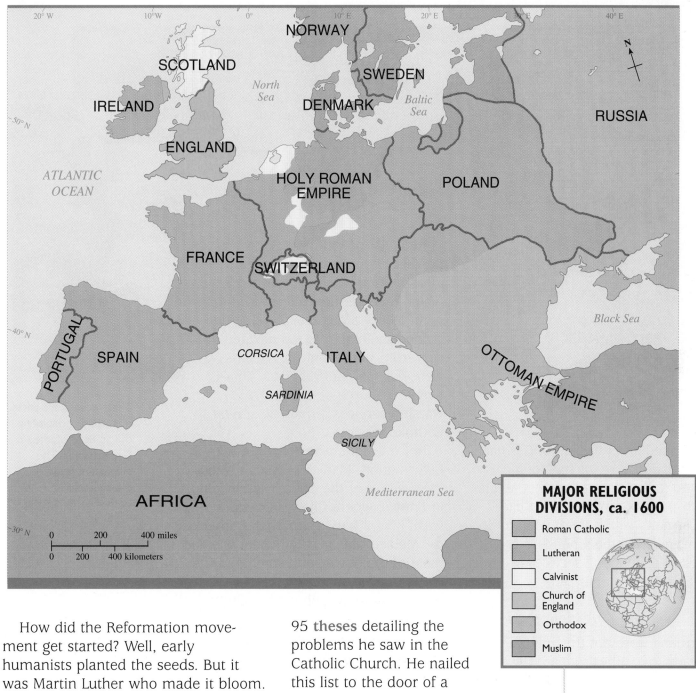

MAJOR RELIGIOUS DIVISIONS, ca. 1600	
Roman Catholic	
Lutheran	
Calvinist	
Church of England	
Orthodox	
Muslim	

How did the Reformation movement get started? Well, early humanists planted the seeds. But it was Martin Luther who made it bloom. Luther, a German monk, did not like certain Church practices. In particular, he didn't like the practice of priests selling forgiveness of sins to anyone with money. So on October 31, 1517, Luther issued a direct challenge to the Catholic Church. He drew up a list of 95 **theses** detailing the problems he saw in the Catholic Church. He nailed this list to the door of a church in Wittenberg, Germany. This simple act set off a firestorm among Christians. Those who agreed with Luther's protests against the Church became known as Protestants.

In Germany, Luther's actions stirred up deep religious feelings. His actions

---

⭐ **thesis** A statement or idea to be defended in a discussion or debate

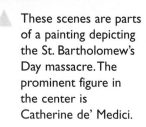

King Henry VIII of England was a devoted Catholic who attacked the ideas of Martin Luther. But in 1529, when Pope Clement VII refused to grant Henry a divorce, the king had second thoughts. He too decided to split from Rome, but his reasons were political, not religious. That is why the Church of England's worship services remain so similar to Catholic services.

Not everyone was delighted with the Reformation. Many Catholics rushed to the defense of the Church, especially in France, where Charles IX was a very weak king. Charles's mother, Catherine de' Medici, (duh MED uh chee) wielded most of the power, and she hated the French Calvinists, known as Huguenots (HYOO guh nahts). On St. Bartholomew's Day in 1572, she launched a surprise attack that killed at least 10,000 Huguenots.

▲ These scenes are parts of a painting depicting the St. Bartholomew's Day massacre. The prominent figure in the center is Catherine de' Medici.

also inspired an upwelling of German **nationalism**. Germans had long resented Italian control of the Catholic Church. Many Germans didn't like non-Germans telling them what to do. They were delighted when Luther suggested conducting services in German rather than in Latin.

John Calvin and King Henry VIII

Germans were not the only ones captivated by Luther's ideas. The Protestant revolt spread quickly to other European countries. Soon the Protestants themselves split into various groups. John Calvin, a French scholar living in Switzerland, broke away from the Catholic Church and started a religious movement known as Calvinism.

The Rise of the Middle Class

In medieval times, the Church, the king, and the nobles had most of the wealth. As Europe moved into the modern age, however, there was a growing class of rich merchants. This group was called the **middle class**.

---

 nationalism A feeling of loyalty and devotion to one's country

⭐ ***middle class*** The social class between the working-class peasants and the wealthy nobles

As the prosperity of merchants grew, kings came to depend on them for loans and for taxes to pay the expenses of government and wars. In return, the middle class demanded more political power from the kings. Middle class people wanted to live like nobles, buying costly furniture, clothing, and jewelry.

Everywhere in Europe the new commerce encouraged the growth of cities. Along with the increase in wealth came a new demand for better education.

Role of Women

The rise of modern Europe brought some significant improvements in the role of women in society. Some women, such as Elizabeth I, Isabella, and Catherine de' Medici, wielded considerable power and helped to shape the policies of their countries.

For most women, their chief role remained that of wife and mother. Still, many women became active participants in activities outside the home. They assumed responsibilities that had once been exclusively reserved for men, and they made major contributions in the fields of commerce, government, and the arts.

▼ Renaissance coins often had portraits of rulers, popes, or nobles.

▼ In this painting titled *The Tax Collector*, the artist portrays the rise of the middle class.

2
Spotlight
KEY TERMS

caravel
Columbian
Exchange

EXPLORING THE WORLD

FOCUS *In the 1400s, European explorers began seeking alternatives to the long, dangerous overland routes to Asia. This led to many changes on maps of the world.*

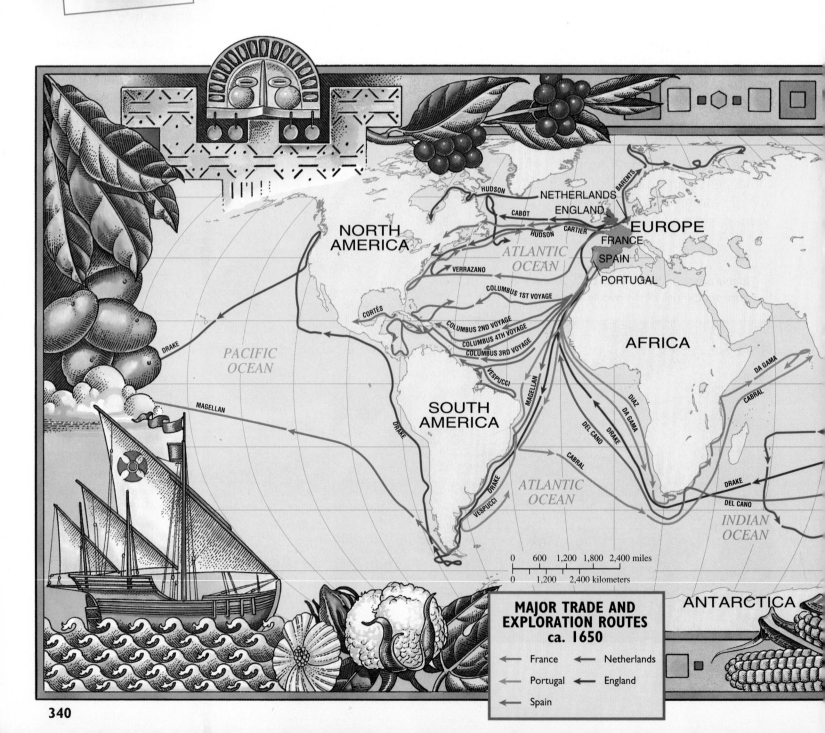

MAJOR TRADE AND
EXPLORATION ROUTES
ca. 1650

⟵ France   ⟵ Netherlands

⟵ Portugal   ⟵ England

⟵ Spain

The Treasures of Asia

Since the days of Marco Polo, Europeans had hungered for the spices and silks of Asia. But the overland routes took years to travel and presented certain dangers. Merchants had to worry about wars, border taxes, and thieves. They also had to worry about the hostile powers that ruled western Asia. Europeans began to think that perhaps there was a better route to the great trading centers of the East.

Going South and West

In the 1400s, Europeans found they could reach Asia by sailing south around Africa. This was possible because of the great strides made in navigation, map making, and shipbuilding. Better ships, such as the Portuguese **caravel**, made sea travel safer and more efficient. Still, mariners had to deal with storms at sea, pirates, and their own fear of sea monsters.

Navigators at the time knew that the world was round. They just thought it was smaller than it really was. They figured that they could reach Asia by sailing west. What they didn't know was that North and South America blocked the way.

The Columbian Exchange

Europeans came to the Americas in increasing numbers. They brought ideas and goods with them and took other goods back, creating the so-called **Columbian Exchange**.

Europeans introduced new farming methods, farm animals, metal tools, and sugar cane. They also brought new diseases, which killed millions of Native Americans. The Europeans received potatoes, tobacco, corn, gemstones, and precious metals, such as gold and silver.

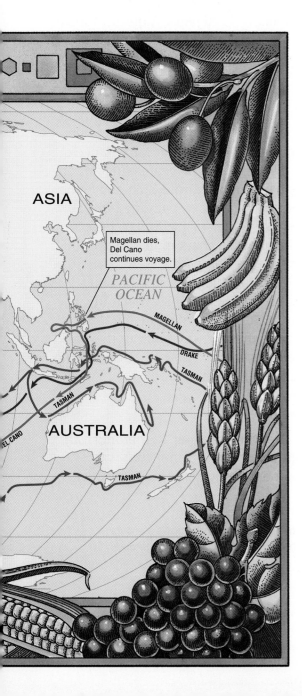

ASIA

Magellan dies, Del Cano continues voyage.

PACIFIC OCEAN

MAGELLAN

DRAKE

TASMAN

TASMAN

EL CANO

AUSTRALIA

TASMAN

⭐ **caravel** A fast, small sailing ship
Columbian Exchange Results of contact between European countries and the Americas

3 **Connections**

KEY TERMS

patron
scaffold
heliocentric
solar system

ART AND SCIENCE OF THE RENAISSANCE

FOCUS *The great artists and scientists of the Renaissance challenged old ideas and created new ways of looking at the world.*

Michelangelo

Michelangelo (mye kul AN juh loh) might be the greatest artist of all time. First, this genius from Italy was a most talented sculptor. His masterpieces include the *Pietà* (pee-AY tah), which shows the Virgin Mary holding the dead body of Christ, and *David*, the slayer of Goliath. Although Michelangelo carved in cold marble, his subjects look alive—as if they are about to spring into action.

◄ A portion of Michelangelo's *David*

Like most artists of his day, Michelangelo depended on the support of **patrons**. One of Michelangelo's patrons was Pope Julius II. One day in 1508 the pope asked him to paint the ceiling of the Sistine Chapel in the Vatican. Michelangelo protested that he was a sculptor, not a painter, but the pope was insistent. Michelangelo spent the next four years lying flat on his back on a **scaffold** high above the floor of the chapel, painting biblical scenes on the ceiling. Today, people willingly wait hours in line to see the stunning results of his efforts.

Michelangelo was also the chief architect of St. Peter's Church in Rome. St. Peter's magnificent dome crowns the largest church in the world. If all this wasn't enough, Michelangelo was also a first-rate poet.

Rembrandt

The Dutch painter Rembrandt van Rijn (REM brahnt vahn ryn) was another artistic genius of the

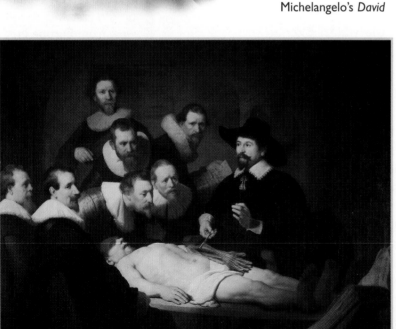

◄ This painting by Rembrandt shows a group of Dutch doctors studying the human body.

★ **patron** A wealthy or important person who helps another person, group, or institution
scaffold A framework for supporting workers

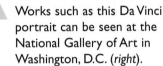

▲ Works such as this Da Vinci portrait can be seen at the National Gallery of Art in Washington, D.C. (*right*).

Renaissance. Unlike Michelangelo, Rembrandt did not have the support of his church. The Dutch Reformed Church looked down on religious art. So Rembrandt turned to rich merchants who wanted portraits painted of themselves and their families. In these portraits, Rembrandt displayed a wide range of emotions and personalities. One of his most famous portraits is *Anatomy Lesson of Professor Tulp*, shown on page 342.

The most revealing of Rembrandt's works is a series of 60 self-portraits. In these he shows himself changing from a brash youth to a confident, middle-aged man to a worn-down old man. These changes reflect the harsh realities of his life—the early death of his wife, the lack of patrons, and the steady loss of his eyesight.

Donatello

One of the earliest Renaissance geniuses was the Italian sculptor Donatello (dah nah TEL loh). He was one of the first to reach back to ancient Rome for inspiration. We see this in his *David* and *St. George*. Donatello carved faces that seemed to be alive. In fact, the artist was heard to demand of one of his works: "Speak then! Why will you not speak?"

Leonardo da Vinci

When people speak of a Renaissance man, they mean someone who is highly skilled in many fields. Perhaps the most notable Renaissance man of all time was Leonardo da Vinci (lee uh NAHR doh duh VIHN chee).

▲ Donatello's *St. George*

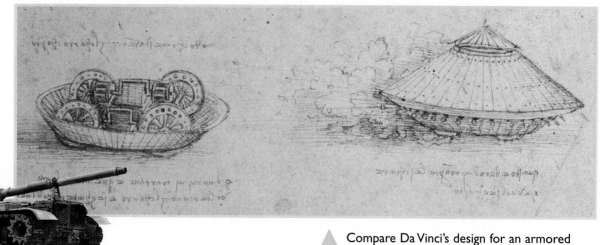

Compare Da Vinci's design for an armored vehicle with today's modern tank.

The idea for this modern tank originated more than 400 years ago.

Like Michelangelo, Da Vinci was a sculptor, a painter, and an architect. His paintings *Mona Lisa* and *The Last Supper* are among the best known in the world. But Da Vinci was more than an artist. He was also an engineer, a scientist, and an inventor. He bridged the gap between Renaissance art and Renaissance science. His scientific sketches of the human body, for example, are also works of art.

Da Vinci's curiosity about the workings of the world led him to design all sorts of things—the first machine gun, an adjustable monkey wrench, and a machine for cutting threads in screws. His active imagination also produced designs for an airplane, a tank, and a submarine.

Copernicus

Nicolaus Copernicus (nihk uh LAY us koh PUR nih kus), a Catholic priest from Poland, was a man with his head in the stars. Copernicus studied religion, of course. But he also studied mathematics, medicine, and astronomy.

Galileo's telescope opened up the heavens for closer observation.

For nearly 1,500 years, people had viewed the universe according to the teachings of Ptolemy (TAHL uh mee). This astronomer of ancient times had claimed that the earth was the center of the universe and that all heavenly bodies moved around it.

As Copernicus studied the sun, the moon, and the planets, a new picture formed in his mind. Using mathematical models, Copernicus determined that all the planets, including Earth, moved around the sun. His model of a **heliocentric solar system** shocked leaders of the Catholic Church. They believed that God had created all things for human beings. So it seemed logical that the earth would be the center of the universe. Many of the Church's beliefs were based on this concept.

Galileo

Many scientists supported the findings of Copernicus. Among them was Galileo Galilei (gal uh LEE oh gal-uh LAY ee), of Italy. Observations that

---

★ **heliocentric solar system**   A model of the solar system with the sun at its center

Galileo made with his new telescope convinced him that Copernicus's model was right.

Despite Galileo's reputation as a scientist and astronomer, the Church condemned him for supporting Copernicus. Today, however, everyone accepts that the earth and the other planets revolve around the sun.

Pascal

Blaise Pascal (blez pas KAL) started his career early. Born in France in 1623, Pascal was only 21 when he built the world's first digital calculator, ancestor to the modern computer.

Like other Renaissance men, Pascal didn't confine himself to one field. His

▲ Compare Pascal's calculator (*above*) with a modern-day version.

The Granger Collection

▲ Isaac Newton had one of the greatest scientific minds of all time.

scientific studies led to the invention of the hypodermic syringe and the hydraulic press. He was also widely respected for his writings on philosophy and religion.

Newton

Sir Isaac Newton is considered to be one of the greatest scientific geniuses of all time. From his fertile mind came an understanding of light, the law of gravity, and the physical laws that govern the motion of all moving bodies. In fact, an entire field of physics bears his name.

To Newton, the universe worked like a finely tuned watch. It ran according to a clear set of laws established at creation by God, the master watchmaker. To understand the laws of nature, thought Newton, was to understand God.

SHOW WHAT YOU KNOW!

REFOCUS
COMPREHENSION

1. Describe some of the works that earned Michelangelo the reputation of the greatest artist of all time.

2. How did Copernicus's idea of a heliocentric solar system differ from the ideas of most people of that time?

THINK ABOUT IT
CRITICAL THINKING

Why can Leonardo da Vinci be considered a man ahead of his time?

WRITE ABOUT IT
ACTIVITY

Most people consider Isaac Newton to be the greatest scientific genius in history. Write a paragraph in support of this belief.

4

Spotlight

★ **KEY TERMS**

Machiavellian
quixotic
satire

📖 **LITERATURE**

Bard of Avon

LITERATURE
OF THE RENAISSANCE

FOCUS *The Renaissance produced some of the greatest writers in human history. Their works still inspire and instruct modern readers.*

▼ Don Quixote and Sancho Panza still inspire artists and playwrights today.

Niccolò Machiavelli

The term **Machiavellian** (mak ee uh-VEL ee un) is often used today as an unflattering adjective to describe political figures. Generally speaking, a Machiavellian person is someone not to be trusted.

Niccolò Machiavelli (nee koh LOH mak ee uh VEL ee) would be upset if he knew what his name has come to mean. As a young man, Machiavelli

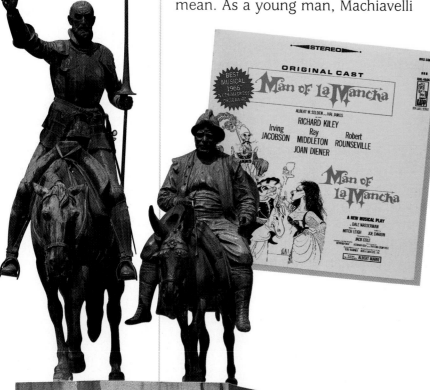

was a civil servant in Florence, Italy. During this period he had dealings with many important men of his time, including the pope, the kings of France and Germany, and several Italian princes.

In 1513, Machiavelli wrote a book titled *The Prince*. The book was based on what he had learned about politics in Italy. In *The Prince*, Machiavelli told how rulers really acted, not how they ought to act. Princes, he wrote, always acted in their own self-interest. This, bad as it was, wasn't the point of the book. The book helped readers take a cold, hard look at how rulers had to act if they wanted to keep their power.

Over the years, *The Prince* has continued to inspire discussion. Some people view it as an immoral guide for evil leaders. Others see it as a powerful insight at how the real world of politics works.

Miguel de Cervantes

The Spanish writer Miguel de Cervantes (mee GEL thhe ther VAHN-tes) also gave rise to the origin of a new word—**quixotic** (kwihks AHT ihk). The word comes from his great novel, *Don Quixote de la Mancha* (dahn kee-HOHT ay duh lah MAHN chuh).

★ *Machiavellian* Crafty, deceitful

★ *quixotic* Foolishly idealistic; impractical

A modern cast in a performance of Shakespeare's comedy *Much Ado About Nothing*

In this book Don Quixote is a knight who rides around the country on a broken-down horse. With Sancho Panza, his good-natured and more practical sidekick, Don Quixote seeks out opponents to fight. One of his more unusual opponents is a windmill, which he attacks, mistaking it for a giant. This encounter led to the coining of the phrase *tilting at windmills*.

Cervantes wrote the book as **satire**, poking fun at Spanish nobility and the cruelty of his time. *Don Quixote* was an immediate success throughout Europe. Today it remains one of the most widely read novels ever written. In fact, in the 1960s it was the inspiration for the popular musical *Man of La Mancha*.

William Shakespeare

If you were to say that William Shakespeare was the best writer ever in the English language, someone might disagree with you. But it's not likely. Shakespeare's plays capture every mood, from knee-slapping comedy and heartbreaking tragedy to flag-waving patriotism. Name any human emotion, and Shakespeare wrote about it. And he wrote about it brilliantly. His use of language set a standard by which playwrights are still judged.

Shakespeare's works have remained immensely popular for nearly 400 years. Operas have been written about the characters Othello and Falstaff. Many of Shakespeare's plays, such as *Hamlet, Macbeth,* and *Much Ado About Nothing*, have been turned into successful motion pictures.

Shakespeare was not only a gifted writer of the English language but also a great inventor of words and phrases. Many of his creations remain a part of our everyday language. *Leapfrog, lonely*, and *hurry* are but three of the nearly 2,000 words he created. Such familiar sayings as *fair play, tongue-tied*, and *melted into thin air* all came from the pen of this Renaissance genius.

This statue of William Shakespeare in Stratford-upon-Avon, England, looks over characters from some of his plays.

 satire The use of ridicule or sarcasm to expose the vices or misbehavior of others

Bard of Avon: The Story of William Shakespeare

By Diane Stanley and Peter Vennema

William Shakespeare was one of the greatest playwrights of all time. For over 300 years, his work has inspired writers, actors, and audiences throughout the world. Read about the kinds of plays Shakespeare wrote and the people and events that inspired him.

Shakespeare wrote three different kinds of plays: tragedies, comedies, and histories. In writing them, he followed many of the customs and fashions of the time.

The main characters in the tragedies, for example, were always doomed to death in the end. The comedies were full of mistaken identities, women disguised as men, miscarried letters, and all sorts of silly complications that were all resolved in the end, with everyone planning weddings. The histories told the stories of kings and great noblemen in exciting situations, such as war and rebellion.

Yet, while he followed all these conventions, he wove humor into his tragedies, put serious problems into his comedies, and brought the issues of the common people into his histories. His characters and the words they spoke were amazing and highly original.

Each of these wonderful plays had a central role for the company's leading man—James Burbage's son, Richard. In the early days, he played such youthful roles as Romeo in *Romeo and Juliet* and Prince

Hal in *Henry IV*. As he grew older, he played Hamlet, Othello, King Lear, and Macbeth. It is unlikely that any other actor in history has been given such a series of great parts to play!

Shakespeare's histories were very popular with the English people, partly because they were about English kings. Most historical plays at that time were about ancient civilizations, such as those of Greece or Rome. While Shakespeare wrote two such plays—*Julius Caesar* and *Anthony and Cleopatra*—most of his histories were about the great (and not so great) kings of England as well as other heroes and villains, plots, murders, and battles out of England's history.

In doing research for *Henry IV*, he read that the king's son, Prince Hal, had been very wild in his youth. And so, with this little hint from history, Shakespeare's wonderful imagination invented Sir John Falstaff, a fat and drunken knight who leads Prince Hal astray. Though Falstaff is a shameless liar, loud, cowardly, and crude, somehow Shakespeare makes us love him. Falstaff is the butt of many jokes, but they never get him down. Even in the tense battle scenes, he is there, a ridiculous figure clanking around in enormous armor, trying to avoid danger at all cost.

The groundlings loved him, and so did everyone else. In fact, Queen Elizabeth asked Shakespeare to write another play about Falstaff, showing him in love. And so he wrote *The Merry Wives of Windsor*, in which Falstaff writes love letters to two different ladies. By chance, the ladies discover what he is up to and decide to get even. The poor fellow winds up hidden in a basket of dirty laundry, which is dumped in the Thames River.

Want to read more about Shakespeare, his work, and the times in which he lived? Check this book out of your school or public library.

SHOW WHAT YOU KNOW!

REFOCUS
COMPREHENSION

1. Identify and define two words that had their origin in Renaissance literature.

2. Why did Cervantes use satire as a means of expressing his ideas?

THINK ABOUT IT
CRITICAL THINKING

What sorts of activities are indicated by the expression *tilting at windmills*?

WRITE ABOUT IT
ACTIVITY

Use the character of Falstaff to illustrate how Shakespeare was able to introduce humor into a play about a serious subject.

THE RISE OF NATIONALISM

FOCUS *As Europe moved into the modern age, some leaders were able to position themselves and their countries to take advantage of changing times. Others were not so successful.*

A CRUSHING DEFEAT

The middle of the fourteenth century marked the beginning of a long period of distrust and hostility between Spain and England. Thus it was that, in May 1588, King Philip II of Spain sent his powerful navy, known as the Spanish Armada (ahr MAH duh), to crush the English.

With more than 130 warships, the Spanish Armada was the greatest fleet in history. But it had flaws. Some ships were heavy and hard to maneuver. Others were not built well enough to handle the rough seas around England.

The smaller but faster English ships smashed the Spanish fleet. Forced to flee north around Scotland, the Spaniards lost more ships to the stormy seas. Only 76 ships of the once-mighty armada made it back to Spain. The English lost no ships, making this perhaps the most one-sided battle in history. It also signaled the beginning of the end for Spain as a world power.

"I AM THE STATE!"

Louis XIV was only four years old in 1643 when he inherited the French throne. So for years the real power was wielded by the prime minister, Cardinal Mazarin.

The French nobles hated Mazarin, and in 1648 they launched a rebellion known as the *Fronde* (frohnd). The nobles were defeated and in 1662 Louis took over the throne, declaring "L'état c'est moi!" or "I am the State!"

Louis was known as the Sun King because he believed he was the center of France, as the sun is the center of the solar system. During his 54-year reign, Louis drained the treasury in a series of senseless wars. He also spent lavishly on Versailles (vur SYE), the most impressive palace in Europe. Louis believed that such a setting was only fitting for the greatest king of the greatest country in Europe.

1588	1662	1688	1689–1725
English fleet defeats the Spanish Armada	Louis XIV takes control of French throne	William and Mary assume English throne	Peter the Great rules as czar of Russia

1550   1600   1650   1700   1750

A BLOODLESS REVOLUTION

In 1688 a son was born to King James II of England. Ordinarily this would be a joyous occasion for the English people. However, James was a Catholic king in a Protestant country. James's new son, who would also be Catholic, was first in line to inherit the throne!

This situation was too much for the English nobles. They asked James's daughter Mary and her husband William III of the Netherlands, who were Protestant, to assume the throne. On December 10, 1688, James was forced to flee England. This bloodless rebellion came to be known as the Glorious Revolution.

During the reign of William and Mary, Parliament assumed greater powers. In 1689 it enacted the Bill of Rights, which spelled out the rights of Parliament. New laws limited the power of the monarchy and protected the rights of the people.

PETER THE GREAT

Peter the Great was the czar (zahr), or ruler, of Russia from 1689 until 1725. Attempting to make Russia more European, he ordered many reforms. He banned the wearing of beards because he saw them as a symbol of Asian backwardness. To make his point, Peter even shaved a few men himself. He also simplified the Russian alphabet, required people to wear Western dress, and gave greater freedom to women.

Peter built a city by the Gulf of Finland, on land captured from Sweden. He named the city St. Petersburg. It replaced Moscow as the capital of Russia. To Peter, this city was his "window into Europe." It stood as a clear symbol that Russia had become a modern European nation.

SHOW WHAT YOU KNOW!

REFOCUS
COMPREHENSION

1. Why was Louis XIV known as the Sun King?

2. What was the most significant event during the reign of William and Mary?

THINK ABOUT IT
CRITICAL THINKING

Explain why this lesson is titled "The Rise of Nationalism."

WRITE ABOUT IT
ACTIVITY

Compare the basic idea of the Bill of Rights enacted by the English Parliament with the Bill of Rights in the Constitution of the United States.

SUMMING UP

1 DO YOU REMEMBER...
COMPREHENSION

1. Where and why was the Hundred Years' War fought?

2. What desire led to the beginning of the Renaissance?

3. What led Henry VIII of England to split with the Catholic Church?

4. What did Europeans unintentionally bring to the Americas as part of the Columbian Exchange?

5. Why is Leonardo da Vinci considered to be a great "Renaissance man"?

6. What important idea did Copernicus and Galileo develop?

7. What was Machiavelli's view of how rulers acted?

8. What three types of plays did William Shakespeare write?

9. How did the power of the monarchy change in England during the rule of William and Mary?

10. How did Peter the Great want Russia to change?

2 SKILL POWER
FORMULATING GENERALIZATIONS

In this chapter you read about making and identifying generalizations. Look back in the chapter and see if you can find any generalizations that the authors have made. Then write a few of your own generalizations about Europe during the Renaissance.

3 WHAT DO YOU THINK?
CRITICAL THINKING

1. In what ways was the Renaissance a rebirth of civilization?

2. In the 1400s, European explorers made many voyages. How was this sense of adventure in keeping with the spirit of the Renaissance?

3. How might Copernicus's discovery have changed people's view of themselves and life on Earth?

4. Why was it appropriate for Renaissance writers like Cervantes to use satire in their writings?

5. Which European monarchs were able to position themselves to take advantage of changing times? Which were less successful? Explain your answers.

4 SAY IT, WRITE IT, USE IT
VOCABULARY

Make a time line of Europe between 1400 and 1750. When listing important events on the time line, use six or more of the vocabulary terms.

caravel	patron
Columbian Exchange	quixotic
heliocentric solar system	Renaissance
Machiavellian	Reformation
middle class	satire
nationalism	scaffold
	thesis

CHAPTER 15

5 GEOGRAPHY AND YOU
MAP STUDY

Identify the major religion in each of the following areas.

1. North Africa
2. Holy Roman Empire
3. Russia
4. England

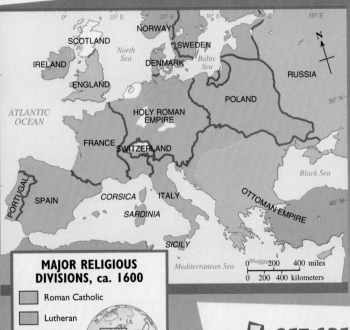

MAJOR RELIGIOUS DIVISIONS, ca. 1600

- Roman Catholic
- Lutheran
- Calvinist
- Church of England
- Orthodox
- Muslim

6 TAKE ACTION
CITIZENSHIP

Think about Martin Luther nailing his 95 theses to the church door in Wittenberg. Sometimes people need to speak out and detail problems they see in their surroundings. What about you? Are there problems in your neighborhood or school that need to be addressed? What improvements or changes do you think are needed? Make a list of your theses—you might have 3 or 30—and tape them to the chalkboard in your class. Later, with a group of classmates, read your theses and discuss what you think should be done.

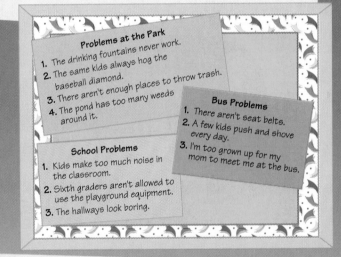

Problems at the Park
1. The drinking fountains never work.
2. The same kids always hog the baseball diamond.
3. There aren't enough places to throw trash.
4. The pond has too many weeds around it.

Bus Problems
1. There aren't seat belts.
2. A few kids push and shove every day.
3. I'm too grown up for my mom to meet me at the bus.

School Problems
1. Kids make too much noise in the classroom.
2. Sixth graders aren't allowed to use the playground equipment.
3. The hallways look boring.

7 GET CREATIVE
LANGUAGE ARTS CONNECTION

Choose a work of art created by one of the artists mentioned in this chapter and research it to find out more about its subject matter and the artist's techniques. Prepare a short oral report to share what you learn with your classmates. If possible, obtain a copy of the art piece you chose and show it as you present your talk.

LOOKING AHEAD As Europe moved into the modern age, find out what changes were taking place in the Americas.

EXPLORE

CHAPTER 16

CHANGING CULTURES

To the Europeans and Africans who came to the Americas, these lands were a new world. How would this attitude affect the Native Americans? Would the groups learn from each other?

CONTENTS

Look on page 369 to find out who made baskets such as the one shown here.

IN THE AMERICAS

You can explore several cultures of the Americas in these books. Read one that interests you and fill out a book-review form.

READ AND RESEARCH

The Diving Bell **by Todd Strasser** (Scholastic, 1992)
Although Culca dreams of diving with the men in her Mexican village, she knows that she cannot. When the Spaniards come to claim the Americas, they capture all the men in Culca's village to make them dive for gold. Can Culca save them before it's too late? *(historical fiction)*

San Rafael: A Central American City Through the Ages **by Xavier Hernández, illustrated by Jordi Ballonga and Jesep Escofet** (Houghton Mifflin Co., 1992)
Observe detailed drawings and read the descriptions to explore a fictional Maya city in Central America. Trace the city's growth and development over 2,000 years to the present. *(nonfiction)*

The Pueblos **by Suzanne Powell** (Franklin Watts, 1993)
The Spanish explorers called them Pueblos for the villages in which they lived. The Pueblo people were Native Americans living in what would become the southwestern United States. Find out how the Pueblos lived hundreds of years ago, and visit Pueblo people who keep the traditions alive today. *(nonfiction)*

SKILL POWER Summarizing Information

Summarizing helps you make large amounts of information easier to understand and remember.

UNDERSTAND IT

Do you ever get so excited about a book or a movie that you can hardly wait to tell your friends about it? You probably tell them about the main characters and about the most important things that happen—except the ending, of course! When you share the main ideas with your friends, you are summarizing the story.

EXPLORE IT

Writing a summary will help you recall the most important points of what you read. To write a summary, follow these steps.

1. Write a title for your summary.
2. Write the main idea for each paragraph.
3. Read your summary. Did you list only the main ideas? Did you leave any out?

Write a summary of this article. The first main idea has been underlined for you.

Houses in Colonial America

<u>When European settlers first came to colonial America, they built houses like the ones they had in Europe.</u> The English built houses with thatched roofs. Swedish settlers built log cabins, and the Dutch used doors with upper and lower parts that opened separately.

As settlers became accustomed to their new surroundings, they began to build with materials that were most plentiful in their area. Wood was available everywhere in colonial America, so it was used most often. In New England, many colonists built houses of stone, which was plentiful in that area. Bricks also were used in all the colonies, but they were more expensive than wood.

Fireplaces were the center of family life in the colonies. Meals were cooked in the fireplace, which also provided most of the heat and light. People gathered in front of the fireplace to eat, sew, relax, and entertain visitors. Wealthy colonists had many fireplaces in their houses.

▲ The fireplace was a family gathering spot in colonial America.

TRY IT

Find a newspaper or magazine article about a topic that interests you. The article might be about pet care, in-line skating, or your favorite author. Write a summary of the article. Then with your classmates make a display of the articles and the summaries.

If you read all the summaries, you will learn a lot about the interests of your friends. The summaries will also tell you which articles you would like to read.

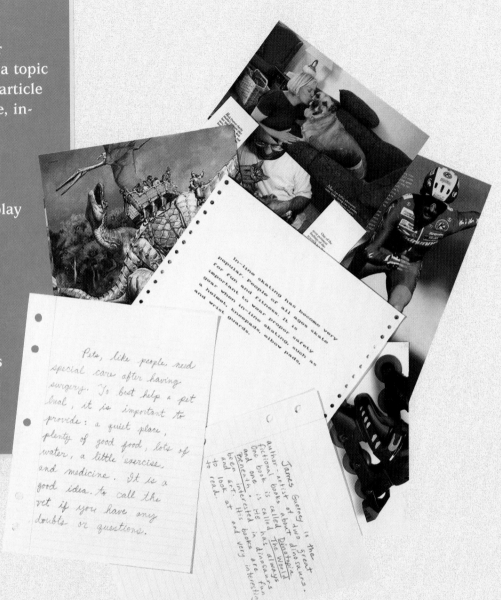

In-line skating has become very popular. People of all ages skate for fun and fitness. It is important to wear proper safety gear when in-line skating, such as a helmet, kneepads, elbow pads, and wrist guards.

Pets, like people, need special care after having surgery. To best help a pet heal, it is important to provide: a quiet place, plenty of good food, lots of water, a little exercise, and medicine. It is a good idea to call the vet if you have any doubts or questions.

James Gurney is the author-artist of two great fictional books about dinosaurs. One book is called Dinotopia: The World Beneath. His books are fun to look at and very interesting to read.

SKILL POWER SEARCH Choose one of the sections in this chapter that you find especially interesting and then practice the skill of summarizing information.

Setting the Scene

KEY TERMS

circumnavigation
viceroy
peninsular
criollo
peonage
pre-Columbian

A HEMISPHERE TRANSFORMED

FOCUS *Colonization of the Americas by Spain and Portugal brought enormous change for the civilizations already there. Eventually many aspects of Native American, African, and European cultures blended into a unique Latin American culture.*

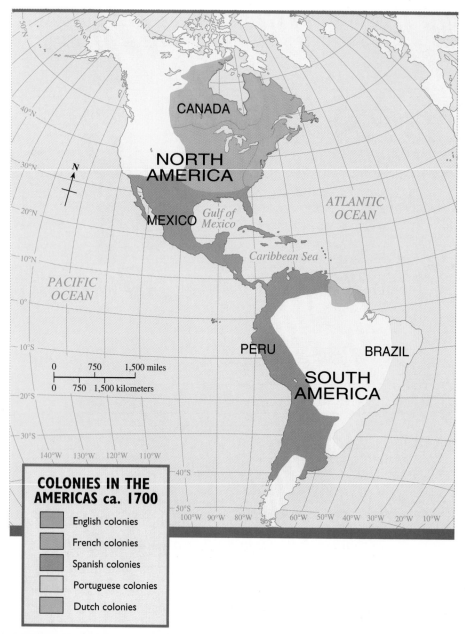

COLONIES IN THE AMERICAS ca. 1700

- English colonies
- French colonies
- Spanish colonies
- Portuguese colonies
- Dutch colonies

Explorers in the Americas

After the arrival of the first explorers and conquerors in North and South America, Europeans continued to learn about the many wonders of the two continents. From bases in the Caribbean and Mexico, explorers fanned out across the continents. Later, Ferdinand Magellan, a Portuguese navigator sailing for Spain, discovered Cape Horn, at the tip of South America, on the first **circumnavigation** of the globe.

After the conquest of the Aztec Empire, Spaniards explored what is now the Southwest of the United States, looking for the fabled cities of gold. Explorers went up the Amazon River to the source of the great rivers of South America.

Though other European nations had gotten a late start, they too sent explorers to the Americas. The English looked for the Northwest Passage, a waterway through North America, to Asia. The French explored the rivers of North America.

 circumnavigation The act of sailing or flying around an area

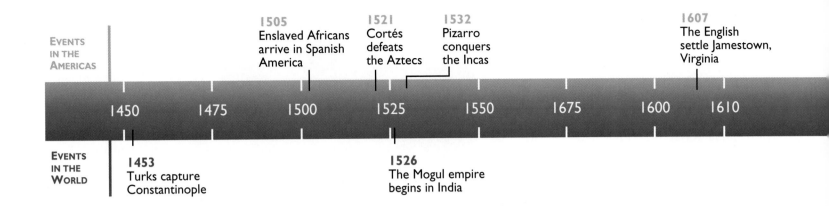

1505
Enslaved Africans arrive in Spanish America

1521
Cortés defeats the Aztecs

1532
Pizarro conquers the Incas

1607
The English settle Jamestown, Virginia

1450   1475   1500   1525   1550   1675   1600   1610

1453
Turks capture Constantinople

1526
The Mogul empire begins in India

Establishing Colonies

As the map shows, the nations of Europe carved out colonies for themselves in the Americas. The French established their power in today's Canada. The English ruled the 13 colonies that would become the United States, as well as some islands in the Caribbean Sea. The French and Dutch also set up colonies in the Caribbean. In the nineteenth century the Russians started trading outposts in Alaska and northern California.

The largest colonized area, however, was in the hands of the Spanish and the Portuguese. These two nations controlled the area from Florida south to the tip of South America.

Spanish and Portuguese rule brought sweeping changes to the Americas. The conquerors did more than just place new rulers in power. They also brought new ways of life and new people to share the land with the original inhabitants. The American lands claimed by Spain and Portugal came to be known as Latin America. The name came from Latin, the root language of Spanish and Portuguese.

Rulers of Great Power

Both Spain and Portugal had powerful monarchs who ruled as they saw fit. This carried over into the Americas. The top officials in the Spanish colonies were called **viceroys**, literally "assistant-kings." Appointed by the king, they were responsible only to him. Layers of lesser officials served under them. At each level, officials held great power. They answered to the officials above them and ultimately to the king in Spain, not to the colonists. Portugal's method of rule was similar. A governor-general in Brazil represented the Portuguese king. He ruled from Bahia, on Brazil's eastern coast.

SOME EARLY EXPLORERS		
Explorer	**Date**	**Territory Explored**
Columbus	1492–1504	Caribbean Islands
Balboa	1513	Central America
Cortés	1519–1521	Mexico
Verrazano	1524	Searched for the Northwest Passage
Pizarro	1531–1535	Peru
Cartier	1535	Canada—St. Lawrence River
De Soto	1539–1542	North American southeast
Estevanico	1539	North American southwest
Coronado	1540–1542	North American southwest
Frobisher	1576–1578	Searched for the Northwest Passage

★ **viceroy** A governor of a colony ruling as the representative of the king

Colonial Society

Spain and Portugal brought to the Americas a style of life that reflected their class-conscious societies. In both countries the kings and nobles formed the upper class. Almost everyone else was a commoner. So, in the Americas, colonial society became divided between upper and lower classes.

Many of the soldiers who helped to conquer the Americas had been commoners back home. In gratitude for their deeds, rulers often granted them noble titles and gave them American lands. Nobles from Spain and Portugal also received lands on which to start colonies.

Settlers from the home country who came to Spanish America were known as **peninsulares** (pay neen soo LAH rez). They became Latin

Sor [Sister] Juana was a scholar and poet in colonial Mexico.

America's upper class. Slightly below them in status were **criollos** (kree OH-yohz). Some criollos became very wealthy, but they could not hold the higher positions in government. Everyone else was part of the lower class. People of European background were better off socially and economically than Native Americans and Africans. People of the various groups intermarried, so there were many combinations. The status-conscious Spaniards had a name for each type.

A Woman's Place in Society

Latin Americans were not only divided by class. There were also strict rules about the roles of men and women. While men moved about the worlds of education, commerce, religion, and government, women had two basic choices—they could marry or become nuns. This is the atmosphere in which a criolla, Juana Inés de la Cruz, the most famous Spanish-speaking poet of the late 1600s, lived. Fearing that marriage would prevent her from studying, she chose to enter a convent at the age of 17. Juana's poems spoke of subjects

SOCIAL STRUCTURE

Viceroy
Peninsulares
Criollos
Lower Class
Slaves

⭐ **peninsular** Spanish, meaning person "from the peninsula" of Iberia, where Spain and Portugal are located
criollo Person of European parents born in the Americas

that were dangerous in a world ruled by tradition and the Church. She questioned the rigid roles of men and women and spoke out in favor of scientific experimentation as a way to understand the world.

A European slave dealer auctions Africans in the Americas.

African Labor Force

When Europeans first arrived, an estimated 50 million people lived in Spanish America. By the 1600s the Native American population had dropped to a mere 4 million. Some died of mistreatment or overwork. However, the great majority perished from European diseases to which they had no natural immunity.

The Europeans found a new source of workers on the west coast of Africa. Under colonial law, enslaved Africans could be bought and sold as property. That was a kind of slavery unknown to the Americas. Aztecs and Incas had used captives as slaves, but they never thought of them as property.

The first enslaved Africans were brought to Spanish America within 13 years after Columbus's arrival. By the late 1500s, there were some 60,000 Africans in Spanish colonies. During the 1700s the number swelled enormously, as economic growth increased the demand for cheap labor.

The Spanish treated Native Americans differently from Africans. Native Americans could be forced to work on farmland or in a mine. But they could not be bought and sold.

A Different Kind of Slavery

The first landholdings in Spanish America were called *encomiendas* (en koh MYEN dahs). With an encomienda the landholder acquired more than land. He or she also got the labor of the Native Americans who lived on it. This practice was later stopped.

In its place a new system, called **peonage**, developed by the 1600s. Landowners now had to pay each worker a wage. However, the colonists found that by lending money to workers, they could bind them in a web of debt. Workers could not take a new job as long as they owed money to their employer. When workers died, their families inherited the debt.

 peonage A system where debtors must work for their creditors until their debts are paid

Missionaries in the Americas

Spain and Portugal were eager to tap the wealth of the Americas. But they were also concerned with a second goal—to convert the Native Americans to Roman Catholicism.

Priests arrived on the earliest Spanish ships. The first Spanish missionaries reached Mexico in 1524. Often barefoot and wearing simple brown robes, they spread through the Americas.

Missionaries not only preached religion but also healed the sick and set up schools. Sympathetic missionaries fought to improve conditions for Native Americans. They set up model communities, helping the people build farms and workshops.

During the 1500s, priests protested the mistreatment of Native Americans. Bartolomé de las Casas (bahr toh loh MAY de lahs KAH sahs) was one of the most outspoken. Las Casas promoted the use of African slaves to ease conditions for Native Americans. He later regretted this suggestion.

Within a short time, many Native Americans became Catholics, but they did not necessarily give up all their old beliefs. Many continued to worship other gods and goddesses alongside the God of the Christians.

A Cultural Mix

As time passed, a unique Latin American culture developed. It blended elements from Spain, Portugal, **pre-Columbian** America, and Africa. Peninsulares and criollos adopted many of the foods and customs of Native Americans. For example, they made a flat corn-and-flour bread called a tortilla and wrapped it around meat and beans. They slept in Maya-style hammocks and adopted Native American words.

Religions also blended. In 1531 a vision of the Virgin Mary appeared to a baptized Aztec named Juan Diego. He saw her at a ruined temple where Aztecs earlier had worshiped a goddess known as Our Mother. Juan Diego's vision was of a brown-skinned Mary. As the Virgin of Guadalupe, she became the patron saint of Mexico.

The African contribution to the new culture was also very important, especially in the Caribbean and Brazil. African foods—yams, black-eyed peas, and bananas—became part of everyday life for all. Africans also brought with them the memories of the instruments they had used at home. They made marimbas (similar to xylophones), drums, and stringed instruments. These instruments produce the distinctive music of Latin America that is popular today.

▼ Missionaries spread throughout Latin America.

 pre-Columbian Before the exploration and conquest of the Americas by Europeans

The family in this painting typifies the cultural mix that was created in Latin America.

Neighbors in Conflict

Spain and Portugal were not the only European nations to seek wealth in the Americas. Besides exploration and settlements, military force played a role in deciding who ruled where. In the late 1500s, English "sea dogs" or pirates, like Sir Francis Drake, harassed the Spaniards. They attacked Spanish ships and towns in the Caribbean and along the Spanish Main—the mainland areas that bordered the Caribbean.

The English, the French, and the Dutch gained control of some Caribbean islands and scattered spots along the coast of the mainland. England started sugar plantations in Jamaica. France had a colony in what is today Haiti. For a short time, the Dutch controlled parts of Brazil's coast. Four separate wars in the late 1600s and 1700s helped to redraw the colonial borders between the American territories of the European nations.

Sea dogs would attack towns and hold officials for ransom.

FALL OF GREAT EMPIRES

FOCUS *The fall of the Aztec Empire occurred because of the Aztec belief that Cortés was a god and because of an alliance between Cortés and other Native Americans. The Inca Empire fell to Pizarro after it had been weakened by a previous war.*

A Legend Comes True

According to an Aztec legend, the god Quetzalcoatl would return someday to claim his kingdom. The god, who was light-skinned, would come across the sea in the east. The prophecy told that he would return in a 1 Reed year of the Aztec calendar.

The Aztec emperor Moctezuma (mawk tay SOO mah) became nervous as the 1 Reed year approached. It was 1519 in the European calendar. That was the year that Hernán Cortés and his Spanish **conquistadors** (kahn KEES tuh-dorz) arrived on the east coast of Mexico. Moctezuma heard that light-skinned people who rode strange beasts had arrived in great ships. Assuming this must be Quetzalcoatl, Moctezuma became fearful.

Two Emperors Are Defeated

Shortly after arriving, Cortés met Malinche (mah LEEN chay), a Native American woman. Her people had been conquered by the Aztecs, and she was willing to serve Cortés as interpreter and guide. As he marched toward the capital city, Cortés picked up more support. Malinche told him the people resented their mistreatment at the hands of the Aztecs. Through her, he offered to free them. Cortés and his men killed the emperor and laid waste the Aztec capital.

Farther south, the conquistador Francisco Pizarro was also lucky. When he reached Peru, Atahualpa (ah tuh WAHL puh), the son of the former Inca ruler, had just defeated his brother in a war for the throne. The fighting had left the Inca Empire in a weakened condition.

▼ This painting portrays the battle for Tenochtitlán.

★ *conquistador* Spanish word for "conqueror"

CONZEDERACION COMOLEMALTRATA

This illustration from that time period shows a Spanish soldier beating a young Incan as his mother begs for mercy.

The victorious Atahualpa was arrogant. He took lightly the threat posed by the small number of Spaniards. When Pizarro invited Atahualpa to a feast in 1532, the Inca ruler accepted. Pizarro took him prisoner and executed him the next year. Without a ruler, the Inca Empire was easy prey for the Spaniards. Pizarro soon captured the Inca capital city of Cuzco.

New Cities

Cortés's men set fire to the Aztec city of Tenochtitlán. The victorious Spaniards built their new capital on the site of the old one. Defeated Aztecs were put to work tearing down the old city's statues and buildings.

The stones of Tenochtitlán were turned into new buildings for the Spanish capital. Catholic churches were built on the sites of Aztec temples. The conquerers built palaces for themselves.

Tenochtitlán was renamed *Mexico*, "the place of the Mexicas," another name for the Aztecs. It became the capital of New Spain. Today it is Mexico City, capital of the nation.

In Peru, Pizarro also ordered a new capital to be constructed. But the Inca stronghold of Cuzco was high in the Andes Mountains, far too remote for the capital of a Spanish colony.

In 1535, Pizarro founded a new city near the Pacific coast. He called it "the City of the Kings." The city was laid out in Spanish style. A large plaza, surrounded by a cathedral and government buildings, formed the heart of the city.

Later called Lima, the city became the headquarters of Spanish viceroys. The vast wealth of Spanish America was used there to build lavish homes and to decorate the churches and monasteries with gold and silver. Today, Lima is the capital of Peru.

SHOW WHAT YOU KNOW!

REFOCUS
COMPREHENSION

1. How were small numbers of Spanish soldiers able to overcome the Aztec and Inca empires?

2. What became of the Aztec and Inca capital cities?

THINK ABOUT IT
CRITICAL THINKING

Which capital city suffered the worse fate—that of the Aztecs or the Incas? Explain your answer.

WRITE ABOUT IT
ACTIVITY

Examine the painting on page 364. Write a paragraph in which you use what you see to compare the Aztec and Spanish cultures. Look at their clothing, tools, weapons, animals, and so on.

THE FRENCH IN THE AMERICAS

FOCUS *French exploration and colonization in the Americas extended from what is now eastern Canada, south along the Mississippi River, and onto the Caribbean island of Hispaniola.*

THE FRENCH IN CANADA

Jacques Cartier (zhahk kahr tee AY), searching for the Northwest Passage, sailed along the Canadian coast in 1534. He claimed that land for France. Around 1600 the French king gave merchants permission to build trading posts in what was called New France. One merchant hired the king's mapmaker, Samuel de Champlain (sham PLAYN), to go to North America.

Champlain made his first trip to New France in 1603. Over the next 30 years, he returned nearly a dozen times. French fur traders and trappers followed. Champlain also started the first permanent French settlement in New France at Quebec in 1608.

The French got along well with most Native Americans. Unlike the Spaniards, the French did not try to conquer them and showed respect for their culture.

Fur traders lived among the Native Americans, learning their languages and ways of life. Many priests went to New France to introduce Christianity to the Native Americans.

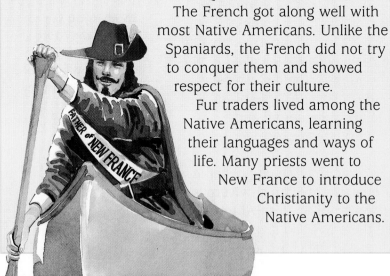

ISLANDS IN THE SUN

The French also colonized some of the islands of the Caribbean. In the 1600s the western part of the island of Hispaniola (hihs pun YOH luh) came under French control. Hispaniola had been the earliest base of the Spaniards in the Americas, established in 1492. French settlers soon came to the western part of the island, where there were few Spanish settlements. The French called their colony Saint Domingue (san duh MANG). Today it is called Haiti.

Here the French established sugar and coffee plantations. The European sweet tooth made Saint Domingue the wealthiest of all of France's colonies.

However, a large number of workers were required to harvest the sugar cane and turn it into sugar. As a result, the French government allowed the importation of enslaved people from Africa. Soon the Africans greatly outnumbered the French.

1534
Jacques Cartier explores the Canadian coast

1608
Samuel de Champlain founds Quebec

1673
Marquette and Joliet explore the Mississippi

1682
French claim the Louisiana Territory

1803
France sells the Louisiana Territory

1550   1600   1650   1700   1750   1800

DOWN THE MISSISSIPPI

Jacques Marquette (mahr KET) was a missionary in New France. He was interested in geography and was a skilled mapmaker. Marquette teamed up with a fur trapper named Louis Joliet (lwee JOH lee et). Both men had heard Native Americans speak of a great river farther to the south. Perhaps this might be the long-sought Northwest Passage.

In 1673, Marquette and Joliet set out to look for the river. After many weeks they reached the Mississippi. They paddled down the river, but as it continued to flow south, not west, they knew they had not found the Northwest Passage.

Nine years later, Robert de La Salle, another explorer, went down the Mississippi to the Gulf of Mexico. La Salle claimed the land along the river for France. He called it Louisiana to honor his king.

LOUISIANA TERRITORY

France strengthened its hold on its Louisiana territory by building a string of trading posts, villages, and forts along the Mississippi River. The two most important ones became the cities of St. Louis and New Orleans.

In 1762, Spain took control of the Louisiana Territory. But in 1800, Napoleon Bonaparte, who was the new ruler of France, forced Spain to give it back.

Napoleon needed money to finance his wars in Europe more than he needed land. He offered to sell Louisiana to the United States. In 1803 the two countries agreed on a price of $15 million. This was a huge sum at the time, and no one really knew how much land there was. As it turned out, the United States had purchased all or part of 13 of its future states—at a cost of about 3 cents an acre.

REFOCUS
COMPREHENSION

1. Why did the French first bring enslaved people from Africa to the Caribbean?

2. Although the Mississippi was not the sought-after Northwest Passage, how was the river important to the French?

THINK ABOUT IT
CRITICAL THINKING

The relationship between French settlers and Native Americans was different from the one between the Spaniards and Native Americans. What conditions may have led to this difference?

WRITE ABOUT IT
ACTIVITY

You are a French explorer along the Mississippi River. Write a diary entry describing your sights and experiences during one day in the wilderness.

367

4

NATIVE AMERICAN CULTURES

FOCUS *The United States was inhabited for thousands of years by Native American peoples. Clues to these varied cultures can be found in the artifacts and structures they left behind.*

Anasazi Farmers

Encouraged by rumors of golden cities, Spanish explorers searched the land that is Arizona and New Mexico today. Here they found Native American farmers who lived in villages with houses of adobe. The Spaniards called these native peoples Pueblos, after the Spanish word for "village." Among them were Hopis (HOH peez) and Zunis (ZOO neez). You can find these names on the map at right.

The ancestors of these Native Americans were known as the Anasazi (ahn uh SAH zee). From about A.D. 100 to 1300, the Anasazi lived in the area where the present-day states of Arizona, New Mexico, Utah, and Colorado meet. They knew how to make the most of a desert environment. Their ancestors were hunters and gatherers. But the spread of agriculture from Middle America changed the Anasazi into farmers. Soon they learned how to use irrigation to water their corn crops.

▼ The largest of the Anasazi cliff dwellings was Mesa Verde in southwestern Colorado.

★ ***adobe*** Sun-dried bricks used for building

Many baskets, such as those shown here, were so tightly woven that they could hold water.

Anasazi Cliff Dwellers

The Anasazi often built their houses in the sides of cliffs for protection from weather and from enemies. These buildings were like apartment houses, with many rooms. The rooms were very tiny, however. The ceilings were so low that the Anasazi had to bend over all the time they were indoors.

One group of Anasazi, the Mesa Verde (MAY suh vurd) people, lived on top of the **mesas** above the cliffs. Around the year 1200 the people shifted to the sides of the cliffs along the Mancos River. Some scholars believe they did this to make more space on top of the mesa for farmland.

The people cut building blocks from the sandstone cliffs and then fashioned rooms that fit tightly into the crevices. To make the best use of the space, the rooms were stacked up, sometimes four levels high. At night, the cliffdwellers huddled around the fire. In the morning the men of Mesa Verde climbed steep steps to get to their fields on the top of the mesa.

Because the Mesa Verde people did not trade much with neighboring people, their supply of goods was small. When pots broke, they had to be fixed with **pitch**, and clothing was usually handed down. The crowded ledges made life more difficult. Human wastes and garbage were deposited close to the living quarters, which harmed the health of the community.

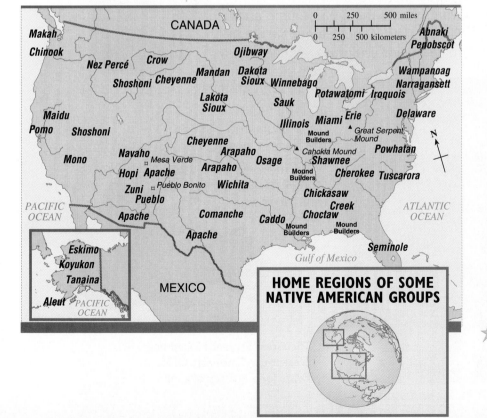

HOME REGIONS OF SOME NATIVE AMERICAN GROUPS

⭐ *mesa* A flat-topped plateau or tableland with steep sides
pitch A sticky substance found in some evergreen trees, coal tar, and petroleum

Leaving the Cliff Dwellings

Around 1275 a drought made farming more difficult. For years the rain rarely fell, and the food supply shrank to almost nothing. There was no alternative but to leave. Some Anasazi left food behind, showing that they hoped to come back some day. But they never returned.

The Mesa Verde people left their cliff dwellings and moved away. Their descendants grew corn and squash, performing dances and songs to their gods so the seeds would grow. They created beautiful pottery, baskets, and blankets that still impress people today.

Mound Builders

In the area that is now called Georgia, the Spaniards found temples and earthen pyramids. They had been built by a Native American people that anthropologists call Mound Builders. They had lived in the region of the Mississippi River for thousands of years. The Cherokees, Natchez, and Creeks are among their descendants.

The first mounds were built about 1000 B.C. Over time the mounds grew in size. Some were shaped to look like animals. To make them, workers carried thousands of baskets of dirt from other places. Many of the mounds must have taken years to create. Often the animal shape can best be appreciated if viewed from above.

Many of the mounds are burial sites. Layers of bodies have been found. As each stage of the mound was completed, bones were added and covered with soil. The biggest mounds have generations of dead.

Cultural Changes

A new mound culture called Hopewell arose around 100 B.C. in what is now the area of Ohio and Illinois. The Hopewell people created magnificent sculpture. Artifacts show that they went as far as Wyoming and Michigan to trade tools and freshwater pearls for copper and stones to use in their artwork.

Artifacts from mounds in present-day Texas *(above)* and Ohio *(center and below)*

The Great Serpent Mound near present-day Cincinnati, Ohio, twists for a quarter of a mile.

▲ A Navajo rock painting of Spaniards and their horses and dogs

Around A.D. 500 the Mississippian culture appeared. It thrived throughout the Mississippi Valley south to the Gulf of Mexico and in the southeastern woodlands. These people built pyramid-shaped mounds with temples and palaces on top. In the thirteenth century some 10,000 people lived in the village at Cahokia (kuh HOH kee-uh). The area had hundreds of mounds. The largest pyramid, built a bit later, rose to a height of 100 feet.

The People of the Plains

Many Native Americans of the Plains lived very simple lives. They settled near streams or rivers to have a source of water. Women were responsible for farming. The men hunted buffaloes. They had no horses.

Buffalo hunting on foot was dangerous and difficult. Though the Plains people had bows and arrows, they could kill a thick-skinned buffalo only if it was already wounded. One way to wound them was to drive a herd off a cliff.

The Culture Changes

Spanish explorers and settlers brought horses to the Americas and changed the way of life of the Plains people forever. Some of the Spanish horses escaped into the wild and, over time, wandered into the plains. During the 1600s the Plains people caught and tamed the horses.

On horseback the Plains people could roam hundreds of miles in search of animals. They brought home more food than ever before. Horses also enabled the Plains people to carry more and heavier goods. Trading with neighboring groups increased. The resulting prosperity caused a great increase in the Plains population.

Other Native Americans began to adopt horses and the Plains way of life. The Comanches (kuh MAN cheez), for example, perfected the art of horseback riding. Riding became as natural as walking. However, the Plains way of life in time would be destroyed by the westward expansion of the United States.

5

Map Adventure

SAILING THE SPANISH MAIN

FOCUS *From the fifteenth to the seventeenth centuries, Spanish fleets sailed the Caribbean Sea, carrying treasures from the Americas back to Spain. Pirates from many nations roamed the waters of the Spanish Main, attacking unsuspecting Spanish ships.*

Adventure on the Spanish Main

Every year two large treasure fleets, protected by royal **galleons**, sailed from Spain to the colonies in the Americas. The New Spain **Flota** sailed to Mexico for Aztec treasures, while the Tierra Firme Flota sailed south for the riches of South America. The fleets traveled to many ports before sailing to Havana and then back to Spain. Everyone, including the pirates who roamed the Spanish Main, knew the routes.

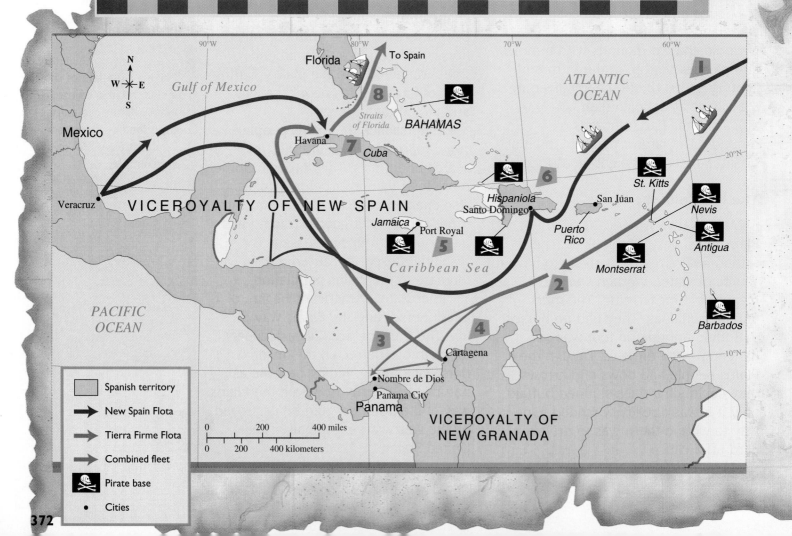

Map legend:

- Spanish territory
- ➡ New Spain Flota
- ➡ Tierra Firme Flota
- ➡ Combined fleet
- ☠ Pirate base
- • Cities

Map Key

1 New Spain Flota This fleet left Spain every spring for ports in Mexico, Honduras, and the northern islands. The ships carried goods such as glass, books, paper, and clothes to be traded with the Spanish colonists. The following February the fleet sailed to Havana.

2 Tierra Firme Flota Every August this fleet sailed toward the port of Cartagena (kahr tuh HAY nuh) in the viceroyalty of New Granada. Some of the ships continued on to Nombre de Dios. The following January the fleet regrouped in Cartagena and sailed for Havana.

3 Nombre de Dios Mule trains carrying Inca silver and gold arrived in this town from Panama City to trade with the Tierra Firme Flota. The town had almost no defenses and was an easy target for pirates.

4 Cartagena Mule trains from the interior brought emeralds, pearls, indigo, and cocoa to Cartagena to trade with the fleet.

5 Port Royal This port was a notorious pirate town. It was a permanent base where pirates gathered to spend their stolen riches and plan attacks against the Spaniards.

6 Hispaniola French pirates established bases along the northern and southern coasts from which to raid Spanish ships or coastal towns.

7 Havana This city had a well-defended harbor. Here the fleets would take on supplies for the long trip back to Spain. Pirates raided ships approaching or leaving the harbor.

8 Straits of Florida Ships leaving Havana for Spain sailed northeast through these dangerous straits. Storms, coral reefs, and shallow water caused many ships to sink, and pirates lurking in the Bahamas were also a constant threat.

★ **galleon** A large, heavily armed ship used for trading and war
flota A fleet of ships
indigo A plant used for making blue dye

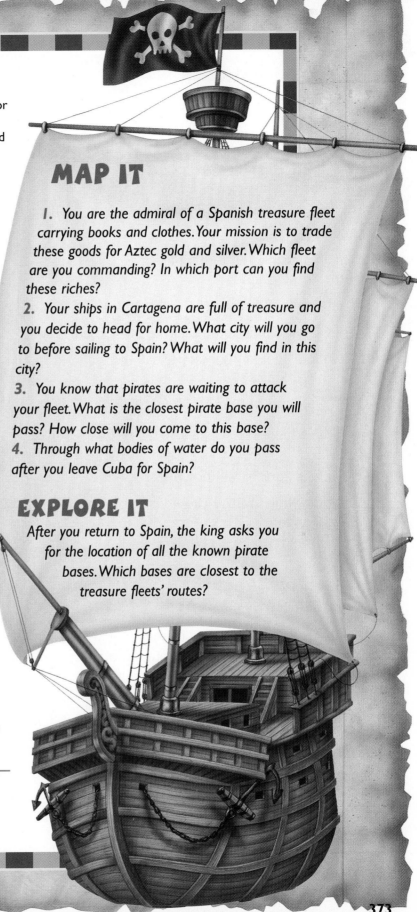

MAP IT

1. You are the admiral of a Spanish treasure fleet carrying books and clothes. Your mission is to trade these goods for Aztec gold and silver. Which fleet are you commanding? In which port can you find these riches?

2. Your ships in Cartagena are full of treasure and you decide to head for home. What city will you go to before sailing to Spain? What will you find in this city?

3. You know that pirates are waiting to attack your fleet. What is the closest pirate base you will pass? How close will you come to this base?

4. Through what bodies of water do you pass after you leave Cuba for Spain?

EXPLORE IT

After you return to Spain, the king asks you for the location of all the known pirate bases. Which bases are closest to the treasure fleets' routes?

SUMMING UP

1 DO YOU REMEMBER...
COMPREHENSION

1. Why were Juana Inés de la Cruz's poems considered dangerous?

2. Who were the English sea dogs, and what did they do?

3. What was expected to happen in a 1 Reed year of the Aztec calendar?

4. What does the name *Mexico* mean?

5. Why is Samuel de Champlain remembered?

6. Why did Napoleon Bonaparte sell Louisiana to the United States?

7. Who were the Anasazi and where did they live?

8. What have anthropologists found in the Mound Builders' mounds?

9. What was Port Royal known as?

10. What did mule trains bring to Nombre de Dios to trade with the Tierra Firme Flota?

2 SKILL POWER
SUMMARIZING INFORMATION

Pick one person described in this chapter whom you would like to know more about. Find an article, book, or encyclopedia article that you could summarize. Remember the following guidelines.

1. Use the title of the article, chapter, or chapter section as the title of your summary.

2. Write the main idea of each paragraph under the summary title.

3. Leave out details and unimportant information.

3 WHAT DO YOU THINK?
CRITICAL THINKING

1. Why do you think the workers under the peonage system did not rebel against the landowners?

2. Why were the conquistadors able to conquer Moctezuma and Atahualpa?

3. Was Napoleon Bonaparte right or wrong to sell Louisiana? Explain your opinion.

4. Why didn't the Anasazi return to their cliff dwellings after the drought ended in the late 1200s?

5. The Spanish conquistadors stole riches from the people of the Americas. The pirates in turn stole the treasures from the Spaniards. Whose side would you be on and why?

4 SAY IT, WRITE IT, USE IT
VOCABULARY

Write a travel brochure about one of the historical places mentioned in this chapter. Use as many of these terms as possible.

adobe	mesa
criollo	peninsular
circumnavigation	peonage
conquistador	pitch
flota	pre-Columbian
galleon	viceroy
indigo	

5 GEOGRAPHY AND YOU

MAP STUDY

The map below shows the viceroyalties of Spain and Portugal in the Americas around 1650. Study the map and answer these questions.

1. Which viceroyalty included part of what is now the United States?

2. Compare this map to maps of North America and South America in the Atlas. Which modern capital cities were once capitals of viceroyalties?

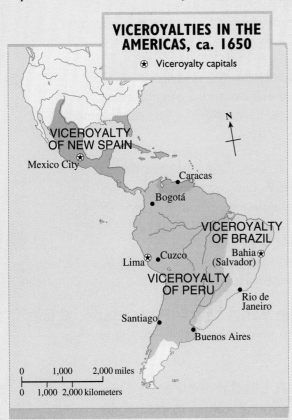

VICEROYALTIES IN THE AMERICAS, ca. 1650

⊛ Viceroyalty capitals

VICEROYALTY OF NEW SPAIN

Mexico City ⊛

Caracas

Bogotá

VICEROYALTY OF BRAZIL

Lima ⊛ Cuzco

Bahia ⊛ (Salvador)

VICEROYALTY OF PERU

Rio de Janeiro

Santiago

Buenos Aires

| 0 | 1,000 | 2,000 miles |
| 0 | 1,000 | 2,000 kilometers |

6 TAKE ACTION

CITIZENSHIP

A number of historical sites were mentioned in this chapter. Most have been preserved for future generations to see. Are there historical sites near where you live? Have they been preserved? Are there places that should be preserved? Find out about people in your area who are trying to protect a historical site. How are they repairing or protecting it? Share your findings in class. Use pictures to illustrate your talk.

7 GET CREATIVE

HEALTH CONNECTION

Do you know what ethnic foods are? They are the foods that are associated with a particular culture. Several ethnic foods are mentioned in this chapter. Make a chart of these foods, using pictures from magazines or drawing your own. On the chart, tell where each food comes from. Explain the nutritional importance the foods played in the health and survival of people in the Americas.

LOOKING AHEAD Turn your attention to Chapter 17, where you will learn about the beauty and culture of Southeast Asia.

EXPLORE

CHAPTER 17

CIVILIZATIONS OF

Perhaps nowhere on earth do ancient traditions operate alongside modern conventions as smoothly as they do in Southeast Asia.

▼ What is the unusual object the boy is holding? You'll find out when you read page 388.

CONTENTS

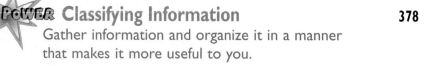

SOUTHEAST ASIA

You can learn more about the countries and cultures of Southeast Asia from these books. Read one that interests you and fill out a book-review form.

READ AND RESEARCH

Thailand: Land of Smiles by Karen Schwabach
(Dillon Press, 1991)
You will find the facts and folklore of this country fascinating. Read about King Mongkut, who is featured in the movie *The King and I.* Learn about schools where children learn sword fighting and flower making, as well as science and math. *(nonfiction)*

A Boat to Nowhere by Maureen Crane Wartski, illustrated by Dick Teicher (Penguin USA, 1981)
The life of their peaceful village changes drastically for Mai and Loc when the new government takes over. Their family must flee Vietnam if Grandfather is to be saved. *(historical fiction)*

The Tiger's Whisker and Other Tales from Asia and the Pacific by Harold Courtlander, illustrations by Enrico Arno (Henry Holt & Co., 1995)
These amusing Asian stories focus on truth, wisdom, and other virtues. *(folk tales)*

Batik and Tie-Dye by Susie O'Reilly
(Thomas Learning, 1993)
Batik, a decorative technique for dyeing cloth, has been around for centuries. You can learn how to design your own batik patterns. *(nonfiction)*

Skill Power

Classifying Information

Knowing how to classify information makes it easier to remember and learn the material you read.

UNDERSTAND IT

How many games did your favorite baseball team win last year? How many touchdown passes did your team's quarterback throw? It's hard to remember facts, even when they're about things that really interest us. Fortunately, there are sports books that classify this type of information. With simple-to-use tables and charts, you can find what you want to know about any player or team.

EXPLORE IT

You can make charts to help you classify information. Read the paragraph that follows.

THE SLOW PACE OF CHANGE IN INDIAN VILLAGES

The coming of European traders did not greatly change the lives of the people of India. They still lived and worked in small farm villages. The people knew little about the change of rulers. The only government officials that villagers knew were tax collectors. The government did not provide schools, post offices, or even village police. Each village had its own leader and council. The council settled disputes and dealt with people who broke the customs of the village. Life followed the old traditions of the village, no matter who ruled the nation.

This chart shows how some of the information from the paragraph can be organized.

VILLAGE LIFE IN INDIA		
History	Economy	Government
Small villages existed before European traders arrived.	small farms	village council

378

TRY IT

With a group of classmates, make a chart that classifies information about a topic that interests you. For example, you might classify information about your favorite sports teams, nearby towns and cities, parks and recreation areas—anything. Label your chart clearly and share it with your classmates.

Our County Parks

	Hiking Trails	Swimming	Play Areas	Camping
Seneca Park	✓	✓	✓	✓
Pod Park	✓		✓	
Jospen Park		✓	✓	
Moose Park	✓		✓	✓

SKILL POWER SEARCH *As you read this chapter, expand the chart on page 378 to include information you learn about Southeast Asia.*

Setting the Scene

KEY TERM
Pacific Rim

CROSSROADS OF ASIA

FOCUS *A crossroads is a place where important pathways intersect. In the case of Southeast Asia, the crossroads lies along the vital trade routes between two great civilizations—India and China.*

A Region of Land and Water

Have you ever been to Southeast Asia, or do you know anyone who has been there? Marco Polo stopped off there in the thirteenth century on his way back from China. Today many people travel to that part of the world for business or sightseeing.

The term *Southeast Asia* refers to the region south of China and east of India. This region of the world is famous for its lush, tropical vegetation, its beautiful art and architecture, and its historic cities. Southeast Asia is home to many different peoples, each with a rich and varied culture.

Nations of Southeast Asia

Ten nations make up Southeast Asia. These nations are: Myanmar (mee ahn MAH), which was formerly called Burma; Thailand (TEYE land); Laos (LAH ohs); Cambodia; Vietnam; Malaysia; Indonesia; the Philippines; Brunei (broo NEYE); and Singapore. At one time, the nations of Cambodia, Laos, and Vietnam together were called Indochina.

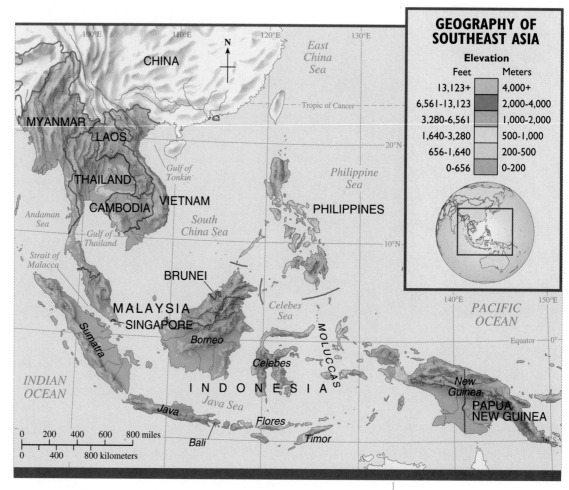

GEOGRAPHY OF SOUTHEAST ASIA

Elevation

Feet	Meters
13,123+	4,000+
6,561-13,123	2,000-4,000
3,280-6,561	1,000-2,000
1,640-3,280	500-1,000
656-1,640	200-500
0-656	0-200

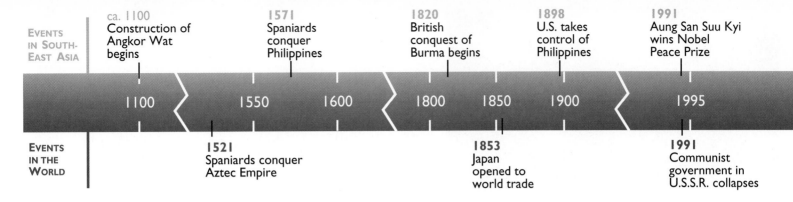

| EVENTS IN SOUTH-EAST ASIA | ca. 1100 Construction of Angkor Wat begins | 1571 Spaniards conquer Philippines | 1820 British conquest of Burma begins | 1898 U.S. takes control of Philippines | 1991 Aung San Suu Kyi wins Nobel Peace Prize |

| 1100 | 1550 | 1600 | 1800 | 1850 | 1900 | 1995 |

| EVENTS IN THE WORLD | 1521 Spaniards conquer Aztec Empire | 1853 Japan opened to world trade | 1991 Communist government in U.S.S.R. collapses |

The varied landscape features found in Southeast Asia include mountains (*above*), tropical rain forests (*right*), and coastlines (*below*).

As the map on page 380 shows, Southeast Asia includes part of the Asian mainland and countless islands. In fact, two nations—Indonesia and the Philippines—include more than 20,000 islands between them. Among the large Indonesian islands are Java and Sumatra. Indonesia also includes the western part of the island of New Guinea. The two largest islands of the Philippines are Mindanao (mihn duh NOU) and Luzon (loo-ZAHN), where the capital city of Manila is located. Singapore is a city-state on an island at the tip of the Malay Peninsula.

The countries of Southeast Asia are among the most prosperous of the **Pacific Rim**. With its population of nearly 500 million people and reserves of many natural resources, this region is destined to become an important element of the world economy in the next century.

Influence of Geography

The cultures and traditions found in different parts of Southeast Asia are as varied as the geography. The island nature of the region made it possible for small isolated communities to develop. The isolation allowed each community to develop a unique lifestyle.

Geography also has a strong influence on climate. The climate of a place is another important factor that affects the type of society that develops there.

 **Pacific Rim**   All nations that border on the Pacific Ocean

In hilly areas, farmers often use a technique called terracing to plant crops.

Tropical Climate

Southeast Asia is located in the tropics. In Chapter 1 you learned that the climate of the tropics is hot and humid. Like India, much of Southeast Asia has a very wet monsoon season.

A large part of the region is covered by rain forests. At one time the vegetation was so dense that people had difficulty passing through the forests. For this reason, the people of Southeast Asia once considered the forests to be home to a variety of gods and spirits.

Because the human population in Southeast Asia today is growing so fast, much of the rain forest is being cut down. The trees are used for lumber, and the cleared land is used for construction and for agriculture.

Highlands Climate

You have learned that elevation can affect climate. The mainland regions of Southeast Asia are mountainous, and the climate is cooler and drier. The lifestyles of people in these regions are different from those in the warmer, wetter regions. For example, people in highlands areas use different farming techniques, wear different clothing, and build different kinds of houses.

Early History of the Region

People have lived in Southeast Asia for a long time. Fossils found on the island of Java indicate that a type of early human lived there about 700,000 years ago. Over the centuries, waves of migrating people from the mainland settled in Southeast Asia.

Traditionally most of the people lived in fishing and farming communities, and rice was the main crop. Most villages were populated by craftworkers and farmers. Trade among neighboring islands was common.

The geography of the region made it impossible for a single ruler to conquer the lands and peoples of Southeast Asia. Over time, however, small kingdoms did develop. The rulers were not only political leaders but were also religious leaders.

The central unit of all societies was the family. Extended families lived together in the same household. A person was expected to place the needs of the family before his or her own interests. Elders were respected throughout every society, and the status of women was very high.

As is true in much of Southeast Asia today, houses were made of water-resistant tropical wood, such as bamboo or teak. As shown in the picture on page 383, the houses were built on stilts, which raised them several feet above the ground. Thus the building was protected from flooding during the monsoon season. Steeply sloped roofs helped to drain off the heavy rains.

Influence of India and China

Southeast Asia is at the crossroads between India and China. These two great civilizations strongly influenced the cultural development of the region.

The map on page 380 shows that a narrow strait separates the Malay Peninsula from the island of Sumatra. This area became the heart of early trading empires. Srivijaya (sree wih JAW yuh), on Sumatra, was the first of these empires.

Srivijaya became powerful in the 600s and 700s. Its capital, Palembang (pah lem BAHNG), served as an exchange point for cargoes from China and India. The people of Palembang also had products to trade. These products included sweet-smelling woods, such as camphor (KAM fur); woven palm mats; and jewelry and other items created from tortoise shells. Over the centuries other trading empires arose in the same area.

Role of Religion

Religion played an important role in the societies that developed in Southeast Asia. Chinese influence was strongest in Vietnam. Confucianism became the foundation of the Vietnamese governmental system. The

▲ Fishing is a major industry in coastal areas of Southeast Asia.

▼ Houses in monsoon areas have steeply sloped roofs and are built on stilts.

Chinese influence was so strong that the emperor of Vietnam took titles and performed rituals similar to those of the Chinese emperor.

Islam made its way to Southeast Asia by Muslim traders from the Middle East. By the 1300s, Islam had been established in Indonesia and had spread to Malaysia and the Philippines. Today, Indonesia has the largest Muslim population in the world.

India also contributed to the religions of Southeast Asia. Hinduism and Buddhism,

383

A monk in traditional robes strolls on a causeway leading to Angkor Wat.

along with the arts and literature associated with these religions, spread throughout the region. These new religions mixed with traditional beliefs in spirits.

The Khmers and Angkor Wat

The Khmer (kuh MER) people in Cambodia offer a perfect example of the mixing of new religious ritual and traditional beliefs. Early in the ninth century, Khmer communities along the Mekong River united into a kingdom. The ruler was a devout Hindu.

The Khmers combined worship of the Hindu gods with their own worship of ancestors. In the 1100s, Suryavarman II came to the throne. Under his leadership, the Khmers built a great temple, or *wat*, in the capital city of Angkor. This temple, known as Angkor Wat (ANG kor waht), is the largest sacred building in the world, covering more than 300 acres. But it was only a small part of a complex that made up the royal city.

Angkor Wat is elaborately decorated inside and out with sculptures of religious figures. Originally it was dedicated to the Hindu god Vishnu. Later it became a Buddhist shrine. Members of both religions made pilgrimages there.

Europeans Arrive

For centuries, traders from the Middle East, India, and China had the rich markets of Southeast Asia pretty much to themselves. Needless to say, Europeans envied the huge profits made by these traders.

After 1500, Europeans began to arrive in Southeast Asia. The first to come were Portuguese traders. They set up trading posts, only to be driven out by the Dutch. The Spaniards, British, and French followed, setting up their own colonies in the region.

From 1800 to the mid-twentieth century, these five European powers controlled much of Southeast Asia and its rich markets. The British ruled in Burma; the Dutch in Indonesia; the French in Laos, Cambodia, and Vietnam; the Spaniards in the Philippines; and the Portuguese in Timor. Only Thailand remained free of colonial control.

During World War II, Japan took over most of the region, driving the Europeans out. After the war ended in 1945, the Europeans tried to reclaim their colonies. However, the people of the region strongly resisted a return to colonization. One by one the countries of Southeast Asia gained their independence.

Balinese women carry offerings to the temple *(below);* a temple in Burma *(right)*

SHOW WHAT YOU KNOW!

REFOCUS
COMPREHENSION

1. Why does much of Southeast Asia have a hot, moist climate?

2. Name the major religions of Southeast Asia and tell where each originated.

THINK ABOUT IT
CRITICAL THINKING

How might the design of houses in the hilly regions of Southeast Asia differ from that of houses in coastal regions?

WRITE ABOUT IT
ACTIVITY

Write a brief paragraph explaining why Southeast Asia is often referred to as the crossroads of Asia.

GAINING INDEPENDENCE

FOCUS *The end of World War II marked the beginning of the end of colonial rule for many nations of Southeast Asia.*

PHILIPPINES

When the Spanish-American War began in 1898, the Spaniards had ruled the Philippines for more than 300 years. After Spain lost the war, a Filipino named Emilio Aguinaldo (ah gee NAHL doh) declared the Philippines to be an independent nation, with himself as president.

American troops were sent to the islands. After two years of fighting, Aguinaldo was captured, and an American governor was appointed. In 1934, Congress agreed to grant the Philippines its independence.

Japan took control of the islands during World War II. After the war, the United States kept its promise. On July 4, 1946, the Philippines became an independent nation.

INDONESIA

In the early 1800s the Dutch established control over Indonesia. Dutch settlers owned profitable coffee, sugar, and indigo plantations. However, most native peoples lived in poverty.

In 1926 the Dutch put down an unsuccessful revolt by native Indonesians. Two leaders of the independence movement—Sukarno (soo KAHR noh) and Muhammad Hatta—were jailed.

In World War II, Japanese invaders were greeted as liberators by the Indonesians. When Japan surrendered in August 1945, Sukarno and Hatta declared Indonesian independence.

The Dutch finally gave up control of most of the islands in 1949. Disputes over the western part of New Guinea continued until 1963, when the United Nations granted it to Indonesia.

BURMA (MYANMAR)

In 1886, Myanmar, which was then called Burma, became a province of British India.

When Japan invaded Burma during World War II, a group of Burmese patriots called the Thirty Heroes helped drive the British from Burma. However, the Japanese treated the Burmese people even worse than the British had. So the Thirty Heroes joined forces with the British and their allies to fight Japan.

After World War II, Britain allowed the Burmese people to vote for a new government. The people chose independence, which was granted in January 1948.

1946
U.S. grants independence to Philippines

1948
Burma (Myanmar) gains independence from Britain

1949
Dutch give up control of Indonesia

1954
Vietnam divided into two parts as it wins its independence

1959
Britain grants independence to Singapore

1945   1950   1955   1960

SINGAPORE

A thousand years ago an Indian prince added an island to his domain and named it Singapore, or "City of Lions." It remained a small settlement of fishers and traders until 1819. In that year an Englishman named Thomas Raffles established a trading post there. Shortly thereafter, Singapore became a British colony.

After World War II the British allowed Singapore to govern itself. In 1959, Singapore was granted its independence. Four years later, Singapore joined Malaysia, a new nation on the peninsula to the north. However, most people in Singapore were of Chinese descent, while the people on the mainland were Malays. Ethnic friction developed between these groups, causing Singapore to become an independent nation again in 1965.

VIETNAM

In 1802, France helped a new emperor take the throne of Vietnam. Over time the French took control of Vietnam. The emperor remained, but French officials ran the government. Vietnam became part of French Indochina, a colony that included present-day Cambodia and Laos.

Vietnamese patriots staged a rebellion in 1908. Though they were unable to defeat the French, rebel groups continued to fight for independence until the outbreak of World War II. After Japanese troops moved into Vietnam, an independence fighter named Ho Chi Minh formed an army to resist them. When the French returned to reclaim their colony after the war, Ho's forces began a guerrilla war for independence that lasted eight years.

In 1954, Vietnam was granted independence but was divided into two parts. Ho Chi Minh became president of North Vietnam, and the former emperor became ruler of South Vietnam. Unhappiness with this arrangement eventually led to the Vietnam War in the 1960s. In 1976 a victorious North Vietnamese government reunited the country.

SHOW WHAT YOU KNOW!

REFOCUS
COMPREHENSION

1. How did the United States come to have control over the Philippines?

2. Why did Singapore break away from Malaysia only two years after becoming part of that nation?

THINK ABOUT IT
CRITICAL THINKING

Why did the conclusion of World War II play such an important role in helping nations of Southeast Asia gain their independence?

WRITE ABOUT IT
ACTIVITY

Read more about one of the independence leaders mentioned in this lesson. Write a brief report telling what you learned about that person.

ARTS AND CRAFTS

FOCUS *A wide variety of art and art forms enrich the lives of people in Southeast Asia. Many of these have their origins in cultures hundreds of years old.*

Indonesian Shadow Plays

One of the most popular arts of Southeast Asia is the *wayang kulit* (wah YANG KOO lit), or "shadow play." Begun in Java centuries ago, shadow plays are still an important part of Indonesian culture.

Originally the puppets represented the spirits of the dead that had come back to earth to help the living solve problems. A tenth-century Javanese poet described the effect of the plays on the audience: "There are people who weep, are sad and aroused watching the puppets, though they know they are merely carved pieces of leather manipulated and made to speak."

The dalang (duh LANG), or puppet master, worked behind a white cotton cloth stretched tightly on a frame. The shadows of the puppets were cast on the cloth by an oil lamp. The audience sat in front of the cotton screen, and the dalang used rods made of rhinoceros horn to manipulate the puppets.

Dalangs also spoke the dialogue and described the action. They had to

▼ A Javanese
shadow puppet

be strong because the puppets were quite heavy and a performance could last as long as nine hours. Many dalangs began to study the art as children, learning it from their fathers.

Preparations for a Show

Making the puppets was an art in itself. The puppets were flat figures made of buffalo hide. The skin was scraped clean and then left to **cure** for as long as ten years.

When it was dry enough, the leather was cut into the shapes of puppets. Each character had a certain style so that the audience could recognize it. A hero, for example, was slender with a long, elegant nose.

The plots of the shadow plays came from several sources. Some were traditional Javanese myths. Also popular were tales from Buddhist folklore and the Hindu epics. These familiar stories were called trunk tales. Puppet masters developed new plots to make branch tales. The branch tales described heroic deeds, romances, and rivalries within the royal courts.

⭐ **cure** To process, as by drying or aging

Balinese Dancers

The island of Bali is famous for its varied art forms. Many Balinese artists devote their lives to creative activities. Dance is one of the most important of the Balinese arts. Dance is also tied to Hinduism, the religion of most Balinese people.

In Bali, practically everyone dances. Dance marks all of life's experiences, from birth to death. However, it takes long training to become a skilled dancer. Dancers must learn to move each part of their bodies—head, neck, arms, hands, legs, and feet—in time with the music.

Many dancers wear masks and tell stories with their performances. In trance dances, the dancer seeks to communicate with gods or ancestors. Another kind of dance portrays battles between good and evil. One of the most famous of these is a dance known as a barong (buh RAHNG). In this dance, good is represented by the mythical lion Barong. He fights an evil being who has bulging eyes and tusks.

Batik—A Craft and an Art

Batik is a technique for decorating cloth with dyes. It started in the islands of present-day Indonesia and the Malay Peninsula. Batik makers put wax on parts of the cloth before dying it. The wax keeps the dye from coloring those parts. Colors are added to the cloth one by one to form elaborate patterns.

In early times the wax was painted on with a stick. Around the 1100s in Java, waxers developed a new technique. They spread the wax on with a copper cup with a spout. This new tool made more complex patterns possible. Sometimes it took months to finish a cloth. Batik making was also an occupation for upper-class women.

Batik cloth is worn today throughout many parts of Southeast Asia. But the beautiful cloth is not just for fashion. Many patterns have ceremonial and religious meanings.

▲ The beautiful pattern was formed by alternately waxing and dying different parts of the cloth.

◄ Balinese dancers performing a traditional dance

Classical Music—Indonesian Style

A distinct kind of music called gamelan (GAM uh lan) developed on the islands of Java and Bali. This classical Indonesian music became an important part of all celebrations and festivals.

The gamelan orchestra uses a variety of instruments. Many are percussion instruments, including different types of gongs. The word *gong* comes from the Malay language. Some musicians play inverted bronze bowls, bronze or wooden xylophones, and finger drums. The orchestra also includes a flutelike instrument and a stringed instrument similar to a two-stringed fiddle.

The music of the gamelan orchestra is quite complex. The instruments produce a texture of sounds and notes to create melodies. The role of the drummers is to keep the sounds all together and in the right tempo. The gamelan orchestras provide the music for both shadow plays and Balinese dance.

Above, this carved elephant head is actually a mask worn by Balinese dancers.

Right, instruments used by a gamelan orchestra

Show What You KNOW!

REFOCUS
COMPREHENSION

1. Name and briefly describe two of the art forms discussed in this lesson.

2. What is the purpose of the wax used in batik?

THINK ABOUT IT
CRITICAL THINKING

Why might staging a shadow play be easier today than it was centuries ago?

WRITE ABOUT IT
ACTIVITY

Adapt a scene from one of your favorite stories for use as a shadow play. Write a script and describe the actions of the puppets.

BANGKOK—AN INTERNATIONAL CITY

FOCUS *Bangkok, the capital of Thailand, is truly an international city. Here tradition rubs elbows with modern technology, and everyone's life is enriched.*

A City of Contradictions

You and a friend are visiting Bangkok, the capital of Thailand. With about 6 million people, Bangkok combines modern and ancient traditions. The main business district is very much a modern city. You can stay in a luxurious hotel, eat in a **gourmet** restaurant, and shop for beautiful Thai silk and cotton goods. Many international businesses have offices in the skyscrapers that tower over downtown Bangkok.

⭐ **gourmet** Involving the preparation of fine or exotic food dishes

You want to get a really good look at the city, so you travel from the airport to your hotel by boat. You ride along the klongs, or canals, that run through the city. This is the way most people get around, for the streets are usually choked with traffic. Your river taxi has a colorful awning to protect you from the hot sun, and the driver points out the city's interesting sights.

A Feast for the Eyes

On your first full day in Bangkok, you and your friend hire a guide. You

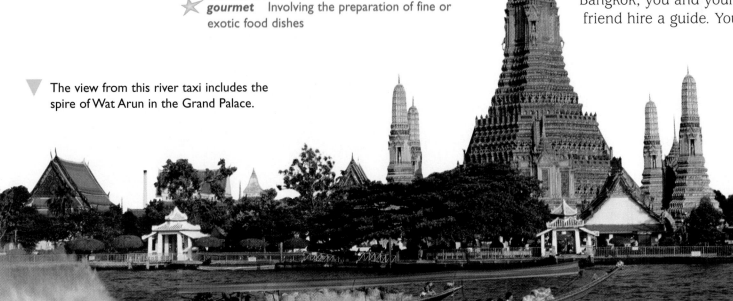

▼ The view from this river taxi includes the spire of Wat Arun in the Grand Palace.

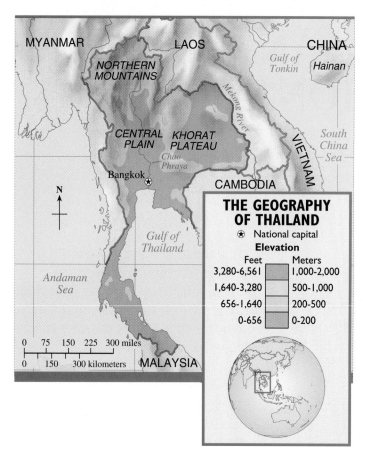

THE GEOGRAPHY OF THAILAND
⊛ National capital
Elevation

Feet		Meters
3,280-6,561		1,000-2,000
1,640-3,280		500-1,000
656-1,640		200-500
0-656		0-200

A Feast for the Body

By now you're getting hungry. Food stands are everywhere, and the food in Bangkok is delicious! You order a mixture of rice and pork wrapped in a banana leaf. At first the hot spices make you gasp, but then the coconut milk that is part of the dish cools your mouth.

You decide to have fruit for dessert. There are some very unusual fruits, such as jackfruit and durian. Your friend orders durian, which has a strong, unfamiliar aroma. You decide to play it safe and have a banana.

Kickboxing and Kites

Later you want to attend one of Bangkok's many sporting events. Perhaps you'll see a Thai kickboxing match at Lumpini Stadium. Your guide explains that the boxers

get an early start, because later in the day the heat and humidity can become overpowering. As you stroll along, you see the Buddhist monks leave their wats to beg. The wats are beautiful structures whose tall spires dot the city. Most Thais are Buddhists, and they earn spiritual merit by giving rice, fruit, and other kinds of food to the monks.

You stop to visit the Wat Arun, the Temple of the Dawn. Its outer walls are covered with thousands of pieces of porcelain. Your guide tells you that when the temple was being built, the supply of porcelain ran out. The people of Bangkok donated all their dishes, which were used to finish the walls.

You can do your grocery shopping by boat at the floating markets of Bangkok.

This elaborate statue stands guard over one of the many temples found in the Grand Palace.

SHOW WHAT YOU KNOW!

REFOCUS
COMPREHENSION

1. Why is a river taxi a good way to travel around Bangkok?

2. Why is Bangkok considered to be an international city?

THINK ABOUT IT
CRITICAL THINKING

What passage implies that the king's role is largely ceremonial?

WRITE ABOUT IT
ACTIVITY

Write a postcard home giving highlights of your visit to Bangkok.

begin by paying homage to Buddha. Then they engage in a fast-paced, exciting contest accompanied by music.

You'd also like to see the kite fights held on the Pramane Ground of the Royal Palace. Teams of handlers control huge kites, defending them against smaller kites that try to cut through their strings.

The Grand Palace

No visit to Bangkok is complete without a visit to the Grand Palace, which is really a small city. Besides the government buildings, the Grand Palace includes many Buddhist shrines with colorful roofs and beautiful carvings and statues.

Thailand's king is still regarded as a god by many of his people. He is descended from Rama I, who built Bangkok 200 years ago. The king no longer lives in the Grand Palace, but he comes there for ceremonies.

You hope someday to visit Bangkok in the spring. Then you can see the king become the Harvest Lord. Using a red and gold plow, he digs a furrow in the ground. He then plants rice to ensure a good harvest for his land.

Your guide explains that this is just one of many holiday celebrations held throughout the year. As you enjoy this vacation, you will find that Bangkok is a modern city that has not forgotten its glorious traditions.

A LEADER FOR PEACE

FOCUS *A young woman carries on the tradition of patriotism passed down from her father. For her efforts she is made a prisoner by her government and is honored by the rest of the world.*

The Nobel Peace Prize

In 1991, Aung San Suu Kyi (awng sahn soo chee) became the eighth woman to receive the Nobel Peace Prize. Until that time, few people around the world had ever heard of her. But they soon learned that in addition to the distinction of receiving the award, she was the first one to receive it while being held prisoner by her own government.

Suu, as she likes to be called, had been arrested by the government of Burma, now named Myanmar, in 1989. She was charged with being married to a foreigner. Her real crime, however, was leading the opposition to Burma's military government.

Independence for Burma

Suu's family had long been active in Burmese politics. Her father, Aung San, was one of the Thirty Heroes who founded the Burma Independence Army in the early 1940s. Their goal was independence from British rule.

During the early stages of World War II, Aung San and his comrades fought on Japan's side against Great Britain. However, after the British were driven out, Burma was treated as a Japanese colony. Aung San and his comrades switched sides and helped drive the Japanese from Burma. Aung San organized a new government but was assassinated in 1947.

In that year his daughter Suu was only two years old. She does not remember the shock of her father's death. While growing up, she attended Buddhist convent schools. When Suu was 18, she decided to go to Oxford University, in Great Britain.

▼ Aung San Suu Kyi speaks with journalists after being freed from house arrest.

★ **house arrest** Confinement to one's home on orders of legal officials

Following News From Home

Suu had led a sheltered life in her native land. In Great Britain she learned about politics and her nation's sad history. By that time, Burma was under the control of a military goverment led by Ne Win, one of her father's old comrades.

Suu met Michael Aris, a young British man who was a student of Asian cultures. Suu was aware that in Burma she would face **prejudice** as the wife of a foreigner. But in 1972 she and Aris were married.

Suu worked for a time at the United Nations in New York. She then moved to Japan. She continued to follow events in her country, which was suffering under Ne Win's dictatorship. She told friends, "It is my destiny to rule Burma."

Working for Democracy

In 1988, Suu flew home to visit her mother. Burma was in chaos. Riots and antigovernment demonstrations spread through the country. Ne Win's soldiers killed many demonstrators.

"The people of my country were demanding independence," Suu said later. "I felt I had a duty to get involved." She toured the country, speaking to huge crowds and calling for the overthrow of the government. She was arrested and confined to her house. Though she was not in prison, Suu suffered greatly. Her husband and two young sons were seldom allowed to visit. Her eyesight began to fail, and she steadily lost weight.

---

prejudice Dislike or distrust of someone because of such characteristics as race, religion, or nationality

This family photo shows baby Suu with her parents and two older brothers.

The government offered to release Suu if she would leave the country. She chose to stay. When Suu received a Nobel Prize, the Myanmar government was embarrassed and finally released her. Suu plans to continue working for democracy in Myanmar. She may yet take her father's place as its leader.

An election official holds up a ballot box at a polling place during the nation's first free elections in 30 years.

SUMMING UP

1 DO YOU REMEMBER...
COMPREHENSION

1. What two great civilizations have most influenced the cultures of Southeast Asia?

2. Name two large islands that are part of Indonesia.

3. For about how long have people lived in Southeast Asia?

4. When did Europeans begin to arrive in Southeast Asia?

5. Which European country colonized Burma? Which European country colonized Vietnam?

6. Why were the Indonesians happy when the Japanese invaded their country in 1942?

7. What do Javanese shadow plays usually tell about?

8. What role does dance play in Balinese life?

9. What is a wat?

10. What is Burma now named?

2 SKILL POWER
CLASSIFYING INFORMATION

Classify the information in "Gaining Independence," the lesson on pages 386–387. Think of four categories that will let you classify details about the colonies described on those pages and how they gained their independence.

3 WHAT DO YOU THINK?
CRITICAL THINKING

1. What role did geography play in preventing Southeast Asia from coming under the rule of a single conqueror?

2. For which Southeast Asian countries did independence come fairly easily? Which countries had a more difficult struggle? Explain.

3. How are the Javanese wayang kulit puppets different from the puppets of our country?

4. Why might Buddhist monks beg for food instead of working for a living?

5. How was Aung San Suu Kyi influenced by her father's experiences?

4 SAY IT, WRITE IT, USE IT
VOCABULARY

Write a story, using as many of these terms as you can. Think about a plot and characters. Be creative!

cure   Pacific Rim
gourmet   prejudice
house arrest

5 GEOGRAPHY AND YOU
MAP STUDY

In this chapter you took a trip to Bangkok, Thailand. Suppose a visitor from Bangkok came to where you live. Draw a map for your guest showing interesting places to see and things to do in your town or city.

6 TAKE ACTION
CITIZENSHIP

Although we can't all win Nobel Peace Prizes like Aung San Suu Kyi, we can be leaders for peace in our homes, schools, and communities. How? That depends on the situation. It might mean not arguing with someone who is looking for a fight or avoiding situations where conflicts are likely. It might mean easing a tense situation by talking it out. Share your ideas with a "Let Peace Begin Here" poster or bulletin board. Use words and art to show ways to be a peacemaker.

Methods of Farming		
Slash and Burn	Terracing	Contour Plowing

ADVANTAGES

DISADVANTAGES

7 GET CREATIVE
SCIENCE CONNECTION

Methods of farming differ around the world. Sometimes a method is chosen because it is the best way to use the land. In other places a method is chosen because it is a tradition that has been used for generations. Do some research to learn about different methods of farming. Organize your ideas and make a chart showing the advantages and disadvantages of each method. The chart here shows some farming methods. You may find others for your chart.

LOOKING AHEAD Find out how an age of imperialism in Europe led to widespread colonialism.

CHAPTER 18

THE AGE OF

Part of the United States once belonged to England. Another part was Spanish. The Dutch and the French were here, too. What happened in the United States also happened in many other parts of the world. Read about how Europe influenced and was influenced by other cultures.

Today you may own clothes, books, and toys made halfway around the world. But in 1851, exhibits like the one shown on page 414 would have made you open your eyes in wonder.

CONTENTS

IMPERIALISM

You can learn more about European expansion from these books. Read one that interests you and fill out a book-review form.

READ AND RESEARCH

Industrial Revolution edited by John D. Clare
(Harcourt Brace & Co., 1994)
Learn about how the inventions of new machines and the opening of factories brought about changes in the way people lived in Europe and the United States in the eighteenth and nineteenth centuries. (*nonfiction*)

Words: A Book About the Origins of Everyday Words and Phrases by Jane Sarnoff and Reynold Ruffin (Macmillan Publishing Co., 1981)
Trade and interaction with people from many parts of the world had a great influence on the English language. Find out the history of many words and phrases that you use. (*nonfiction*)

An Adventure in New Zealand by The Cousteau Society Staff (Simon & Schuster Books, 1992)
See how the traditions of New Zealand's first settlers are still alive today. Color photographs help you appreciate the people, unique animals, and scenery of this beautiful land. (*nonfiction*)

SKILL POWER Recognizing Word Origins

Recognizing the origins of words and word parts can help you learn about the influence of other cultures.

UNDERSTAND IT

English is a rather hungry language. Some of our words have roots in Greek and Latin. You probably know many of these words. *Uni,* as in *United,* comes from the Latin word for "one." *Geo* comes from a Greek word meaning "earth." A quick look in a dictionary can show how many words in English have a *geo* beginning. English has also gobbled up whole words from other languages. They are called loan words or borrowed words, but English really has no intention of returning them!

EXPLORE IT

American place names provide a good example of the way English borrows words from other languages. Look at this map of Indiana. Indiana is also a borrowed name. Can you match the clues below with some of the place names shown on the map?

1. A river with a Native American name

2. A city with the same name as a country that was part of the Inca Empire

3. A city with a name that ends with the Greek word for *city*

4. A city named for the Italian explorer who sailed to the Americas in 1492

5. A city named for a French hero of the American Revolution

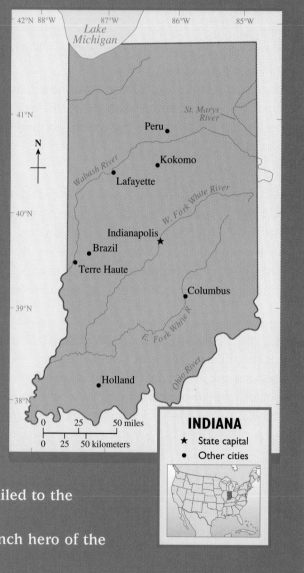

INDIANA
★ State capital
● Other cities

TRY IT

You will need a dictionary and a world map to complete this activity. Study the list of words below. Do you know most of them? They are all words borrowed from other cultures.

Copy the words on a sheet of paper. Look in a dictionary for the derivation, or source, of these words. Write the culture or country of origin next to each word on your list.

With your classmates, make a bulletin-board display of borrowed words. Write each word on an index card. Attach a piece of yarn to the card. Attach the other end of the yarn to the map on the country or area from which the word was borrowed.

algebra	piano
alphabet	petunia
bungalow	pumpkin
caravan	shawl
curfew	syrup
goober	turquoise
indigo	tycoon
jungle	yam

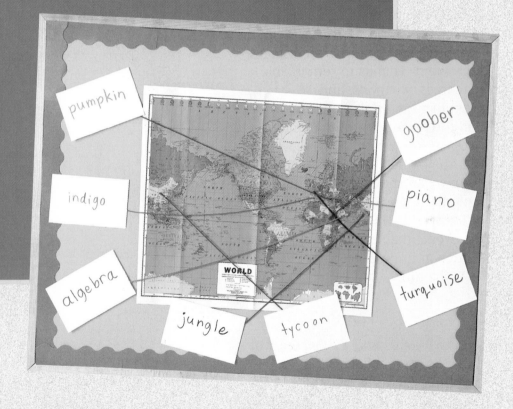

Find out about borrowed words on page 407 in this chapter.

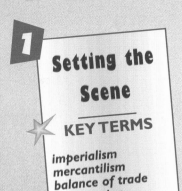

Setting the Scene

★ KEY TERMS

imperialism
mercantilism
balance of trade
exploitation
Industrial Revolution

EUROPEAN EXPANSION

FOCUS *Inventions in agriculture and industry led Europeans to search for new markets and new sources of raw materials in other parts of the world.*

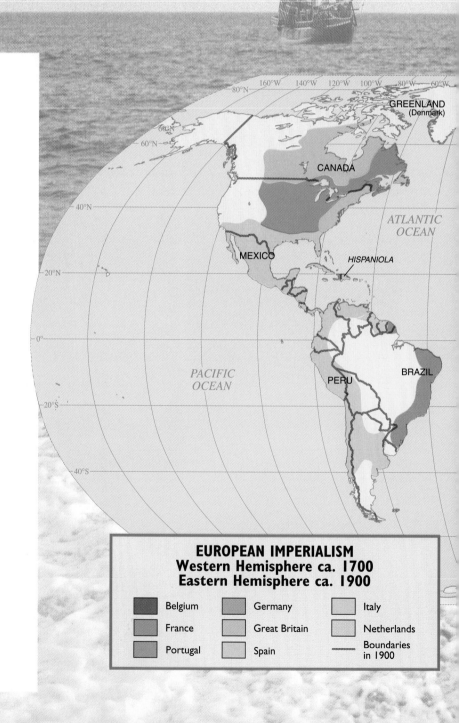

A Duty to Expand

In the late 1800s, Europeans were in control of lands and seas around the world wherever their economic and political interests took them. Thanks to remarkable machines, weapons, and manufacturing skills, the Europeans had the power to dominate other peoples. The Europeans believed that their way of life was superior.

The map shows how European nations expanded into other parts of the world. This chapter will trace the events that led up to this European **imperialism** (ihm PIHR-ee ul ihz um).

Trade Leads to Wealth

In the 1600s and 1700s, most of Europe's leaders believed in an economic theory known as **mercantilism**. It was based on the idea that there was only so much wealth in the world. And, of course, as everyone knew, wealth was power. This was one reason that

---

imperialism The economic, political, and cultural domination of another country
mercantilism A system of policies designed to build the wealth of a country

EUROPEAN IMPERIALISM
Western Hemisphere ca. 1700
Eastern Hemisphere ca. 1900

■ Belgium	■ Germany	□ Italy
■ France	□ Great Britain	□ Netherlands
■ Portugal	□ Spain	— Boundaries in 1900

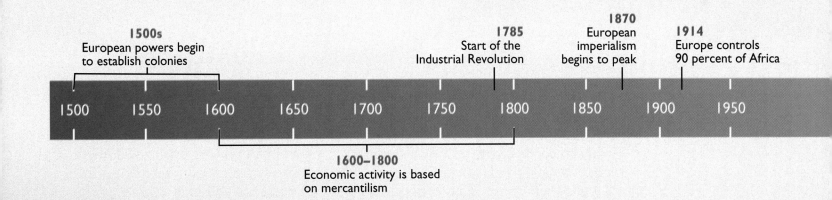

1500s
European powers begin
to establish colonies

1785
Start of the
Industrial Revolution

1870
European
imperialism
begins to peak

1914
Europe controls
90 percent of Africa

| 1500 | 1550 | 1600 | 1650 | 1700 | 1750 | 1800 | 1850 | 1900 | 1950 |

1600–1800
Economic activity is based
on mercantilism

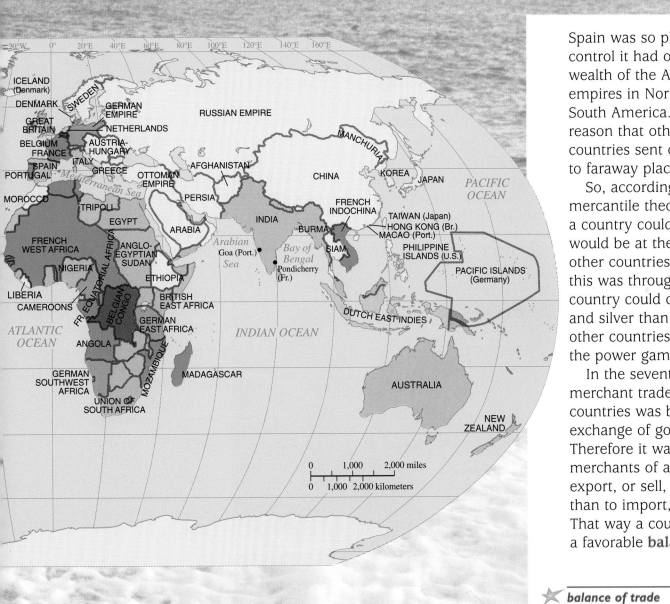

Spain was so pleased with the control it had over the great wealth of the Aztec and Inca empires in North America and South America. It was also the reason that other European countries sent out explorers to faraway places.

So, according to the mercantile theory, the only way a country could grow richer would be at the expense of other countries. One way to do this was through trade. If a country could collect more gold and silver than it sent out to other countries, it was ahead in the power game.

In the seventeenth century, merchant trade between countries was based on the exchange of gold and silver. Therefore it was vital for the merchants of a country to export, or sell, more products than to import, or buy, them. That way a country would have a favorable **balance of trade**.

⭐ ***balance of trade***   A comparison between the value of a country's exports and imports

Government Control of Trade

This kind of economic setup would work only if there were rules and regulations made by the government to control its country's trade. Imported goods had special taxes on them to make them more costly than products made in the home country. Some governments even went to war to protect their nation's economy.

People could become rich under this economic system. This was the time in Europe when kings and nobles built grand palaces. Some merchants also made vast fortunes. But for the people who lived in the villages and farms of the countryside, the mercantile system made little difference in their lives. In fact, rural life in much of Europe had changed very little since the Middle Ages.

A Need for Markets

One way a country could gain economic power was to have colonies. Starting in the 1500s all the major European powers practiced some form of colonialism. Spain and Portugal established colonies in the Americas. England and France set up colonies in North America, in the Caribbean, and later in Asia and in Africa. The Dutch secured colonies and trading posts in North America, along the coast of Africa, and in the Pacific Ocean region.

For the most part, these early colonies were not meant for settlement but for economic **exploitation**. They were set up by trading companies made up of merchants and other investors. Governments would give the companies monopolies, or complete control, in the colonies. The trading companies took the risks of establishing and supplying the colonies, and reaped the profits, if there were any.

In time, colonies were taken over by governments. The colonies provided a cheap new source of raw materials and new markets for finished goods. As far as

In the Amsterdam harbor of the late 1600s, ships were loaded with goods to trade with Dutch colonies around the world.

★ **exploitation** The use of people or things in a selfish or unfair way governments were concerned, these colonies existed solely for the benefit of the home country. People in the colonies were not allowed to make their own finished goods or compete with the home country.

Home Countries Change

Since the dawn of time, people have been making the things they needed by hand. The **Industrial Revolution**, which began in England in the late 1700s, changed that. New inventions, such as the steam engine, helped make these changes. Up until this time most people, nobles and peasants alike, were supported by agriculture. By the middle of the 1800s, that had changed, not only in Great Britain but in western Europe and the United States as well. Industry was becoming the main economic activity.

If you had to pick one date as the start of the Industrial Revolution, a good choice would be 1785. In that year, Richard Arkwright adapted James Watt's steam engine to fit a spinning machine. Suddenly the making of cloth was no longer the business of a skilled worker.

Wood was being replaced by iron as a building

▲ The invention of the steam engine led to new forms of transportation, in addition to the building of factories.

▼ Well-off Europeans began to visit colonies in large numbers in the 1800s. Here tourists explore Egypt.

material and by coal as a fuel. New industries sprang up everywhere. Mining, especially coal and iron mining, became a major industry. The steam engine changed the way people and goods were transported. Steamships and railroads replaced sailing ships and stagecoaches. And then there were the new industries that built the machines that made the goods produced during the Industrial Revolution. The newly industrialized countries began to search for even larger world markets for their products.

Building Empires

Imperialism was a high-powered form of colonialism that reached its peak between 1870 and 1914. It wasn't just an economic theory. It was also a political and cultural policy.

⭐ **Industrial Revolution** The period of great change brought about by the invention of power-driven machinery

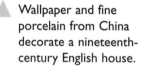

Wallpaper and fine porcelain from China decorate a nineteenth-century English house.

Europeans of the late 1800s truly believed that they had developed the best way of life. They wanted other peoples to adopt it.

Africa and Asia were key targets for imperialism in the nineteenth century. By 1914, Europeans controlled about 90 percent of Africa. Great Britain and France had most of the colonies. But Spain, Germany, Portugal, Belgium, and Italy all had pieces of the African landscape.

In Asia, the British took over India, part of the Malay Peninsula, and Burma, today called Myanmar. The French had colonies in Southeast Asia and in the South Pacific. The Dutch took over the East Indies, now called Indonesia. The Philippines became a colony of the United States after the Spanish-American War.

Influence from Abroad

While Europeans were bringing what they felt were the benefits of their way of life to their colonies, they were being influenced in return. For example, around 1700, fewer than 1 million pounds of tea were imported to England. By 1800, the British were importing nearly 15 million pounds a year. Textile mills were turning out brightly colored cotton cloth called

Brighton Pavilion

▼ A trip through the dictionary will tell you where these words come from.

boomerang

origami

ketchup

tulip

banana

dandelion

calico and woolens in paisley prints. The original designs had come from India. The Pavilion in Brighton, England, built by King George IV when he was Prince of Wales, certainly shows the influence of foreign architecture.

Borrowed Words

The British did not import only raw materials and ideas from other countries. They also borrowed many words from other languages.

sleigh

Beginning with the explorations of the 1400s and continuing into the colonialism of the 1800s, travelers and traders brought back exotic foods, goods, and words. Sailors who visited Asia brought back a fish sauce called *ke-tsiap*. This word became *ketchup*— a very familiar sauce to you. The word *canoe* came to us from a Spanish version of a West Indian word that Christopher Columbus recorded.

rodeo

canoe

circus, comedy

SHOW WHAT YOU KNOW!

REFOCUS
COMPREHENSION

1. Why did countries want to amass great amounts of gold and silver?

2. How were the aims of early colonialism different from those of imperialism?

THINK ABOUT IT
CRITICAL THINKING

Was the imperialism of European countries beneficial or harmful to other countries? Explain your answer.

WRITE ABOUT IT
ACTIVITY

You live in England in the 1700s. Your government is looking for people to form colonies in other parts of the world.

Write an advertisement for the government to attract colonists. Explain how new colonies will help your country.

EUROPEAN EMPIRES

FOCUS *From the 1500s to the 1800s, the nations of Europe tried to increase their economic strength by building colonial empires.*

THE PORTUGUESE

The Portuguese wanted to join Spain in exploring what would be called the New World. In 1494, the two countries signed the Treaty of Tordesillas (tward uh SEE-us). This gave Portugal the land that would become Brazil. Portugal also set up the colony of Angola on the West African coast. A nation of traders, Portugal established strategic trading posts there, as well as in India, China, and on some Pacific islands.

Portugal's population was very small—the nation could not afford to lose too many people to colonies. In any event, most Portuguese were not attracted to the tropical lands in the rest of its empire. These colonies existed only to support commerce.

THE DUTCH

Like the Portuguese, the Dutch were a trading people. They too had a tiny population and could not occupy vast new lands. Using trading companies, such as the Dutch East India Company, they settled for a small empire. The Dutch established key colonies in the West Indies, South America, Africa, and the East Indies.

The Dutch Empire was centered in the East Indies. In the 1600s the Dutch drove out the Portuguese and gained control of the surrounding seas. To protect their ocean trade routes to this part of the world, the Dutch set up a colony at the Cape of Good Hope, on the southern tip of Africa.

1494	1600s	1600s	1763	1776
Treaty of Tordesillas	Portuguese lose East Indies to the Dutch	French colony in Canada set up	French lose Canada to Great Britain	British lose American colonies

1450   1500   1550   1600   1650   1700   1750   1800

THE FRENCH

The French were dreaming dreams of a vast empire. In the 1600s they set up colonies in eastern Canada, the West Indies, and South America. Like the Portuguese and Dutch, the French were traders. They had little interest in large-scale colonial settlements. Few French people had any desire to swap a life in France for a life in the frozen wilds of North America or the steamy jungles of Guiana (gee AHN uh) in South America.

The French lost their colony in Canada in 1763. In the 1800s, though, they added colonies in Africa and Southeast Asia.

THE BRITISH

The greatest empire builders of all were the British. In the 1800s they liked to boast that "the sun never sets on the British Empire." Although the British lost their American colonies in 1776, they still had colonies spanning the globe. From Australia to India to Egypt to South Africa to Canada, the British flag flew high.

Like everyone else, the British had colonies to make money. Using trading companies, which were granted special monopolies, the British exploited the wealth of their colonies. But the British were settlers as well as traders. For a variety of reasons, many British families left home to live in the new colonies and build permanent settlements.

REFOCUS
COMPREHENSION

1. What large colony did Portugal gain by signing the Treaty of Tordesillas?

2. What was the main reason these European nations first set up colonies in other parts of the world?

THINK ABOUT IT
CRITICAL THINKING

What do you think the Europeans thought about the native peoples in their colonies?

WRITE ABOUT IT
ACTIVITY

You want to sign on with a British group that will set up a colony in the Americas, but you must have your parents' permission.

Write a letter to your parents that will convince them that this will be a worthwhile experience for you.

EFFECTS OF THE INDUSTRIAL REVOLUTION

FOCUS *The nineteenth century was a time of great industrial growth. People's lives changed, not always for the better.*

One Revolution Leads to Another

Major changes in agriculture helped set the stage for the Industrial Revolution in Great Britain. New inventions such as the horse-drawn hoe and the mechanical seeder would not work efficiently on small, narrow strips of land that had been rented to poor farmers. In the 1700s, wealthy landowners had Parliament pass a series of **enclosure acts**. Soon neat fences, hedges, and stone walls dotted the English landscape. Because of the new machinery, fewer workers were needed to farm the large fields.

What happened to the poor farmers kicked off the land? Many headed for towns and cities in search of work. They were willing to do anything. This willingness was tested by the **factory system** which was just emerging.

The Need for Workers

Steam engines were big and heavy. Special buildings, called mills or factories, were constructed to house the engines. The mills needed workers and many farmers filled these jobs. Steam engines had a huge appetite for fuel. Iron ore and coal were mined to build and fuel the new machines. These mines also needed workers.

Working on the farm had been back-breaking labor for the entire family. But at least it was outdoors where people could breathe fresh air. Work in the mills or mines, on the other hand, was often unhealthy and dangerous. Men, women, and children labored long days for low wages.

The machines set the pace in the factories. And the machines never seemed to need a rest. It was easier to replace a worker than a

After the English Parliament allowed open fields to be walled in, many poor farmers had to find other work.

⭐ **enclosure acts** Laws that allowed wealthy farmers to close off all the common land

---

⭐ **factory system** The practice of having workers use machines in one large place instead of working at home or in small workshops

Factories filled the air of industrial towns with smoke and soot.

machine. So workers who became sick were fired. People went hungry and lived in the streets if they could not find work.

Child Labor

Another dark side of the factory system was **child labor**. Most work in the textile mills was tedious and didn't require any skill. As a result, children made up nearly 50 percent of the work force in many mills. Some children were only six years old.

Child labor took children away from their parents and helped to undermine family life. Children who worked all day, of course, didn't go to school. Factory work dulled their minds and endangered their health. Many

⭐ **child labor**   The practice of employing children to work in factories, mills, and mines

◀ Children were also put to work in mines, where their small size allowed them to fit into tunnels too small for adults.

children came home covered with black-and-blue marks from beatings they received for working too slowly. Their poor working parents dared not complain. They feared their children would lose their jobs.

Attempts at Reform

A few people wanted something done about the children's working conditions. One was Michael Thomas Sadler, a member of Parliament. He formed a committee to hear what life was really like for the poor children of the Industrial Revolution. Many children appeared before the committee to tell their stories.

The Sadler Committee's published report shocked many upper-class English people. Most had had no idea how miserable life was for children in the mills. They demanded immediate action. Within a year, Parliament passed the Factory Act of 1833. It stated that children under the age of 9 could not be hired to work in the mills. The law also limited the working hours of children. Children under the age of 13 could not work more than 8 hours a day. Older children could not work more than 12 hours.

Another reform law was passed in 1842. It prevented employers from hiring boys under the age of 13 to work in the mines.

4

THE GREAT EXHIBITION OF 1851

FOCUS *People from around the world came to London in 1851 to examine the wonders inside the Crystal Palace. What they saw gave them hope that the world was becoming a much better place in which to live.*

A Giant Greenhouse

You round the street corner in Hyde Park, London, in 1851. There, gleaming in the bright sunshine, you see Joseph Paxton's Crystal Palace—home of the Great **Exhibition** of 1851. How would you describe this building? You might call it a giant greenhouse. You might use words like "immense" and "breathtaking." But the Crystal Palace is more than that. It is more spectacular than anything you have ever seen before.

Like all visitors, you enter the Palace through a big glass door. Then there you are inside the largest building ever constructed out of cast iron and glass, more than a third of a mile long. Looking up, it is easy to believe that it took nearly 300,000 panes of glass to build the roof and walls!

---

exhibition A display for the public of industrial and agricultural achievements

Genius on Display

When you manage to take your eyes away from the ceiling, you probably want to dash off in several directions at once. Everywhere you turn, you see fantastic displays from nations all over Europe and many countries around the world. Each country is proud to show off its new inventions and economic progress. That, after all, was one reason for holding the Great Exhibition in the first place.

The American display catches your eye first. There you see Colt revolvers,

▼ Like most visitors to the Crystal Palace, you would probably find yourself tilting your head back and staring at the glass roof towering 66 feet above your head.

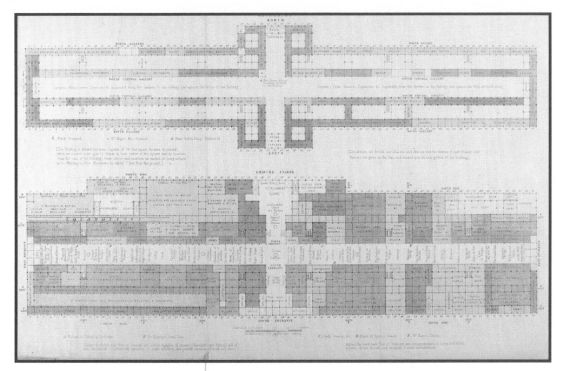

This floor plan makes clear what a marvel the Crystal Palace was.

a new sewing machine, McCormick's reaper, and a whole group of new and fascinating products for the home. The French, meanwhile, are showing off decorative silks, a gadget for folding envelopes, and a small submarine. The Austrians have a display of luxury handicrafts, and the Russians are exhibiting their raw materials. But it is the British who really steal the show. They have better steam machines than anyone else. These marvels of technology are what gave the Industrial Revolution its base of power.

Prince Albert's Hopes

The Great Exhibition was the brainchild of Prince Albert, husband of Great Britain's Queen Victoria. He had an optimistic view of the future. He saw the unlimited potential of science and industry. If people continued to work hard and apply their knowledge, Albert believed, everyone around the world would have a happy and abundant future.

"The exhibition of 1851," he declared, "is to give us a true test and a living picture of the point of development at which the whole of mankind has arrived in this great task, and a new starting point from which all nations will be able to direct their further exertions [efforts]."

A Special Motto

It probably won't take you long to figure out that the Great Exhibition is about something more than steam engines and new inventions. After all, the motto of the exhibition is "Progress, Work, Religion, Peace." The part about progress and work is easy to understand. But you wonder what part religion and peace will play.

For some people, the wonders of science and technology are replacing religion. These people are now focusing on the power of people, not the power of God. Others, however, remain loyal to their religious beliefs. They see the Industrial Revolution as the final proof of God's power. It is these people who have put together the Great Exhibition. If you glance at

Exhibits of toys and other goods came from places far away.

A season ticket allowed a visitor to return to the exhibition many times.

the cover of your Crystal Palace catalog, you notice these words: "WE ARE CARRYING OUT THE WILL OF THE GREAT AND BLESSED GOD."

A New Field of Competition

Just as religion is important in the exhibition's motto, peace is part of the picture, too. The people in charge of the exhibition believe that the Industrial Revolution will lead to world peace. They believe that when people have more of everything, they will be more content and less warlike. In addition, they feel that competition involved in making better products will replace war, which only destroys things. Victory will no longer mean destroying an enemy but will mean making a new invention or solving a technical problem.

Wandering through the exhibits, you overhear people talking about their hopes for a peaceful future. You think about what one English writer said, "In a few inches of cotton, there are tales of conquests requiring more skill than Napoleon's greatest battle. Such skillful victories cost no tears and they are for the good of the human race."

SHOW WHAT YOU **KNOW!**

REFOCUS
COMPREHENSION

1. What did the Great Exhibition of 1851 have to do with the Industrial Revolution?

2. What did the English writer mean by "in a few inches of cotton, there are tales of conquests requiring more skill than Napoleon's greatest battle"?

THINK ABOUT IT
CRITICAL THINKING

Why do you think the organizers of the Great Exhibition went to the effort and expense to build such a spectacular building as the Crystal Palace?

WRITE ABOUT IT
ACTIVITY

You are an American journalist visiting the Great Exhibition of 1851. Write an article for your newspaper describing the event.

AUSTRALIA AND NEW ZEALAND

FOCUS *Convicts, missionaries, gold miners, and farmers were the first European settlers in Australia and New Zealand. Land ownership was a source of conflict between the colonists and native peoples.*

Unknown Southern Land

About 1,900 years ago the Greek geographer Ptolemy had a theory that there had to be landmasses south of Asia and Europe to balance those great continental areas. This area that no European had ever seen came to be called *Terra Australis Incognita*, the "Unknown Southern Land."

Spanish, Portuguese, and Dutch explorers all sailed in the area of the unknown land before 1650. It was not until the next century, however, that the Australian coastline was explored and mapped by Europeans. On his first voyage in 1770, Captain James Cook claimed the eastern part of the continent for Great Britain.

The First People

The first people to settle Australia came from the Asian mainland over 40,000 years ago. In time, Europeans were to call their descendants

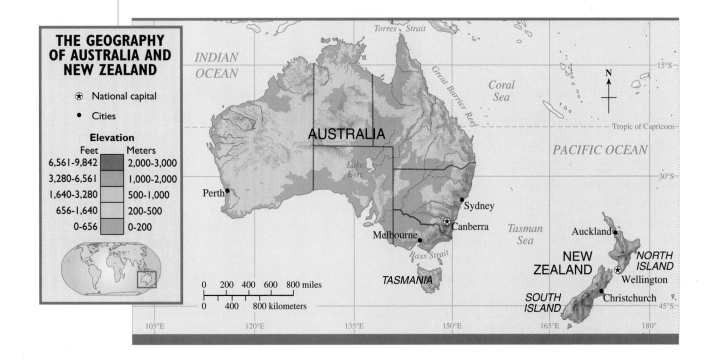

THE GEOGRAPHY OF AUSTRALIA AND NEW ZEALAND

⊛ National capital
• Cities

Elevation

Feet	Meters
6,561-9,842	2,000-3,000
3,280-6,561	1,000-2,000
1,640-3,280	500-1,000
656-1,640	200-500
0-656	0-200

Aborigines (ab uh RIHJ un neez). The name comes from Latin and means "from the beginning."

The Aborigines did not live in permanent settlements. They roamed through specific tribal lands. They used digging sticks for grubbing insects from the soil. Their hunting weapons consisted of **boomerangs**, wooden spears, and stone axes.

The British settlers did not recognize Aboriginal rights to their land. It has only been in the 1990s that Australian courts have recognized some of the land claims made by the descendants of Australia's first people.

From Colony to Commonwealth

British prisons in the eighteenth century were badly overcrowded. Judges sentenced people to long terms, even for minor offenses. One solution was to send convicts with other settlers to colonize the new territory. Their fleet arrived in Australia in 1788. Life was hard for these early

Today Sydney, Australia, is a high-tech city recognized by its harborside opera house.

A descendant of Australia's first people, the Aborigines, displays a traditional painting on tree bark.

settlers, but they made a success of their colony near what is today the city of Sydney. More and more people from Great Britain followed and established other colonies along the coasts. Eventually settlers also moved inland and established the great sheep and cattle **stations**.

The colonies grew slowly until 1851, when gold was discovered. Suddenly everyone wanted to go to Australia. Newcomers came not only from Great Britain but from the rest of Europe and Asia as well.

In 1901, six former Australian colonies became states in the **Commonwealth** of Australia. Australians decided to build a new capital city. It was named Canberra—an Aboriginal word meaning "meeting place."

Land of the Maori

The map on page 415 shows that New Zealand consists of two main islands and a number of smaller ones.

---

 boomerang A flat, curved wooden weapon that returns to the thrower when hurled

---

station A huge Australian ranch where sheep and cattle are raised
commonwealth An independent nation governed by its people

Snowcapped peaks, lakes, geysers, rain forests, and beaches make New Zealand attractive to tourists.

The scenery of the country draws many tourists to New Zealand. The Maori (MAH oh ree) culture also attracts tourists.

The Maori arrived in New Zealand over many hundreds of years, beginning in about the year 700. It is believed that they came from the islands in the Pacific Ocean. Today the Maori make up about nine percent of New Zealand's population.

On the same voyage in which he explored Australia, James Cook claimed New Zealand for the British. British settlers, mainly missionaries, began arriving around 1814.

Two Versions of a Treaty

In 1840, British settlers and a group of Maori signed the Treaty of Waitangi (WEYE tahng ee). The Maori agreed to accept Queen Victoria as their ruler and sell their land only to the government. In return, the British government agreed to protect Maori land and rights. Unfortunately there were two conflicting versions of the treaty—the English and the

Maori translation. Conflict over land ownership arose between the government and the Maori, who owned land as tribes, not individuals.

Land ownership is important to all New Zealanders because so little of the islands is suitable for farming. Although some colonists were lured by a gold rush in 1862, the country's wealth was built on its dairy and cattle farming and the wool from its sheep.

REFOCUS
COMPREHENSION

1. How is the arrival of the Maori in New Zealand different from that of the Aborigines in Australia?

2. What factors brought newcomers to Australia and New Zealand?

THINK ABOUT IT
CRITICAL THINKING

How did the Aborigine and Maori ideas of land ownership differ from European ideas of land ownership? How could this difference cause problems?

WRITE ABOUT IT
ACTIVITY

Make and label a time line to show the events described in this lesson in Australia and New Zealand.

The Maori people have a tradition of carving and painting wood.

417

SUMMING UP

1 DO YOU REMEMBER...
COMPREHENSION

1. What inventions made large textile factories possible?

2. Why did coal mining become more important in the 1700s?

3. On what false belief was mercantilism based?

4. What is a favorable balance of trade?

5. Where was the Dutch Empire centered?

6. From which European country were people most likely to settle in colonies?

7. What did the Factory Act of 1833 accomplish?

8. What British devices at the Great Exhibition stole the show?

9. Why did the organizers of the Great Exhibition think improvements in industry would lead to world peace?

10. Which explorer claimed parts of Australia and New Zealand for Great Britain?

2 SKILL POWER
RECOGNIZING WORD ORIGINS

You know that English words come from many different sources. Choose three of the words you learned or read about in this chapter and find out about their origins. Some possibilities include *industry, factory, labor, Australia, merchant, New Zealand, aborigine,* and *imperialism.*

3 WHAT DO YOU THINK?
CRITICAL THINKING

1. Do you think the poor in England were better off working on the land or in the new factories?

2. How do you think the desire for colonies affected relations between the countries of Europe?

3. Do you, like Prince Albert, think that science and industry are producing a happy and abundant future? Explain your answer.

4. Describe a reform law that you think our Congress should pass soon.

5. Why do you think Australia grew so slowly as a colony at first?

4 SAY IT, WRITE IT, USE IT
VOCABULARY

Suppose you are running for Parliament in Great Britain in the early 1800s. Write a position paper that tells how you stand on the issues that concern people. Try to use as many of these terms as you can in your position paper.

balance of trade	exploitation
boomerang	factory system
child labor	imperialism
commonwealth	Industrial Revolution
enclosure acts	mercantilism
exhibition	station

5 GEOGRAPHY AND YOU
MAP STUDY

Study the map below and answer this question.

1. Why did industrial cities such as Birmingham, Sheffield, Manchester, and Glasgow develop where they did?

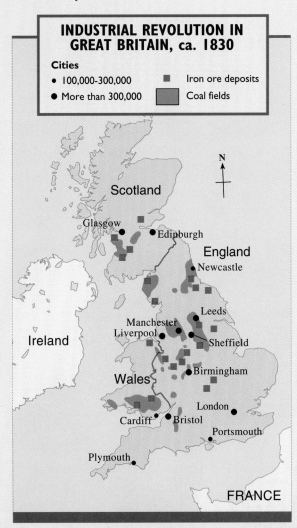

INDUSTRIAL REVOLUTION IN GREAT BRITAIN, ca. 1830

Cities
- 100,000–300,000
- More than 300,000

■ Iron ore deposits
▨ Coal fields

N

Scotland
Glasgow
Edinburgh
England
Newcastle
Leeds
Manchester
Liverpool
Sheffield
Ireland
Wales
Birmingham
London
Cardiff · Bristol
Portsmouth
Plymouth
FRANCE

6 TAKE ACTION
CITIZENSHIP

Life was very hard for children who worked in British industries in the 1800s. As the Industrial Revolution continued to expand, attempts were made to reform child labor. Today, in the United States, there are definite child labor laws in all 50 states. With a group of friends, research what the laws are in your state. Make a chart that shows what kind of work young people are allowed to do and at what age they can do it.

7 GET CREATIVE
LANGUAGE ARTS CONNECTION

One reason that English is such a rich language is that it borrows new words from many different sources. See if you can make up some new words to lend to English. Create three new words for things that just don't have names now. For example, what could you name a pizza that has exactly three toppings? Include a definition for each word, and a picture, if you like.

LOOKING AHEAD In the next chapters, find out what effects European imperialism will have on the rest of the world.

UNIT 5

Times OF GREAT Change

How Is the World Changing?

Do you listen to the news reports about what is happening around the world? What you hear on the news tonight could be the result of something that happened 10, 20, or even 100 years ago. Learn how great changes of the past affect the way we live today.

THE SPREAD

Over the last 200 years, national pride often led governments to overstep their bounds. The resulting nationalism always triggered conflict.

CONTENTS

How does this radio compare with ones used by people in the 1920s? Find out on page 431.

OF NATIONALISM

These books can help you learn more about the relationship between nationalism and imperialism and how these attitudes can lead to war. Read one that interests you and fill out a book-review form.

READ AND RESEARCH

. . . I never saw another butterfly . . .
edited by Hana Volakova (Schocken Books, 1993)
In 1941 the Nazis turned Terezin into a Jewish ghetto. Although most of the children eventually perished, two suitcases full of children's drawings and poetry were found there. *(poetry and art)*

Florence Nightingale by Donna Shore
(Silver Burdett Press, 1990)
Read this inspiring story of the young English woman who made nursing a respectable profession and dedicated her life to improving the care given to wounded soldiers. *(biography)*

War Game by Michael Foreman (Arcade Publishing, 1993)
While playing soccer on a hot summer day in 1914, a group of British boys decides to join the army. Their friendship lasts even as World War I rages around them. *(historical fiction)*

A World War Two Submarine by Richard Humble and Mark Bergin (Peter Bedrick Books, 1991)
The importance of submarines in World War II becomes clear when you read this book. You'll see how these early submarines looked, both inside and out, and you'll find out how they operated. *(nonfiction)*

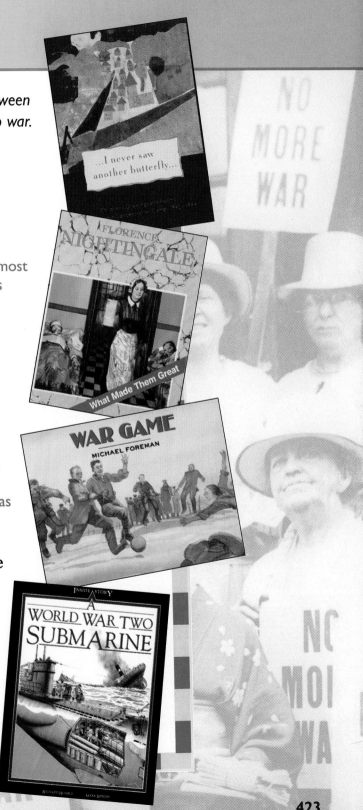

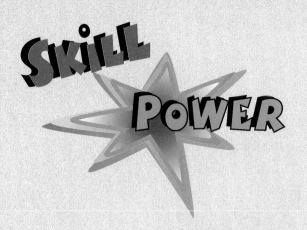

SKILL POWER

Recognizing Fact and Opinion

Knowing the difference between fact and opinion will help you become a critical thinker.

UNDERSTAND IT

Is everything you read in a book or newspaper a fact? Some of the statements may be facts, but others are the writer's opinions. It is important that you know the difference.

A fact is information that can be proved to be true. This is a fact: *In some countries coins are shaped like polygons rather than circles.*

An *opinion* tells what the writer or speaker believes or feels. Here is an opinion: *Round coins are easier to use than multisided ones.*

You can decide whether or not you agree with an opinion. Well-thought-out opinions are supported by facts. But watch out for opinions that are based on inaccurate information or faulty reasoning. Here is an example: *Polygon-shaped coins are worth more than round coins.*

EXPLORE IT

Sometimes it is hard to tell opinions from facts. An opinion may be stated very strongly and, at first glance, it may seem like a fact. To see if a statement is a fact, give it one of these tests.

- Check the statement against what you know. Are you sure from your own experience or knowledge that it is true?

- Test the statement yourself to see if it is true. Or check it against information from other sources, especially reference books. You could also ask an expert.

- If there is no way to test the statement, consider it an opinion rather than a fact.

Use the tests above to help you decide whether these statements are fact or opinion.

The first known coins were made in the Middle East about 2,600 years ago.

By the year 2600, credit cards will have completely replaced coins and bills as money.

With a partner, write ten statements. Some should be facts. Some should be opinions. You and your partner are going to run a quiz show called "Is That a Fact?" Your classmates will be the contestants on the quiz show.

Write your statements out on large sheets of paper. As you and your partner hold them up, the contestants decide if the statement is a fact or an opinion.

Is That a Fact?

The most important invention of all time was the steam engine.

SKILL

POWER SEARCH This chapter is filled with facts. Select four or five of those facts and form opinions about each.

★ **KEY TERMS**

natural rights
unalienable rights
barricade
communism

NATIONS IN CONFLICT

FOCUS *Europe's growth in wealth and military power led to an upsurge in nationalism and a series of conflicts. Internal upheavals and social changes also rocked the nations of Europe.*

The Enlightenment

If the Middle Ages can be called the Age of Faith, the eighteenth century can be called the Age of Reason. New discoveries led many Europeans to reject old ideas about themselves and their world. These people now felt confident that they could make a better world by using the power of the human mind. This new outlook became known as the Enlightenment.

John Locke, an English writer, felt that people had certain **natural rights**. Locke argued that these rights existed in nature just as surely as Isaac Newton's law of gravity. But how could people get governments to let them exercise these rights? It wasn't easy. In some cases, people decided to protect their natural rights by force of arms.

★ **natural rights** Basic human rights, such as life, property, and freedom

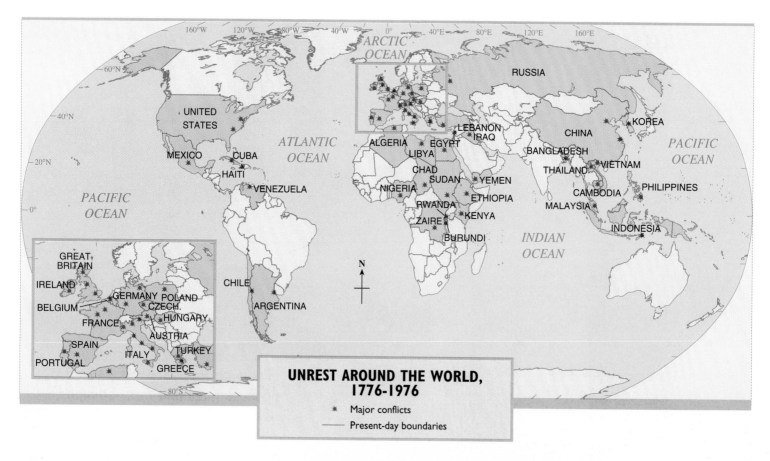

UNREST AROUND THE WORLD, 1776-1976

★ Major conflicts

— Present-day boundaries

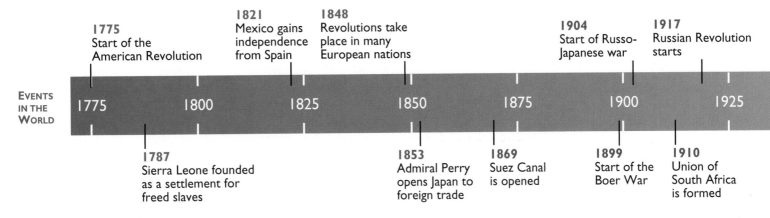

1775 Start of the American Revolution

1821 Mexico gains independence from Spain

1848 Revolutions take place in many European nations

1904 Start of Russo-Japanese war

1917 Russian Revolution starts

1775 · 1800 · 1825 · 1850 · 1875 · 1900 · 1925

1787 Sierra Leone founded as a settlement for freed slaves

1853 Admiral Perry opens Japan to foreign trade

1869 Suez Canal is opened

1899 Start of the Boer War

1910 Union of South Africa is formed

Start of an Era of Revolution

When the English Parliament denied Americans their natural rights, the Americans rebelled. The Declaration of Independence, which listed the reasons for the American Revolution, specifically identifies life, liberty, and the pursuit of happiness as being **unalienable rights** of all people.

In July 1789 the people of France rose up against their king. The people may have been inspired by the success of the Americans in their struggle for independence. But they were also angered by their king's refusal to address their problems.

During the French Revolution, many people, including the king and queen of France, were executed as traitors. The guillotine (GIHL uh teen), a machine used to behead people, became a gory symbol of the revolution. You will read more about the American and French revolutions on page 432.

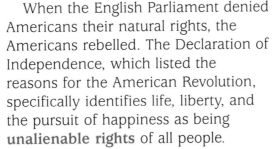

The guillotine claimed many victims during the French Revolution.

Revolutionary Ideals

While the American Revolution was a success, the French Revolution was in many ways a failure. The American Revolution paved the way for democracy and the presidency of George Washington. The French Revolution simply paved the way for the dictator Napoleon Bonaparte (nuh-POH lee un BOH nuh part). Still, the democratic ideals behind these revolutions gave hope to people elsewhere. As the table on page 429 shows, people in other lands were also ready to fight for an end to oppressive governments.

Revolutions in the Western Hemisphere

In the 1790s people on the island of Haiti revolted against their colonial French rulers. Led by a freed slave named Toussaint L'Ouverture (too SAHN loo ver TOOR), the Haitians fought valiantly for several years. The French gave up in 1803, and Haiti became the second nation in the Western Hemisphere, after the United States, to gain its independence.

In 1821 the people of Mexico won their 11-year struggle with Spain for independence. In the years that followed, peoples in other countries of the Western Hemisphere also fought and won revolutions. Sadly, none of these revolutionary movements had the same democratic outcome as the American Revolution.

★ **unalienable rights** Rights that cannot be taken away from a person

What happened in most countries was that revolutionary leaders became dictators who denied political freedom to the vast majority of the people. As a result, the government formed after a revolution was little better than the one it replaced.

Revolutions in Europe

In 1830 and again in 1848, many European countries were beset by revolution. In both cases the people were angered by government's failure to respond to their needs, which were largely economic. The rate of unemployment was very high, and the situation was made worse by high food prices following poor harvests.

In the revolutions of 1848, working-class men, women, and children put up **barricades** in the streets. From behind the barricades, ordinary people bravely fought against government forces, and many died. In the end, all the revolutions of 1848 failed.

 barricade   A barrier or obstruction

Revolutions in China and Russia

Early in the twentieth century, uprisings occurred in two of the largest countries in the world. In 1911, revolutionaries in China overthrew a dynasty that had ruled the country for more than two centuries.

In 1917 the Russian people rose up against their czar. A temporary government was established, but it lacked the support of the people. Many working-class people in Russia had embraced the idea of **communism**. Leaders of the Communist movement took advantage of the unstable situation. In a second revolution, the Communists took over the government and remained in power until 1991.

You will read more about the Chinese and Russian revolutions on page 433.

The Spirit of Nationalism

The effects of the American and French revolutions were like those of

 communism   Ideally, a political system in which most property is owned by the government and shared by those governed

This painting depicts a scene from the revolution in Vienna.

TURMOIL AND CONFLICT	
DATES	REVOLUTIONS
1775–1783	American Revolution
1789–1799	French Revolution
1791–1804	Revolution in Haiti
1810–1821	Mexican Revolution
1830s	Revolutions in France, Belgium, Russia, and the Italian states
1848	Revolutions in Ireland, France, some German and Italian states, Greece, Austrian Empire
1889	Bloodless revolution in Brazil
1911	Chinese Revolution
1917	Russian Revolution

tossing rocks into a pond. They had a ripple effect that spurred other oppressed people to fight for their natural rights.

If we stretch the pond and rock image a bit, we can think of the pond as nationalism. You may recall from Chapter 15 that nationalism is a strong sense of pride in one's country. All the revolutions discussed in these pages were nationalist movements. They all involved the rising up of citizens in protest against an oppressive government.

Unification of Germany and Italy

The spirit of nationalism also stirred the Germans and the Italians. Neither group had its own nation at the beginning of the nineteenth century. Germans lived in a number of small states and tiny kingdoms. Most Italian people were under Austrian rule.

The unification of Germany began with Prussia. This large German state slowly took over the smaller German states and became the modern nation

of Germany in 1871. Meanwhile, Italians were waging a series of wars. From these conflicts the modern nation of Italy emerged in 1870.

Nationalism Oversteps Its Bounds

In some ways nationalism was a good idea. The problem was that nationalism didn't always end at a nation's borders. More often than not, nationalism led to imperialism.

Even the United States yielded to the temptation to expand its influence. Many Americans thought that their ideals were so good that American control should extend as far as possible. They called this imperialistic feeling *manifest destiny*. It led Americans to expand across North America and the Pacific Ocean to the Hawaiian Islands and the Philippines.

In the nineteenth century, the desire to take more than what was rightfully theirs led European nations into a series of wars. Imperialism also set the stage for the great world wars of the twentieth century.

◄ The Eiffel Tower has been a symbol of French national pride since 1889.

429

This painting by Monet reflects the nationalistic spirit of France.

Two More Wars

In 1870, Prussia attacked France. In the Franco-Prussian War, German troops occupied Paris and took control of the French provinces of Alsace and Lorraine. It was at this point that Prussia dominated the German Empire.

In 1904 the Japanese victory over Russia in the Russo-Japanese War shocked the world. No Asian nation had ever before beaten a modern European power. But Japan was not like other Asian nations. In less than 50 years it had developed along the European model into a powerful industrial and military state. The Japanese, like the Germans, now swelled with an aggressive sense of national pride.

World War and an Uneasy Peace

The forces of overheated national pride eventually led to World War I. In 1914 most leaders thought their side would win the war easily. Within a few months, they realized their mistake. World War I became the bloodiest conflict up to that time.

At the end of the war, four horrible years later, the British and the French wanted to punish their German enemies. Under the Treaty of Versailles, which ended the war, Germany lost some of its territories. The Germans were forced to admit their war guilt and were required to pay the victors $32 billion, an unbelievable sum in those days. These harsh terms created deep resentment and made for an uneasy peace that would last just 20 years.

Humanitarian Efforts

War causes terrible suffering and loss. Fortunately, war can also bring out the best in people. The result can be thought of as a positive outcome for a very negative situation.

For example, in two different wars the reports of poor medical treatment for wounded soldiers led to humanitarian action. In 1854, Florence Nightingale, an English nurse, almost singlehandedly established guidelines to ensure that all military hospitals would provide sanitary conditions and adequate care for wounded soldiers.

In a second case, Jean-Henri Dunant, a Swiss banker, wrote a book about the poor treatment of sick and wounded soldiers during the war for Italian independence. In his book, Dunant presented a suggestion that eventually led to the formation of the International Red Cross.

This scene from a jazz club in Berlin, Germany, catches the flavor and excitement of the Jazz Age.

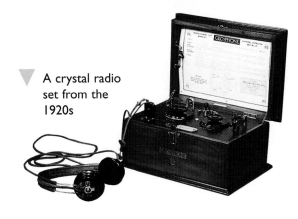

▼ A crystal radio set from the 1920s

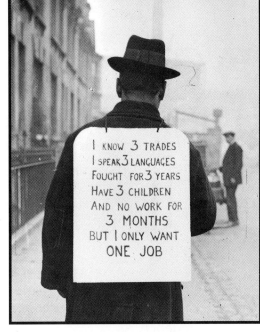

▲ As the sign on this man's back indicates, unemployment was a major problem during the Great Depression.

The Jazz Age and the Depression

At the beginning of the 1920s no one was thinking about another world war. Most people just wanted to have a good time and forget about the war. Young people in the United States and Europe listened to radios like the one shown here, and they danced to the hot new American music called jazz. People began calling the 1920s the Jazz Age. The United States, now the most powerful nation in the world, also set trends in fashion, theater, literature, art, and sports.

Another tag put on the decade was the Roaring Twenties. This referred not only to the fast pace of life but also to the booming American economy. People in all walks of life were making

a great deal of money in the stock market. More people enjoyed wealth and luxury than ever before.

The good times came to an abrupt end when the American stock market crashed in October 1929. This crash helped to trigger the Great Depression of the 1930s. It was the worst economic disaster in modern history, and eventually this depression would contribute to the downfall of governments around the world.

Max de Groot's Dancing Band

REVOLUTIONARY TIMES

FOCUS *If citizens are deprived of certain rights and things they need to live in dignity, the citizens will rise up against their government or ruler. Evidence in support of this idea can be found in the accounts on these pages.*

THE AMERICAN REVOLUTION

American colonists thrived under British rule for almost 150 years. In fact, it was probably their success that led to the War of Independence. As local assemblies became more powerful in America, the British Parliament felt it necessary to pass laws to maintain control over the colonies. Many of these laws involved taxing the colonies.

Since the colonies were not represented in Parliament, they had no voice in the matter. So the colonists followed a natural course—they rebelled. "No taxation without representation" became the rallying cry of the colonies.

On April 19, 1775, colonists engaged British troops in battle. The ensuing war, led by General George Washington (*left*), ended in victory for an independent America. By 1789 the United States of America had been established, the first democratic government in history with a written constitution.

THE FRENCH REVOLUTION

On July 14, 1789, an angry mob in search of weapons stormed the Bastille (bas TEEL), a prison fortress in Paris. This incident marked the start of the French Revolution. The Bastille became the rallying symbol of this great struggle.

In 1791 a constitution was drawn up, limiting the powers of the king and establishing a legislature. However, few people were satisfied with the new government. In January 1793 the king was found guilty of treason and was executed. This event sent shockwaves through other European nations.

Under the leadership of Maximilien Robespierre (mak see MEE lyen ROHBZ pyer), shown above, the revolution turned into a sea of blood known as the Reign of Terror. In little more than a year, thousands of people, including the monarchs, died by the guillotine. The bloodshed ended in 1794 with the execution of Robespierre. However, the revolution was not over. It would last another 10 years, ending with the dictator Napoleon Bonaparte in power.

1775
Start of the American Revolution

1789
Storming of the Bastille

1911
Manchu dynasty falls

1917
Czar Nicholas II steps down

1775   1800   1900   1925

THE CHINESE REVOLUTION

The Manchu (man CHOO) dynasty ruled China for more than 200 years. However, by the mid-1800s the government had become weak and corrupt. Beginning in the 1840s, a series of uprisings took place. The most serious of these was the Boxer Rebellion.

In 1900 the Boxers, a revolutionary group, launched a series of attacks against all foreigners and Chinese Christians. The rebellion was put down by an international army. But in 1911, revolutionaries finally overthrew the Manchu government. The leading figure in the revolution was Dr. Sun Yixian (SUN yee-shee YEN), shown here. He was named the first president of the new Chinese Republic.

THE RUSSIAN REVOLUTION

By the spring of 1917, the threat of revolution had hung over the government of Czar Nicholas II for decades. Russia suffered terrible losses in the early years of World War I. As the war dragged on, shortages of food and other necessities in Russia led to unrest and eventual uprisings. In March 1917, angry mobs rampaged through the streets of Petrograd demanding "bread and peace." A temporary government was set up and Czar Nicholas stepped down as ruler on March 15.

The unstable government that followed was challenged by the Communists. A civil war broke out, and it was won by the Communists in 1920. After their victory the Communists, under the leadership of Lenin, dismantled the old capitalist society and began building a new state.

REFOCUS
COMPREHENSION

1. What actions by the British Parliament incited the American colonists to rebel?

2. What was the Boxer Rebellion?

THINK ABOUT IT
CRITICAL THINKING

What did all of the revolutions described in this lesson have in common?

WRITE ABOUT IT
ACTIVITY

Make a list of five questions you would like to ask one of these people if you had the chance to interview him.

RISE OF DICTATORSHIP

FOCUS *Many European countries, their governments weakened by war and the economic depression, were ideal breeding grounds for takeover by powerful leaders.*

Opening the Door

During the 20-year period between the two world wars, much of Europe was in disarray. Millions of lives had been lost during the war, and the economies of many nations were in shambles. Unemployment was high and people were very unhappy. Governments on both sides of the conflict—winners and losers—had a hard time justifying the terrible costs of the war.

The combination of weak leadership and a restless citizenry provided an ideal breeding ground for the rise of dictatorships. In 1920, 26 European states were democracies. By 1940 only 5 democracies remained—the United Kingdom, Ireland, Sweden, Finland, and Switzerland. The rest of the nations were governed by some form of dictatorship.

Joseph Stalin—"Man of Steel"

In 1917, Lenin became the leader of the newly formed Union of Soviet Socialist Republics (U.S.S.R.). On Lenin's death in 1924, a power struggle took place among several high-ranking Communists for Soviet leadership. The winner of that struggle was Joseph Stalin. Stalin, which means "steel," was the revolutionary name chosen by this tough, unyielding man, who would rule as dictator of the Soviet Union until his death in 1953.

True to his chosen name, Joseph Stalin ruled with an iron fist. He drove his people without mercy to build up Soviet industry and agriculture. Anyone who resisted Stalin was killed. Millions of Soviets died during the 1930s as a result of Stalin's policies.

Stalin's toughness and strong leadership proved to be an asset to the victorious powers during World War II. However, these same qualities, combined with a suspicious nature, contributed greatly to world tension, especially between the Soviet Union and the United States. These tensions would continue to plague both nations for decades after Stalin's death.

▲ Stalin was a powerful dictator.

Mussolini—Italy's New Leader

Even though Italy was on the winning side in World War I, the country gained little from the victory. The Italian people were unhappy with their government and its handling of the peace settlement. Benito Mussolini (be NEE toh moos uh LEE nee) took advantage of the unsettled situation.

Mussolini became the leader of the Fascist (FASH ihst) party in Italy. The Fascists believed in a political system made up of a single party, a single ruler, and total government control of all vital activities.

Mussolini promised the Italian people strong leadership and unity, two qualities that were sadly lacking in Italy at the time. In 1922, Mussolini declared himself to be dictator of Italy. He liked to be called *Il Duce* (eel DOO-chay), which means "the leader."

The Rise of Adolf Hitler

No country suffered greater losses as a result of World War I than did Germany. The new German government, called the Weimar (WEYE-mahr) Republic, was faced with the task of rebuilding its once-great nation. The Germans also carried the burden of meeting the harsh terms of the Versailles treaty. These obstacles proved to be too great for a weak government to overcome.

The German people were devastated by the loss of the war and the economic problems that followed. They blamed the government for their misery. Once again, the stage was set for a dictator to take control. In this case the dictator was Adolf Hitler.

Actually, Hitler had been trying to seize control of Germany since the early 1920s. He had become head of the National Socialist, or Nazi, party. The Nazi party had philosophies and goals similar to those of the Fascists in Italy. Unemployment and inflation caused by the economic depression helped pave the way for Hitler's rise to power.

▼ *Il Duce*, Benito Mussolini

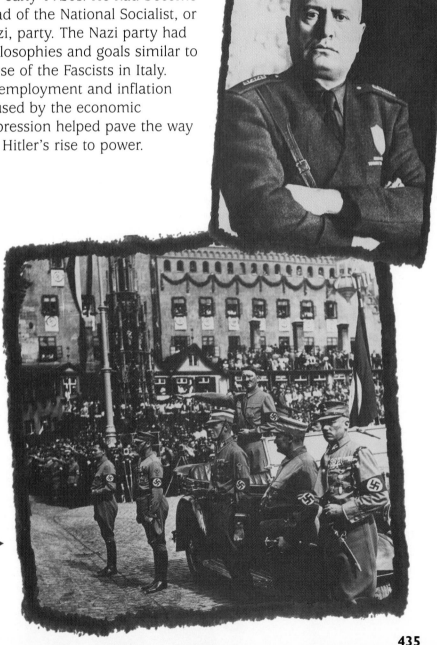

Adolf Hitler was one of the most powerful and most hated dictators in the world. ▶

In 1933, Hitler assumed power in Germany. He put his people to work building up industries and the military. At the same time, Hitler provided the people with a **scapegoat**. He claimed that the Jews were to blame for Germany's defeat in World War I and for all of Germany's economic troubles. This allowed the rest of the German people to forgive themselves and gave them a special target for revenge.

Japan's Ruler—Hirohito

Japan prospered as a result of World War I. While European nations were locked in combat, Japan's industries were producing war supplies for the winning side. By the end of the war, Japan had become an industrial power with a strong economy. In addition, democratic ideals had made some real progress.

Japan's ruler was Emperor Hirohito (hihr oh HEE toh). But the generals wielded the real power. Hirohito went along with just about everything the generals wanted. He was a dictator in name only; in truth, the generals dictated to him and to the nation.

When the worldwide economic depression crippled Japan's economy, a weak parliament did little to help. It was the same old story. The Japanese government exchanged democratic ideals for strong leadership that promised prosperity and stability. By 1932 the generals had taken control and set out to make Japan the most feared military force in Asia.

⭐ *scapegoat* A person or group blamed for the mistakes or crimes of others

These children are greeting ▶ Allied soldiers who have come to free them from a Nazi death camp.

▲ This drawing was done by a young prisoner at Terezin, a Nazi concentration camp. Most likely the artist was killed.

Beyond Evil

The cruel ambitions of Hitler, Mussolini, and the Japanese generals led directly to World War II. In the case of Adolf Hitler, his vision of world dominance also led to an evil beyond words.

After preaching hatred of Jews for so long, Hitler began to believe his own lies. He and his staff developed a plan for what they called the "final solution" to the Jewish problem. The rest of the world called it genocide.

Throughout the war, the Nazis rounded up Jews and other groups they considered to be inferior and transported them to prison camps. At the camps the prisoners were forced to exist in terrible conditions and were subjected to inhuman treatment.

Hitler's final solution was mass execution. An incredible number of men, women, and children were murdered in Nazi death camps. The victims included about 6 million Jews, as shown in the table at the left. Millions of other people, including Slavs, Gypsies, Russians, Magyars (MAG-yahrz), and Poles were also victims of this mass murder, which is known as the Holocaust.

JEWISH POPULATION		
	1939	1945
Austria	60,000	7,000
Belgium	90,000	40,000
Bulgaria	50,000	47,000
Czechoslovakia	315,000	44,000
France	270,000	200,000
Germany	240,000	80,000
Greece	74,000	12,000
Hungary	400,000	200,000
Italy	50,000	33,000
Netherlands	140,000	20,000
Poland	3,350,000	50,000
Romania	800,000	430,000
USSR	3,020,000	2,500,000
Yugoslavia	75,000	12,000

★ *genocide* The planned destruction of a whole group of people because of their race, religion, or nationality
Holocaust The mass murder of millions of Jews and other people by the Nazis

REFOCUS
COMPREHENSION

1. How did economic depression contribute to the rise of dictatorships in Europe?

2. Why was Japan's economy in better shape than the economies of most European nations in 1920?

THINK ABOUT IT
CRITICAL THINKING

What effect can a nation's economic well-being have on its politics?

WRITE ABOUT IT
ACTIVITY

Use books in your school or local library to learn more about one of the dictators or events described in this lesson. Write a brief report about your findings.

WORLD WARS I AND II

FOCUS *The forces of nationalism and imperialism combined with technology to make World War I and World War II the bloodiest conflicts in history.*

World War I Begins

Who's to blame for World War I? Most historians agree that no one nation was responsible. Years of tension had contributed to a climate of war. The nationalism of the 1800s led to a huge buildup of military forces. It also led to military **alliances**. If one nation in an alliance was attacked, all the others would come to its aid. It was like a row of dominoes: One small push and the whole row falls down.

That small push came on June 28, 1914. On that day a Serbian nationalist shot and killed the Austrian archduke and his wife as they drove through Sarajevo, Bosnia (sar uh YAY-voh BAHZ nee uh). Soon Austria, supported by its ally Germany, declared war on Serbia. Shortly after, in accordance with their alliances, Russia, France, and Great Britain declared war on those countries at war with Serbia.

Other Nations Enter the War

As time passed, other nations entered the war. On one side were Germany, Austria-Hungary, and later the Ottoman Empire and Bulgaria. These countries were called the

Central Powers because of their central location in Europe, as shown on the map. On the other side were the Allies. By the end of the war, the Allies included Great Britain, France, Russia, Italy, the United States, and more than two dozen other countries.

Germany, the strongest of the Central Powers, faced the Russians in the east and the French and British in the west. The war in the west quickly turned into a **stalemate**. Neither side could defeat the other. Soldiers on both sides dug trenches from the North Sea to Switzerland. For the next four years, huge armies blasted away at each other, with neither side gaining an advantage.

---

stalemate A situation in which further action is impossible or useless

---

alliance An agreement among persons, groups, or nations to act together

EUROPE DURING WORLD WAR I

- Allies
- Central Powers
- Neutral countries

Map of Europe during World War I showing NORWAY, SWEDEN, DENMARK, North Sea, Baltic Sea, Ireland (Br.), GREAT BRITAIN, NETH., BELG., GERMAN EMPIRE, LUX., RUSSIAN EMPIRE, ATLANTIC OCEAN, FRANCE, SWITZ., AUSTRO-HUNGARIAN EMPIRE, ROMANIA, BOSNIA, Black Sea, PORTUGAL, SPAIN, Corsica (Fr.), Balearic Is., Sardinia (It.), ITALY, SERBIA, MONTENEGRO, BULGARIA, ALBANIA, GREECE, OTTOMAN EMPIRE, Mediterranean Sea, Sicily, SP. MOROCCO, ALGERIA, TUNISIA (Fr.)

EUROPE AFTER WORLD WAR I

New nations

NORWAY
SWEDEN
FINLAND
ESTONIA
LATVIA
LITHUANIA
IRISH FREE STATE (1922)
GREAT BRITAIN
DENMARK
North Sea
Baltic Sea
UNION OF SOVIET SOCIALIST REPUBLICS
ATLANTIC OCEAN
NETH.
BELG.
LUX.
GERMANY
POLAND
CZECHOSLOVAKIA
FRANCE
SWITZ.
AUSTRIA
HUNGARY
ROMANIA
YUGOSLAVIA
Black Sea
PORTUGAL
Corsica (Fr.)
ITALY
BULGARIA
SPAIN
Balearic Is.
Sardinia
ALBANIA
GREECE
TURKEY
Gibraltar (Br.)
Mediterranean Sea
Sicily
SP. MOROCCO
ALGERIA (Fr.)

0 200 400 miles
0 200 400 kilometers

However, some people had a more somber outlook. Sir Edward Grey, a British statesman, expressed this view when he said, in 1914, "The lamps are going out all over Europe. We shall not see them lit again in our lifetime."

By the end of the war, Europe lay in ruins. About 10 million men had died, and 20 million more had been wounded. The monarchies in Russia, Germany, and Austria-Hungary had been toppled. As the map shows, their empires were divided up to create the new nations of Poland, Czechoslovakia, Yugoslavia, Finland, Estonia, Latvia, and Lithuania. Turkey was also created from part of the Ottoman Empire.

The sinking of American ships by German submarines brought the United States into the war in 1917. The fresh American troops and supplies helped to tip the balance of the war in favor of the Allies.

The League of Nations

By the end of this "war to end all wars," President Woodrow Wilson of the United States developed a plan known as the Fourteen Points. The last point called for establishment of the League of Nations. Wilson hoped the League would allow nations to settle their disputes at a conference table.

Much to Wilson's dismay, Congress voted to keep the United States from becoming a member of the League of Nations. In fact the United States entered a period of **isolationism**, during which Americans left the countries of Europe to solve their own problems. And there were plenty of problems to solve!

▼ These children are being given a tea party in a London street to celebrate the end of World War I.

Europe Before and After the War

On the eve of World War I, Europe was peaceful and prosperous. For the previous 400 years it had been the center of world power. Many Europeans believed their situation would not be changed by the war.

⭐ **isolationism** A policy of opposing involvement of one's country in alliances or agreements with other nations

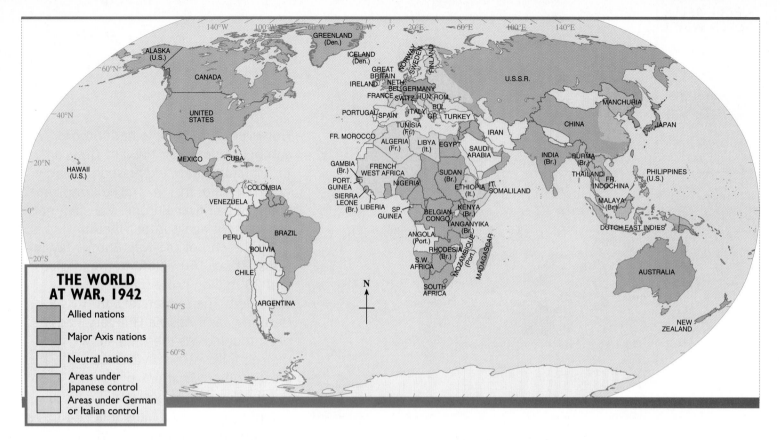

**THE WORLD
AT WAR, 1942**

- Allied nations
- Major Axis nations
- Neutral nations
- Areas under Japanese control
- Areas under German or Italian control

Harsh peace demands of the Allies made the Germans resentful. In addition, the war so weakened Russia that it fell to the Communists. Fear that communism would spread to the rest of Europe raised tensions during the 1920s and 1930s. This increased fear and suspicion helped pave the way for the rise of the dictatorships of Hitler and Mussolini.

Meanwhile any high hopes for the League of Nations fizzled. It did not have the military force or diplomatic power to stop an aggressor. So the League sat by helplessly when Japan invaded Manchuria in 1931. It also did little to prevent the Italian dictator, Mussolini, from conquering the African nation of Ethiopia in 1936.

On to World War II

Nothing was ever done to stop Hitler from rearming Germany, even though this action violated terms of the Treaty of Versailles. This lack of action encouraged Hitler to become bolder. In 1938 he occupied Austria. In March 1939 he took over Czechoslovakia. Only after Germany invaded Poland on September 1, 1939, did the Allies decide to fight. And so World War II began.

Back in 1936, Hitler had formed an alliance with Mussolini. Germany and

◄ These members of a British women's military unit are comparing notes after a briefing session.

This plate is one of a set made to honor members of the Allied air forces.

Members of a French underground unit prepare to carry the fight to the Germans.

SHOW WHAT YOU KNOW!

REFOCUS
COMPREHENSION

1. What event triggered the outbreak of World War I?

2. What historic event brought World War II to a close?

THINK ABOUT IT
CRITICAL THINKING

How might American membership in the League of Nations have helped to promote peace?

WRITE ABOUT IT
ACTIVITY

Make a list of questions you would like to ask of someone who recalls World War II.

Italy became known as the Axis Powers. Japan joined this alliance later in 1940. Against the Axis Powers stood the Allies. By 1942, World War II was in full swing. The map on page 440 shows the countries aligned on both sides of this global conflict.

Global War

World War II was a total war. Entire populations were mobilized for the war effort. Russian women and children fought beside men in the battle of Stalingrad. In the United States and Britain, women worked in shipyards and airplane factories, and many joined the armed services.

The Allies gained the upper hand in Europe in 1944. On April 30, 1945, Hitler killed himself. A week later, Germany surrendered and the war in Europe was over. Japan, however, showed no signs of giving up.

A historic event brought World War II to an end. On August 6, 1945, the United States dropped an atomic bomb on Hiroshima, Japan. In a flash this powerful new weapon killed more than 78,000 people. Three days later, a second atomic bomb was dropped on Nagasaki, and Japan surrendered. The end of the bloodiest war in history had ushered in one of its most frightening eras—the nuclear age.

Hope for the Future

In six short years, World War II caused incredible suffering. The total number of dead and wounded exceeded 50 million. And due to bombings, invasions, and Hitler's death camps, more civilians than soldiers died in the war.

Yet people did not lose faith in the future. In 1945 the Allies created the United Nations. They hoped this new international organization would succeed where the League of Nations had failed. But could it succeed? Tension was already building between two powerful wartime allies—the United States and the Soviet Union.

5

Connections

KEY TERMS

suffrage
pacifist

WOMEN DEMAND THEIR RIGHTS

FOCUS *Starting in the nineteenth century, women in Europe and the United States began to demand that their voices be heard and that their rights be granted.*

Inequality in the Nineteenth Century

In the nineteenth century, men had mixed feelings about women. On one hand, they thought women weren't very intelligent. On the other hand, they realized that women were in charge of family life—and the family was the bedrock on which society was built. Men believed that if women left the home and entered the workplace, civilization would collapse.

So in most parts of the world, women were expected to stay home. They couldn't own property or work as engineers, doctors, or lawyers. Women couldn't run for public office or vote for the men who did.

Opposition to Equal Rights

By the mid-1800s some women began to demand reform. They wanted equal rights with men. These demands, of course, didn't please most men. Men fought back, quoting the Bible, the Qur'an, and other holy books to claim that men were superior to women.

The women reformers also had trouble in their own ranks. Poor working women were worried about earning enough money to survive. To them, it seemed that "women's rights"

were only for middle-class women. Even Queen Victoria scoffed at women's rights and called the idea "this mad, wicked folly."

The Right to Vote

The women reformers didn't back down. In 1848, Elizabeth Cady Stanton, Susan B. Anthony, and Lucretia Coffin Mott held the first women's rights convention in Seneca Falls, New York. These American women campaigned for woman **suffrage** in national elections. In Great Britain, Emmeline Pankhurst and her two daughters founded the Women's Social and Political Union in 1903.

▼ To make her point, this reformer chained herself to a fence in front of the prime minister's house in London, England.

⭐ *suffrage*   The right to vote

As this poster shows, women in Britain had strong arguments when it came to the right to vote.

The long, bitter struggle of these "suffragettes," as they were laughingly called in the press, finally began to pay off. In 1893, New Zealand became the first nation to give women the right to vote. Women in Great Britain won suffrage in 1918. And two years later the Nineteenth Amendment to the Constitution granted the vote to American women. It would be decades before women in most other nations would be able to vote.

Women's Rights in the Workplace

Meanwhile, women were also fighting for their rights in the

In recognition of her work, Susan B. Anthony's face appears on a one-dollar coin.

workplace. Florence Nightingale, who was mentioned briefly on page 430, became a nurse at a time when nursing was not a respectable profession. Nightingale trained at a Lutheran hospital in Germany. She returned to England and helped to train other nurses.

In America, Elizabeth Blackwell became the first woman doctor. Gradually, women broke into other professions as well. During World War II, women took over skilled factory jobs that in the past had been held only by men. Despite these advances, women were paid much less than men for doing the same work. Even today, women often receive lower wages than men for the same job or profession.

Continuing to Fight

Women reformers were on the front lines of other struggles as well. Some women, like Emma Goldman, were revolutionaries, fighting for the rights of poor working men and women.

Other women fought for peace. Bertha von Suttner, an Austrian writer, was a dedicated **pacifist**. A close friend of Alfred Nobel, Suttner urged him to include peace as a category for his Nobel prizes. A famous American pacifist was Jeannette Rankin, the first woman to be elected to the United States Congress. She was the only member of Congress to vote against American participation in both World War I and World War II.

⭐ *pacifist*   A person opposed to all wars

REFOCUS
COMPREHENSION

1. Why were men in the nineteenth century reluctant to recognize women's rights?

2. What was a suffragette?

THINK ABOUT IT
CRITICAL THINKING

Why were women denied equal rights with men?

WRITE ABOUT IT
ACTIVITY

You are assigned to interview one of the women in this article for your school paper.

Name the woman you would interview and make up a list of questions you would ask her.

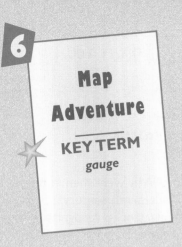

Map Adventure

⭐ **KEY TERM**

gauge

THE GREAT LONDON-TO-AUSTRALIA AIR DERBY

FOCUS *In 1919, Australia sponsored a race to link its commonwealth with Great Britain by air. Two brothers and their crew flew over four continents and 11,000 miles in a quest for victory.*

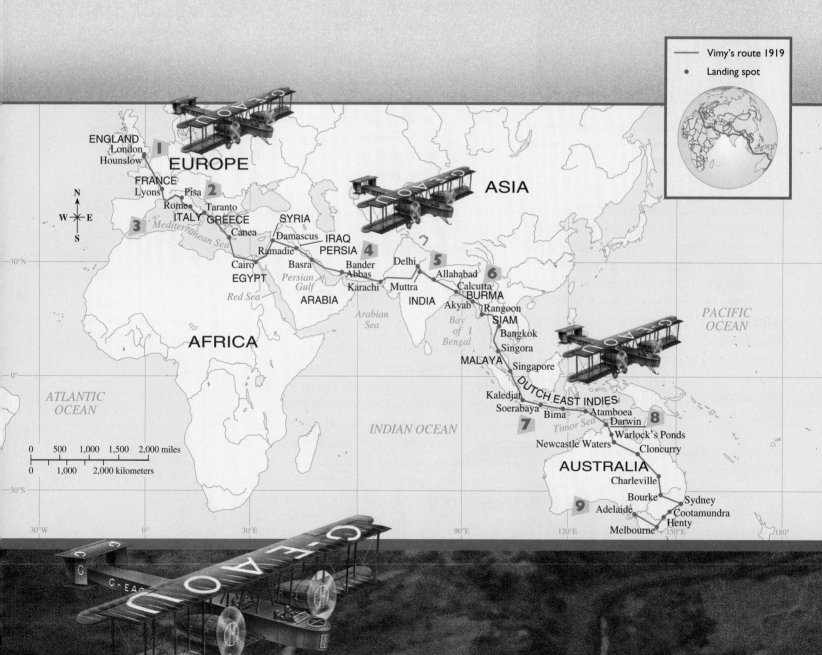

—— Vimy's route 1919

• Landing spot

ENGLAND
London
Hounslow
1

EUROPE

FRANCE
Lyons
Pisa
Rome
Taranto
2
ITALY
GREECE
Canea
SYRIA
Damascus
IRAQ
Ramadie
PERSIA
4
Delhi
5
Allahabad
6
Cairo
Basra
Bander Abbas
Karachi
Muttra
Calcutta
BURMA
EGYPT
Persian Gulf
Akyab
Rangoon
ARABIA
INDIA
SIAM
Red Sea
3
Mediterranean Sea

ASIA

Arabian Sea

Bay of Bengal

Bangkok
Singora
MALAYA
Singapore

AFRICA

PACIFIC OCEAN

ATLANTIC OCEAN

Kaledjat
DUTCH EAST INDIES
Soerabaya
Bima
7
Timor Sea
Atamboea
Darwin
8
Warlock's Ponds
Newcastle Waters
Cloncurry

INDIAN OCEAN

AUSTRALIA

Charleville

Bourke
9
Adelaide
Sydney
Cootamundra
Henty
Melbourne

N W E S

| 0 | 500 | 1,000 | 1,500 | 2,000 miles |
| 0 | 1,000 | | 2,000 kilometers | |

30°N
0°
30°S
30°W
0°
30°E
90°E
120°E
150°E
180°

Adventure in a Vimy Plane

The Great London-to-Australia Air Derby offered a large cash prize to the first Australian team to fly from Hounslow, England, to Darwin, Australia, in 30 days or less. Six teams entered the race. Pilot Ross Smith, his brother Keith Smith, Jim Bennett, and Wally Shiers chose a Vickers Vimy twin-engine plane and prepared for the race of their lives.

Map Key

1 Hounslow The Vickers Vimy took off on November 12, 1919, with 516 gallons of fuel. Snow covered the runway, and a thick fog quickly enveloped the plane.

2 Pisa Because of winds, the crew could not reach Rome on the second day. They landed at Pisa and were grounded by rain and mud until the fifteenth. A broken oil gauge then forced them to stop briefly.

3 Mediterranean Sea Crossing the Mediterranean, the Vimy flew 250 miles over open sea. Four hours later, the plane passed over the African coastline.

4 Bander Abbas After leaving Bander Abbas, the Vimy flew its longest leg of the trip—730 miles nonstop—to Karachi. It took the team eight and a half hours.

5 Allahabad As the team prepared for takeoff, an angry bull suddenly charged the Vimy. A boy ran onto the runway to distract the bull, and the Vimy took off safely.

6 Calcutta The crew expected an easy flight from Calcutta to Akyab. Suddenly a hawk hit the left propeller, only inches from the pilots' heads. Luckily the propeller did not break apart, and the Vimy flew on.

7 Soerabaya The Vimy's wheels became trapped in mud at Soerabaya. People helped the crew cover the runway with bamboo. The Vimy took off, scattering bamboo everywhere.

8 Darwin Gliding over the Indian Ocean, the crew spotted Australia's coastline. On December 10 at 3 P.M., they landed at the crowded Darwin airfield. Twenty-seven days and 20 hours after they began their quest, the prize was theirs.

9 Adelaide Adelaide was the Smith brothers' hometown. After receiving their prize in Melbourne, the crew flew the Vimy to Adelaide, where they received a hero's welcome.

★ *gauge* An instrument for measuring

MAP IT

1. You are a navigator aboard the Vimy plane. You leave Hounslow, headed for Rome. In what direction should you fly?

2. To prepare for the difficult water crossings, the pilot, Ross Smith, asks you for a list of bodies of water you might encounter on the route to Australia. Consult the map to create the list.

3. After a long flight to Karachi, your crew must reach the east coast of India. Is it shorter to fly south around the coast or east across the land?

4. Victory greets your crew in Darwin. How many miles have you flown? How many stops did you make on the trip?

EXPLORE IT

Use a current world map to retrace the Smiths' historic flight. What are the present-day nations along the route?

SUMMING UP

1 DO YOU REMEMBER . . .
COMPREHENSION

1. What unalienable rights of people did the leaders of the American Revolution identify?

2. How was the outcome of other revolutions in the Western Hemisphere different from that in the United States?

3. How did nationalism affect the Germans and Italians during the early 1800s?

4. What goals did Stalin set for the Russian people?

5. What dictator rose in Italy in the 1920s? What dictator rose in Germany in the 1930s?

6. How was Hirohito's leadership of Japan different from that of the European dictators?

7. How did military alliances make large-scale wars more likely?

8. Why wasn't the League of Nations able to prevent World War II?

9. When did women in Great Britain win suffrage? When did American women?

10. On what continents did the Vimy land?

2 SKILL POWER
RECOGNIZING FACT AND OPINION

Explain why the sentence below, which appears on page 427, is an opinion. Then write three facts from Lesson 1 that support this opinion.

While the American Revolution was a success, the French Revolution was in many ways a failure.

3 WHAT DO YOU THINK?
CRITICAL THINKING

1. Why has the United States been able to avoid dictatorships over the last two centuries?

2. How might creating a scapegoat have helped Hitler unite the German people?

3. Why might World War I and World War II be described as two halves of the same war?

4 Do you think women today have equal rights with men? Give examples to support your answer.

5. Why would Australians want to establish the fact that their country could be reached by air travel?

4 SAY IT, WRITE IT, USE IT
VOCABULARY

Write a paragraph about the causes and effects of World War II. Use five or more of the terms below in your writing.

alliance	natural rights
barricade	pacifist
communism	scapegoat
gauge	stalemate
genocide	suffrage
Holocaust	unalienable rights
isolationism	

446

5 GEOGRAPHY AND YOU
MAP STUDY

The map below shows the nations that were created from the German, Austro-Hungarian, and Russian empires at the end of World War I.

Compare this map with the map of Europe in the Atlas. Which countries shown on this map also appear on the map in the Atlas?

FINLAND

ESTONIA

LATVIA

LITHUANIA

Baltic Sea

POLAND

CZECHOSLOVAKIA

Adriatic Sea

YUGOSLAVIA

6 TAKE ACTION
CITIZENSHIP

A flag is a very important symbol of national pride. The flag of the United States has a long history. There are rules about displaying the flag properly and regulations about disposing of old worn-out flags. Work in groups to make a display featuring the U.S. flag, its history, and how it should be treated.

7 GET CREATIVE
COMPUTER CONNECTION

The artwork on page 437, done by a child in a concentration camp, is a symbol of the outrages of the Nazis. Think of an issue that concerns you. Check the Internet to see if there are groups that have the same concerns you do. Learn as much as you can about these groups and share your findings with your classmates.

LOOKING AHEAD
As Europe moved into the modern age, find out what changes were taking place in the Americas.

THE NATIONS OF

After the people in the United States and France gained their independence, the people of Latin America wanted similar freedoms. Read this chapter to learn what happened during Latin America's struggle for independence.

CONTENTS

▼ This girl's cup is a traditional one used in parts of Latin America. Look at page 468 to find out who uses the cup.

LATIN AMERICA

You can learn more about Latin America and its culture from these books. Read one that interests you and fill out a book-review form.

READ AND RESEARCH

Cowboy by David H. Murdoch, photographed by Geoff Brightling (Alfred A. Knopf, 1993)

The South American pampas are home to many gauchos. These Argentinian cowboys have a rich history that goes back three centuries. Here you will see photos of their equipment and clothing. You can also read about cowboys of other countries. *(nonfiction)*

Grab Hands and Run by Frances Temple (HarperTrophy, 1993)

After his father disappears, Felipe, his mother, and his sister must escape the turmoil in El Salvador. Follow their exciting but fearful journey to Canada. Find out if hope alone can help them reach their destination. *(historical fiction)*

The Amazon Rain Forest and Its People by Marion Morrison (Thomson Learning, 1993)

Find out why the survival of the Amazon rain forest is important to its native people and also to the rest of the world. Learn about the problems in our ecosystem and how each person can make a difference. *(nonfiction)*

Simón Bolívar: Latin American Liberator by Frank De Varona (The Millbrook Press, 1993)

Growing up in an empire ruled by Spain, Simón Bolívar came to admire the liberty and justice he saw on his travels to the United States. Find out how his patriotism influenced the development of Latin America. *(biography)*

SKILL POWER

Reading Resource Maps

Knowing how to read a resource map is a skill that will allow you to get a lot of information about a place.

EXPLORE IT

Here are two resource maps of Canada. The map below shows Canada's population density. Colors are used to show where people live—and don't live—in Canada. Most people in Canada live in the purple areas. The yellow areas have very few people. What does the second map of Canada show? What symbols are used to show information? Use the maps to find answers to these questions.

- In which colored areas of Canada would you expect to find farms and small villages?

- How many people live in each square mile where Ottawa is located?

- Are most oil fields in Canada located in the eastern or western part of the country?

- What can you say about the number of people living in areas that have a lot of oil fields?

UNDERSTAND IT

Assume that you are going on a fossil hunt. How would you find out where fossils might be located? A resource map could help you decide where to dig.

A resource map shows you at a glance where resources can be found. It may use dots, different-colored areas, numbers, or small pictures to pinpoint locations.

POPULATION DENSITY IN CANADA

Population Density

⊛ National capital

People per square mile	People per square kilometer
Over 250	Over 100
126–250	51–100
26–125	11–50
1–25	1–10
Less than 1	Less than 1

0   200   400 miles
0   400 kilometers

Ottawa ⊛

N

TRY IT

Think of a resource you would like to know about—maybe all the places in your neighborhood where you can rent videotapes or play basketball. Make a resource map showing the locations of the places you select. You may want to trace a map of an area and add dots or numbers and a map key of its resources. Or draw a large map freehand and use pictures as markers. Be as creative as you wish, but remember that your goal is to show someone else where certain resources can be found.

Prepare a group display of resource maps. Be sure that each map is labeled so that viewers can appreciate the display.

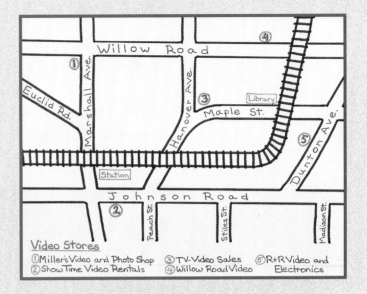

Video Stores
①Miller's Video and Photo Shop   ③TV-Video Sales   ⑤R+R Video and
②Show Time Video Rentals   ④Willow Road Video   Electronics

OIL FIELDS IN CANADA

✪ National capital

⚒ Oil fields

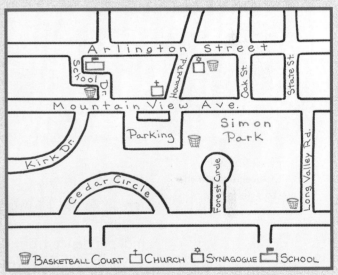

🗑BASKETBALL COURT   †CHURCH   📿SYNAGOGUE   📖SCHOOL

SKILL POWER SEARCH *Look at the resource map on page 461. How else might that same information be shown?*

451

INDEPENDENCE AND ITS CONSEQUENCES

FOCUS *The countries of Latin America struggled for independence from the domination of European powers.*

▲ Pierre Toussaint L'Ouverture led the struggle for independence in Haiti.

Freedom in the Air

In 1776 the 13 British colonies in North America declared their independence from Great Britain. In 1792 the French overthrew their king and formed a republic. These events sent a thrill of excitement through many Latin Americans. They too began to plot ways of gaining freedom.

Upper-class Latin Americans—*criollos* and *peninsulares*—were very cautious. They feared that a war for independence might set off uprisings among Native Americans and enslaved Africans. That, in turn, might threaten their own wealth and even their lives.

Since the social structure was unequal, Africans and Native Americans saw things differently. They were eager to throw off unwanted masters and gain their freedom. As you read this lesson, refer to the map on page 453 to follow the progress of independence.

The Haitian Revolution

Latin America's first revolution was started by enslaved Africans on the Caribbean island of Hispaniola. During the 1600s the western part of the island had come under French control. It was called Saint Domingue. By the time of the French Revolution, its sugar, coffee, and indigo plantations had made it the richest of all the French colonies.

Excited by the revolution in France, Saint Domingue's slave-owning planters wanted independence. But quarrels broke out within their ranks. Taking advantage of the discord among the planters, enslaved Africans rose in revolt. Bloody slaughter and chaos followed. Under the leadership of Pierre Toussaint L'Ouverture (pee AIR too SAN loo ver TOOR) and Jean Jacques Dessalines (zhahn zhahk day sah-LEEN)—both born into slavery—the

452

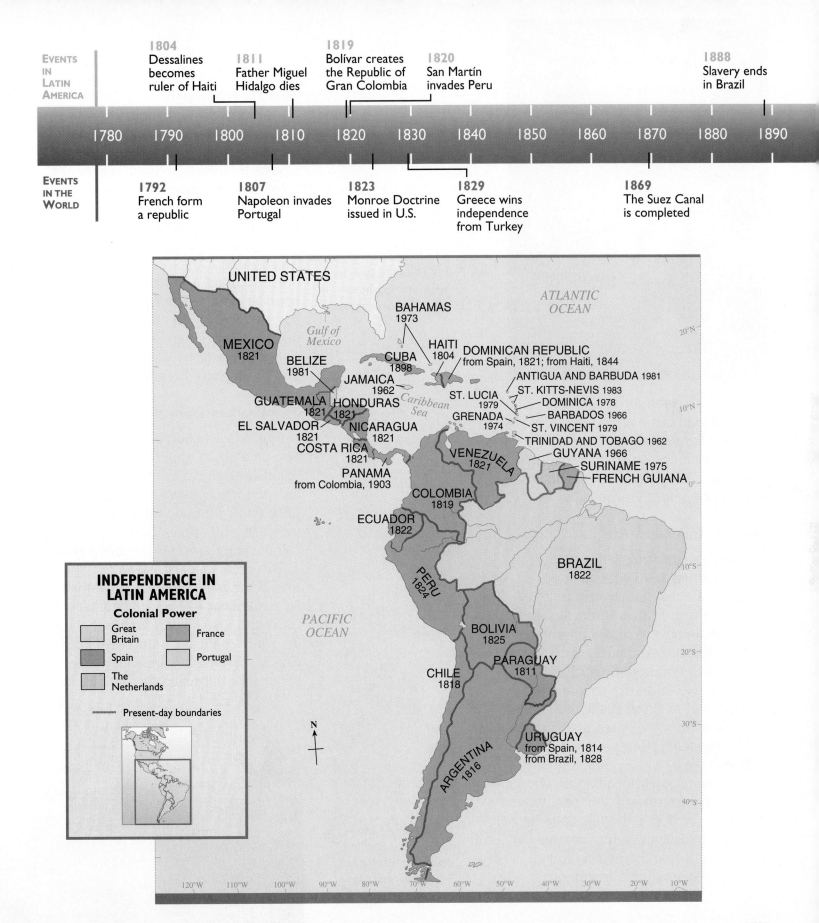

EVENTS IN LATIN AMERICA

1804 Dessalines becomes ruler of Haiti

1811 Father Miguel Hidalgo dies

1819 Bolívar creates the Republic of Gran Colombia

1820 San Martín invades Peru

1888 Slavery ends in Brazil

1780 1790 1800 1810 1820 1830 1840 1850 1860 1870 1880 1890

EVENTS IN THE WORLD

1792 French form a republic

1807 Napoleon invades Portugal

1823 Monroe Doctrine issued in U.S.

1829 Greece wins independence from Turkey

1869 The Suez Canal is completed

UNITED STATES

ATLANTIC OCEAN

BAHAMAS 1973

Gulf of Mexico

MEXICO 1821

BELIZE 1981

CUBA 1898

HAITI 1804

DOMINICAN REPUBLIC from Spain, 1821; from Haiti, 1844

JAMAICA 1962

ANTIGUA AND BARBUDA 1981

ST. KITTS-NEVIS 1983

GUATEMALA 1821

HONDURAS 1821

Caribbean Sea

ST. LUCIA 1979

DOMINICA 1978

EL SALVADOR 1821

NICARAGUA 1821

GRENADA 1974

BARBADOS 1966

ST. VINCENT 1979

COSTA RICA 1821

VENEZUELA 1821

TRINIDAD AND TOBAGO 1962

GUYANA 1966

PANAMA from Colombia, 1903

COLOMBIA 1819

SURINAME 1975

FRENCH GUIANA

ECUADOR 1822

PACIFIC OCEAN

PERU 1824

BRAZIL 1822

BOLIVIA 1825

PARAGUAY 1811

CHILE 1818

URUGUAY from Spain, 1814 from Brazil, 1828

ARGENTINA 1816

INDEPENDENCE IN LATIN AMERICA

Colonial Power

Great Britain

France

Spain

Portugal

The Netherlands

Present-day boundaries

N

20°N
10°N
0°
10°S
20°S
30°S
40°S

120°W 110°W 100°W 90°W 80°W 70°W 60°W 50°W 40°W 30°W 20°W 10°W

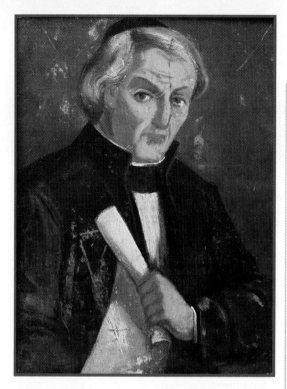

Father Miguel Hidalgo led an army that fought for Mexico's independence.

rebels finally won. In 1804, Saint Domingue became an independent nation, with Dessalines as ruler. The island was renamed Haiti (HAY tee), which was the name used by Native Americans before French rule.

Mexican Independence

The Mexican struggle for independence began in 1810 when a criollo priest in the town of Dolores issued a call to arms to Native Americans and mestizos, people of mixed parentage. Father Miguel Hidalgo (mee GEL ee-THHAHL goh) was not afraid of social upheaval. He said, "My children, will you be free? Will you make the effort to recover from the hated Spaniards the lands stolen from your forefathers 300 years ago?"

Soon Hidalgo was leading an army of 80,000 men toward Mexico City. But most criollos, as well as Catholic Church officials, did not relish the thought of losing their lands and prestige. They refused to support

Hidalgo. Peninsulares and Spanish troops crushed the rebels.

Events in Spain encouraged Mexico's push toward independence. Liberal reformers in Spain ousted the king. They planned to give more rights to the people of Spanish America. But Mexico's criollos feared that this would mean greater power for mestizos and Native Americans. A criollo army officer named Agustín de Iturbide (ah-goo STEEN de ee toor BEE thhay) led a successful revolt in 1821. He then declared himself emperor of Mexico. Two years later he was overthrown, and the country became a republic.

Two Leaders Emerge

France's invasion of Spain in 1808 also created an opportunity for Spanish Americans who wanted independence. Revolutions began in 1810 and continued for 15 years. By the year 1825, Spain had lost all its colonies on the American mainland.

Two great leaders played a major role in the independence movement—Simón Bolívar (see MAWN baw LEE-vahr) and José de San Martín (hoh SAY de sahn mahr TEEN). In 1813, Bolívar won a short-lived independence for Venezuela, but when the fighting in

This painting shows workers on a Brazilian plantation more than 300 years ago.

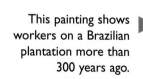

Europe ended, Spain regained control of this colony.

In 1817, Bolívar returned to Venezuela with a small invasion force. *Llaneros* (yah NER ohz), or cowboys, from the countryside swelled the ranks of Bolívar's army. He marched his soldiers across the Andes toward the city of Bogotá. The army won a great victory in 1819. When Bolívar rode into the city, cheers of "Our liberator!" greeted him. In December 1819, Bolívar announced the creation of a new nation, the Republic of Gran Colombia, which included the present-day countries of Ecuador, Colombia, and Venezuela.

Meanwhile, San Martín led the fight for independence in the south. Born in Argentina, he returned from Spain after a revolt broke out in Argentina in 1811. Five years later Argentina won its independence. Then San Martín entered Chile, leading an army through the high mountain passes. He joined forces with the rebels there and ousted the Spaniards. Next he moved against the colonial powers in Peru. In 1821 his troops entered the capital, Lima. San Martín became "protector" of the newly independent territory. However, a Spanish army still held large portions of Peru.

A Dream of Unity

Who would lead the final revolt against the Spaniards in South America? Bolívar and San Martín met in Ecuador to make plans. San Martín bowed out, letting Bolívar take command. Bolívar and his generals defeated the Spaniards and freed northern Peru.

Bolívar dreamed of uniting all of South America into one great confederation, or union. But few others shared his dream. Instead the new nations split farther apart with independence. Uruguay and Paraguay split from Argentina, and Gran Colombia divided into three

▲ Colombian folk art captures a bit of life in the countryside.

Curing Scene Molas. Artist Unknown. San Blas Islands, Panama c, 1965
Cloth 14.5 x 20.25" Museum of American Folk Art, New York

▲ Molas—decorative pieces from Central America—are made by cutting through layers of fabric to reveal different colors. This mola shows a harvest scene.

nations. Bolívar's dream of a united South America never came true.

Brazil's Way

Brazil's road to independence took a different course. After Napoleon's troops invaded Portugal in 1807, the Portuguese court fled to Brazil. When the wars in Europe ended, Portugal's king returned home. He left his son, Pedro, in Brazil to keep an eye on things. In 1822 the Brazilians' demands for independence increased, so Pedro declared Brazil independent—with himself as emperor. However, he did accept a constitution that gave the people of Brazil some basic rights.

Slavery continued longer in Brazil than it did anywhere else in South America. Pedro's son, Pedro II, was helpful in bringing about its end in 1888. This increased his unpopularity with the powerful people in the country, and he was ousted the next year. Brazil then became a republic.

Relations With the United States

In 1823, United States President James Monroe issued what became known as the Monroe Doctrine. It declared that the United States would not allow European nations to acquire any new colonies in the Americas. Since then the United States has frequently intervened in the affairs of Latin American nations.

The United States applauded when Texas won its independence from Mexico in 1836. When Texas joined the United States in 1845, war broke out between the United States and Mexico. After winning the war, the United States took the land that is now California, Arizona, New Mexico, Utah, Colorado, and Nevada.

Two remaining Spanish colonies, Cuba and Puerto Rico, were freed from European control after the Spanish-American War of 1898. But the United States kept soldiers in Cuba for years.

Puerto Rico came under the direct rule of the United States. Today it is a commonwealth of the United States and is self-governing. Although Puerto Ricans are citizens of the United

▼ The destruction of an American warship, the *Maine,* marked the beginning of the Spanish-American War.

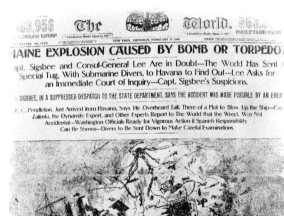

THE BIG STICK IN THE CARIBBEAN SEA

◀ Theodore Roosevelt is shown carrying a big stick as he faces Latin America.

SHOW WHAT YOU
KNOW!

REFOCUS
COMPREHENSION

1. Why were criollos and peninsulares often cautious about independence?

2. How did caudillos threaten independence in Latin America?

THINK ABOUT IT
CRITICAL THINKING

Explain how events in Spain, France, and Portugal affected independence movements in Latin America.

WRITE ABOUT IT
ACTIVITY

Write a letter to the editor explaining how you would feel if Latin American countries started enforcing a big-stick policy in the United States.

States, they cannot vote in presidential elections and have no voting representatives in Congress. But Puerto Ricans have voted not to become a state or an independent country.

Roosevelt's Big-Stick Policy

In the early twentieth century, the United States flexed its muscles in Latin America. President Theodore Roosevelt developed a **big-stick policy** toward Latin America that was patterned after a West African proverb: "[If you] speak softly and carry a big stick, you will go far."

Roosevelt helped Panama break away from Colombia in 1903. Panama then granted the United States the right to construct a canal across its territory. The United States controlled the canal and a strip of land on either side. The United States has promised to give control of the canal to Panama in 1999.

Any Chance for Democracy?

The wars for independence shook up the old social order in Latin America. Criollos, mestizos, Native Americans, and people of African descent had all played a part in gaining independence, and they wanted to share its benefits.

Many of the people who had fought for independence formed armies that later battled among themselves for territory. Some of the armies were led by powerful leaders called **caudillos** (kou THHEE yawz). Often these leaders made alliances with powerful landowners and wealthy merchants.

In each new country, civilians wrote their own constitutions and tried to set up stable governments. But they could not always control the caudillos. Dictatorships have been common in many Latin American nations well into the twentieth century.

⭐ **big-stick policy** A policy of acting from a position backed with a show of strength

⭐ **caudillo** A leader, especially a military dictator

457

THEY LED THE WAY

FOCUS *Although it takes many people to make independence possible, there are always a few leaders whose accomplishments stand out.*

TOUSSAINT L'OUVERTURE

When Pierre Toussaint L'Ouverture was a boy, he sat under a tree to read. A Frenchman, enraged by the sight of a slave reading, beat the boy. No African slave in Saint Domingue was allowed to learn to read.

It took years for Toussaint L'Ouverture to avenge the beating. He led a rebellion that overthrew the French colonial government.

Although Toussaint L'Ouverture died in 1803, before Saint Domingue became independent, he is credited with leading his country to independence. Today Toussaint L'Ouverture is considered the George Washington of Haiti.

SIMÓN BOLÍVAR

Although Simón Bolívar was born into a wealthy family, his early life was full of sorrow. Both his parents died when he was still a boy. When he was 16, Bolívar went to Spain, where he fell in love. Two years later Bolívar brought his bride to Venezuela. Tragically she caught yellow fever and died within a year.

Grief-stricken, Bolívar decided to devote his life to helping free his country from Spanish rule. He succeeded, winning independence for Venezuela and many other countries. Yet people refused to accept his dream of a united South America. Bolívar died at age 47, convinced that he was a failure.

JOSÉ DE SAN MARTÍN

The father of José de San Martín was a Spanish soldier in Argentina. Young José decided to have a military career, too. When he was 33, San Martín joined the fight for Argentina's independence.

He proved to be a brilliant military commander, leading his troops to victory after victory. After driving the Spaniards from Argentina, he marched to Chile and Peru, liberating them as well.

However, San Martín had no wish to lead the nations he freed. In 1822, San Martín turned over his troops to Bolívar. San Martín never explained why.

1803
Toussaint
L'Ouverture
dies in France

1807
Bolívar joins
Venezuelan
revolutionaries

1822
San Martín turns
over his troops
to Bolívar

1867
Juárez restores
government in
Mexico

1898
Cuba gains
independence
from Spain

1800   1825   1850   1875   1900

BENITO JUÁREZ

The year was 1862. Benito Juárez (be NEE toh HWAH res), president of Mexico, prepared to leave Mexico City. He kissed the Mexican flag and shouted to a cheering crowd, "¡Viva, México!" Although a French army was heading for the city, Juárez wanted the people to know he would support them.

The French took control of the country and named Maximilian I as emperor. Juárez eluded capture by traveling through the countryside, rallying his people. Mexicans formed bands of fighters that attacked the French soldiers.

Finally, in 1867 the French troops withdrew. Juárez's forces executed Maximilian, restoring the constitutional government. Today Juárez is revered as the man who saved Mexico's independence.

JOSÉ MARTÍ

In a life that lasted only 42 years, José Martí had enough careers for several lifetimes. His poetry and essays helped establish a new and modern style in Latin American literature. His countless newspaper articles were read throughout the Americas.

Martí's greatest achievement, however, was his leadership of the Cuban independence movement. He took part in his first rebellion in 1868, when he was only 15. After the revolt failed, Martí was deported and spent most of the rest of his life outside Cuba. For many years he lived in the United States, gathering funds from Cuban immigrants to supply an army to fight for Cuba's independence.

When the rebellion began in 1895, Martí left for Cuba. He was killed in the fighting. His followers carried on the struggle, and in 1898, Cuba at last became free of Spanish rule.

SHOW WHAT YOU KNOW!

REFOCUS
COMPREHENSION

1. What does it mean to say that Toussaint L'Ouverture was the George Washington of Haiti?

2. What are three contributions that José Martí made to Cuba?

THINK ABOUT IT
CRITICAL THINKING

Why did Bolívar think he was a failure? Explain your reasons for agreeing or disagreeing with him.

WRITE ABOUT IT
ACTIVITY

Put yourself in José de San Martín's place. Make up a list of advantages and disadvantages of being the leader of a freed nation.

459

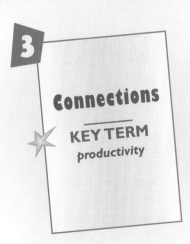

LATIN AMERICAN ECONOMIES

FOCUS *Latin America's decisions about what goods and services to produce are based on factors such as its geography, its natural resources, and the skills of its workers.*

Why Do Countries Trade?

You have learned about trade throughout history, such as the trade between Egypt and Kush and between China and India. Have you ever thought about the reasons why countries produce and trade the goods and services they do?

Sometimes the reasons have to do with geography and the skills of the workers in the country. The quality of a country's transportation systems and even the number of its telephones have an effect on its trade. What a country produces also depends upon what other countries want to buy.

What Affects Trade?

You can see from the map on page 461 that Latin America produces a variety of goods. When each country decides what it wants to produce, it takes many things into consideration.

What is the geography of the country? If it has high mountains and a cold climate, it may not be a good place to grow food crops. But it might be a perfect place to mine silver or grow trees. Since Chile has a mountainous and rugged landscape, only about 7 percent of its land is suitable for farming. However, it's rich in mineral resources such as copper,

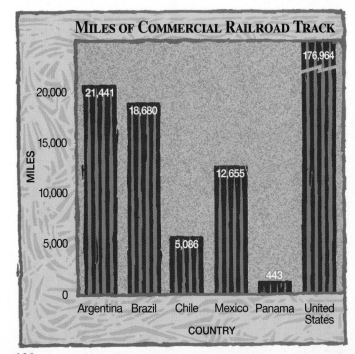

MILES OF COMMERCIAL RAILROAD TRACK

Country	Miles
Argentina	21,441
Brazil	18,680
Chile	5,086
Mexico	12,655
Panama	443
United States	176,964

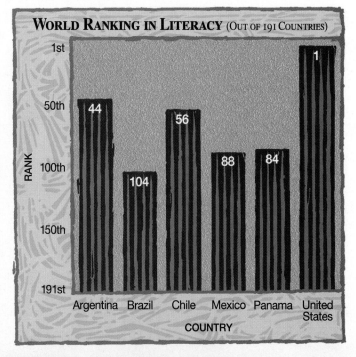

WORLD RANKING IN LITERACY (OUT OF 191 COUNTRIES)

Country	Rank
Argentina	44
Brazil	104
Chile	56
Mexico	88
Panama	84
United States	1

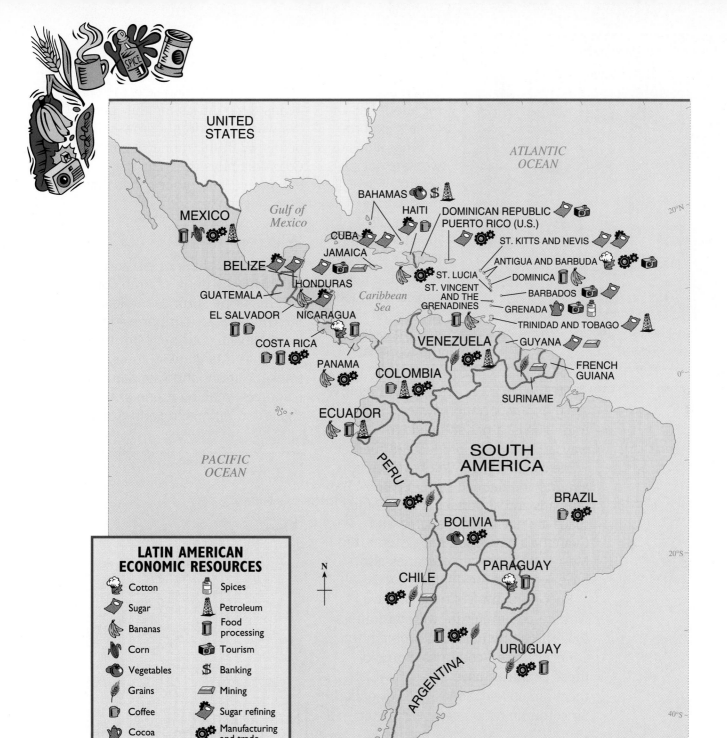

LATIN AMERICAN ECONOMIC RESOURCES

UNITED STATES

ATLANTIC OCEAN

Gulf of Mexico

MEXICO

BAHAMAS

HAITI

DOMINICAN REPUBLIC
PUERTO RICO (U.S.)

CUBA

JAMAICA

ST. KITTS AND NEVIS

BELIZE

ANTIGUA AND BARBUDA

HONDURAS

GUATEMALA

ST. LUCIA

DOMINICA

ST. VINCENT
AND THE
GRENADINES

BARBADOS

Caribbean Sea

GRENADA

EL SALVADOR

NICARAGUA

TRINIDAD AND TOBAGO

COSTA RICA

VENEZUELA

GUYANA

PANAMA

COLOMBIA

FRENCH
GUIANA

SURINAME

ECUADOR

PACIFIC OCEAN

PERU

SOUTH AMERICA

BRAZIL

BOLIVIA

PARAGUAY

CHILE

URUGUAY

ARGENTINA

LATIN AMERICAN ECONOMIC RESOURCES

Cotton		Spices	
Sugar		Petroleum	
Bananas		Food processing	
Corn		Tourism	
Vegetables		Banking	
Grains		Mining	
Coffee		Sugar refining	
Cocoa		Manufacturing and trade	

N

0   500   1,000   1,500   2,000 miles

0   1,000   2,000 kilometers

80°W   60°W   40°W   20°W   0°

20°N

0°

20°S

40°S

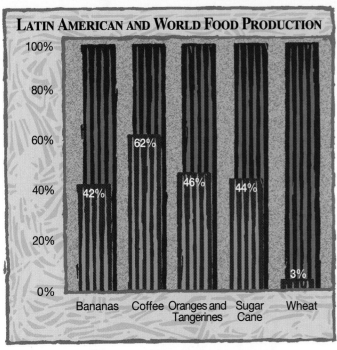

LATIN AMERICAN AND WORLD FOOD PRODUCTION

Bananas: 42%
Coffee: 62%
Oranges and Tangerines: 46%
Sugar Cane: 44%
Wheat: 3%

■ World ■ Latin America

which accounts for about half of Chile's exports.

What kinds of workers does a country have? If most workers are unskilled, high-technology industries would not be the best choice. But food processing may suit the skills of the workers perfectly.

How modern are the transportation systems? To trade goods, a nation needs to have ways of getting its products to market.

Mexico and Argentina have modern airports and railroad systems. Brazil has railroads and airports, but most of its roads are not paved. Panama and Guatemala have good rail systems, too. Most Latin American countries also have seacoasts for shipping goods.

Successful traders need to have ways to communicate with customers, too. This sometimes is a problem for Latin American countries. Some of these countries have areas in which there are no telephones, TVs, or radios. So communication can be difficult.

Who Wants to Trade?

When countries make a product, they try to trade with other countries that do not make the same product. For example, Colombia grows coffee beans because it has the right climate and enough people to handpick the

coffee beans. It then sells the coffee beans to countries in other parts of the world that do not grow coffee beans. With the money it earns, Colombia buys the industrial equipment and other goods that it does not make.

Who Trades What?

When you think of oil, do you automatically think of Arab countries? You might be surprised to learn that the United States imports a lot of oil from Mexico. Our neighbor to the south has a large work force, good transportation, and vast natural resources, making it one of the wealthier nations in Latin America.

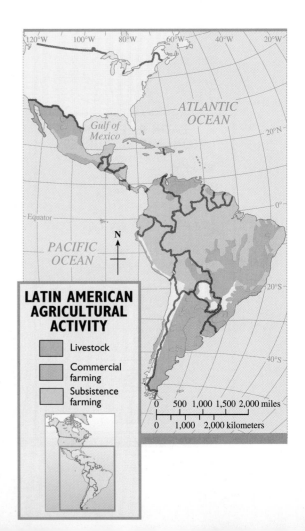

LATIN AMERICAN AGRICULTURAL ACTIVITY
- Livestock
- Commercial farming
- Subsistence farming

In addition to oil, Mexico exports beautiful jewelry. It is produced there because silver is one of Mexico's natural resources.

Argentina and Uruguay have lands that are suitable for grazing livestock. So it is logical that they export a lot of cattle, meat products, and leather. Ecuador's climate makes it ideal for growing bananas. It is the leading banana exporter in Latin America.

Coffee and bananas are the largest sources of income for the nations of Central America. The United States is their best customer for these products.

The Problem of Single Industries

Some countries are very good at producing one thing, so they concentrate on that. Honduras and Costa Rica rely on the export of bananas, and more than half of Cuba's farmland is used for growing sugar cane. These countries suffer when diseases infect plants or droughts cause plants to die.

While a large part of the Latin American economy is devoted to

Diamonds, emeralds, and sapphires are mined in Brazil.

agriculture, as shown on the map on page 461, many countries are increasing manufacturing. This can help their economies if crops fail.

Looking to the Future

As Latin America continues to advance in literacy, transportation, communication, and industrialization, its **productivity** most likely will increase, too. This means that the region will be likely to have more exports and therefore be able to import more.

▼ Mining and manufacturing are important parts of the Latin American economy.

★ *productivity* The producing of goods or wealth

SHOW WHAT YOU
KNOW!

REFOCUS
COMPREHENSION

1. What are three things that countries need in order to trade?

2. Why is it risky for a country to rely heavily on one crop or product for trade?

THINK ABOUT IT
CRITICAL THINKING

Explain how the literacy rate of a country can affect its economy.

WRITE ABOUT IT
ACTIVITY

Invent a new product or service. Write a summary of the resources you would need to produce it and the communication systems and means of transportation you would need to sell it.

Spotlight

IMMIGRANTS IN LATIN AMERICA

FOCUS *People have been moving to new places since ancient times. Convincing people to move to Central and South America was important to the development of those areas.*

The Need for Workers

South America has great natural resources—minerals, fertile land, and forests. But in the nineteenth century, the continent did not have enough people to provide workers to develop those resources. Many Latin American nations needed to attract immigrants from Europe and Asia.

The vast **pampas** of Argentina were sparsely populated in 1850. The nation's leaders realized that by attracting settlers they could turn these areas into farms and ranches. Starting in 1853 the government offered immigrants free seed and animals so that they could start farms. Between 1853 and 1914, nearly 6 million immigrants arrived in Argentina, most coming from Italy and Spain.

Similarly, Chile had large deposits of minerals and fertilizer that were potential sources of wealth. But its population was too small to provide workers to mine them. In the 1890s the Chilean government began to offer free passage by boat to immigrants who would move there.

▲ Bernardo O'Higgins— the son of an Irish immigrant—helped Chile win its independence.

Brazil freed its enslaved African population in 1888. Before long the owners of the country's immense coffee, cotton, and sugar plantations needed to find new workers. At the same time, **emigration** companies were formed in Japan to send laborers overseas. Thousands of Japanese people began to arrive in Brazil.

Peru also sought to solve its labor shortage by making agreements with Japanese emigration companies. In 1873 the first Japanese workers arrived in Peru and began working on the cotton and sugar plantations there. Almost 25,000 Japanese citizens emigrated from Japan to Peru between 1873 and 1930.

Why Immigrants Came

Immigrants from both Europe and Asia came to South America in search of a better life. People were fleeing from war, poverty, and religious discrimination at home.

Italy's unification in 1861 did little to help the peasant farmers in the south of the country and on Sicily. Floods and earthquakes in the late

---

 pampas The extensive, treeless plains of Argentina and some other parts of South America

 emigration The leaving of one country or region to settle in another

nineteenth century caused widespread crop failures and starvation. The industrious Italian peasants looked overseas for opportunities to build a better life. Millions of them made the decision to cross the Atlantic in search of jobs.

The situation was similar in Spain and Portugal, where the loss of overseas colonies caused an economic decline at home. It was an easy decision for landless and unemployed peasants to move to Latin America, where the language and customs were familiar to them.

Germans also came to South America in the nineteenth century.

▼ The Lerner family (*left, below left*) emigrated from Russia and settled in Argentina. These children of German immigrants to Venezuela attended a German school (*below*).

Many of them were descendants of people who had settled in the Volga River region of Russia. When the Russian government began to pass laws restricting their freedoms, these Russian Germans joined the other Europeans who migrated to the Americas.

Jews within the Russian empire were systematically persecuted. They often endured **pogroms**, in which non-Jews attacked and killed them, also burning their homes and businesses. In the 1880s, Baron Maurice de Hirsch, a wealthy German Jewish banker, contributed a huge sum of money to help Russian Jews settle elsewhere. He purchased land in South America for farming colonies. By 1914 about 25,000 immigrant Jews lived in such colonies in Argentina.

Immigrants From Asia

In 1868, when Japan began a program of modernization, the island nation suffered from overpopulation. Soon workers began to go overseas. Many were sponsored by Japanese emigration companies, who promised to protect their interests and guarantee their return passage.

China experienced a major civil war from 1850 to 1864. Millions of people were killed, and large areas

⭐ **pogrom** An organized persecution of a minority group

Mexico, and Peru, most went to Cuba to work on the sugar plantations. About 126,000 Chinese immigrants arrived in Cuba between 1847 and 1877. Conditions under which they worked were so bad that only about one third of them survived.

India sent thousands of contract laborers to British colonies in the Caribbean area. By 1917, British Guiana had imported over 238,000 Indian laborers. Trinidad and Jamaica also saw a major influx of Indians. International protests after 1917 finally brought an end to the contract labor system.

▲ Laborers—including immigrant Chinese men—load sugar cane.

were devastated in the fighting. The resulting poverty caused many to seek work overseas.

Contract Laborers

After slavery was banned in the New World, European nations that still controlled colonies in the Caribbean looked for a new source of labor. They found it in China and India, where desperate poverty caused many people to agree to work overseas.

Virtually all Chinese and Indians who came to Latin America before 1874 were contract laborers. They signed contracts that required them to work for a certain number of years. Known as coolies, from a Chinese word that means "bitter strength," the contract laborers were treated almost as slaves.

Although some Chinese workers also went to British Guiana, Brazil,

Immigrants Aid the Economy

Immigrants transformed the economies of many Latin American nations. Settlers in Argentina plowed the pampas, sowing wheat, corn, and barley. Much of the grain harvest was exported, bringing enormous wealth to the country.

Italian immigrants planted vineyards, as they had in their native country, creating major winemaking industries in Chile and Argentina. Chinese and Indian immigrants in the Caribbean, once they were freed from labor contracts, established businesses, such as restaurants, laundries, grocery stores, and boarding houses. Jews from Russia also opened stores and markets. These and many other immigrant groups formed a middle class that bridged the gap between the rich and the poor in Latin America.

Alberto Fujimori symbolizes the blending of cultures in Latin America. ▶

Blending Cultures

Newcomers also contributed to the cultures of their adopted countries. Throughout Central America, South America, and the Caribbean, immigrants have influenced their new nations' styles of cooking, music, and literature. Everywhere in Latin America, immigrants and their descendants have become leaders in business, journalism, and government.

Today, Argentina is a diverse nation, in which many languages are spoken alongside Spanish. Buenos Aires is a cosmopolitan city that resembles other modern cities in the world.

Brazil has more citizens of Japanese descent than any other country outside Japan. A majority of the population of Guyana, formerly British Guiana, is of Asian descent.

In 1990 the people of Peru elected Alberto Fujimori as the country's president. His name reflects both his Latino and Japanese heritage. Fujimori's parents were Japanese immigrants. His election symbolizes the influence that immigrants have had on Latin America.

▼ Many cultures blend in Argentina's capital, Buenos Aires.

5

THE LIFE OF A GAUCHO

FOCUS *An independent way of life and a free spirit are characteristic of the gauchos living on the South American pampas.*

Cowboy Legends

If you are a gaucho living on the pampas of South America, you are following a tradition that is hundreds of years old. Novels, poems, and songs portray you as a brave frontiersman, like the cowboys of the United States.

Your family tells you about the most famous gaucho—Martín Fierro, the hero of two epic poems written by the Argentine author José Hernández. Fierro deserted the Spanish army because he had been cruelly treated. He roamed the pampas on his horse, making friends with others who lived as they pleased.

Are Gauchos the Good Guys?

People today admire the gauchos' defiance of authority and independent way of life. If you had lived in Fierro's time, you would have been thought of as an outlaw. The Spaniards who ruled your country would have looked upon you as lazy and dishonest.

Gauchos of Fierro's time had many reasons for escaping from society. Like Fierro, they might have been deserters

from the army. They could have been enslaved Africans who escaped from their masters. Or they might have been Native Americans who resisted the Spanish conquest of their lands. There are gauchos from all different races, but race doesn't matter on the pampas.

Ride 'Em, Gaucho!

As a gaucho your life depends on two animals—the horse and the cow. Thousands of these animals roam wild on the vast pampas. If you can capture a horse, you can use it to chase a cow. That is all you need to survive.

When you are hungry, you roast the cow's meat over a fire. You use its hide to make your clothing, boots, and bedding. If you need to buy something at a **pulpería**, you trade some of your cowhides for goods.

Your life isn't always a lonely one. Gauchos gather for big cattle hunts and for contests of their horse-racing skills. Gauchos love music, too. They sing and play guitars late into the night.

▲ *Above,* a gaucho holds a cup of maté, a drink made from the leaves of an evergreen tree; *right,* a silver-trimmed maté cup.

 pulpería   A country store

468

A Frenchman, Jean Baptiste Debret, painted gauchos of Brazil.

Skill at riding is important to the gaucho way of life. As soon as you were able to walk, your gaucho father began teaching you to ride a horse. You learned to lasso cattle by practicing on chickens and dogs. You had to learn to survive and defend yourself on the pampas.

My Hero!

So how did gauchos get to be heroes? Gauchos eagerly joined the cause of independence. Their skills, like yours, made them feared fighters. They staged raids on Spanish forts and then retreated into the pampas, where no soldier could catch them. They needed no supplies, for they

lived off the land, as you always have.

After the war, many of the gauchos found that their achievements had made them respected. Some gauchos became *caudillos*, or military leaders. Others served in the caudillos' armies.

New Guys on the Pampas

Later, when new immigrants settled in South America, they adopted gaucho customs. Like you, they wore the high leather boots, the long ponchos or cloaks, and the small black hats that gauchos wear. In doing so, the immigrants paid tribute to the gauchos' heroism and spirit.

Gauchos relax at a rodeo near Buenos Aires.

Silver is often used for everyday items, such as this stirrup.

SHOW WHAT YOU KNOW!

REFOCUS
COMPREHENSION

1. Why is the skill of riding important in the gaucho's life?

2. What do you know about gauchos that tells you they did not always like to be alone?

THINK ABOUT IT
CRITICAL THINKING

Why was it particularly appropriate for gauchos to fight for the cause of independence?

WRITE ABOUT IT
ACTIVITY

Work with a partner to make two lists: one showing what you would like about the life of a gaucho and one showing what you would not like.

SUMMING UP

1 DO YOU REMEMBER...
COMPREHENSION

1. Where was Latin America's first revolution for independence? Who led it?

2. What was the Monroe Doctrine?

3. What event in Europe in 1808 helped Latin Americans who wanted independence?

4. In which South American countries did San Martín lead the struggle for independence from Spain?

5. What is one country that Simón Bolívar helped free from Spanish rule?

6. What are the largest sources of income for the nations of Central America?

7 What are some factors that make Mexico a wealthy nation?

8. What were contract laborers? Where did they mainly come from?

9. How did immigrants change the pampas?

10. What groups of people became the first gauchos?

2 SKILL POWER
READING RESOURCE MAPS

Choose one of the following resources. Make a resource map showing that resource in your state.

Farming   A mineral resource

Forests   A major industry

Livestock

3 WHAT DO YOU THINK?
CRITICAL THINKING

1. Why did the United States want Panama to break away from Colombia?

2. How might South America be different today if Simón Bolívar's dream had come true?

3. Look at the map of economic resources on page 461. Which country, in your opinion, has the greatest potential for economic success?

4. Do you think most immigrants moved to Latin America because they wanted to or because they had to? Explain.

5. How might the arrival of immigrant farmers on the pampas have affected the gauchos?

4 SAY IT, WRITE IT, USE IT
VOCABULARY

Picture yourself as a visitor to Latin America in the late nineteenth century. Write a letter to a friend, describing some of the things you see. Use at least six of these terms in your letter, and show that you know their meanings.

big-stick policy	pogrom
caudillo	productivity
emigration	pulpería
pampas	

5 GEOGRAPHY AND YOU
MAP STUDY

Study the map below. Make a list of Mexico's mineral resources. Which resource do you think is Mexico's most important export? Explain your answer.

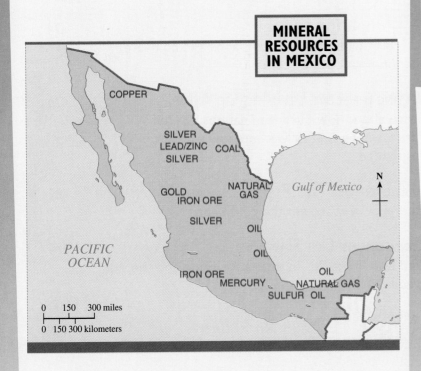

MINERAL RESOURCES IN MEXICO

COPPER

SILVER
LEAD/ZINC   COAL
SILVER

GOLD   NATURAL   *Gulf of Mexico*   N
IRON ORE   GAS

SILVER

OIL

PACIFIC OCEAN   OIL

IRON ORE   OIL
MERCURY   NATURAL GAS
SULFUR OIL

0   150   300 miles

0   150 300 kilometers

6 TAKE ACTION
CITIZENSHIP

One of the factors that affects economies in Latin America and the United States is the skill of workers. Without a skilled and educated work force, industries aren't able to work at peak efficiency, produce high-quality goods, or compete with other trading nations. Do research to find the three major industries in your state or region that export products around the world. List three different occupations that are available in each industry. Then show the kind of education that you would need to work at each occupation.

7 GET CREATIVE
MUSIC CONNECTION

Every nation or region has music that belongs to its culture. Some areas also have musical instruments that are typically used. Do research to find out what music and musical instruments are characteristic of a Latin American nation or region. You might even find recordings of Latin American music. Then plan a show with your classmates to demonstrate the types of music you found in your research.

LOOKING AHEAD
Independence fever spread around the world. In the next chapter you will learn how independence came to Africa.

CHAPTER 21

INDEPENDENCE

The story of European involvement in Africa is not a pleasant one. From the Atlantic slave trade to the colonization of their continent, Africans have been faced with a constant battle to control their own destinies. Today they are succeeding.

CONTENTS

▼ Warriors of a great African nation used shields like the one the girl is holding. Read about this nation on pages 478–479.

IN AFRICA

You can learn more about the history and culture of Africa from these books. Read one that interests you and fill out a book-review form.

READ AND RESEARCH

Door of No Return: The Legend of Gorée Island
by **Steven Barboza** (Dutton Children's Books, 1994)
Read about Gorée Island, a quiet West African resort. Less than 200 years ago, it was a place where dungeons held captured Africans waiting to be boarded onto slave ships. *(nonfiction)*
• *You can read a selection from this story on page 486.*

Shaka: King of the Zulus by **Diane Stanley** and **Peter Vennema** (William Morrow & Co., 1994)
As a young boy, Shaka, son of a Zulu chief, was banished from the clan, along with his mother. Follow the years of struggle and growth as Shaka fulfills his dream of becoming a great nineteenth-century military leader. *(biography)*

Nelson Mandela: Voice of Freedom by **Libby Hughes** (Macmillan Publishing Co., 1992)
In South Africa, the rights and freedoms of black people had been denied for centuries. Read about Nelson Mandela, the lawyer who has worked tirelessly for justice and equality for his people. *(biography)*

One Day We Had to Run! by **Sybella Wilkes** (The Millbrook Press, 1994)
Read the personal accounts of children from the war-torn countries of Sudan, Somalia, and Ethiopia as they fled their homelands in order to survive. *(nonfiction)*

Comparing Graphs

Knowing how to read graphs can help you understand facts and the relationships between them.

UNDERSTAND IT

Have you ever heard the expression "A picture is worth a thousand words"? Sometimes that picture is a graph. A graph can show you at a glance a thousand words' worth of information!

Here are the four kinds of graphs you will see most often.

- A pie graph compares parts of a whole. The whole pie stands for 100 percent, and each slice represents a percentage of the pie.

- A bar graph also compares facts. It lets you see how much more there is of one thing than there is of another.

- A line graph is used to show changes over time.

- A pictograph uses picture symbols to show amounts. People, trees, and dollar signs are often used as picture symbols.

EXPLORE IT

Franklin Township wanted to build sports areas for its residents. To learn the sports that townspeople preferred, the mayor conducted a survey. The four graphs on these pages show what she found out.

1. According to the pie graph, which sport do the residents like most? Which is their second favorite?

2. The township has 8,400 square meters of land available. What sport or sports could be played on that land?

3. Which sport is rising in popularity? Which graph shows that fact?

4. Which sport area would cost the least to build and maintain?

5. Based on the information in the graphs, what would you recommend be built on the land?

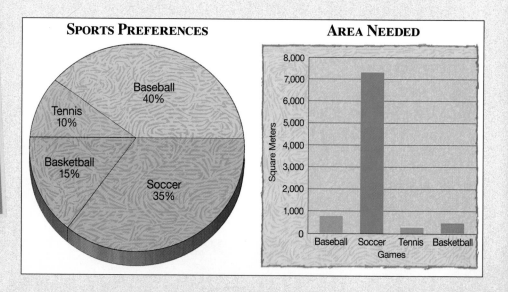

TRY IT

With a small group of classmates, take a survey to find out more about the other students in your class. You may wish to survey them about their favorite hobbies, magazines, television shows, snacks, or sports.

Then show the findings of your survey in one or more of the following: a pie graph, bar graph, line graph, or pictograph. Give your graphs titles and display them on a class bulletin board.

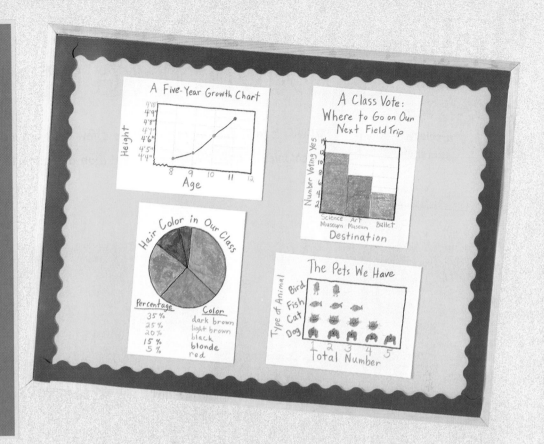

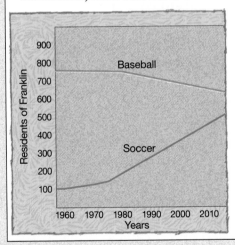

INTEREST IN SOCCER AND BASEBALL, PAST AND EXPECTED

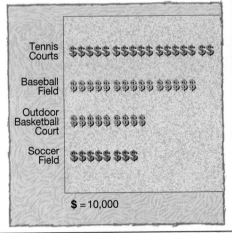

COST, INCLUDING MAINTENANCE

SKILL POWER SEARCH *Choose a topic in this chapter that contains facts you think could be shown well in a graph. Then put the information in a graph.*

DIVIDING UP AFRICA

FOCUS *It took the European nations a few days around a conference table to divide Africa into colonies. It took the Africans more than a century to regain their independence.*

▲ This painting shows European merchant ships off the southern coast of Africa.

Europeans Reach Africa

As you learned in Chapter 11, many early African societies had links with other people across the Sahara and the Indian Ocean. Arabs, for example, crossed the Sahara as traders. In these dealings the Africans kept control of their own societies.

The first direct contact between Africans and Europeans took place early in the fifteenth century, when Portuguese sailors explored the African coastline. Over the next 500 years, European involvement in Africa increased and resulted in Africans losing control of their societies.

There were two major reasons for European involvement in Africa. At first there was the Atlantic slave trade. Later an increased spirit of nationalism spurred a wave of European colonialism. As the map on the next page shows, by the end of the nineteenth century, most of Africa was divided into European colonies.

Early European-African Relationships

Europe's early interest in Africa was mainly in supplying slaves for trade, which you will learn more about on pages 484–485. In fact, until the 1800s, Europeans knew little about Africa. Several countries built trading centers along the west coast of Africa, but they depended on Africans to bring slaves and trading goods to these posts from the interior.

As the Industrial Revolution took root in Europe, nations began looking for new markets for their products. Africa was one of those markets. In addition, Africa had many desirable resources that Europeans wanted.

EVENTS
IN AFRICA

1787
Sierra Leone founded
as a colony for
freed slaves

1879
War breaks out
between Britain
and Zulu nation

1885
European nations
"divide up" Africa

ca. 1945
Many African
colonies launch
independence
movements

1994
Nelson Mandela
elected president
of South Africa

1785   1825   1865   1905   1955   1995

EVENTS
IN THE
WORLD

1812
Start of war between
America and Britain

1865
End of Civil War
in United States

1869
Suez Canal
opens

1945
United Nations
organized

1957
U.S.S.R. launches
Sputnik

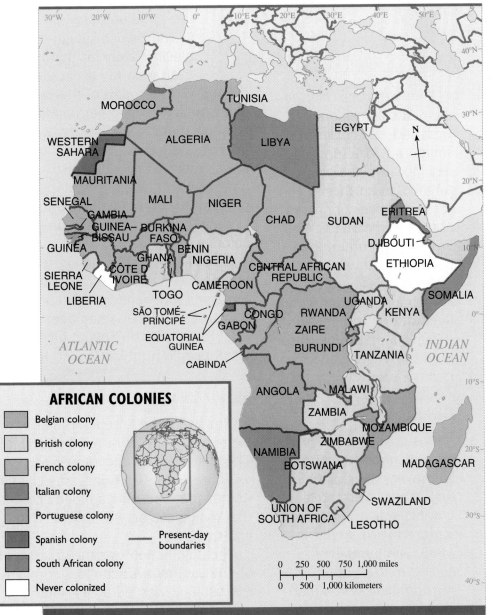

AFRICAN COLONIES

- Belgian colony
- British colony
- French colony
- Italian colony
- Portuguese colony
- Spanish colony
- South African colony
- Never colonized
- Present-day boundaries

0   250 500 750 1,000 miles
0   500 1,000 kilometers

These included precious woods, palm oil, gold, ivory, and agricultural products.

Many African kingdoms grew rich trading with the Europeans. Some African leaders traded for guns, which made them stronger than their neighbors. It became an advantage to be a trade partner with Europe. Over time, Africans became increasingly dependent on European trade.

Colonization of Africa

Increased involvement in Africa led Europeans to begin exploring the interior of this great continent. This exploration led to serious problems for native Africans.

European explorations in Africa revealed rich deposits of copper and other valuable metals. Soon European nations were no longer satisfied with African trade and markets. European governments wanted colonies that they could take advantage of for their resources. The Europeans believed that having colonies was a sign of strength and prestige.

477

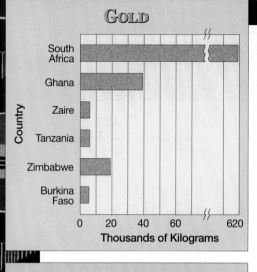

GOLD

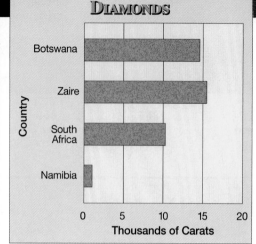

DIAMONDS

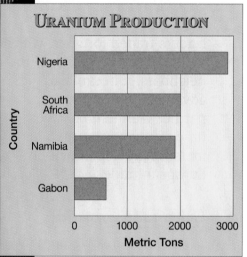

URANIUM PRODUCTION

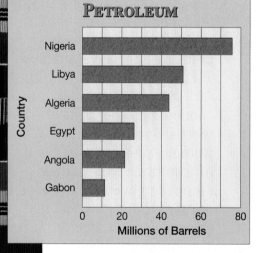

PETROLEUM

These graphs provide information about some of Africa's most valuable natural resources.

The Portuguese started the first colonies on the west and east coasts of southern Africa (present-day Mozambique and Angola). In northern Africa, France conquered Algeria in the 1830s. The French government had been insulted when the Algerian ruler hit the French ambassador with a fly swatter. France used this incident as an excuse to invade Algeria and turn it into a colony.

Dividing Up Africa

The urge to colonize became a race to conquer. To prevent the scramble for colonies from breaking out into war, 15 European nations met in Berlin in 1885. The Europeans agreed to draw up territorial lines on a map of Africa. These borders paid little attention to the identity of the people who lived in the area. African ethnic groups were either divided into different colonies or grouped with others within the same borders.

The French sought to have a block of colonies that reached from west to east across the northern part of the continent. The British, on the other hand, wanted colonies that reached north along Africa's east coast from the Cape of Good Hope to Egypt. These two nations were the largest colonial powers, but Germany, Belgium, Italy, and Portugal also held African colonies.

By 1914 only Ethiopia and Liberia had not been colonized. Ethiopia remained independent by defeating Italy in 1896. Liberia had been established as a homeland for free black people from the United States.

Shaka Zulu—Warrior and Leader

How were the Europeans able to exert such authority over the Africans? The answer lay in their superior weapons. This superiority was clearly demonstrated during a bloody conflict that took place between the British and the Zulu.

The Zulu nation was the greatest of all the southern African kingdoms. In the 1800s it was led by a military genius named Shaka (SHAHK uh) Zulu.

As a young man, Shaka was fascinated by war. He was trained in using the African spear and developed tactics that made his soldiers more effective.

Rise of the Zulu Nation

When Shaka Zulu became ruler in 1818, he turned the Zulu into a warrior nation. For ten years the Zulu empire expanded. No neighboring nation could withstand Shaka's armies.

As defeated enemies fled the Zulu, they incited wars and disruption in their path. From this period of disorder, called the *Mfecane,* or "smashing up," new national groupings arose.

In 1840 a group known as the Shona was invaded and beaten by a branch of the Zulu that was

A seventeenth-century bronze statue of a Portuguese soldier

This painting shows a British officer falling in a battle with the Zulu.

A Zulu chieftain

A Zulu officer reviewing his troops

fleeing Shaka's rule. Later, Europeans moved into Shona territory from the Cape Colony at the southern tip of Africa. The Shona people were so poor and disorganized that the Europeans found it difficult to believe they had built the Great Zimbabwe.

Territories occupied by the Shona were easily overrun by European settlers in the 1890s. The settlers named the territory Rhodesia, after Cecil Rhodes, its British founder.

Defeat of the Zulu Nation

Meanwhile the Zulu nation continued to enjoy great prosperity. This prosperity ended when the British decided to expand its colonies into Zulu territory. In 1879, war broke out between the Zulu and the British. In the first month of the war, the Zulu won a major victory, killing 800 British soldiers.

The British answered the challenge by bringing in fresh troops and heavy **artillery**. The Zulu had no weapons to match the British cannons. British soldiers and their African allies slaughtered most of the Zulu armies and captured the Zulu capital. The independent Zulu kingdom came to an end in 1887.

⭐ **artillery** Guns of large caliber; cannons

479

Mission schools played an important role in colonial Africa. In these schools, African children learned European languages and customs, making them eligible for posts in the colonial government. Thus it became an advantage for an African to become "Europeanized." You will read more about life in a mission school on pages 489–491.

▲ Ceremonial opening of parliament in the independent nation of Ghana

Life Under Imperialism

European nations governed their African colonies in different ways. The French sent administrators who tried to make their subjects as French in culture as possible. The British, on the other hand, governed by indirect rule. Whenever the British could deal with an existing system of government, they allowed it to remain in place. Although British officials held the highest colonial offices, the British hired qualified Africans to fill less important positions.

Independence and Afterward

After World War II ended in 1945, African leaders began to demand freedom. They pointed to the fact that thousands of Africans had fought on the side of the victorious European nations in the war. But the Europeans were reluctant to give up the source of so much of their wealth.

In the long run the Africans' desire for independence could not be denied. In many colonies the struggle was carried on through nonviolent protests. In others, warfare cost the lives of thousands of Africans and Europeans.

▼ These photographs show people taking part in multiracial elections in South Africa (left) and Tunisia.

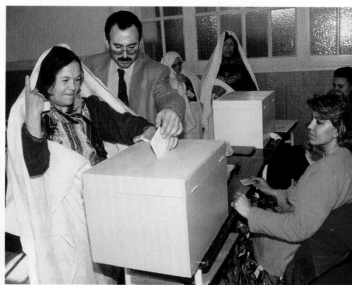

But the result was the same. After Ghana won its independence from Britain in 1957, freedom spread through the continent. In 1990, Namibia (nuh MIHB ee uh) became the last of the sub-Saharan African nations to attain self-government.

Separatist Policies in South Africa

In South Africa, a white-controlled government refused to allow equal rights to the nation's majority black population. Since 1948 a system called **apartheid** (uh PAHR tayt) had separated the two races, keeping blacks in poverty.

The African National Congress (ANC), an organization of South Africans who wanted to end apartheid, was banned. Its leader, Nelson Mandela, was sentenced to life in prison.

⭐ **apartheid**   Separation of races by law in South Africa

Nelson Mandela ▶

South Africa became isolated, since many nations of the world protested apartheid by refusing to trade with the nation. In 1990 the government lifted its ban of the ANC and released Mandela. Four years later the ANC won the nation's first election in which all citizens could vote. Mandela became president of the country.

Mandela, like other leaders throughout Africa, still faces many problems. Africa's history of colonization has weakened it. Many people suffer from poverty and disease. Rivalries between different ethnic groups within the same country remain a source of trouble.

Yet Africa has abundant natural resources that today enrich the countries where they are found. Having thrown off foreign rule, Africans look toward a future in which they will determine their own destiny.

◀ These signs show the types of activities that were segregated under apartheid.

SHOW WHAT YOU KNOW!

REFOCUS
COMPREHENSION

1. What effect did the Industrial Revolution in Europe have on trade with Africa?

2. What was apartheid and what was its effect on black South Africans?

THINK ABOUT IT
CRITICAL THINKING

Why did Europeans feel it was important to divide Africa into colonies?

WRITE ABOUT IT
ACTIVITY

Would you rather have lived in an African colony under French control or British control? Give reasons for your selection.

Map Adventure

★ **KEY TERM**
headwaters

THE EXPLORATION OF AFRICA

FOCUS At their closest points, Africa and Europe are only eight miles apart. However, until brave explorers risked their lives in the late nineteenth century, Europeans knew very little about the interior of Africa.

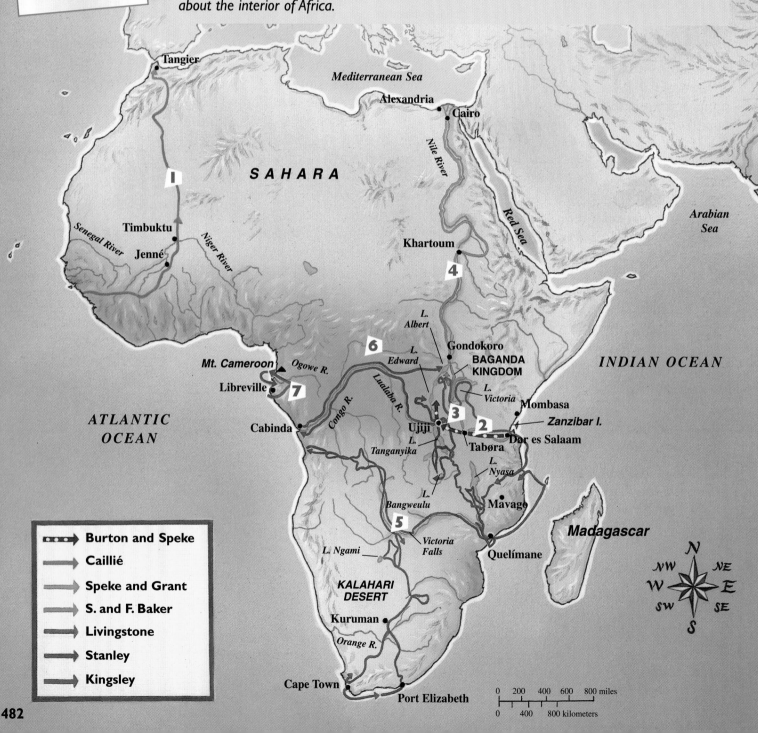

Legend:
- ▣▣▣▶ Burton and Speke
- ▶ Caillié
- ▶ Speke and Grant
- ▶ S. and F. Baker
- ▶ Livingstone
- ▶ Stanley
- ▶ Kingsley

Map labels: Tangier, Mediterranean Sea, Alexandria, Cairo, Nile River, Red Sea, Arabian Sea, SAHARA, Timbuktu, Jenné, Senegal River, Niger River, Khartoum, L. Albert, L. Edward, Gondokoro, BAGANDA KINGDOM, INDIAN OCEAN, Mt. Cameroon, Ogowe R., Libreville, L. Victoria, Mombasa, Lualaba R., Congo R., Ujiji, L. Tanganyika, Tabora, Zanzibar I., Dar es Salaam, Cabinda, ATLANTIC OCEAN, L. Nyasa, L. Bangweulu, Mavage, Madagascar, L. Ngami, Victoria Falls, Quelímane, KALAHARI DESERT, Kuruman, Orange R., Cape Town, Port Elizabeth

Compass: N, NW, NE, W, E, SW, SE, S

Scale: 0 200 400 600 800 miles / 0 400 800 kilometers

African Adventures

Where are the **headwaters** of the Nile? Do the Nile and the Congo rivers meet? Who lives in the heart of Africa? These are questions that pushed explorers into dense jungles, through deserts, and down dangerous rivers. Their adventures would make them famous and unlock the mysteries of this vast continent.

Map Key

1 Caillié's route In 1827, René Caillié joined a caravan headed for the city of Timbuktu. He suffered illness, but he crossed the Sahara and reached Tangier. He was the first European to visit Timbuktu and live.

2 Burton and Speke Richard Burton and John Hanning Speke left Zanzibar in August 1857 to find the source of the Nile River. Surviving diseases and dangerous insects, they crossed dense jungles, bogs, and vast plains to explore Lake Tanganyika.

3 Speke and Grant Speke returned to Africa in 1860 with Captain James Grant to prove Lake Victoria was the source of the Nile. The explorers visited the Baganda kingdom and found Ripon Falls, where Lake Victoria spills into the Nile River.

4 The Baker expedition Samuel and Florence Baker set out from Egypt to find Speke and Grant. After meeting them in the village of Gondokoro, the Bakers continued south and investigated Lake Albert.

5 Livingstone's journeys From 1849 to 1860, Dr. David Livingstone explored Lake Ngami and the 600-mile Zambezi River. Next he searched East Africa for the source of the Nile. In 1868, Livingstone vanished. The world wondered where in Africa he was.

6 Stanley's search Henry Morton Stanley began his search for Dr. Livingstone in 1871 and found him in the village of Ujiji. Stanley led two more expeditions between 1873 and 1889 and proved that Lake Victoria was the source of the Nile.

7 Kingsley's voyages Mary Kingsley made three trips to West Africa from 1892 to 1895. Kingsley became the first European woman to sail up the Ogowe River and climb the 13,000-foot Mount Cameroon.

MAP IT

1. It is 1866, and you and Dr. Livingstone are trying to find the source of the Nile. First, you leave Zanzibar and head toward Lake Nyasa. Which direction are you marching in?

2. Heading northwest toward the Lualaba River, you pass two lakes. What lakes are these? Is either of them the source of the Nile?

3. Eight years later you return to Africa with Henry Morton Stanley. As you sail up the Lualaba River, you notice that it connects to another river. If you travel west on this river, where will it take you?

4. In Cabinda, Stanley asks you to measure the distance between Cabinda and Zanzibar. How far away is Zanzibar?

EXPLORE IT

You are in charge of your own expedition. In your notebook, explain where you will explore. Be sure to include the names of rivers and towns.

★ **headwaters** The beginning, or source, of a large stream or river

THE SLAVE TRADE

FOCUS *The Atlantic slave trade resulted in millions of Africans being removed from their homes and forced to settle in foreign lands thousands of miles away.*

The Atlantic Slave Trade Begins

The Atlantic slave trade began in the late 1400s when Portuguese ships bought a few Africans to be sold as slaves in Europe. This practice lasted for more than three centuries. In the 1700s alone, 6 million Africans were wrenched from their homes and shipped across the Atlantic to European colonies in the Americas and the Caribbean.

Slavery had been part of African society before the Atlantic slave trade. But those earlier slaves had usually been prisoners of war. They had eventually been allowed to take their place as free, full-fledged members of society. Slaves also had been part of the trans-Sahara trade with the Arabs.

However nothing in history compares in scope to the Atlantic slave trade. Portugal, Great Britain, France, and Spain were the major participants in this trading of human beings. These nations had posts along the west coast of Africa that served as "factories" for processing African slaves.

The Trade Increases

Wealthy landowners had established large plantations in colonies on the Caribbean islands and in North and South America. The major crops, sugar and coffee, brought great profits to the

Slave ships like the one shown in this picture carried millions of Africans from their homelands.

Store Room.

owners. But many laborers were needed to keep these huge operations running. The cheapest source of labor, of course, was slaves.

African Involvement

As the demand for slaves grew, Europeans encouraged Africans living in coastal regions to raid villages in the interior to capture new slaves. Africans took part in the slave trade for many reasons. Some, like the Dahomey (duh HOH mee) people of West Africa, received European guns in exchange for slaves. Such weapons enabled the Dahomey to increase their economic, political, and military power.

Other African societies obtained desirable goods and wealth. In most cases the West African societies had little choice. They had to raid inland villages for slaves or be raided and enslaved themselves.

End of the Trade

In the nineteenth century, opposition to slavery grew. **Abolitionists** recognized slavery as a social evil. Many people felt that slavery weakened the character of slaveholders. In the face of such strong opposition, slavery and the slave trade were outlawed by governments on both sides of the Atlantic.

Attempts were made to resettle freed slaves in Africa. In 1787 the British established Sierra Leone as a colony for freed slaves. In 1822 the American Colonization Society organized Liberia, which became an independent African nation in 1847. But a majority of free African Americans rejected resettlement. They demanded a voice in the nations they had helped to build.

★ *abolitionist*   A person who advocates an end to slavery

As this notice shows, slaves were considered property.

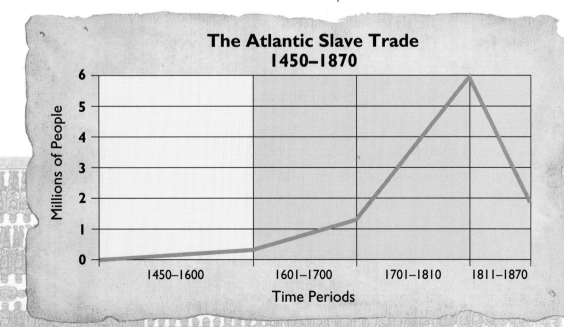

**The Atlantic Slave Trade
1450–1870**

Millions of People — Time Periods: 1450–1600, 1601–1700, 1701–1810, 1811–1870

The drawing behind the graph shows the lower deck of a slave ship.

Door of No Return

by Steven Barboza

Accounts of the Atlantic slave trade tell the story of one of history's most tragic periods. In this book the author visits an island that played a prominent role in the events of that time.

In 1619, a Dutch "man of warre" sailed to Jamestown, Virginia. Aboard were some twenty African slaves—the first to land in the English colony in North America. The ship may well have set sail from Gorée Island, starting slave shipments to England's mainland colony.

Some thirty years earlier, in 1588, the Dutch settled Gorée and built two forts: Nassau, by the shore, and Orange, on the mountain. They renamed the island *Goede Reade*, which meant "good harbor." The island became known as Gorée.

From Gorée, Europeans shipped slaves to the West Indies, and according to one historian, more than 13 percent of the slaves imported to the North American mainland were from the region of Africa near where Gorée lies.

As competition for slaves heightened, Gorée grew in value as a slave post. Wars were fought for it. In 1629, João Pereira-Corte Real, the Portuguese governor of the Cape Verde Islands, destroyed the Dutch forts. A year later, the Dutch recaptured the island. In 1645, the Portuguese and then the French seized Gorée. The Dutch retook the island two years later. The British occupied it in 1664. The Dutch regained it again. Finally, in 1677, the French drove out the Dutch permanently and kept it for most of the next two centuries. They leveled the Dutch forts and built their own, Saint-Michel and Saint-François, on the same sites.

In the 1600s and 1700s, some fifty European fortresses were built along 300 miles of the Gold Coast—the shoreline of what is today Ghana, on the Gulf of Guinea. The larger forts were called "castles." One of them, Cape Coast Castle, housed more than 1,000 slaves at a time. Slaves from there were packed like spoons, sometimes 350 to 400, aboard slave ships bound for the New World.

Gorée never housed as many slaves as Cape Coast Castle, but the island remained an active and important port from which some 60,000 slaves were delivered to the Americas, and its slave quarters are among the best preserved.

Ships arrived on the Gold Coast and at Gorée, and were loaded with slaves for the journey to the New World. In the "triangular slave trade," European ships brought manufactured goods to the African coast to be traded for slaves. The slaves were then transported for sale in the West Indies and the Americas. Finally, the ships carried molasses and other West Indian products to Europe on the final leg of their voyage.

Accurate records were not kept, so we will never know precisely how many children of Africa became slaves. Historians say millions died on slave ships, but perhaps 10 million to 12 million Africans survived the voyages—as many people as there are living today in Illinois or Ohio or Pennsylvania. Until about 1820, for every European that came to the New World, five Africans were brought.

Of the 700 million people in the New World today, one scholar estimates that about 100 million are of African ancestry.

Slavery touched every tribe in Africa, splintering families. But not every slave was shipped to the West. Many remained on the African continent. By the late 1800s, slaves made up two-thirds of many African societies.

Meanwhile, on Cape Verde, a mixed race of people emerged: Cape Verdeans. Their roots were in both Africa and Portugal. My grandparents were Cape Verdean. Their ancestors—and of course, mine—were probably slaves who stopped on Gorée on their way to Cape Verde.

Want to read more about the history of Gorée and the author's visit to that island? Check the book out of your school or public library.

SHOW WHAT YOU KNOW!

REFOCUS
COMPREHENSION

1. How did the establishment of plantations influence the Atlantic slave trade?

2. Why did some African people help supply slaves to European traders?

THINK ABOUT IT
CRITICAL THINKING

Why were the slave trading posts established along Africa's west coast?

WRITE ABOUT IT
ACTIVITY

Make up a list of questions you would have asked an abolitionist in 1850.

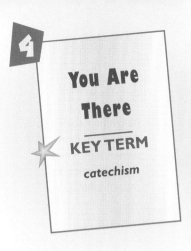

You Are There

KEY TERM

catechism

LIFE IN A MISSION SCHOOL

FOCUS *With the European colonization of much of Africa, acquiring a formal education became an important step along the road to self-government.*

You Must Go to School

It's a very tense day in your young life. You graduated from a mission school in your African colony about a week ago. Now you and your parents are waiting to hear if you have been chosen to go on to high school.

As you wait, you pace the floor and think about your experience at the mission school. You remember that you really didn't want to go to school. You wanted to learn skills from your parents. This is how most African children have been brought up.

Your parents sat you down and told you how things have changed. Your country is now a colony under the control of a European country. To get ahead, you must learn the language and customs of that country. If you do well in school, you may qualify to work for the colonial government.

Your parents had to pay a small fee to send you to the mission school. The fee didn't cover the costs of your schooling. It was more of an insurance policy. The missionaries knew that your parents didn't have any money to waste. Once they had paid the fee to the school, they would make sure you were at school every day.

Your First School

On your first day of school, you were surprised to see that your teacher was African. You had expected a European teacher. You later found out that the teacher was trained by the missionaries. The village leaders provide a house for him because he is an honored guest.

You recall being fascinated by the method of teaching used by your

A Sunday-school class at a Methodist mission school in Angola in 1925

Religious rituals like the baptism shown here were part of a mission-school education.

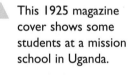

This 1925 magazine cover shows some students at a mission school in Uganda.

teacher. He gathered you and your classmates under a tree. On the branches were hung several cloths painted with the letters of the alphabet. You remember sitting under the shady tree, chanting "a-e-i-o-u" and then using your fingers to form the letters in the sand.

As soon as you learned all the letters on one cloth, you moved on to the second cloth. Once you had learned the letters on all the cloths, you were promoted to the first class. Being in the first class was special because you were allowed to use slates.

Language and Religion

All subjects in a mission school are taught in the language of the European country that controls your colony. In your school that language was French. So as you learned a new language, you also studied arithmetic, science, geography, and history. The history, however, was not that of your own people. It was the history of the Europeans.

The missionaries, of course, wanted you to be a Christian. So the teacher spent time each day reading from a book called a **catechism** (KAT ih kihz-um). He also read stories from the Bible, which were more interesting.

The best part of religion class was learning to sing hymns. You have always enjoyed music, even though hymns sound different from the songs you learned in your village.

Learning a Lesson the Hard Way

You discovered that it was wise not to anger the teacher. He had a stick that he used to punish children who misbehaved. You learned this lesson the hard way—you and your classmates played a trick on your teacher. An inspector was coming from the mission to visit your school, and all the children played hooky on the day he came.

The next day the teacher was waiting for you and your classmates with his stick, which he applied with some vigor to your backsides. You smile as you think about it now, but it was several days before any of you could sit at your desks.

 catechism A handbook of questions and answers for teaching the principles of a religion

Going Away to School

Your daydreams are broken by a messenger who arrives with the news. You have been chosen to go to the secondary school at the mission headquarters many miles away!

You have never been away from home before. But you have talked with a friend in your village who went to the same school you will attend. So you have some idea of what life is like at a secondary school.

You will be trained as a teacher, a translator, or some other government official. All your classmates will be boys. Girls and boys go to separate secondary schools. Fewer girls go to secondary school because they are often needed to help at home.

You will live in a dormitory with other students. You can be sure that the food will be nothing like your mother's cooking. You might even want to run away. But the thought of your parents' high hopes will keep you in school.

Learning for Your People

If you do well at the secondary school, it is possible that you might go on to college. You know of a young man named Nelson Mandela who is attending a college for African students. The college is operated by the Methodist Church. Mandela's education has inspired him to devote his life to the freedom of his people.

You also know of several other fine young men who are beginning to speak of freedom. The spark of learning has inspired each of them. Perhaps you too can join with them and many others to lead your beloved Africa to freedom and independence in the twentieth century.

▼ A present-day elementary school class in Nigeria

▼ A high school class at a girls' school in Zimbabwe

SHOW WHAT YOU KNOW!

REFOCUS
COMPREHENSION

1. Why did your parents insist that you attend a mission school?

2. Why aren't classes at a mission school taught in native African languages?

THINK ABOUT IT
CRITICAL THINKING

In what sense did the education of African colonists help lead to the end of colonialism in Africa?

WRITE ABOUT IT
ACTIVITY

Write a letter to a friend, describing a typical day at your mission school.

INDEPENDENCE

FOCUS *During World War II, African colonies supported their colonial rulers. As payment for their services, some colonies demanded their independence.*

African Independence

Angola	1975	Madagascar	1960
Benin	1960	Malawi	1964
Botswana	1966	Mali	1960
Burkina Faso	1960	Mauritania	1960
Burundi	1962	Mozambique	1975
Cameroon	1960	Namibia	1990
Central African Republic	1960	Niger	1960
		Nigeria	1960
Chad	1960	Rwanda	1962
Congo	1960	Senegal	1960
Djibouti	1977	Sierra Leone	1961
Egypt	1922	Somalia	1960
Equatorial Guinea	1968	South Africa	1961
		Sudan	1956
Gabon	1960	Swaziland	1968
Gambia	1965	Tanzania	1961
Guinea	1958	Togo	1960
Guinea-Bissau	1974	Tunisia	1956
Ivory Coast	1960	Uganda	1962
Kenya	1963	Zaire	1960
Lesotho	1966	Zambia	1964
Libya	1951	Zimbabwe	1980

GHANA

On March 6, 1957, bells rang, drums thundered, and people chanted "Free-DOM! Free-DOM!" throughout the new nation of Ghana. British flags in the former colony of the Gold Coast were lowered and replaced by the new flag of Ghana. Ghana had become the first black-ruled African nation to win its independence in the twentieth century.

The leader of the new nation, Kwame Nkrumah (KWAHM e en KROO muh), was born in a small village in 1909. He attended college in the United States and Great Britain, learning about the nonviolent freedom movement led by Mohandas Gandhi in India. In 1947, Nkrumah returned to his native land with a similar program he called Positive Action.

Though Nkrumah was often jailed for leading strikes and protests, he persevered. He declared, "We believe in the freedom of the peoples of all races." When the British allowed free elections for a new legislature, Nkrumah's party won a majority. He chose the name Ghana for the nation in honor of the early African empire you read about in Chapter 11.

| 1947 | | 1952 | 1957 | 1962 | 1963 |
Nkrumah returns to Ghana from India | | British arrest Kenyatta | Ghana gains its independence | Algeria gains its independence | Kenya gains its independence |

1945   1950   1955   1960   1965

ALGERIA

Algeria, which is just across the Mediterranean Sea from France, became more than a French colony. It was divided into three departments, or states, of the nation of France. More French people settled there than in any other part of the French empire. But the vast majority of the population was made up of African Muslims. These people were not granted the same rights enjoyed by French Algerians.

During World War II, Algerian Muslims helped to liberate France from Nazi Germany. In gratitude, France gave them voting rights. But the Muslims wanted independence, and a revolt broke out in 1954. When the French government began to negotiate with the Muslims, French settlers in Algeria started their own rebellion. Bloody fighting devastated the country, and thousands of settlers fled to France. In 1962 a nationwide vote in France on Algerian independence was approved by an overwhelming majority.

KENYA

As young Jomo Kenyatta tended his family's herds, he saw that the best land was owned by white farmers. He learned that his people, the Kikuyu (kee KOO yoo), were part of the British colony of Kenya. Kenyatta wanted to regain the land for Africans. He became head of the first nationalist movement in East Africa in 1923. By speaking in villages all over Kenya, Kenyatta gradually won the support of most Africans.

In 1952 the British arrested Kenyatta. They accused him of leading the Mau Mau (mou mou), a terrorist group that had killed white settlers. He was sentenced to a labor camp.

Kenyatta's imprisonment only increased support for his cause. People rallied around the cry *"Uhuru na Kenyatta!"* ("Freedom and Kenyatta!"). When the British released him, thousands of people were waiting to cheer him. In 1963, Kenyatta became the first president of the independent nation of Kenya.

REFOCUS
COMPREHENSION

1. What was Ghana's colonial name?

2. Why did the Algerian Muslims feel that France owed them their independence?

THINK ABOUT IT
CRITICAL THINKING

What influence did World War II have on the independence movements in Africa?

WRITE ABOUT IT
ACTIVITY

Do library research about the independence of another African nation. Write a brief report about your findings.

SUMMING UP

1 DO YOU REMEMBER...
COMPREHENSION

1. Which was the last of the sub-Saharan African nations to win self-government?

2. When did African leaders begin to demand independence from Europe?

3. What was John Hanning Speke trying to find on his expeditions to Africa?

4. Who finally proved that Lake Victoria was the source of the Nile?

5. When did the Atlantic slave trade begin and how long did it last?

6. Why were Sierra Leone and Liberia established?

7. Why did parents send their children to mission schools?

8. Why did the missionaries want children to attend the mission schools?

9. What was the first black-ruled African nation to win its independence in the twentieth century?

10. Who led the nationalist movement in the British colony of Kenya?

2 SKILL POWER
COMPARING GRAPHS

Find out more about an African nation that interests you. Read about the population, the weather, the number of people who live in cities and on farms, the economy, or the wildlife of the area.

Use a pie graph, bar graph, line graph, or pictograph to show your information. Give your graph a title and display it in the classroom.

3 WHAT DO YOU THINK?
CRITICAL THINKING

1. How did the French and the British differ in the ways they controlled their African colonies?

2. Why were expeditions through Africa so difficult for the Europeans who attempted them?

3. Do you think the European explorers who searched for the source of the Nile but failed deserve as much credit as the explorers who succeeded? Explain your opinion.

4. Why have citizens of South Africa become more aware of the importance of church-operated schools in their country?

5. How did the influence of Mohandas Gandhi save lives in Ghana?

4 SAY IT, WRITE IT, USE IT
VOCABULARY

Assume that you are visiting one of the African nations mentioned in this chapter. You have been asked to help children in a mission school learn these terms. For each term, write a sentence that will help the children understand how the term is used. Be sure your sentences are examples of the terms' use, not definitions.

abolitionist   catechism
apartheid   headwaters
artillery

5 GEOGRAPHY AND YOU
MAP STUDY

Cecil Rhodes, the British imperialist, said that he wished to see Great Britain's African empire spread from Cape Town in South Africa to Cairo in Egypt. Look at the map. Did Rhodes' wish come true?

What modern African nations were once part of Great Britain's empire? The map on page 477 will help you with your answer.

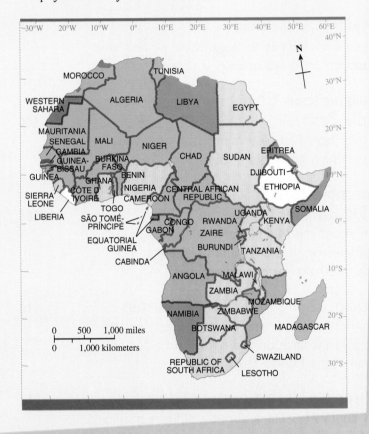

6 TAKE ACTION
CITIZENSHIP

As you read in this chapter, the right to vote has been very important to African nations since their independence. Remind citizens of your country to use their right to vote. Make posters, bumper stickers, and fliers that encourage people to get out and vote for the candidates of their choice.

The first **TUESDAY** after the first Monday in **NOVEMBER** is an **IMPORTANT DAY !**

P L E A S E

V O T E !!

A GOOD CITIZEN ☺
☺ V O T E S !

7 GET CREATIVE
SCIENCE CONNECTION

Zoologists from all over the world go to Africa to study animals in their native environments. Trace a map of Africa. Using an encyclopedia for reference, write the name of each of the following animals on the map in an area where it is found. You may want to include pictures of the animals.

lion	elephant	gorilla
giraffe	ostrich	cheetah
hyena	rhinoceros	hippopotamus
bongo	mandrill	zebra

LOOKING AHEAD   **Read the next chapter to learn how conflicting interests have affected countries in the Middle East.**

CHAPTER 22

THE MIDDLE EAST

Because the Middle East supplies oil to much of the world, has some countries with close ties to the West, and has a people seeking a homeland, it is an area of ongoing conflict. Its struggles toward peace concern people worldwide.

This girl is practicing a modern version of an old craft. Look at page 509 to see another way of doing it.

CONTENTS

IN MODERN TIMES

You can learn more about the Middle East from these books. Read one that interests you and fill out a book-review form.

READ AND RESEARCH

Kiss the Dust by Elizabeth Laird (Penguin USA, 1994)
Here is a story of a desperate Kurdish family running for their lives from the Iraqi government. The mountainous trail to freedom is a dangerous one. Find out what lies ahead for Tara and her family. *(historical fiction)*

Hafiz al-Asad of Syria by Charles Patterson
(Julian Messner, 1991)
Since 1970, Hafiz al-Asad has been president of Syria, a politically important Middle Eastern country. Coming from a poor family, he used his talent, ambition, and a thirst for power to become a leader in this part of the world. *(biography)*

A Young Person's History of Israel by David Bamberger (Behrman House, 1994)
As David Bamberger traces the history of Israel, learn about its conflicts of the past and present. Notice how the author's perspective is reflected in the tone of his book. *(nonfiction)*

Skill POWER

Making an Outline

Knowing how to make and use outlines will help you organize information you are reading or writing about.

UNDERSTAND IT

Taking notes is a good way to remember information. When you have many notes on a topic, you need to organize them. That's when an outline comes in handy. An outline is an orderly list of important points that summarize a subject.

Placing notes in an outline helps you see how different facts and ideas relate to each other. An outline is also a helpful study tool. What's more, making an outline is an excellent way to organize information in the order in which you'll use it in a written report.

EXPLORE IT

To make an outline, first identify the main topics, or main ideas. Show these with Roman numerals. Then list the subtopics that support a main topic. Subtopics are shown with capital letters beneath the main topic they support. Below each subtopic, list details that support it. Use numbers for details below the subtopics they support.

This is an outline for a report on Anwar el-Sadat (AHN-wahr el sah DAHT), a leader in the Middle East.

I. Early Years
   A. Birth
      1. Village in Nile River delta
      2. Born in 1918
   B. Schooling
      1. Egyptian military academy
      2. Graduated in 1938

II. Military and Government Career
   A. Young militant
      1. Jailed for revolutionary activities
      2. Helped overthrow King Farouk
   B. President
      1. Succeeded Gamal Abdel Nasser
      2. Held office from 1970 to 1981
   C. Peacemaker
      1. Camp David accord
      2. Nobel Peace Prize

As you can see from the outline, there's a period after each letter or numeral. The first word of each topic, subtopic, or detail is capitalized, too. If you have Roman numeral I for a main topic, you should also have II; if you have *A* for a subtopic, you need to have *B*; and if you have the numeral 1 for a detail, you must have 2.

Egypt's Anwar el-Sadat addresses Israel's legislature.

TRY IT

The Middle East is one of our globe's hot spots. Newspapers and news magazines run many stories about the people and events there. Find one article about the Middle East. Read it carefully and take notes. Then organize your notes in outline form as shown below.

Post a copy of the article and your outline of it on a classroom bulletin-board display called "An Outline of the Middle East." For the background of your display, prepare a large outline map showing the countries of the Middle East.

A Proud Heritage

I. Historical Views
    A. Marco Polo's opinions on Arab shipbuilders
        1. Marco Polo was astonished to find that Arab shipbuilders used no nails.
        2. Polo believed that boats sewn together with rope were "wretched affairs."
    B. Marco Polo was wrong.
        1. Arab merchants and sailors had some of the best trade routes in the world.
        2. The Arabs' knowledge of astronomy and the monsoons allowed them to travel long distances in their sewn boats.
II. Threats of Extinction
    A. Discoveries in Oman
        1. Wooden boats in Oman show careful use of scarce wood.
        2. Dhows and mashuas
    B. Saving the Past
        1. Researchers find old boats and study how they are built.
        2. They are trying to preserve the past by establishing a national maritime museum.

SKILL POWER SEARCH *Look at the lesson on pages 506 to 509. Make an outline that is like the one the writers of this book might have used.*

CHANGING LIFE IN THE MIDDLE EAST

FOCUS *The countries of the Middle East, like others around the world, sought and won independence. But the struggle was not always easy, and uncertainty still remains.*

The Ottoman Empire

From the 1500s the Middle East and much of North Africa were part of the Ottoman Empire. The Ottomans, or Turks from central Asia, emerged in what is now Turkey. By 1453 the Ottomans conquered Constantinople, in the Byzantine Empire, and renamed it Istanbul.

By the middle of the sixteenth century, the Ottoman Empire extended from central Europe to Greece around the Mediterranean to Algeria. Although Ottoman rulers were Muslims, they allowed Christian and Jewish subjects to practice their religions freely.

By the early 1600s the Ottoman Empire reached the size shown on the map. Around that time, the Ottomans began to fall behind Europe's economic and technological progress. This growing gap led to a series of military defeats in the 1700s.

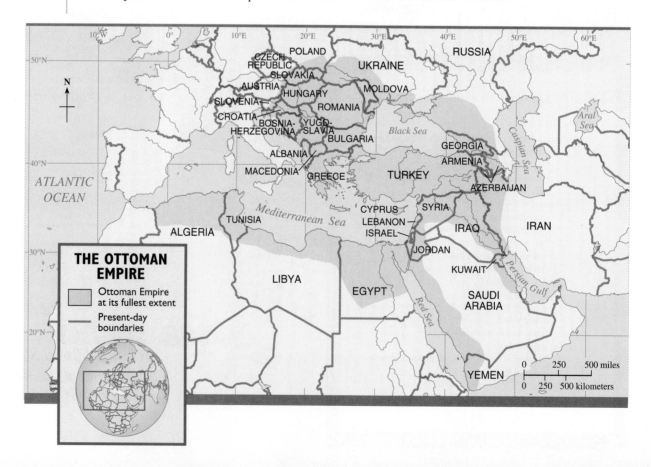

THE OTTOMAN EMPIRE

- Ottoman Empire at its fullest extent
- Present-day boundaries

500

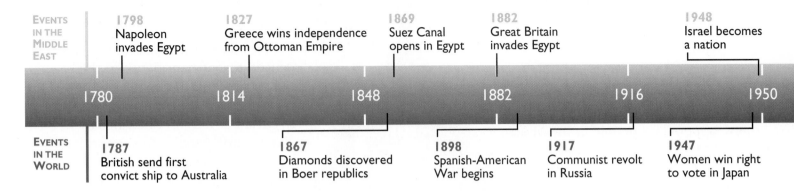

EVENTS IN THE MIDDLE EAST

1798 Napoleon invades Egypt

1827 Greece wins independence from Ottoman Empire

1869 Suez Canal opens in Egypt

1882 Great Britain invades Egypt

1948 Israel becomes a nation

1780   1814   1848   1882   1916   1950

EVENTS IN THE WORLD

1787 British send first convict ship to Australia

1867 Diamonds discovered in Boer republics

1898 Spanish-American War begins

1917 Communist revolt in Russia

1947 Women win right to vote in Japan

Napoleon Invades Egypt

The Ottoman Empire's loss of power became obvious when Napoleon Bonaparte and a French army invaded Egypt in 1798. When the Mamluks, or Egyptian leaders, heard this, they were not concerned. They believed that the Egyptian army was so strong that it would crush the Europeans. Such boasts were soon silenced.

The French easily defeated the Mamluks at the Battle of the Pyramids. Within weeks, Napoleon's army conquered most of Egypt.

Napoleon's troops patrolled the streets of Cairo. His engineers surveyed Egypt. This showed that Europe was more advanced than the Middle East. According to some scholars, this realization began a struggle over the definition of Middle Eastern identity.

An artist's impression of Napoleon's invasion of Egypt

Middle Eastern Economy Falters

By the Middle Ages, Europe was expanding its agriculture and its population. The Middle East was not able to grow at the same rate. Europe's growth gave it increasingly greater power than the Middle East had.

Europe was going through the Industrial Revolution in the nineteenth century. This advance in industrialization enabled Europeans to produce large quantities of goods to export all around the world. The Europeans took advantage of this advance.

Europe's Industrial Advantage

In the Middle East, Europeans bought locally raised material, such as cotton or the cocoons from which silk was made. They took the goods back to their own countries, where they made them into cloth or other products. Then the Europeans sold the finished products in the Middle East or in North Africa. Because their factories turned out such large quantities of goods, Europeans could charge lower prices for these goods than the Middle Eastern natives could charge for their locally produced goods.

This led to unhappy economic results in the Middle East. The lower-priced imported goods drove many local manufacturers out of business. Farmers became overly dependent on Europeans to buy their products.

European Culture Moves In

At the same time, Western culture began to spread through the Ottoman Empire. In the late nineteenth century, many upper-class people in the Middle East began to adopt European fashions, books, clothes, and food.

The people of the multiethnic Ottoman Empire spoke several languages. But now some upper-class people wanted to learn French or English, perhaps to impress powerful Europeans. Among the places where people of the Middle East studied were colleges set up by Christian missionaries from Europe and the United States. For example, the American University of Beirut was founded in 1866 as the Syrian Protestant College. Schools were also established by Jewish societies to teach French in Jewish communities of the Ottoman Empire.

▲ This Turkish helmet shows ornamentation that is typical of that part of the world.

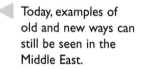

◄ Today, examples of old and new ways can still be seen in the Middle East.

Sometimes these cultural influences caused resentment between the Europeans and the people of the Middle East. Europeans believed that they had a mission to civilize a "backward" people. To support such claims, Europeans tried to draw a false picture of Muslim societies. They portrayed Muslims as corrupt people who treated women no better than cattle. They looked down on Muslim practices that were different from their own, such as the practice of veiling women and secluding them from public life.

Carving Up the Ottoman Empire

European ideas of nationalism and the policies of the Ottomans also helped destroy the fabric of the multiethnic Ottoman Empire. For years, the leaders of the Ottoman Empire had allowed different ethnic groups within the empire to manage their own internal affairs. But only Turks could hold important posts in the government of the empire itself.

As the Ottoman Empire tried to modernize, it grew more harsh in collecting taxes. Peasants rarely saw any benefit from the taxes they paid. Even though they supported the **sultan** in Istanbul, the lower classes did not share the interest in European ideas that the upper classes had.

Religion also played a role in dividing the empire. Christian Serbs and Greeks began to demand national independence in the early nineteenth century. In 1821 a major revolt against Ottoman rule broke out on the Greek

 ★ **sultan** A Muslim ruler

mainland. By 1830, British and Russian warships had helped the Greeks win their independence. More than four decades later, Serbia also gained its independence from the empire.

The Effect of European Imperialism

Farther south, European imperialism cost the Ottoman Empire many of its territories. Egypt, after Napoleon's invasion, was just barely part of the Ottoman Empire. In 1830 the French occupied Algeria. Fifty years later France also dominated Tunisia.

Both Great Britain and France played important roles in Egypt's economy. In 1882, fearing they were losing control over their economic interests, the British invaded Egypt and later claimed it as a **protectorate**.

In World War I the Ottomans sided with Germany against Great Britain and France. Germany lost the war. So the British and the French, without consulting local inhabitants, carved the Middle East into **mandates**. Suddenly, countries were governed by people who knew little about them.

New Homelands

The end of the Ottoman Empire changed the map of the Middle East. After World War I the Ottoman heartland around Istanbul became the nation of Turkey. Other states won their independence later. In 1922, Great Britain announced that Egypt was independent. But Egypt did not gain complete independence until 1956, when it took control of the Suez Canal. A similar policy brought independence to Iraq, although British influence lasted until 1958. Lebanon and Syria became independent from France by the end of World War II. Jewish settlers in Palestine formed the new nation of Israel in 1948.

The architecture and people of Istanbul reflect a mixture of influences.

protectorate A weak country or territory protected and controlled by a stronger country
mandate A territory placed under the governing powers of another country

Other nations emerged on the Arabian Peninsula. Yemen declared itself independent. Abdul Aziz, who ruled a kingdom in the interior of the peninsula, absorbed Mecca, Medina, and other territory to found the kingdom of Saudi Arabia.

Independence opened a new era for the Middle East. It was often one of conflict and confusion, but it also led to achievement.

Attempts at Arab Unity

Many Arabs felt that the new national borders were artificial ones. They called for a unified Arab state that would extend from Morocco to Iraq. In the 1960s, Egypt led a movement for Arab unity.

In 1952 a young Egyptian army officer, Gamal Abdel Nasser, rose to power. Coming from a modest background—his father was a postman—Nasser worked hard. Under his leadership, Egypt finally removed all remaining British control. Nasser set out to strengthen the nation.

He started by taking over the Suez Canal. Designed by a French engineer and built between 1859 and 1869 by Egyptian workers, the canal had been under British control since 1875. Because the canal linked the Indian Ocean and the Mediterranean Sea, it was very important to world trade. In 1956, Nasser declared that the canal was a national treasure that Egypt should control. In response, the British and the French sent troops to capture the canal. Israel also moved its army into Egyptian territory.

Under pressure from the United Nations and the United States, the three invading nations were forced to withdraw. Nasser emerged as an Arab hero who dared to confront what many referred to as "the imperialist West." After that, Nasser strengthened his position as leader of the Arabs.

Nasser's Dreams Die With Him

In 1958, Egypt and Syria merged into a new nation called the United Arab Republic. This was a step toward Arab unity, but three years later Syria withdrew.

In the early 1960s, Radio Cairo, called the voice of the Arabs, broadcast Nasser's messages throughout the region. Millions also listened to its popular entertainment programs. Radio made the Egyptian dialect of Arabic more widely understood in the Middle East.

Unfortunately, after Nasser's death in 1970, no one took his place as a leader that all Arabs could accept. Disputes among

The opening of the Suez Canal is shown in this engraving.

The shah of Iran and his wife lost their thrones when Iranians revolted against their oppression of the people and their efforts to westernize Iran.

the Arab nations have continued to disrupt attempts to achieve unity in the Middle East.

The Influence of New Ideas

Since the early nineteenth century, the people of the Middle East—like most of the world's population—have struggled with modernization. Modern science, technology, and democracy were appealing in many ways, but they also have caused problems.

For example, American and European television shows can be received in the Middle East by satellite dishes. Such programs portray a lifestyle that differs from the traditional Middle Eastern ways of living. The West's focus on the importance of wealth causes resentment among some Middle Eastern people. Much of the dress and behavior of Westerners is condemned as immodest by Muslims.

New ideas threatened existing social structures, which provided people of the Middle East with a sense of

security. This conflict between modern and traditional ideas remained after Middle Eastern countries gained independence, and it continues to exist today.

Conflicting Ideas

Today some people want to emphasize local values and traditions and exclude all others. Iran has tried to stamp out Western influence in all aspects of life there. The country now has an Islamic government that rules according to the teachings of Islam.

Other people in the Middle East believe that a return to the past would weaken society. Instead they want to keep local traditions alive, but they also want to adopt new ideas they think are useful. In this way some people believe they can encourage the use of computer technology and also promote notions of democracy. At the same time, they believe they can keep traditional ideas alive by continuing religious practices and national celebrations that encourage a sense of cultural identity. As is true in most of the world, people of the Middle East do not agree on everything. But Middle Easterners do want to maintain their identity.

505

NEW NATIONS FROM AN OLD EMPIRE

FOCUS *The breakup of the Ottoman Empire left many people wondering who they were and where their loyalties lay.*

A Crisis of Identity

The last 200 years have brought many changes to the Middle East. The challenge of the West has forced people of the region to find new identities and loyalties.

Western nations conquered the area with their weapons and technology. This forced Muslim thinkers to ask why Allah would allow Europeans to surpass the Muslims in technology, to defeat them in battle, and to occupy their land. Some people believed that these events were signs that Muslims had failed to follow their religious duties properly. A stricter practice of Islam would solve the problem.

Others adopted Western dress and ideas rather than cling strictly to Islam. They believed that Muslims would succeed if they adopted Western ways as quickly as possible.

Most Muslims took a middle course. They wanted to keep their heritage but also wanted to adopt science and technology from the West.

COUNTRIES THAT WERE FORMED FROM THE OTTOMAN EMPIRE

Entirely in the Ottoman Empire		Partly in the Ottoman Empire	
Albania	Israel	Algeria	Libya
Armenia	Kuwait	Austria	Poland
Bosnia and Herzegovina	Lebanon	Azerbaijan	Russia
	Macedonia	Croatia	Saudi Arabia
Bulgaria	Moldova	Czech Republic	Slovenia
Cyprus	Romania	Egypt	Syria
Georgia	Slovakia	Iran	Tunisia
Greece	Turkey	Iraq	Ukraine
Hungary	Yugoslavia	Jordan	Yemen

Use the map on page 500 to locate the countries that were entirely in the Ottoman Empire.

Building New Loyalties

When nations were created, the people of the Middle East had to form new loyalties. In many cases the new borders were artificial ones that showed no concern for the people who lived there. A family in Aleppo might have traded, intermarried, and visited with friends in nearby Antioch. But now Aleppo was in Syria, and Antioch was in Turkey. The family was separated from its relatives and friends by a border drawn by Europeans.

Moreover the family was told they were citizens of the new nation of Syria. They were no longer part of the Ottoman Empire. No one knew for certain what it meant to be a Syrian.

People also wondered what it meant to be an Arab in the modern world. How was it the same or different from being an Iraqi or a Jordanian or an Egyptian? There were differences in culture within the Arab world. In Morocco the culture was a blend of Arabian and African customs.

Trade divided the Arab world, too. Tunisians traded more with Italy than with any Arab state. Oman, on the eastern tip of the Arabian Peninsula, had stronger trading links with India than it had with the Arab world.

Leaders of each new nation took steps to form a national identity. First each country adopted a new flag and a national anthem. The anthem praised the beauties of the country and its unique heritage. In addition, national holidays were named that celebrated the end of foreign rule. Schools created a sense of national feeling by teaching children about the past national glories of the people.

▲ Women in traditional Muslim dress participate in the opening of the First Islamic Countries' Women's Sports Games in Tehran, Iran.

Ataturk Westernizes Turkey

At the end of World War I, a revolution ended the rule of the Ottoman sultans. Turkey became an independent republic. It was no longer the center of the Islamic religion, as the Ottoman Empire had been. Mustafa Kemal (moos tah FAH ke MAHL), the leader of the new nation, set his people on a whole new path.

Mustafa Kemal came to be called Ataturk, or Father of the Turks. His title was President of the Republic, but he was in fact a dictator. He moved the capital from Istanbul to Ankara. Then he set out to modernize the country, using Europe as a model.

Mustafa Kemal, wearing a Western-style uniform and his military medals

Wearing a fez was a tradition in Turkey until Ataturk insisted on Western dress.

He introduced the Roman alphabet for writing Turkish, replacing the Arabic script that had previously been used for five centuries. Three months later, Kemal ordered that all newspapers, books, and street signs in Turkey be printed in the new alphabet.

Ataturk believed that Turks should dress like modern Europeans. One of his targets was the Turkish **fez**. A fez is a hat that Turkish men had worn for more than a century. The custom began when an Ottoman sultan ordered his soldiers and officials to wear fezzes. The fezzes made it easier for them to touch their foreheads to the ground when they prayed.

In 1925, Ataturk appeared in public wearing a Western hat and suit. He told all Turkish men that they too must wear such hats. To make sure that they did, Ataturk created a law forbidding anyone to wear a fez. This law upset many Turkish men. They associated the fez with prayer. Some people felt that not wearing a fez was a sign that a man had given up the religion of Islam.

New Laws for Women

New laws also changed the lives of women in Turkey. Turkish women wore veils to hide their faces in public places. But Kemal said that veils could no longer be worn.

Kemal wanted Turkish women to change in more ways than just in dress. He said that men and women in a modern nation should be equal. In the past, girls in Turkey had only been educated in their homes. Kemal ordered them to go to public schools. For the first time, women could take jobs in business and government. They were also given the right to vote.

---

 fez   A brimless hat shaped like a cone but with a flat top, usually red with a flat black tassel hanging from the top

National Foods

In many Arab lands, finding a national identity was tied to trying to feel unique, or different from others. Food was one way for people to show their uniqueness. People were proud of their national foods. For example, a national dish of Egypt is *ta'miyah*, or deep-fried vegetarian burgers.

Just across the border, Israelis—and farther north, Lebanese and Syrians—have a similar dish that they call *falafel* (fuh LAHF ul). Is falafel better than ta'miyah? A Lebanese may tell you that it is. Even when people know that food like theirs is found elsewhere, they may believe that their version is better. Such attitudes are meant to increase national pride in one's own country.

Radio Spreads National Music

Finally, nationalism also found expression in music and song. Each country in the Middle East has its favorite singer. Music stars such as Fairuz in Lebanon became well-known because of the radio. In the 1950s, 1960s, and 1970s, radios became cheaper, thanks to Japanese mass production. As a result, even people without much money were able to purchase them.

Families gathered to listen to the news and their favorite singers. People in Lebanon liked Fairuz not just for her

▲ A woman uses traditional means to weave a carpet.

music but also for the fact that she was Lebanese. However, the same song that makes the Lebanese proud of Fairuz is equally popular among Arabs from Morocco to Iraq. So elements of national identity are not always as distinct as people like to think they are. What some see as a symbol of one nation is seen by others as something that unites all Arabs.

Television has replaced the radio in most places in the Middle East. Satellite dishes now let people all over the world learn about one another. This technology will continue to expose the Middle East to Western influence, but it also may help Westerners understand the Middle East.

SHOW WHAT YOU KNOW!

REFOCUS
COMPREHENSION

1. What are two problems that resulted from the breakup of the Ottoman Empire into new countries?

2. How did people express their loyalty to their new country?

THINK ABOUT IT
CRITICAL THINKING

Compare life in Turkey after Ataturk's changes with life in the United States today.

WRITE ABOUT IT
ACTIVITY

Suppose your state decided to join with a state next to it to form a new nation. What might people do to increase their national pride?

Make a list of the things you would suggest for the national song, the national flag, the national anthem, and the national food. What would you name the country? What occasions would you celebrate as national holidays?

CHANGING ROLES OF WOMEN

FOCUS *The influence of Western ideas led to changes in the roles of Middle Eastern women. These changes sometimes led to confusion for both women and men.*

Western Attitudes

Europeans explained imperialism in the Middle East by arguing that they were civilizing a "backward" region. To support their claims, they used **stereotypes** of Muslim societies. They pictured Middle Eastern life as decaying and immoral. They depicted the veiling of women and their exclusion from public life as abusive. Yet many people of the Middle East claimed that Muslim women were better off than were Western women. They pointed to Islam's guarantees of "equal but separate" places for women in society. The truth, as usual, lies somewhere between these arguments.

Women Defining Their Roles

By the end of the nineteenth century, after educated Muslims began to learn about Europe, they believed that women in Europe had more rights than those in the Middle East. Writers began to argue that for society to progress, women had to be freed from tradition.

In 1923 a group of upper-class women, led by Huda al-Sha'rawi, (HOO-duh ahl shah RAH wee) formed the Egyptian **Feminist** Union. She declared that her goal was to free women but remain faithful to Islam.

This balance was difficult to achieve. An attempt to raise the age of marriage for girls from 12 years to 16 years led conservative religious leaders to claim that this was against Islam. When feminists

Modern women in the Middle East dress according to their own ideas and beliefs.

---

stereotype A way of thinking about a person or group that follows a fixed pattern, paying no attention to individual differences
feminist A supporter of the principle that women should have political, economic, and social rights equal to those of men

Israeli women serve in the military. ▶

REFOCUS
COMPREHENSION

1. How did Huda al-Sha'rawi try to change the status of women in the Middle East?

2. List ways in which traditional and modern roles of women in the Middle East differ.

THINK ABOUT IT
CRITICAL THINKING

Explain why you agree or disagree with this statement: Perhaps women working together will have better results than men have had.

WRITE ABOUT IT
ACTIVITY

Write a few paragraphs about a woman you know. Describe how she dresses and what she does. How is she like or different from other women you know?

wanted education for girls to be equal to that for boys, conservatives objected.

Women were caught in the middle. Westerners ridiculed their traditions. But their own society regarded any changes as being against their religion.

Necessity Forces Changes

In the twentieth century, economic necessity forced many Muslim women to work. According to traditional practices, men and women who were not related were not supposed to come in contact with each other. Differences such as these between necessity and traditions led to a crisis in most Middle Eastern societies.

Several responses to this crisis emerged. In the more conservative countries, women who did not wear traditional clothing and stay at home could be threatened. Many women wore Islamic clothing while continuing to work. Yet many women often refused to give up their right to wear what they wanted. So it is very common today to see traditional and Western styles of clothing side by side.

Israel's Women

Even in Israel, where there is a great deal of Western influence, women do not have clear-cut roles. They serve beside men in the military, and they are similarly educated. Some Israeli boys and girls grow up in **kibbutzim**, where men and women share work. Even in Israel, however, equality is not firmly established. It sometimes conflicts with traditions of Orthodox Judaism, which sees a woman's role as that of a man's helper.

Women's Contributions

Despite the conflicting roles of women today, the Middle East has had many women in powerful positions. Golda Meir (me IHR) became Israel's prime minister in 1969, leading the nation in a war with Egypt and Syria. Hanan Ashrawi (hah NAHN ahsh RAH-wee) is a spokesperson for Palestinians.

Ashrawi and Naomi Chazan (nay OH-mee khah ZAHN) of Israel have organized a women's group. Perhaps women working together will have better results than men have had.

---

 kibbutz   An Israeli settlement in which people live in groups as a family

UNREST
IN THE MIDDLE EAST

FOCUS *Different religions, different points of view, and nationalistic interests have bred conflict in the Middle East.*

LEBANON

National unity has been a difficult goal for Lebanon. Religion is one thing that has separated the population. When Lebanon became independent in 1943, its leaders agreed to a religious division of power. Christians were then the majority, so it was agreed that a Christian would be president. A Sunni Muslim would hold the office of prime minister, and a Shi'i Muslim would be the speaker of the national legislature.

However, the Muslim population grew faster than the Christian and became the majority. There also was a growing economic gap between the upper and lower classes. These things led to quarrels about the division of power. In 1975, civil war broke out and lasted until 1990, when an agreement was signed between the warring communities.

IRANIAN REVOLUTION

The shah of Iran used some of the country's oil wealth to modernize the nation, but he wasted much of the nation's wealth. The shah ruled with an iron fist, and his secret police jailed and killed his opponents. Muslim clergymen were among the shah's most powerful critics.

In 1979, demonstrations forced the shah to flee the country. A Muslim cleric named Ruhollah Khomeini (roo-HOH luh koh MAYN ee) came to power and took the title of Ayatollah, which means "sign of God." He established a republic based on the teachings of Islam.

Khomeini hated the United States for its support of the shah. In 1979, Iranians took 52 Americans hostage for more than a year. The hostages were freed in 1981. However, relations between the two nations remain hostile.

| 1943 | 1979 | 1980 | 1991 |
| Lebanon gains independence | Khomeini assumes power in Iran | Iraq invades Iran | The U.S. and its allies attack Iraq |

| 1940 | 1951 | 1962 | 1973 | 1984 | 1995 |

IRAN-IRAQ WAR

When Iran was in turmoil, Saddam Hussein was president of neighboring Iraq. Hussein worried about the spread of the Islamic revolution from Iran to southern Iraq. He also saw an opportunity to seize an oil-rich area of Iran. In 1980, Iraq invaded Iran.

The Iraqi army swiftly moved into the oil-rich area, but Iran fought back. Both sides bombed each other's oil tankers in the Persian Gulf. This brought U.S. and European warships into the gulf to protect their oil interests. Even so, the war severely damaged the oil-producing capacity of both Iran and Iraq.

In 1988, Iran and Iraq finally accepted a United Nations-sponsored cease-fire. More than 1 million people lost their lives in the war.

GULF WAR

After the war with Iran, Iraq was left with a very large debt. Saddam Hussein needed money to maintain his army, which he used to control the country. He turned his attention to neighboring Kuwait, a small land rich in oil. Hussein claimed that Kuwait had been illegally taken from Iraq after World War I. In 1990, Iraqi troops invaded and overran Kuwait.

On January 17, 1991, the United States and its allies began an air attack on Iraq. Later they sent in ground troops. Within 100 hours of the ground attack, the Iraqi army was defeated and Iraq was further devastated.

SHOW WHAT YOU
KNOW!

REFOCUS
COMPREHENSION

1. What led to the civil war in Lebanon?

2. Why did Iraq see an opportunity to seize oil-rich land in Iran?

THINK ABOUT IT
CRITICAL THINKING

Much of the land in the Middle East is rich in oil. Why is this so important to Western nations?

WRITE ABOUT IT
ACTIVITY

Make a list of the reasons that war broke out in the areas shown on these two pages. Then write a few sentences about each item on the list, expressing your opinion about the reason.

BRIDGING THE GAP

FOCUS *From its beginning in 1948, Israel has had differences with its Arab neighbors. Attempts to reach peace agreements are still going on.*

Jerusalem: A Holy Place for Many

Jerusalem has places that are holy to Christians, Jews, and Muslims. This has made it a focus for the modern struggle between Israelis and Arabs.

Jews trace their claim on Jerusalem to about 1000 B.C., when King David captured the city and made it his capital. His son, Solomon, built a splendid temple in the city. It stood until 587 B.C., when it was destroyed by the Babylonians. A second temple was built in 516 B.C. During this time, Babylonians, Persians, and Greeks took turns ruling Jerusalem. After many Jewish revolts, Romans destroyed Jerusalem and drove its people into exile. The Roman emperor Hadrian built a new city on the ruins of Jerusalem.

In the fourth century A.D. Emperor Constantine, a Christian, constructed the Church of the Holy Sepulcher in Jerusalem. It honored the place where Jesus Christ's body is believed to have rested after his crucifixion.

In 638 a Muslim caliph captured the city of Jerusalem. Later, one of his successors built a magnificent shrine called the Dome of the Rock.

It is where Muhammad is said to have ascended to heaven. Under Muslim rule, the remaining part of the second Jewish temple became a pilgrimage site for Jews.

The Ottoman Turks brought Jerusalem into their domain in 1517. It remained part of the Ottoman Empire

▼ The Dome of the Rock can be seen behind the Western Wall, where Jews come to pray.

until British troops captured it during World War I. The British assumed control of the surrounding area, which was called Palestine.

Zionism

During the nineteenth century, Jews in Europe faced vicious discrimination. Theodor Herzl (TAY oh dor HER tsul), a Hungarian-born Jew, wrote a book called *The Jewish State* in 1896. Herzl declared that the solution to Jewish persecution would be the establishment of a homeland for the Jews. That homeland, Jews decided, should be Palestine, the site of the ancient kingdoms of Judah and Israel. This idea became known as Zionism, after the hill near where Solomon's temple had stood. Jews in many nations became supporters of Zionism.

In 1917 the British government declared its support for a Jewish homeland in Palestine. At the time, only about 50,000 Jews lived in Palestine, compared with about 568,000 Arab Muslims and 74,000 Christians.

In the 1920s the British began to allow large numbers of Jewish immigrants to settle in Palestine. The Arab

A Jewish man and his children praying at the Western Wall.

population revolted, and British troops defended the Jewish settlers. In 1936, Arabs staged a nationwide strike and attacked British government buildings and Jewish settlements. Nevertheless, by 1939 almost 500,000 Jews lived in Palestine.

The Holocaust, in which German Nazis killed 6 million European Jews, increased worldwide Jewish demands for a homeland. After World War II, Zionists in Palestine began a military struggle against the British and Arabs.

The British turned the problem over to the United Nations, which decided to **partition** Palestine into two sections. One would be Jewish, and the other would be Arab. On May 14, 1948, Jews in Palestine proclaimed the establishment of the state of Israel.

On the following day, Egypt, Jordan, Syria, Lebanon, and Iraq launched a war against Israel. The Arabs failed to conquer the Jewish state, and the United Nations negotiated a truce. Jerusalem was divided into Jewish and Arab sections. During the war, about 700,000 Palestinian Arabs were forced to live in exile.

The Six-Day War

In 1967, Egypt, Jordan, and Syria again threatened Israel by moving troops to its borders. On June 5 the Israeli army attacked the three nations. The war ended six days later with a decisive Israeli victory.

Israel gained possession of Gaza and the Sinai Peninsula, which was formerly part of Egypt. It also took the

partition To divide into parts

Palestinian children celebrate the anniversary of the declaration of a Palestinian homeland.

Maryland. The three men worked out a peace **accord** that was signed in 1979. But the other Arab nations and the Palestinians did not join in the peace accord because they did not think it treated them equally. In 1981, Sadat was assassinated by people who did not support his peace efforts because they felt he was giving in to pressure from the West.

The PLO

Palestinians formed the Palestinian Liberation Organization (PLO) in 1964 to regain the land that had become part of Israel. Later the PLO and Israel attacked each other again and again. The cycle of violence cost many lives on both sides.

In addition to the military aspect of the conflict, the PLO tried to gain the support of the Palestinian people. In 1977 the PLO's leader, Yasir Arafat, won recognition from the United Nations. By the early 1980s, Arafat began to seek a negotiated solution with Israel.

In 1982, Israel invaded Lebanon to wipe out PLO bases there. Many civilians and PLO fighters were killed. Afterward, Israeli troops occupied southern Lebanon.

Palestinian nationalism continued to be a strong force. Young Arabs in the Israeli-occupied West Bank began to attack Israeli soldiers with rocks. Others staged demonstrations and strikes. These uprisings, which became increasingly violent, came to be known as the **intifada**.

West Bank from Jordan and the Golan Heights from Syria. Its territory was now about four times greater than it had been after its war for independence. But about 1.5 million Arabs lived in the conquered territories. Governing them presented a problem.

The Camp David Accords

Egypt and Syria launched a war on Israel in 1973. It was called the Yom Kippur War because the Arabs attacked during the holiest Jewish holiday. Israel again won, but victory came at great cost in lives and money.

In November 1977 the Egyptian president, Anwar el-Sadat, made a surprise visit to Jerusalem. He addressed the Knesset, the Israeli parliament, and called for peace between the two nations.

President Jimmy Carter of the United States invited Sadat and Israel's leader, Menachem Begin (muh NAHK-um BAY gihn), to Camp David in

accord A mutual agreement
intifada An uprising of Palestinian Arabs against Israeli military forces in occupied territories of the Gaza Strip and the West Bank

Rabin and Arafat Agree

An Israeli government headed by Yitzhak Rabin (yihts KHAHK rah BEEN) came into office in 1992. Rabin took bold steps toward solving the Palestinian problem. After secret negotiations, he and Arafat flew to Washington, D.C., in 1993.

There they signed a treaty in which the PLO acknowledged Israel's right to exist. Israel agreed to allow Palestinian self-rule, first in the Gaza Strip and the West Bank town of Jericho, and later in other areas of the West Bank. The long struggle between Palestinians and Israelis seemed to be at an end.

▲ Yitzhak Rabin and Yasir Arafat shake hands at the White House in 1995 as King Hussein of Jordan, President Clinton of the U.S., and President Mubarak of Egypt look on.

However, Rabin was killed in 1995 by an Israeli Jew who did not agree with his ideas. So the struggle for peace in the Middle East continues.

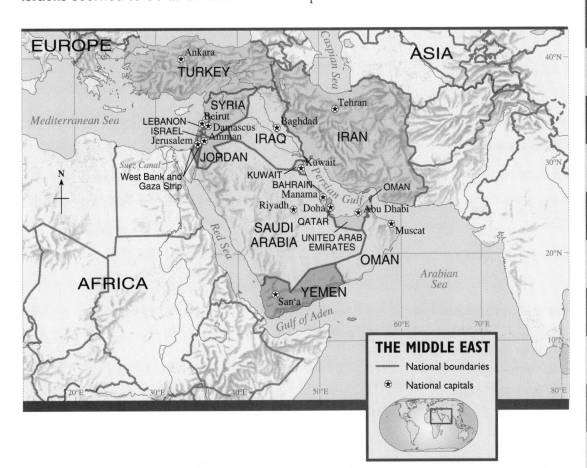

THE MIDDLE EAST
- - - National boundaries
✪ National capitals

SUMMING UP

1 DO YOU REMEMBER...
COMPREHENSION

1. Who were the Ottomans? What areas did the Ottomans eventually control?

2. Why was the outcome of Napoleon's 1798 invasion a surprise to the Egyptians?

3. How did World War I lead to the breakup of the Ottoman Empire?

4. What important goal did Gamal Abdel Nasser call for?

5. How did many Muslims feel about Western science and technology?

6. What are some things that Mustafa Kemal, or Ataturk, did to change Turkey?

7. How has exposure to Western ideas changed the way women dress in the Middle East?

8. How did Ayatollah Khomeini's view of government in Iran differ from that of the shah?

9. Why did Saddam Hussein invade neighboring Kuwait in 1990?

10. What idea became known as Zionism?

2 SKILL POWER
MAKING AN OUTLINE

Outline the main ideas of "Unrest in the Middle East," the lesson on pages 512–513. Use the heading of each section as a main topic of your outline. Then use two or three main ideas in each section as subtopics. Fill in details where you can.

3 WHAT DO YOU THINK?
CRITICAL THINKING

1. Do you think it's wise for Muslim leaders to eliminate Western influences and return to traditional values? Explain your thinking.

2. Why was it important for each new Arab nation to form a national identity?

3. Are women in the Middle East overcoming stereotypes?

4. How was oil a factor in both the Gulf War and the Iran-Iraq War?

5. What suggestions for living in peace could you give to Israel and its Arab neighbors?

4 SAY IT, WRITE IT, USE IT
VOCABULARY

Summarize three conflicts that have occurred in the Middle East in modern times. See how many of the terms you can use in your summary.

accord	mandate
feminist	partition
fez	protectorate
intifada	stereotype
kibbutz	sultan

5 GEOGRAPHY AND YOU

MAP STUDY

Study the map. Refer to it as you answer the following questions.

1. What two oceans are connected by the Suez Canal?

2. How does this affect travel by ship from Europe to Asia?

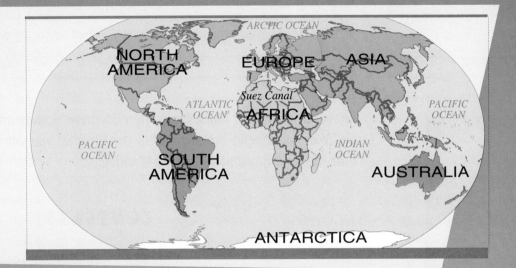

ARCTIC OCEAN

NORTH AMERICA

EUROPE

ASIA

ATLANTIC OCEAN

Suez Canal

PACIFIC OCEAN

AFRICA

PACIFIC OCEAN

INDIAN OCEAN

SOUTH AMERICA

AUSTRALIA

ANTARCTICA

6 TAKE ACTION

CITIZENSHIP

On a kibbutz, everyone shares the cleaning, cooking, and sewing. In our country, with more and more women working full time outside the home, all the members of a family need to do their share of homemaking. Discuss some methods that can help a family work together to get the housework done. List the best suggestions on a chart or bulletin-board display.

7 GET CREATIVE

HEALTH CONNECTION

Food was one of the ways in which new Arab countries showed their uniqueness. Although people may argue whether falafel or ta'miyah is better (see page 509), many people agree that Middle Eastern food is delicious. Do research to plan a menu for a Middle Eastern meal. You might find recipes for vegetable burgers and other Arab fare, such as shish kebab, couscous, and tabouli. If your school has a kitchen you can use, your class may want to serve a Middle Eastern meal.

LOOKING AHEAD

Change is seldom easy for individuals or nations. In the next chapter you will learn about changes that came to Asia.

EXPLORE

CHAPTER 23

ASIA IN MODERN

Japan, China, Korea, India. How often do these names appear in newspaper headlines or on TV or radio news broadcasts? In this chapter you will learn about the modern nations of Asia that are so important in the world today.

CONTENTS

Look at page 527 to see how robots function in modern factories.

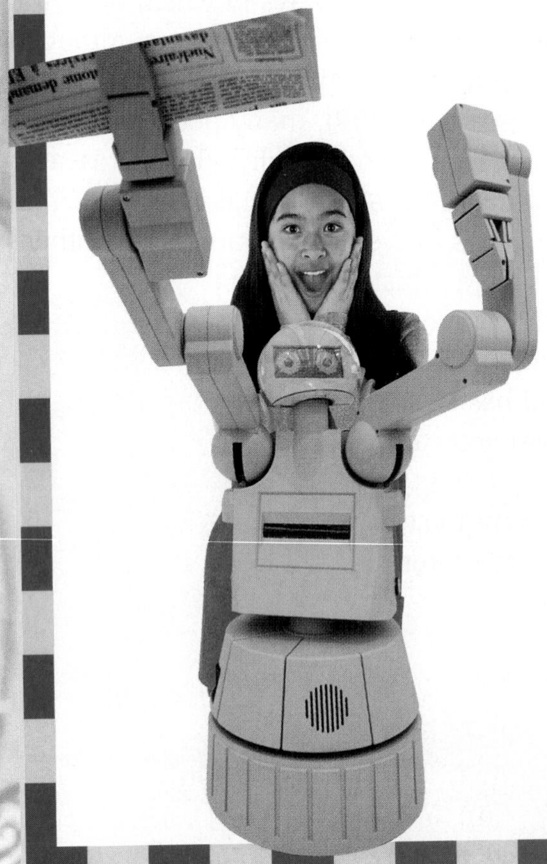

TIMES

You can learn more about Asia today from these books. Read one that interests you and fill out a book-review form.

READ AND RESEARCH

China Past—China Future by Alden R. Carter (Franklin Watts, 1994)
This history of China will take you back to the ancient dynasties and bring you through periods of invasions and revolution into modern times. *(nonfiction)*

The Children of India by Jules Hermes (Carolrhoda Books, 1993)
This rich photo essay shows the amazing diversity among the people and cultures of India. Read about the lives of desert nomads, farmers, and city dwellers. *(nonfiction)*

Goodbye, Vietnam by Gloria Whelan (Random House, 1993)
When Mai's grandmother is in danger of being arrested, her family chooses to flee their village rather than let the police take her. What follows is a gripping story of courage and sacrifice. *(historical fiction)*

Young Fu of the Upper Yangtze by Elizabeth Foreman Lewis (Dell Publishing, 1990)
Political turmoil is everywhere since the empress has died. Will Young Fu succeed as a coppersmith's apprentice or will he fall into danger in the city? *(historical fiction)*

SKILL POWER Drawing Conclusions

Drawing conclusions is a way to use the information you read and the information you already know to get a better understanding of a selection.

UNDERSTAND IT

Look at the photograph of rush-hour traffic in Beijing. What conclusion can you draw about transportation in China's capital? That's right, unlike Americans, the Chinese rely more on bicycles than cars to get to work.

When you read text, you can also fill in some information for yourself. Authors can't explain every fact and idea. There just isn't enough space. So good readers read between the lines and draw their own conclusions. Drawing conclusions helps you understand what you read.

EXPLORE IT

Drawing conclusions isn't hard. Just pay attention to the facts and ideas you read—selection information. Then add whatever facts and ideas you know—known information. Together, they add up to a conclusion.

SELECTION INFORMATION	+	KNOWN INFORMATION	=	CONCLUSION

Read the paragraph that follows and think about a conclusion you might draw.

During the 1950s, Chairman Mao Zedong said China should let "a hundred flowers bloom." He meant that the Chinese people should feel free to discuss any ideas at all. For the first time, teachers and government workers began to speak openly about problems in China. Those who criticized the Chinese government, however, soon found themselves in jail or sent to work in factories.

What might you conclude from this paragraph?

SELECTION INFORMATION	+	KNOWN INFORMATION	=	CONCLUSION
The Chinese were encouraged to speak freely. Those who criticized the government were punished.		Most people don't like criticism. Leaders like to stay in power.		Mao Zedong decided that free speech might weaken his government.

TRY IT

Find a news article in a newspaper or magazine that tells about something that interests you. Read the article and draw a conclusion from it. Use a diagram like the ones on page 522 to show the information on which you base your conclusions.

Display your article and diagram. Encourage your classmates to tell whether they agree or disagree with your conclusions.

SKILL POWER SEARCH *As you read this chapter, draw a conclusion about each lesson.*

Setting the Scene

KEY TERMS

tenant farmer
Opium War
embassy
commune
Cultural
Revolution

THE GROWTH OF ASIAN POWER

FOCUS *Until the mid-nineteenth century, much of Asia was isolated from the West. In the following 150 years, war, revolution, and modernization swept the continent.*

The Changing Picture of Asia

Asia, with more than 3 billion people, is home to almost 60 percent of the world's population. As you can see from the map, modern Asia is divided into many nations. There are different peoples, cultures, religions, and political systems. Sometimes this diversity brings

conflict. The clash between Buddhists and Hindus led to a civil war in Sri Lanka. In the Philippines, Christians and Muslims are fighting one another.

The civil war in Afghanistan today began with the Soviet Union's invasion of the country in 1979. Muslim rebels were resisting the Soviet-supported Communist government. Even after

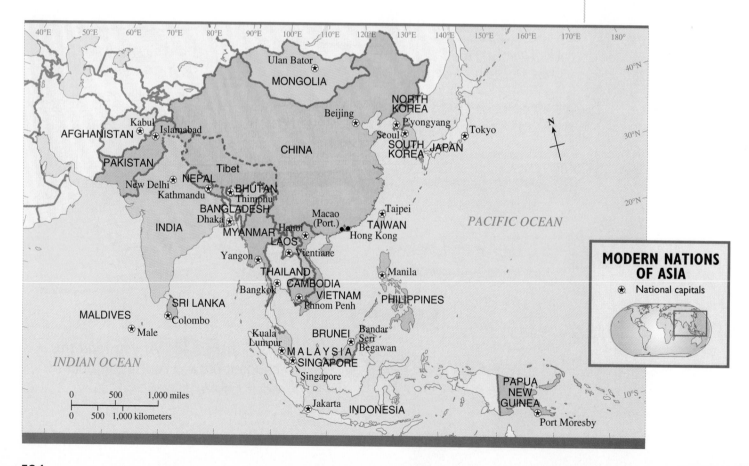

MODERN NATIONS OF ASIA

⊛ National capitals

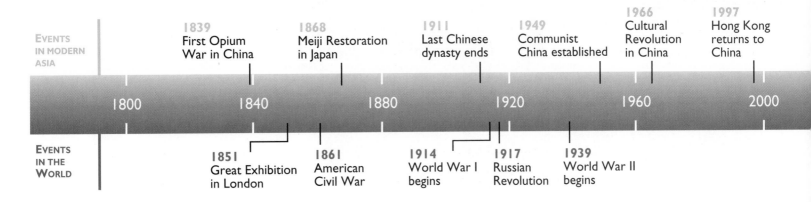

EVENTS IN MODERN ASIA	1839 First Opium War in China	1868 Meiji Restoration in Japan	1911 Last Chinese dynasty ends	1949 Communist China established	1966 Cultural Revolution in China	1997 Hong Kong returns to China	

1800   1840   1880   1920   1960   2000

EVENTS IN THE WORLD   1851 Great Exhibition in London   1861 American Civil War   1914 World War I begins   1917 Russian Revolution   1939 World War II begins

the Soviets withdrew in 1988, fighting between the government and the Muslim rebels has continued.

Yet parts of Asia have experienced great prosperity. Many Asian countries along the Pacific Ocean have built modern industries. These Pacific Rim nations have the world's fastest-growing economies.

The Westernization of Japan

On a July day in 1853, four American steamships entered Japan's Edo Bay. Commodore Matthew Perry requested that Japan open its ports to trade with the United States.

The arrival of the "black ships" caused an upheaval. Japan had been closed to the outside world since the 1600s. When the shogun agreed to Perry's demands, many Japanese saw it as a sign of weakness. Rallying behind the emperor, they overthrew the shogun. In 1868 a new Japanese government came to power, headed by the young emperor Meiji (MAY jee).

The Meiji Restoration, as the change in government was called, caused an upheaval in Japanese society. The samurai lost their privileges. A new constitution set up a Japanese legislature. In addition, a school system was founded to ensure an education for both boys and girls.

Japan began to modernize. The government sent students to European countries and to the United States to learn Western technology, military tactics, and political ideas. The government financed the construction of factories to produce export goods. It also built railroads and port facilities.

▼ Modern Japan combines the old and the new.

▲ Many Japanese eagerly took on Western ways.

A Military Power

Japan's growing wealth and strength made it the most powerful nation in east Asia. It set out to build an empire through military conquest. In 1894, Japan attacked China, capturing the island of Taiwan. Ten years later, Japan amazed the world by winning a war with Russia. In 1910, Japan annexed Korea entirely. Japanese aggression continued during the 1930s with further attacks on China. This was one of the events that led to World War II, and crushing defeat.

Occupied Japan

In 1945, Japan lay in ruins. Its cities, ports, and factories had been bombed to rubble. The country was stripped of its colonies and had to make payments to the nations it had occupied. For the first time in their history, the Japanese saw their country occupied by a foreign power.

General Douglas MacArthur, the "American shogun," dictated public policy from 1945 until 1952. He distributed plots of land to many former **tenant farmers**. A new constitution that outlawed war was written, and it also gave all citizens the right to vote.

Japan Today

The Korean War in 1950 put Japan on the road to an economic miracle that had its roots in the Meiji period. The United States needed supplies for the war, and Japan was the nearest source. To fill the demand, Japan built new up-to-date factories.

The 1960s brought even greater prosperity. Japan's economy grew at the astounding rate of over ten percent per year. Japan started to export automobiles to the United States. By the 1980s, consumers in many nations were driving Japanese cars and buying Japanese television sets.

 tenant farmer One who farms land owned by another and pays rent in cash or crops

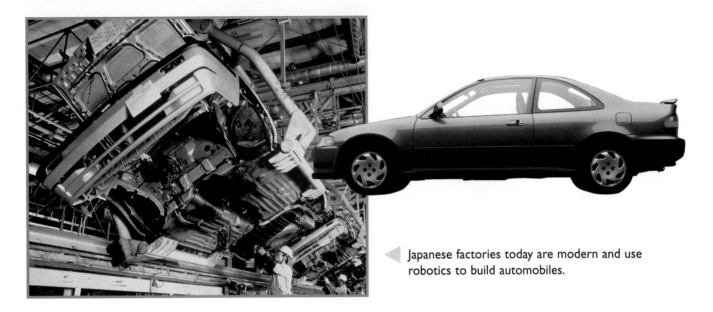

Japanese factories today are modern and use robotics to build automobiles.

China: A Giant Is Challenged

When the Manchus, a tribe from the north, conquered China in 1644, they established the Ch'ing (chihng) dynasty. Under their rule, imperial China reached its largest area. During the first 150 years of the dynasty, China prospered, and the population expanded greatly.

Beginning around 1800, the people of China faced challenges from the West. European nations and the United States sought to expand trade with China. The British introduced opium, a drug that was grown in their colony in India. As its use spread, the Chinese government became alarmed at the effect the drug was having on the population.

In 1839 a Chinese official at the port of Canton, now called Guangzhou (GWAHNG joh), seized and destroyed opium from British ships. In response, the first **Opium War** was declared by Great Britain. Western weapons proved to be superior. China was forced to give Great Britain the island of Hong Kong and to open its ports to Western ships. The Chinese felt humiliated.

More military defeats followed, resulting in further Western influence on China. Worst of all, Japan easily defeated China in a war in 1894. This loss to a much smaller Asian nation was a shock. Many Chinese felt that Westerners were to blame for China's weakness and had to be driven out.

In 1900 a secret society of patriotic Chinese called the Boxers killed Western missionaries and attacked the **embassies** of Western nations in Beijing. Troops from Western nations and Japan fought their way to Beijing and put down the Boxer Rebellion.

The Last Dynasty

The defeat of the Boxers made many Chinese realize that they had to learn

An American magazine cover shows the two sides in the Boxer Rebellion of 1900.

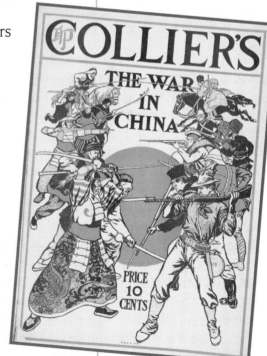

 Opium War   Wars between China and Great Britain, fought over trade in the habit-forming drug

 embassy   The official headquarters of an ambassador

527

from the West. In 1905, China ended the imperial examination system that had lasted almost 1,500 years. Western science was now taught instead of the Confucian classics. The Manchu rulers were discredited as well. In 1911, a revolution broke out, bringing the last Chinese dynasty to an end.

The most beloved figure in the new Chinese Republic was President Sun Yixian. He spent much of his efforts trying to unify the country. Military leaders known as warlords controlled many areas of China. After Sun's death in 1925, his brother-in-law Jiang Jieshi (jee AHNG jee ESH ee) took over.

The People's Republic of China

Helped by members of the Chinese Communist party, Jiang defeated the warlords. Immediately he turned on his Communist allies. Led by Mao Zedong (mou dzuh DOONG), Communists retreated across China on what came to be known as the Long March.

During World War II, Jiang's Nationalist government and the Chinese Communists concentrated on defeating the Japanese. After the war, civil war between the two sides resumed. The Communists were victorious in 1949.

Mao Zedong revolutionized daily life in China. Private ownership of land was ended. Peasant families were organized into huge **communes**

▲ Mao Zedong celebrates Chinese National Day.

▼ Students rally in Beijing in 1989 to protest their government's policies.

to tend crops and set up small factories. In 1966, Mao called upon China's young people to launch the **Cultural Revolution**. Students who were called Red Guards investigated everyone suspected of lacking a revolutionary spirit. Many officials were fired, jailed, or killed.

China's Policies in Tibet

Mao's policies caused turmoil in Tibet. His troops took control of the region in 1951. Chinese officials replaced the Buddhist priests. The Chinese government crushed all dissent and sent many Chinese people to live in Tibet, which had been renamed Xizang (shee DZAHNG). The Dalai Lama (dahl eye LAH muh), the spiritual leader of Tibet, escaped. Since then he has worked with little success for Tibet's independence.

After Mao's death in 1976, conditions in China improved a bit. The new

 commune A group of people who share possessions and responsibilities

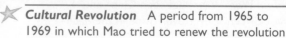 *Cultural Revolution* A period from 1965 to 1969 in which Mao tried to renew the revolution

Jiang Jieshi and Jiang Song Meilin, his wife, established Taipei as the capital of the Chinese Nationalist government on Taiwan.

SHOW WHAT YOU KNOW!

REFOCUS
COMPREHENSION

1. How were Japan's and China's relations with the rest of the world similar until the 1800s?

2. What are the current governments of China and Taiwan, and how are they related?

THINK ABOUT IT
CRITICAL THINKING

How might the Chinese attitude toward non-Chinese people have affected the way they handled challenges from Japan and the West?

WRITE ABOUT IT
ACTIVITY

Look back at the information and pictures about Japan. Then make a travel brochure that describes what a visitor to Japan can expect to see of the "old" or "new" Japan.

leader, Deng Xiaoping (dung sheeow-PIHNG), began economic reforms. However, there has been little progress toward democracy. In May 1989, over 100,000 students gathered in Tiananmen (tee EN ahn muhn) Square, in Beijing, to demand political freedom. In June the government used tanks to drive off the unarmed students. When other countries protested China's handling of the Tiananmen Square situation, China told them not to meddle in the affairs of the country. In spite of criticism, China's leaders have kept a tight hold on the nation.

Taiwan and Hong Kong

After Mao's forces took over China in 1949, Jiang Jieshi and many of his followers fled to the island of Taiwan. Here the Nationalists formed a new government, which claimed authority to rule all of China. Backed by the United States, Taiwan represented China in the United Nations. In 1971 the U.N. expelled Taiwan and admitted Communist China.

Today Taiwan still trades with the United States and many other countries. With a highly educated population, Taiwan has experienced great economic prosperity. Many of its people want to give up claim to China and be recognized as a separate state.

The future of the British colony of Hong Kong is also uncertain. Though small in area, Hong Kong is an economic powerhouse of banking and manufacturing. In 1984, Great Britain agreed to return Hong Kong to China in 1997. Hong Kong will be allowed to keep its capitalist system for 50 years. But no one knows how the Communist rulers of China will treat it.

2

Connections

KEY TERMS

collective farm
guerrilla

**NATIONS OF
SOUTHEAST ASIA**

SOUTHEAST ASIA

FOCUS *The former European colonies in Southeast Asia have found independence in the twentieth century difficult. Their challenges include conflicts between Communists and Nationalists, ethnic rebellions, and economic development.*

One Vietnam

After the Vietnam War, Vietnam's Communist rulers worked to rebuild the economy. They tried to resettle city dwellers on huge **collective farms**. Large businesses were placed under state control.

As a result, thousands of Vietnamese, many of Chinese descent, fled the country. Millions of farmers resisted the government's attempts to bring their lands under group control.

Faced with economic collapse, the government allowed farmers to work family-sized plots of land. Farmers were allowed to sell their excess production on the free market.

A new generation of leaders came to power in the late 1980s. The country's free-market economy expanded, and Vietnam patched up its relations with the United States.

★ **collective farm** A farm that is operated by a group of people who share the products

Cambodia and Laos

You can see on the map that Laos and Cambodia were likely to become involved in the Vietnam War. Cambodia, used as a shelter by North Vietnamese troops, was bombed by the United States. Communist **guerrillas** (guh RIHL-uz) seized power in 1975 and killed over 1 million non-Communist Cambodians.

Vietnam invaded Cambodia in 1978, setting up a rival government. Many Cambodians moved into refugee camps in Thailand. After Vietnam withdrew its forces, the U.N. conducted nationwide elections in Cambodia in 1993. The voters supported Norodom Sihanouk (NOR uh dum SEE hahn ook), who had been the nation's king. But guerrillas still plague the government.

★ **guerrilla** A member of a military force that organizes the local population and attacks in small bands

Map: Nations of Southeast Asia

100°E 110°E 120°E 130°E 140°E 150°E 160°E

0   500   1,000 miles
0   500   1,000 kilometers

20°N

MYANMAR (BURMA)
LAOS
THAILAND
VIETNAM
CAMBODIA
South China Sea
PHILIPPINES
PACIFIC OCEAN

10°N

N

BRUNEI
MALAYSIA
SINGAPORE
I N D O N E S I A
PAPUA NEW GUINEA

0°

10°S

INDIAN OCEAN

Tea harvester in the mountains of Malaysia ▶

Laos was also devastated by both sides during the Vietnam War. In 1975, Communist guerrillas overthrew the government. Many Laotians fled to Thailand, but some were forced back.

The Laotian government failed to establish a socialist economy. By the 1990s it was trying to attract investment from Western nations.

Malaysia and Singapore

The former British colony of Malaya became independent in 1957. Six years later, it combined with Singapore and several smaller states on the island of Borneo to form the nation of Malaysia.

Singapore, with its mostly Chinese population, broke away from Malaysia in 1965. Since then, Singapore has prospered. Its excellent harbor makes it the region's major port. Its economy also includes banking, communications, manufacturing, and tourism. Workers in Singapore have the highest standard of living of any country in Southeast Asia.

Malaysia continues to suffer from unrest among its ethnic groups as well as guerrilla revolts. But Malaysia's economy is booming, largely due to its exports of rubber and tin.

Indonesia

Indonesia won its independence from the Netherlands in 1949. Sukarno, a leader of the freedom movement, became president. Sukarno wanted Indonesia and other former colonial nations to remain neutral in the struggle between Communist nations and the West.

In practice, however, Indonesia became increasingly dependent on aid from the Soviet Union and Communist China. Sukarno faced rebellions among the various ethnic groups within Indonesia. Inflation caused widespread suffering.

The Indonesian Communist party attempted to overthrow the government in 1965. The army, led by General Suharto, put down the rebellion. Afterward, hundreds of thousands of suspected Indonesian Communists were killed.

General Suharto became president in 1967. He has allowed foreign companies to invest in Indonesia's industrial development. The economy has prospered under his rule.

531

3

Spotlight

KEY TERMS

Hangul

subsidy

KOREA

FOCUS *Ancient Korea had a highly developed culture, influenced by the Chinese and by Buddhists. Because of its location, this country has suffered many wars.*

Accomplishments of the Past

By ancient tradition, the godlike figure Tangun (TAHNG gun) united several ethnic groups to form Korea in 2333 B.C. The nation was called Chosŏn, which means "land of the morning calm."

Korea was influenced in many ways by its neighbor China. Koreans adopted a writing system based on Chinese characters. Confucianism formed the ideals of the Korean government. Buddhism came to Korea in the fourth century A.D.

The Korean people showed great talent for science and technology. In the 600s they built an astronomical observatory. It was used to create an accurate calendar. In the 1500s, military engineers built the world's first armored warships. Some were called turtle ships because they had "shells" to protect them.

In the 1440s, the Koreans created their own 40-letter alphabet called **Hangul** (HAHNG gool). Each year on October 9, the country celebrates Hangul Day.

Resisting Japan and China

Korea is located on a peninsula on the eastern coast of Asia. China is on Korea's northern border, and Japan is only 125 miles to the east. Throughout their history, Koreans have had to fight domination by these two nations.

In 1231, when the Mongols ruled China, they conquered Korea. For more than a century, the Koreans remained under Mongol control.

Japan first invaded Korea in 1592. But the Korean armored ships drove the Japanese away. After that, Korea's kings barred all foreigners from the nation. Korea became known as the Hermit Kingdom.

During the nineteenth century, Korea faced threats from the West. In order to gain a strong ally, Korea signed a treaty with Japan in 1876. But in 1910, Japan annexed Korea.

The years of Japanese rule were grim. Japanese became Korea's official language. Koreans were forbidden to use their own language. Anti-Japanese protests broke out in 1919. Although the protestors were unarmed, Japanese police killed 5,000 of them.

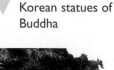

Korean statues of Buddha

★ ***Hangul*** The alphabet that King Sejong presented to the Korean people as a gift

532

The Country Divides

After Japan's defeat at the end of World War II, Koreans looked forward to getting their independence. Allied leaders agreed that U.S. troops would supervise Japan's withdrawal from the southern part of Korea. The Soviet Union's forces would do the same in the north. The dividing line was the 38th parallel, or line of latitude, across the peninsula. This line was meant to be a temporary one, for Korea had been a united nation.

But tensions between the Americans and the Soviets kept Korea from being unified. In the south, the Republic of Korea declared its independence in the summer of 1948. Soon the Democratic People's Republic of Korea in the north, led by a Communist government, followed with its own announcement.

In June 1950, North Korea invaded South Korea. The North's forces swept down the peninsula. South Korea was saved by the arrival of a U.N. military force under the leadership of U.S. generals.

When U.N. troops drove North Koreans back toward the Chinese border, China entered the war. A truce ended the fighting in 1953. The new line separating North Korea from South Korea was at almost the same place as before. The two Koreas have not yet signed a peace treaty, but the truce has held.

▲ A South Korean practicing the ancient art of calligraphy

▼ Towns and families were divided by the 38th parallel.

Self-Sufficiency in the North

North Korea's leader, Kim Il Sung, set out to rebuild his shattered country. North Korea had the advantage of rich natural resources, including most of the peninsula's coal and iron.

Kim wanted to create a self-sufficient economy. That meant using all the available land for farming. Terracing and irrigation boosted rice production. North Korea also developed state-owned industries.

Wages are low in North Korea, but health care and housing are free. Government **subsidies** keep the price of rice very low. Education is free for the first 11 years. When Kim Il Sung died in 1994, his son Kim Jong Il succeeded him.

⭐ *subsidy*   A grant of money

▲ Industry and agriculture in South Korea

Industrial South

South Korea was devastated in the war. Only a few houses stood in Seoul, its capital. South Korea had relatively few resources and depended on U.S. aid. In 1961, an army commander named Park Chung Hee seized power.

As president, Park led the nation to economic success. He believed that South Korea could make products for export. He placed his hopes on a well-educated and low-paid work force that would attract foreign investment.

In the 1960s many foreign companies did open factories in the country. From them, South Koreans learned high-technology techniques. The government borrowed money to develop a textile industry.

By the 1970s, Korean families founded several large businesses. South Korea began to manufacture cars, ships, and steel. In the 1980s, exports included computers and computer chips.

Economic success did not bring about a more democratic society. The country was shaken by strikes for higher pay and antigovernment demonstrations. In 1987 the government agreed to allow elections. Today the president is a civilian rather than someone from the military.

SHOW WHAT YOU KNOW!

REFOCUS
COMPREHENSION

1. Why were Korea's armored warships called turtle ships?

2. How did North Korea and South Korea differ in their development of industry?

THINK ABOUT IT
CRITICAL THINKING

What aspects of Korea's history are similar to those of China and Japan?

WRITE ABOUT IT
ACTIVITY

Choose five important events in Korea's history. Write a newspaper headline for each one.

THE SUBCONTINENT DIVIDES

FOCUS *In casting off the yoke of imperialism, India faced internal conflict over government control. Ethnic, religious, and political differences continue to plague India and the other countries of the subcontinent.*

The New Nation of India

In 1915, Mohandas K. Gandhi returned to India, his homeland. Since 1893, he had practiced law in South Africa, which, like India, was part of the British colonial empire.

In South Africa, Gandhi had developed his philosophy of nonviolence. He believed that peaceful protests would force the British to allow Indians to rule themselves. Gandhi's reputation spread around the world when he led a 200-mile march to the shores of the Indian Ocean to make salt from seawater. This was in protest of British taxation of Indian salt.

During the 1920s and 1930s, Gandhi led strikes, demonstrations, and **boycotts** of British products. He practiced **civil disobedience**. Though the British government jailed him and thousands of his followers, it was forced to grant India a new constitution in 1935.

Not all Indians recognized Gandhi as their leader. Muslims made up a sizable minority of India's population. They feared that Hindus, who were the majority, would control the government of an independent India. Led by Muhammad Ali Jinnah, Muslims demanded an independent state of their own.

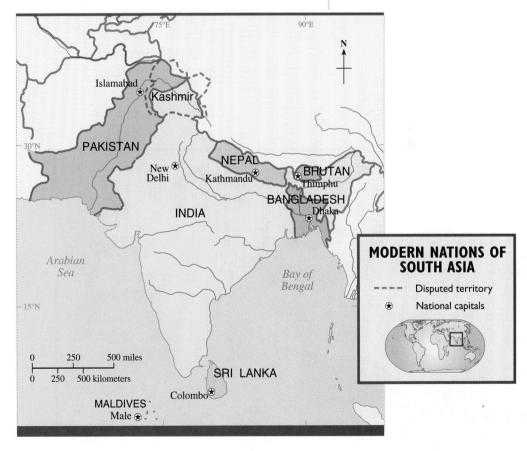

MODERN NATIONS OF SOUTH ASIA

---- Disputed territory

⊛ National capitals

⭐ **boycott** A campaign in which people refuse to deal with a particular group or business

civil disobedience The refusal to obey unjust civil laws

Mohandas Gandhi—called *Mahatma* or "great soul"—with his granddaughters

Muhammad Ali Jinnah *(right center)* is called the father of modern Pakistan.

In August 1947, India gained its independence. Gandhi took no great joy in the victory. For as you can see on the map on the previous page, India had been partitioned into two countries. One country, called India, consisted of territory in which the majority of the people were Hindus. The other country was Pakistan, which became a homeland for India's Muslims.

Gandhi was assassinated in 1948 by a Hindu who was enraged by the kindness Gandhi had shown to Muslims. Gandhi's closest follower, Jawaharlal Nehru (juh WAH hur lahl NAY roo), became the first prime minister of India.

A Muslim Pakistan

The creation of India and Pakistan resulted in a mass migration of about 15 million people. Hindus in Pakistan made their way to India, while Muslims in India marched in the other direction.

Almost immediately a war broke out between India and Pakistan. Both claimed the state of Kashmir. Though Indian troops finally occupied the area, it remains in dispute today.

As a nation, Pakistan was severely weakened by being divided into two parts, separated by over 1,000 miles of Indian territory. Though East Pakistan held a majority of the nation's population, it had little say in the military-controlled government. In 1971, East Pakistan declared itself independent and renamed itself Bangladesh.

Problems for Bangladesh

Independence did not bring prosperity to Bangladesh. Overcrowding continues to be a major problem. Though the nation is slightly smaller than Wisconsin, its population is almost half that of the entire United States.

Much of Bangladesh suffers from typhoons that blow in from the Bay of Bengal. Floods have sometimes driven hundreds of thousands of people from their homes. With few natural resources, Bangladesh is one of the world's poorest countries.

A Troubled Island Nation

Ceylon, a large island off the southeast coast of India, won its independence from Great Britain in 1948. The nation later took back its old name Sri Lanka.

Sri Lankan people belong to two major ethnic groups. About 74 percent of Sri Lankans are Sinhalese (sihn huh-LEEZ), who are Buddhists. The Tamils, who make up 18 percent of the population, are Hindus. Since 1983 a guerrilla group, the Tamil Tigers, has carried on a rebellion against the government. The Tamil Tigers want to create an independent Tamil state in Sri Lanka.

▼ Nepalese villagers of the Himalayan lowlands lead isolated lives.

The Kingdom of Nepal

Located between China and India, Nepal contains the world's highest mountains, the Himalayas. Siddhartha Gautama, the founder of Buddhism, was born in Nepal over 2,500 years ago. Today, however, most of the nation's people are Hindus.

In 1816, Nepal lost part of its territory in a war with the British. As a result, Nepal followed a policy of isolation from the outside world until 1951. In that year, Nepal's king declared his support for a democratic form of government.

A constitution was adopted in 1959. But three years later the king dissolved the legislature and banned political parties. Protests plagued the country until 1990, when the king gave up most of his power and allowed nationwide elections.

WOMEN LEADERS IN MODERN ASIA

FOCUS *A number of women have served as heads of government in modern Asia. Many of them were members of political families.*

INDIRA GANDHI

Indira Gandhi's family was deeply involved in India's independence movement. Her father was the nation's first prime minister. In 1966, Gandhi herself became prime minister. In 1975, however, when riots broke out against her policies, Gandhi declared an emergency and took dictatorial powers. She jailed thousands of her political opponents. When she later allowed free elections, Indians voted her out of office. Gandhi returned to office in 1980. Four years later she was assassinated, and her son Rajiv became prime minister.

EMPRESS CI XI

In 1851, 16-year-old Ci Xi (tzuh shee) was chosen to be a member of the Chinese emperor's household. Ci Xi gained honor when she gave birth to the emperor's first son.

The emperor died in 1861, and Ci Xi's 5-year-old son took the throne. Ci Xi became one of the advisors for the child and gradually gained total control of the government.

Ci Xi dominated China until her death in 1908. She opposed Western influences. However, her policy weakened China. Two years after she died, a rebellion overthrew the last emperor of China.

CORAZON AQUINO

Corazon Aquino (KAWR uh zohn uh KEEN oh) was the daughter of a wealthy sugar planter in the Philippines. She married Benigno Aquino, a young Filipino politician.

Benigno led the opposition to the corrupt government of Ferdinand Marcos. Marcos had him assassinated in 1983. Three years later, Corazon bravely ran against Marcos for president. When Marcos manipulated the elections, Corazon began a "people power" campaign. Marcos was forced to flee, and Aquino became president.

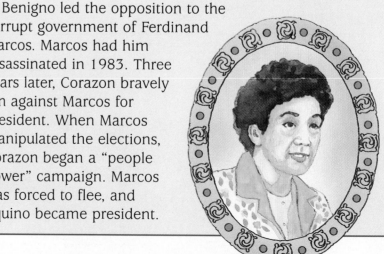

1861
Empress Ci Xi comes to power in China

1960
Sirimavo Bandaranaike becomes prime minister of Sri Lanka

1966
Indira Gandhi becomes prime minister of India

1986
Corazon Aquino runs for president of the Philippines

1988
Benazir Bhutto becomes prime minister of Pakistan

1860 — 1960 — 1965 — 1985 — 1990

SHOW WHAT YOU KNOW!

REFOCUS
COMPREHENSION

1. How did Ci Xi come to power?

2. Why can these women leaders be described as members of political dynasties?

THINK ABOUT IT
CRITICAL THINKING

Compare the number of women heads of state in Asia with the United States. How can you explain the difference?

WRITE ABOUT IT
ACTIVITY

What makes a man or woman want to lead a country? Write a paragraph expressing your ideas.

BENAZIR BHUTTO

Zulfikar Bhutto (ZOOL fih kahr BOO toh) became prime minister of Pakistan in 1971. His daughter Benazir, then only 18, witnessed her father's struggle to solve the nation's many problems. In 1977, Pakistan's voters reelected Zulfikar. But the country's military leaders took over and put President Bhutto to death in 1979.

For the next six years, Benazir was under house arrest. After her release, she went to Great Britain and formed a coalition to oppose Pakistan's military dictatorship. She returned to Pakistan in 1986 to campaign for free elections. Two years later, the dictator who executed her father died, and Benazir Bhutto became prime minister.

SIRIMAVO BANDARANAIKE

Sirimavo Bandaranaike (see ree MAH vaw bahn drah NEE kee) is the first woman ever to become leader of a democratic nation. Her husband, Solomon, had been prime minister of Ceylon, now Sri Lanka, from 1956 until his assassination in 1959.

Bandaranaike entered politics to keep alive the political party her husband had founded. Her opponents said that she had no experience. She replied, "People forget I had twenty years of political education from my husband." Showing her political skills, Sirimavo forged alliances with other parties. Her emotional speeches also swayed the voters. She became Ceylon's prime minister in 1960.

She followed a nationalist policy, working to end British domination of her country. In 1965 she lost a reelection bid. But she returned to office in 1970, serving until 1977. Her daughter became Sri Lanka's prime minister in 1994.

539

SUMMING UP

1 DO YOU REMEMBER...
COMPREHENSION

1. What changes occurred in Japan as the result of the Meiji Restoration?

2. What did the Boxers hope to achieve in China in 1900?

3. When did the Communists take power in China?

4. Why does Hong Kong face an uncertain future?

5. What economic policies failed in Vietnam after the Vietnam War?

6. What natural features and resources help Singapore and Malaysia prosper?

7. Why was the defeat of Japan in 1945 especially important to the Koreans?

8. What did Mohandas Gandhi hope to achieve with his philosophy of nonviolence?

9. Why was the Indian subcontinent divided into India and Pakistan?

10. What woman, as president of the Philippines, brought democratic changes to that island nation?

2 SKILL POWER
DRAWING CONCLUSIONS

Draw a conclusion about which country in modern Asia you would most like to live in. Use details from this chapter as well as what you already know about the countries of Asia.

3 WHAT DO YOU THINK?
CRITICAL THINKING

1. What similarities do you see between Japan following the Meiji Restoration (1868) and Japan following the American occupation (1945–1952)?

2. How successful has communism been in Southeast Asia? Give examples to support your opinion.

3. Has North Korea or South Korea, in your opinion, been more successful in meeting its people's needs?

4. Why didn't Gandhi take great joy in the events of 1947?

5. How do the careers of Indira Gandhi, Corazon Aquino, and Benazir Bhutto suggest that instability and violence are a fact of life in the politics of some parts of modern Asia?

4 SAY IT, WRITE IT, USE IT
VOCABULARY

Make a time line of important events in modern Asian history. In the descriptions of the events you list on the time line, use as many of these vocabulary terms as possible.

boycott	guerrilla
civil disobedience	Hangul
collective farm	Opium War
commune	subsidy
Cultural Revolution	tenant farmer
embassy	

5 GEOGRAPHY AND YOU
MAP STUDY

Study the map of the geography of the Korean peninsula. Then answer these questions.

1. Which country, North Korea or South Korea, is more mountainous?

2. Approximately how long is the total coastline of North Korea and South Korea?

3. Between what degrees of latitude is South Korea located?

4. Between what degrees of latitude is North Korea located?

5. Are the capitals of North Korea and South Korea located on the east coast or the west coast of the peninsula?

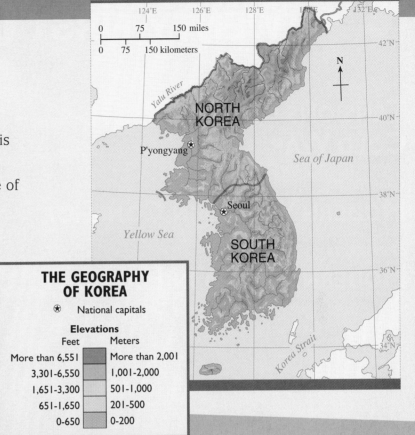

THE GEOGRAPHY OF KOREA

⊛   National capitals

Elevations

Feet	Meters
More than 6,551	More than 2,001
3,301-6,550	1,001-2,000
1,651-3,300	501-1,000
651-1,650	201-500
0-650	0-200

6 TAKE ACTION
CITIZENSHIP

In his work for Indian independence, Gandhi popularized the use of nonviolent civil disobedience. Since then, American citizens have used this technique in many ways. At the library, research one example of civil disobedience in our country. In an oral report explain why, how, where, and when the event occurred. Tell whether you think it was nonviolent. Also decide whether civil disobedience was an effective way for organizers to achieve their goals.

7 GET CREATIVE
MATH CONNECTION

Over 3 billion people live in Asia—almost 60 percent of the world's population. Make a map of Asia that shows this population density. A recent almanac will give you the population and land area of each country you have read about. Divide the area by the population to find the average population per square mile. Then show these densities on a map, coding each country by color according to its density. Be sure to include a key that shows the density represented by each color.

LOOKING AHEAD   As the world moved toward the twenty-first century, its desire for peace and stability was tested in the cold war.

Toward THE TWENTY-FIRST Century

What Will the New Century Bring?

You are going to spend most of your life in the twenty-first century. What do you think your future will be like? Learn about the events today that are shaping the future for you and other people around the world.

TENSIONS OF THE

Why did the United States and the Soviet Union distrust each other in the decades following World War II? What did the space race have to do with the cold war? How did young people influence the culture of the 1960s? Read this chapter to find answers to these questions.

CONTENTS

▲ Turn to page 558 to find out how the outfit this girl is wearing relates to the cold war.

COLD WAR

These books tell about the people, places, and events that made the cold war so chilling. Read one that interests you and fill out a book-review form.

READ AND RESEARCH

Living in Space **by Larry Kettelkamp** (William Morrow & Co., 1993)
If you're wondering what lies ahead in the space program, this book will help you prepare for the future. Read about plans for the space shuttle, spaceports, and a blueprint for colonizing Mars. *(nonfiction)*

The Russian Federation **by David C. Flint** (Millbrook Press, 1992)
For years the cold war between the United States and the U.S.S.R. kept these two nations apart. As you read about the breakup of the Union of Soviet Socialist Republics, think of ways that the two countries are now able to work together. *(nonfiction)*

The Berlin Wall **by Lisa Mirabile** (Silver Burdett Press, 1991)
Trace the history of the Berlin Wall, Germany's concrete symbol of conflict, from the morning when it first appeared to the day it came down. *(nonfiction)*

Recognizing Propaganda

Learning how to recognize and evaluate propaganda can help you understand when someone is trying to influence your thinking.

UNDERSTAND IT

You probably encounter propaganda every day. Advertising is propaganda. An election poster is propaganda. Your brother's plea for you to take over his paper route on Saturday morning probably also is propaganda.

Propaganda is a way of presenting information that is designed to make you agree with what it says. Although propaganda has come to suggest that ideas are false or misleading on purpose, this is not necessarily so. Propaganda may support ideas that are true or false.

EXPLORE IT

When you see an advertisement, you know the advertiser is trying to convince you to buy a product. But other kinds of propaganda are not always so obvious. Look at the propaganda techniques below and see how they are used in the poster.

- Loaded words are often used in propaganda. A loaded word is one that is meant to carry a meaning beyond the obvious one. For example, words such as *baby, mom, honesty,* and *luxurious* often make people think of positive things. Words such as *un-American, drab, materialistic,* and *unfair* often make people think of negative things.

- Pictures can be loaded, too. A loaded picture is one that is intended to make you think of things in a certain way. For example, a picture of a scenic view on a beautiful day most likely will make people think of something positive. But a dark picture of an old factory on a dismal day probably will provoke negative feelings.

- Colors also can serve different purposes for propaganda. During the cold war, red signified communism. Red, white, and blue symbolized American ideals.

◀ This Chinese poster tried to show that Mao Zedong's leadership gave strength to Chinese communism. Which propaganda techniques can you identify in this poster?

TRY IT

Working with a partner, decide on an issue that interests you and has two sides. For example, your town might be planning to pave over part of a park to make a parking lot for people who come to the park. Some people probably think it is a good idea, while others do not.

Use propaganda techniques to make two posters—one supporting one side of the issue and another supporting the opposite side. Include your posters in a class display and ask your classmates to identify the propaganda techniques you used.

SKILL POWER SEARCH

Find a picture in this chapter and explain how it could be used for the purposes of propaganda.

THE COLD WAR

FOCUS *The cold war between the United States and the Soviet Union dominated the world from 1945 until 1990. Events of this period reflected the struggle between these superpowers.*

▼ Checkpoints on the boundary between East and West Germany were used to keep people where they belonged.

A Dangerous World

People called World War I "the war to end all wars." They didn't have such false hopes at the end of World War II. Hitler, Mussolini, and the Japanese generals were gone. But the ruthless Soviet dictator Joseph Stalin was still in power.

At the end of the war, the Soviet Union and the United States were the superpowers of the world. These two former allies found they couldn't get along. The Soviets hoped to spread communism around the world. The Americans wanted to stop the Soviets and have a **capitalist** world economy. Both sides feared nuclear war, so each did everything it could to advance its goals without actually fighting. Americans and Soviets fought what became known as the **cold war**.

The Soviet Empire

The Soviets, who occupied Eastern Europe, quickly supported Communist governments there.

★ *capitalist* Describing a system in which land, factories, and materials used in making goods are privately owned and operated for profit
cold war A bitter political, economic, and intellectual rivalry among nations, without actual military conflict

By the late 1940s, Communists controlled Hungary, Bulgaria, Albania, Czechoslovakia, Poland, and Yugoslavia. Stalin wanted these nations, which you can see on the map, to be Communist so that they would be a buffer to protect the Soviet Union from invasion.

The Soviet buffer frightened people. As Winston Churchill warned in a speech in 1946, "an **iron curtain** [had] descended across the continent."

A Divided Germany

After World War II the United States, Great Britain, France, and the Soviet Union divided Germany into four zones. They also divided the German capital—Berlin—into four zones. Berlin was located inside the Soviet German zone. The Soviet Union kept its German zone and its part of Berlin separate. The other three countries combined their zones into one. In 1949, West Germany—the Federal Republic of Germany—was set up with a democratic government. The Soviets created a Communist government— the German Democratic Republic—in what was called East Germany.

★ *iron curtain* A barrier of secrecy that isolated the Soviet Union and the countries it controlled

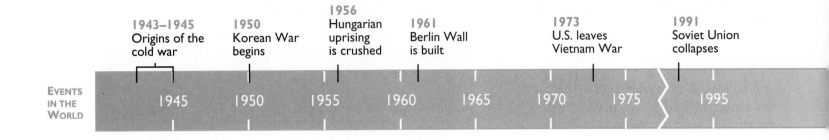

1943–1945	1950	1956	1961	1973	1991
Origins of the cold war	Korean War begins	Hungarian uprising is crushed	Berlin Wall is built	U.S. leaves Vietnam War	Soviet Union collapses

EVENTS IN THE WORLD

1945   1950   1955   1960   1965   1970   1975   1995

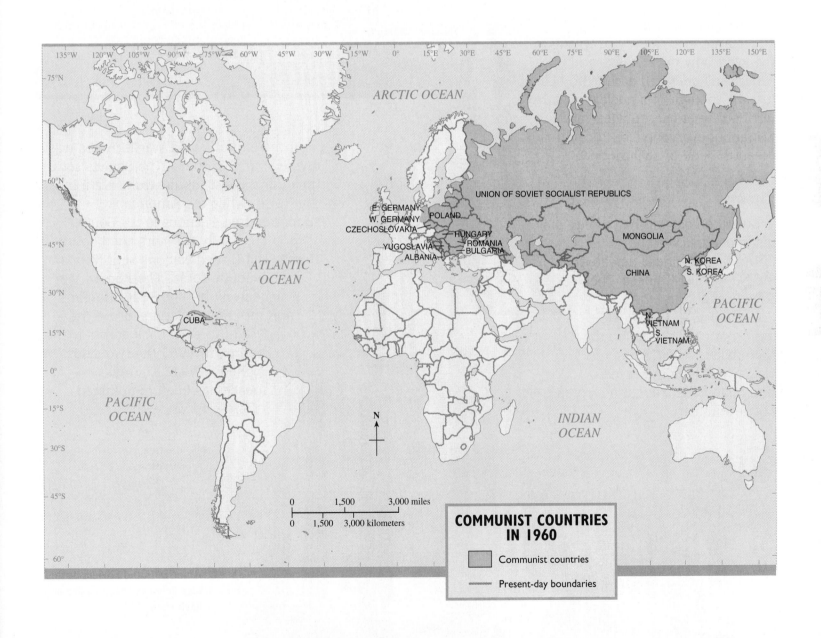

ARCTIC OCEAN

UNION OF SOVIET SOCIALIST REPUBLICS

E. GERMANY
W. GERMANY
CZECHOSLOVAKIA
POLAND
HUNGARY
YUGOSLAVIA
ROMANIA
BULGARIA
ALBANIA

MONGOLIA

CHINA

N. KOREA
S. KOREA

N. VIETNAM
S. VIETNAM

CUBA

ATLANTIC OCEAN

PACIFIC OCEAN

PACIFIC OCEAN

PACIFIC OCEAN

INDIAN OCEAN

N

0   1,500   3,000 miles
0   1,500   3,000 kilometers

COMMUNIST COUNTRIES IN 1960

Communist countries

Present-day boundaries

The Soviet Threat

Why were Americans so afraid of communism? After all, it wasn't a better economic system. American capitalism easily outproduced Soviet communism. The threat was really political. Americans saw the Soviet Union as a dictatorship determined to take over the world.

Yet Americans were not willing to risk war. Why not? Soviets and Americans both had atomic bombs. Just the thought of a nuclear war terrified Americans, Soviets, and just about everyone else. It could mean the end of civilization.

Communism in China and Korea

Still, the cold war had plenty of hot spots. In 1949 the Communist Chinese defeated the Nationalist Chinese. The Soviets supported the Communists in China, while the Americans supported the Nationalists. The Communist victory in China increased Americans' fears about the spread of communism.

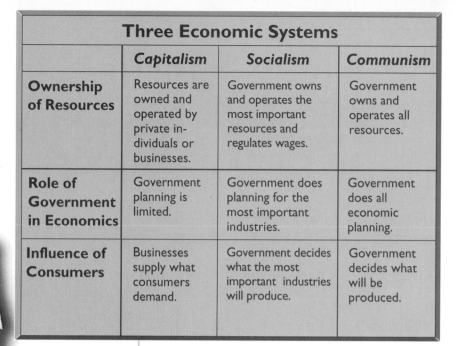

Three Economic Systems			
	Capitalism	*Socialism*	*Communism*
Ownership of Resources	Resources are owned and operated by private individuals or businesses.	Government owns and operates the most important resources and regulates wages.	Government owns and operates all resources.
Role of Government in Economics	Government planning is limited.	Government does planning for the most important industries.	Government does all economic planning.
Influence of Consumers	Businesses supply what consumers demand.	Government decides what the most important industries will produce.	Government decides what will be produced.

At the end of World War II, Korea was divided into two zones. The Soviets set up a Communist **regime** (ruh ZHEEM) in the North, while the Americans supported free elections in the South.

In 1950, North Korea invaded South Korea. The United Nations sent troops to help South Korea. The Korean War dragged on until the South Koreans and the United Nations drove the North Koreans back across the border. In 1953 the two sides signed a truce. An uneasy peace has been maintained there ever since.

⭐ **regime** A form of government or rule

◀ Americans and Soviets both kept missiles ready to fire at each other.

An End to Colonial Empires

Not all countries faced a threat of communism after World War II. In Asia and Africa, one colony after another gained independence. The United States, for example, gave the Philippines its independence on July 4, 1946, but it supported a pro-Western dictator there.

Some colonies, however, gained their independence only after long struggles. This was the case in India. Indians had hoped that their loyalty to Great Britain in World War I would be rewarded with independence, but it wasn't. It took many years of nonviolent protests by people such as Mohandas Gandhi and Vijaya Pandit to convince the British. In 1947, Great Britain granted India its independence.

Fierce civil wars broke out in the Philippines and in India. People in those countries went through a bitter process of learning how to create stable democracies.

Communism in Vietnam

At other times, countries gained independence only after bloody wars. This happened in the French colony of Vietnam. The French refused to give the Vietnamese their independence, and the United States backed the French. Why? It wasn't because Americans loved French colonialism. It was because the Vietnamese were led by the Communist Ho Chi Minh (hoh chee mihn). Americans at the time believed in the **domino theory**. They thought that if Vietnam fell to the Communists, the rest of Southeast Asia would fall like a row of dominoes.

By 1954, the French were defeated in Vietnam. Communists ran the northern part of Vietnam, and non-Communists ran the southern part. When Communists tried to take over South Vietnam, war broke out. Then Americans sent troops to support South Vietnam. The Vietnam War (1963–1973) ended in a Communist victory. It was the first American military defeat ever.

The Berlin Wall

Perhaps the most powerful symbol of the cold war was the Berlin Wall. During the 1950s, thousands of people who lived in Communist East Berlin fled to democratic West Berlin. In 1961 the Communists decided to stop this escape by building a wall dividing Berlin. In doing so, they turned the eastern half of the city into a prison. People who had been neighbors before the wall went up between them could no longer visit each other. Relatives were separated from one another. Dozens of people were killed trying to escape from East Germany to West Germany.

▲ Hungarians showed their displeasure with the Soviet invasion in 1956 by burning pictures of Stalin.

★ **domino theory**   The idea that if a nation becomes a Communist state, the nations nearby will also

HOT SPOTS

1. 1946: Communists revolt against Greek government.
2. 1947: Turkey fights off Communists.
3. 1948: U.S.S.R. refuses to allow Czechoslovakia and Poland to participate in Marshall Plan.
4. 1948: Yugoslavia splits with U.S.S.R.
5. 1948: U.S.S.R. blockades Berlin.
6. 1949: Chinese Communists take over government.
7. 1950–1953: Korean War
8. 1953: U.S.S.R. puts down revolt in East Germany.
9. 1954: Chinese Communists attack Nationalist Chinese.
10. 1956: U.S.S.R. puts down revolt in Hungary.
11. 1956: Polish demonstrations against government
12. 1958: Lebanon requests U.S. aid to fight revolt.
13. 1960: U.S. spy plane shot down over U.S.S.R.
14. 1960: U.S.S.R. cuts off aid to China.
15. 1961: U.S. invades Cuba.
16. 1961: Berlin Wall is built.
17. 1962: Cuban missile crisis
18. 1962: China attacks India.
19. 1965: U.S. supports anti-Communists in Dominican Republic.
20. 1963–1973: U.S. participates in Vietnam War.
21. 1966: Cultural Revolution in China
22. 1969: U.S.S.R. and Chinese border clashes
23. 1968: U.S.S.R. invades Czechoslovakia.
24. 1973: U.S. helps overthrow pro-Communist government in Chile.
25. 1979: U.S.S.R. invades Afghanistan.
26. 1980s: U.S. supports anti-Communists in Nicaragua.

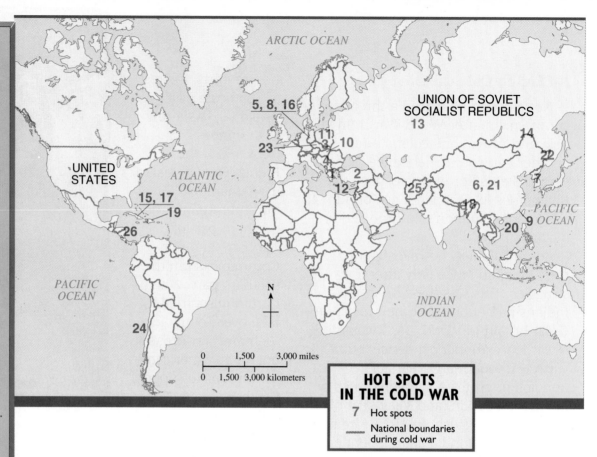

HOT SPOTS IN THE COLD WAR

7 Hot spots
——— National boundaries during cold war

Frustration in Eastern Europe

In 1956, Hungarians cut ties to the Soviet Union and wanted to restore democracy. Nikita Khrushchev (KROOS-chawf), the new Soviet ruler, sent tanks into Hungary to crush the uprising.

In 1968 the Communist government in Czechoslovakia wanted to grant people more freedom. This government wanted to allow non-Communist political parties and freedom of the press. Again, Soviet tanks moved in and crushed the hopes of the Czech people.

The greatest challenge to Soviet authority came from Poland. In the 1980s a protest movement was led by a workers' union called Solidarity.

The union was outlawed by the government, and many of its leaders were thrown into jail. Finally, in 1989, the government legalized the union and called for free elections. So where were the Soviet tanks this time?

Inside the Soviet Union

The answer could be found in the Soviet Union. Things were changing there. The Soviet social and economic fabric was breaking down. Mikhail Gorbachev (mee kah EEL gor buh-CHAWF), the new Soviet leader, saw this and tried to correct it.

Gorbachev began a policy called *glasnost* (GLAHS nust). He announced that Soviets could now see movies and read books that had once been

 glasnost A policy of openness in the Soviet Union that resulted in less secrecy about problems and weaknesses in Soviet society

forbidden. Soviets were also given freedom of speech. Gorbachev wanted people to speak out about social problems in the Soviet Union so that these problems could be corrected. He even suggested that non-Communist candidates be allowed to run for office.

The End of the Communist Empire

These changes rocked the foundations of communism in Europe. There was no stopping change now.

In November 1989 the East German government announced that it would no longer stop people from entering West Germany. The gates in the Berlin Wall were opened. Millions of East Germans rushed into West Germany. Many paused long enough to help smash the hated wall to bits. Eleven months later, on October 3, 1990, East Germany and West Germany were joined to form the democratic Federal Republic of Germany. All the other Communist regimes in Eastern Europe fell as well.

The end came to Communist rule in the Soviet Union, too. Gorbachev had given Soviet citizens a taste of freedom. The Communists were kicked out of power, and the Soviet Union itself collapsed. In 1991 the 15 Soviet republics declared their own independence. The cold war between the Soviet Union and Western nations was over. The West had won because it was better governed, more prosperous, and more able to deal with change.

▼ During the move away from communism in the Soviet Union, people tore down statues that reminded them of past leaders, such as Lenin.

SHOW WHAT YOU KNOW!

REFOCUS
COMPREHENSION

1. Explain what Churchill meant when he said that an iron curtain had descended across the European continent.

2. What are two ways in which nations gained independence during the cold war? Give an example for each way.

THINK ABOUT IT
CRITICAL THINKING

Write a paragraph or two explaining how you think people in Hungary felt when Soviet tanks rolled into their country in 1956.

WRITE ABOUT IT
ACTIVITY

Put yourself in the place of a person living in East Berlin after the Berlin Wall was built. Write a letter to a friend, explaining how your life has changed.

CHALLENGE TO AMERICAN VALUES

FOCUS *In the late 1940s, Stalin's broken promises and the growing Soviet threat forced the United States to build up its defense against the "Communist menace."*

Stalin's Broken Promises

Joseph Stalin was not a man of his word. He would promise one thing and then do something else. Americans discovered this the hard way.

In 1945, President Franklin D. Roosevelt went to Yalta, in southern Russia, to meet with Stalin and Great Britain's Winston Churchill. The three leaders discussed the fate of Eastern Europe after the war. At the time, the Soviet army occupied Eastern Europe.

▼ The hammer and sickle on the Soviet flag stand for united peasants and workers. The star is a symbol of communism.

Stalin argued that the Soviet Union needed to control the area for its own protection. Roosevelt and Churchill, however, wanted the people of Eastern Europe to have free elections to choose their leaders and form of government. In the end the Soviet dictator agreed to hold free elections as soon as possible.

It didn't take Stalin long to break his promise. He did not trust Churchill and Roosevelt, fearing that they planned to invade the Soviet Union. Just 13 days after the Yalta agreement was signed, the Soviets set up a Communist government in Romania. By the late 1940s the Soviets had forcefully installed Communist governments throughout Eastern Europe.

The Truman Doctrine

Things looked bad in southern Europe as well. Communists threatened to take over Greece and Turkey. The new American President, Harry S Truman, thought that it was important for communism to be kept within its existing borders. So he proposed to give military aid to any country that faced a Communist takeover.

"I believe," Truman told Congress, "that it must be the policy of the United States to support free peoples who are resisting [Communist] pressure." This new policy, called the Truman Doctrine, gave support to Greece and Turkey and helped to keep them out of Communist hands.

The Marshall Plan

What about Western Europe? The economies of these countries were in ruins after the war. How would Americans react to the Communist menace there? The answer was the Marshall Plan, named after U.S. Secretary of State George Marshall.

Under this plan, American taxpayers spent billions of dollars rebuilding Western Europe. Americans wanted to help their allies and West Germany recover from the war. They also wanted to share their American ideals, maintain democratic institutions, and provide markets for Western capitalism. The plan worked. Western Europe did not fall to the Communists.

Americans also offered aid to Eastern Europe and the Soviet Union. Stalin, however, flatly turned down the offer of aid. He saw the Marshall Plan as an attempt by the United States to lure Eastern Europeans away from communism. The air was now chillier than ever.

The Berlin Airlift

In 1948, Stalin tried to drive the Western powers out of West Berlin. Remember that West Berlin was inside

▲ Winston Churchill, Franklin Roosevelt, and Joseph Stalin met at Yalta in 1945.

▼ The stripes on the flag of the United States stand for the original 13 colonies. The stars represent the 50 states.

East Germany—behind the iron curtain. All of its supplies had to be brought into the city by truck or train through East Germany. Stalin, breaking yet another promise, blockaded all of the roads and railroads into West Berlin, which prevented the delivery of any supplies to the city.

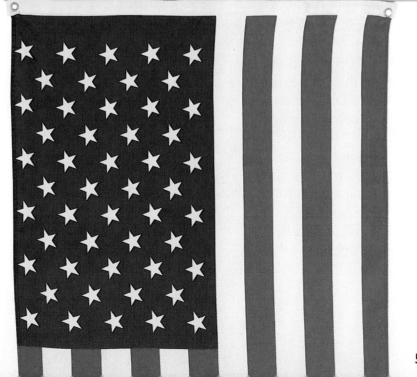

What could the Americans do? They could fight the Soviets, but that might cost the lives of countless Americans. They could give in and let Stalin have his way, but that would be an act of cowardice. Or they could fly supplies in over the blockade. For nearly a year, that's what planes did. In the end, the Soviets realized that the Western powers were going to keep up the Berlin airlift indefinitely. So in May 1949 they lifted the blockade of roads and railroads.

The United States Builds Alliances

To make sure that it had the support of other countries in its fight against communism, the United States began to put together alliances. In 1949 the United States, Canada, and ten Western European nations formed the North Atlantic Treaty Organization (NATO). Members of NATO agreed that an attack on one member would be considered an attack on all members. The United States also set up the Southeast Asian Treaty Organization (SEATO) to defend democracy in Asia. The Soviet Union followed with its own alliance, the Warsaw Pact, which included the Soviet Union and the nations it dominated in Eastern Europe.

(Below) Flowers in front of the Airlift Memorial in Berlin honor pilots who lost their lives when they delivered supplies.

(Right) The Voice of America broadcast propaganda supporting Western views. ▶

War of Words and Money

As we have seen, the cold war was fought largely with words and money. Each side wanted to win the hearts and minds of people around the world. The United States used radio broadcasts through the Voice of America and Radio Free Europe to bring its message to people in Eastern Europe and elsewhere. It established the **Peace Corps** (kor), an organization of mostly young volunteer workers, to help people in developing countries around the world.

Americans also used money to fight communism. The Alliance for Progress was set up in 1961. This program, a kind of Marshall Plan for Central and South America, offered aid to countries in Central and South America to encourage them not to accept communism. The United States sent billions of dollars to help those areas. Still, many Americans thought it was worth the price if it reduced the appeal of communism.

The Cost of Victory

The cold war cost the Americans dearly. Trillions of dollars were spent preparing for a possible war with the Soviet Union. This money might have been spent on other things. But most Americans were willing to make

⭐ **Peace Corps** A U.S. agency that provides skilled volunteers to assist people in developing areas abroad

A Peace Corps volunteer works with young children. ▶

whatever sacrifices were needed to defeat communism.

The Soviet Union, in turn, spent vast sums of money on its military. But while the American economy could take the strain, the Soviet economy couldn't. This **arms race** helped to destroy the Soviet economy. When the cold war ended, it was Western ideals—democracy and economic freedom—that Eastern European countries chose to embrace.

⭐ *arms race*   A competition between the United States and the U.S.S.R. to have a superior military force

In 1989 the most visible symbol of communism—the Berlin Wall—fell. Joyous crowds of people tore it down while puzzled East German soldiers stood by. By the 1990s virtually all of the European countries had chosen their own form of government or were working toward that goal.

▼ Joyful Germans celebrate the fall of the Berlin Wall.

1. What were two promises that Joseph Stalin broke?

2. Explain how the Truman Doctrine, the Marshall Plan, and the Alliance for Progress helped in the fight against communism.

THINK ABOUT IT
CRITICAL THINKING

How would life in the United States have been different if Americans had not spent so much money to fight communism?

WRITE ABOUT IT
ACTIVITY

With a partner, make a poster that could have been used to support the American point of view on communism or the Soviet point of view on American democracy.

THE SPACE RACE

FOCUS *The competition between the Soviet Union and the United States extended into space. The space race became a test to see whether a dictatorship or a democracy would put a man on the moon first.*

"ONE GIANT LEAP"

After losing early rounds, the Americans scored a knockout punch by putting the first man on the moon. On July 16, 1969, *Apollo 11* was launched. Aboard it were three astronauts—Neil Armstrong, Edwin "Buzz" Aldrin, and Michael Collins.

Four days later, Armstrong stepped out of his landing craft and onto the surface of the moon. The world watched on TV as he said, "That's one small step for a man, one giant leap for mankind." Armstrong and Aldrin planted an American flag on the landing site. The moon landing was a scientific success. It was a pretty good political victory, too.

FIRST IN SPACE

On October 4, 1957, the Soviets launched *Sputnik*, the first artificial Earth satellite, into space. The news shocked Americans, who started asking tough questions. Were the Soviets smarter than we were? Was the Soviet Union using *Sputnik* to spy on us? Had we grown too soft to win the cold war?

Americans didn't like to play second fiddle to anyone. So they pressed harder with their own space program. They wanted to catch up to the Soviets. In 1958 the United States launched its own satellite. Round one of the space race, however, had been won by the Soviets.

FIRST MAN IN SPACE

Round two also went to the Soviets. On April 12, 1961, they put the first man in space aboard *Vostok I*. The man was Yuri Gagarin, a 27-year-old cosmonaut. News of Gagarin's successful Earth orbit delighted the Soviets. However, it was a bitter disappointment to Americans. They had wanted to be the first to put a person in orbit.

On February 20, 1962, astronaut John Glenn was launched into orbit. Aboard the *Friendship 7*, Glenn orbited Earth three times. Americans danced in the streets. They honored Glenn with a ticker-tape parade through New York City. The space race was getting closer.

1957
Soviets launch first satellite

1961
Yuri Gagarin is first man in space

1969
Americans put first man on moon

1975
Soviets and Americans link up in space

1983
Sally Ride is first American woman in space

1955   1960   1965   1970   1975   1980   1985

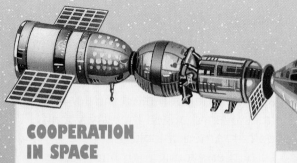

COOPERATION IN SPACE

The United States and the Soviet Union may have been cold war enemies on Earth, but they were becoming friends in space. On July 15, 1975, the Americans launched a three-man Apollo spaceship. On the same day, the Soviets sent up a two-man Soyuz spaceship. Two days later, the spacecraft linked up in space. The three astronauts and the two cosmonauts worked together to conduct a series of scientific experiments.

Known as the Apollo-Soyuz Test Project, it was the first time the two superpowers had held a joint space mission. People hoped that such international cooperation would promote more peaceful relations back on Earth.

THE SPACE SHUTTLE AND WOMEN

On April 12, 1981, the space shuttle *Columbia* blasted into space. The shuttle was the first reusable American spaceship. When the mission was over, *Columbia* flew back to Earth and landed just like a jet plane.

Later, in 1983, the space shuttle *Challenger* carried Sally Ride into orbit. She was the first American woman in space. The Soviets, on the other hand, had always included women in their space program. The first Soviet woman in space was Valentina Tereshkova, way back in 1963. It seems that the Americans had finally caught up to the Soviets on that score as well.

SHOW WHAT YOU KNOW!

REFOCUS
COMPREHENSION

1. Why were Americans upset when the Soviets launched *Sputnik*?

2. Why was the moon landing of *Apollo 11* so important to Americans?

THINK ABOUT IT
CRITICAL THINKING

Explain why you think a joint Soviet-American space mission might help promote more peaceful relations on Earth.

WRITE ABOUT IT
ACTIVITY

Talk to adults who were alive in 1957 or 1969. Ask them to tell you how they felt when *Sputnik* was launched or when astronauts first landed on the moon. Write a summary of what they tell you.

THE CULTURE OF THE SIXTIES

FOCUS *The decade of the 1960s was a time of cultural upheaval. Everything—from music to fashion to politics to civil rights—changed greatly.*

A Look Back

One of the top songs from the year 1960 was "What's the Matter With Kids Today?" Adults laughed at the song's lyrics: *Why can't they be like we were, perfect in every way?* These adults didn't know how lucky they were. Young people in 1960 were pretty tame and respectful toward authority.

To many people, the song would have been far more appropriate in 1970. By that time, adults *really* didn't know what was the matter with kids. In ten short years, young people had helped turn the world upside down. The **youth culture** of the 1960s changed many people's taste in music, clothes, art, and food. Young people also challenged old ideas about race, war, patriotism, and women.

Beatlemania

The Beatles didn't just come to the United States in 1964, they *invaded* it. These four mop-haired rock singers came from Liverpool, England. They brought with them "Beatlemania," a craze that had already swept Europe. Everywhere the Beatles went, young people flocked to hear their socially challenging and fun-filled music. The Beatles even changed the way young people in America looked.

Until then, young men had worn their hair above their ears. Now they started wearing it longer, just like the Beatles did. Long hair became the fashion for both men and women in the 1960s. Young people saw it as a sign of youth and independence. Many young people also began to wear clothes like those that the Beatles wore.

▲ In the 1960s, buttons were used to express opinions. Can you guess what these buttons stand for?

▼ The Beatles—John Lennon, Ringo Starr, Paul McCartney, and George Harrison—were popular with young people who enjoyed the bright colors and zany patterns of the animated Beatle movie shown here.

⭐ **youth culture** The ideas, customs, skills, and arts of young people

Fashion and Food

Actually, the Beatles' hair was quite short—at least compared with hair in the late 1960s. By then, many young men wore their hair so long it fell over their shoulders and down their backs. Many African Americans let their hair grow in a natural style called an Afro. Some worried barbers rented billboard space that screamed the message "Get a Haircut!"

The fashion slogan for the late 1960s was "Anything goes." T-shirts, stockings, jackets, and body paint came in every imaginable color. Many young people—often called hippies or flower children—wore beads, Navajo headbands, and flowers in their hair. They wore floppy bell-bottomed pants and long skirts. Some daring young women wore shorter and shorter skirts. Some young people of the 1960s deliberately wore clothes and colors that shocked the older generation.

Young people even rejected the food their parents ate. Many of them didn't want meat and potatoes anymore. Some young people became vegetarians because eating meat meant killing animals, which they thought was wrong. Some demanded all-natural food—without added chemicals, preservatives, or artificial color. And some began eating foods that their parents had never heard of—yogurt, granola, and bean curd.

▲ Young people wore buttons to protest the war in Vietnam.

Race and Protest

In the 1960s, some young people—both black and white—fought for **civil rights**. This battle took place largely in the South. Black Americans there were being denied many of their civil rights. For example, they were often denied the right to vote. Some restaurants wouldn't serve them. African Americans could not swim in "whites-only" sections of public beaches or drink from "white" drinking fountains.

People of all ages fought for civil rights, but young people often played a key role. Black college students staged a **sit-in** demonstration at a lunch counter in North Carolina. White college students rode freedom buses with black students to protest laws

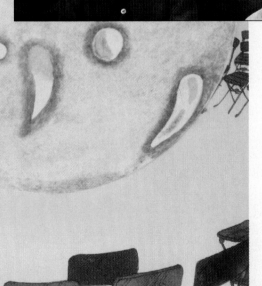

⭐ **civil rights** Rights guaranteeing equal treatment of all U.S. citizens with respect to life, liberty, and property, and to the protection of the law
sit-in A method of protesting a policy in which demonstrators sit in, and refuse to leave, a public place

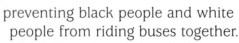

preventing black people and white people from riding buses together. They also held wade-ins at "white" beaches and read-ins at "white" libraries. Such efforts helped to produce the Civil Rights Act of 1964 and the Voting Rights Act of 1965.

War and Protest

When the United States first sent troops into Vietnam, most Americans thought it was a good idea. After all, Americans had been able to contain communism in Greece, Turkey, Korea, and West Berlin. But Vietnam was different. By 1968 the war was out of control. Thousands of Americans and Vietnamese were dying.

Again, some young people took a stand. They sang peace songs. They staged sit-ins to show their disapproval of the war. Many young men refused to serve in the armed forces. In November 1969, more than 250,000 people marched on Washington, D.C. At the time, it was the largest protest in American history. Young people in Europe also demonstrated against the war.

Many young people were committed to peace, but they went to college and held jobs. Others simply dropped out. Feeling that they couldn't change society, they just washed their hands of it. Some lived in communes. Others left the country to live in Canada, Europe, or Asia. Still others chose to live on the fringes of society, taking odd jobs here and there to support themselves.

▲ Casual dress, unconventional transportation, and protest marches were typical of young people of the 1960s.

The Role of Television

Television played a huge role in turning people against the Vietnam War. Never before had people seen a real war on TV. But there it was—wounded soldiers,

burning villages, and dead bodies. Across the country, night after night, it was the same thing. Before the Vietnam War, television had been used for entertainment. Suddenly in the 1960s it was providing a front-row seat to a bloody and seemingly endless war. By 1969, many Americans who had once supported the war were against it.

Protest marches and candlelight vigils in the 1960s helped influence American attitudes toward the Vietnam War.

Women and Protest

Women also began to protest. They believed that they had been denied their civil rights. Women, many of whom fought against racism and the Vietnam War, began thinking about their own lives. Beginning in the late 1960s, women demanded rights that were equal to those of men.

In 1966 a group of feminists began challenging old ideas. They formed the National Organization for Women (NOW), which worked to improve the lives of women. One of the goals of feminists was to give women and men equal opportunities by overcoming the stereotypes of women's roles and men's roles. Feminists started demanding jobs that only men had done before— driving trucks, building skyscrapers, or working as managers and executives. They also fought for equal pay for doing the same kind of work as men. The great decade for women's rights was the 1970s, but the seed was planted in the protest movements of the 1960s.

For almost anyone who was a young person then, the 1960s marked a turning point. By using protests, young people were able to influence many aspects of life. In a number of cases, it was young people who changed the thinking of people around the world.

SHOW WHAT YOU KNOW!

REFOCUS
COMPREHENSION

1. What are two areas in which the Beatles influenced young people?

2. What are two ways in which race protests and war protests were alike?

THINK ABOUT IT
CRITICAL THINKING

Explain why you agree or disagree with the idea that the song title "What's the Matter With Kids Today?" accurately describes the young people of the 1960s.

WRITE ABOUT IT
ACTIVITY

Take yourself back to the 1960s. Write a newspaper editorial explaining your views on a topic such as civil rights, women's rights, war, or Beatlemania.

SUMMING UP

1 DO YOU REMEMBER. . .
COMPREHENSION

1. Why weren't Americans willing to risk all-out war with the Soviet Union?

2. What were some "hot spots" of the cold war?

3. What was the purpose of the Berlin Wall?

4. What event symbolized the end of the cold war?

5. What was the purpose of NATO?

6. What effect did the arms race have on the Soviet economy?

7. What did the Peace Corps, the Voice of America, and the Alliance for Progress all have in common?

8. What did people hope the Apollo-Soyuz Test Project might lead to?

9. What were some of the ideas that young people in the 1960s challenged?

10. How did television affect America's support for the war in Vietnam?

2 SKILL POWER
RECOGNIZING PROPAGANDA

Use old newspapers or magazines as resources to find two examples of propaganda. For each example you find, explain how it tries to convince you to believe something. Share your examples of propaganda with your classmates.

3 WHAT DO YOU THINK?
CRITICAL THINKING

1. Why did the Allies divide Germany and Berlin after World War II?

2. Why didn't the Soviets send their tanks into Poland to stop the free elections there in 1989?

3. How did the United States' experiences with Joseph Stalin after World War II affect our later relationships with the Soviet Union?

4. Does the space race with the Soviets remind you of any competitions that the United States is now involved in with other countries? Explain.

5. In your opinion what was the most important change that young people of the 1960s brought about?

4 SAY IT, WRITE IT, USE IT
VOCABULARY

Select at least six terms from the list below. For each term you choose, write a few sentences telling how the term relates to the 1960s.

arms race	iron curtain
capitalist	Peace Corps
civil rights	regime
cold war	sit-in
domino theory	youth culture
glasnost	

5 GEOGRAPHY AND YOU
MAP STUDY

1. Which countries controlled Germany at the end of World War II?

2. Which zone did not border the Soviet zone?

3. How far inside the Soviet zone was Berlin?

4. Compare this map with a map of Germany today. What differences do you see?

GERMANY AFTER WW II

Berlin Airlift, 1948–1949

6 TAKE ACTION
CITIZENSHIP

The 1960s were a time of protests, both peaceful and violent. While peaceful protests can be a good way to publicize issues and influence events, violent protests lead to bloodshed and destruction. Make up a list of rules that you think will keep a protest peaceful. What should protesters do? What shouldn't they do? Does your town or city government already have guidelines? If possible, describe a protest that actually occurred recently, telling what the participants did to keep it peaceful.

7 GET CREATIVE
MUSIC CONNECTION

With a group of classmates, find and play Beatles songs or other songs from the 1960s that influenced youth culture. Study the lyrics of these songs. Then give an oral report on one or more of these songs, telling how they might have led people to change their tastes or challenge old ideas. If possible, have the songs playing in the background as you speak.

LOOKING AHEAD The end of the cold war did not bring peace to the world. In the next chapter, find out what conflicts are continuing.

THE WORLD

Worldwide wars broke out twice in this century. As the twentieth century draws to a close, there is still war around the world. But it's of a different sort. In this chapter you'll learn what factors have contributed to conflict within nations.

CONTENTS

Read page 571 to see how conflicts have led to tensions around the world.

IN CONFLICT

These books give you a close-up look at how people are affected by conflict around the world. Read one that interests you and fill out a book-review form.

READ AND RESEARCH

I Dream of Peace by children of former Yugoslavia
(Harper Collins Publishers, 1994)
The children of former Yugoslavia have seen the darkness of war. Their relatives have been killed and their homes have been destroyed. In this book the children share their dreams of peace through writing and art. *(nonfiction)*
• *You can read a selection from this book on page 578.*

New Kids in Town: Oral Histories of Immigrant Teens by Janet Bode (Scholastic, 1989)
Meet Amitabh from India, Anna from Greece, Abdul from Afghanistan, and other immigrant teens from around the world. Read their stories about the successes and hardships they face in the United States. *(biography)*

Water Wars by Olga Cossi (Silver Burdett Press, 1993)
Read all about a worldwide environmental and economic issue—preserving water. Discover the different ways in which people everywhere can conserve this precious natural resource. *(nonfiction)*

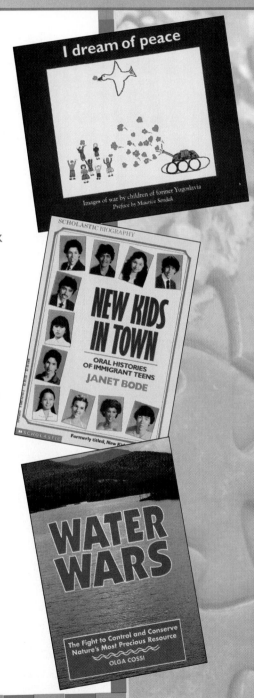

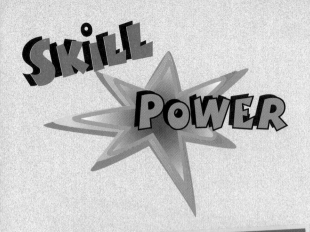

SKILL POWER

Evaluating Arguments

Deciding whether information and opinions are relevant and consistent will help you evaluate arguments.

UNDERSTAND IT

Have you ever argued with someone and not been able to come up with good reasons to support your ideas? Did you ever want to kick yourself the next day because you came up with a great argument—or realize that the person you had been arguing with had not used correct information to support his or her ideas? If so, you know the importance of taking some time to evaluate both sides of an argument.

EXPLORE IT

When people disagree over issues, they should support their arguments with factual information. Some facts are relevant because they support the main point of an argument. Other facts are irrelevant because they have little or nothing to do with the point of the argument.

Some information is consistent, which means it is logical and agrees with the other ideas presented. Inconsistent information does not agree with other ideas presented. Deciding whether information is relevant and consistent helps us evaluate, or judge the worth of, an argument.

In the paragraphs below, irrelevant and inconsistent arguments are underscored. Can you tell which is which?

The United Nations is working on a global disaster-reduction plan. Experts from all over the world would predict, monitor, and prevent disasters whenever possible. Some people are opposing this important plan. They need to be persuaded to support it.

Over the past 20 years, natural disasters have killed more than 3 million people. Because the world population is increasing, there has been a steady increase in the number of deaths these disasters cause. <u>That is why everyone agrees that a global strategy is needed to predict, prevent, and relieve disaster-related suffering</u>.

Improved monitoring and communications are already limiting the damage done by hurricanes. Environmental scientists know how to prevent flooding in some areas, too. Earthquakes are difficult to escape, but better monitoring devices and building codes are helping to save lives. <u>Wars also cause mass movements of people, bringing on medical disasters</u>. However, the U.N. plan is needed to expand research to find even better ways of saving lives.

▲ Floods are one kind of natural disaster.

Work with a partner to decide on a topic that has two sides. Go to the library to learn all you can about both sides of your topic. Then write a summary supporting one side of the argument, while your partner writes a summary supporting the opposite side.

Ask your partner to read your summary to check for irrelevant ideas or inconsistencies. Then use a computer or your best handwriting to copy your summary to share with the class.

CHILDREN SHOULD GET ALLOWANCES THAT EQUAL THEIR AGES

Some financial experts believe that children should get allowances that equal their ages. This means that a 12-year-old would get $12 a week. This doesn't mean that the child would get to spend all that money. It would be put into three accounts.

1. *Long-term savings* This money would be for big things, such as college.
2. *Short-term savings* This money would be saved for special things, such as a new bike.
3. *Spending money* This is the money you could spend on anything, such as video games or snacks.

Children would have to earn the money. They would have a list of jobs that had to be done every week. If they didn't do the jobs, they wouldn't get paid. It would be just like a real job. That's why experts think it is a good idea. It teaches kids to be responsible with work and money.

Side B

CHILDREN SHOULD NOT GET BIG ALLOWANCES

Should children get big allowances? Many experts say no. They believe that

1. Children should do chores because they are members of a family, not because they are being paid.
2. Most families, particularly those with several children, cannot afford to give children a lot of allowance money.
3. Children can learn to manage money with a small amount. Most children do not need their own money until they are teenagers. Then they can get real experience with money by working at a part-time job.

Side A

SKILL POWER SEARCH *This chapter discusses issues that affect our world. Give your opinion on one of these issues, using consistent and relevant arguments.*

Setting the Scene

★ KEY TERMS

global culture
global village
refugee
terrorism

A SHRINKING WORLD

FOCUS *As the world grows smaller and smaller, strong forces tend to bring people and cultures closer together. At the same time, other powerful forces are pulling them apart.*

Cultures Intermingle

The world is getting smaller, much smaller. It is not, of course, physically shrinking. It just seems that way. A Concorde jet now zips from Washington, D.C., to Paris, France, in about three hours. A fax sent from Cairo gets to Chicago seconds later. A personal computer can link you to the rest of the world through networks such as the World Wide Web.

The world is shrinking in other ways as well. Whether you're in Beijing, Bangkok, or Boston, you can find a McDonald's restaurant. Under the golden arches, you can order the same Big Mac in China as in the United States. This is an example of our **global culture**.

Music and fashion are parts of global culture, too. The music of top rock bands from the United States and Great Britain tumbles out of boom boxes from Tokyo to Johannesburg to Prague. People around the world stand in line for the same concerts. From New York to New Delhi, many young people wear the same uniform of T-shirts and jeans. At the same time, world music from Africa, Asia, and

Latin America influences the sound that musicians create in Europe and the United States.

 Beijing, China, has the largest McDonald's restaurant in the world.

Tension in the Global Village

People once thought that the spread of a global culture would wipe out regional and national differences. Faster communication and transportation would turn the world into a kind of **global village**. The people of the global village would live in friendship and harmony.

In some ways the world has become a global village. Thanks to technology, people in many nations

 global culture Ways of living that are shared by many people around the world

★ *global village* The idea that people across the world can interact as easily as do people in a small town

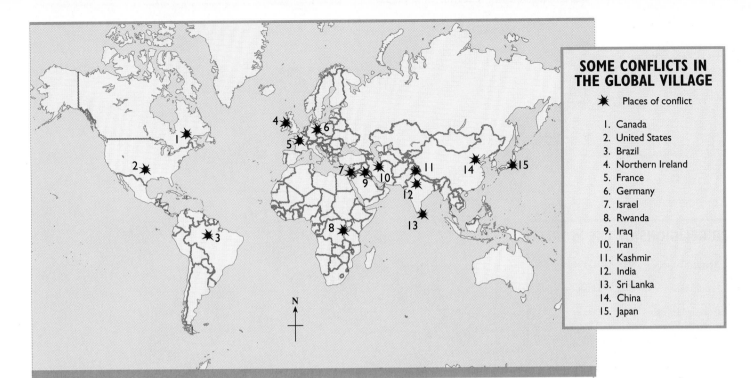

can share the same experiences. For example, millions of people around the globe can watch the same World Cup soccer game at the same time.

In other ways, the world isn't a global village at all. Often the meeting of different cultures has created tensions and has led to violence. The map on this page shows some of the places throughout the world where conflicts between cultures have occurred.

A Clash of Cultures

In many places and to many local leaders, the new global culture does not look global at all. It looks American—in food, in clothes, in ideas. In fact, much of this culture comes from western Europe. But to people in Asia, the Middle East, and Africa, the culture looks American. Some call it McWorld.

Like U.S. rock music, U.S. films and television programs are popular around the world. Again this has two sides. For example, as apartheid was ending in South Africa in the 1980s, one of the most popular imported TV programs was *The Cosby Show*. It was a story about an upper middle class African American family that lived in New York City.

On the other hand, leaders in many countries are angry and disturbed by the changes. They fear that their own cultural values have been invaded and taken over by ideas from the West—especially from the United States.

Defending Traditional Ways

Resistance to global culture is strong in some parts of the non-Western world. In Iran, for example, the 1979 revolution was led by religious leaders.

People around the world may eat the same fast foods you do. ▶

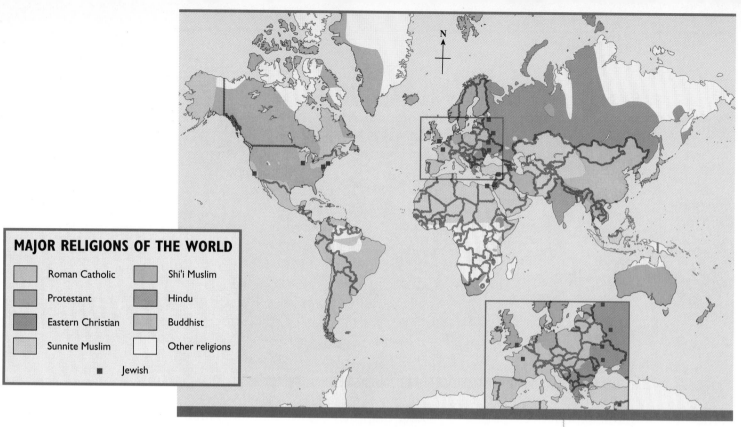

MAJOR RELIGIONS OF THE WORLD

- Roman Catholic
- Protestant
- Eastern Christian
- Sunnite Muslim
- Shi'i Muslim
- Hindu
- Buddhist
- Other religions
- ■ Jewish

One of the revolt's main goals was to end Western influence and return to Islamic tradition. Iranian women, many of whom wore Western clothes, now had to wear the traditional veil and long robes. The leaders regarded Western ways as evil. The revolt was necessary to protect their culture.

Similarly, China's Communist officials have harshly suppressed students and others who want Western-style democracy. They also resist Western cultural influences such as rock music.

Making a Living

Around the world, people want to live in peace and provide for their families. In many countries this has become very difficult.

Up to the mid-1950s, most people in the world lived by farming. Now fast-growing populations demand more food and need more jobs. To make a living, people flock from farming areas to cities. Mexico City, for example, is the fastest-growing city in the world. In 1990 it had 20 million people. By the year 2000 it may have 30 million. As a result, housing, services, and jobs are harder to find.

As poorer nations try to develop their economies, other conflicts arise. For centuries, small bands of people have lived in the Amazon rain forest of Brazil. In the last decade, when farmers and mining companies went to work there, many of the native people were killed or died from disease. Their ancient cultures were destroyed as large parts of the rain forests were cut down.

People on the Move

Millions of people in the world's poorer countries have left their

PACIFIC NATIONS

AUSTRALIA
NEW ZEALAND
51,039

homes. The graph below shows immigration from Asia, Africa, and Latin America to the United States. Europe and Canada have also sent large numbers of immigrants. These people hope for a better way of life in the richer industrial countries. Another huge group of people move around the world as **refugees**, escaping war or political unrest.

In 1990, foreigners made up 3.3 percent of the population of Great Britain. In the United States, the number was 8.5 percent. It was 16.3 percent in Switzerland. Sometimes the newcomers are welcomed. In many places, though, their increasing numbers cause conflict.

About 5 million North African immigrants live and work in France.

⭐ *refugee*   A person who flees war or political or religious persecution

Most are Muslims from France's former colonies. Many non-Muslim people fear that French Muslim influences will weaken French culture.

In Germany, dislike of foreign workers has exploded into violence. Some young Germans have attacked Turkish workers and burned their homes. In the United States, conflicts arise between local workers and immigrants from Latin America or Southeast Asia. Local people are sometimes angry at those who enter the country illegally and take low-paying jobs, appearing to deprive citizens of work.

Conflicts Over Religion

The map on page 572 shows the major religions practiced by people around the world. For many people, religion is one of the most important parts of their culture. They are willing

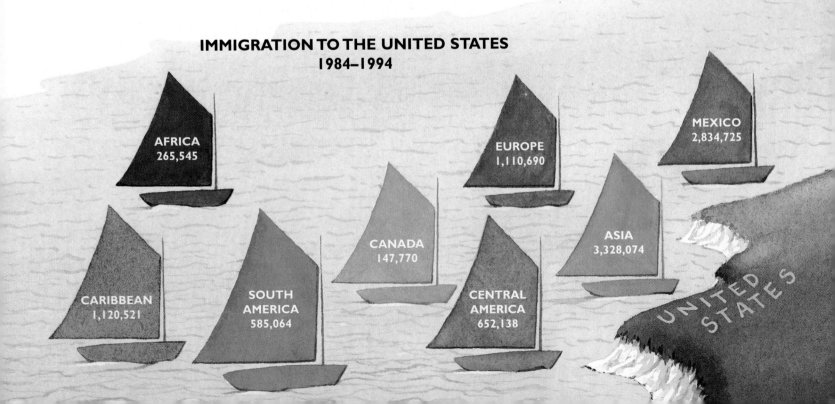

IMMIGRATION TO THE UNITED STATES
1984–1994

AFRICA 265,545

EUROPE 1,110,690

MEXICO 2,834,725

CANADA 147,770

ASIA 3,328,074

CARIBBEAN 1,120,521

SOUTH AMERICA 585,064

CENTRAL AMERICA 652,138

UNITED STATES

to fight to protect beliefs. Often religious beliefs become a part of political conflicts.

In Northern Ireland, fighting between Catholics and Protestants has gone on for centuries. Besides religion, the two sides disagree on the country's ties with Great Britain.

Conflicts and violence between Hindus and Muslims in India continue. Muslims in the Kashmir region of northern India are fighting for an independent state. Elsewhere in India, Hindu militants have attacked Muslims and destroyed their mosques.

Violence as a Weapon

Extreme beliefs, both political and religious, have been the cause of much violence in recent decades. Extremists often use violence simply to show their power. This is called **terrorism**. For example, in 1995 a federal building in Oklahoma City was destroyed by American terrorists. Some extreme Muslim groups use terrorism against those they consider enemies of Islam. One group was charged with the 1993 bombing of the

▲ Religious conflict caused destruction in the once beautiful Kashmir region of India.

▼ Many world leaders attended the funeral of Israel's prime minister.

World Trade Center in New York City.

In the Middle East, Arab and Israeli leaders have moved slowly toward peace. Yet to some Israelis, such plans seem like treason. In 1995 a young Israeli law student who wanted to stop the peace movement shot and killed Prime Minister Yitzhak Rabin.

In Japan the leader of a religious cult was charged with releasing poison gas in the Tokyo subway. It killed 12 people and sickened thousands more.

Nations Torn Apart

Differences between ethnic groups within nations have often literally torn the countries apart. Rival groups fight to control the government and to maintain their own cultures.

Several African nations have seen bloody civil wars between different peoples. One of the worst broke out in Rwanda (roo AHN duh). In 1994, Hutu soldiers there killed thousands of the rival Tutsis. More than 2 million

★ **terrorism** The use of force or threats to terrify and coerce

574

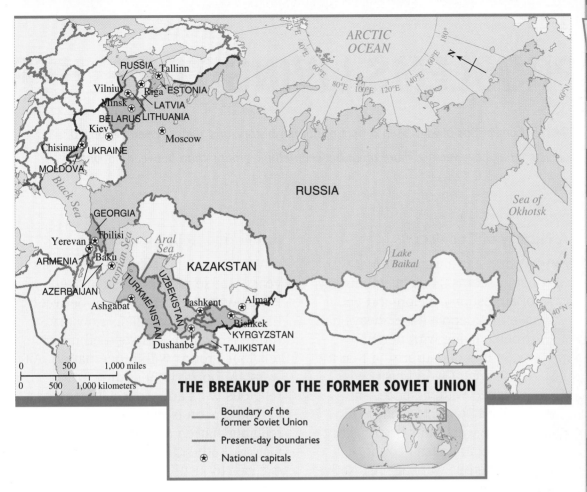

THE BREAKUP OF THE FORMER SOVIET UNION

- Boundary of the former Soviet Union
- Present-day boundaries
- ⊛ National capitals

REFOCUS
COMPREHENSION

1. What is it about American music, foods, clothes, and television that other cultures may find threatening?

2. Why has an increase in immigration led to resentment in the countries that take in the newcomers?

THINK ABOUT IT
CRITICAL THINKING

What might be the effects if some ethnic groups tried to separate from the United States?

WRITE ABOUT IT
ACTIVITY

Write a letter to the manager of a fast-food restaurant about to open in another country. Suggest actions he or she can take to avoid cultural problems.

Rwandans escaped to neighboring countries as refugees.

Around the world, groups of people have tried to establish separate ethnic identities. In Sri Lanka, fighting goes on between the government and Tamil separatists, who want their own nation. In Spain, Basques continue their fight for independence.

The former Soviet Union was made up of many ethnic groups. As the map shows, when it broke apart, many of those groups became independent nations. Sometimes splitting up is done peacefully. Czechs and Slovaks once lived together as the country of Czechoslovakia. Then, in 1993, the country divided. Today the Czech people live in the Czech Republic and the Slovaks live in Slovakia.

In Canada, people have turned to law instead of violence. Many of the French-speaking people in Quebec would like to separate themselves from the English-speaking part of Canada. A number of elections have been held, and more and more people are voting for separation.

A Tug of War

Clearly, many people are being pulled in two directions at once. As the world gets smaller, a global culture develops. It can bring many benefits. However, people still want to hold on to their traditions and independence.

PROBLEMS LIVING TOGETHER

FOCUS *Conflict has always been a part of human history, and things haven't changed. Conflicts today, however, are more often between ethnic groups than between nations.*

A History of Conflicts

The world has always been at war, or so it seems. Look at the history of almost any region and you'll see that people have always had trouble living with neighbors.

So it is not surprising that the time line of world history is studded with violence. The United States has fought nine major wars in its brief history. And that doesn't count numerous wars against Native Americans.

Most conflicts in the past few centuries have been between or among nations. The United States fought Great Britain twice. Russia fought Japan. Israel fought its Arab neighbors four times in a span of 25 years. Germany has fought France three times since 1870. And the French and British have probably lost track of the number of times they have gone to war with each other.

Ethnic and Religious Conflicts

Wars have not decreased in recent years. But something has changed. Fewer wars are being fought between nations. Instead, conflicts now are more likely to be between ethnic or religious groups within one nation. All wars are horrible. But ethnic or religious wars are especially heartless.

One reason is that ethnic or religious hatred often has a long history. Both sides can find plenty of excuses to justify their cruelty. Each side is forever getting even for something the other side did.

Many ethnic or religious conflicts have broken out in recent years. The list is depressingly long. It includes Ethiopia, Somalia, Iraq, Northern Ireland, Rwanda, India, and Sri Lanka.

Yugoslavia—A Case Study

One classic example of ethnic conflict is Yugoslavia. This country was unified in 1918 under Peter I, a Serbian king. The new nation combined six ethnic groups—Bosnian Muslims, Croats, Serbs, Macedonians, Montenegrins, and Slovenes. The people within this nation were also split along religious lines—Roman

◄ As the pictures on these pages show, children suffer the most when people can't live together in peace.

Catholic, Eastern Orthodox, and Muslim.

After World War II, Yugoslavia became a Communist country. It was then organized as a **federal republic**. The republics were divided more or less along ethnic lines. Marshal Tito, the Communist leader, kept a lid on ethnic differences.

Tito died in 1980. After that, things began to fall apart. The economy worsened. Unemployment hit 20 percent and inflation soared by 250 percent. Some ethnic groups began complaining that the federal government was favoring the other ethnic groups.

Ethnic Violence

Finally, in 1990, communism collapsed. Without its dictatorial rule, Yugoslavia quickly broke up along ethnic lines. Croatia and Slovenia declared independence in 1991. Serbia and Montenegro joined to create the new Federal Republic of Yugoslavia.

But old ethnic and religious divisions—long buried—began to surface again. Although the Serbs clashed with the Croats, the biggest trouble spot was Bosnia and Herzegovina (hert suh goh VEE nuh). Here Serbs lived with Muslims.

The Serbs tried to drive the Muslims out of Bosnia. Suddenly Serbs felt justified in attacking someone just because that person was a Bosnian Muslim. The scale of the violence shocked the rest of the world.

In 1995, at the prodding of the United States, representatives of the warring states met in Dayton, Ohio. A treaty was hammered out and later signed in Paris, with the hope that it would solve many of the problems.

⭐ *federal republic*   A government in which power is divided between a central authority and individual states

I Dream of Peace

By children of former Yugoslavia

I dream of peace

Images of war by children of former Yugoslavia
Preface by Maurice Sendak

Children in the war-torn areas of former Yugoslavia were asked to tell how they felt about the war. They expressed themselves in letters, poetry, and drawings. UNICEF (United Nations Children's Fund) collected the work from schools and refugee camps. Read what some of the children had to say.

War is here, but we await peace. We are in a corner of the world where nobody seems to hear us. But we are not afraid, and we will not give up.

Our fathers earn little, just barely enough to buy five kilos of flour a month. And we have no water, no electricity, no heat. We bear it all, but we cannot bear the hate and the evil.

Our teacher has told us about Anne Frank, and we have read her diary. After fifty years, history is repeating itself right here with this war, with the hate and the killing, and with having to hide to save your life.

We are only twelve years old. We can't influence politics and the war, but we want to live! And we want to stop this madness. Like Anne Frank fifty years ago, we wait for peace. She didn't live to see it. Will we?

Students from a fifth-grade class in Zenica

I am not a refugee, but I understand the fear and the suffering of the children.

My father is a Croat, my mother is a Serb, but I don't know who I am.

My brothers, my sisters, my grandparents, my aunts, and my uncles, all are in Croatia. I have not seen them since the start of this horrible war.

More than a year has passed since I heard their voices. And the only link between us are the letters, letters, only letters. . . .

Lepa, 11, from Belgrade

If I were President,
the tanks would be playhouses for the kids.
Boxes of candy would fall from the sky.
The mortars would fire balloons.
And the guns would blossom with flowers.

All the world's children
would sleep in a peace unbroken
by alerts or by shooting.

The refugees would return to their villages.
And we would start anew.

Roberto, 10, from Pula

If you want to read more about the feelings of these children and look at their artwork, check the book out of your school or public library.

SHOW WHAT YOU KNOW!

REFOCUS
COMPREHENSION

1. How are the borders of ethnic and religious conflicts different from those of other wars?

2. What problems in Yugoslavia led to war in the 1990s?

THINK ABOUT IT
CRITICAL THINKING

Why would other countries be reluctant to try to stop religious and ethnic wars?

WRITE ABOUT IT
ACTIVITY

Make your own page to add to the book *I Dream of Peace*. Create a painting or drawing and write a few lines to express your feelings about conflicts around the world.

CHANGING ECONOMIC DISTRIBUTION

FOCUS *Today, goods may be produced in factories on the opposite side of the world from where they will be sold. This new global economy has not changed the fact that there are rich and poor nations.*

Business Goes Worldwide

Just a few hundred years ago, almost everything a person needed was made locally. Then, slowly, national economies emerged as a result of the Industrial Revolution. Further improvements in production, transportation, and communication led to today's global economies.

Look at the example of bicycles. You might buy a mountain bike at your local cycle shop. But the labor and

SOME INTERNATIONAL TRADE GROUPS

Asia-Pacific Economic Co-operation (APEC)

European Union (EU)

Organization of Petroleum Exporting Countries (OPEC)

North American Free Trade Agreement (NAFTA)

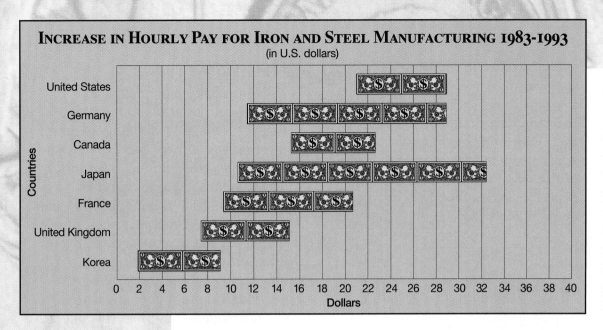

INCREASE IN HOURLY PAY FOR IRON AND STEEL MANUFACTURING 1983-1993
(in U.S. dollars)

Seeking Profits

Multinational corporations, like other businesses, want to make profits—the higher, the better. One way they can do this is to reduce the cost of labor. In today's global markets, that isn't hard to do.

Multinational corporations are almost always headquartered in **developed countries**, such as the United States, Germany, or Japan. These multinational corporations can move their factories to developing countries, such as Brazil, Guatemala, or the Philippines. Workers in such countries get paid much lower wages than workers in developed countries.

Jobs on the Move

This process of moving factories and jobs has been made easier by trade agreements such as the North America Free Trade Agreement (NAFTA). Under NAFTA, U.S. and Canadian companies can now easily move their operations south to Mexico. And there are good profit-making reasons to do so.

In Mexico, companies can hire a factory worker for $6 an hour. A

materials for this bike did not come from the local community. Instead this bike is the result of an international manufacturing effort. The steel alloy frame may have been made in Taiwan. The tires might have been manufactured in Singapore or India. The parts were assembled by workers in either China, Korea, or Mexico. Later, the bike was shipped to the company in the United States that put its name on it. Finally, the bike was shipped to your local shop.

As your bike zigzagged across the world, it tied together a number of economies. The result is a global economy. In such an economy, decisions that affect a person's job are no longer made by that person's neighbor. They are made by the managers of **multinational corporations** who might live on the other side of the world.

 multinational corporation   A company that does business in more than one country

developed country   A country with access to natural resources, an industrial base, an educated population, and advanced technology

similar worker in the United States or Canada might cost $20 an hour. Such a wage difference means that some U.S. and Canadian workers will lose their jobs to Mexican workers. This story is repeated in many other parts of the world. As part of a global economy, factory workers no longer enjoy the job security they once had.

Rich and Poor Nations

With factory jobs moving to developing nations, you might think that these nations would grow rich. But that is not the case. As the map shows, the **gross domestic product** varies greatly between nations.

First, the total number of new jobs usually isn't very high. Also, the wages paid for these workers are relatively low. So the wealth flowing into the developing country isn't that great. Second, the profit goes right back to the developed countries. This happens

gross domestic product The total value of all the goods and services produced in a year within the borders of a nation

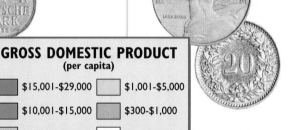

GROSS DOMESTIC PRODUCT
(per capita)

■ $15,001–$29,000	■ $1,001–$5,000
■ $10,001–$15,000	■ $300–$1,000
■ $5,001–$10,000	□ No data

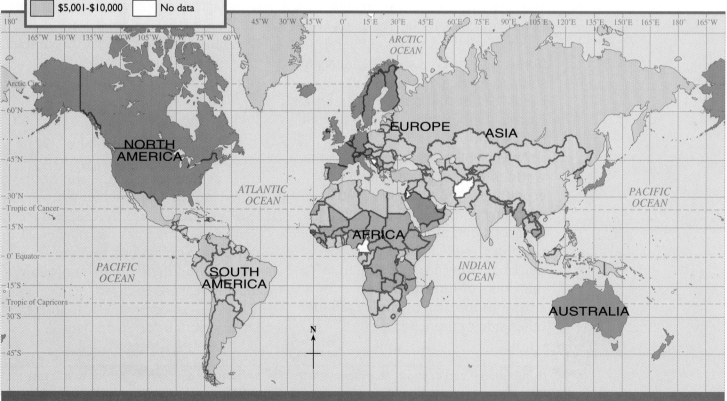

▲ There is a worldwide market for multinational products.

SHOW WHAT YOU
KNOW!

REFOCUS
COMPREHENSION

1. Why do factory workers in developed countries no longer have the job security they once had?

2. How is it that poor countries stay poor if jobs are moving there?

THINK ABOUT IT
CRITICAL THINKING

Why is it that developed countries tolerate immigrants in good economic times and resent them in hard economic times?

WRITE ABOUT IT
ACTIVITY

Write a letter to the editor of your school newspaper. Express your views on whether students should buy products made in the United States or in other parts of the world.

because people in the developing countries buy imported goods from the developed countries. These imported goods might include such items as televisions, cassette players, and electric fans. As a result the economic gap between high-income nations and low-income nations remains huge.

The Effects of Poverty

The effect of this gap between rich and poor nations can be seen in human terms. The average person in Japan can expect to live until the age of 79. The average person in Ethiopia, where poverty is widespread, can expect to live until the age of 47.

The crushing poverty felt in low-income countries hits women and children especially hard. It is estimated that 70 percent of the world's poor people are women. Each year, millions of them die of starvation or disease. Millions of their children also die. It is estimated that 5 million children under age 5 die each year from the devastating effects of poverty.

Sadly most poor nations are doomed to remain poor. One of the main reasons is overpopulation. No nation can grow richer if every gain in income is wiped out by a gain in population. The situation is getting worse, not better. In 1950 about 33 percent of the world's people lived in high-income countries. By the early twenty-first century, that number will drop to about 15 percent.

These are the harsh facts of economic life that have driven so many people to seek work in developed nations. These facts have also caused increased tension between the so-called haves and the have-nots of the world.

SUMMING UP

1 DO YOU REMEMBER...
COMPREHENSION

1. Why do the leaders of some countries oppose the move toward a global culture?

2. What aspects of Western culture have Chinese Communist officials suppressed?

3. How has the need to make a living affected the rain forests in Brazil?

4. In 1990, what percentage of the U.S. population was made up of newcomers?

5. What religious groups are in conflict in Northern Ireland? What groups are warring in India?

6. How have wars changed in recent years?

7. What six ethnic groups were combined when Yugoslavia was unified in 1918?

8. Why do multinational corporations tend to locate their factories in developing countries?

9. Why are some Americans and Canadians likely to lose their jobs because of NAFTA?

10. How is the percentage of the world's people in wealthy nations likely to change in the future?

2 SKILL POWER
EVALUATING ARGUMENTS

Choose one of the statements below. Then find information in this chapter to build a consistent argument to support the opinion.

- The development of a world culture will break down barriers between people.

- Ethnic differences can lead to violence when a country does not have a strong government.

- Only controlling population increase will close the gap between rich and poor nations.

3 WHAT DO YOU THINK?
CRITICAL THINKING

1. Why is traditional farming unlikely to support the economy of a country with a fast-growing population?

2. People of different religions generally get along in the United States. Why is this true when serious religious conflict is common in many other countries?

3. Do you think multinational corporations should have the right to make more money by firing workers in wealthy countries and hiring low-wage workers in developing countries? Why?

4. Why might limiting population growth help a developing nation become wealthier sooner?

5. Do you think it's important to narrow the gap between the rich and the poor nations? Why?

4 SAY IT, WRITE IT, USE IT
VOCABULARY

What do you think the world will be like in the year 2100? Assuming current trends continue, what might you see? Write a world forecast, using as many of the terms below as possible.

developed country gross domestic product
federal republic multinational corporation
global culture refugee
global village terrorism

5 GEOGRAPHY AND YOU
MAP STUDY

Study the map below to answer these questions.

1. Which is the northernmost country?

2. Which state is the southernmost country?

3. Which country has been divided by the 1995 peace plan?

THE FORMER YUGOSLAVIA

— Yugoslavia, 1990

— New boundary under peace plan, December 1995

⊛ National capitals

• Other cities

6 TAKE ACTION
CITIZENSHIP

For the most part, people of different religions and ethnic groups get along pretty well in the United States. Still, conflicts do arise from time to time. At the library, find magazine and newspaper stories about ethnic, racial, and religious conflicts in your region of the United States. Think about ways that these conflicts might be resolved. Keep in mind that members of groups usually want to keep their own traditions intact.

7 GET CREATIVE
LANGUAGE ARTS CONNECTION

Create a plan for a pen-pal organization that can reduce tensions between ethnic groups. Draw a flowchart to show what groups of children you might convince to correspond with each other. Write a sample letter to a pen pal, explaining your plan.

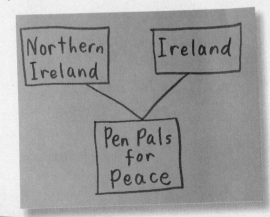

LOOKING AHEAD World peace has been a goal throughout history. In the next chapter you will learn about people working together.

THE WORLD

Our world has become smaller in many ways through international cooperation, communication, travel, and technology. In this chapter, find out how you fit into the world of today and of tomorrow.

▼ Turn to page 600 to read about virtual reality, which may affect the way we view the world.

CONTENTS

IN HARMONY

These books tell about the world we live in today. Read one that interests you and fill out a book-review form.

READ AND RESEARCH

Talking Peace **by Jimmy Carter** (Penguin USA, 1995)
Read how our former President Jimmy Carter continues to work for world peace through the Carter Center, which he established in Atlanta, Georgia. Try to accept his challenge to become involved in one project that will make the world a better place. *(nonfiction)*

The Endangered World **edited by Scott E. Morris**
(Chelsea House Publishers, 1993)
Learning to read the special-purpose maps in this atlas will help you to understand the global effects of population growth, endangered species, toxic waste, and other serious environmental problems. *(reference)*

Computers of the Future **by David Darling** (Dillon Press, 1996)
In the twenty-first century, computers will affect our lives even more than they do today. Read about the possibilities for intelligent robots and computer chips that will give us instant knowledge. *(nonfiction)*

Rescue Mission: Planet Earth **by Children of the World in association with the United Nations** (Kingfisher Books, 1994)
Our planet is in trouble—this fact is clear to the children around the world who contributed to this book. Find out how you can join the rescue mission outlined in the 1992 Earth Summit document. *(nonfiction)*

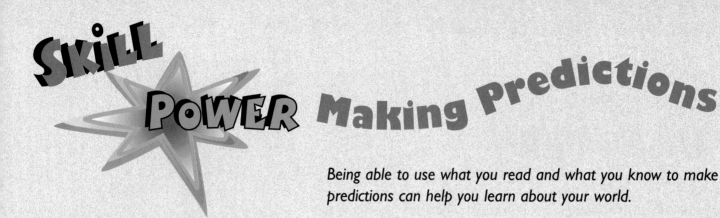

SKILL POWER Making Predictions

Being able to use what you read and what you know to make predictions can help you learn about your world.

UNDERSTAND IT

Think about all the predictions you hear or make every day. Perhaps your local TV, radio, or newspaper predicts rain for tomorrow. You may predict that you are going to do well on a test because you've done a lot of studying. Perhaps your dad predicts that your mom will be late getting home from work because she has an important meeting.

Logical predictions are based in part on what a person reads or learns from other sources. They also are based on experiences a person has had that can be applied to the future.

EXPLORE IT

Here are some steps you can follow to make predictions when you read.

- Read this paragraph and think about what is happening. Then predict what will happen next.

  Many people of the Canadian province of Quebec had a heritage that differed from that of other Canadians. Nearly everyone in Quebec spoke French and wanted to preserve French traditions. Outside of Quebec, most Canadians spoke English and had a culture based on British traditions. Conflicts between the two cultures led the people of Quebec to consider separating from Canada and becoming an independent country.

- As you make your prediction, think about what you know from your own experience, from what you have read before, or from what you know about the way people act. Can you guess what happened in Canada? Read the next paragraph.

  The government of Canada made efforts to support Quebec. It allowed Quebec to make French its official language and to preserve its French culture. However, some French-speaking Canadians still wanted to separate from Canada. In 1995 a resolution for separation was narrowly defeated. But separatists planned to put another resolution to a vote soon.

- Now verify your prediction. Was it correct?

- If your prediction was incorrect, how might you change it?

You can see the French influence in the old part of the city of Quebec.

Girls' Swimming Coach Considers Move to College

AURORA Insiders at Aurora High School speculate that girls' swimming coach Rachel Chan may be considering a move to the head coach position for State University's women's swimming program. Chan could not be reached for comment, but reliable sources believe that State University has offered her the position, to begin January 1.

Chan's record at Aurora has been outstanding. During the past three years, her team has won two state championships, and swimmer Krystal Meredith is expected to participate in Olympic trials next spring. Some sources believe that Chan would not leave Aurora until after Meredith graduates.

State University's search for a new coach developed after coach Victoria Leigh announced her plans to relocate to Utah. State's women's swimming program has attracted talented swimmers in the past few years, but they have not reached their potential. Chan's ability to motivate swimmers would be an asset to the State team.

Huskies Lead Region in 2nd Round of Play

OAK PARK Continuing their winning streak, the Oak Park Huskies pulled off an extraordinary 68–67 win over the Belville Broncos in overtime play last night. The Huskies move to the third round against La Grange on Saturday.

Last night, Husky forward Dwayne Johnson led the scoring with 23 points. However, his free-throw performance was off the mark, missing 4 out of 6 tries. Teammates Russ DeOrio and Steve Golden picked up the slack with 12 points each.

The Huskies are favorites to win against the La Grange Bobcats on Saturday. During the preseason, the Huskies trounced La Grange 74–40. Husky coach Jeff Miller warns, however, that "La Grange has matured this year. They are not a team to be taken lightly."

Coach Chan will go to State University because she wants to make a name for herself.

The Huskies will win the state championship because they're on a winning streak.

SKILL POWER SEARCH

Choose one of the topics covered in this chapter and make a prediction about what will happen by the time you are an adult.

A SHRINKING WORLD THROUGH COOPERATION

FOCUS *While modern technology has made our lives more complex, it has also enhanced cooperation and closeness among world cultures.*

Closeness Through Transportation

In 1620 it took two months for the *Mayflower* to sail from England to America. Today supersonic jet aircraft can travel that same distance in about three hours! As the map shows, such advances in transportation have made it relatively easy to go anywhere in the world in a short time.

Jet planes have done more than cut the time it takes to go from one place to another. They have brought the cultures of the world into closer contact. Nations now have to cooperate on standards for emergency procedures, access to airspace, and a common language used by pilots.

▼ Some modern high-speed trains have been nicknamed bullet trains.

There have been improvements in other forms of transportation as well. In France and Japan, railways that once carried trains at 40 or 50 miles per hour now carry trains at well over 100 miles per hour. And the United Kingdom and France have been linked since 1994 by a railway traveling through the underwater Channel Tunnel.

Sea travel is also faster than it used to be. The two months it took the Pilgrims to cross the Atlantic on the *Mayflower* must have seemed like an eternity. Thirty years ago, that same crossing took less than a week and was considered fast. Today, the fastest ships are capable of crossing the Atlantic in less than four days. And where land-masses block passage between bodies of water, canals have been built to create shortcuts. It's enough to make a Pilgrim's head swim.

Closeness Through Communication

Improved systems of communication also have tied the world's nations closer together. In the days of the cold war, a telephone "hot line" between the President of the United

States and the Premier of the Soviet Union was used whenever there were misunderstandings that might have led to World War III.

The speed of communication continues to improve. A phone call placed in the United States can be transmitted to a satellite that then sends the call to almost anyplace else in the world.

Computer Technology

The development of computer technology has provided people all over the world with the potential for nearly instantaneous communication. Not long ago, no one would have thought that fax machines, E-mail, and satellite hookups would have been possible in anything but science fiction. And the idea of a personal computer would have been considered a joke. Most people believed that only huge companies and the federal government could ever afford computers. Besides, who could afford a home big enough to house a computer the size of an entire room? But today's personal computers

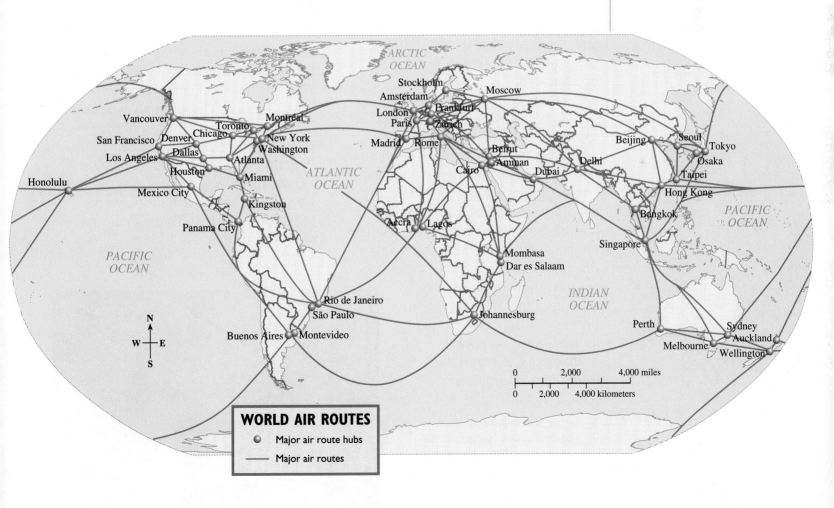

WORLD AIR ROUTES

● Major air route hubs

— Major air routes

Representatives of member nations at the fiftieth anniversary celebration of the United Nations

are not only small enough and light enough to fit on your lap, they are also faster and more powerful than any of those old computers that were the size of a large room!

Personal computers have made it possible for any individual to be wired to the world. With the proper telephone hookup, you can send an electronic letter to a pen pal in China. Or you might fax your A+ world history test to your grandmother hundreds of miles away. By using the Internet, you can obtain information on just about any topic.

Only a few decades ago, the future of computer use in homes and schools seemed limited. Now, computer availability has made that future almost limitless.

After an earthquake in Japan, electronic communication helped people monitor relief cooperation.

Closeness Through Cooperation

In some ways, people today cooperate with each other the old-fashioned way—by working together. They do this through international organizations. These organizations can be made up of just two nations, several nations, or all nations. Regardless of how the organizations are set up, they all have basically the same goal. Member nations work together to find common solutions to common problems.

The United Nations

The most famous international organization is the United Nations (U.N.). Founded in 1945 at the close of World War II, the organization's main purpose is to promote peace and to develop friendly relations between the nations of the world. But it also works to solve economic, social, and **humanitarian** problems and to promote human rights and freedoms. The success of the United Nations' efforts is directly dependent on the goodwill and cooperation of its members.

For more than 50 years, the United Nations has worked to improve relationships between nations and to better the living conditions of people all over the world. But because of its size, the United Nations frequently works through smaller organizations, such as UNESCO, UNICEF, WHO, and IMF.

Sometimes cooperation between nations exists regionally rather than

⭐ **humanitarian** Promoting the elimination of human pain and suffering

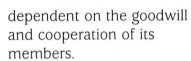

International Organizations of Cooperation	
ORGANIZATION	GOAL
United Nations Educational, Scientific, and Cultural Organization **(UNESCO)**	Works for world peace by focusing on education and the international exchange of scientific information
United Nations Children's Fund **(UNICEF)**	Uses donated money to provide health care for needy children
World Health Organization **(WHO)**	Promotes research dedicated to the treatment and elimination of disease
International Monetary Fund **(IMF)**	Protects the value of the world currencies and promotes the expansion of international trade
European Union **(EU)**	Promotes economic and political cooperation among the nations of Europe; richer members pledge to increase aid to poorer members
Organization of African Unity **(OAU)**	Promotes economic development; works to guarantee human rights and find peaceful solutions to conflicts between members
Organization of American States **(OAS)**	Promotes economic development; works to guarantee human rights and find peaceful solutions to conflicts between members
Commonwealth (formerly the British Commonwealth of Nations)	Members cooperate to find common policies on financial, scientific, educational, and military matters

▲ World peace is the goal of individual nations working together.

globally. Throughout history, nations that neighbor each other or that have similar interests and goals form alliances or create trade agreements for mutual benefit. Organizations and agreements such as the European Union, the Organization of American States, the Commonwealth, the North American Free Trade Agreement, (NAFTA), and the Asia-Pacific Economic Cooperation (APEC) were created to solve regional rather than global problems.

Good Health Through Cooperation

Perhaps the greatest achievements of international cooperation have been in the field of health. Until recently, families around the world knew firsthand the horror of diseases such as smallpox, polio, yellow fever, and measles. Without vaccines, people had

▲ The members of the U.N. realize children are the world's future.

▼ Adult literacy is a concern of all nations in the world.

no way to prevent these diseases. Each year, millions fell victim to them.

Now, however, doctors and scientists have unlocked the mysteries of many diseases. In some cases they have developed vaccines that prevent diseases such as smallpox, polio, and measles. In other cases they have found that simple

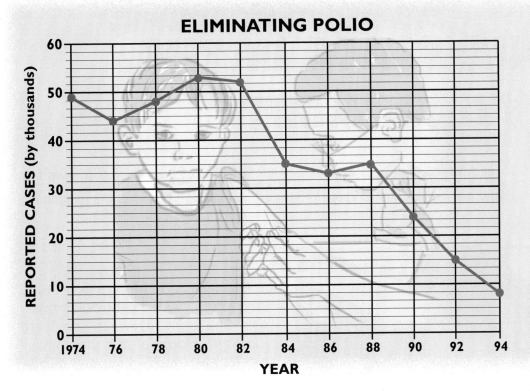

ELIMINATING POLIO

Graph: REPORTED CASES (by thousands) vs YEAR

Y-axis: REPORTED CASES (by thousands) — 0, 10, 20, 30, 40, 50, 60

X-axis: YEAR — 1974, 76, 78, 80, 82, 84, 86, 88, 90, 92, 94

SHOW WHAT YOU KNOW!

REFOCUS
COMPREHENSION

1. What has made worldwide travel faster?

2. What international organization was created at the end of World War II?

THINK ABOUT IT
CRITICAL THINKING

What are two ways in which the U.N. has helped to promote peace in the world?

WRITE ABOUT IT
ACTIVITY

Smallpox was eliminated as a disease in the 1980s. Polio soon may be eliminated. What disease would you like to see eliminated next?

Write a paragraph or two explaining your reasons for choosing that disease.

sanitation procedures prevent the spread of diseases, such as yellow fever and typhoid fever.

Thanks to international cooperation, lifesaving medical advances have been carried around the globe. In the 1980s, the World Health Organization (WHO) succeeded in eliminating all cases of smallpox worldwide. Now, WHO has set a goal of eliminating polio worldwide by the year 2000. Statistics indicate that WHO is well on its way to success.

Vaccination Equals Prevention

More recently, UNICEF led a successful campaign to vaccinate (VAK-suh nayt) 80 percent of the world's children against diseases ranging from measles to diphtheria to whooping

cough. And the Centers for Disease Control in Atlanta, Georgia, works with other centers around the world to control the spread of viruses such as the flu. Without this worldwide cooperation, such successes would not have been possible.

▼ By vaccinating children around the world, we are controlling the spread of disease.

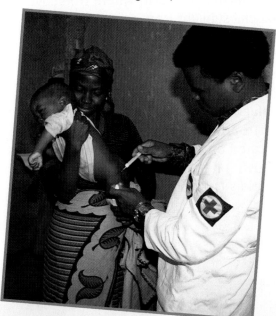

★ **sanitation** The practice of creating healthful living conditions

595

OUR PLACE IN THE ENVIRONMENT

FOCUS *The stress on the world's environment has increased as the human population has grown. People are now learning to cooperate to save such vital resources as the rain forests.*

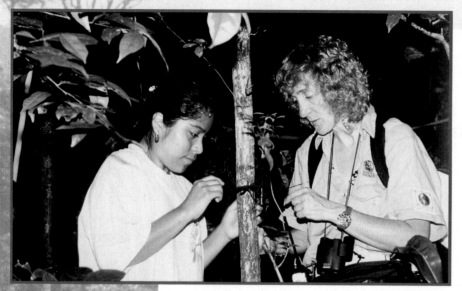

▲ Plants in the rain forest produce chemicals that are used as medicines.

The Wonders of the Rain Forest

Think about a place where the air is warm and moist, where tree cover blocks sunlight from the ground, and where all kinds of strange and wonderful animals live. Such places do exist. They are called **tropical rain forests**, and they are among the most valuable resources on our planet.

Tropical rain forests are areas located on or near the equator, as shown on the map. Over half of the world's tropical rain forests are located in Central and South America. The rest are located in Africa and Southeast Asia. The name *rain forest* comes from the large amount of rain these areas receive each year—up to 400 inches in some places.

The Benefits of the Rain Forest

Although rain forests cover less than 10 percent of the earth, they provide most of the oxygen needed to sustain life on Earth. They are home to about 50 percent of all the world's trees and at least 40 percent of the world's total plant and animal life. There are no other places on Earth that have a higher degree of plant and animal diversity.

Rain forests are a bit like a living laboratory. Certain chemical compounds, found no place else on Earth, are found in the rain forests. Researchers are constantly searching the rain forests for new chemical compounds that might someday prove beneficial to humans.

Some of the rain forest compounds, such as **curare** (kyoo RAH ree), are

---

⭐ **tropical rain forest** A dense, evergreen forest found in tropical regions and having large amounts of yearly rainfall

⭐ **curare** A poison that is used during surgery to relax a patient's muscles

already being used to help people. Curare is a poison taken from the bark and sap of trees in South America. At one time it was used by hunters to paralyze their prey. Now it is used by doctors to relax the muscles of patients during surgery. Who knows what other wonder drugs may yet be discovered in the world's tropical rain forests?

Farms or Forests

Until recently, nobody thought much about rain forests. A few small groups of people lived in them. And once in a while, a scientist or two would venture through them. But for the most part, rain forests were unexplored. Millions of plants and animals lived out their life cycles there without any interference from the outside world.

As the world's population grew, however, all that changed. Farmers began to move into the rain forests. In order to grow crops and graze cattle, these farmers cleared many acres of rain forest. Unfortunately, the soil is not well suited for farming. It quickly loses its fertility and is unable to sustain crops or cattle.

▼ The golden toad is endangered because of rain forest destruction.

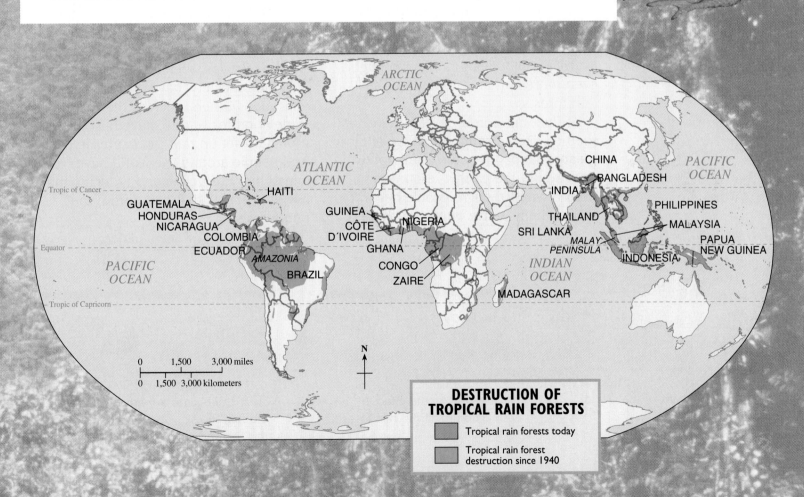

DESTRUCTION OF TROPICAL RAIN FORESTS

- Tropical rain forests today
- Tropical rain forest destruction since 1940

RICE PRODUCTION

Pounds of Rice per Acre (y-axis): 6,000 / 5,750 / 5,500 / 5,250 / 5,000 / 4,750 / 4,500 / 4,250 / 4,000

Year (x-axis): 1965 / 1975 / 1985 / 1995

▲ Greater yields per acre may be one solution to the problem of increasing need for farmland.

Farmers found that they needed to constantly clear more and more acres to keep their farms going.

Meanwhile, other people moved into the rain forests. Loggers began to harvest the valuable hardwood trees found there. Miners began to collect valuable minerals, including iron, aluminum, copper, oil, natural gas, and gold. With all this development came roads, such as the Trans-Amazon Highway in Brazil. Road-building projects brought even more human activity into the rain forests.

At first, rain forest development seemed like a good thing. After all, it meant that people were finding new ways to use the earth's resources. After a while, though, people began to realize the negative impact of these actions. Recent estimates indicate that as much as 50 million acres of rain forest are being cut down each year. Countless species of plants and animals are also being destroyed. As these facts have become more widely known, there has been a growing movement to save the rain forests from further destruction.

Saving the Rain Forests

Once again, cooperation is the key. In the case of the rain forests, the cooperation has been worldwide. Organizations such as the World Wildlife Fund and the Environmental Defense Fund have coordinated efforts to preserve rain forests.

Some groups, such as the Cousteau (koo STOH) Society, have emphasized education. Others, such as the World Wide Fund for Nature, have raised money to set up rain forest preserves. And people around the world have joined in by recycling and reducing the use of products that come from the rain forests.

SHOW WHAT YOU KNOW!

REFOCUS
COMPREHENSION

1. Where are most of the world's rain forests located?

2. Why are the rain forests so important?

THINK ABOUT IT
CRITICAL THINKING

What would be the effect of the destruction of all the rain forests?

WRITE ABOUT IT
ACTIVITY

Slash-and-burn is a method of clearing the rain forests. Find out more about this method and write a short report on why it is used and what the problems are with this method.

COMING TOGETHER THROUGH TECHNOLOGY

FOCUS *Advances in technology have created new opportunities to bring the people of the world together.*

◄ Current technology enables people to have access to the information superhighway.

The Information Superhighway

What is the **information superhighway**? Comprised of computers and telephone lines worldwide, it is a complex electronic communications network that can connect you to people and places all around the world. To those who use the information superhighway, its development and existence is a revolution in worldwide communications.

The Internet is part of the information superhighway. If you have access to a personal computer and a telephone line, you, too, can get on the Internet and cruise along the information superhighway. You can send messages to people in faraway countries. You can obtain speeches, announcements, and articles that would otherwise never make it to your hometown. And that's just the beginning. Scientists predict all sorts

---

★ *information superhighway* Worldwide, computer-accessed information database

of exciting uses for the information superhighway in the years to come.

One possibility is the electronic mall. You would sit in front of your computer and browse through stores anywhere in the world as though you were actually there. The computer could tell you what merchandise was available—and might even show how a shirt would look on a lifelike image of you!

Businesses, too, are finding ways to benefit from the superhighway. Corporate meetings, for example, can be held through videoconferencing, which enables people in different cities to meet with each other using computers and TV screens. Chances are good that as technology spreads, the superhighway will continue to offer new ways to bring people together.

Education might also be revolutionized by the superhighway. Already in use in some communities, computers can transmit lessons taught in one part of the country to every other part of the country—or the world.

Training for a Safer Tomorrow

People often say, "Seeing is believing." But in the case of **virtual reality**, seeing is more than believing; it is experiencing! Virtual reality is the

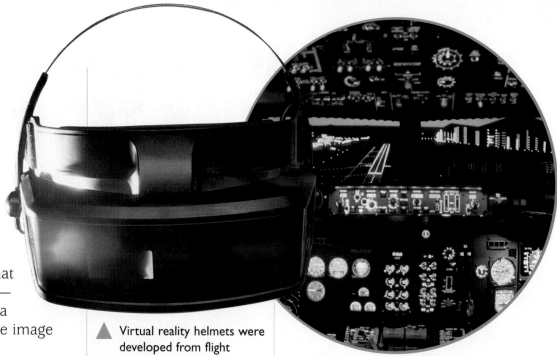

▲ Virtual reality helmets were developed from flight simulators used for pilot training.

name given to interaction with special computer programs. During this interaction, a three-dimensional environment that looks real is projected before your eyes. Better still, the environment reacts to your every move!

It works like this. First, you put on special goggles, a headset, and gloves. These allow you to see, hear, and move in an environment that the computer has created. Suppose you are training to be a doctor. The computer can simulate the environment of an operating room, complete with a patient who needs surgery. You can practice surgery on this patient image. As you move your gloved hands, you can see the incision you are making. You can complete the entire operation on the computer. In this way you can gain valuable surgical experience without ever really cutting into anything or anyone.

★ **virtual reality**   Computer-controlled, three-dimensional 360° images that appear to be real

Virtual reality holds great promise for training other specialists as well. It can help pilots learn to fly. It can show architects what their planned buildings look like. It can help police officers sharpen their responses in hostile situations. And, yes, there can be virtual reality games for kids. Virtual reality games might let you tour the pyramids of Egypt, enter a valley filled with dinosaurs, or explore the Amazon.

Exploring the Past With Technology

Modern technology can also help us understand more about the past. Dr. Robert Ballard proved this dramatically when he explored the wreck of the ocean liner *Titanic*. Everyone knew this mighty ship had sunk in the North Atlantic on April 14, 1912. But no one knew exactly where it lay. In 1985, Ballard used sophisticated sonar and video equipment to locate the remains of the *Titanic*.

Ballard didn't stop there. The next year, he used a remote-controlled, underwater robot named *Jason, Jr.* to search through the ruins. His findings gave historians important new insights into the *Titanic's* tragic end.

Robots and other new devices are now being used to explore other underwater ruins. Discoveries made by these high-tech tools will provide valuable clues to our past.

▼ Using technology such as this underwater vehicle, Robert Ballard explores the past.

SHOW WHAT YOU KNOW!

REFOCUS
COMPREHENSION

1. What is the information super-highway?

2. How can virtual reality be used to train pilots and doctors?

THINK ABOUT IT
CRITICAL THINKING

How have computers changed the way people live, work, and play?

WRITE ABOUT IT
ACTIVITY

Think of a profession or career that might have its training process improved by virtual reality. Then write a paragraph or two describing how virtual reality might be used to train someone interested in that profession or career.

CARRYING THE PAST INTO OUR FUTURE

FOCUS *Throughout history the human race has built on the achievements of those who went before. So, too, the children of tomorrow will build on the achievements we make today.*

Using Our Heritage

As we have seen, history began about 6,000 years ago, when the Sumerians began drawing pictures on clay tablets. After that, ancient peoples went on to develop full alphabets, calendars, paper, and improved farming techniques. These and other inventions made life easier and more productive for people.

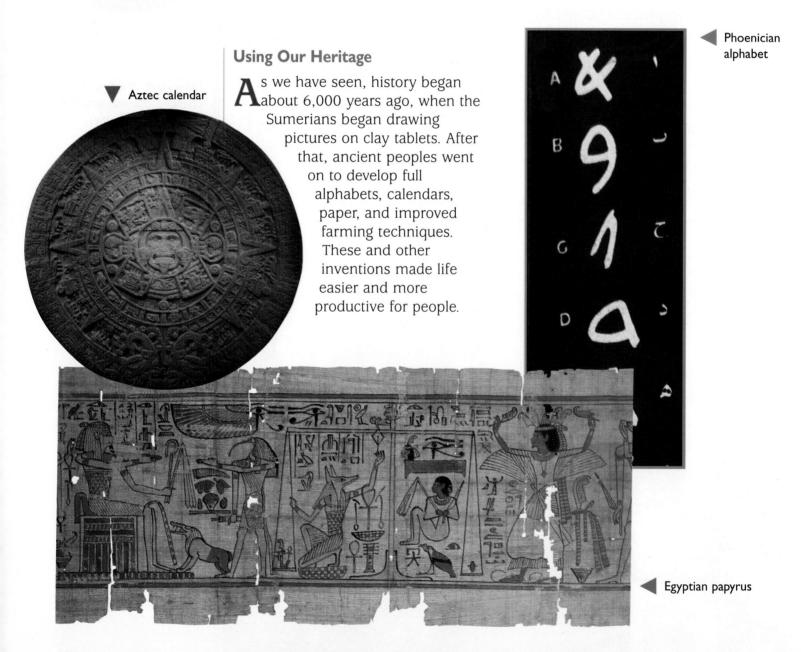

▼ Aztec calendar

◀ Phoenician alphabet

◀ Egyptian papyrus

▼ The Standard of Ur

Where We Are Now

Ancient inventions and cultures have laid the foundations on which modern society has been built. We have taken ideas and observations from the past and carried them to exciting new levels in the present.

Agronomists (uh GRAHN uh mihsts) have applied knowledge acquired in years past to farm with amazing efficiency. Other scientists have learned to prevent or treat many diseases, to replace certain body parts when the need arises, and to create new chemical compounds that make

▲ Greek ruins at Delphi

life safer and easier. We have even built vehicles that carry people into space.

Into the Twenty-first Century

Future generations will build on what we accomplish today. As we have seen, worldwide communications have already become almost instantaneous, and our transportation and engineering skills have created a society that has touched the sky. Others will build on these accomplishments to shape the future in ways we cannot yet describe.

A laser disc, a CD-ROM, and a compact disc (CDs) ▶

⭐ **agronomist** A scientist specializing in efficient crop production

SHOW WHAT YOU KNOW!

REFOCUS
COMPREHENSION

1. What are some ancient inventions that have made life easier?

2. How have we improved on these ancient inventions?

THINK ABOUT IT
CRITICAL THINKING

Which inventions of the past have contributed the most to modern life?

WRITE ABOUT IT
ACTIVITY

Choose a modern invention and, in a paragraph or two, describe how you think people of the future might build on that invention to improve their lives.

SUMMING UP

1 DO YOU REMEMBER...
COMPREHENSION

1. What is the purpose of international organizations?

2. When was the United Nations founded?

3. How does the organization called UNESCO work for world peace?

4. What disease was eliminated in the 1980s through the efforts of the World Health Organization?

5. Why are rain forests so important in sustaining life on Earth?

6. What do researchers hope to find when they search the rain forests?

7. What two things do you need to access the information superhighway?

8. What equipment lets you see, hear, and move in virtual reality?

9. In what situations have robots proved to be a useful tool for scientific discoveries?

10. Why was the development of writing an important milestone in history?

2 SKILL POWER
MAKING PREDICTIONS

Look back at Chapter 26 and make three predictions about how our society and world will change over the next 25 years. List the factual information and personal experiences on which you base each prediction.

3 WHAT DO YOU THINK?
CRITICAL THINKING

1. What do you think are the three most important ways in which high-speed transportation and communications link different nations and cultures?

2. When or why might a member nation choose not to cooperate with the United Nations?

3. Do you think the nations of the world could ever eliminate all diseases? Explain.

4. Who gets to access the information superhighway? How might the superhighway tend to widen the gap between wealthy and poor people and nations?

5. What invention of the last 100 years do you think has done the most to make our lives today better? Why?

4 SAY IT, WRITE IT, USE IT
VOCABULARY

Write a short essay telling how the nations of the world might cooperate and use high technology to save endangered environments. Use as many of the terms as possible in your essay.

agronomist
curare
humanitarian
information
superhighway

tropical rain forest
sanitation
virtual reality

5 GEOGRAPHY AND YOU
MAP STUDY

In 1995 the United Nations celebrated its fiftieth anniversary. In 1945 the U.N. had 51 members. These members are listed below. On an outline map of the world, locate and color the U.N. members of that time.

Argentina	Iraq
Australia	Lebanon
Belgium	Liberia
Bolivia	Luxembourg
Brazil	Mexico
Belorussian S.S.R.	The Netherlands
Canada	New Zealand
Chile	Nicaragua
China	Norway
Colombia	Panama
Costa Rica	Paraguay
Cuba	Peru
Czechoslovakia	Philippines
Denmark	Poland
Dominican Republic	Saudi Arabia
Ecuador	South Africa
Egypt	Syria
El Salvador	Turkey
Ethiopia	Ukrainian S.S.R.
France	U.S.S.R.
Greece	United Kingdom
Guatemala	United States
Haiti	Uruguay
Honduras	Venezuela
India	Yugoslavia
Iran	

6 TAKE ACTION
CITIZENSHIP

Think Globally, Act Locally—that's what the button suggests. But how can ordinary people do that? Brainstorm with a group of classmates to come up with a list of suggestions for how to work toward important world goals by acting here and now in your own community. For example, to help save the rain forest, you might list products that people could substitute for products from the rain forest.

7 GET CREATIVE
COMPUTER CONNECTION

Find out more about virtual reality. Then work with a group of classmates to come up with a proposal for a new way to use this amazing technology. Your suggestions can be educational or purely for entertainment. Be sure to explain how your idea takes full advantage of both seeing and moving in a three-dimensional environment.

LOOKING BACK

Look back at the Contents page at the front of this book. Which time in history did you find to be the most interesting? Why?

REFERENCE

CONTENTS

SECTION

RESEARCH AND REFERENCE

You are studying about the world and its people. These books present many facts and statistics about the countries that have developed throughout history. Learn about maps and mapmakers from ancient times to the present.

The Kingfisher Reference Atlas: An A-Z Guide to Countries of the World
by Brian Williams (Kingfisher Books, 1993)
Visit each country of the world to discover its population, geography, climate, and economics. Comprehensive statistics in easy-to-use tables will give you a quick access to the facts.

The Young Oxford Companion to Maps and Mapmaking
by Rebecca Stefoff (Oxford University Press, 1995)
Learn how and why maps are made. Read about the earliest mapmakers from all around the globe and study the history of cartography up to the present day. You might even accept the challenge to make a map of your own.

The Children's Atlas of the 20th Century
by Sarah Howarth (The Millbrook Press, 1995)
The 20th century has seen more change than any other time in history. Using photos, maps, and time lines, follow the political, cultural, and scientific progress around the world.

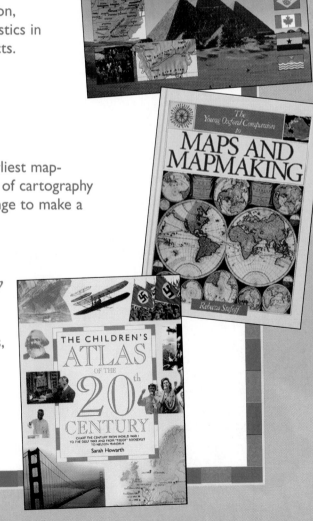

160°W 140°W 120°W 100°W 80°W 60°W

ARCTIC OCEAN

Greenland
(Den.)

Arctic Circle

Alaska (U.S.)

80°N

60°N

ALEUTIAN IS. (U.S.)

CANADA

NORTH

AMERICA

40°N

UNITED STATES

See inset below

Bermuda (U.K.)

AZORES
(Port.)

ATLANTIC OCEAN

Midway I. (U.S.)

Tropic of Cancer

MEXICO

20°N

HAWAII (U.S.)

Caribbean Sea

CAPE VERDE

VENEZUELA

GUYANA

SURINAME

French Guiana
(Fr.)

COLOMBIA

Equator

0°

GALÁPAGOS IS.
(Ecuador)

ECUADOR

SOUTH

AMERICA

BRAZIL

PACIFIC OCEAN

PERU

WESTERN
SAMOA

*AMERICAN
SAMOA (U.S.)*

FRENCH POLYNESIA
(Fr.)

BOLIVIA

TONGA

20°S

COOK IS. (N.Z.)

Pitcairn I. (U.K.)

Tropic of Capricorn

PARAGUAY

CHILE

URUGUAY

Easter I.
(Chile)

ARGENTINA

N
W — E
S

International Date Line

40°S

**WEST INDIES AND
CENTRAL AMERICA**

0   150   300 miles
0 150 300 kilometers

UNITED STATES

30°N

N
W — E
S

ATLANTIC OCEAN

Gulf of Mexico

25°N

60°S

Antarctic Circle

FALKLAND IS.
(U.K.)

80°S

Tropic of Cancer

B
A
H
A
M
A
S

CUBA

TURKS AND
CAICOS IS. (U.K.)

MEXICO

20°N

*CAYMAN
ISLANDS
(U.K.)*

Hispaniola

GREATER ANTILLES

HAITI

DOMINICAN
REPUBLIC

BR. VIRGIN IS.
(U.K.)

Puerto Rico
(U.S.)

ANTIGUA
AND BARBUDA

BELIZE

JAMAICA

VIRGIN ISLANDS (U.S.)

Guadeloupe (Fr.)

GUATEMALA

ST. KITTS AND NEVIS

15°N

HONDURAS

Caribbean Sea

DOMINICA

Martinique (Fr.)

ST. LUCIA

EL SALVADOR

NICARAGUA

NETH. ANTILLES (Neth.)

ARUBA

ST. VINCENT AND
THE GRENADINES

LESSER ANTILLES

BARBADOS

GRENADA

10°N

COSTA
RICA

TRINIDAD
AND
TOBAGO

PANAMA

COLOMBIA

VENEZUELA

90°W   85°W   80°W   75°W   70°W   65°W   60°W

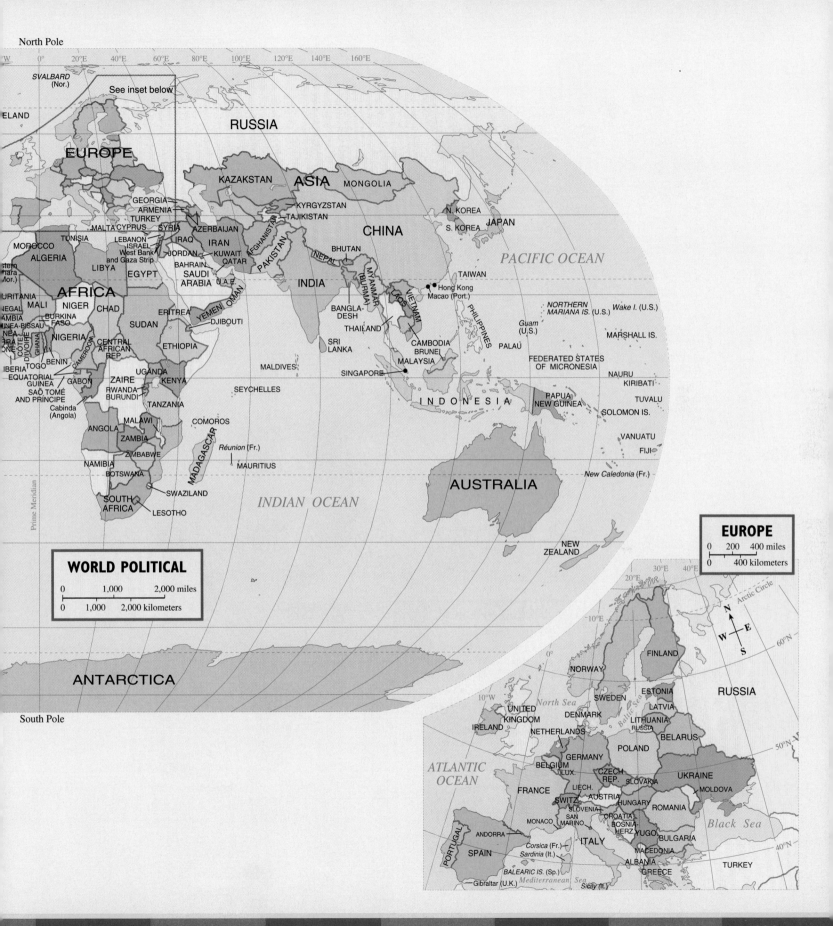

North Pole

SVALBARD (Nor.)

See inset below

ELAND

EUROPE

RUSSIA

ASIA

KAZAKSTAN

MONGOLIA

GEORGIA
ARMENIA
TURKEY
MALTA CYPRUS
SYRIA
AZERBAIJAN
LEBANON
ISRAEL
West Bank
and Gaza Strip
JORDAN
IRAQ
IRAN

KYRGYZSTAN

TAJIKISTAN

N. KOREA

S. KOREA
JAPAN

CHINA

PACIFIC OCEAN

AFGHANISTAN

PAKISTAN

NEPAL

BHUTAN

TAIWAN

TUNISIA

MOROCCO

ALGERIA

LIBYA

EGYPT

BAHRAIN
KUWAIT QATAR
SAUDI
ARABIA
U.A.E.

YEMEN OMAN

DJIBOUTI

INDIA

BANGLA-
DESH

MYANMAR
(BURMA)

LAOS

VIETNAM

Hong Kong
Macao (Port.)

NORTHERN
MARIANA IS. (U.S.)

Wake I. (U.S.)

stern
hara
Mor.)

URITANIA
NEGAL
MALI
AMBIA
GUINEA-BISSAU
NEA
RA
ONE
IBERIA
COTE
D'IVOIRE
TOGO
BENIN
GHANA
CAMEROON
NIGER

NIGERIA

CHAD

CENTRAL
AFRICAN
REP.

ERITREA

SUDAN

ETHIOPIA

AFRICA

THAILAND

SRI
LANKA

MALDIVES

CAMBODIA
BRUNEI
MALAYSIA

SINGAPORE

PHILIPPINES

PALAU

Guam
(U.S.)

MARSHALL IS.

FEDERATED STATES
OF MICRONESIA

NAURU

KIRIBATI

EQUATORIAL
GUINEA
GABON
SAO TOMÉ
AND PRÍNCIPE
Cabinda
(Angola)

ZAIRE

RWANDA
BURUNDI

UGANDA

KENYA

TANZANIA

SEYCHELLES

INDONESIA

PAPUA
NEW GUINEA

TUVALU

SOLOMON IS.

ANGOLA

ZAMBIA

MALAWI

ZIMBABWE

COMOROS

MADAGASCAR

Réunion (Fr.)

MAURITIUS

VANUATU

FIJI

NAMIBIA

BOTSWANA

New Caledonia (Fr.)

SWAZILAND

SOUTH
AFRICA

LESOTHO

INDIAN OCEAN

AUSTRALIA

Prime Meridian

WORLD POLITICAL

0   1,000   2,000 miles

0   1,000   2,000 kilometers

NEW
ZEALAND

ANTARCTICA

South Pole

EUROPE

0   200   400 miles

0   400 kilometers

30°E   40°E

20°E

Arctic Circle

N
W   E
S

60°N

10°E

FINLAND

NORWAY

0°

North Sea

SWEDEN

ESTONIA

RUSSIA

10°W

UNITED
KINGDOM

DENMARK

LATVIA

LITHUANIA

Baltic Sea

RUSSIA

IRELAND

NETHERLANDS

GERMANY

POLAND

BELARUS

ATLANTIC
OCEAN

BELGIUM
LUX.

LIECH.

CZECH
REP.

SLOVAKIA

UKRAINE

50°N

FRANCE

SWITZ.

AUSTRIA

SLOVENIA

HUNGARY

MOLDOVA

ROMANIA

PORTUGAL

MONACO

SAN
MARINO

CROATIA
BOSNIA-
HERZ.
YUGO.

Black Sea

ANDORRA

ITALY

BULGARIA

SPAIN

Corsica (Fr.)
Sardinia (It.)

MACEDONIA

ALBANIA

40°N

TURKEY

BALEARIC IS. (Sp.)

GREECE

Gibraltar (U.K.)

Mediterranean Sea

Sicily (It.)

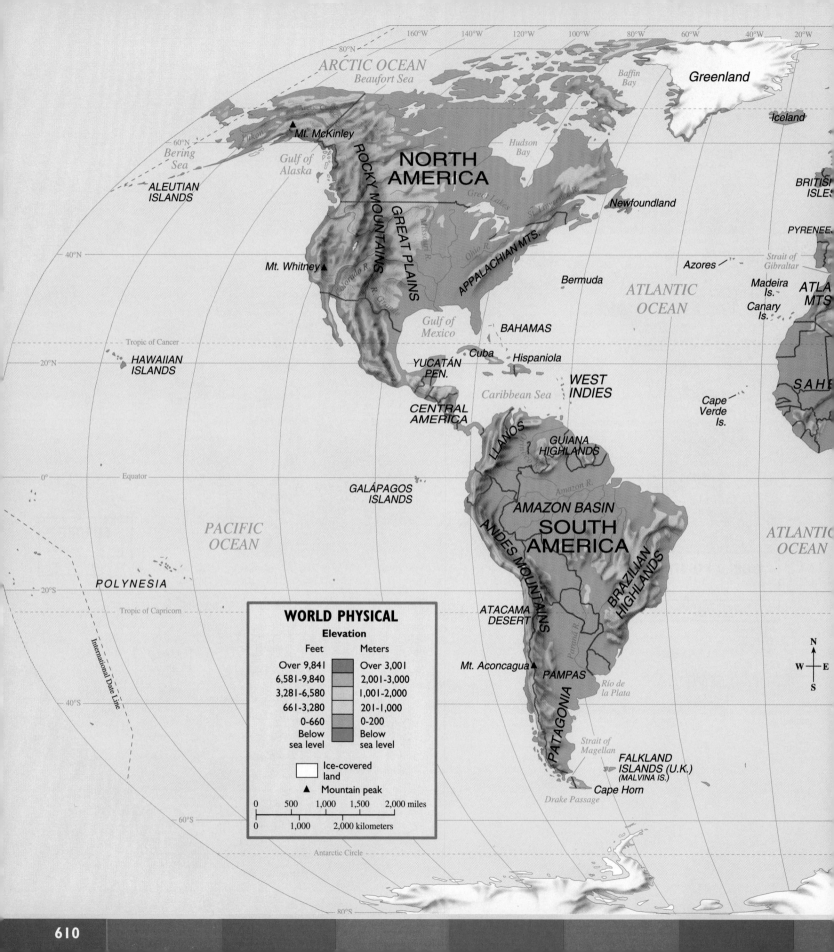

WORLD PHYSICAL

Elevation

Feet	Meters
Over 9,841	Over 3,001
6,581-9,840	2,001-3,000
3,281-6,580	1,001-2,000
661-3,280	201-1,000
0-660	0-200
Below sea level	Below sea level

Ice-covered land

▲ Mountain peak

0   500   1,000   1,500   2,000 miles

0   1,000   2,000 kilometers

ARCTIC OCEAN
Beaufort Sea

Greenland

Iceland

NORTH AMERICA

Baffin Bay

Hudson Bay

Bering Sea

Gulf of Alaska

▲ Mt. McKinley

ALEUTIAN ISLANDS

ROCKY MOUNTAINS

GREAT PLAINS

Great Lakes

St. Lawrence R.

Newfoundland

BRITISH ISLES

PYRENEE

Missouri R.

Ohio R.

APPALACHIAN MTS.

Azores

Strait of Gibraltar

Mt. Whitney ▲

Colorado R.

Bermuda

ATLANTIC OCEAN

Madeira Is.

Canary Is.

ATLA MTS

Rio Grande

Gulf of Mexico

BAHAMAS

Cuba

Hispaniola

WEST INDIES

SAHE

HAWAIIAN ISLANDS

YUCATÁN PEN.

Caribbean Sea

Cape Verde Is.

CENTRAL AMERICA

LLANOS

GUIANA HIGHLANDS

GALÁPAGOS ISLANDS

Amazon R.

PACIFIC OCEAN

AMAZON BASIN

SOUTH AMERICA

ATLANTIC OCEAN

ANDES MOUNTAINS

BRAZILIAN HIGHLANDS

POLYNESIA

ATACAMA DESERT

Paraná R.

Mt. Aconcagua ▲

PAMPAS

Rio de la Plata

N
W   E
S

PATAGONIA

Strait of Magellan

FALKLAND ISLANDS (U.K.)
(MALVINA IS.)

Cape Horn

Drake Passage

160°W   140°W   120°W   100°W   80°W   60°W   40°W   20°W

80°N

60°N

40°N

Tropic of Cancer

20°N

0° Equator

20°S   Tropic of Capricorn

International Date Line

40°S

60°S

Antarctic Circle

80°S

20°E 40°E 60°E 80°E 100°E 120°E 140°E 160°E

SVALBARD

ARCTIC OCEAN

Barents Sea

Novaya
Zemlya

*Baltic
Sea*

North
Sea

URAL MTS.

Ob R.

Yenisey R.

SIBERIA

Lena R.

*Sea of
Okhotsk*

KAMCHATKA
PENINSULA

EUROPE

Volga R.

Irtysh R.

Ural R.

ALTAI MTS.

ASIA

GOBI

L.
Baikal

Sakhalin

CARPATHIANS

Danube R.

▲ALPS

Mt. Blanc

CAUCASUS
MTS.

*Aral
Sea*

Caspian Sea

Hokkaido

BALKAN
PEN.

Black Sea

Mt. Ararat ▲

▲
Mt. Damavand

TIBETAN
PLATEAU

Honshu

*Sea of
Japan*

*Mediterranean
Sea*

▲Mt.
Everest

Huang He

Yangtze R.

Shikoku
Kyushu

*East
China
Sea*

SAHARA

Nile R.

ARABIAN
PENINSULA

THAR
DESERT

Ganges R.

Taiwan

NUBIAN
DESERT

*Persian
Gulf*

Red Sea

DECCAN
PLATEAU

Hainan

*South
China
Sea*

PHILIPPINE
ISLANDS

SUDAN

*Arabian
Sea*

*Bay of
Bengal*

MICRONESIA

AFRICA

GREAT RIFT VALLEY

Sri
Lanka

MALAY
PEN.

PACIFIC OCEAN

Zaire (Congo) R.

L. Victoria

▲ Mt. Kenya

▲ Mt. Kilimanjaro

Sumatra

Borneo

INDONESIA

ZAIRE
BASIN

SEYCHELLES

Celebes

New Guinea

INDIAN
OCEAN

Java

Timor

MELANESIA

Zambezi R.

Madagascar

KALAHARI
DESERT

GREAT SANDY
DESERT

Orange R.

AUSTRALIA

NULLARBOR
PLAIN

Darling R.

Cape of
Good Hope

North
Island

Tasmania

South
Island

NEW ZEALAND

ANTARCTICA

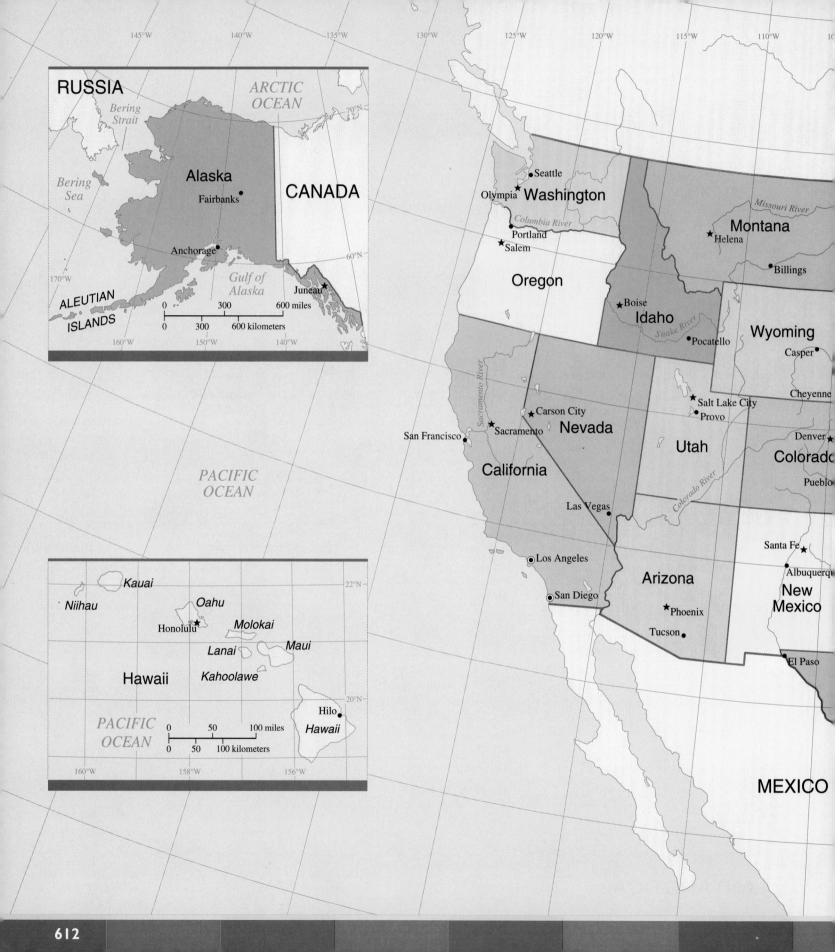

RUSSIA

Bering Strait

ARCTIC OCEAN

70°N

Alaska

Fairbanks

CANADA

Bering Sea

Anchorage

60°N

170°W

ALEUTIAN ISLANDS

Gulf of Alaska

Juneau

| 0 | 300 | 600 miles |
| 0 | 300 | 600 kilometers |

160°W   150°W   140°W

PACIFIC OCEAN

Kauai

22°N

Niihau

Oahu

Honolulu   Molokai

Lanai   Maui

Hawaii   Kahoolawe

20°N

PACIFIC OCEAN

Hilo

Hawaii

| 0 | 50 | 100 miles |
| 0 | 50 | 100 kilometers |

160°W   158°W   156°W

145°W   140°W   135°W   130°W   125°W   120°W   115°W   110°W   10

Seattle

Olympia   Washington

Columbia River

Missouri River

Montana

Helena

Portland

Salem

Billings

Oregon

Boise

Idaho

Snake River

Wyoming

Pocatello

Casper

Sacramento River

Salt Lake City

Provo

Cheyenne

Carson City

Nevada

Denver

San Francisco   Sacramento

Utah

Colorado

California

Pueblo

Las Vegas

Colorado River

Santa Fe

Los Angeles

Albuquerqu

Arizona

New Mexico

San Diego

Phoenix

Tucson

El Paso

MEXICO

CANADA

North Dakota
• Fargo
• Bismarck

Minnesota

South Dakota
• Pierre ★

Sioux Falls •

Nebraska

Lincoln •
Omaha •

Kansas
Topeka ★
• Wichita

Oklahoma
★ Oklahoma City

Texas

Austin ★
Houston ⊙
San Antonio •

Minneapolis •   St. Paul ★

Wisconsin
Milwaukee •
Madison ★

Iowa
Dubuque •
Des Moines ★

Illinois
Springfield ★

Missouri
Kansas City •
Jefferson City ★
St. Louis ⊙

Arkansas
Fort Smith •
Little Rock ★

Mississippi
Greenville •
Jackson ★

Louisiana
Baton Rouge ★
New Orleans ⊙

Lake Superior

Michigan

Lake Michigan

Lansing ★
Chicago ⊙

Fort Wayne •

Indiana
Indianapolis ★

Cincinnati •

Louisville •

Kentucky
Frankfort ★

Nashville •

Tennessee

Memphis •

Alabama
Montgomery ★

Mobile •

Lake Huron

Detroit ⊙

Cleveland •

Lake Erie

Ohio
Columbus ★

Pittsburgh •

West
Virginia
Charleston •

Atlanta ★

Birmingham •

Georgia

Tallahassee ★

St. Lawrence River

Lake Ontario

Buffalo •

New
York

Albany ★
Springfield •

Pennsylvania
Harrisburg ★
Philadelphia ⊙
Wilmington •
Baltimore •
Washington, D.C. ⊛ Annapolis •

Virginia
Richmond ★ Norfolk •

North Carolina
Raleigh ★
• Charlotte

South
Carolina
Columbia ★
Charleston •
Savannah •

Florida
Tampa •

Miami •

Maine
Augusta ★

Burlington •   Portland •
Montpelier ★ New
Vermont Hampshire
Manchester • Concord ★
Boston ★
Massachusetts
Hartford ★ Providence ★
Bridgeport • Rhode Island
Connecticut
New York City ⊙
Trenton ★
New
Jersey
Dover ★
Delaware
Maryland

ATLANTIC
OCEAN

BAHAMAS

CUBA

Lake Superior
Missouri River
Platte River
Arkansas River
Mississippi River
Red River
Ohio River
Rio Grande
Gulf of Mexico
St. Lawrence River

UNITED STATES
POLITICAL

⊛ National capital

★ State capitals

⊙ Cities with populations
    over 1 million

• Other cities

—— National boundaries

—— State boundaries

0   150   300 miles
0   150   300 kilometers

N
W   E
S

613

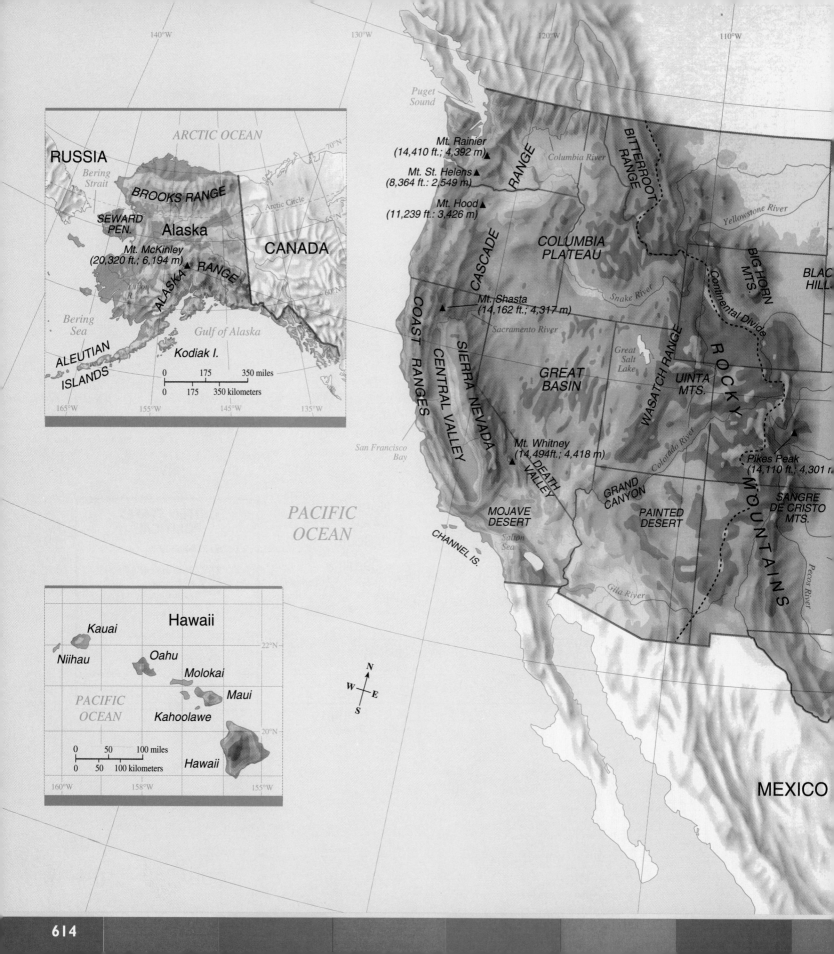

ARCTIC OCEAN

RUSSIA

Bering Strait

BROOKS RANGE

Arctic Circle

70°N

SEWARD PEN.

Alaska

CANADA

65°N

Mt. McKinley
(20,320 ft.; 6,194 m) ▲

ALASKA RANGE

Yukon R.

60°N

Bering Sea

Gulf of Alaska

ALEUTIAN ISLANDS

Kodiak I.

| 0 | 175 | 350 miles |
| 0 | 175 | 350 kilometers |

165°W   155°W   145°W   135°W

Puget Sound

Mt. Rainier
(14,410 ft.; 4,392 m) ▲

Mt. St. Helens
(8,364 ft.; 2,549 m) ▲

Mt. Hood ▲
(11,239 ft.; 3,426 m)

Columbia River

BITTERROOT RANGE

CASCADE RANGE

COLUMBIA PLATEAU

Yellowstone River

Snake River

BIG HORN MTS.

Continental Divide

BLACK HILL

Mt. Shasta
(14,162 ft.; 4,317 m) ▲

Sacramento River

COAST RANGES

SIERRA NEVADA

CENTRAL VALLEY

GREAT BASIN

Great Salt Lake

WASATCH RANGE

UINTA MTS.

ROCKY

San Francisco Bay

Mt. Whitney
(14,494 ft.; 4,418 m) ▲

DEATH VALLEY

Colorado River

GRAND CANYON

Pikes Peak
(14,110 ft.; 4,301 m)

MOUNTAINS

MOJAVE DESERT

PAINTED DESERT

SANGRE DE CRISTO MTS.

PACIFIC OCEAN

CHANNEL IS.

Salton Sea

Gila River

Pecos River

Kauai

Niihau

Hawaii

Oahu

Molokai

22°N

PACIFIC OCEAN

Maui

Kahoolawe

20°N

| 0 | 50 | 100 miles |
| 0 | 50 | 100 kilometers |

Hawaii

160°W   158°W   155°W

N
W — E
S

MEXICO

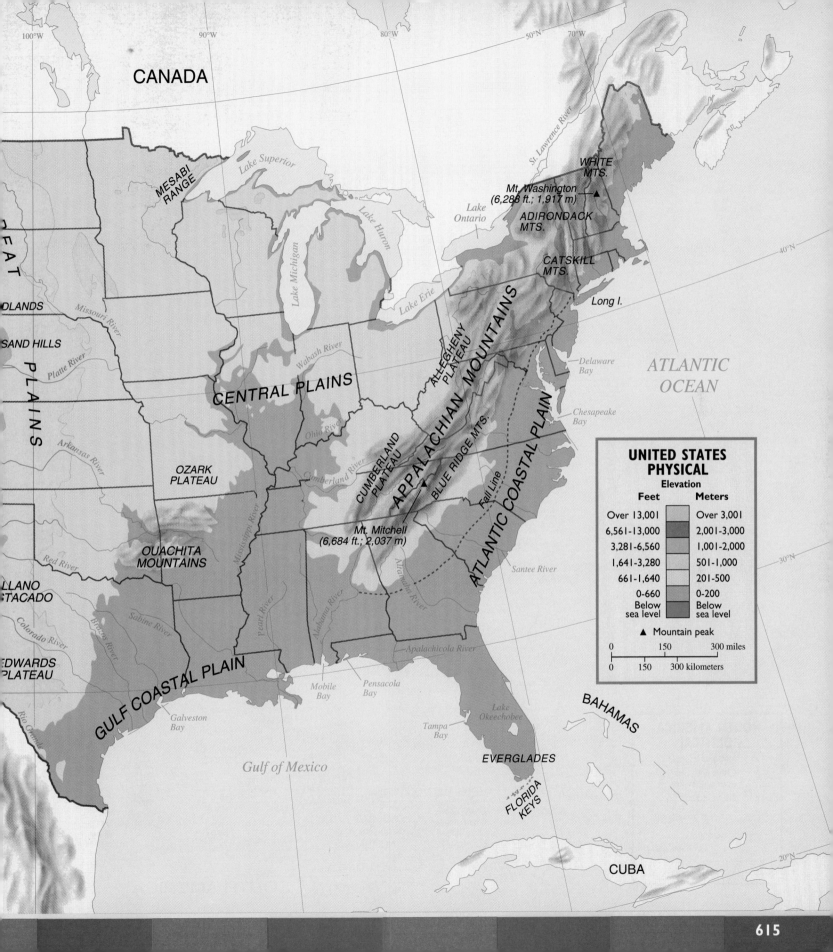

CANADA

MESABI
RANGE

Lake Superior

Lake Michigan

Lake Huron

Lake Ontario

Lake Erie

WHITE
MTS.

Mt. Washington
(6,288 ft.; 1,917 m) ▲

ADIRONDACK
MTS.

CATSKILL
MTS.

Long I.

St. Lawrence River

ATLANTIC
OCEAN

Missouri River

DLANDS

SAND HILLS

P L A I N S

G R E A T

Platte River

Arkansas River

OZARK
PLATEAU

OUACHITA
MOUNTAINS

Red River

*LLANO
STACADO*

*EDWARDS
PLATEAU*

Colorado River

Rio Grande

Brazos River

Sabine River

Wabash River

CENTRAL PLAINS

Ohio River

Cumberland River

ALLEGHENY
PLATEAU

CUMBERLAND
PLATEAU

APPALACHIAN MOUNTAINS

BLUE RIDGE MTS.

Mt. Mitchell
(6,684 ft.; 2,037 m) ▲

Mississippi River

Pearl River

Alabama River

Altamaha River

Fall Line

ATLANTIC COASTAL PLAIN

Delaware
Bay

Chesapeake
Bay

Santee River

GULF COASTAL PLAIN

Galveston
Bay

Mobile
Bay

Pensacola
Bay

Apalachicola River

Tampa
Bay

Lake
Okeechobee

EVERGLADES

Gulf of Mexico

FLORIDA
KEYS

BAHAMAS

CUBA

UNITED STATES PHYSICAL

Elevation

Feet	Meters
Over 13,001	Over 3,001
6,561–13,000	2,001–3,000
3,281–6,560	1,001–2,000
1,641–3,280	501–1,000
661–1,640	201–500
0–660	0–200
Below sea level	Below sea level

▲ Mountain peak

0   150   300 miles

0   150   300 kilometers

ASIA

EUROPE

Bering Sea

ARCTIC OCEAN

Barrow

Qaanaaq

Greenland (Kalaalit Nunaat) (Den.)

Beaufort Sea

Baffin Bay

Alaska (U.S.)

Anchorage

Gulf of Alaska

Yukon R.

Arctic Circle

Mackenzie R.

Whitehorse

Juneau

Great Bear Lake

Yellowknife

Great Slave Lake

Nuuk

Iqaluit

Labrador Sea

PACIFIC OCEAN

Victoria

Vancouver

Seattle

Portland

Spokane

Edmonton

Calgary

Saskatoon

Regina

Winnipeg

CANADA

Churchill

Hudson Bay

Lake Winnipeg

Goose Bay

Sept-Îles

Gander

St. John's

ST. PIERRE-MIQUELON (Fr.)

Columbia R.

Missouri R.

Great Lakes

Quebec

Montreal

St. John

Halifax

San Francisco

Great Salt Lake

Salt Lake City

Denver

Colorado R.

Arkansas R.

Minneapolis

St. Paul

Omaha

Milwaukee

Kansas City

Chicago

Detroit

Cleveland

St. Louis

Cincinnati

Toronto

Ottawa

Buffalo

Pittsburgh

Boston

New York

Philadelphia

Washington, D.C.

ATLANTIC OCEAN

Los Angeles

San Diego

Phoenix

UNITED STATES

Memphis

Norfolk

El Paso

Dallas

Rio Grande

Mississippi R.

Ohio R.

Atlanta

Tropic of Cancer

San Antonio

Monterrey

Houston

New Orleans

MEXICO

Gulf of Mexico

Bermuda (U.K.)

Guadalajara

Mexico City

Orizaba

Miami

Havana

Nassau

BAHAMAS

N
W   E
S

CUBA

CAYMAN ISLANDS (U.K.)

Santiago

HAITI

Port-au-Prince

JAMAICA

Kingston

DOMINICAN REPUBLIC

Santo Domingo

Puerto Rico (U.S.)

VIRGIN IS. (U.S.-U.K.)

ANTIGUA AND BARBUDA

ST. KITTS AND NEVIS

Guadeloupe (Fr.)

DOMINICA

Martinique (Fr.)

ST. LUCIA

BARBADOS

Clipperton Island (Fr.)

Belmopan

BELIZE

GUATEMALA

Guatemala

San Salvador

EL SALVADOR

HONDURAS

Tegucigalpa

Managua

San José

COSTA RICA

NICARAGUA

Caribbean Sea

ARUBA

NETH. ANTILLES (Neth.)

GRENADA

ST. VINCENT AND THE GRENADINES

TRINIDAD AND TOBAGO

Panama Canal

PANAMA

Panama

SOUTH AMERICA

NORTH AMERICA POLITICAL

⊛ National capitals

◉ Cities with populations over one million

• Major cities

— National boundaries

— State boundaries

0   300   600 miles

0   300   600 kilometers

ASIA

EUROPE

ARCTIC OCEAN

Bering Sea

St. Lawrence I.

ALEUTIAN ISLANDS

Nunivak I.

ALASKA PEN.

Kodiak I.

SEWARD PEN.

BROOKS RANGE

ALASKA RANGE

Mt. McKinley ▲
(20,320 ft.; 6,194 m)

Point Barrow

Beaufort Sea

QUEEN ELIZABETH ISLANDS

Ellesmere Island

Greenland (Kalaalit Nunaat)

Arctic Circle

60°N

Gulf of Alaska

YUKON PLATEAU

Yukon R.

Barrow Strait

Victoria Island

BOOTHIA PEN.

Baffin Bay

Baffin Island

Davis Strait

ALEXANDER ARCHIPELAGO

Mackenzie R.

Great Bear Lake

COAST MTS

QUEEN CHARLOTTE ISLANDS

Great Slave Lake

Southampton I.

Hudson Strait

Labrador Sea

50°N

Vancouver I.

Peace R.

Athabasca R.

CANADIAN SHIELD

Hudson Bay

LABRADOR

30°W

PACIFIC OCEAN

N. Saskatchewan R.

ROCKY MOUNTAINS

CASCADE RANGE

Columbia R.

LAURENTIAN HIGHLANDS

Newfoundland

Prince Edward I.

40°N

Cape Mendocino

Mt. Rainier
(14,410 ft.; 4,392 m) ▲

Snake R.

Great Salt Lake

Missouri R.

Lake Winnipeg

Lake Superior

St. Lawrence R.

Great Lakes

Cape Breton I.

40°W

COAST RANGES

SIERRA NEVADA

GREAT BASIN

North Platte R.

GREAT PLAINS

BLACK HILLS

Lake Michigan

Lake Huron

Lake Ontario

APPALACHIAN MTS.

Cape Cod

Long I.

Point Conception

Mt. Whitney
(14,494 ft.; 4,481 m) ▲

COLORADO PLATEAU

Colorado R.

South Platte R.

▲ Mt. Elbert
(14,433 ft.; 4,399 m)

CENTRAL LOWLANDS

Lake Erie

Ohio R.

ATLANTIC OCEAN

40°W

Guadalupe I.

LOWER CALIFORNIA

OZARK PLATEAU

Arkansas R.

Mississippi R.

Tennessee R.

▲ Mt. Mitchell

Cape Hatteras

30°N

Eugenia Point

Rio Grande

Red R.

COASTAL PLAIN

Bermuda I.

NORTH AMERICA PHYSICAL

Land Elevation

Feet	Meters
Over 13,001	Over 4,001
6,501–13,000	2,001–4,000
3,001–6,500	1,001–2,000
1,501–3,000	501–1,000
701–1,500	201–500
0–700	0–200
Below sea level	Below sea level

▲ Mountain peak

SIERRA MADRE OCCIDENTAL

SIERRA MADRE ORIENTAL

False Cape

Gulf of California

FLORIDA PEN.

Cape Canaveral

N
W · E
S

Tropic of Cancer

0   300   600 miles

0   300   600 kilometers

110°W

Citlaltépetl ▲
(18,696 ft.; 5,700 m)

YUCATÁN PEN.

Gulf of Mexico

FLORIDA KEYS

BAHAMAS

CAYMAN ISLANDS

Cuba

GREATER ANTILLES

WEST INDIES

Hispaniola

Jamaica

VIRGIN IS.

Puerto Rico

St. Kitts and Nevis

Guadeloupe

Martinique

St. Lucia

St. Vincent

Barbuda
Antigua

LEEWARD ISLANDS

Dominica

WINDWARD ISLANDS

Barbados

Grenada

LESSER ANTILLES

20°N

CENTRAL AMERICA

ISTHMUS OF PANAMA

Aruba Curaçao

Bonaire

Tobago

Trinidad

10°N

Caribbean Sea

SOUTH AMERICA

100°W   90°W   80°W   70°W   60°W   50°W

Caribbean Sea

Barranquilla
Cartagena
Maracaibo
Valencia Caracas
Cúcuta Barquisimeto
San VENEZUELA
Cristóbal
Bucaramanga *Orinoco R.*
Medellín
Bogotá
Cali
COLOMBIA

GUYANA SURINAME

Georgetown French Guiana
(Fr.)
Paramaribo Cayenne

ATLANTIC OCEAN

Mapelo I.
(Colombia)

Equator
Quito
ECUADOR
GALÁPAGOS IS.
(Ecuador)
Guayaquil
Iquitos

Belém
Manaus *Amazon R.*
São Luís
Fortaleza

Madeira R.

Trujillo

B R A Z I L

Recife
Maceió

PERU

Lima
Callao
Cuzco

L. Titicaca
La Paz
BOLIVIA
Sucre

Arequipa

Xingu R.
Tocantins R.
Araguaia R.
São Francisco R.

Brasília
Salvador

N
W E
S

Belo
Horizonte

Chuquicamata

Tropic of Capricorn
Antofagasta

PARAGUAY
Asunción

Paraguay R.
Paraná R.

Rio de Janeiro
São Paulo
Niterói
Santos
Curitiba

San Felix I.
(Chile)
San Ambrosio I.
(Chile)

Tucumán

CHILE

Córdoba
Valparaíso
Santiago

Santa Fe
Rosario Paraná

Uruguay R.

Pôrto Alegre

ATLANTIC OCEAN

Juan Fernández Is.
(Chile)

Buenos Aires
La Plata

URUGUAY
Montevideo

Concepción

ARGENTINA

Bahía Blanca

Mar del Plata

PACIFIC OCEAN

SOUTH AMERICA POLITICAL
⊛ National capitals
◉ Cities with populations over one million
• Other cities
International boundaries

0   400   800 miles
0   400   800 kilometers

*Strait of
Magellan*

FALKLAND IS. (U.K.)
(MALVINAS IS.)

Punta Arenas

Caribbean Sea

GUAJIRA PEN.

Margarita I.

ORINOCO RIVER DELTA

Lake Maracaibo

Orinoco R.

C. Orange

▲ Mt. Tolima
(17,105 ft.; 5,215 m)

LLANOS

GUIANA HIGHLANDS

Gulf of Panama

Mapelo I.

AMAZON RIVER DELTA

Marajó Island

Equator 0°

GALÁPAGOS IS.

Río Negro

Amazon R.

C. São Roque

▲ Mt. Chimborazo
(20.561 ft.; 6,267 m)

AMAZON

BASIN

Gulf of Guayaquil

Marañón R.

Ucayali R.

Negra Pt.

ANDES   MOUNTAINS

10°S

SOUTH
AMERICA

Xingú R.

Araguaia R.

Tocantins R.

São Francisco R.

▲ Mt. Huascarán
(22,205 ft.; 6,763 m)

MATO
GROSSO
PLATEAU

**PACIFIC
OCEAN**

ANDES

L. Titicaca

▲ Mt. Ancohuma
(20,958 ft.; 6,388 m)

Madeira R.

L. Poopó

Paraguay R.

Paraná R.

BRAZILIAN   HIGHLANDS

20°S

▲ Mt. Bandeira
(9,479 ft.; 2,890 m)

MOUNTAINS

ATACAMA DESERT

C. Frio

Tropic of Capricorn

San Felix I.

San Ambrosio I.

GRAN CHACO

**ATLANTIC
OCEAN**

Paraná R.

Uruguay R.

30°S

Juan Fernández Is.

▲ Mt. Aconcagua
(22,831 ft.; 6,959 m)

PAMPAS

Río de
la Plata

Blanca Bay

SOUTH AMERICA PHYSICAL

Land Elevation

Feet	Meters
Over 13,121	Over 4,001
6,561-13,120	2,001-4,000
3,281-6,560	1,001-2,000
661-3,280	201-1,000
0-660	0-200

▲ Mountain peak

San Matías Gulf

Chiloé I.

VALDÉS PEN.

CHONOS
ARCHIPELAGO

TAITAO PEN.

N
W   E
S

PATAGONIA

*Gulf of
San Jorge*

C. Tres Puntas

0   400   800 miles
0   400   800 kilometers

FALKLAND IS. (U.K.)
(MALVINAS IS.)

Grande Bay

40°S

*Strait of
Magellan*

Tierra Del Fuego
Cape Horn

South Georgia

50°S

90°W   80°W   70°W   60°W   50°W   40°W   30°W   20°W   10°W   0°

AFRICA POLITICAL

★ National capitals

⊙ Cities with populations over one million

• Other cities

—— International boundaries

- - - Disputed boundaries

| 0 | | 500 | | 1,000 miles |
| 0 | 500 | | 1,000 kilometers | |

EUROPE

ASIA

Mediterranean Sea

TUNISIA

Tunis

Algiers

Oran

Tangier

Rabat

Casablanca

MOROCCO

Marrakech

MADEIRA IS. (Port.)

CANARY IS. (Sp.)

El Aaiún

Western Sahara (Morocco)

ALGERIA

LIBYA

Tripoli

Benghazi

Alexandria

Cairo

EGYPT

Suez Canal

Nile R.

L. Nasser

Red Sea

Port Sudan

MAURITANIA

Nouakchott

MALI

Timbuktu

Niger R.

NIGER

CHAD

Khartoum

SUDAN

White Nile R.

Blue Nile R.

ERITREA

Asmara

DJIBOUTI

Djibouti

Gulf of Aden

Dakar

SENEGAL

Banjul

GAMBIA

Bissau

GUINEA-BISSAU

GUINEA

Conakry

Freetown

SIERRA LEONE

Monrovia

LIBERIA

Bamako

BURKINA FASO

Ouagadougou

Niamey

BENIN

TOGO

GHANA

CÔTE D'IVOIRE

Yamoussoukro

Accra

Lomé

Porto-Novo

NIGERIA

Abuja

Lagos

N'Djamena

L. Chad

CENTRAL AFRICAN REPUBLIC

Bangui

CAMEROON

Yaounde

Malabo

EQUATORIAL GUINEA

SÃO TOMÉ AND PRÍNCIPE

São Tomé

Libreville

GABON

CONGO

Cabinda (Angola)

Brazzaville

Kinshasa

ZAIRE

Zaire (Congo) River

ETHIOPIA

Addis Ababa

SOMALIA

Mogadishu

UGANDA

Kampala

KENYA

Nairobi

L. Turkana

L. Victoria

RWANDA

Kigali

BURUNDI

Bujumbura

TANZANIA

Mombasa

Dar es Salaam

L. Tanganyika

L. Nyasa

SEYCHELLES

Victoria

INDIAN OCEAN

Luanda

Ascension (Br.)

ATLANTIC OCEAN

St. Helena (Br.)

ANGOLA

ZAMBIA

Lusaka

L. Kariba

Zambezi River

MALAWI

Lilongwe

COMOROS

Moroni

MOZAMBIQUE

ZIMBABWE

Harare

Antananarivo

MADAGASCAR

MAURITIUS

Port Loui

Réunion (Fr.)

NAMIBIA

Windhoek

BOTSWANA

Gaborone

Pretoria

Johannesburg

Maputo

Mbabane

SWAZILAND

SOUTH AFRICA

Maseru

LESOTHO

Durban

Umtata

Cape Town

Port Elizabeth

Tropic of Cancer

Tropic of Capricorn

Equator

0°

15°N

15°S

30°S

30°N

15°W

0°

15°E

30°E

45°E

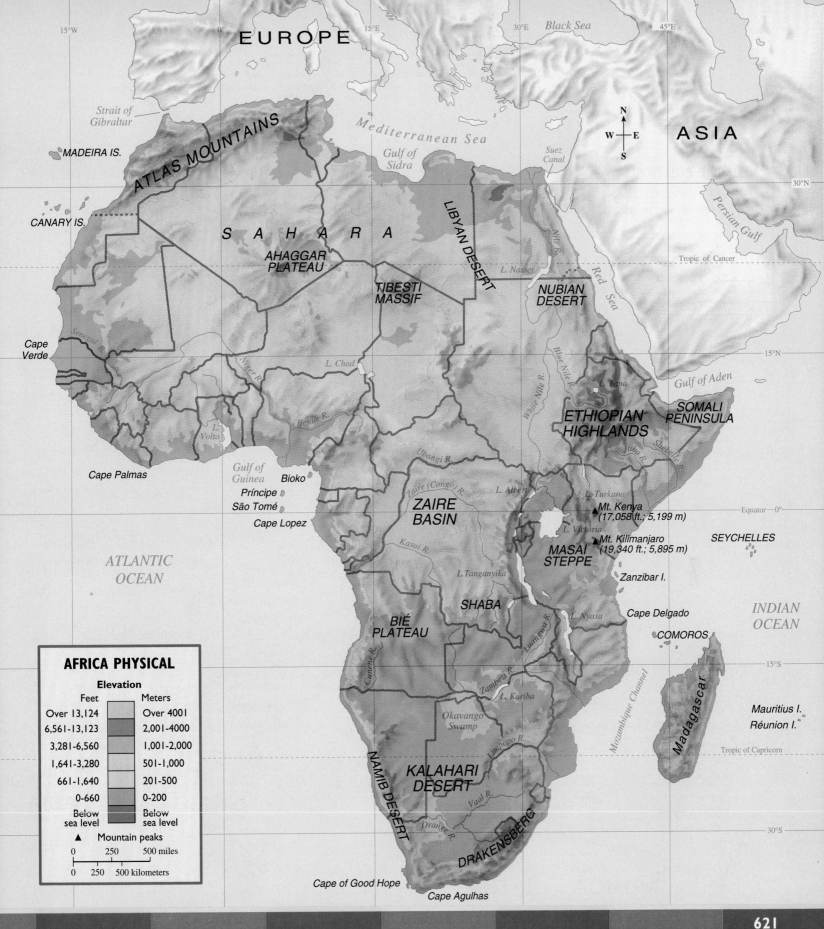

EUROPE

ASIA

Strait of Gibraltar

MADEIRA IS.

Mediterranean Sea

Gulf of Sidra

Suez Canal

Black Sea

Persian Gulf

ATLAS MOUNTAINS

CANARY IS.

SAHARA

AHAGGAR PLATEAU

TIBESTI MASSIF

LIBYAN DESERT

Nile R.

L. Nasser

NUBIAN DESERT

Red Sea

Tropic of Cancer

30°N

15°N

Cape Verde

Senegal R.

Niger R.

L. Chad

Benue R.

L. Volta

Blue Nile R.

White Nile R.

L. Tana

Gulf of Aden

SOMALI PENINSULA

ETHIOPIAN HIGHLANDS

Cape Palmas

Gulf of Guinea

Bioko

Príncipe

São Tomé

Cape Lopez

Ubangi R.

Zaire (Congo) R.

ZAIRE BASIN

Kasai R.

L. Albert

L. Turkana

▲ Mt. Kenya (17,058 ft.; 5,199 m)

▲ Mt. Kilimanjaro (19,340 ft.; 5,895 m)

Juba R.

Shebelle R.

L. Victoria

MASAI STEPPE

Zanzibar I.

SEYCHELLES

Equator—0°

ATLANTIC OCEAN

L.Tanganyika

SHABA

BIÉ PLATEAU

Cunene R.

Luangwa R.

Cape Delgado

L. Nyasa

COMOROS

INDIAN OCEAN

Mozambique Channel

Madagascar

15°S

Zambezi R.

L. Kariba

Mauritius I.

Réunion I.

Okavango Swamp

Limpopo R.

Tropic of Capricorn

NAMIB DESERT

KALAHARI DESERT

Vaal R.

Orange R.

DRAKENSBERG

30°S

Cape of Good Hope

Cape Agulhas

AFRICA PHYSICAL

Elevation

Feet		Meters
Over 13,124		Over 4001
6,561-13,123		2,001-4000
3,281-6,560		1,001-2,000
1,641-3,280		501-1,000
661-1,640		201-500
0-660		0-200
Below sea level		Below sea level

▲ Mountain peaks

0   250   500 miles

0   250   500 kilometers

EUROPE POLITICAL

- ⊛ National capitals
- ⊙ Cities with populations over one million
- • Other cities
- ⌇⌇ International boundaries

0   150   300 miles
0   150   300 kilometers

Barents Sea

Murmansk

ICELAND
Reykjavík
Kópavogur

Arctic Circle

Narvik

FINLAND

White Sea

Arkhangel'sk

Norwegian Sea

L. Onega

FAROE IS.
(Den.)

Trondheim

NORWAY

Tampere

L. Ladoga

SHETLAND IS.
(U.K.)

Bergen

Oslo

Helsinki

St. Petersburg

RUSSIA

Yaroslav

SWEDEN

Stockholm

Tallinn

ESTONIA

Göteborg

Gulf of Bothnia

Baltic Sea

Riga

LATVIA

Moscow

UNITED
KINGDOM

Glasgow

North Sea

DENMARK

Aarhus

LITHUANIA

Vilnius

Tula

Belfast

Leeds

Copenhagen

Kaliningrad

RUSSIA

Minsk

Dublin

Liverpool

Manchester Sheffield

Birmingham

IRELAND

Cork

London

NETHERLANDS

Gdańsk

POLAND

BELARUS

Amsterdam

Hamburg

Bremen

Berlin

Poznań

Warsaw

Kiev

Antwerp
The Hague
Rotterdam

Hannover Leipzig

Łódź

Thames R.

Ghent

Cologne

Kraków

Lviv

Kharkiv

ATLANTIC
OCEAN

English Channel

Brussels

BELGIUM LUXEMBOURG

GERMANY

Dresden

Wrocław

UKRAINE

Dnieper R.

Paris

Luxembourg

Frankfurt

Prague

Ostrava

Kirovograd

Dnepropetrovsk
Zaporizhzhya

Seine R.

Stuttgart

CZECH REP.

SLOVAKIA

Dniester R.

LIECHTENSTEIN

Munich

Bratislava

Miskolc

MOLDOVA

Loire R.

Zürich
Vaduz

Vienna

Graz

Budapest

Cluj

Chisinau

Kryvyy
Rog

FRANCE

Bern

SWITZERLAND

AUSTRIA

HUNGARY

Odesa

Lyon

Rhône R.

Ljubljana

ROMANIA

Bay of
Biscay

Milan

SLOVENIA

Timisoara

Bucharest

Bordeaux

Turin

Po R.

San
Marino

Zagreb

CROATIA

Black Sea

Toulouse

Genoa

BOSNIA–
HERZEGOVINA

Belgrade

Andorra-
La Vella

MONACO

Florence

Ebro R.

Marseille

Nice

SAN MARINO

Sarajevo

Danube R.

YUGOSLAVIA

BULGARIA

Oporto

PORTUGAL

Douro R.

ANDORRA

Monaco

ITALY

Adriatic Sea

Sofia

Plovdiv

Madrid Saragossa

Tagus R.

Barcelona

Corsica
(Fr.)

VATICAN
CITY

Vatican City

Rome

Durrës

Skopje

MACEDONIA

Istanbul

Lisbon

SPAIN

Tiranë

ALBANIA

Thessaloníki

TURKEY

Seville

Valencia

BALEARIC IS. (Sp.)

Sardinia
(It.)

Naples

Aegean
Sea

Ankara

Strait of
Gibraltar

Gibraltar (U.K.)

Mediterranean Sea

Palermo

Sicily

GREECE

Athens

ASIA

AFRICA

MALTA
Valletta

Crete (Gr.)

622

EUROPE PHYSICAL

Elevation

Feet	Meters
13,120+	4001+
6,561–13,120	2,001–4,000
3,281–6,560	1,001–2,000
1,641–3,280	501–1,000
661–1,640	201–500
0–660	0–200

▲ Mountain peaks
● Cities

0   150   300 miles
0   150   300 kilometers

Iceland

Arctic Circle

LOFOTEN IS.

LAPLAND

Norwegian Sea

FAROE IS.

KJØLEN MTS.

SCANDINAVIAN PENINSULA

Glittertinden
(8,104 ft.; 2,470 m)▲

White Sea

Barents Sea

L. Onega

L. Ladoga

Gulf of Bothnia

SHETLAND IS.

HEBRIDES IS.

ORKNEY IS.

L. Vänern

L. Vättern

Saaremaa I.
Gotland I.

Gulf of Finland

L. Peipus

JUTLAND PENINSULA

BALTIC PLAINS

Baltic Sea

North Sea

Ireland
Great Britain
BRITISH ISLES

Thames R.

Elbe R.

Oder R.

Vistula R.

Dnieper R.

ATLANTIC OCEAN

English Channel

Ruhr R.

Seine R.

NORTH EUROPEAN PLAIN

CARPATHIAN MTS.

Dniester R.

Loire R.

Danube R.

Bay of Biscay

Garonne R.

Matterhorn
(14,692 ft.; 4,478 m)▲

A L P S

Po R.

Danube R.

CRIMEAN PEN.

PYRENEES

Mt. Blanc
(15,771 ft.; 4,807 m)▲

APENNINES

ITALIAN PENINSULA

Adriatic Sea

DINARIC ALPS

Black Sea

Douro R.

Ebro R.

BALKAN MTS.

Bosporus

IBERIAN PENINSULA

Tagus R.

Guadiana R.

Corsica

Tyrrhenian Sea

Sardinia

BALEARIC IS.

Mt. Vesuvius
(4,190 ft.; 1,277 m)▲

BALKAN PENINSULA

Mt. Olympus
(9,570 ft.; 2,917 m)▲

PINDUS MTS.

Aegean Sea

Strait of Gibraltar

Mediterranean Sea

Sicily ▲ Mt. Etna
(11,122 ft.; 3,390 m)

Ionian Sea

AFRICA

ASIA POLITICAL

⊛ National capitals

◉ Cities with populations over one million

• Other cities

⸻ International boundaries

---- Disputed boundary

0 250 500 750 1,000 miles
0 500 1,000 kilometers

PACIFIC OCEAN

Bering Sea

Magadan

KAMCHATKA PENINSULA

Sea of Okhotsk

Aldan R.

Sakhalin I. (Russia)

KURIL IS. (Russia)

Amur R.

Khabarovsk

Sapporo

Harbin

Vladivostok

Inner Mongolia

Fushun
enyang

NORTH KOREA

Sea of Japan

Tokyo

Yokohama

P'yongyang

Kyoto Nagoya
Kobe

ijing
Dalian

Seoul
Osaka

Tianjin

SOUTH KOREA
Pusan

JAPAN

Qingdao

Kitakyushu

Yellow Sea

East China Sea

Korea Strait

Tropic of Cancer

MARSHALL ISLANDS

Majuro

Nanjing

Shanghai

RYUKYU IS. (Japan)

Wuhan

KIRIBATI

Bairiki

Taipei

TAIWAN

NORTHERN MARIANA IS. (U.S.)

Palikir

TUVALU

Yaren

Funifuti

ang
st R.

Guangzhou

NAURU

Luzon Strait

Philippine Sea

FIJI

cao
ort.)

Hong Kong

FEDERATED STATES OF MICRONESIA

Suva

South China Sea

Guam (U.S.)

Manila

a Nang

Koror

Equator

SOLOMON ISLANDS

ETNAM

PALAU

Honiara

Davao

VANUATU

Bandar Seri Begawan

Celebes Sea

Jayapura

Lae

Port-Vila

BRUNEI

Irian Jaya

PAPUA NEW GUINEA

AYSIA

Manado

New Guinea

New Caledonia (Fr.)

I N D O N E S I A

Port Moresby

Samarinda

Pontianak

Borneo

Celebes

Banda Sea

Arafura Sea

Coral Sea

Banjarmasin

Ujung Pandang

Java Sea

East Timor (Indo.)

karta

Surabaya

Timor

AUSTRALIA

Java
andung

120°E   140°E   160°E   180°E

ARCTIC OCEAN

NORTH
LAND

*Barents
Sea*

Novaya
Zemlya

*Kara
Sea*

*Laptev
Sea*

NEW
SIBERIAN
IS.

TAYMYR
PEN.

VERKHOYANSK

YAMAL
PEN.

CENTRAL
SIBERIAN
PLATEAU

EUROPE

WEST
SIBERIAN
PLAIN

S I B E R I A

Lower Tunguska R.

Angara R.

L. Baikal

Black Sea

ANATOLIAN

KIRGIZ
STEPPE

KAZAK
UPLANDS

Aral Sea

Ishim R.

SAYAN
MTS.

Cyprus

Caspian Sea

Mt. Ararat
(17,011 ft.; 5,185 m)

TURAN LOWLAND

L. Balqash

MONGOLIAN
PLATEAU

Suez
Canal

SYRIAN
DESERT

ELBURZ MTS.

PLATEAU
OF IRAN

Amu Darya

TIAN SHAN

TARIM
BASIN

NAN SHAN

Mediterranean Sea

Tigris R.

Euphrates R.

ZAGROS MOUNTAINS

PAMIRS

ALTUN SHAN

HINDU KUSH

KUNLUN SHAN

ASIA

AFRICA

Persian Gulf

TIBETAN PLATEAU

Red Sea

ARABIAN
PENINSULA

Sutlej R.

HIMALAYAS

Chang Jiang

GREAT
INDIAN
DESERT

Mt. Everest
(29,028 ft.; 8,848 m)

RUB AL'KHALI
DESERT

*Gulf of
Oman*

Brahmaputra R.

Gulf of Aden

*Arabian
Sea*

INDIAN PENINSULA

Xijiang

WESTERN GHATS

DECCAN
PLATEAU

EASTERN GHATS

*Bay of
Bengal*

INDOCHINA
PENINSULA

INDIAN
OCEAN

ANDAMAN
IS.

*Andaman
Sea*

*Gulf of
Thailand*

LAKSHADWEEP

Sri
Lanka

NICOBAR
IS.

Strait of Malacca

MALDIVES

MALAY
PENINSULA

N

MENTAWAI IS.

40°E 60°E 80°E 100°E

80°N

626

HERSKI
RANGE

RANGE

*Bering
Sea*

CENTRAL RANGE

**KAMCHATKA
PENINSULA**

*Sea of
Okhotsk*

Sakhalin

KURIL IS.

Amur R.

Hokkaido

MANCHURIAN
PLAIN

*Sea of
Japan*

Honshu

▲Mt Fuji
(12,388 ft.; 3,776 m)

KOREAN
PEN.

JAPANESE
ARCHIPELAGO

Korea Strait

Shikoku

*Yellow
Sea*

Kyushu

NORTH
CHINA
PLAIN

*East
China
Sea*

RYUKYU IS.

Okinawa

BOHEA HILLS

Taiwan

Luzon Strait

*Philippine
Sea*

inan

*South
China
Sea*

Luzon

PHILIPPINE IS.

Samar

Panay
Negros

Palawan

Mindanao

ATUNA

*Celebes
Sea*

Halmahera

MOLUCCAS

New Guinea

MAOKE
MTS.

Ceram

Buru

ARU
IS.

Borneo

Celebes

Banda Sea

*Arafura
Sea*

ngka

Java Sea

EAST INDIES

Flores

Timor

AUSTRALIA

Sumbawa

Sumba

Java

Bali

Lombok

*PACIFIC
OCEAN*

Tropic of Cancer

Equator

20°N

40°N

20°N

0°

20°S

20°S

120°E

140°E

160°E

180°E

AUSTRALIA AND NEW ZEALAND
POLITICAL AND PHYSICAL

Elevation

Feet	Meters
Over 6,561	Over 2,001
3,281–6,560	1,001–2,000
1,641–3,280	501–1,000
661–1,640	201–500
0–660	0–200

——— State or territorial boundaries
⊛ National capitals
★ State or territorial capitals
• Other cities
▲ Mountain peaks

0   500   1,000 miles
0   500   1,000 kilometers

MALAYSIA

INDONESIA

PAPUA
NEW
GUINEA

New Guinea

BISMARCK ARCHIPELAGO

Bougainville

New Britain

SOLOMON ISLANDS

Honiara ⊛

VANUATU

Port-Vila ⊛

FIJI

Suva ⊛

PACIFIC OCEAN

Equator

Banda Sea

Timor Sea

Arafura Sea

Torres Strait

Cape York Peninsula

Gulf of Carpentaria

Coral Sea

Great Barrier Reef

New Caledonia (Fr.)

Norfolk I. (Aust.)

Tasman Sea

INDIAN OCEAN

Darwin ★

Northern Territory

MACDONNELL RANGES
Alice Springs •

MUSGRAVE RANGES

SIMPSON DESERT

GREAT SANDY DESERT

GIBSON DESERT

Western Australia

GREAT VICTORIA DESERT

A U S T R A L I A

GREAT ARTESIAN BASIN

Queensland

Mount Isa •

Townsville •

Rockhampton •

Toowoomba •

Brisbane ★
Ipswich •

South Australia

NULLARBOR PLAIN

Great Australian Bight

L. Eyre

L. Torrens

Spencer Gulf

Port Augusta •
Whyalla •

Broken Hill •

Adelaide ★

New South Wales

Darling R.

Murray R.

Bathurst •
Wagga Wagga •

Newcastle •
Sydney ★
Wollongong •
Port Kembla •
Canberra, A.C.T. ⊛
Mt. Kosciusko
(7,316 ft.; 2,230 m) ▲

GREAT DIVIDING RANGE

AUSTRALIAN ALPS

Victoria

Ballarat •
Geelong •
Melbourne ★

Bass Strait

Launceston •

Hobart ★

Tasmania

Perth ★

Albany •

Kalgoorlie •

Geraldton •

Carnarvon •

NEW ZEALAND

North I.

North Cape

Whangarei •
Auckland •
Hamilton •

Gisborne •
Napier •
Wellington ⊛

Cook Strait

SOUTHERN ALPS

South I.

Christchurch •

Mt. Cook
(12,349 ft.; 3,764 m) ▲

Dunedin •

Invercargill •

Port Moresby ⊛

Tropic of Capricorn

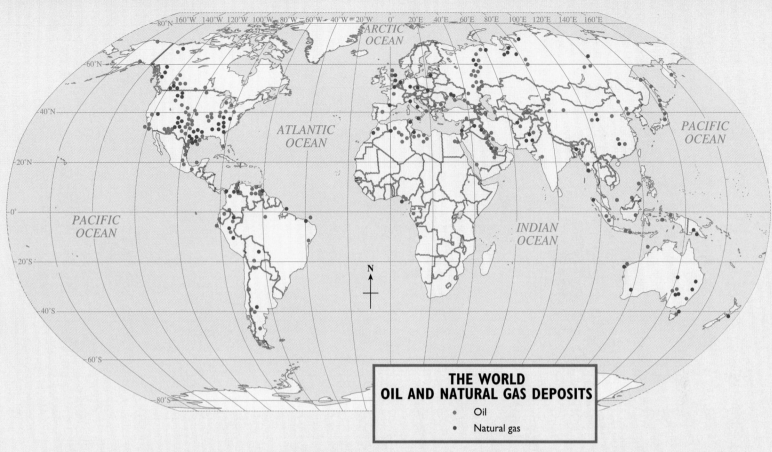

THE WORLD
OIL AND NATURAL GAS DEPOSITS

- Oil
- Natural gas

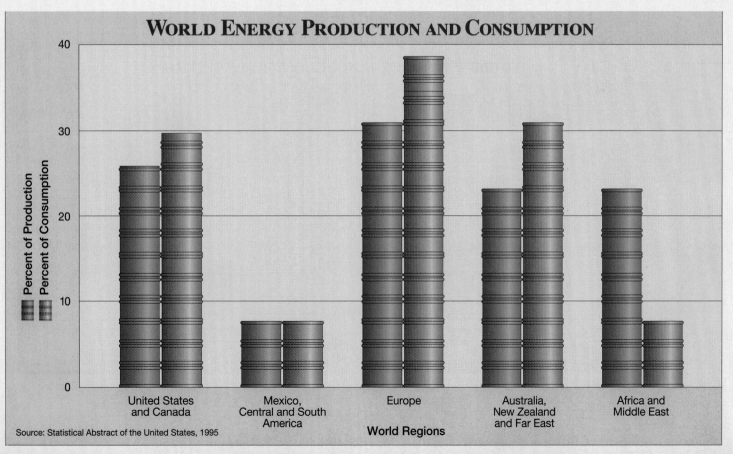

WORLD ENERGY PRODUCTION AND CONSUMPTION

Percent of Production
Percent of Consumption

40

30

20

10

0

United States
and Canada

Mexico,
Central and South
America

Europe

Australia,
New Zealand
and Far East

Africa and
Middle East

World Regions

Source: Statistical Abstract of the United States, 1995

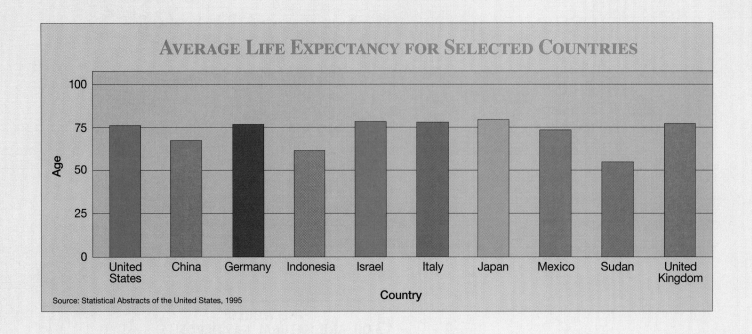

AVERAGE LIFE EXPECTANCY FOR SELECTED COUNTRIES

Source: Statistical Abstracts of the United States, 1995

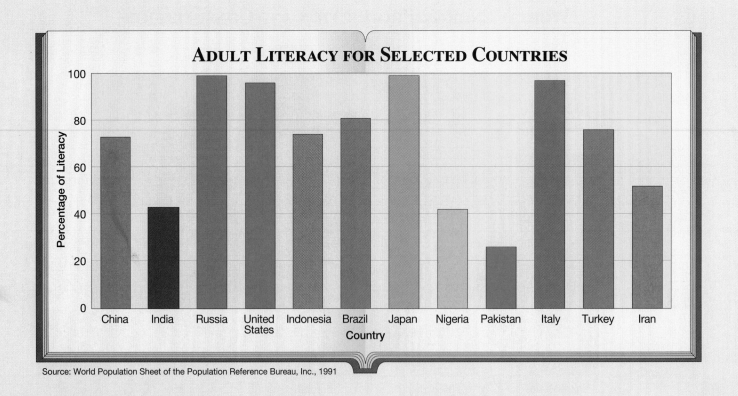

ADULT LITERACY FOR SELECTED COUNTRIES

Source: World Population Sheet of the Population Reference Bureau, Inc., 1991

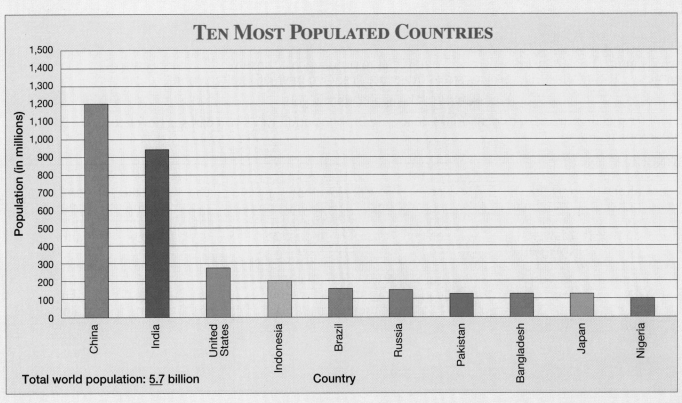

TEN MOST POPULATED COUNTRIES

Population (in millions)

1,500
1,400
1,300
1,200
1,100
1,000
900
800
700
600
500
400
300
200
100
0

China | India | United States | Indonesia | Brazil | Russia | Pakistan | Bangladesh | Japan | Nigeria

Country

Total world population: 5.7 billion

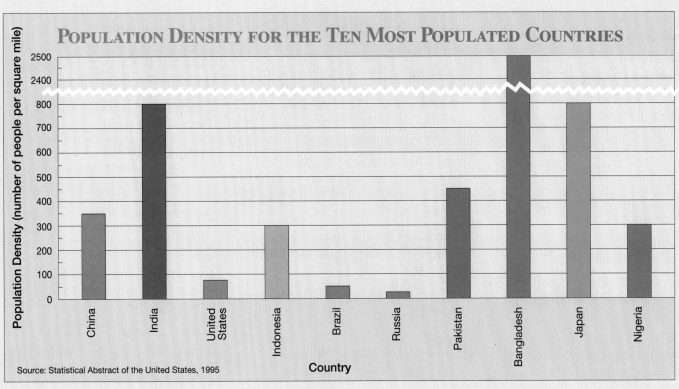

POPULATION DENSITY FOR THE TEN MOST POPULATED COUNTRIES

Population Density (number of people per square mile)

2500
2400

800
700
600
500
400
300
200
100
0

China | India | United States | Indonesia | Brazil | Russia | Pakistan | Bangladesh | Japan | Nigeria

Country

Source: Statistical Abstract of the United States, 1995

Some words in this book may be new to you or difficult to pronounce. Those words have been spelled phonetically in parentheses. The syllable that receives stress in a word is shown in small capital letters.

For example: Chicago (shuh KAH goh)

Most phonetic spellings are easy to read. In the following Pronunciation Key, you can see how letters are used to show different sounds.

PRONUNCIATION KEY

a	after	(AF tur)	oh	flow	(floh)	ch	chicken	(CHIHK un)
ah	father	(FAH thhur)	oi	boy	(boi)	g	game	(gaym)
ai	care	(kair)	oo	rule	(rool)	ing	coming	(KUM ing)
aw	dog	(dawg)	or	horse	(hors)	j	job	(jahb)
ay	paper	(PAY pur)	ou	cow	(kou)	k	came	(kaym)
						ng	long	(lawng)
e	letter	(LET ur)	yoo	few	(fyoo)	s	city	(SIHT ee)
ee	eat	(eet)	u	taken	(TAYK un)	sh	ship	(shihp)
				matter	(MAT ur)	th	thin	(thihn)
ih	trip	(trihp)	uh	ago	(uh GOH)	thh	feather	(FETHH ur)
eye	idea	(eye DEE uh)				y	yard	(yahrd)
y	hide	(hyd)				z	size	(syz)
ye	lie	(lye)				zh	division	(duh VIHZH un)

A

abolitionist (ab uh LIHSH un ihst) A person who advocates an end to slavery. p. 485.

absolute power (AB suh loot POW ur) Power of a ruler that is not limited by a constitution, parliament, or other similar form of government. p. 32.

accord (uh KORD) A mutual agreement. p. 516.

adobe (uh DOH bee) Sun-dried bricks used for building. p. 368.

agronomist (uh GRAHN uh mihst) A scientist specializing in efficient crop production. p. 603.

algebra (AL juh bruh) A form of mathematics that uses letters and numbers to solve problems. p. 228.

alliance (uh LYE uns) An agreement among persons, groups, or nations to act together. p. 438.

alms (ahmz) A donation to the poor. p. 226.

ambassador (am BAS uh dur) An official who represents his or her government in a foreign land. p. 108.

anthropologist (an throh PAHL uh-jihst) A person who studies humans, especially the physical and cultural characteristics, customs, and social relationships. p. 34.

apartheid (uh PAHR tayt) Separation of races by law in South Africa. p. 481.

applied science (uh PLYD SYE uns) Science put to practical use. p. 230.

apprentice (uh PREN tihs) A person learning a trade by working with a master skilled in that trade. p. 209.

aqueduct (AK wuh dukt) A structure made for bringing water from one place to another. p. 173.

archaeologist (ahr kee AHL uh jihst) A person who studies the life and culture of the past, especially ancient peoples. p. 34.

archipelago (ahr kuh PEL uh goh) A chain of islands in a sea. p. 286.

architect (AHR kuh tekt) A person who designs buildings and is in charge of their construction. p. 277.

architecture (AHR kuh tek chur) A style or special way of building. p. 147.

armorer (AHR mur ur) A person who makes armor for a lord and his knights. p. 213.

arms race (ahrmz rays) A competition between the United States and the U.S.S.R to have a superior military force. p. 557.

artillery (ahr TIHL ur ee) Guns of large caliber; cannons. p. 479.

B

balance of trade (BAL uns uv trayd) A comparison between the value of a country's exports and imports. p. 403.

barbarian (bahr BER ee un) An uncivilized or crude person. p. 118.

barricade (BAR ih kayd) A barrier or obstruction. p. 428.

Bedouin (BED oo ihn) An Arab who lives in the desert and moves between established grazing areas. p. 220.

big-stick policy (bihg stihk PAHL uh-see) A policy of acting from a position backed with a show of strength. p. 457.

boomerang (BOOM ur ang) A flat, curved, wooden weapon that returns to the thrower when hurled. p. 416.

boycott (BOI kaht) A campaign in which people refuse to deal with a particular group or business. p. 535.

brush (brush) Low, shrublike vegetation. p. 131.

bulla (BUL uh) A charm worn for protection. p. 176.

C

caliph (KAY lihf) A Muslim religious and political leader. p. 222.

calligraphy (kuh LIHG ruh fee) The art of fine handwriting. p. 121.

capitalist (KAP ut tul ihst) Describing a system in which land, factories, and materials used in making goods are privately owned and operated for profit. p. 548.

caravan (KAR uh van) A group of people and goods traveling together. p. 53.

caravel (KAR uh vel) A fast, small sailing ship. p. 341.

carnelian (kahr NEEL yun) A clear red gemstone. p. 65.

cartogram (KAHR tuh gram) A map in which country size is based on some value other than land area. p. 11.

caste (kast) Any one of the Hindu social classes into which a person was born and which ruled his or her relations with others. p. 97.

castellan (KAS tuh lun) The governor of a castle. p. 213.

catapult (KAT uh pult) An ancient weapon used to throw rocks or arrows. p. 109.

catechism (KAT uh kihz um) A handbook of questions and answers for teaching the principles of a religion. p. 490.

caudillo (kou THHEE lyoh) A leader, especially a military dictator. p. 457.

causeway (KAWZ way) A raised roadway above a body of water. p. 318.

centrism (SEN trihz um) A way of looking at the world from the point of view of one's own country or region. p. 38.

child labor (chyld LAY bur) The practice of employing children to work in factories, mills, and mines. p. 411.

circumnavigation (sur kum nav uh-GAY shun) The act of sailing or flying around an area. p. 358.

citadel (SIHT uh del) A fort built on a high point for defending a town. p. 140.

city-state (SIHT ee stayt) A city that governs itself as well as the land and people around it. p. 51.

civil disobedience (SIV ul dihs oh-BEE dee uns) The refusal to obey unjust civil laws. p. 535.

civil rights (SIV ul ryts) Rights guaranteeing equal treatment of all U.S. citizens with respect to life, liberty, and property and to the protection of the law. p. 561.

cold war (kohld wor) A bitter political, economic, and intellectual rivalry among nations, without actual military conflict. p. 548.

collective farm (kuh LEK tihv fahrm) A farm that is operated by a group of people who share the products. p. 530.

Columbian Exchange (kuh LUM bee-un eks CHAYNJ) Results of contact between European countries and the Americas. p. 341.

commonwealth (KAHM un welth) An independent nation governed by its people. p. 416.

commune (KAHM yoon) A group of people who share possessions and responsibilities. p. 528.

communism (KAHM yoo nihz um) Ideally, a political system in which most property is owned by the government and shared by those governed. p. 428.

confederation (kun fed ur AY shun) Groups joined together for a specific purpose; a league or alliance. p. 268.

conquistador (kahn KEES tuh dor) Spanish word for "conqueror." p. 364.

constitution (kahn stuh TOO shun) A document that contains the laws or rules of government. p. 288.

contiguous (kun TIHG yoo us) Sharing an edge or boundary. p. 242.

corporal punishment (KOR puh rul PUN ihsh munt) A whipping or beating. p. 108.

counselor (KOUN suh lur) A person who advises. p. 242.

covenant (KUV uh nunt) An agreement. p. 58.

criollo (kree OH yoh) Person born in Latin America of European parents. p. 360.

Crusade (kroo SAYD) Any of the wars fought during three centuries by the Christians of Europe against the Muslims. p. 199.

cultivate (KUL tuh vayt) To dig, fertilize, and remove weeds before planting seeds. p. 119.

Cultural Revolution (KUL chur ul rev uh LOO shun) A period from 1965 to 1969 in which Mao tried to renew the revolution. p. 528.

culture region (KUL chur REE jun) Division of people based on a variety of factors, such as language, religion, or customs and traditions. p. 9.

cuneiform (kyoo NEE uh form) A form of writing with wedge-shaped symbols. p. 61.

curare (kyoo RAH ree) A poison that is used during surgery to relax a patient's muscles. p. 596.

curator (kyoo RAYT ur) A person in charge of a museum. p. 17.

cure (kyoor) To process, as by drying or aging. p. 388.

D

decimal (DES uh mul) Based on the number 10. p. 313.

defendant (dee FEN dunt) A person who is being accused. p. 179.

delta (DEL tuh) Land formed by mud and sand in the mouth of a river. p. 72.

demand (dih MAND) The amount of goods people are ready and able to buy at a certain price. p. 30.

developed country (dih VEL upt KUN tree) A country with access to natural resources, an industrial base, an educated population, and advanced technology. p. 581.

dhow (dou) A small wooden ship used by traders. p. 249.

dialect (DEE uh lekt) A variety of a language, used only in a certain region or among a certain people. p. 117.

dictator (DIHK tayt ur) A person who takes complete charge of the government. p. 167.

direct democracy (duh REKT duh-MAHK ruh see) Participation in government by all citizens directly, not through representatives. p. 150.

disciple (dih SYE pul) A follower of a teacher or leader. p. 171.

dogma (DAHG muh) A body, or collection, of beliefs. p. 344.

domino theory (DAHM uh noh THEE-uh ree) The idea that if a nation becomes a Communist state, the nations nearby will also. p. 551.

dowry (DOU ree) The property a woman brings to a marriage. p. 54.

E

ebony (EB uh nee) A dark, hard wood found in Asia. p. 279.

Egyptologist (ee jihp TAHL uh jihst) A scientist who studies the remains of ancient Egypt. p. 83.

elevation (el uh VAY shun) Height above the surface of the earth or above sea level. p. 15.

embassy (EM buh see) The official headquarters of an ambassador. p. 527.

emigration (em ih GRAY shun) The leaving of one country or region to settle in another. p. 464.

empire (EM pyr) Many different lands brought under one government. p. 54.

enclosure acts (en KLOH zhur akts) Laws that allowed wealthy farmers to close off all the common land. p. 410.

epistle (ee PIHS ul) A letter. p. 171.

erosion (ee ROH zhun) Wearing away of rocks and soil by the action of water, wind, or moving ice. p. 13.

excommunicate (eks kuh MYOO nih-kayt) To punish by revoking the right to take part in church rituals. p. 194.

exhibition (ek suh BIHSH un) A display for the public of industrial and agricultural achievements. p. 412.

exile (EKS eyel) A forced living away from one's country. p. 105.

exploitation (eks ploi TAY shun) The use of people or things in a selfish or unfair way. p. 404.

F

factory system (FAK tuh ree SIHS-tum) The practice of having workers use machines in one large place instead of working at home or in small workshops. p. 410.

fast (fast) Going without food or drink. p. 226.

federal republic (FED ur ul rih PUB-lihk)   A government in which power is divided between a central authority and individual states. p. 577.

feminist (FEM uh nihst)   A supporter of the principle that women should have political, economic, and social rights equal to those of men. p. 510.

feudalism (FYOOD uh lihz um)   A political and economic system prevalent in Europe in the Middle Ages. p. 197.

fez (fez)   A brimless hat shaped like a cone but with a flat top, usually red with a flat black tassel hanging from the top. p. 508.

flota (FLOH tuh)   A fleet of ships. p. 373.

forge (forj)   To shape metal by heating and pounding. p. 251.

fresco (FRES koh)   A painting made with watercolors on wet plaster. p. 139.

G

galleon (GAL ee un)   A large, heavily armed ship used for trading and war. p. 373.

gauge (gayj)   An instrument for measuring. p. 445.

genocide (JEN uh syd)   The planned destruction of a whole group of people because of their race, religion, or nationality. p. 437.

geographer (jee AHG ruh fur)   A person who studies the earth's surface and how living and nonliving things interact with it. p. 7.

geologist (jee AHL uh jihst)   A person who studies the earth's crust and the way in which its layers were formed. p. 35.

glasnost (GLAHS nust)   A policy of openness in the Soviet Union that resulted in less secrecy about problems and weaknesses in Soviet society. p. 552.

global culture (GLOH bul KUL chur)   Ways of living that are shared by many people around the world. p. 570.

global village (GLOH bul VIHL ihj)   The idea that people across the world can interact as easily as do people in a small town. p. 570.

gourd (gord)   A family of plants that includes squash and pumpkin. p. 323.

gourmet (GOR may)   Involving the preparation of fine or exotic food dishes. p. 391.

griot (gree OH)   A person who memorizes and tells the oral history of the people. p. 242.

gross domestic product (grohs doh-MES tihk PRAHD ukt)   The total value of all the goods and services produced in a year within the borders of a nation. p. 582.

guerrilla (guh RIHL uh)   A member of a military force that organizes the local population and attacks in small bands. p. 530.

guild (gihld)   An organization of people in a craft or trade. p. 198.

H

haiku (HYE koo)   A three-line poem that has 17 syllables. p. 296.

hajj (haj)   A Muslim pilgrimage. p. 226.

Hangul (HAHNG gool)   The alphabet King Sejong presented to the Korean people as a gift. p. 532.

headwaters (HED wawt urz)   The beginning, or source, of a large stream or river. p. 483.

heliocentric solar system (hee lee-oh SEN trik SOH lur SIHS tum)   A model of the solar system with the sun at its center. p. 344.

helot (HEL ut)   A person forced to work for another person. p. 141.

heritage (HER ih tihj)   A system of ways and beliefs handed down from one generation to another. p. 147.

hieroglyphic (hye ur oh GLIHF ihk)   A picture or symbol representing a word, syllable, or sound. p. 72.

Hijrah (hihzh RAH)   The journey from Mecca to Medina. p. 222.

Holocaust (HAHL uh kawst)   The mass murder of millions of Jews and other people by the Nazis. p. 437.

house arrest (hous uh REST)   Confinement to one's home on orders of legal officials. p. 394.

human feature (HYOO mun FEE-chur)   Evidence of human presence in an area. p. 16.

humanitarian (hyoo man uh TER ee-un)   Promoting the elimination of human pain and suffering. p. 593.

I

icon (EYE kahn)   A sacred image or picture. p. 193.

ideograph (IHD ee oh graf)   A symbol representing a thing or idea. p. 121.

imperialism (ihm PIHR ee ul ihz um)   The economic, political, and cultural domination of another country. p. 402.

635

indigo (IHN dih goh)   A plant used for making blue dye. p. 373.

Industrial Revolution (ihn DUS tree-ul rev uh LOO shun)   The period of great change brought about by the invention of power-driven machinery. p. 405.

infantry (IHN fun tree)   Soldiers who are trained and armed for fighting on foot. p. 153.

intifada (ihn tih FAH duh)   An uprising of Palestinian Arabs against Israeli military forces in occupied territories of the Gaza Strip and the West Bank. p. 516.

information superhighway (ihn fur-MAY shun soo pur HYE way)   Worldwide, computer-accessed, information database. p. 599.

initiation rite (ih nihsh ee AY shun ryt)   The period of instruction and the ceremony with which a person is admitted into a group. p. 253.

iron curtain (EYE urn KURT un)   A barrier of secrecy that isolated the Soviet Union and the countries it controlled. p. 548.

isolationism (EYE suh LAY shun ihz-um)   A policy of opposing involvement of one's country in alliances or agreements with other nations. p. 439.

J

jujitsu (joo JIHT soo)   Japanese system of unarmed combat. p. 300.

jury (JOOR ee)   A group of people called into court to give a verdict in a dispute. p. 151.

K

Kaaba (KAH buh)   The central shrine of Islam. p. 221.

karma (KAHR muh)   All the actions in a person's life that affect the next life. p. 100.

kendo (KEN doh)   A Japanese form of fencing. p. 300.

kibbutz (kih BOOTS)   An Israeli settlement where people live in groups as a family. p. 511.

L

lapis lazuli (LAP ihs LAZ yoo lee)   A dark blue gemstone. p. 65.

lentil (LENT ul)   A plant, with seeds growing in pods, used as food. p. 103.

libation (lye BAY shun)   The ceremony of pouring wine or oil to honor a god. p. 85.

lineage (LIHN ee ihj)   All the people who share a common known ancestor. p. 250.

lingua franca (LIHNG gwuh FRAHN-kuh)   A Latin term used to describe a language used by people whose first languages are different. p. 232.

llama (LAH muh)   A South American animal used for work and for its wool. p. 320.

loess (LOH es)   A yellowish, fine-grained soil that is very fertile. p. 117.

long house (lawng hous)   A shelter for six to seven families built by Native Americans. p. 41.

M

Machiavellian (mak ee uh VEL ee un)   Crafty, deceitful. p. 346.

magnet (MAG niht)   An object that can attract iron or steel. p. 128.

mandate (MAN dayt)   A territory placed under the governing powers of another country. p. 503.

marathon (MAR uh thahn)   A footrace of 26 miles, 385 yards. p. 144.

martial arts (MAHR shul ahrts)   Artistic forms of movement related to self-defense or attack. p. 125.

mausoleum (maw suh LEE um)   A large tomb. p. 277.

medieval era (med EE vul IHR uh)   The time period between A.D. 500 and 1500. p. 195.

meditate (MED uh tayt)   To spend time thinking quietly. p. 295.

mercantilism (MUR kun tihl ihz um)   A system of policies designed to build the wealth of a country. p. 402.

mesa (MAY suh)   A flat-topped plateau or tableland with steep sides. p. 369.

Mesoamerica (mez oh uh MER ih-kuh)   The area extending southward from central Mexico to include most of Central America. p. 308.

middle class (MIHD ul clas)   The social class between the working class peasants and the wealthy nobles. p. 338.

militant (MIHL ih tunt)   Ready and willing to fight in support of a cause. p. 269.

minaret (mihn uh RET)   A high tower on a mosque. p. 226.

mineralogy (mihn ur AHL uh jee)   The science of metals. p. 229.

mortar (MORT ur)   A mixture of lime, sand, and water used to cement, or hold, bricks or stones together. p. 312.

mosque (mahsk)   Muslim house of worship. p. 226.

mummy (MUM ee)   A body treated for burial with preservatives to keep it from decaying. p. 78.

multinational corporation (MUL tee-NASH uh nul kor puh RAY shun)   A company that does business in more than one country. p. 581.

myth (mihth)   A traditional story about the origins and activities of the gods. p. 143.

N

nationalism (NASH uh nul ihz um)   A feeling of loyalty and devotion to one's country. p. 338.

natron (NAY trahn)   A mineral salt found in soil from dry lake beds. p. 78.

natural rights (NACH ur ul ryts)   Basic human rights, such as life, property, and freedom. p. 426.

nomad (NOH mad)   A person who keeps moving around looking for food or pasture for his or her animals. p. 40.

nonconformist (nahn kun FORM ihst)   A person who does not follow the beliefs and practices of society. p. 298.

novel (NAHV ul)   A long story with a plot that has a beginning, a middle, and an end. p. 297.

O

oasis (oh AY sihs)   A fertile area in the desert. p. 220.

obelisk (AHB uh lihsk)   A four-sided pillar with a top shaped like a pyramid. p. 72.

observatory (ub ZURV uh tor ee)   A building equipped with instruments to study the stars. p. 229.

ocean current (OH shun KUR unt)   Narrow band of fast-moving ocean water. p. 21.

Opium War (OH pee um wor)   Wars between China and Britain, fought over trade in the habit-forming drug. p. 527.

P

Pacific Rim (puh SIHF ihk rihm)   All nations that border on the Pacific Ocean. p. 381.

pacifist (PAS uh fihst)   A person opposed to all wars. p. 443.

paleontologist (pay lee un TAHL uh-jihst)   A person who studies the life forms of the past, especially prehistoric life forms, using animal and plant fossils. p. 35.

pampas (PAHM puz)   The extensive, treeless plains of Argentina and some other parts of South America. p. 464.

papyrus (puh PYE rus)   A tall reed that grows in the Nile Valley, the pith (spongy center part) of which was used to make a paperlike substance. p. 73.

parable (PAR uh bul)   A brief story that teaches a moral lesson. p. 171.

partition (pahr TIHSH un)   To divide into parts. p. 515.

patrician (puh TRIHSH un)   A member of the upper class. p. 166.

patron (PAY trun)   A wealthy or important person who helps another person, group, or institution. p. 342.

Peace Corps (pees kor)   A U.S. agency that provides skilled volunteers to assist people in developing areas abroad. p. 556.

peninsula (puh NIHN suh luh)   A piece of land almost surrounded by water and connected to a larger body of land. p. 138.

peninsulare (pen ihn soo LAHR ay)   Spanish, meaning "person from the peninsula" of Iberia, where Spain and Portugal are located. p. 360.

peonage (PEE uh nihj)   A system where debtors must work for their creditors until their debts are paid. p. 361.

persecute (PUR sih kyoot)   To treat cruelly and unfairly. p. 171.

pharmacist (FAHR muh sihst)   A person trained to prepare drugs and medicines. p. 128.

philosophy (fuh LAHS uh fee)   The study of what people think about the meaning of life. p. 148.

pilot (PYE lut)   A person who steers a ship. p. 128.

pitch (pihtch)   A sticky substance found in some evergreen trees, coal tar, and petroleum. p. 369.

plaintiff (PLAYN tihf)   A person making a complaint against another in court. p. 179.

plait (playt)   A braid of hair. p. 321.

plateau (pla TOH)   A broad stretch of high, level land. p. 15.

plebeian (plee BEE un)   One of the common people. p. 166.

pogrom (poh GRAHM)   An organized persecution of a minority group. p. 465.

polygamy (puh LIHG uh mee)   The practice of having two or more spouses at the same time. p. 251.

portcullis (port KUL ihs)   An iron and hardwood gate that can be quickly lowered during an attack. p. 213.

precipitation (pree sihp uh TAY shun) Water that falls from clouds in the form of rain, snow, sleet, or hail. p. 12.

pre-Columbian (pree kuh LUM bee-un) Before the exploration and conquest of the Americas by Europeans. p. 362.

prehistory (pree HIHS tuh ree) History before recorded history, as learned from archaeology and other areas of study. p. 29.

prejudice (PREJ oo dihs) Dislike or distrust of someone because of their race or religion. p. 395.

productivity (proh duk TIHV uh tee) The producing of goods or wealth. p. 463.

protectorate (proh TEK tur iht) A weak country or territory protected and controlled by a stronger country. p. 503.

province (PRAHV ihns) A region of a country, usually having a local government. p. 288.

pulpería (pool pay REE ah) A country store. p. 468.

Q ▬▬▬▬▬▬▬▬▬▬▬▬▬

quixotic (kwihks AHT ihk) Foolishly idealistic; impractical. p. 346.

R ▬▬▬▬▬▬▬▬▬▬▬▬▬

Reformation (ref ur MAY shun) Sixteenth-century religious movement aimed at reforming the Catholic Church. p. 336.

refugee (ref yoo JEE) A person who flees war or political or religious persecution. p. 573.

regime (ruh ZHEEM) A form of government or rule. p. 550.

region (REE jun) An area of the earth's surface whose parts have one or more common characteristics. p. 7.

reign (rayn) A period of royal power, authority, or rule. p. 98.

reincarnation (ree ihn kahr NAY-shun) The continuation of a soul, upon the death of one body, into another body or form. p. 100.

Renaissance (ren uh SAHNS) Refers to the great revival of art and learning in Europe in the 1300s, 1400s, and 1500s. p. 335.

republic (rih PUB lihk) A form of government that allows citizens to choose representatives to rule. p. 165.

reservoir (REZ ur vwahr) A place where water is collected and stored for use. p. 318.

rote learning (roht LURN ihng) Learning by heart, often without understanding. p. 295.

S ▬▬▬▬▬▬▬▬▬▬▬▬▬

sack (sak) To rob a captured city. p. 85.

samisen (SAM uh sen) A musical instrument somewhat like a guitar, that has a long neck and three strings. p. 298.

sanitation (san un TAY shun) The practice of creating healthful living conditions. p. 595.

satire (SA tyr) The use of riducule or sarcasm to expose the vices or misbehavior of others. p. 347.

savanna (suh VAN uh) A flat, dry grassland of the tropics, dotted with shrubs and trees. p. 243.

scaffold (SKAF uld) A framework for supporting workers. p. 342.

scapegoat (SKAYP goht) A person or group blamed for the mistakes or crimes of others. p. 436.

scribe (skryb) A person who copies information and keeps records. p. 51.

seasonal migration (SEE zun ul mye GRAY shun) The moving of herds of animals from pasture to pasture according to the seasons of the year. p. 265.

sediment (SED uh munt) Any matter set down by wind or water, such as sand or soil. p. 15.

seismograph (SYZ muh graf) An instrument used to measure the strength of earthquakes. p. 129.

shifting cultivation (SHIHFT ing kul-tuh VAY shun) To clear and farm land for a short period and then move on to another plot. p. 244.

shogun (SHOH gun) A military leader. p. 289.

sit-in (siht ihn) A method of protesting a policy in which demonstrators sit in, and refuse to leave, a public place. p. 561.

spiritual (SPIHR ih choo ul) A religious folk song. p. 256.

stalemate (STAYL mayt) A situation in which further action is impossible or useless. p. 438.

station (STAY shun) A huge Australian ranch where sheep and cattle are raised. p. 416.

status (STAT us) Position, rank, or standing in a group. p. 253.

steppe (step) A great plain of grassland with few trees. p. 264.

stereotype (STER ee uh typ)   A way of thinking about a person or group that follows a fixed pattern, paying no attention to individual differences. p. 510.

Stone Age (stohn ayj)   An early period in the history of human beings when stone tools and weapons were used. p. 40.

stylus (STYE lus)   A pointed tool used in writing on a soft surface. p. 63.

subcontinent (sub KAHNT un unt)   A large land mass that is smaller than a continent. p. 94.

subsidy (SUB suh dee)   A grant of money. p. 533.

suburb (SUB urb)   A town, village, or other district on the outskirts of a city. p. 19.

suffrage (SUF rihj)   The right to vote. p. 442.

sultan (SULT un)   A Muslim ruler. p. 502.

supply (suh PLYE)   The amount of goods available for purchase at a given price. p. 30.

sustenance (SUS tuh nuns)   That which sustains life; food or nourishment. p. 28.

T

tabernacle (TAB ur nak ul)   A shrine or place of worship. p. 59.

tapestry (TAP us tree)   A rich, heavy cloth with designs and scenes woven into it. p. 205.

technician (tek NIHSH un)   A person trained in a certain job or science. p. 128.

technology (tek NAHL uh jee)   A method for dealing with technical problems. p. 230.

tenant farmer (TEN unt FAHR mur)   One who farms land owned by another and pays rent in cash or crops. p. 526.

terrain (ter RAYN)   Ground or area of land. p. 131.

terrorism (TER ur ihz um)   The use of force or threats to terrify and coerce. p. 574.

thesis (THEE sihs)   A statement or idea to be defended in a discussion or debate. p. 337.

till (tihl)   To plow and plant land. p. 244.

toga (TOH guh)   A loose garment worn in public. p. 174.

tribute (TRIHB yoot)   A payment given by subjects to rulers. p. 84.

tropical rain forest (TRAHP ih kul rayn FOR ihst)   A dense, evergreen forest found in tropical regions and having large amounts of yearly rainfall. p. 596.

U

unalienable rights (un AYL yen uh-bul ryts)   Rights that cannot be taken away from a person. p. 427.

untouchable caste (un TUCH uh bul kast)   A group of families who were considered low in status and were discriminated against. p. 97.

V

viceroy (VYS roi)   A governor of a colony ruling as the representative of the king. p. 359.

virtual reality (VUR choo ul ree AL-uh tee)   Computer-controlled, three-dimensional, 360 degree images that appear to be real. p. 600.

vizier (vih ZIHR)   A chief minister. p. 75.

W

wadi (WAH dee)   A valley formed by heavy flooding. p. 81.

water clock (WAWT ur klok)   A device for measuring time by the flow of water. p. 273.

work song (wurk song)   A song sung to match the rhythm of the work. p. 256.

Y

yamb (yam)   An inn and government station house along a busy road. p. 273.

yoga (YOH guh)   Indian exercises and postures designed to discipline the body and clear the mind. p. 101.

youth culture (yooth KUL chur)   The ideas, customs, skills, and arts of young people. p. 560.

yurt (yoort)   A structure of felt or hides stretched over a round frame. p. 264.

Z

ziggurat (ZIHG uh rat)   A temple tower. p. 51.

INDEX

Page numbers in italics indicate illustrations.

and inventions, 53, 54
Persians in, 55
Phoenicians in, 54–55
Sumerians in, 52–54
Mestizos, 454
Metalwork, 315
Mexica, 311, 365
Mexico, 365
economy in, 581–582
immigrants in, 466
independence in, 427, 454, 458, 459
and trade, 462
Mexico City, 18, *18,* 365, 454, 458, 572
Mfecane, 479
Michael VIII Palaeologus of Nicaea, 202
Michelangelo, 342, *342*
Middle Ages, 195, 196, 208, 332
education in, 204
literature in, 205–206
religion in, 199
See also Medieval Europe.
Middle class, rise of, 338–339, *339*
Middle East, 39, 517
building loyalties in, 507
Camp David Accords in, 516
changing life in, 500–505, 511
claims for Jerusalem, *514, 515,* 514–515
conflicting ideas in, 505, 506
crisis of identity in, 501, 506
faltering of economy in, 501–502
geography of, *517*
independence in, 503–504
music in, 509
national foods in, 509
nationalism in, 507
new ideas in, 505
PLO in, 516
Rabin-Arafat agreement in, *517*
role of religion in, 503
Six-Day War in, 515–516
television in, 509
terrorism in, 574
trade in, 507
unrest in, 512–513
western influences in, 507–508
women in, 508, 510–511
Yom Kippur War, 516
Zionism in, 515
See also individual countries.
Militant, 269
Military history, 32–33
Minarets, 226
Mindanao, 381
Mineralogy, 229
Ming dynasty, 131, 266, 270
Minoans, 139

Minos, King, 139
Missionaries, 292–293, 417
in Americas, 362, *362,* 366
in Middle East, 502
Mission schools, 480, *489, 490, 491,* 489–491
Mississippian culture, 371
Mississippi River, French exploration of, *367, 367*
Moctezuma, 312, 364
Mogul Empire, in India, 267, *268,* 268–269, 271
Mohenjo-Daro, 95
Monasteries, 199
Monet, painting by, *430*
Money, *30*
paper, 127
Mongols, 123, 264–266
Monotheism, 58
Monroe Doctrine, 456
Monsoons, 94
in India, 92, 94
summer, 249
winter, 249
Monte Cassino, 200
Montenegro, 577
Moon, exploration of, 558
Moors, and Reconquista, 334, *334*
Morocco, 507
Moscow, 351
Moses, 59, *59,* 87
Mosques, 226, 232
Mother Goddess, 100
Mott, Lucretia Coffin, 442
Mound builders, 370, *370*
Mountain barrier passes, 20, 20–21
Mozambique, 478
Muawiya, 234
Muhammad, 39, 220, 221–222, 231, 232, *226–227*
Multinational corporations, 581
Mummies, 78, *78-79, 80,* 313
Murasaki, 297
Music
of the Beatles, 560, *560*
in Indonesia, 380, *380*
Jazz Age in, 431, *431*
in Middle East, 509
in Renaissance, *335*
in sub-Saharan Africa, *256, 257,* 256–257
Muslim empire
downfall of, 225
expansion of, 222–224
in Spain, 225
trade in, 225
See also Islam.
Muslims, 223, 334
and Algebra, 228
Algerian, 493

and applied sciences, 230, *230*
Arabic language of, 232–233
architecture of, 231
art of, 230–231
and building of Baghdad, 234
calligraphy of, 231, *231*
centers of learning of, 228
claims on Jerusalem, 514
contribution of, 229
and Crusades, 199, 225
divisions among, 227
formation of Pakistan, 536
in Iran, 512
in Lebanon, 512
literature of, 233, *233*
and practice of medicine, 228–230
resistance of, to global culture, 571–572
in Spain, 224
and spread of Islam, 222–224
in sub-Saharan Africa, 246, 247, 254
trade routes of, 221
Umayyad dynasty of, 224, 234
and women, 510–511
See also Moors and Islam.
Mussolini, Benito, 435, *435,* 437, 548
and alliance with Hitler, 440–441
Mwene Mutapa, 254
Myanmar, 380, 386, 394, 406
Aung San Suu Kyi, 394–395
British in, 385
See also Burma.
Mycenaean civilization, 140
Myths, Greek, 143, 147

N ▬▬▬▬▬▬

Nadir ul Asar, 277
Nagasaki, 441
Nalanda, 267
Nalanda, University of, *108, 109*
Namibia, 481
Nanak, Guru, 269
Nanjing, 270
Napoleon, invasion of Egypt, 501, *501*
Nara, 288
Nasser, Gamal Abdul, 504
Nationalism
European ideas of, 502
German, 338
in Middle East, 507
Palestinian, 516
problems with, 429
rise of, 350–351
spirit of, 428–429
National Organization for Women (NOW), 563

National Socialist (Nazi) party, 435
Native Americans
Anasazi as, *368,* 368–369
decline in population of, 361
Mound Builders, 370, 371
Plains people, 371
Pueblos, 368
and slavery, 361
Spanish treatment of, 360
Spanish attempts to convert to Christianity, 362
Natron, 78
Natural resources in Africa, 477, 478
Natural resources in rain forest, 598
Natural rights, 426
Nazis
and holocaust, *436, 437,* 441
as political party, 435
Nebuchadnezzar, King, 57
Nefertiti, 86
Nehru, Jawaharlal, 536
Nepal, 94, 537
New France, 366
New Guinea, 381, 386
Ne Win, 395
New Testament, 171
Newton, Isaac, 345, *345*
New Zealand
British in, 417
Maori in, 416–417
women's rights in, 443
Nicholas II, Czar of Russia, 433
Niger River Valley, development of agriculture in, 245
Nightingale, Florence, 430, 443
Nkrumah, Kwame, 492
Nile River, 72, 73, *82, 83,* 243
Nineteenth Amendment, 443
95 Theses, 337
Nobel, Alfred, 443
Nobel Peace Prize, 394, 395, 443
Noh drama, *297,* 297–298
Nomads, 40
Nonconformists, 298
Nonviolent freedom movement, 492
Norsemen, 201
North America
agriculture in, 341
Vikings in, 201
North American Free Trade Agreement (NAFTA), 581–582, 594
North Atlantic Treaty Organization (NATO), 556
Northern Ireland, religious conflict in, 574

ACKNOWLEDGMENTS

Grateful acknowledgment is made to the following publishers, authors, and agents for their permission to reprint copyrighted material. Every effort has been made to locate all copyright proprietors; any errors or omissions in copyright notice are inadvertent and will be corrected in future printings as they are discovered.

from *Bard of Avon: The Story of William Shakespeare* by Diane Stanley and Peter Vennema. Text copyright ©1992 by Diane Stanley and Peter Vennema. Cover illustration copyright ©1992 by Diane Stanley. Reprinted by permission of Morrow Junior Books, a division of William Morrow & Company, Inc.

from *Catherine, Called Birdy* by Karen Cushman. Copyright ©1994 by Karen Cushman. Cover art copyright ©1995 by Bryan Leister. Cover design by Stephanie Rosenfield. Cover copyright ©1995 by HarperCollins Publishers. Reprinted by permission of Clarion Books/Houghton Mifflin Co, and of HarperCollins Publishers. All rights reserved.

from *Digging to the Past: Excavations in Ancient Lands* by W. John Hackwell. Copyright ©1986 by W. John Hackwell. Reprinted with the permission of Simon & Schuster.

from *Door of No Return: The Legend of Gorée Island* by Steven Barboza. Copyright ©1994 by Steve Barboza. Used by permission of Dutton Children's Books, a division of Penguin Books USA Inc.

from "Evolution of African-American Music" by Portia K. Maultsby, Ph.D. Copyright ©1992 by Portia K. Maultsby, Ph.D. All rights reserved. Revised 1995.

from *The Great Alexander the Great* by Joe Lasker. Copyright ©1983 by Joe Lasker. Used by permission of Puffin Books, a division of Penguin Books USA Inc.

from *I Dream of Peace* by children of former Yugoslavia. Copyright ©1994 by UNICEF. Reprinted by permission of HarperCollins Publishers, Inc.

CREDITS

Front Cover *Design, Art Direction, and Production:* Design Five, NYC; *Photo* Dana Sigall. *Details* © Alain Evrard/Photo Researchers, Inc.; Steve Elmore/Tom Stack & Associates; © J. Cochin/Photo Researchers, Inc.; C.M. Dixon; Jim Rudnick/The Stock Market; M.L. Sinibaldi/The Stock Market; Wendy Shattil/Bob Rozinski/Tom Stack & Associates; © Will & Deni McIntyre/Photo Researchers, Inc.; NASA.

Maps Mapping Specialists Limited

All photographs by Silver Burdett Ginn (SBG) unless otherwise noted.

Photographs 1: *bkgd.* © Brian Parker/Tom Stack & Associates/Digital Image Build; Tom Young/The Stock Market; NASA; Jean–Marie Chauvet/Sygma. 5: *b.* AP/Wide World Photos. 7: *l.* Superstock; *r.* R. Van Der Meer/Tony Stone Images. 8: *t.l.* David DeVries/Bruce Coleman; *t.r.* Keren Su/Stock Boston; *b.l.* Raga/The Stock Market; *b.m.* Ron Sanford/The Stock Market; *b.r.* Lauren Goodsmith/The Image Works. 11: James Hackett/Leo de Wys. 13: *l.* Cameramann International; *m.* M. Thonig/H. Armstrong Roberts; *r.* Paul Harris/Tony Stone Images. 14: *l.* Chad Ehlers/Tony Stone Images; *r.* Ed Mullis/Aspect Picture Library/The Stock Market. 15: *l.* David R. Frazier/Tony Stone Images; *r.* Tom Bean/The Stock Market. 18: Robert Frerck/Odyssey Productions. 19: *t.l.* Patrick Ward/Stock Boston; *t.r.* Wolfgang Kaehler; *b.l.* M. Thonig/H. Armstrong Roberts; *b.r.* M.W. Hoar/Bruce Coleman. 20: *t.* Viviane Holbrooke/The Stock Market; *b.l.* Elliott Smith; *b.m.* Patrick Ward/Stock Boston; *b.r.* Flavio Del Mese/The Image Bank. 24–25: *bkgd.* Jean Clottes/Ministere de la Culture/Sygma. 27: Courtesy, Elsie Davis. 28: Superstock. 29: The Philbrook Museum of Art, Tulsa, OK. 30: *m.l.* Christopher Liu/ChinaStock; *m.r.* James P. Blair/© National Geographic Society; *b.l.* Otis Imboden/© National Geographic Society; *b.r.* Superstock. 31: *t.* Superstock; *b.* Ron Edmonds/AP/Wide World Photos. 32: *t.* Cheltenham Art Gallery & Museums, Glos./The Bridgeman Art Library; *m.* The Bridgeman Art Library; *b.* Louvre, Paris/The Bridgeman Art Library. 33: *t.* F.L. Kenett/Robert Harding Picture Library; *m.* Ancient Art & Architecture; *b.* George Rainbird Ltd./Robert Harding Picture Library. 34: Photography by Egyptian Expedition/The Metropolitan Museum of Art . 35: *t.l.* Erich Lessing/Israel Museum (IDAM), Jerusalem, Israel/Art Resource, NY; *t.r.* The Granger Collection, New York; *b.* Ian Berry/Magnum. 36: *bkgd.* Rosen/Saba. 38: Scala/Art Resource, NY. 39: Giraudon/Art Resource, NY. 41: *t.* Jean-Marie Chauvet/Sygma; *b.* Erich Lessing/National Museum, Budapest, Hungary/Art Resource, NY. 44–45: *l.* Adam Woolfitt/Robert Harding Picture Library; *m.l.* E.T. Archive; *m.r.* Wellcome Institute/Michael Holford; *r.* C.M. Dixon. 48: *t.* Judi Benvenuti; *b.* British Museum/Michael Holford. 50: Superstock. 50–51: Superstock. 51: Copyright Trustees of the British Museum. 52: *t.* The Iraq Museum/Scala/Art Resource, NY; *b.* British Museum/Michael Holford. 53: Ancient Art & Architecture. 54: Erich Lessing/Art Resource, NY. 55: Ancient Art & Architecture. 58: The Pierpont Morgan Library, New York, B.34. 59: Dahlem Staatliche Gemaldegalerie, Berlin/The Bridgeman Art Library. 60: Jewish Museum/Art Resource, NY. 61: *bkgd.* C.M. Dixon; *l.* C.M. Dixon; *r.* Hirmer Fotoarchiv. 62: Oriental Museum, Durham University/The Bridgeman Art Library. 63: British Museum/Michael Holford. 67: British Museum, London/The Bridgeman Art Library. 68–69: *bkgd.* Robert Frerck/Odyssey Productions. 71: *t.r.* Grant Heilman Photography; *b.l.* Christi Carter/Grant Heilman Photography; *b.r.* Runk/Schoenberger/Grant Heilman Photography. 75: Max Hunn/FPG International. 76–77: Ancient Art & Architecture. 77: British Museum/Bridgeman Art Library/Art Resource, NY. 78: The Children's Museum of Indianapolis. 78–79: Michael Holford. 79: The Field Museum, Chicago, IL. Neg # A111057c. Photo: Ron Testa. 80: Ancient Art & Architecture. 85: Museum Expedition, courtesy of Museum of Fine Arts, Boston. 94–95: *bkgd* Borromeo/Art Resource, NY. 96: *t.* C.M. Dixon; *b.* Courtesy, Museum of Fine Arts, Boston. 98: Courtesy, The Board of Trustees of the Victoria & Albert Museum/The Bridgeman Art Library. 99: *t.r.* ARTEPHOT/Vision; *b.* Musee De Calcutta/ARTEPHOT/Roland. 100: National Museum/Borromeo/Art Resource, NY. 101: *t.* John Elk III/Stock Boston; *b.* Adam Woolfitt/Robert Harding Picture Library. 102: John Elk/Stock Boston. 103: *t.* Victoria Ginn; *b.* Boltin Picture Library. 104: *t.* © 1997 Lindsay Hebberd/Woodfin Camp & Associates; *b.* Victoria Ginn. 105: *t.l., t.r.* Robert Harding Picture Library; *b.* Victoria Ginn. 108: *t.* Copyright British Museum; *b.* © 1997 Lindsay Hebberd/Woodfin Camp & Associates. 110: Dinodia Picture Agency. 117: Royal Ontario Museum, Canada. 119: *t.* Laurie Platt Winfrey/Carousel Research; *b.* Robert Harding Picture Library. 120: *t.* Wellcome Institute/Michael Holford; *b.* Fujii Saiseikai/The Yurinkan Museum. 121: *t.* Robert Harding Picture Library; *b.* ChinaStock. 124: Wang Lu/ChinaStock. 125: Royal Ontario Museum, Canada. 127: Victoria & Albert Museum/E.T. Archive. 128: ChinaStock. 129: *b.* Michael Holford. 134: *inset* Aaron Haupt/Frazier Photolibrary. 134–135: *bkgd.* Ancient Art & Architecture. 136: *b.* Ancient Art & Architecture. 137: Bob Martin/Allsport. 139: Museo Mandralisca Cefalu/Scala/Art Resource. 140: Athens National Museum/Nimatallah/Art Resource. 141: *t.* Ancient Art & Architecture; *b.* C.M. Dixon. 142: *t.* Antonio M. Rosario/The Image Bank; *b.* Werner Krutein/Liaison International. 143: The Mansell Collection. 144: *t.l.* David Bartruff/FPG International; *t.r.* British Museum/Michael Holford; *b.* Bob Daemmrich/The Image Works. 145: *t.* Ancient Art & Architecture; *b.* National Archaeological Museum/The Bridgeman Art Library. 147: Phil Degginger/Tony Stone Images. 148: *t.* Scala/Art Resource, NY; *m.* Joan Marcus; *b.* Jean Pragen/Tony Stone Images. 149: Scala/Art Resource, NY. 150: © 1997 Nubar Alexanian/Woodfin Camp & Associates. 151: *t.* Agora Excavations/American School of Classical Studies Athens/Laurie Platt Winfrey, Inc.; *b.* Museo Pio Clementino, Vatican Museums, Vatican State/SCALA/Art Resource, NY. 153: Museo Archeologica Naples, Italy/Superstock. 154–155: *bkgd.* Ancient Art & Architecture. 160–161: *bkgd.* National Historical Museum, Bucharest/Superstock. 162: © Bonnie Sue/Photo Researchers, Inc. 165: Firenze, Museo Archeologica/Scala/Art Resource, NY. 166: Copyright British Museum. 167: *t.* National Historical Museum, Bucharest/Superstock; *b.* Luis Castaneda/The Image Bank. 169: J. Gordon Miller/Superstock. 171: *l.* British Museum/Michael Holford; *r.* Palatine Library, Parma/Superstock. 172–173: Superstock. 175: *t.l.* Museo Nazionale Romano delle Terme, Rome, Italy/Scala/Art Resource; *t.r.* British Museum/Michael Holford; *m.* Museo Teatrale, Milano/Scala/Art Resource, NY; *b.* Paris, Louvre/Giraudon/Art Resource, NY. 176: Ancient Art & Architecture. 176–177: Superstock. 177: Museo Nazionale, Naples/Art Resource, NY. 178: *t.* Jean Pragen/Tony Stone Images; *b.* C.M. Dixon. 179: Superstock. 180: *t.* Phyllis Picardi/Stock Boston; *b.* Gaetani/Prisma/Photoreporters.

434: Archive Photos. 435: *t.* Popperfoto; *b.* Laurie Platt Winfrey. 436: *t.* The Bettmann Archive; *b.* Hulton Deutsch Collection Limited. 437: Scala/Art Resource, NY. 438: © 1997 BBC Hulton Picture Library/Woodfin Camp & Associates. 439: Hulton Deutsch Collection Limited. 440: © 1997 BBC Hulton Picture Library/Woodfin Camp & Associates. 441: *l.* © 1997 Hulton Picture Company/Woodfin Camp & Associates; *r.* SBG/Courtesy, Jane Heelan. 442: *r.* Mary Evans Picture Library. 443: *t.* Mary Evans Picture Library. 444–445: *bkgd.* James L. Stanfield/© National Geographic Society. 448–449: SBG/Courtesy, Jane Heelan. 450: SBG/Courtesy, The Gregg Collection. 452: The Granger Collection, New York. 454: Laurie Platt Winfrey/Carousel Research. 454–455: Harold Samuel Collection, Corporation of London/The Bridgeman Art Library. 456: *t.* Gavin Ashworth/Museum of American Folk Art; *b.* The Bettmann Archive. 457: The Granger Collection, New York. 463: *bkgd.* John Burwell/Folio, Inc.; *inset* E.R. Degginger/Bruce Coleman; *b.* Miguel Rio Branco/Magnum. 464: Hulton Deutsch Collection Limited. 465: *t.l., b.l.* Courtesy, Susan Freeman; *r.* Deutsche Schule, Caracas/Courtesy, Alice Firgau. 466: Culver Pictures. 467: *t.* Alejandro Balaguer/Sygma; *b.* Superstock. 468: *l.* Michael Moody/D. Donne Bryant. 469: *t.* Superstock; *b.* Robert Frerck/Odyssey Productions. 472–473: *bkgd.* Lee Foster/FPG International. 476: British Library, London/The Bridgeman Art Library. 479: *t.* Robert Frerck/Odyssey Productions; *m., b.l.* Mary Evans Picture Library; *b.r.* E.T. Archive. 480: *t.* AP/Wide World Photos; *b.l.* Brooks Kraft/Sygma; *b.r.* Abdelfatteh Belaid/Sygma. 481: *t.* D. Aubert/Sygma; *m.* Robert Frerck/Odyssey Productions; *b.* Popperfoto. 484: The Granger Collection, New York. 485: *t.* North Carolina Collection/University of N.C. Library at Chapel Hill, photo by Billy Barnes; *b.* The Bettmann Archive. 486–488: *bkgd.* Lee Foster/FPG International. 489: The Bettmann Archive. 490: *l., r.* Mary Evans Picture Library. 491: *l.* © 1997 Betty Press/Woodfin Camp & Associates; *r.* Sue Dorfman/Stock Boston. 496–497: *bkgd.* Yuri Dojc/The Image Bank. 498: David Rubinger/Time/Sygma. 501: © 1997 Woodfin Camp & Associates. 502: *t.* The Bridgeman Art Library; *b.* Superstock. 503: © 1997 Robert Frerck/Woodfin Camp & Associates. 504: The Granger Collection, New York. 505: Sygma. 507: Farnood/Sipa Press. 508: *l.* Culver Pictures; *r.* Yuri Dojc/The Image Bank. 509: Arthur Hustwitt/Leo de Wys. 510: *l.* Patrick David/Sipa Press; *r.* Geopress/H. Armstrong Roberts. 511: M. Milner/Sygma. 514–515: Steve Vidler/Leo de Wys. 515: AP/Wide World Photos. 516: Rula Halawani/Sygma. 517: Trippett/Sipa Press. 520: *inset* © Philippe Plailly/Science Photo Library/Photo Researchers, Inc. 520–521: *bkgd.* E.R. Degginger/H. Armstrong Roberts. 522: © Chromosohm/Sohm/Photo Researchers, Inc. 525: Vladpans/Leo de Wys. 526: Laurie Platt Winfrey/Carousel Research. 527: *t.l.* Jean Kugler/FPG International; *t.r.* Doug Finley; *b.* Laurie Platt Winfrey/Carousel Research. 528: *t.* Christopher Liu/ChinaStock; *b.* J. Langevin/Sygma. 529: *l.* J.P. Laffont/Sygma; *r.* George Hunter/H. Armstrong Roberts. 531: Bob Krist/Leo de Wys. 532: Fridmar Damm/Leo de Wys. 533: *t.* © 1997 Kim Newton/Woodfin Camp & Assoc.; *b.* Anthony Suau/Liaison International. 534: *l.* Jean-Paul Nacivet/Leo de Wys; *r.* Cameramann International. 536: *t.* The Bettmann Archive; *b.* Sygma. 537: *bkgd.* Bruce Stewart/Bruce Coleman; *inset* Bill Wassman/The Stock Market. 542–543: *bkgd.* © Brian Parker/Tom Stack & Associates; *t.* Simmon/Stock Imagery; *m.l.* © Farrell Grehan/Photo Researchers, Inc.; *m.r.* © Louis Goldman/Photo Researchers, Inc.; *b.l.* Robert Frerck/Odyssey Productions; *b.r.* Rogers/Monkmeyer Press. 544: *inset* Richard T. Nowitz. 544–545: *bkgd.* Michael Pasdzior/The Image Bank. 546: Christopher Liu/ChinaStock. 548: Archive Photos/Express Newspaper. 550: Archive Photos/American Stock. 551: Hulton Deutsch Collection Limited. 553: The Bettmann Archive.

555: *t.* Keystone Paris/Sygma. 556: The Bettmann Archive. 557: *t.* John Moss/Black Star; *b.* Eric Bouvet/Liaison International. 560: Ken Karp for SBG. 560–561: The Kobal Collection. 561: *t., m.* Ken Karp for SBG; *b.* Photofest. 562: *t.* Ed Bailey/Black Star; *b.* Eloy Hernandez/Sygma. 562–563: Dennis Brack/Black Star. 563: Paul Fusco/Magnum. 565: SBG/Courtesy, Jane Heelan. 568: Paul Brown/Seattle Post-Intelligencer/Sygma. 570: Wolfgang Kaehler. 571: *t.* Ken Ross/FPG International; *b.* F. Hibon/Sygma. 574: *t.l.* John Moore/AP/Wide World Photos; *t.r.* Jackie Foryst/Bruce Coleman; *b.* Vladimir Sichov/Sipa Press. 576: *t.* © 1997 Enrico Dagino/Woodfin Camp & Associates; *b.* © 1997 Betty Press/Woodfin Camp & Associates. 577: *t.l.* Paul Lowe/Magnum Photos; *t.r.* Malanca/Sipa Press; *b.* © 1997 Enrico Dagino/Woodfin Camp & Associates. 578–579: *bkgd.* P. Vauthey/Sygma. 583: © 1997 Barry Iverson/Woodfin Camp & Associates. 586–587: *bkgd.* John Chiasson/Liaison International. 588: Marc Romanelli/The Image Bank. 590: Romilly Lockyer/The Image Bank. 592: *t.* United Nations/Sygma; *b.* R.Vogel/Liaison International. 593: *t.* Cameramann International; *b.* SBG/Courtesy, Phoenix Stamp House. 594: *t.l.* The Bettmann Archive; *t.r.* John Chiasson/Liaison International; *b.* William Campbell/Sygma. 595: © 1997 Betty Press/Woodfin Camp & Associates. 596: Courtesy, JASON Foundation/Tricom Associates. 596–597: *bkgd.* Carol Hughes/Bruce Coleman. 597: Michael Fogden/Bruce Coleman. 599: *bkgd.* Lloyd Wolf/Folio; *inset* Robert Burgess/Folio. 600: *l.* Larry Keenan/The Image Bank; *r.* © James King–Holmes/Science Photo Library/Photo Researchers, Inc. 601: Courtesy, JASON Foundation/Tricom Associates. 602: *t.l.* National Museum Anthropology/Odyssey Productions; *t.r.* Ancient Art & Architecture; *b.* Louvre, Paris/The Bridgeman Art Library. 603: *t.* British Museum/Michael Holford; *m.r.* Superstock. 606–607: Photo data gathered by Hank Brandli/Mosaic photographed by Trent Chase.

Illustrations M2–M23: John Margeson. 16–17: Robert LoGrippo. 56–57: John Holder. 62: Elizabeth Brady. 64–65: Sarah Jane English. 70: Wendy Smith-Griswold. 71: Lisa Pomerantz. 73: Patrick O'Brien. 74: Sarah Jane English. 75: Elizabeth Brady. 76: Joe Scrofani. 77: Elizabeth Brady. 80: Jackie Geyer. 81: Sarah Jane English. 82–83: Sarah Jane English. 86–87: Ethan Long. 106–107: David McCall Johnston. 114–115: Linda Richards. 115: Roger Roth. 122: Mou-Sien Tseng. 123: Jean & Mou-Sien Tseng. 126: Patrick O'Brien. 130–131: Gary Torrisi. 133: Neecy Twinem. 147: Toni H. Kurrasch. 156–157: Bill Basso. 159: Amy Bryant. 166: Tungwai Chau. 174: Mike Jaroszko. 179: David McCall Johnston. 182–183: Nina Laden. 196: Jackie Geyer. 196–197: Robert LoGrippo. 200–203: David Wenzel. 215: David Wenzel. 218: Eldon Doty. 222–223: Judith Sutton. 234–235: Pamela Becker. 242: Quentin Webb. 248: Rodica Prato. 251: John Holder. 254–255: Eldon Doty. 270–271: Peter Bono. 276: Joe Scrofani. 287: David Johnston. 289: Kristen Miller. 292–293: Joe Boddy. 311: Jim Frazier. 314–315: Kevin O'Malley. 317: Mee Wha Lee. 332: Stephen Wells. 340–341: Joe Scrofani. 350–351: Rob McDougall. 360: Don Stewart. 366–367: Denny Bond. 372–373: Phil Wilson. 386–387: Bradley H. Clark. 397: Phil Wilson. 407: Amy Bryant. 408–409: David Wenzel. 432: John Gampert. 433: John Gampert. 444: Phil Wilson. 458–459: Jim Trusilo. 460: Martucci Studio. 461: Amy Bryant. 462: Martucci Studio. 474–475: Martucci Studio. 478: Martucci Studio. 482–483: Sarah Jane English. 485: Stephen Wells. 492: Mike Reagan; Irena Roman. 493: Irena Roman. 512–513: Irena Roman. 538: Gary Torrisi. 539: Gary Torrisi. 558–559: Tony Randazzo. 572–573: Lee Steadman. 581: Martucci Studio,T/Maker Co. 595: Anthony Cericola. 598: Anthony Cericola.629: Martucci Studio. 630–631: Martucci Studio.